Lecture Notes in Computer Science 13877

Founding Editors

Gerhard Goos
Juris Hartmanis

The series Lecture Notes in Computer Science (LNCS), including its subseries Lecture Notes in Artificial Intelligence (LNAI) and Lecture Notes in Bioinformatics (LNBI), has established itself as a medium for the publication of new developments in computer science and information technology research, teaching, and education.

LNCS enjoys close cooperation with the computer science R & D community, the series counts many renowned academics among its volume editors and paper authors, and collaborates with prestigious societies. Its mission is to serve this international community by providing an invaluable service, mainly focused on the publication of conference and workshop proceedings and postproceedings. LNCS commenced publication in 1973.

Guy-Vincent Jourdan · Laurent Mounier ·
Carlisle Adams · Florence Sèdes ·
Joaquin Garcia-Alfaro
Editors

Foundations and Practice of Security

15th International Symposium, FPS 2022
Ottawa, ON, Canada, December 12–14, 2022
Revised Selected Papers

 Springer

Editors
Guy-Vincent Jourdan 🆔
University of Ottawa
Ottawa, ON, Canada

Laurent Mounier 🆔
Université Grenoble Alpes
Grenoble, France

Carlisle Adams 🆔
University of Ottawa
Ottawa, ON, Canada

Florence Sèdes 🆔
University Toulouse III Paul Sabatier
Toulouse, France

Joaquin Garcia-Alfaro 🆔
Telecom SudParis
Palaiseau, France

ISSN 0302-9743　　　　　　ISSN 1611-3349 (electronic)
Lecture Notes in Computer Science
ISBN 978-3-031-30121-6　　ISBN 978-3-031-30122-3 (eBook)
https://doi.org/10.1007/978-3-031-30122-3

This Springer imprint is published by the registered company Springer Nature Switzerland AG
The registered company address is: Gewerbestrasse 11, 6330 Cham, Switzerland

Preface

This volume contains the papers presented at the 15th International Symposium on Foundations and Practice of Security (FPS 2022), which was hosted by University of Ottawa in Ottawa, Canada, on December 12–14, 2022.

FPS 2022 received 83 submissions from countries all over the world. The Program Committee selected 26 regular papers and 2 short papers for presentation. The agenda was complemented with a panel on the use of CyberRanges and three keynotes. The panel included the participation of Emmanuel Druon (Université du Québec à Chicoutimi), Guy-Vincent Jourdan (University of Ottawa), Paul Berthier (RHEA Group), Reda Yaich (IRT SystemX), and Marc-Antoine Faillon (Polytechnique Montréal). Keynotes included Alexandra Boldyreva (Professor of Computer Science and the Associate Chair for Graduate Studies in the School of Cybersecurity and Privacy at the Georgia Institute of Technology), Reihaneh Safavi-Naini (Professor of Computer Science and the NSERC/Telus Industrial Research Chair in Information Security at the University of Calgary), and Stephanie Carvin (Associate Professor of International Relations at the Norman Paterson School of International Affairs at Carleton University). Many thanks to all of them for their participation in the program of FPS 2022!

The best paper award of FPS 2022 was granted to the contribution "Security Analysis of Improved EDHOC Protocol" by Baptiste Cottier and David Pointcheval, from the Ecole Normale Supérieure in Paris, France. The best paper runner-up award of FPS 2022 was granted to the contribution "Towards Characterizing IoT Software Update Practices" by Conner Bradley and David Barrera, from Carleton University in Ottawa, Canada.

Many people contributed to the success of FPS 2022. First and foremost, we would like to thank all the researchers who submitted their research to the conference. The selection was a challenging task, and we sincerely thank all the Program Committee members, as well as the external reviewers, who volunteered to read and discuss the papers.

We are very grateful to our local organization chairs Paula Branco and Paria Shirani, to our publicity chair Paria Shirani, to our publication chair Joaquin Garcia-Alfaro, and to our Steering Committee, in particular to Nora Cuppens and Frédéric Cuppens for their guidance.

We also want to express our gratitude to all the volunteers that have helped us make this edition of the conference a success: William Aiken, Bernard Asare, Mayukh Bhattacharjee, Samuel Brie, Jean-Gabriel Gaudreault, Asmaa Hailane, Md Sabbir Hossein, Alireza Toghiani Khorasgani, Paul Mvula, Ehsan Nazari, David Owusu, and Sam Yuen.

Finally, special thanks to Latifa El Bargui for her help and incredible support before, during, and after the conference.

We hope the articles contained in this proceedings volume will be valuable for your professional activities in the area.

This year's edition of FPS was made possible thanks to the generous sponsorship received from the University of Ottawa, the Faculty of Engineering of the University of Ottawa, Fortinet, IBM, and SystemX.

December 2022

Guy-Vincent Jourdan
Laurent Mounier
Carlisle Adams
Florence Sèdes
Joaquin Garcia-Alfaro

Organization

General Chairs

Carlisle Adams — University of Ottawa, Canada
Florence Sèdes — Université Toulouse III Paul Sabatier, France

Program Committee Chairs

Guy-Vincent Jourdan — University of Ottawa, Canada
Laurent Mounier — Université Grenoble Alpes, France

Local Organization Chairs

Paula Branco — University of Ottawa, Canada
Paria Shirani — University of Ottawa, Canada

Publications Chair

Joaquin Garcia-Alfaro — Institut Polytechnique de Paris, France

Publicity Chair

Paria Shirani — University of Ottawa, Canada

Program Committee

Carlisle Adams — University of Ottawa, Canada
Furkan Alaca — Queen's University, Canada
Esma Aïmeur — Université de Montréal, Canada
Ken Barker — University of Calgary, Canada
David Barrera — Carleton University, Canada
Abdelmalek Benzekri — Université Toulouse 3 Paul Sabatier, France
Anis Bkakria — IRT SystemX, France

Gregory Blanc   Institut Polytechnique de Paris, France
Guillaume Bonfante   Université de Lorraine, LORIA, France
Paula Branco   University of Ottawa, Canada
Ana Rosa Cavalli   Institut Polytechnique de Paris, France
Xihui Chen   University of Luxembourg, Luxembourg
Frédéric Cuppens   Polytechnique Montréal, Canada
Nora Cuppens-Boulahia   Polytechnique Montréal, Canada
Xavier de Carné de Carnavalet   Hong Kong Polytechnic University, China
Mourad Debbabi   Concordia University, Canada
Steven Ding   Queen's University, Canada
Benoit Dupont   Université de Montréal, Canada
Amy Felty   University of Ottawa, Canada
Sébastien Gambs   Université du Québec à Montréal, Canada
Joaquin Garcia-Alfaro   Institut Polytechnique de Paris, France
Arash Habibi Lashkari   York University, Canada
Talal Halabi   Laval University, Canada
Abdessamad Imine   University of Lorraine, France
Jason Jaskolka   Carleton University, Canada
Mathieu Jaume   Sorbonne University, France
Houda Jmila   Institut Polytechnique de Paris, France
Guy-Vincent Jourdan   University of Ottawa, Canada
Raphaël Khoury   Université du Québec à Chicoutimi, Canada
Hyoungshick Kim   Sungkyunkwan University, South Korea
Evangelos Kranakis   Carleton University, Canada
Romain Laborde   Université Toulouse III Paul Sabatier, France
Pascal Lafourcade   Université Clermont Auvergne, France
Maryline Laurent   Télécom SudParis, France
Olivier Levillain   Institut Polytechnique de Paris, France
Luigi Logrippo   Université du Québec en Outaouais, Canada
Taous Madi   King Abdullah University of Science and
                                           Technology, Saudi Arabia

Suryadipta Majumdar   Concordia University, Canada
Jean-Yves Marion   Université de Lorraine, France
Ashraf Matrawy   Carleton University, Canada
Daiki Miyahara   University of Electro-Communications, Japan
Benoît Morgan   University Toulouse III Paul Sabatier, France
Djedjiga Mouheb   Laval University, Canada
Paliath Narendran   University at Albany, USA
Guillermo Navarro-Arribas   Autonomous University of Barcelona, Spain
Omer Landry Nguena Timo   Université du Québec en Outaouais, Canada
Jun Pang   University of Luxembourg, Luxembourg
Karthik Pattabiraman   University of British Columbia, Canada

Marie-Laure Potet	Université de Grenoble Alpes, VERIMAG, France
Isabel Praça	Instituto Superior de Engenharia do Porto, Portugal
Silvio Ranise	Fondazione Bruno Kessler, Italy
Jean-Marc Robert	École de technologie supérieure, Canada
Michaël Rusinowitch	LORIA-INRIA Nancy, France
Kazuo Sakiyama	The University of Electro-Communications, Japan
Khosro Salmani	Mount Royal University, Canada
Rei Safavi-Naini	University of Calgary, Canada
Florence Sèdes	University Toulouse III Paul Sabatier, France
Paria Shirani	Concordia University, Canada
Renaud Sirdey	Commissariat à l'Energie Atomique, France
Natalia Stakhanova	University of Saskatchewan, Canada)
Chamseddine Talhi	École de Technologie Supérieure, Canada
Nadia Tawbi	Université Laval, Canada
Valérie Viet Triem Tong	Centrale Supelec, France
Sadegh Torabi	George Mason University, USA
Ahmad Samer Wazan	Zayed University, Abu Dhabi
Reda Yaich	IRT SystemX, France
Jun Yan	Concordia University, Canada
Nicola Zannone	Eindhoven University of Technology, The Netherlands
Mengyuan Zhang	Hong Kong Polytechnic University, China
Lianying Zhao	Carleton University, Canada

Steering Committee

Frédéric Cuppens	Polytechnique Montréal, Canada
Nora Cuppens-Boulahia	Polytechnique Montréal, Canada
Mourad Debbabi	University of Concordia, Canada
Joaquin Garcia-Alfaro	Institut Polytechnique de Paris, France
Evangelos Kranakis	Carleton University, Canada
Pascal Lafourcade	University of Clermont Auvergne, France
Jean-Yves Marion	Mines de Nancy, France
Ali Miri	Toronto Metropolitan University, Canada
Rei Safavi-Naini	Calgary University, Canada
Nadia Tawbi	Université Laval, Canada

Additional Reviewers

Abdulaziz Abdulghaffar
Tahir Ahmad
Emmanuel Alalade
Walid Arabi
Sepideh Avizheh
Beatrice Berard
Stefano Berlato
Julien Cassagne
Romain Dagnas
Sabyasachi Dutta
Vaibhav Garg
Therese Hardin
Vinh Hoa La
Daniel S. Hono
Md Nazmul Hoq
Padmavathi Lyer
Alvi Jawad
Majid Khabazin

Gildas Kouko
Riccardo Longo
Wissam Mallouli
Souha Masmoudi
Manh-Dung Nguyen
Huu Nghia Nguyen
Charles Olivier-Anclin
Hélène Orsini
Somnath Panja
Md Wasiuddin Pathan Shuvo
Andrew Pulver
Vincent Raulin
Leo Robert
Khaled Sarieddine
Sofya Smolyakova
Shiva Sunar
Ziming Zhao

Contents

Cybercrime and Privacy

Physical-Layer Security

Blockchain

IoT and Security Protocols

Short Papers

Cryptography

Security Analysis of Improved EDHOC Protocol

Baptiste Cottier[(⊠)] and David Pointcheval

DIENS, École normale supérieure, CNRS, Inria, PSL University, Paris, France
`baptiste.cottier@ens.fr`

Abstract. Ephemeral Diffie-Hellman Over COSE (EDHOC) aims at being a very compact and lightweight authenticated Diffie-Hellman key exchange with ephemeral keys. It is expected to provide mutual authentication, forward secrecy, and identity protection, with a 128-bit security level.

A formal analysis has already been proposed at SECRYPT '21, on a former version, leading to some improvements, in the ongoing evaluation process by IETF. Unfortunately, while formal analysis can detect some vulnerabilities in the protocol, it cannot evaluate the actual security level.

In this paper, we study the protocol as it appeared in version 15. Without complete breaks, we anyway exhibit attacks in 2^{64} operations, which contradict the expected 128-bit security level. We thereafter propose improvements, some of them being at no additional cost, to achieve 128-bit security for all the security properties (i.e. key privacy, mutual authentication, and identity-protection).

1 Introduction

A key agreement is under analysis by IETF [10], under the name *Ephemeral Diffie-Hellman Over COSE* (EDHOC). EDHOC aims at being a very compact and lightweight authenticated Diffie-Hellman key exchange with ephemeral keys. It is expected to provide mutual authentication, forward secrecy, and identity protection, with a 128-bit security level.

This protocol is deeply inspired from SIGMA [7] and OPTLS [8] and targets constrained devices over low-power IoT radio communication technologies. For this reason, very aggressive parameters are proposed to minimize the communications. This paper follows a request from the LAKE working group to study the computational security of the EDHOC protocol with such aggressive parameters.

1.1 Related Work

A formal analysis of the May 2018 version has already been proposed by Bruni *et al.* in [2] and later completed and updated by [3,6,9], leading to some improvements. But such a formal analysis, when successful, does not give any insight about the actual security level, in terms of time complexity of the best possible

G.-V. Jourdan et al. (Eds.): FPS 2022, LNCS 13877, pp. 3–18, 2023.
https://doi.org/10.1007/978-3-031-30122-3_1

attack. While our computational analysis covers the MAC-based authentication method, other ongoing works cover other authentication methods based on signatures.

1.2 Contributions

In this paper, we analyse the August 2022 version of EDHOC proposal [10]. We are able to prove the three expected security properties in the random oracle model, under a Diffie-Hellman assumption and with secure encryption primitives. However, because of the aggressive settings, we exhibit attacks in 2^{64} operations, against authentication, which is not acceptable for a 128-bit security level.

We thereafter propose some improvements to get better security, at no communication cost. Firstly, adding more inputs to some hash value allows to speed-up the simulator when searching in some tables. Secondly, one converts an authenticated encryption scheme into a simple one-time secure encryption scheme, for hiding the identity of the Initiator, and sends a larger tag together with the External Authorization Data, in plaintext. We convert an authenticated ciphertext into a smaller ciphertext encrypting only a part of the message, and the remaining of the message is sent as plain values rather than encrypted, but with better authentication. This conversion globally has no communication impact, but increases from 64 to 128-bit security level for initiator-authentication. Last, we confirm that a fourth message provides a 128-bit security level for responder-authentication.

2 Preliminaries

2.1 Computational Assumptions

For security analysis in the computational setting, we rely on some computational assumptions: the Gap Diffie-Hellman problem and some properties of symmetric encryption.

Gap Diffie-Hellman (GDH). The Gap Diffie-Hellman problem aims to solve a Diffie-Hellman instance $(U = g^u, V = g^v)$, in a group $\mathbb{G}$ with generator g, where $u, v \xleftarrow{\$} \mathbb{Z}_p$, by computing g^{uv}, with access to a Decisional Diffie-Hellman oracle DDH returning 1 if a tuple-query (g^a, g^b, g^c) is a Diffie-Hellman tuple, and 0 otherwise. We define the advantage $\mathbf{Adv}_{\mathbb{G}}^{\mathsf{gdh}}(t, q_{\mathsf{ddh}})$, as the maximum advantage over all algorithms $\mathcal{A}$ in outputting g^{uv}, with time-complexity at most t and making at most q_{ddh} queries to the DDH oracle.

One-Time Pad Encryption. We will use several symmetric encryption schemes, such as the one-time pad: given a random key $\mathsf{sk} \in \{0,1\}^k$, the encryption of the message $m \in \{0,1\}^k$ is $c = \mathcal{E}(\mathsf{sk}, m) \leftarrow m \oplus \mathsf{sk}$, while the decryption just consists in $m = \mathcal{D}(\mathsf{sk}, c) \leftarrow c \oplus \mathsf{sk}$. It satisfies the injective property:

$$\forall \mathsf{sk}, m_0, m_1 \in \{0,1\}^k, \mathcal{E}(\mathsf{sk}, m_0) = \mathcal{E}(\mathsf{sk}, m_1) \implies m_0 = m_1.$$

It also guarantees perfect privacy: for a random secret key sk, c does not leak any information about the plaintext. We stress this is of course for a one-time use only, as there is no additional oracle access.

Authenticated Encryption with Associated Data (AEAD). We will also use an Authenticated Encryption with Associated Data scheme $\Pi' = (\mathcal{E}', \mathcal{D}')$, with a key sk and initialisation vector IV. For a message $m \in \mathcal{M}$ and some associated data $a \in \mathcal{A}$, the ciphertext is $c = \mathcal{E}'(\mathsf{sk}, \mathsf{IV}; m; a)^1$, while the decryption process provides $m = \mathcal{D}'(\mathsf{sk}, \mathsf{IV}; c; a)$ in case of valid ciphertext c with respect to sk, IV, and a, or $\perp$ otherwise. Two security properties are expected from such an AEAD.

Indistinguishability. $\Pi' = (\mathcal{E}', \mathcal{D}')$ should protect message-privacy (IND-CPA, for Indistinguishability under Chosen-Plaintext Attacks). More precisely, we consider the Experiment $\mathbf{Exp}_{\Pi'}^{\mathsf{ind\text{-}cpa}}(\mathcal{A})$ in which we randomly choose $b \in \{0, 1\}$ and a secret key sk, $\mathcal{A}$ can ask multiple queries $(\mathsf{IV}, a, m_0, m_1)$, all with different IV, and for each we compute and send $c = \mathcal{E}'(\mathsf{sk}, \mathsf{IV}; m_b; a)$ to $\mathcal{A}$. Let $b' \in \{0, 1\}$ be the output of $\mathcal{A}$. Then, the Experiment $\mathbf{Exp}_{\Pi'}^{\mathsf{ind\text{-}cpa}}(\mathcal{A})$ outputs 1 if $b' = b$ and 0 otherwise. We define the advantage of $\mathcal{A}$ in violating IND-CPA security of Π' as $\mathbf{Adv}_{\Pi'}^{\mathsf{ind\text{-}cpa}}(\mathcal{A}) = \Pr[\mathbf{Exp}_{\Pi}^{\mathsf{ind\text{-}cpa}}(\mathcal{A}) = 1]$ and the advantage function $\mathbf{Adv}_{\Pi'}^{\mathsf{ind\text{-}cpa}}(t)$, as the maximum value of $\mathbf{Adv}_{\Pi'}^{\mathsf{ind\text{-}cpa}}(\mathcal{A})$ over all $\mathcal{A}$ with time-complexity at most t. We stress that c only aims at protecting the message-privacy, but does not provide any security for the associated data. Thanks to multiple queries, we are in the chosen-plaintext setting, and not a one-time security as before.

Authentication. An AEAD scheme is also expected to guarantee some unforgeability property (UF-CMA, for Unforgeability under Chosen-Message Attacks), also for the associated data (not encrypted). More precisely, we consider the Experiment $\mathbf{Exp}_{\Pi'}^{\mathsf{uf\text{-}cma}}(\mathcal{A})$ in which $\mathcal{A}$ is given access to the encryption oracle $\mathcal{E}'(\mathsf{sk}, \cdot; \cdot; \cdot)$, for a random secret key sk. The Experiment returns 1 if $\mathcal{A}$ outputs some data a, an initialisation vector IV and a ciphertext c accepted with respect to IV and a, which means that $\mathcal{D}'(\mathsf{sk}, \mathsf{IV}; c; a) \neq \perp$, while c has not been obtained as the output of an encryption query to $\mathcal{E}'(\mathsf{sk}, \cdot; \cdot; \cdot)$. We define the advantage of $\mathcal{A}$ in violating UF-CMA security of Π' as $\mathbf{Adv}_{\Pi'}^{\mathsf{uf\text{-}cma}}(\mathcal{A}) = \Pr[\mathbf{Exp}_{\Pi'}^{\mathsf{uf\text{-}cma}}(\mathcal{A}) = 1]$ and the advantage function $\mathbf{Adv}_{\Pi'}^{\mathsf{uf\text{-}cma}}(t)$ as the maximum value of $\mathbf{Adv}_{\Pi'}^{\mathsf{uf\text{-}cma}}(\mathcal{A})$ over all $\mathcal{A}$ with time-complexity at most t.

2.2   Brief Description of EDHOC

As with any key exchange protocol, EDHOC aims to provide a common session key to two parties. We briefly sketch the key elements of the EDHOC protocol. Due to the page limitations, we refer the reader to [10] for a detailed description. EDHOC protocol can be instantiated with several settings:

- *Authentication Method*: Each party (Initiator and Responder) can use an authentication method: either with a signature scheme (SIG), or with a static Diffie-Hellman key (STAT).

---

^{1} We use semicolons here to distinguish keying material, message and Additional Data.

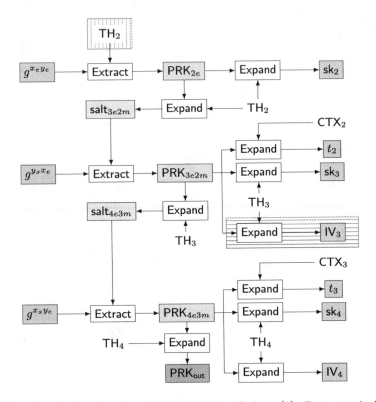

Fig. 1. Key Derivation (for the STAT-STAT Method) from [9]. Green vertical hatchs denote additions and red horizontal hatchs denote removals compared to the initial version. (Color figure online)

- *Cipher Suites*: Ordered set of protocol security settings. Initial paper offers many possible suites, but we focus on the most aggressive cipher suites setting the MAC length to 8 bytes, while still using SHA-256 as a hash function, with 256-bit outputs.
- *Connection Identifiers*: Data that may be used to correlate between messages and facilitate retrieval of protocol state in EDHOC and application.
- *Credentials and Identifiers*: They are used to identify and optionally transport the authentication keys of the Initiator and the Responder.

We suppose both the Initiator and the Responder are aware that the authentication method is STAT/STAT. Also, we ignore the Cipher Suite ID Suites_I (as it appears in [10]) in the first message of the protocol.

Extract and Expand. In the EDHOC Key-Schedule, recalled in Fig. 1 (ignoring the vertically hatched patterns for the initial protocol), the pseudorandom keys (PRK) are derived using an extraction function. In our context, Extract(salt, IKM) = HKDF-Extract(salt, IKM) is defined with SHA-256, where IKM holds for Input Keying Material (in our context, this will be some Diffie-Hellman keys) and Expand(PRK, info, len) = HKDF-Expand(PRK, info, len) where

$\mathbb{G} = <g>$	Cyclic group generated by g, of size p		
$\mathcal{H}$	Hash function SHA-256 (256 bits digest)		
X_e, x_e	Initiator Ephemeral DH Public and Secret Key		
X_s, x_s	Initiator Static DH Public and Secret Key		
Y_e, y_e	Responder Ephemeral DH Public and Secret Key		
Y_s, y_s	Responder Static DH Public and Secret Key		
EAD	External Authorization Data		
$\mathcal{E}, \mathcal{D}$	One-time Pad Encryption and Decryption		
$\mathcal{E}', \mathcal{D}'$	AEAD Encryption and Decryption		
sk	Secret key	t_2, t_3	MAC tags
TH	Transcript Hash	$\perp$	Protocol abortion
C_R, C_I	Connection Identifiers	κ_{sec}	Expected bit-security

Lengths

ℓ_C	Connection Identifiers	ℓ_{mac}, ℓ_{hash}	MAC and Hash output
ℓ_2, ℓ_{id}	m_2 and ID	ℓ_{key}, ℓ_{iv}	Key and IV

Fig. 2. Notations

info contains the transcript hash (TH_2, TH_3 or TH_4), the name of the derived key and some context, while len denotes the output length.

Transcript hashes, denoted TH_i, are used as input to the HKDF-Expandfunction. More precisely, with SHA-256 as $\mathcal{H}$, we have:

$$TH_2 = \mathcal{H}(Y_e, C_R, \mathcal{H}(m_1)) \quad TH_3 = \mathcal{H}(TH_2, m_2) \quad TH_4 = \mathcal{H}(TH_3, m_3[, m_3'])$$

where m_1 is the first message sent by the Initiator, m_2 and m_3 (possibly concatenated to m_3' in our improvement, to preserve the authentication property) respectively are the plaintexts respectively encrypted in the message 2 and message 3. More notations are provided in Fig. 2.

Protocol. The detailed description of the initial protocol is given in Fig. 3, ignoring the gray highlights which will be for our improvements. The final session key is $SK = PRK_{out}$.

3   Our Improvements

We here make some remarks on the initial protocol, with some improvements, that appear in gray highlights in Fig. 3, and to the removed/additional hatched patterns in Fig. 1.

3.1   On Mutual Authentication

The encryption key sk_3, used by the initiator to encrypt its second message m_3, is computed by calling HKDF-Expandon PRK_{3e2m}. However, even an adversary that plays in the name of a non-corrupted user, is able to compute PRK_{3e2m},

Initiator	Responder
$x_s, X_s = g^{x_s}$	$y_s, Y_s = g^{y_s}$

InitRun1($\mathsf{ID_I}$)
$x_e \xleftarrow{\$} \mathbb{Z}_p, X_e \leftarrow g^{x_e}; \mathsf{C_I} \xleftarrow{\$} \{0,1\}^{\ell_C}$
$m_1 \leftarrow (X_e \| \mathsf{C_I} \| \mathsf{EAD_1})$

$\xrightarrow{\quad m_1 \quad}$

RespRun1($\mathsf{ID_R}, y_s, m_1$)
Parse m_1 as $(X_e \| c \| \mathsf{EAD_1})$
$y_e \xleftarrow{\$} \mathbb{Z}_p, Y_e \leftarrow g^{y_e}; \mathsf{C_R} \xleftarrow{\$} \{0,1\}^{\ell_C}$
$\mathsf{sid} \leftarrow (\mathsf{C_I}, \mathsf{C_R}, X_e, Y_e)$
$\mathsf{PRK}_{2e} \leftarrow \mathsf{HKDF\text{-}Extract}(\boxed{""\ |\ \mathsf{TH_2}}, X_e^{y_e})$
$\mathsf{TH_2} \leftarrow \mathcal{H}(Y_e, \mathsf{C_R}, \mathcal{H}(m_1))$
$\mathsf{sk_2} \leftarrow \mathsf{HKDF\text{-}Expand}(\mathsf{PRK}_{2e}, 0, \mathsf{TH_2}, \ell_2)$
$\mathsf{salt}_{3e2m} \leftarrow \mathsf{HKDF\text{-}Expand}(\mathsf{PRK}_{2e}, 1, \mathsf{TH_2}, \ell_{\mathsf{hash}})$
$\mathsf{PRK}_{3e2m} \leftarrow \mathsf{HKDF\text{-}Extract}(\mathsf{salt}_{3e2m}, X_e^{y_s})$
$\mathsf{CTX_2} \leftarrow (\mathsf{ID_R} \| \mathsf{TH_2} \| Y_s \| \mathsf{EAD_2})$
$t_2 \leftarrow \mathsf{HKDF\text{-}Expand}(\mathsf{PRK}_{3e2m}, 2, \mathsf{CTX_2}, \ell_{\mathsf{mac}})$
$m_2 \leftarrow (\mathsf{ID_R} \| t_2 \| \mathsf{EAD_2}); c_2 \leftarrow \mathcal{E}(\mathsf{sk_2}, m_2)$

InitRun2($\mathsf{ID_I}, x_s, Y_s, (Y_e, c_2, \mathsf{C_R})$)

$\xleftarrow{\quad Y_e, c_2, \mathsf{C_R} \quad}$

$\mathsf{PRK}_{2e} \leftarrow \mathsf{HKDF\text{-}Extract}(\boxed{""\ |\ \mathsf{TH_2}}, Y_e^{x_e})$
$\mathsf{TH_2} \leftarrow \mathcal{H}(Y_e, \mathsf{C_R}, \mathcal{H}(m_1))$
$\mathsf{sk_2} \leftarrow \mathsf{HKDF\text{-}Expand}(\mathsf{PRK}_{2e}, 0, \mathsf{TH_2}, \ell_2)$
Set $m_2 \leftarrow \mathcal{D}(\mathsf{sk_2}, c_2)$; parse as $(\mathsf{ID_R} \| t_2 \| \mathsf{EAD_2})$
$\mathsf{CTX_2} \leftarrow (\mathsf{ID_R} \| \mathsf{TH_2} \| Y_s \| \mathsf{EAD_2})$
$\mathsf{salt}_{3e2m} \leftarrow \mathsf{HKDF\text{-}Expand}(\mathsf{PRK}_{2e}, 1, \mathsf{TH_2}, \ell_{\mathsf{hash}})$
$\mathsf{PRK}_{3e2m} \leftarrow \mathsf{HKDF\text{-}Extract}(\mathsf{salt}_{3e2m}, Y_s^{x_e})$
$t_2' \leftarrow \mathsf{HKDF\text{-}Expand}(\mathsf{PRK}_{3e2m}, 2, \mathsf{CTX_2}, \ell_{\mathsf{mac}})$
if $t_2' \neq t_2 : \mathbf{return} \perp$
$\mathsf{TH_3} \leftarrow \mathcal{H}(\mathsf{TH_2}, m_2)$
$\mathsf{sk_3} \leftarrow \mathsf{HKDF\text{-}Expand}(\mathsf{PRK}_{3e2m}, 3, \mathsf{TH_3}, \boxed{\ell_{\mathsf{key}}\ |\ \ell_{\mathsf{id}}})$
$\boxed{\mathsf{IV_3} \leftarrow \mathsf{HKDF\text{-}Expand}(\mathsf{PRK}_{3e2m}, 4, \mathsf{TH_3}, \ell_{\mathsf{iv}})\ |\ \emptyset}$
$\mathsf{salt}_{4e3m} \leftarrow \mathsf{HKDF\text{-}Expand}(\mathsf{PRK}_{3e2m}, 5, \mathsf{TH_3}, \ell_{\mathsf{hash}})$
$\mathsf{PRK}_{4e3m} \leftarrow \mathsf{HKDF\text{-}Extract}(\mathsf{salt}_{4e3m}, Y_e^{x_s})$
$\mathsf{accepted} \leftarrow 1$
$\mathsf{CTX_3} \leftarrow (\mathsf{ID_I} \| \mathsf{TH_3} \| X_s \| \mathsf{EAD_3})$
$t_3 \leftarrow \mathsf{HKDF\text{-}Expand}(\mathsf{PRK}_{4e3m}, 6, \mathsf{CTX_3}, \boxed{\ell_{\mathsf{mac}}\ |\ \kappa_{\mathsf{sec}}})$
$m_3 \leftarrow \boxed{(\mathsf{ID_I} \| t_3 \| \mathsf{EAD_3})\ |\ \mathsf{ID_I}}, m_3' \leftarrow (t_3 \| \mathsf{EAD_3})$
$c_3 \leftarrow \boxed{\mathcal{E}'(\mathsf{sk_3}, \mathsf{IV_3}; m_3; "")\ |\ \mathcal{E}(\mathsf{sk_3}, m_3)}$

$\xrightarrow{\quad c_3, m_3' \quad}$

RespRun2($\mathsf{ID}, \mathsf{st}, \mathsf{peerpk}, c_3$)
$\mathsf{TH_3} \leftarrow \mathcal{H}(\mathsf{TH_2}, m_2)$
$\mathsf{sk_3} \leftarrow \mathsf{HKDF\text{-}Expand}(\mathsf{PRK}_{3e2m}, 3, \mathsf{TH_3}, \boxed{\ell_{\mathsf{key}}\ |\ \ell_{\mathsf{id}}})$
$\boxed{\mathsf{IV_3} \leftarrow \mathsf{HKDF\text{-}Expand}(\mathsf{PRK}_{3e2m}, 4, \mathsf{TH_3}, \ell_{\mathsf{iv}})\ |\ \emptyset}$
$m_3 \leftarrow \boxed{\mathcal{D}'(\mathsf{sk_3}, \mathsf{IV_3}; c_3; "")\ |\ \mathcal{D}(\mathsf{sk_3}, c_3)}$
parse m_3 as $\boxed{(\mathsf{ID_I} \| t_3 \| \mathsf{EAD_3})\ |\ \mathsf{ID_I}}$ and m_3' as $(t_3 \| \mathsf{EAD_3})$
$X_s \leftarrow \mathsf{peerpk}[\mathsf{ID_I}]$
$\mathsf{salt}_{4e3m} \leftarrow \mathsf{HKDF\text{-}Expand}(\mathsf{PRK}_{3e2m}, 5, \mathsf{TH_3}, \ell_{\mathsf{hash}})$
$\mathsf{PRK}_{4e3m} \leftarrow \mathsf{HKDF\text{-}Extract}(\mathsf{salt}_{4e3m}, X_s^{y_e})$
$\mathsf{accepted} \leftarrow 1$
$\mathsf{CTX_3} \leftarrow (\mathsf{ID_I} \| \mathsf{TH_3} \| X_s \| \mathsf{EAD_3})$
$t_3' \leftarrow \mathsf{HKDF\text{-}Expand}(\mathsf{PRK}_{4e3m}, 6, \mathsf{CTX_3}, \boxed{\ell_{\mathsf{mac}}\ |\ \kappa_{\mathsf{sec}}})$
if $t_3' \neq t_3 : \mathbf{return} \perp$
$\mathsf{TH_4} \leftarrow \mathcal{H}(\mathsf{TH_3}, m_3, m_3')$
$\mathsf{sk_4} \leftarrow \mathsf{HKDF\text{-}Expand}(\mathsf{PRK}_{4e3m}, 8, \mathsf{TH_4}, \ell_{\mathsf{key}})$
$\mathsf{IV_4} \leftarrow \mathsf{HKDF\text{-}Expand}(\mathsf{PRK}_{4e3m}, 9, \mathsf{TH_4}, \ell_{\mathsf{iv}})$
$m_4 \leftarrow "", m_4' \leftarrow \mathsf{EAD_4}$
$c_4 \leftarrow \mathcal{E}'(\mathsf{sk_4}, \mathsf{IV_4}; m_4; m_4')$

$\xleftarrow{\quad c_4, m_4' \quad}$

$\mathsf{TH_4} \leftarrow \mathcal{H}(\mathsf{TH_3}, m_3, m_3')$
$\mathsf{sk_4} \leftarrow \mathsf{HKDF\text{-}Expand}(\mathsf{PRK}_{4e3m}, 8, \mathsf{TH_4}, \ell_{\mathsf{key}})$
$\mathsf{IV_4} \leftarrow \mathsf{HKDF\text{-}Expand}(\mathsf{PRK}_{4e3m}, 9, \mathsf{TH_4}, \ell_{\mathsf{iv}})$
if $\mathcal{D}'(\mathsf{sk_4}, \mathsf{IV_4}; c_4; m_4') = \perp : \mathbf{return} \perp$
$\mathsf{PRK_{out}} \leftarrow \mathsf{HKDF\text{-}Expand}(\mathsf{PRK}_{4e3m}, 7, \mathsf{TH_4}, \ell_{\mathsf{hash}})$ $\mathsf{PRK_{out}} \leftarrow \mathsf{HKDF\text{-}Expand}(\mathsf{PRK}_{4e3m}, 7, \mathsf{TH_4}, \ell_{\mathsf{hash}})$
$\mathsf{terminated} \leftarrow 1$ $\mathsf{terminated} \leftarrow 1$
$\mathsf{SK} \leftarrow \mathsf{PRK_{out}}$ $\mathsf{SK} \leftarrow \mathsf{PRK_{out}}$

Fig. 3. Optimized EDHOC with four messages in the STAT/STAT Authentication Method. Our modifications compared to [10] (draft-ietf-lake-edhoc-15) are represented by $\boxed{\text{previous}\ |\ \textbf{new}}$ and additions by gray highlights

when knowing the Initiator ephemeral key x_e, as PRK_{3e2m} does not depend on x_s, the long term secret key of the Initiator. In order to break the Initiator authentication, with respect to a Responder, an adversary can play on behalf of any user as an Initiator. It will be able to compute sk_3, but not t_3, for which value it will need some luck, but this is only 64-bit long! Which is not enough for a 128-bit security.

To get around this issue, we suggest to modify the construction of Initiator's second message as follows: Initial message $m_3 = (\mathsf{ID}_\mathsf{I}\|t_3\|\mathsf{EAD}_3)$ is split as $m_3 \leftarrow (\mathsf{ID}_\mathsf{I})$ and $m_3' \leftarrow (t_3\|\mathsf{EAD}_3)^2$. Thus, m_3 is encrypted using sk_3 (with a one-time pad encryption scheme $\Pi = (\mathcal{E}, \mathcal{D})$, under sk_3 still depending on PRK_{3e2m}) into c_3. Then m_3' does not need to be encrypted. We introduce the value κ_{sec}, always set as the expected bit-security parameter, independently of the ℓ_{mac} value. Then, we set the length of t_3 to be κ_{sec}, as it already authenticates $\mathsf{CTX}_3 = (\mathsf{ID}_\mathsf{I}\|\mathsf{TH}_3\|X_s\|\mathsf{EAD}_3)$. Concretely, the second message sent by the initiator to the responder is: $c_3\|m_3'$, where $c_3 = \mathcal{E}(\mathsf{sk}_3, m_3), m_3' = t_3\|\mathsf{EAD}_3$. Once the Responder receives (c_3, m_3'), he first decrypts c_3, retrieves X_s using m_3, computes PRK_{4e3m} and is then able to verify the tag t_3, allowing to check the authenticity of ID_I, as well as all the other values is $\mathsf{CTX}_3 = \mathsf{ID}_\mathsf{I}\|\mathsf{TH}_3\|X_s\|\mathsf{EAD}_3$. The extra required length for the tag t_3 is perfectly compensated by the absence of the tag jointly sent when using Authenticated Encryption, and the plaintext length of m_3 is the same as the encryption of m_3. Therefore, this does not impact the communication cost of the protocol, until $\kappa_{\mathsf{sec}} \leq 2 \times \ell_{\mathsf{mac}}$, but improves to κ_{sec}-bit security for Initiator-Authentication.

About the Responder-Authentication, t_2 also provides a 64-bit security level only: by guessing it, any active adversary can make the initiator terminate, and thus breaking the responder-authentication, if one does not wait for the fourth flow c_4, m_4'. However, with this fourth flow, we can show the $2 \times \ell_{\mathsf{mac}}$-bit security level is achieved.

3.2   On Reduction Efficiency

After analysis, we also notice another improvement: the key PRK_{2e} is computed according to $g^{x_e y_e}$ only, as the salt used in HKDF-Extractis an empty string. When considering several parellels sessions, this allows an adversary to find a collision with any of the session making a single call to HKDF-Extract. Therefore, we replace the empty string used as salt with TH_2 that depends on the session variables and is different for each session. Thus, an adversary has to make a call to HKDF-Extract with a chosen TH_2, linked to a specific session. This makes the reduction cost of the key-privacy game independent of the number of sessions.

4   Security Analysis

Security Goals. The security goals of an authenticated key exchange protocol are:

---

[2] One can move EAD_3 in m_3, if privacy is required. It is still secure with any one-time secure encryption, but increasing the key size in the particular case of one-time pad.

- *Key Privacy*: Equivalent to Implicit Authentication. **At most both** participants know the final session key, which should remain indistinguishable from random to outsiders. With additional *Perfect Forward Secrecy*, by compromising the long-term credential of either peer, an attacker shall not be able to distinguish past session keys from random keys. In our context, this will rely on a Diffie-Hellman assumption.
- *Mutual Authentication*: Equivalent to explicit authentication. **Exactly both** participants have the material to compute the final session key.
- *Identity Protection*: **At most both** participants know the identity of the Initiator and the Responder. While the identity of the Initiator should be protected against active adversaries, the identity of the Responder should be protected against passive adversaries only.

Random Oracle Model. For the security analysis, we model Hash and Key Derivation Functions as random oracles. Respectively, the random oracles RO_T and RO_P will model HKDF-Extract and HKDF-Expand functions as perfect random functions.

4.1   Key Privacy

We describe in Fig. 4 the security game introduced in [5] following the framework by Bellare *et al.* [1]. After initializing the game, the adversary $\mathcal{A}$ is given multiple access to the following queries:

- NewUser: Generates a new user by generating a new pair of keys.
- Send: Controls activation and message processing of sessions
- SessionKeyReveal: Reveals the session key of a terminated session.
- LongTermKeyReveal: Corrupts a user and reveals its long term secret key.
- Test: Provides a real-or-random challenge on the session key of the queried session.

Then, the adversary makes a single call to the Finalize algorithm, which returns the result of the predicate $[b' = b]$, where b' is the guess of $\mathcal{A}$ and b is the challenge bit, after succeeding through the Sound and Fresh predicates.

The advantage of an adversary $\mathcal{A}$ against the key privacy is its bias in guessing b, from the random choice: $\mathbf{Adv}^{\mathsf{kp-ake}}(\mathcal{A}) = \Pr[b' = b] - 1/2$. A formalized description of the EDHOC protocol can be found in the full version [4]. It is compliant with the security game made in Fig. 4. The protocol is analyzed in the random oracle model, therefore, HKDF can be substituted by respective random oracles.

Theorem 1. *The above EDHOC protocol satisfies the key privacy property under the Gap Diffie-Hellman problem in the Random Oracle model. More precisely, with q_{RO} representing the global number of queries to the random oracles, N the number of users, and ℓ_{hash} the hash digest length, $\mathbf{Adv}^{\mathsf{kp-ake}}_{\mathsf{EDHOC}}(t; q_{RO}, N)$ is upper-bounded by*

$$(2N + 1) \cdot \mathbf{Adv}^{\mathsf{GDH}}_{\mathbb{G}}(t, q_{RO}) + \frac{q_{RO}^2 + 4}{2^{\ell_{\mathsf{hash}}+1}}$$

Initialize ()

1 : time ← 0
2 : users ← 0
3 : $b \leftarrow\$ \{0,1\}$

NewUser ()

1 : users ← users + 1
2 : $(\mathsf{pk}_{\mathsf{users}}, \mathsf{sk}_{\mathsf{users}}) \leftarrow\$ \mathsf{KGen}$
3 : $\mathsf{revltk}_{\mathsf{users}} \leftarrow \infty$
4 : $\mathsf{peerpk}[\mathsf{users}] \leftarrow \mathsf{pk}_{\mathsf{users}}$
5 : return $\mathsf{pk}_{\mathsf{users}}$

LongTermKeyReveal(u)

1 : time ← time + 1
2 : $\mathsf{revltk}_u \leftarrow$ time
3 : return sk_u

SessionKeyReveal(u, i)

1 : if $\pi_u^i = \bot$ or
       $\pi_u^i.\text{status} \neq$ accepted :
2 :   return $\bot$
3 : $\pi_u^i.revealed \leftarrow$ **true**
4 : return $\pi_u^i.\text{SK}$

Finalize(b')

1 : if ¬Sound :
2 :   return 1
3 : if ¬Fresh :
4 : $b' \leftarrow 0$
5 : return $[b = b']$

Send(u, i, m)

1 : if $\pi_u^i = \bot$:
2 :   (peerid, role) ← m
3 : $(\pi_u^i, m') \leftarrow\$ \mathsf{Activate}(u, \mathsf{sk}_u, \text{peerid}, \text{peerpk}, \text{role})$
4 : $\pi_u^i.t_{acc} \leftarrow 0$
5 : else :
6 : $(\pi_u^i, m') \leftarrow\$ \mathsf{Run}(u, \mathsf{sk}_u, \pi_u^i, \text{peerpk}, \text{role})$
7 : if $\pi_u^i.\text{status} =$ accepted :
8 :   time ← time + 1
9 : $\pi_u^i.t_{acc} \leftarrow$ time
10 : return m'

Test(u, i)

1 : if $\pi_u^i = \bot$ or
       $\pi_u^i.\text{status} \neq$ accepted or $\pi_u^i.\text{tested}$:
2 :   return $\bot$
3 : $\pi_u^i.\text{tested} \leftarrow$ **true**
4 : $T \leftarrow T \cup \{\pi_u^i\}$
5 : $k_0 \leftarrow \pi_u^i.\text{SK}$
6 : $k_1 \leftarrow\$ \mathsf{KE.KS}$
7 : return k_b

Sound

1 : if ∃ distinct $\pi_u^i, \pi_v^j, \pi_w^k$ with $\pi_u^i.\text{sid} = \pi_v^j.\text{sid} = \pi_w^k.\text{sid}$:
2 :   return false
3 : if $\exists \pi_u^i, \pi_v^j$ with
4 : $\pi_u^i.\text{status} = \pi_v^j.\text{status} =$ accepted
5 :   and $\pi_u^i.\text{sid} = \pi_v^j.\text{sid}$
6 :   and $\pi_u^i.\text{peerid} = u$ and $\pi_v^j.\text{peerid} = v$
7 :   and $\pi_u^i.\text{role} \neq \pi_v^j.\text{role}$, but $\pi_u^i.\text{SK} \neq \pi_v^j.\text{SK}$
8 :   return false
9 : return true

Fresh

1 : $\forall \pi_u^i \in T$
2 :   if $\pi_u^i.\text{revealed}$
          or $\mathsf{revltk}_{\pi_u^i.\text{peerid}} < \pi_u^i.t_{acc}$:
3 :   return false
4 :   if $\exists \pi_v^j \neq \pi_u^i$ s.t.
          $\pi_u^i.\text{sid} = \pi_u^i.\text{sid}$ and
          ($\pi_v^j.\text{tested}$ or $\pi_v^j.\text{revealed}$) :
5 :   return false
6 : return true

Fig. 4. Authenticated Key Exchange Key Privacy Security Game $G_{\mathsf{AKE},\mathcal{A}}^{\mathsf{kp-ake}}$

Game G_0. This game is the key privacy security game $G_{\mathsf{AKE},\mathcal{A}}^{\mathsf{kp-ake}}$ (defined in Fig. 4) played by $\mathcal{A}$ using the KeyGen, Activate and Run algorithms. The KeyGen algorithm generates a long term pair of key, calling Activate with an user with identity u, $\mathcal{A}$ creates its i-th session with u, denoted π_u^i.

$$\Pr[\textsc{Succ}_0] = \Pr[G_{\mathsf{AKE},\mathcal{A}}^{\mathsf{kp-ake}}],$$

where the event $\textsc{Succ}$ means $b' = b$.

We stress that in this security model, with Perfect Forward Secrecy, we use the weak definition of corruption, meaning that a query to LongTermKeyReveal only reveals the long-term key, while the ephemeral key remains unrevealed. We say a party/session is non-corrupted if no query to LongTermKeyReveal has been made before the time of acceptance t_{acc}, where we consider each block (InitRun1, InitRun2, RespRun1, RespRun2) as atomic. Then corruptions can only happen between two calls to simulated players.

Game G_1. In this game, we simulate the random oracles by lists that are empty at the beginning of the game. As RO_T and $\mathcal{H}$ always return a digest of size ℓ_{hash}, we simply use the simulation oracle SO_T and $SO_{\mathcal{H}}$ respectively. However, RO_P may return values of several lengths. We thus define a simulation oracle by digest size: SO_P^{size}, for size in $\{\ell_2, \ell_{\mathsf{id}}, \ell_{\mathsf{hash}}, \ell_{\mathsf{key}}, \ell_{\mathsf{iv}}, \ell_{\mathsf{mac}}, \kappa_{\mathsf{sec}}\}$

The simulation oracles SO_P and $SO_{\mathcal{H}}$ work as the usual way of simulating the answer with a new random answer for any new query, and the same answer if the same query is asked again. For the simulation oracles SO_T, the oracle consists in a list that contains elements of the form $(\mathsf{str}, Z, (X, Y); \lambda)$, where when first set, either Z or (X, Y) is non-empty. Indeed, when making a call to a random oracle, the official query is of the form (str, Z), where str is any bit string, that can be empty or a pseudo-random key, and Z is a Diffie-Hellman value. Then, the simulator checks in the list for an entry matching with $(\mathsf{str}, Z, *; \lambda)$. If such an element is found, one outputs λ, otherwise one randomly set $\lambda \xleftarrow{\$} \{0, 1\}^{\kappa}$ and append $(\mathsf{str}, Z, \bot; \lambda)$ to the list. But later, the simulator will also ask queries of the form $(\mathsf{str}, (X, Y))$, where (X, Y) is a pair of group elements. Then one checks in the list for an entry matching with either $(\mathsf{str}, *, (X, Y); \lambda)$ or $(\mathsf{str}, Z, *; \lambda)$ such that $\mathsf{DDH}(g, X, Y, Z) = 1$. If such an element is found, one outputs λ, otherwise one randomly set $\lambda \xleftarrow{\$} \{0, 1\}^{\kappa}$ and append $(\mathsf{str}, \bot, (X, Y); \lambda)$ to the list. When such new kinds of elements exist in the list, for the first kind of queries (str, Z), one checks in the list for an entry matching with either $(\mathsf{str}, Z, *; \lambda)$ as before, or $(\mathsf{str}, *, (X, Y); \lambda)$ such that $\mathsf{DDH}(g, X, Y, Z) = 1$. Thanks to the DDH oracle, this simulation is perfect, and is thus indistinguishable to the adversary: $\Pr[\mathrm{Succ}_0] = \Pr[\mathrm{Succ}_{-1}]$.

Game G_2. In order to prevent collisions in the future PRK generation, we modify the simulation oracles $SO_T, SO_P^{\ell_{\mathsf{hash}}}$ and $SO_{\mathcal{H}}$, such that if a collision occurs, the simulator stops. From the birthday paradox bound, we have:

$$\Pr[\mathrm{Succ}_0] - \Pr[\mathrm{Succ}_{-1}] \leq \frac{q_{SO_T}{}^2 + q_{SO_P^{\ell_{\mathsf{hash}}}}{}^2 + q_{SO_{\mathcal{H}}}{}^2}{2^{\ell_{\mathsf{hash}}+1}}.$$

Game G_3. One can note that thanks to the above simulation of the random oracles, the simulator does not need anymore to compute Diffie-Hellman values. Then, for every simulated player, the simulator generates X_e or Y_e at random in the group, and the simulation is still performed as in the previous game. As corruption queries only reveal long-term secret, still known to the simulator, the view of the adversary is perfectly indistinguishable of the previous game and we have: $\Pr[\mathrm{Succ}_0] = \Pr[\mathrm{Succ}_{-1}]$.

Game G_4. In this game, when simulating any **initiator** receiving a forged tuple $(Y_e, c_2, \mathsf{C_R})$ from the adversary in the name of a **non-corrupted user**, one simulates PRK_{3e2m} thanks to a private oracle $SO_{\mathsf{PRK}_{3e2m}}$, which makes it perfectly unpredictable to the adversary. If the pair $(Y_e, \mathsf{C_R})$ is forged, TH_2 and salt_{3e2m} are different from the values obtained by a possibly simulated responder, thanks to the absence of collisions as they are respectively computed using $\mathsf{SO}_{\mathcal{H}}$ and $\mathsf{SO}_P^{\ell_{\mathsf{hash}}}$. Otherwise, sk_2 is not modified. So if the ciphertext c_2 is forged, thanks to the injective property of the one-time pad encryption scheme $(\mathcal{E}, \mathcal{D})$ when the key is fixed, m_2, then TH_3 and salt_{4e3m} are different from the values obtained by a possibly simulated responder. In order to detect the inconsistency of PRK_{3e2m} with respect to the public oracle answer, the adversary must have asked SO_T on the correct Diffie-Hellman value $X_e{}^{y_s}$. We denote the event F_1, that query $X_e{}^{y_s}$ is asked whereas y_s is the long-term secret key of a non-corrupted user and X_e has been generated by the simulator. If this event happens (which can easily be checked as the simulator knows y_s), one stops the simulation: $|\Pr[\mathrm{Succ}_0] - \Pr[\mathrm{Succ}_{-1}]| \leq \Pr[F_1]$.

Game $\mathbf{G}_{4'}$. We now provide an upper-bound on $\Pr[F_1]$: given a GDH challenge $(X = g^x, Y = g^y)$, one simulates all the X_e as $X_e = X \cdot g^r$, for random $r \overset{\$}{\leftarrow} \mathbb{Z}_p$, but chooses one user to set $Y_s = Y$. Even if y_s is therefore not known, simulation is still feasible as the simulator can make query to the SO_T oracle with input (X_e, Y_s). Then, one can still answer all the corruption queries, excepted for that user. But anyway, if F_1 happens on that user, this user must be non-corrupted at that time: one has solved the GDH problem, and one can stop the simulation. If the guess on the user is incorrect, one can also stop the simulation: $\Pr[F_1] \leq N \cdot \mathbf{Adv}_{\mathbb{G}}^{\mathsf{GDH}}(t, q_{\mathsf{RO}})$, where N is the number of users in the system.

Game $\mathbf{G}_5$. In this game, when simulating any **responder** receiving a forged message m_1 from the adversary in the name of a **non-corrupted user**, still non-corrupted when sending c_3 to RespRun2, one simulates PRK_{4e3m} thanks to a private oracle $\mathsf{SO}_{\mathsf{PRK}_{4e3m}}$, which makes it perfectly unpredictable to the adversary. Since m_1 is forged, thanks to the absence of collisions, $\mathsf{TH}_2, \mathsf{TH}_3$, and salt_{4e3m} are different from the values obtained by a possibly simulated responder. In order to detect the inconsistency of PRK_{4e3m} with respect to the public oracle answer, the adversary must have asked SO_T on the correct Diffie-Hellman value $Y_e{}^{x_s}$. We denote the event F_2, that query $Y_e{}^{x_s}$ is asked whereas x_s is the long-term secret key of a non-corrupted user and Y_e has been generated by the simulator. If this event happens, as above, one stops the simulation: $|\Pr[\mathrm{Succ}_0] - \Pr[\mathrm{Succ}_{-1}]| \leq \Pr[F_2]$.

Game $\mathbf{G}_{5'}$. We now provide an upper-bound on $\Pr[F_2]$: given a GDH challenge $(X = g^x, Y = g^y)$, one simulates all the Y_e as $Y_e = Y \cdot g^{r'}$, for random $r' \overset{\$}{\leftarrow} \mathbb{Z}_p$, but chooses one user to set $X_s = X$. Then, one can still answer all the corruption queries, excepted for that user. But anyway, if F_2 happens on that user, this user must be non-corrupted at that time: one has solved the GDH problem, and one can stop the simulation. If the guess on the user is incorrect, one can also stop the simulation: $\Pr[F_2] \leq N \cdot \mathbf{Adv}_{\mathbb{G}}^{\mathsf{GDH}}(t, q_{\mathsf{RO}})$.

Game $\mathbf{G}_6$. In this game, we simulate the key generation of PRK_{2e}, for all the passive sessions (m_1 received by a simulated responder comes from a simulated initiator, or $(Y_e, c_2, \mathsf{C_R})$ received by a simulated initiator comes from a simulated responder, and both used the same m_1 as first message), thanks to a private oracle $\mathsf{SO}_{\mathsf{PRK}_{2e}}$, acting in the same vein as SO_T, but not available to the adversary. This makes a difference with the previous game if the key PRK_{2e} has also been generated by asking SO_T on the correct Diffie-Hellman value $Z = g^{x_e y_e}$. We denote by F_3 the latter event, and stop the simulation in such a case: $|\Pr[\text{Succ}_0] - \Pr[\text{Succ}_{-1}]| \le \Pr[F_3]$.

Game $G_{6'}$. We now provide an upper-bound on $\Pr[F_3]$. Given a GDH challenge $(X = g^x, Y = g^y)$, one simulates all the X_e as $X_e = X \cdot g^r$, for random $r \xleftarrow{\$} \mathbb{Z}_p$, and all the Y_e as $Y_e = Y \cdot g^{r'}$, for random $r' \xleftarrow{\$} \mathbb{Z}_p$. As the key PRK_{2e} now depends on the session context, any query Z to the SO_T oracle can make F_3 occurs on a single pair $(X_e = X \cdot g^r, Y_e = Y \cdot g^{r'})$. Hence, q_{RO} DDH-oracle queries might be useful to detect F_3 on an input $Z = \text{CDH}(X_e, Y_e) = g^{xy} \cdot X^{r'} \cdot Y^r \cdot g^{rr'}$, solving the GDH challenge (X, Y): $\Pr[F_3] \le \mathbf{Adv}_{\mathbb{G}}^{\text{GDH}}(t, q_{\text{RO}})$.

Game G_7. In this game, when simulating any **initiator** receiving the second message $(Y_e, c_2, \mathsf{C_R})$, from the adversary in the name of a **non-corrupted user**, one simulates PRK_{3e2m} thanks to a private oracle $\text{SO}_{\text{PRK}_{3e2m}}$. This makes a difference with the previous game only if this is a passive session, in which case PRK_{2e} is unpredictable, and thus different from the public one excepted with probability $2^{-\ell_{\text{hash}}}$. As there are no collisions, salt_{3e2m} is different from the value obtained by a possibly simulated responder. In order to detect the inconsistency of PRK_{3e2m} with respect to the public oracle answer, the adversary must have asked SO_T on the correct Diffie-Hellman value $X_e^{y_s}$, which is not possible as event F_1 already stops the simulation. Hence, we just have $|\Pr[\text{Succ}_0] - \Pr[\text{Succ}_{-1}]| \le 2^{-\ell_{\text{hash}}}$.

Game G_8. In this game, when simulating any **initiator** receiving the second message $(Y_e, c_2, \mathsf{C_R})$, from the adversary in the name of a **non-corrupted user**, one simulates PRK_{4e3m} thanks to a private oracle $\text{SO}_{\text{PRK}_{4e3m}}$. In this case, PRK_{3e2m} is unpredictable, as well as salt_{4e3m} and PRK_{4e3m}: $\Pr[\text{Succ}_0] = \Pr[\text{Succ}_{-1}]$.

Game G_9. In this game, when simulating any **responder** receiving c_3, from the adversary in the name of a **non-corrupted user**, one simulates PRK_{4e3m} thanks to the private oracle $\text{SO}_{\text{PRK}_{4e3m}}$. This makes a difference with the previous game only if this is not a passive session, in which case PRK_{2e} is unpredictable, and thus different from the public one excepted with probability $2^{-\ell_{\text{hash}}}$. As there are no collisions, salt_{3e2m}, PRK_{3e2m}, and salt_{4e3m} are different from the values obtained by a possibly simulated responder. In order to detect the inconsistency of PRK_{4e3m} with respect to the public oracle answer, the adversary must have asked SO_T on the correct Diffie-Hellman value $Y_e^{x_s}$, which is not possible as event F_2 already stops the simulation: $|\Pr[\text{Succ}_0] - \Pr[\text{Succ}_{-1}]| \le 2^{-\ell_{\text{hash}}}$.

Game G_{10}. In this game, for any fresh session, one simulates PRK_{out} thanks to the private oracle $\text{SO}_{\text{PRK}_{\text{out}}}$. A session being fresh means that no corruption of the party or of the partner occurred before the time of acceptance: the initiator is not corrupted before receiving $(Y_e, c_2, \mathsf{C_R})$ and the responder is not corrupted before receiving c_3. By consequent, they are not corrupted before PRK_{4e3m} was computed. We have seen above that in those cases, the key PRK_{4e3m} is generated using the private oracle $\text{SO}_{\text{PRK}_{4e3m}}$: it is unpredictable. The use of the private oracle $\text{SO}_{\text{PRK}_{\text{out}}}$ can only be detected if the query PRK_{4e3m} is asked to SO_P: $|\Pr[\text{Succ}_0] - \Pr[\text{Succ}_{-1}]| \le q_{\text{SO}_P^{\ell_{\text{hash}}}} \times 2^{-\ell_{\text{hash}}}$.

Globally, one can note that the gap between the initial and the last games is upper-bounded by

$$(2N+1) \cdot \mathbf{Adv}_{\mathbb{G}}^{\mathsf{GDH}}(t, q_{\mathsf{RO}}) + \frac{q_{\mathsf{SO}_T}^2 + q_{\mathsf{SO}_P}^{\ell_{\mathsf{hash}}} + q_{\mathsf{SO}_{\mathcal{H}}}^2}{2^{\ell_{\mathsf{hash}}+1}} + \frac{2 + q_{\mathsf{SO}_P}^{\ell_{\mathsf{hash}}}}{2^{\ell_{\mathsf{hash}}}}$$

$$\leq (2N+1) \cdot \mathbf{Adv}_{\mathbb{G}}^{\mathsf{GDH}}(t, q_{\mathsf{RO}}) + \frac{q_{\mathsf{RO}}^2 + 4}{2^{\ell_{\mathsf{hash}}+1}}$$

Eventually, for all the fresh sessions, in the real case ($b = 0$), the private oracle is used, and outputs a random key, while in the random case ($b = 1$), the session key is random too: $\Pr[\mathrm{SUCC}_0] = 1/2$. This concludes the proof.

4.2   Explicit Authentication

Explicit authentication (or mutual authentication) aims to ensure each participant has the material to compute the final session key (accepts) when the partner terminates. In the EDHOC protocol, this means the responder (resp. the initiator) owns the private long-term key y_s (resp x_s) associated to the long-term public key Y_s (resp. X_s), and the private ephemeral keys, when the partner terminates (Fig. 5).

Finalize

1:    **return** :

$$\forall \pi_u^i \text{ s.t.} \begin{cases} \pi_u^i.\mathsf{status} = \mathsf{terminated} \\ \pi_u^i.t_{acc} < \mathsf{revltk}_{\pi_u^i.\mathsf{peerid}} \end{cases}, \exists \pi_v^j \text{ s.t.} \begin{cases} \pi_u^i.\mathsf{peerid} = v \\ \pi_v^j.\mathsf{peerid} = u \\ \pi_u^i.\mathsf{sid} = \pi_v^j.\mathsf{sid} \\ \pi_u^i.\mathsf{role} \neq \pi_v^j.\mathsf{role} \\ \pi_v^j.\mathsf{status} = \mathsf{accepted} \end{cases}$$

Fig. 5. Finalize Function for the Explicit Authentication Security Game

To do so, the responder uses y_s in RespRun1 to compute PRK_{3e2m} used for the tag t_2 and the key sk_3. In the same way, the initiator uses x_s to compute PRK_{4e3m}, used for the tag t_3. Furthermore, they both have to use their ephemeral keys to compute PRK_{2e}, used for sk_2.

Responder Authentication. Consider a simulated **initiator** receiving a forged message $(Y_e, c_2, \mathsf{C_R})$ from the adversary in the name of a **non-corrupted user**. In such a case, consider the modifications made in the key privacy proof up to the game G_7. Hence, we have replaced the generation of PRK_{3e2m} with a private oracle. Then the advantage of the adversary in breaking the explicit authentication of the responder in this game is bounded by $2^{-\ell_{\mathsf{mac}}}$, added to the gap induced by the modifications made up to the game G_7. This leads to the following theorem:

Theorem 2. *The above EDHOC protocol satisfies the responder-authentication property under the Gap Diffie-Hellman problem in the Random Oracle model. More precisely, with q_{RO} representing the global number of queries to the random oracles, N the number of users, ℓ_{hash} the hash digest length and ℓ_{mac} the MAC digest length, we have $\mathbf{Adv}_{EDHOC}^{auth-resp}(t; q_{RO}, N)$ is upper-bounded by*

$$(2N + 1) \cdot \mathbf{Adv}_{\mathbb{G}}^{GDH}(t, q_{RO}) + \frac{q_{RO}^2 + 2}{2^{\ell_{hash}+1}} + \frac{1}{2^{\ell_{mac}}}.$$

Optimal Reduction. One cannot expect more after these three flows, as the adversary can play the role of the responder with known y_e. Without knowing y_s, it just gets stuck to compute PRK_{3e2m} and thus t_2. But it can guess it (with probability $2^{-\ell_{mac}}$), breaking authentication. But it will not know SK. However, by waiting for the fourth message containing an authenticated encryption c_4, as said in the documentation, this will add a factor $\mathbf{Adv}_{\Pi'}^{uf\text{-}cma}(t) \approx 2^{-\ell_{mac}}$ to the Responder Authentication security: $\mathbf{Adv}_{EDHOC}^{auth-resp}(t; q_{RO}, N)$ is upper-bounded by

$$(2N + 1) \cdot \mathbf{Adv}_{\mathbb{G}}^{GDH}(t, q_{RO}) + \frac{q_{RO}^2 + 2}{2^{\ell_{hash}+1}} + \frac{1}{2^{\ell_{mac}}} \times \mathbf{Adv}_{\Pi'}^{uf\text{-}cma}(t).$$

Initiator Authentication. We now consider any **responder** receiving a forged message c_3 from the adversary in the name of a **non-corrupted user**. As above, considering the modifications made in the key privacy proof up to the game G_8, we have replaced the generation of PRK_{4e3m} with a private oracle. Then the advantage of the adversary in breaking the explicit authentication of the initiator in this game is bounded by $\frac{1}{2^{\kappa_{sec}}}$. Added to the gap induced by the modifications made up to the game G_7. This leads to the following theorem:

Theorem 3. *The above EDHOC protocol satisfies the initiator-authentication property under the Gap Diffie-Hellman problem in the Random Oracle model. More precisely, with q_{RO} representing the global number of queries to the random oracles, N the number of users, ℓ_{hash} the hash digest length and κ_{sec} the expected bit-security, we have $\mathbf{Adv}_{EDHOC}^{auth-init}(t; q_{RO}, N)$ upper-bounded by*

$$(2N + 1) \cdot \mathbf{Adv}_{\mathbb{G}}^{GDH}(t, q_{RO}) + \frac{q_{RO}^2 + 4}{2^{\ell_{hash}+1}} + \frac{1}{2^{\kappa_{sec}}}.$$

4.3   Identity Protection

Let us now consider anonymity, with identity protection. More precisely, we want to show that the initiator's identity ($\mathsf{ID_I}$) is protected against active adversaries, while responder's identity ($\mathsf{ID_R}$) is protected only against passive adversaries.

The values $\mathsf{ID_I}$ and $\mathsf{ID_R}$ are the authentication credentials containing the public authentication keys of the Initiator and the Responder, respectively.

Both those values are sent to the other respective party using One-Time Pad encryption, that perfectly protects the privacy. Then, in one hand we have $\mathsf{ID_R}$ that is part of $\mathsf{CTX_2}$ used to compute t_2 and in the other hand, we have $\mathsf{ID_I}$ that is part of $\mathsf{CTX_3}$ used to compute t_3. We thus define the similar responder and initiator identity protection experiment as follows:

$\mathbf{Exp}_{\mathsf{EDHOC}}^{\mathsf{ID-resp}-b}$

1 : $\mathsf{ID}_{\mathsf{R}_0}, \mathsf{ID}_{\mathsf{R}_1} \leftarrow \mathcal{A}(\mathsf{peerid})$
2 : $m_1 \leftarrow \mathcal{A}(\mathsf{InitRun1}(.))$
3 : $b \leftarrow \{0,1\}$
4 : $\mathsf{ID}_{\mathsf{R}} \leftarrow \mathsf{ID}_{\mathsf{R}_b}$
5 : $y_s \leftarrow \mathsf{sk}_{\mathsf{ID}_{\mathsf{R}}}$
6 : $(Y_e, c_2, \mathsf{C}_{\mathsf{R}}) \leftarrow \mathsf{RespRun1}(\mathsf{ID}_{\mathsf{R}}, y_s, m_1)$
7 : $b' \leftarrow \mathcal{A}(c_2)$
8 : $\mathbf{return}\ b = b'$

$\mathbf{Exp}_{\mathsf{EDHOC}}^{\mathsf{ID-init}-b}$

1 : $\mathsf{ID}_{\mathsf{I}_0}, \mathsf{ID}_{\mathsf{I}_1} \leftarrow \mathcal{A}(\mathsf{peerid})$
2 : $(Y_e, c_2, \mathsf{C}_{\mathsf{R}}) \leftarrow \mathcal{A}(\mathsf{RespRun1}(.))$
3 : $b \leftarrow \{0,1\}$
4 : $\mathsf{ID}_{\mathsf{I}} \leftarrow \mathsf{ID}_{\mathsf{I}_b}$
5 : $x_s \leftarrow \mathsf{sk}_{\mathsf{ID}_{\mathsf{I}}}$
6 : $Y_s \leftarrow \mathsf{peerpk}[\mathsf{ID}_{\mathsf{I}}]$
7 : $c_3 \leftarrow \mathsf{InitRun2}(\mathsf{ID}_{\mathsf{I}}, x_s, Y_s, (Y_e, c_2, \mathsf{C}_{\mathsf{R}}))$
8 : $b' \leftarrow \mathcal{A}(c_3)$
9 : $\mathbf{return}\ b = b'$

In both cases, we consider the modifications made in the key privacy proof up to the game G_7, making PRK_{2e} and PRK_{3e4m} random, and by consequent, so are sk_2 and sk_3.

Responder Identity Protection. The responder's identity has to be protected against passive adversaries only. To distinguish $\mathbf{Exp}_{\mathsf{EDHOC}}^{\mathsf{ID-resp}-0}$ and $\mathbf{Exp}_{\mathsf{EDHOC}}^{\mathsf{ID-resp}-1}$, one must distinguish between an encryption of $\mathsf{ID}_{\mathsf{R}_0}$ and $\mathsf{ID}_{\mathsf{R}_1}$, as sk_2 is random, this implies breaking the injective property and the indistinguishability of $\Pi = (\mathcal{E}, \mathcal{D})$, both being perfect with the one-time pad.

Initiator Identity Protection. The initiator's identity has to be protected against active adversaries. However, if the adversary plays in the name of a responder, he will be detected with high probability with the tag t_2 before reaching game G_7. Therefore, distinguish between $\mathbf{Exp}_{\mathsf{EDHOC}}^{\mathsf{ID-init}-0}$ and $\mathbf{Exp}_{\mathsf{EDHOC}}^{\mathsf{ID-init}-1}$ also implies breaking the injective property and the indistinguishability of $\Pi = (\mathcal{E}, \mathcal{D})$, both being perfect with the one-time pad.

Theorem 4. *The above* EDHOC *protocol protects Initiator and Responder's Identity under the Gap Diffie-Hellman problem in the Random Oracle model. More precisely, with q_{RO} representing the global number of queries to the random oracles, N the number of users, and ℓ_{hash} the hash digest length, both advantages $\mathbf{Adv}_{\mathsf{EDHOC}}^{\mathsf{ID-init}-b}(t; q_{\mathsf{RO}}, N)$ and $\mathbf{Adv}_{\mathsf{EDHOC}}^{\mathsf{ID-resp}-b}(t; q_{\mathsf{RO}}, N)$ are upper-bounded by*

$$(2N + 1) \cdot \mathbf{Adv}_{\mathbb{G}}^{\mathsf{GDH}}(t, q_{\mathsf{RO}}) + \frac{q_{\mathsf{RO}}^2 + 2}{2^{\ell_{\mathsf{hash}}+1}}.$$

5   Conclusion

Our computational analysis proved the EDHOC protocol instantiated with the STAT-STAT authentication method, with $\ell_{\mathsf{mac}} = 64$ and $\kappa_{\mathsf{sec}} = 128$, provides nearly a 128-bit security level for key privacy and identity protection for both the responder and the initiator. In a three-flow scenario, Initiator Authentication reaches a 128-bit security level, using our improvements without extra-cost in our settings, but only a 64-bit security level for the responder. However, as suggested in their documentation, a fourth message using authenticated encryption (AEAD) from the responder to the initiator increases this security up to a 128-bit level. Hence, our improvement of EDHOC, at no communication cost, provides a global 128-bit security level.

Acknowledgments. This work was supported in part by the French ANR Project Crypto4Graph-AI.

References

1. Bellare, M., Rogaway, P.: The security of triple encryption and a framework for code-based game-playing proofs. In: Vaudenay, S. (ed.) EUROCRYPT 2006. LNCS, vol. 4004, pp. 409–426. Springer, Heidelberg (2006). https://doi.org/10.1007/11761679_25
2. Bruni, A., Sahl Jørgensen, T., Grønbech Petersen, T., Schürmann, C.: Formal verification of ephemeral Diffie-Hellman over COSE (EDHOC). In: Cremers, C., Lehmann, A. (eds.) SSR 2018. LNCS, vol. 11322, pp. 21–36. Springer, Cham (2018). https://doi.org/10.1007/978-3-030-04762-7_2
3. Cheval, V., Jacomme, C., Kremer, S., Künnemann, R.: SAPIC+: protocol verifiers of the world, unite! In: USENIX Security Symposium (USENIX Security) (2022)
4. Cottier, B., Pointcheval, D.: Security Analysis of Improved EDHOC Protocol. https://hal.inria.fr/hal-03772082
5. Davis, H., Günther, F.: Tighter proofs for the SIGMA and TLS 1.3 key exchange protocols. Cryptology ePrint Archive, Report 2020/1029 (2020). https://eprint.iacr.org/2020/1029
6. Jacomme, C., Klein, E., Kremer, S., Racouchot, M.: A comprehensive, formal and automated analysis of the EDHOC protocol. In: USENIX Security Symposium (USENIX Security) (2023, to appear)
7. Krawczyk, H.: SIGMA: the "SIGn-and-MAc" approach to authenticated Diffie-Hellman and its use in the IKE protocols. In: Boneh, D. (ed.) CRYPTO 2003. LNCS, vol. 2729, pp. 400–425. Springer, Heidelberg (2003). https://doi.org/10.1007/978-3-540-45146-4_24
8. Krawczyk, H., Wee, H.: The OPTLS protocol and TLS 1.3. In: 2016 IEEE European Symposium on Security and Privacy (EuroS&P 2016), pp. 81–96. IEEE Computer Society (2016). https://doi.org/10.1109/EuroSP.2016.18. https://eprint.iacr.org/2015/978
9. Norrman, K., Sundararajan, V., Bruni, A.: Formal analysis of EDHOC key establishment for constrained IoT devices. In: Proceedings of the 18th International Conference on Security and Cryptography (SECRYPT 2021), pp. 210–221. INSTICC, SciTePress (2021). https://doi.org/10.5220/0010554002100221. https://arxiv.org/abs/2007.11427
10. Selander, G., Mattsson, J.P., Palombini, F.: Ephemeral Diffie-Hellman over COSE (EDHOC). Internet-Draft draft-ietf-lake-edhoc-15, Internet Engineering Task Force (2022). https://datatracker.ietf.org/doc/html/draft-ietf-lake-edhoc-15. https://datatracker.ietf.org/doc/draft-ietf-lake-edhoc/

A Survey on Identity-Based Blind Signature

Mirko Koscina[1] , Pascal Lafourcade[2] , Gael Marcadet[2] ,
Charles Olivier-Anclin[1,2(✉)] , and Léo Robert[3]

[1] be ys Pay, Paris, France
[2] Université Clermont-Auvergne, CNRS, Mines de Saint-Étienne, LIMOS,
Saint-Étienne, France
`charles.olivier-anclin@uca.fr`
[3] Université de Limoges, XLIM, Limoges, France

Abstract. Blind signatures are well-studied building blocks of cryptography, originally designed to enable anonymity in electronic voting and digital banking. Identity-based signature were introduced by Shamir in 1984 and gave an alternative to prominent Public Key Infrastructure. An identity-based blind signature (IDBS) allows any user to interact directly with the signer without any prior interaction with a trusted authority. The first IDBS has been proposed in 2002 and several schemes were proposed since then. Seeking for a full comparison of these primitives, we propose a survey on IDBS and list all such primitives that seems to maintain some security. We also classify their security assumptions based on the existing security expectation that have not been formalized yet in the literature. Moreover, we empirically evaluate the complexity of all the operations used in those schemes with modern cryptographic libraries. This allows us to perform a realistic evaluation of their practical complexities. Hence, we can compare all schemes in terms of complexity and signature size.

Keywords: Identity-based Blind Signature · Survey · Complexity Evaluation

1 Introduction

Since the creation of the Internet, physical cash is progressively replaced through digitization by electronic payments methods like smart card or phone using NFC technology. Within this transformation, specific properties of cash were lost such as anonymity or unlinkability of the customer. In 1982, D. Chaum introduced a cryptographic response to this problem, called *blind signature* [13]. He described this concept as an analogue of an envelope composed of carbon paper that could be signed from the outside where the signature is engraved on a message inside.

For a concrete example, consider the following case where blind signature is helpful. Suppose that a customer wishes to buy a product at 10€ in a store. It asks to its bank a (blind) signature which is worth 10€[1]. The customer then gives this signature to the shopkeeper against the 10€ worth product. The latter sends the signature back to the bank for payment. In this setting double spending is checked by the bank since each payment corresponds to a signature. Moreover, unlinkability is ensured since the bank knows that the customer has withdrawn 10€ but it cannot link it with the inquiry from

---

[1] In this example, a signature defines a given amount of money.

G.-V. Jourdan et al. (Eds.): FPS 2022, LNCS 13877, pp. 19–37, 2023.
https://doi.org/10.1007/978-3-031-30122-3_2

the shopkeeper. Another well-known application for this primitive is the voting scheme in order to ensure that only registered voter can actually vote [42,49].

One of the first scheme using blind signature was developed by D. Chaum, A. Fiat, M. Naor in 1988 [14]. In 1992, S. Von Solms and D. Naccache [80] described a hostage taking that could lead to a crime without possibility to trace down a ransom pay to the criminal through coins made of blind signatures. It shows the necessity to extend the definition of blind signature to give more power to the signer. The goal is to be able to apply blind signature without threat. Therefore, extensions of blind signature such as partially blind signature [3], signer-friendly blind signature, fair blind signature [71] and many others were developed. Those properties allow more control for the signer by adding information or putting constraints on the use of a signature.

Before 1994, factorization was the only hard problem that yield to blind signature. That year was a turnover for the domain, J.L. Camenisch *et al.* [12] introduced the first a blind signature scheme based on the discrete logarithm problem. This scheme was an adaptation of the Nyberg-Rueppel scheme [61] leading to a relatively efficient blind signature. This scheme was also the first blind signature to have an additional property: *message recovery* (signed message is recovered from the public key and the signature).

Following A. Shamir's introduction of identity-based cryptography [68], signature and blind signature schemes were developed using this paradigm. The first ID-based blind signature was introduced by F. Zang and K. Kim [90] in 2002, only one year after the first use of pairing. In 2004, C. Sherman *et al.*[18] opened up the way to ID-based partially blind signature with a new scheme achieving partial restrictive blindness. The next year D. Galindo *et al.* [24] gave a general construction of IDBS only requiring a secure signature and a secure blind signature. This general framework achieved relatively good efficiency, but the signatures generated are about twice as large as a signature of made out schemes (the signature is the concatenation of both signature schemes).

There exist numerous properties proposed by a variety of IDBS schemes with the same practical applications as blind signature. Each situation has specific requirements and depending on the context one may use one schemes or another. Our main goal in this survey is to answer the question of how to choose an IDBS (with which property) for practical use. We list all existing schemes, classify them accordingly to their properties and security assumption; we also compare them using an empirical evaluation. We have included all IDBS[2] as they are for a vast majority independent works. Some does not meet the requirement to be use in practice, but we mention them for exhaustiveness as this may be of interest for authors trying to design new schemes. In such cases we have written the mentions "No reduction", "No proof" or "Not formal" depending on the category the fall within. The authors do not recommend usage of any schemes with one of these mentions in the upcoming table. Their evaluation is not included as this would be irrelevant to compare them with scheme that have guaranteed security.

Contributions. Our contribution aims at bringing new considerations on IDBS. Our first contribution is a survey presenting the existing portfolio to someone seeking to implement these primitives. In this paper, we evaluate all existing IDBS, this is not less than 71 schemes. We classify them within several categories that we discuss throughout this paper. Some reach additional properties that we all present in here. This allows us

---

[2] The authors apologies if any scheme have been omitted in this survey.

to give a full overview of the literature in the field and the existing properties reached by some existing IDBS scheme. We notice that among the existing schemes, some of them (at least 24 schemes) do not reach today's security requirements as no formal security argument have been given by their authors or in the literature we have investigated. We point them out without going into further details on them. Scheme with existing security arguments are investigated further. We start by empirically evaluate the cost of all operations used in existing IDBS schemes. It allows us to establish a metric to evaluate the time efficiency of each part of the given signatures. This answers our goal *i.e.*, obtaining a taxonomy of the reliable schemes in terms of efficiency and cryptographic assumption. This enables us to give insights on the schemes that actually reach the best efficiency in practice.

Seeking for more formalism and security consideration. The long version of this paper provides some formal security definitions for all type of the scheme we are investigating in this paper. These results are given in the appendix of the long version of the paper [5]. We hope it will bring up the security of the new ID-based blind signature that will be designed in the future or at least help giving some further formalization of their security as this has never been achieved for some of them.

Related Work. A few surveys related to blind signature schemes have been presented. To the best of the authors' knowledge, we noticed three of them. The first one [6], gives an overview of 8 existing blind signature schemes and other notions that are directly related to blind signature. It also presents some properties of blind signatures. A second short paper called survey on IDBS was proposed in 2015 by Girish *et al.* [30], but it does not give insights on the existing schemes instead it presents the concept and some existing property without much formalism. In 2018, M. Khater *et al.* [48] compared some blind signatures based on ElGamal. Only 5 schemes derived from the well-known signature are presented and evaluated. They compare the influence of modification in the scheme parameters, such as the number of blinding factor and its influence on the complexity. We include their signatures in our Survey.

All the above cited works only offer a partial view of existing identity-based blind signature schemes and yet it is hard to get a realistic view of the state of the art of the existing literature. Moreover, they do not compare the performance of the schemes in the literature. Our objective is to present a full overview of the existing literature, while our achievement is a detailed taxonomy of all existing IDBS schemes and of the numerous sub-properties. Unlike the above cited papers, we ambition to be exhaustive and to give a full description of field of IDBS.

Outline: Section 2 introduces the security assumptions and the definitions of an ID-based blind signature schemes and its additional properties. Details about our evaluation process are given in Sect. 3. In Sect. 4.1, we are comparing the existing schemes. Finally, in Sect. 5 we give insights of some work that should be done to put forward the domain. In Sect. 6 we conclude our study.

2 Cryptographic Definitions

Blind signature schemes rely on hard mathematical problems for their security. Those assumptions should be well-studied, and assumed to be intractable in reasonable time. The Discrete Logarithm problem (DL) relies on the difficulty to compute the discrete logarithm of an element in some groups. The Decision Diffie-Hellman (DDH), Computational Diffie-Hellman (CDH), Gap Diffie-Hellman (GDH) and the Chosen Target Accompanied Computational Diffie-Hellman problems (CT-ACDH) [15] result directly from it. There are also some variants such as the q-Strong Diffie-Hellman (q-SDH), the k-Bilinear Diffie-Hellman Inversion (k-BDHI), the One-more Bilinear Diffie-Hellman Inversion (1m-BDHI) or the Collusion Attack Algorithm with k traitors (k-CAA). These problems are mostly used for schemes based on elliptic curves. Recently, a polynomial time (PT) algorithm was disclosed solving the Over-determined Solvable System of Linear Equations modulo q with Random inhomogeneity problem (ROS). This led to attacks on many schemes [8] and some IDBS were relying on it.

Alternatives to elliptic curves have been investigated aiming at post-quantum security. Those solutions are essentially based on lattices, notably the Short Integer Solution problem (SIS), the Shortest Vector problem (SV) and its variant on quotient ring the Ring Short Integer Solution problem (R-SIS). One last rather unusual problem that we need here is the Chebyshev Polynomial Computation problem (CPC) [73]. This problem is known to have a reduction to the discrete logarithm in a finite group $GF(p)$, for some prime p [72]. These assumptions are formally defined in the long version of this paper [5]. All existing IDBS are based on one of these problems, we formally introduce the concept of IDBS and informally present the multiple properties that have been put based on this definition.

Definition 1 (IDentity-based Blind Signature - IDBS). *An IDBS with security parameter $\mathfrak{K}$ is a 4-tuple of polynomial-time algorithms* (Setup, Extract, $\langle S, U \rangle$, Verif) *involving an authority $\mathcal{M}$, a signer S and a user U. Algorithms are as follows:*

- Setup($1^\mathfrak{K}$) $\rightarrow$ (mpk, msk) *calls $\mathfrak{K}$ to generate a master key pair* (mpk, msk).
- Extract(msk, ID) $\rightarrow$ $sk[ID]$ *on input S's identity and a master key msk. It returns a secret key $sk[ID]$ later sent to S via a secure channel.*
- $\langle S(sk[ID]), U(mpk, m, ID) \rangle$ $\rightarrow$ σ *is the signature issuing protocol between the signer S and the user U for a message $m \in \{0, 1\}^*$. It generates the signature σ.*
- Verif(mpk, ID, m, σ) *outputs 1 if the signature σ is valid for m, otherwise 0.*

Secure IDBS must meet the three following security properties. *Correctness*, meaning that for any keys and any messages, the signature must always be accepted if all algorithms are honestly executed. *Blindness* requires that no information about the message could be revealed to the signer during the protocol. Finally, *unforgeability* requires that a user cannot forge new signatures from any set of existing signatures. Any of the upcoming schemes will have to meet these three basic properties. For their formal definition see the extended version of this paper [5].

We now describe in turn the other primitives based on IDBS.

ID-Based Proxy Blind Signature - IDPrBS. An original signer S delegates its right to sign to a proxy signer $\mathcal{P}$. After being provided with a key and a public agreement, $\mathcal{P}$ is allowed to sign any message coming from a user U and falling within the agreement. IDPrBS should satisfy the security properties of correctness, blindness and unforgeability. But should also meet additional properties [11]: *Prevention of misuse*: proxy signing key cannot be used for purposes other than generating valid proxy signatures. In case of misuse, the responsibility of the proxy signer should be determined explicitly. *Verifiability*: From a proxy signature, a verifier can be convinced of the original signer's agreement on the signed message. *Strong Identifiability*: Anyone can determine the identity of the proxy signer from a proxy signature. *Strong Undeniability*: A proxy signer cannot repudiate a proxy signature it created.

ID-Based (Restrictive) Partially Blind Signature - IDPBS/IDPRBS [3]. Prior to the protocol, the user and the signer have to agree on a common part denoted info. Instead of signing the usual message, $m||$info is signed. Restrictiveness is an additional constraint put by the signer on the user. $\mathcal{U}$ is only able to get a signature on a message of a certain form, specified by the signer. Those schemes have almost the same security properties as IDBS schemes. The only added difference is the inability of the user to modify the common part unilaterally. We also have a modified version of blindness called *partial blindness* where the signer always knows the common part of the message.

ID-Based Fair Blind Signature - IDFBS [71]. *Fairness* gives the capability to a trusted entity to perform one or two types of link recoveries:

Type I: The trusted entity can output information that enables the signer to recognize the corresponding message-signature pair.
Type II: The trusted entity can output information that enables the signer to efficiently identify the sender or to find the corresponding view of the signing protocol.

ID-Based Blind Signature with **Message Recovery - IDBSMR.** For a given signature and public key pair, there exists a verification algorithm that outputs the signed message. This property is useful to reduce the size of exchanged information. It requires a bijection between the possible messages and the group elements that will be used during the signing process.

ID-Based Forward-Secure Blind Signature - IDFSBS [94]. Consider the lifetime of a system divided into N time periods. In a blind signature context, forward secrecy means that unforgeability of signatures is valid in previous time periods even if current signing secret key of the signer is compromised. Thus, if the private key is compromised, only the signature for the current time period are forgeable. No signature for any previous time period can be forged, hence they remain safe to use.

ID-Based Blind Signature with Batch Verification - IDBSBV [7]. Batch verification has been designed to allow fast verification of multiple signatures. In practice a specific algorithm of verification VerifMult allows to verify a list of message-signature pair $\{(m_1, \sigma_1), \ldots, (m_n, \sigma_n)\}$ with the public key pk and output 1 if all signatures are valid, otherwise 0. We can allow this verification to be probabilistic with negligible probability of failure. Yet we want this verification to run significantly faster than n computations of the Verif algorithm.

ID-Based Weak Blind Signature - IDWBS [96]. This type of scheme does not achieve unlinkability when the signature is revealed to the signer *i.e.,* the signer is able to link the revealed signature to a user when it has a clear view of the message-signature pair.

3 Evaluation Process

We have evaluated all known IDBS schemes with a proven security to choose the most practical one. Here we present a metric to evaluate their complexity. An evaluation of all secure schemes is given in the full version of this paper [5].

Table 1. Conversion in $T_{MUL_{3072}}$.

Operation	256	512	3072	Operation	256	512	3072
$T_{Pairing}$	89.72	698.53		T_{GCD}	0.62	1.19	8.69
T_{TR}	52.12			T_{INV}	0.30	1.14	4.03
T_{EXP}	3.34	18.52	712.15	T_{ECADD}	0.16	0.67	
T_{PH}	3.99	4.65		T_{MUL}	0.08	0.10	1.00
T_{ECMUL}	2.99	12.14		T_{CHEBY}	0.05		
T_H	1.05	1.71		T_{ADD}	0.04	0.07	0.20
T_{GCD}	0.63	1.19	8.64				

In order to evaluate the schemes we had to choose concrete evaluation parameters. Our chosen parameters follow the recommendations of the ECRYPT's reports on key length [22]. These are similar to the more recent NIST's recommendations. We use 3072 bits integers and equivalent 256-bits elliptic curves *i.e.*, over finite field $\mathbb{F}_q$, with q of size 256 bits. In practice, it provides around 128 bits of security. Notice that recommendations for parameters of lattice differ from scheme to scheme, moreover, almost none of the authors of the listed papers gave concrete parameters for there schemes. Based on these elements, we chose to left out reduction for lattice based scheme as parameters for these schemes are still imprecise. However, we evaluate the number of operations that each existing scheme requires.

In order to compare all the existing scheme, we first compare the execution time of each operation with the execution time of a standard 3072 bits integer multiplication. Based on these result we can reduce the complexity of each signature scheme in terms of an unified unit: $T_{MUL_{3072}}$. Table 1 expresses the execution time of relevant operation *op* with the proposed conversion. T_{op} corresponds to the ratio between the execution time of each operation and a 3072 bits integer multiplication.[3] Our results are based on benchmarks on an Intel Core i7-1065G7 CPU @ 1.30 GHz processor without parallelism and generated using modern cryptographic libraries like GMP library [31] (arithmetical operations on integers), MPHELL library [1] (elliptic curve's operations), PBC library [59] (pairing functions) and OpenSSL/Crypto [2] library (hash functions) using state-of-the-art speed up.

We use the notations Minv, Mmul, Mtran, Madd for associated arithmetical operations on matrices. MVmul denotes a multiplication between a matrix and a vector. SVmul is the multiplication of a vector by a scalar. Vadd stands for the addition of two vectors. Vh and Mh are hash functions returning respectively a vector or a matrix. Sample is a sampling operation defined in [29]. We also use the following notations for usual scalar operations: EXP, MUL, ADD, INV. Moreover, ECMUL[4] and ECADD hold for multiplication and addition on elliptic curve. PAIR is the evaluation of a pairing function. H is for evaluation of a hash function and PH holds for hash function mapping on elliptic curve. Less common operation as CHEBY denotes the evaluation of a Chebyshev polynomial. TR denotes the trace function $TR(h) = h + h^2 + h^4$ in $GF(p^6)$ in the context of XTR (Efficient and Compact Subgroup Trace Representation [55]) schemes.

---

[3] Note that our conversion are relatively similar to some existing literature [46,60,76].

[4] It is not clear whether authors recommend symmetric or asymmetric pairing for their schemes. Based on that, we chose to unified the execution time for the two based group G_1 and G_2.

We summarize our results in two types of tables. The first type of table (*e.g.,* Table 2) gives a quick overview of a scheme with the following characteristics: mathematical setting (EC, pairing, *etc.*), security assumptions (CDH, ECDL, *etc.*), number of needed interactions and the number of random elements generated by a user to blind a message, also called *blinding factor*.

The second type of table evaluates and compare the complexity of the schemes. It is postponed to the full version [5] due to length limitation.

4 Schemes Presentation

4.1 ID-Based Blind Signature - IDBS

We have identified 32 IDBS schemes in the literature, they are listed in Table 2. The table gives the mathematical setting, the hard problem when a reduction is provided for the signature, the number of communications and the blinding factor. We chose these characteristics because communication between two distant machines can sometime be longer than running time of any algorithm of the signature edition. On another hand, we specify the number of random parameters to be generated each time. Generating cryptographically-secure randomness is costly, hence a low number of blinding factors can speed up the signature issuing and requires less resources.

Most schemes rely on pairing function and the CDH problem. Some such as [33,52] are pairing free and consequently faster to execute. Due to the increasing development of post-quantum cryptography, new IDBS schemes have been designed based on the SIS problem. Another base concept is XTR. Introduced by Lenstra *et al.* [55], this cryptographic basis leads to smaller signatures for the same security level. For instance, one would need 512-bits prime integers to achieve equivalent security to discrete logarithm problem with prime of 3072 bits. We have used the conversions from [55] to evaluate the operation of scheme from [75] as parameters of the scheme in [92] are not clear. Thus, we cannot propose a rigorous evaluation for this scheme. However, we can infer its relatively slow speed since a zero-knowledge proof procedure is used to sign a message.

Complexity evaluations and further details on the schemes are provided in the full version [5]. From this evaluation we note that the execution of an elliptic curves based signature gives better complexity than evaluation of a pairing function. Thus, pairing based signatures are less efficient. We have observed that Chebyshev polynomials are fast to evaluate, hence it produces an efficient scheme. Chaotic maps can be efficient, but their security needs to be more studied, yet a reduction to the discrete logarithm problem is given [73].

We conclude that the fastest pairing based scheme is 4 times faster than the slowest one. And again, the best pairing free scheme is 5 times faster than the best pairing based scheme. The complexity of [52] and [33] is close, and the difference might be negligible regarding time needed for cache affectation during the execution of properly implemented scheme. The only advantage is for [33], it uses less random values, but it might be compensated by the lowest complexity of the former scheme. Elliptic curve schemes still remain the most efficient schemes relying on a well-studied problem.

Table 2. Identity-Based Blind Signature. (* Weak Linkability)

Ref	Year	Mathematical base	Security reduction	Interactions	Blinding factor
[52]	2018	Elliptic curve	ECDL	3	4
[33]	2011				3
[21]	2020	Pairing	CDH	3	3
[92]	2010				1
[67]	2010				2
[4]	2010				
[41]	2009				
[40]	2005				
[90]	2002				
[90]	2002				
[39]	2010			2	4
[63]	2009				1
[28]	2012		1m-BDHI	2	2
[28]	2012				
[27]	2008				1
[51]	2017		ECDL	2	1
[38]	2011		Q-SDH	4	5
[53]	2017		GDH	3	1
[75]	2013		No reduction	3	2
[95]	2014				
[87]	2013				
[44]	2013				
[41]	2009				
[41]	2009				
[47]	2008				
[91]	2003				
[96]*	2007				3
[57]	2020	Lattice	SIS	4	3
[25]	2016			2	1
[26]	2017				
[69]	2018	Modular Groups	No reduction	3	3
[73]	2020	Chaotic map	CPC	3	1

4.2 ID-Based Proxy Blind Signature - IDPrBS

Sorting the scheme by type of underlying problem, we give an overview of the existing IDPrBS in Table 3. Part of the existing schemes lack of formal security arguments. Three schemes are still recorded in our survey, but this is specified in the table. There

Table 3. ID-based Proxy Blind Signature Scheme.

Scheme	Year	Mathematical base	Security proof	Interactions	Blinding factor
[46]	2020	Elliptic curve	ECDL	3	2
[74]	2013				
[62]	2016		No proof	3	3
[64]	2013				
[34]	2012	Pairing	ECDL	3	2
[35]	2008		k-BDHI	3	2
[89]	2008		No proof	3	2
[54]	2004				
[66]	2017		Not formal	3	2
[81]	2009				
[88]	2008				
[86]	2005				
[83]	2012			4	2
[93]	2014	Lattice	Attacked	2	3
[97]	2018				2

Table 4. ID-based Partially Blind Signature Scheme. (*Scheme with Restrictiveness)

Scheme	Year	Mathematical base	Security proof	Interactions	Blinding factor
[20]*	2019	Elliptic curve	ECDL	3	4
[43]	2016				2
[56]	2013	Pairing	CDH	2	2
[84]	2007			3	4
[85]*	2008				4
[17]	2007				4
[37]*	2007				4
[17]*	2007				7
[16]*	2005				7
[18]*	2004				3
[15]	2009		CT-ACDH	2	2
[36]	2007		Attacked	3	2
[77]	2009		Not formal	3	2
[82]*	2008				7

exist IDPrBS based on the tree prominent type of problems: elliptic curves, pairing and lattice. Proxyness is the most studied property for IDBS, a generic construction exist for this primitive as highlighted in Sect. 4.5. The first scheme was introduced in 2003, only two years after the first appearing of pairing in cryptography in [54]. Ten years later was published the first paring-free scheme [74]. It led to one of the most efficient schemes of this survey and was proven as hard as the well-studied ECDL problem. With the development of quantum computer and the growing threat on classical assumptions, two lattice based schemes were developed [65,70]. Sadly, attacks were found on both primitives. Thus, finding a lattice based IDPrBS is still an open problem.

Complexity evaluation of pairing based schemes are reported in the extended version [5]. With our comparison, we claim that the most efficient, proven secure, ID-based proxy blind signature is the one from S. James *et al.* [46].

4.3   ID-Based Partially Blind Signature - IDPBS

IDPBS sometime with restrictiveness as described in Sect. 2 are exposed in Table 4. These signatures allow adding auxiliary information to the message making them relevant for practical usages. This common information put in context improves management of signature and security. For example, it allows the signer to add an expiration date to its signatures. Up to today, 14 IDPBS have been published. As explained before, restrictiveness requires the user to fit its message to a specific structure. The user has fewer capabilities while the signer has more control. Due similarities between restrictive IDPBS and classical IDPBS, we are evaluating them all together.

As usual we let the reader refer to the full version [5] for in depth evaluation of the schemes. IDPBS were published from 2004. The first published scheme had restrictiveness and was based on pairing. Only later, in 2016, a first scheme was proposed avoiding the use of pairing based cryptography, published by H. Islam *et al.* [43] it introduced the first elliptic curve based scheme leading to better efficiency when issuing signatures. Pairing free schemes are faster than pairing based by a factor of 1.5 to more than 10. Up to now, no lattice based or quantum resistant blind signature has been proposed with the aforementioned properties. The scheme's signature sizes varies from 2 elements (*i.e.*, 514 bits), being relatively short, up to 6 elements (*i.e.*, 1542 bits) clearly leading to more computation during the verification process.

Scheme from [43] seems to be the best fitted algorithms as it is one of the most efficient schemes that we have recorded in our survey. Although its security is proven in the random oracle model, it is an efficient signature algorithm with a short signature, thus could be use in practice.

4.4   ID-Based Blind Signature with Other Properties

We describe and evaluate IDBS schemes with additional properties: message recovery, fairness, forward security and batch verification. These notions are quickly introduced in Sect. 2. Fewer signatures have been presented in the literature with these properties. A brief overview of their usefulness is given, followed by the usual evaluation routine (see Sect. 3). For a short overview of the characteristics of the schemes see Table 5. For their evaluation refer to the full version [5].

ID-Based Blind Signature with Message Recovery - IDBSMR

IDBS schemes with message recovery allow to recover the message from the signature and the public key. The six existing schemes are presented in Table 5. They rely for the most recent one on elliptic curves and on pairing function for the rest of them. Efficiency of these schemes are comparable to the most efficient of this survey. The best known pairing based IDBSMR here only requires half of the computation expected toward the best pairing based IDBS. For their evaluation refer to the full version [5].

A scheme with message recovery has to handle carefully the verification phase. All schemes with message recovery have a small signature only composed of two group elements. The size of the signature can be reduced to 514 bits via a simple compression algorithm. It is still an open problem to present a round-optimal IDBS with message recovery. The existing IDBS with message recovery all need 3 communications. This is an essential point for a blind signature scheme as communication comes at a cost in terms of time efficiency of the protocol.

ID-Based Fair Blind Signature - IDFBS

With a moderate cost, Wand et al. [83] where able to introduce an ID-based Fair Blind Signature. Moreover, it has two additional properties: enabling proxy signature and weak linkability. The drawbacks consist in a relatively long signature (1028 bits) and 4 communications to obtain the signature. Note that the weak linkability property could also be considered as a weakness of the scheme. Latter, an alternative was proposed by Verma et al. [78]. The scheme relies on a Fiat-Shamir signature and is based on oblivious transfer, which is known to be a relatively expensive primitives. Hence, the scheme has a low efficiency and needs many communications. We are not providing a complexity analysis of the latest as one willing to put such a signature in practice may not consider it due to its deficiency of proven security. The authors want to highlight that none of the schemes have been proven secure. In [83], discussion of the security of the scheme is provided, but no attention is given to unforgeability. Security proofs are almost mandatory in today's development of cryptography and here no model has ever been proposed for these schemes. Despite the real practicality provided by fairness, none of the scheme would be considered as reliable enough. We conclude that some work remains to do to propose to the community an efficient and secure IDFBS. We propose a security model for IDFBS in the full version of the paper [5].

ID-Based Forward-Secure Blind Signature - IDFSBS

Forwards security is gradually becoming a central property in cryptography. In the context of signature scheme is allows to divide the lifetime of a key pair into N periods. The secret key is modified for each period while keeping the same public key, thus providing additional security as on leakage of a secret key, previous signature are no longer affected by this security breach. Thus, signatures made during the $N-1$ others are still reliable. This increase the global security of signatures.

IDFSBS are not possible to compare since the authors of [94] were the only one to propose such a signature. It relies on the well-studied SIS problem over lattices and requires 3 communications and 2 blinding factor. The signature is composed of one vector of size m (the message) with elements in $\mathbb{Z}_q$. Lattice based signatures known to produce relatively long outputs which is a drawback compensated by the absence of known algorithm to be efficient against them even on quantum computers. We further evaluate this signature in the full version of the paper [5].

ID-Based Blind Signature with Batch Verification - IDBSBV

Batch verification allows faster signature verification. For signatures with batch verification it is possible to specify an algorithm verifying multiples instance in the same time and significantly faster than the normal verification.

Table 5. IDBS with properties.

Ref	Year	Mathematical base	Security reduction	Interactions	Blinding factor
Message Recovery					
[50]	2019	Elliptic curve	ECDL	3	4
[32]	2005	Pairing	ECDL	3	2
[79]	2018		k-CAA		
[19]	2018		Q-SDH		
[23]	2008		CDH		
[45]	2017		Not formal	3	2
Fairness					
[83]	2012	Pairing	No reduction	4	2
[78]	2016			2 with Oblivious Transfer	$2\hat{\kappa}+1$
Forward-Security					
[94]	2016	Lattice	SIS	3	2
Batch Verification					
[58]	2006	Pairing	k-CAA	2	2

We have observed only one such scheme by Li *et al.* [58]. The scheme is efficient, still relying on pairing function known to be costly. They proposed an efficient signature process leading a relatively short signature with fast verification. Note also that the scheme has a costly verification process, based on pairing. The batch verification allows to drastically reduce the need of pairing function for the verification and thus gives scheme that is comparable to the best pairing free algorithm of the literature.

4.5 Comparison to the Generic Construction

Generic construction of IDBS have been introduced by D. Galindo *et al.* [24]. It gives a generic framework based on a signature scheme $\mathcal{S} = (KG_\mathcal{S}, SGN_\mathcal{S}, VFY_\mathcal{S})$ and a blind signature scheme $\mathcal{BS} = (KG_{\mathcal{BS}}, SGN_{\mathcal{BS}}^{com}, SGN_{\mathcal{BS}}^{blind}, SGN_{\mathcal{BS}}^{sgn}, SGN_{\mathcal{BS}}^{unb}, VFY_{\mathcal{BS}})$. Combining these two structures we can construct a IDBS scheme. In order to accomplish their roles the three entities (user, signer, verifier) have to execute the following algorithm to output and verify a signature: User: $VFY_\mathcal{S}, SGN_{\mathcal{BS}}^{blind}, SGN_{\mathcal{BS}}^{unb}$; Signer: $SGN_{\mathcal{BS}}^{com}, SGN_{\mathcal{BS}}^{sgn}$; Verifier: $VFY_\mathcal{S}, VFY_{\mathcal{BS}}$.

The authors of [24] proposed an instantiation for their ID-based blind signature construction based on two schemes: the Boneh-Lynn-Shacham (BLS) signature [10] and Boldyreva's blind signature [9]. At the time D. Galindo *et al.* idea was published, they claimed to be among the most efficient schemes. We detail the cost of their proposed instantiation in the full version [5].

Based on our reduction, we can deduce that the total complexity of the generated scheme is barely the addition of the cost of both schemes and is around the average of the observed complexity for the existing IDBS schemes. Relying on secure pairing free schemes would lead to a secure IDBS with improved complexity.

A more recently study [11] introduced a new generic construction for IDPBS. As in the previous construction, they rely on a signature and a blind signature. They are organized in a manner reaching an acceptable complexity as explained in the article, with approximately the same complexity as the previous construction.

5   Synthesis of the Current Literature

There exists an extensive literature on IDBS, numerous schemes have been presented by multiple authors. In total 71 schemes are presented in this survey. We noticed that the literature is mostly independent and that no global courses of action was followed by the authors of these schemes. Only few works mostly based on lattices were following previous work due to some attacks found on them: the latest schemes were made to fix some security breach in the existing work. This survey aims at putting some coherence in future work in the field, it brings up formalism for security assumption based on the existing security expectation for each of the properties. In the long version of this paper [5], we have tried to formalize these securities properties for the various security that such a scheme was expected to withdraw when an attack comes in place through security games. Even if these experiments needs further discussion before being fully adopted by the community, we believe it as a step forward in the study of the security of these primitives.

This is motivated by the fact that no security proofs or formal arguments have been disclosed for 22 of the investigated schemes. It implies that it may remain unknown vulnerabilities for existing schemes and possible attacks might be found in the future. We do not recommend using any unproven schemes for practical purposes. Also, some authors provided a reduction for their scheme. Yet, the security may not be ensured as their assumption are weak *e.g.,* IDBS rely on quite unusual hypothesis and some other schemes rely on the broken ROS problem. The later should no longer be used as they do not bring any security to their users.

While exploring the literature, we noticed that it lacks pairing free IDFBS, IDFSBS or IDBSBV schemes. Further studies could potentially improve efficiency and quantum resistance of such primitives. No pairing free IDFBS or IDBSBV yet exists and no post quantum assumption was ever used to design an IDPBS, IDPrBS, IDBSMR, IDFBS or IDBSBV that withdraw proven security until today. A big step forward on the development of new schemes on post quantum assumptions is necessary to guarantee the future of these primitives.

On another hand, minimizing the number of transmission to obtain round optimal IDBS is also of interest for the field as it brings a non-negligible speedup as most construction achieves a computational cost comparable of to the order of magnitude of a Round Trip Time. For example, no round optimal IDBSMR have ever been introduced, combined with this type of primitive that seems to achieve efficient computational time would be of interest.

As highlighted in [90], numerous schemes had issues while being performed in parallel execution. This is mostly due to a polynomial time algorithm capable of solving the

ROS problem [8]. Other studies could focus on bringing an IDBS with proven security under parallel execution.

We see that some works are still to be done in this domain to guarantee the future security and the practicality of the IDBS and other signature schemes evoked in this paper.

6 Conclusion

In this survey we review the literature on ID-based blind signature with several existed properties presented throughout this paper. We show that depending on the case of use, there exist several IDBS schemes to consider. The studied schemes have specific properties and their efficiency relies on manifold requirements. In this survey we answer the question: how to choose an IDBS scheme? For that we have listed all existing IDBS schemes, we present them all with their most notable properties and a reproducible, bias free evaluation of their complexity. Providing a time reduction of all arithmetical operations used for IDBS schemes in order to evaluate them all at the same security level is our first contribution. We directly exploit it to give a metric on the complexity of any these scheme. With this metric we can compute the total computational cost of a signature issuing and verification process. Hence, it is easy to compare their efficiencies.

We can conclude thanks to our study that the most computationally efficient IDBS scheme using EC is [52]. But schemes can be chosen from other kind of feature such as number of communications, number of blinding factors or the size of the signature. We enable anybody to quickly choose from the existing literature the best feted properties and signature for its use based on their characteristics. In the extended version [5], we also give new insights by proposing formal security experiment and open axes of research for these primitives.

References

1. MPHELL: Multi-Precision (Hyper) Elliptic curve Library (2020)
2. OpenSSL library (2021)
3. Abe, M., Fujisaki, E.: How to date blind signatures. In: Kim, K., Matsumoto, T. (eds.) ASI-ACRYPT 1996. LNCS, vol. 1163, pp. 244–251. Springer, Heidelberg (1996). https://doi.org/10.1007/BFb0034851
4. Ajmath, K.A., Reddy, P.V., Gowri, T.: An ID-based blind signature scheme from bilinear pairings (2010)
5. Anonymous. A survey on identity-based blind signature. https://anonymous.4open.science/r/ano_blind-2422
6. Asghar, N.: A survey on blind digital signatures (2015). https://nabihach.github.io/co685.pdf
7. Bellare, M., Garay, J.A., Rabin, T.: Fast batch verification for modular exponentiation and digital signatures. In: Nyberg, K. (ed.) EUROCRYPT 1998. LNCS, vol. 1403, pp. 236–250. Springer, Heidelberg (1998). https://doi.org/10.1007/BFb0054130
8. Benhamouda, F., Lepoint, T., Loss, J., Orrù, M., Raykova, M.: On the (in)security of ROS. Cryptology ePrint Archive, Report 2020/945 (2020)
9. Boldyreva, A.: Threshold signatures, multisignatures and blind signatures based on the gap-Diffie-Hellman-group signature scheme. In: Desmedt, Y.G. (ed.) PKC 2003. LNCS, vol. 2567, pp. 31–46. Springer, Heidelberg (2003). https://doi.org/10.1007/3-540-36288-6_3

10. Boneh, D., Lynn, B., Shacham, H.: Short signatures from the Weil pairing. In: Boyd, C. (ed.) ASIACRYPT 2001. LNCS, vol. 2248, pp. 514–532. Springer, Heidelberg (2001). https://doi.org/10.1007/3-540-45682-1_30

11. Bultel, X., Lafourcade, P., Olivier-Anclin, C., Robert, L.: Generic construction for identity-based proxy blind signature. In: Aïmeur, E., Laurent, M., Yaich, R., Dupont, B., Garcia-Alfaro, J. (eds.) FPS 2021. LNCS, vol. 13291, pp. 34–52. Springer, Cham (2022). https://doi.org/10.1007/978-3-031-08147-7_3

12. Camenisch, J.L., Piveteau, J.-M., Stadler, M.A.: Blind signatures based on the discrete logarithm problem. In: De Santis, A. (ed.) EUROCRYPT 1994. LNCS, vol. 950, pp. 428–432. Springer, Heidelberg (1995). https://doi.org/10.1007/BFb0053458

13. Chaum, D.: Blind signatures for untraceable payments. In: Chaum, D., Rivest, R.L., Sherman, A.T. (eds.) Advances in Cryptology, pp. 199–203. Springer, Boston (1983). https://doi.org/10.1007/978-1-4757-0602-4_18

14. Chaum, D., Fiat, A., Naor, M.: Untraceable electronic cash. In: Goldwasser, S. (ed.) CRYPTO 1988. LNCS, vol. 403, pp. 319–327. Springer, New York (1990). https://doi.org/10.1007/0-387-34799-2_25

15. Chen, W., Qin, B., Wu, Q., Zhang, L., Zhang, H.: ID-based partially blind signatures: a scalable solution to multi-bank e-cash. In: International Conference on Signal Processing Systems (2009)

16. Chen, X., Zhang, F., Liu, S.: ID-based restrictive partially blind signatures. In: Hao, Y., et al. (eds.) CIS 2005. LNCS (LNAI), vol. 3802, pp. 117–124. Springer, Heidelberg (2005). https://doi.org/10.1007/11596981_17

17. Chen, X., Zhang, F., Liu, S.: ID-based restrictive partially blind signatures and applications. J. Syst. Softw. **80**, 164–171 (2007)

18. Chow, S.S.M., Hui, L.C.K., Yiu, S.M., Chow, K.P.: Two improved partially blind signature schemes from bilinear pairings. In: Boyd, C., González Nieto, J.M. (eds.) ACISP 2005. LNCS, vol. 3574, pp. 316–328. Springer, Heidelberg (2005). https://doi.org/10.1007/11506157_27

19. Cui, W., Jia, Q.: Efficient provably secure ID-based blind signature with message recovery. In: 4th Workshop on Advanced Research and Technology in Industry (WARTIA 2018). Atlantis Press (2018)

20. Cui, W., Jia, Q.: Provably secure pairing-free identity-based restrictive partially blind signature scheme. In: Information Technology, Networking, Electronic and Automation Control Conference. IEEE (2019)

21. Deng, L., He, X., Xia, T.: Secure identity-based blind signature scheme for online transactions. Wirel. Pers. Commun. **116**, 1525–1537 (2021)

22. ECRYPT-CSA. Algorithms, Key Size and Protocols Report. Technical report (2018)

23. Elkamchouchi, H.M., Abouelseoud, Y.: A new blind identity-based signature scheme with message recovery. IACR Cryptology ePrint Archive (2008)

24. Galindo, D., Herranz, J., Kiltz, E.: On the generic construction of identity-based signatures with additional properties. In: Lai, X., Chen, K. (eds.) ASIACRYPT 2006. LNCS, vol. 4284, pp. 178–193. Springer, Heidelberg (2006). https://doi.org/10.1007/11935230_12

25. Gao, W., Hu, Y., Wang, B., Xie, J.: Identity-based blind signature from lattices in standard model. In: Chen, K., Lin, D., Yung, M. (eds.) Inscrypt 2016. LNCS, vol. 10143, pp. 205–218. Springer, Cham (2017). https://doi.org/10.1007/978-3-319-54705-3_13

26. Gao, W., Hu, Y., Wang, B., Xie, J., Liu, M.: Identity-based blind signature from lattices. Wuhan Univ. J. Nat. Sci. **22**(4), 355–360 (2017). https://doi.org/10.1007/s11859-017-1258-x

27. Gao, W., Wang, G., Wang, X., Li, F.: One-round ID-based blind signature scheme without ROS assumption. In: Galbraith, S.D., Paterson, K.G. (eds.) Pairing 2008. LNCS, vol. 5209, pp. 316–331. Springer, Heidelberg (2008). https://doi.org/10.1007/978-3-540-85538-5_21

28. Gao, W., Wang, G., Wang, X., Li, F.: Round-optimal ID-based blind signature schemes without ROS assumption. J. Commun. (2012)
29. Gentry, C., Peikert, C., Vaikuntanathan, V.: Trapdoors for hard lattices and new cryptographic constructions. In: Proceedings of the Fortieth Annual ACM Symposium on Theory of Computing, STOC (2008)
30. Girish, K., Phaneendra, D.: Survey on identity based blind signature (2015)
31. Granlund, T.: GNU MP: The GNU Multiple Precision Arithmetic Library (2020)
32. Han, S., Chang, E.: A pairing-based blind signature scheme with message recovery. Int. J. Inf. Technol. **2**, 187–192 (2005)
33. He, D., Chen, J., Zhang, R.: An efficient identity-based blind signature scheme without bilinear pairings. Comput. Electr. Eng. **37**, 444–450 (2011)
34. He, J., Qi, C., Sun, F.: A new identity-based proxy blind signature scheme. In: IEEE International Conference on Information Science and Technology. IEEE (2012)
35. Heng, P., Ke, K., Gu, C.: Efficient ID-based proxy blind signature schemes from pairings. In: International Conference on Computational Intelligence and Security. IEEE (2008)
36. Hu, X., Huang, S.: An efficient ID-based partially blind signature scheme. In: Eighth ACIS International Conference on Software Engineering, Artificial Intelligence, Networking, and Parallel/Distributed Computing (SNPD). IEEE (2007)
37. Hu, X., Huang, S.: An efficient ID-based restrictive partially blind signature scheme. In: Eighth ACIS International Conference on Software Engineering, Artificial Intelligence, Networking, and Parallel/Distributed Computing (SNPD) (2007)
38. Hu, X., Wang, J., Yang, Y.: Secure ID-based blind signature scheme without random oracle. In: International Conference on Network Computing and Information Security. IEEE (2011)
39. Hu, X.-M., Huang, S.-T.: Secure identity-based blind signature scheme in the standard model. J. Inf. Sci. Eng. **26**, 215–230 (2010)
40. Huang, Z., Chen, K., Wang, Y.: Efficient identity-based signatures and blind signatures. In: Desmedt, Y.G., Wang, H., Mu, Y., Li, Y. (eds.) CANS 2005. LNCS, vol. 3810, pp. 120–133. Springer, Heidelberg (2005). https://doi.org/10.1007/11599371_11
41. Huang, Z., Chen, Q., Huang, R., Lin, X.: Efficient Schnorr type identity-based blind signatures from bilinear pairings. In: WRI World Congress on Computer Science and Information Engineering. IEEE (2009)
42. Ibrahim, S., Kamat, M., Salleh, M., Aziz, S.: Secure e-voting with blind signature. In: 4th National Conference of Telecommunication Technology (2003)
43. Islam, S.H., Amin, R., Biswas, G., Obaidat, M.S., Khan, M.K.: Provably secure pairing-free identity-based partially blind signature scheme and its application in online e-cash system. Arabian J. Sci. Eng. **41**, 3163–3176 (2016)
44. Jain, R., Patel, A.A.: Computationally efficient ID-based blind signature scheme in e-voting. Int. J. Sci. Res. Dev. (2013)
45. James, S., Gowri, T., Babu, G., Reddy, P.V.: Identity-based blind signature scheme with message recovery. Int. J. Electr. Comput. Eng. (2017)
46. James, S., Thumbur, G., Reddy, P.: An efficient pairing-free identity based proxy blind signature scheme with message recovery. ISC Int. J. Inf. Secur. (2021)
47. Kalkan, S., Kaya, K., Selcuk, A.A.: Generalized ID-based blind signatures from bilinear pairings. In: International Symposium on Computer and Information Sciences. IEEE (2008)
48. Khater, M.M., Al-Ahwal, A., Selim, M.M., Zayed, H.H.: Blind signature schemes based on ELGamal signature for electronic voting: a survey. Int. J. Comput. Appl. (2018)
49. Kucharczyk, M.: Blind signatures in electronic voting systems. In: Kwiecień, A., Gaj, P., Stera, P. (eds.) CN 2010. CCIS, vol. 79, pp. 349–358. Springer, Heidelberg (2010). https://doi.org/10.1007/978-3-642-13861-4_37

50. Kumar, M., Chand, S.: A pairing-less identity-based blind signature with message recovery scheme for cloud-assisted services. In: Liu, Z., Yung, M. (eds.) Inscrypt 2019. LNCS, vol. 12020, pp. 419–434. Springer, Cham (2020). https://doi.org/10.1007/978-3-030-42921-8_24

51. Kumar, M., Katti, C., Saxena, P.: An identity-based blind signature approach for e-voting system. Int. J. Mod. Educ. Comput. Sci. (2017)

52. Kumar, M., Katti, C.P., Saxena, P.C.: An untraceable identity-based blind signature scheme without pairing for e-cash payment system. In: Kumar, N., Thakre, A. (eds.) UBICNET 2017. LNICST, vol. 218, pp. 67–78. Springer, Cham (2018). https://doi.org/10.1007/978-3-319-73423-1_7

53. Kumar, M., Katti, C.P., Saxena, P.C.: A secure anonymous e-voting system using identity-based blind signature scheme. In: Shyamasundar, R.K., Singh, V., Vaidya, J. (eds.) ICISS 2017. LNCS, vol. 10717, pp. 29–49. Springer, Cham (2017). https://doi.org/10.1007/978-3-319-72598-7_3

54. Lang, W., Tan, Y., Yang, Z., Liu, G., Peng, B.: A new efficient ID-based proxy blind signature scheme. In Ninth International Symposium on Computers and Communications. IEEE (2004)

55. Lenstra, A.K., Verheul, E.R.: The XTR public key system. In: Bellare, M. (ed.) CRYPTO 2000. LNCS, vol. 1880, pp. 1–19. Springer, Heidelberg (2000). https://doi.org/10.1007/3-540-44598-6_1

56. Li, F., Zhang, M., Takagi, T.: Identity-based partially blind signature in the standard model for electronic cash. Math. Comput. Model. **58**, 196–203 (2013)

57. Li, Q., Hsu, C., He, D., Choo, K.-K.R., Gong, P.: An identity-based blind signature scheme using lattice with provable security. Math. Probl. Eng. (2020)

58. Li, R., Yu, J., Li, G., Li, D.: A new identity-based blind signature scheme with batch verifications. In: International Conference on Multimedia and Ubiquitous Engineering. IEEE (2007)

59. Lynn, B.: PBC library: The Pairing-Based Cryptography Library (2021)

60. Nikooghadam, M., Zakerolhosseini, A.: An efficient blind signature scheme based on the elliptic curve discrete logarithm problem. ISC Int. J. Inf. Secur. (2009)

61. Nyberg, K., Rueppel, R.A.: A new signature scheme based on the DSA giving message recovery. In: Proceedings of the 1st ACM Conference on Computer and Communications Security, CCS (1993)

62. Padhye, S., Tiwari, N.: An efficient ID-based proxy blind signature with pairing-free realization. In: International Conference on Innovative Engineering Technologies (2016)

63. Phong, L.T., Ogata, W.: New identity-based blind signature and blind decryption scheme in the standard model. IEICE Trans. Fundam. Electron. Commun. Comput. Sci. **92**, 1822–1835 (2009)

64. Prabhadevi, S., Natarajan, A.: Utilization of ID-based proxy blind signature based on ECDLP in secure vehicular communications. Int. J. Eng. Innov. Technol. (2013)

65. Rawal, S., Padhye, S.: Cryptanalysis of ID based proxy-blind signature scheme over lattice. ICT Express (2020)

66. Sarde, P., Banerjee, A.: A secure ID-based blind and proxy blind signature scheme from bilinear pairings. J. Appl. Secur. Res. **12**, 276–286 (2017)

67. Shakerian, R., MohammadPour, T., Kamali, S.H., Hedayati, M.: An identity based public key cryptography blind signature scheme from bilinear pairings. In: International Conference on Computer Science and Information Technology. IEEE (2010)

68. Shamir, A.: Identity-based cryptosystems and signature schemes. In: Blakley, G.R., Chaum, D. (eds.) CRYPTO 1984. LNCS, vol. 196, pp. 47–53. Springer, Heidelberg (1985). https://doi.org/10.1007/3-540-39568-7_5

69. Shuang, W., Hao, Y., Dongnan, L.: A new identity based blind signature scheme and its application. In: Advanced Information Technology, Electronic and Automation Control Conference. IEEE (2018)

70. Singh, S., Padhye, S.: Identity based blind signature scheme over NTRU lattices. Inf. Process. Lett. (2020)

71. Stadler, M., Piveteau, J.-M., Camenisch, J.: Fair blind signatures. In: Guillou, L.C., Quisquater, J.-J. (eds.) EUROCRYPT 1995. LNCS, vol. 921, pp. 209–219. Springer, Heidelberg (1995). https://doi.org/10.1007/3-540-49264-X_17

72. Tahat, N., Abdallah, E.: Hybrid publicly verifiable authenticated encryption scheme based on chaotic maps and factoring problems. J. Appl. Secur. Res. 13, 304–314 (2018)

73. Tahat, N., Tahat, A.A., Albadarneh, R.B., Edwan, T.A.: Design of identity-based blind signature scheme upon chaotic maps. Int. J. Online Biomed. Eng. (2020)

74. Tan, Z.: Efficient pairing-free provably secure identity-based proxy blind signature scheme. Secur. Commun. Netw. 6, 593–601 (2013)

75. Tang, Q., Shen, F.: Identity-based XTR blind signature scheme. Intell. Autom. Soft Comput. 19, 143–149 (2013)

76. Thu, A.A., Mya, K.T.: Implementation of an efficient blind signature scheme. Int. J. Innov. Manag. Technol. (2014)

77. Tian, X.-X., Li, H.-J., Xu, J.-P., Wang, Y.: A security enforcement ID-based partially blind signature scheme. In: International Conference on Web Information Systems and Mining. IEEE (2009)

78. Verma, G.K., Singh, B.: New ID-based fair blind signatures. In: Futuristic Trends in Engineering, Science, Humanities, and Technology FTESHT-16 (2016)

79. Verma, G.K., Singh, B.: Efficient identity-based blind message recovery signature scheme from pairings. IET Inf. Secur. 12, 150–156 (2018)

80. Von Solms, S., Naccache, D.: On blind signatures and perfect crimes. Comput. Secur. 11, 581–583 (1992)

81. Wang, B., Liu, W., Wang, C.: ID-based proxy blind signature scheme with proxy revocation. In: International Workshop on Computer Science and Engineering, WCSE (2009)

82. Wang, C., Lu, R.: An ID-based transferable off-line e-cash system with revokable anonymity. In: International Symposium on Electronic Commerce and Security (2008)

83. Wang, C.H., Fan, J.-Y.: The design of ID-based fair proxy blind signature scheme with weak linkability. In: International Conference on Information Security and Intelligent Control (2012)

84. Wang, C.-J., Tang, Y., Li, Q.: ID-based fair off-line electronic cash system with multiple banks. J. Comput. Sci. Technol. 22, 487–493 (2007)

85. Wang, S., Han, P., Zhang, Y., Wang, X.: An improved ID-based restrictive partially blind signature scheme. In: Ninth ACIS International Conference on Software Engineering, Artificial Intelligence, Networking, and Parallel/Distributed Computing. IEEE (2008)

86. Wei-min, L., Zong-kai, Y., Wen-qing, C., Yun-meng, T.: A new ID-based proxy blind signature scheme. Wuhan Univ. J. Nat. Sci. 10, 555–558 (2005)

87. Xu, G., Xu, G.: An ID-based blind signature from bilinear pairing with unlinkability. In: International Conference on Consumer Electronics, Communications and Networks. IEEE (2013)

88. Yang, M., Wang, Y.: A new efficient ID-based proxy blind signature scheme. J. Electron. 25, 226–231 (2008)

89. Yu, Y., Zheng, S., Yang, Y.: ID-based blind signature and proxy blind signature without trusted PKG. In: Sarbazi-Azad, H., Parhami, B., Miremadi, S.-G., Hessabi, S. (eds.) CSICC 2008. CCIS, vol. 6, pp. 821–824. Springer, Heidelberg (2008). https://doi.org/10.1007/978-3-540-89985-3_111

90. Zhang, F., Kim, K.: ID-based blind signature and ring signature from pairings. In: Zheng, Y. (ed.) ASIACRYPT 2002. LNCS, vol. 2501, pp. 533–547. Springer, Heidelberg (2002). https://doi.org/10.1007/3-540-36178-2_33

91. Zhang, F., Kim, K.: Efficient ID-based blind signature and proxy signature from bilinear pairings. In: Safavi-Naini, R., Seberry, J. (eds.) ACISP 2003. LNCS, vol. 2727, pp. 312–323. Springer, Heidelberg (2003). https://doi.org/10.1007/3-540-45067-X_27

92. Zhang, L., Hu, Y., Tian, X., Yang, Y.: Novel identity-based blind signature for electronic voting system. In: Second International Workshop on Education Technology and Computer Science. IEEE (2010)

93. Zhang, L., Ma, Y.: A lattice-based identity-based proxy blind signature scheme in the standard model. Math. Probl. Eng. (2014)

94. Zhang, Y., Hu, Y.: Forward-secure identity-based shorter blind signature from lattices. Am. J. Netw. Commun. **5**, 17–26 (2016)

95. Zhao, B., Yang, S.: Anonymous identity-based blind signature in the performance evaluation. In: International Conference on Mechatronics, Control and Electronic Engineering. Atlantis Press (2014)

96. Zhao, Z.-M.: ID-based weak blind signature from bilinear pairings. IJ Netw. Secur. **7**, 265–268 (2008)

97. Zhu, H., Tan, Y.-A., Zhu, L., Zhang, Q., Li, Y.: An efficient identity-based proxy blind signature for semioffline services. Wirel. Commun. Mob. Comput. (2018)

Do Not Rely on Clock Randomization: A Side-Channel Attack on a Protected Hardware Implementation of AES

Martin Brisfors, Michail Moraitis$^{(\boxtimes)}$, and Elena Dubrova

Royal Institute of Technology (KTH), Electrum 229, 196 40 Stockholm, Sweden
{brisfors,micmor,dubrova}@kth.se

Abstract. Clock randomization is one of the oldest countermeasures against side-channel attacks. Various implementations have been presented in the past, along with positive security evaluations. However, in this paper we show that it is possible to break countermeasures based on a randomized clock by sampling side-channel measurements at a frequency much higher than the encryption clock, synchronizing the traces with pre-processing, and targeting the beginning of the encryption. We demonstrate a deep learning-based side-channel attack on a protected FPGA implementation of AES which can recover a subkey from less than 500 power traces. In contrast to previous attacks on FPGA implementations of AES which targeted the last round, the presented attack uses the first round as the attack point. Any randomized clock countermeasure is significantly weakened by an attack on the first round because the effect of randomness accumulated over multiple encryption rounds is lost.

Keywords: Side-channel attack · Random Execution Time · Randomized Clock · Countermeasure · Oversampling · Deep Learning · FPGA · AES · Correlation Power Analysis

1 Introduction

The idea of randomizing the execution time of cryptographic algorithms to protect implementations against side-channel attacks is as old as the attacks themselves [1,2]. There have been numerous papers exploring the topic in the past, mostly for software implementations [3]. Several papers have also suggested ways of implementing randomized clocks to protect FPGA implementations. Their security evaluations have shown that the proposed countermeasures are resistant

---

M. Brisfors and M. Moraitis—Both authors contributed equally to this manuscript. This work was supported in part by the research grant 2021-02426 from Vinnova, the research grant 2020-11632 from the Swedish Civil Contingencies Agency, and the Vinnova Competence Center for Trustworthy Edge Computing Systems and Applications at KTH Royal Institute of Technology.

G.-V. Jourdan et al. (Eds.): FPS 2022, LNCS 13877, pp. 38–53, 2023.
https://doi.org/10.1007/978-3-031-30122-3_3

to Differential Power Analysis (DPA)/Correlation Power Analysis (CPA) [4–16], or Deep Learning (DL)-based EM analysis [16].

However, in this paper, we show that it is possible to break countermeasures based on clock randomization by using a sampling frequency that is much higher than the clock of the cryptographic implementation, synchronizing the traces with pre-processing, and carefully selecting the attack point. The main contributions of the paper are:

- We highlight the importance of oversampling in side-channel analysis by demonstrating how a seemingly secure countermeasure can be broken when the oversampling rate is sufficiently high. Ignoring oversampling may lead to an overestimation of the security of randomized clock countermeasures.
- We present a deep learning-based side-channel attack on a protected FPGA implementation of AES which targets the first round. To the best of our knowledge, all previous attacks on an FPGA implementation of AES with randomized clock targeted the last round [4–16]. Attacking the first round significantly weakens any randomized clock countermeasure because the effect of randomness accumulated over the multiple encryption rounds is lost.
- We propose a randomized clock implementation in which the varying frequency is achieved by an asynchronous switching between four stable frequencies using a fifth frequency and a random number generator.

The rest of the paper is organized as follows. Section 2 reviews the previous work on randomized clock countermeasures. Section 3 presents our randomized clock implementation. Section 4 describes the methods which we use to break the randomized clock countermeasure. Section 5 summarizes the experimental results. Finally, Sect. 6 concludes the paper.

2   Previous Work

Various techniques for randomizing the execution time of cryptographic algorithms have been proposed over the years to protect implementations against side-channel attacks, including using randomized clocks, the addition of random delays or dummy operations, random execution re-ordering, and random branching [3]. In hardware, the majority of countermeasures focus on inserting random delays or randomizing the clock.

To the best of our knowledge, the first hardware-based random delay insertion method was presented in [4]. The main idea is to insert random delays in the datapath of a cryptographic processor in order to randomize its power consumption profile. To realize that, a gate-level implementation of a random delay and a random wait flip-flop was proposed. In [5] the concept is transferred to FPGAs and the resistance of the resulting countermeasure to Differential Power Analysis (DPA) is evaluated.

In [8] a key scheduler controlled by a True Random Number Generator (TRNG) is introduced to create the effect of a randomized clock. To achieve that, the scheduler randomly selects between the output of a set of positive edge and negative edge flip-flops. The approach is further extended in [9] by injecting dummy data during the idle periods.

In [6] a design that uses a different frequency to encrypt each 128-bit plaintext block of an AES-128-CTR FPGA implementation is presented (CTR stands for the counter mode operation of a block cipher). In this design, multiple frequencies $f_1, \ldots, f_n$ are generated by dividing a base frequency f given by a single-input ring oscillator. In addition, four out of the n generated frequencies are phase shifted using Digital Clock Managers (DCMs) to obtain their phase shifted copies $\{f_{i\_0°}, f_{i\_90°}, f_{i\_180°}, f_{i\_270°}\}$, for $i \in \{1, 2, 3, 4\}$. The selection among multiple frequencies is performed pseudo-randomly using a multiplexer controlled by a Linear Feedback Shift Register (LFSR). Later, in [7] it is suggested that performing frequency switching in every clock cycle instead of every new plaintext block offers greater security. In [10], following the same idea, a base clock frequency f is phase shifted through DCMs to create n new frequencies, each shifted by $360/n$ degrees. The selection among multiple frequencies is performed using a clock multiplexer tree controlled by a TRNG. In [11], the design presented in [10] is improved by incorporating the floating mean method [12,13] to generate uniform random numbers.

In [14], four generated frequencies that are multiples of a base clock frequency are used. The selection among frequencies is performed using a multiplexer controlled by an LFSR which is polled at the end of each clock cycle.

In [15] an implementation that leverages the ability of MMCMs to be reconfigured at runtime is presented. The FPGA Block RAMs (BRAMs) are utilized to store different MMCM configurations that define selected sets of frequencies. For each MMCM, m possible configurations, with n output frequencies defined in each, are stored. The implementation proposed in [15] uses $n = 3$ and $m = 1024$, resulting in 3,072 different clock frequencies in total. Since the reconfiguration of MMCMs takes a considerable amount of time (equivalent to 82 encryptions in their case), at least two MMCMs have to be deployed so that one is working while the other one is being reconfigured to achieve runtime frequency tuning. As in [10], the selection among frequencies is performed using a multiplexer controlled by an RNG. The authors use the number of different *cumulative completion times* generated by their approach as a metric of its resilience. With an AES-128 implementation that takes $r = 10$ clock cycles to complete an encryption, the number of different cumulative times to completion is calculated as $_{r+n-1}C_r \times m = 66 \times 1024 = 67,584$[1].

In [16] a more lightweight and scalable solution that can generate even more different times to completion is presented. To generate different frequencies, MMCMs apply a scaling factor to an input clock. Thus, in a constant MMCM configuration, different input frequencies produce different output frequencies. Taking that into consideration, the authors of [16] propose a design that consists of a software-based clock randomizer that generates frequencies in a given range that are fed into an MMCM with constant configuration. The clock randomizer module consists of a processing system core (available in modern FPGAs

---

[1] Note that $_nC_r$ is an alternative notation of $\binom{n}{r}$.

such as Xilinx Ultrascale) that controls the configuration of two programmable clock dividers. A Phase-Locked Loop (PLL) creates a stable clock frequency that passes through the clock dividers and is subsequently fed into an MMCM through a glitch-free clock gate. The MMCM generates n different frequencies by applying the preset scaling factors to the input frequency. Finally, the selection among these n frequencies is done using an RNG-controlled clock multiplexer (that allows glitch-free switching between clocks) which outputs the randomized clock used for the encryption.

The advantage of this approach over the one in [15] is that it does not require the use of BRAMs to store different MMCM configurations[2] and that it is more agile since the input frequencies are controlled in software. The authors adopted the *number of cumulative completion times* metric to evaluate their approach. They tested two implementations, one with $n = 4$ MMCM output frequencies and one with $n = 8$. Their AES-128 implementation takes $r = 13$ clock cycles to complete an encryption and uses $m = 257$ different base frequencies. This results in $_{r+n-1}C_r \times m = 560 \times 257 = 143,920$ for $n = 4$ and $77,520 \times 257 = 19,922,640$ different cumulative times to completion for $n = 8$.

In [17], a lightweight countermeasure offering resistance to remote power attacks for up to one million encryptions is presented. The idea is to add noise to the timing measurements of digital converters which are used in remote attacks. This is realized by adding a random delay in the magnitude of picoseconds to each clock cycle.

3   Proposed Randomized Clock Implementation

The block diagram of the proposed randomized clock is shown in Fig. 1. It consists of an MMCM block, five global clock simple buffers (BUFG), two FDRE D flip flops, a 4-to-1 multiplexer and a 2-input AND gate. A detailed description of the Xilinx 7 series FPGA components referenced in this work is available in the user guide UG953 [18].

The MMCM block has one clock input, four clock outputs and a locked signal to indicate when the generated clocks are ready to be used. The generated clocks pass through one BUFG each and then connect to the 4-to-1 multiplexer. In the implementations presented in the related work [15,16], the multiplexers are implemented through a tree of 2-to-1 global clock MUX buffers (BUFG-MUX_CTRL). A BUFGMUX_CTRL is a primitive of Xilinx 7 series FPGAs that allows a clean, glitch-free switching between two input frequencies. To achieve that, whenever setup/hold conditions are about to be violated by the switching of the select signal, the output clock appears one clock later. In our implementation, we do not want to have this functionality because our aim is to have the selector signal forcefully change between frequencies to create a randomized clock. Such a design choice leads to a clock whose cycles are occasionally too

---

[2] An alternative design with dynamically reconfigurable MMCMs is mentioned, but not implemented.

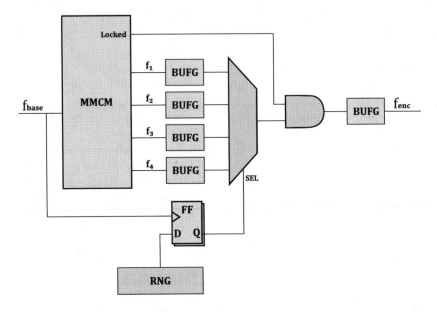

Fig. 1. The block diagram of the proposed randomized clock implementation.

short for the AES core to complete the encryption in time. Therefore, the multiplexer in our design can be implemented either by three BUFGMUXs set to asynchronous switching,[3] or a single 6-input 2-output look-up table (LUT6).

The selector signal comes from two FDRE D flip flops that are clocked with the base frequency and store values from a random number generator (RNG). The RNG can be a TRNG or a PRNG (e.g. an LFSR). In our experiments, we used a set sequence of pre-generated pseudo-random numbers. By adding these two registers, the random numbers arrive at the multiplexer with half the frequency of the base clock, regardless of the frequency of the RNG implementation. This assures a stable select signal.

Finally, the randomized frequency created at the output of the multiplexer is combined with the locked signal of the MMCM (high when the MMCM frequencies are ready to be used) using a 2-input AND gate. Its output passes through a BUFG which outputs the randomized clock used for encryption.

In Fig. 2 the randomized clock generation of the presented implementation is illustrated. On every positive edge of the base clock, f_{base}, the randomized clock's value, f_{enc}, switches asynchronously to the value of one of the four clocks, f_1, f_2, f_3, f_4, depending on the value of the select signal, SEL, generated by the TRNG. To assess how many different frequencies our implementation can generate, we performed a simulation. In the simulation, each base clock cycle

---

[3] A BUFGMUX_CTRL is a Global Clock Control Buffer (BUFGCTRL) with the clock enable (CE) inputs set to constant 1 and select inputs (S) connected to the selection signal. When the select signal is connected to the CE inputs, the glitch-free functionality is lost and the switching occurs asynchronously.

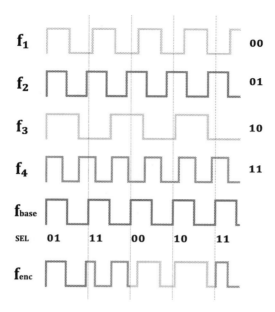

Fig. 2. Proposed randomized clock generation.

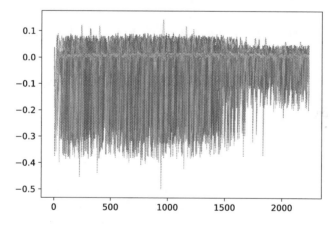

Fig. 3. 100 randomly selected power traces captured with 80× oversampling representing a complete encryption. A lack of gaps implies good randomization.

is represented with a precision of 100K samples and the clocks are simulated 3.7M times. The results show that our randomized clock implementation can generate pulses of at least 403 different frequencies. Therefore, assuming an AES implementation with $r = 10$, the number of cumulative completion times of our randomized clock is $_{r+n-1}C_r \times m = {}_{10+403-1}C_{10} \times 1 \approx 3.478 \times 10^{19}$.

4 Side-Channel Analysis in the Presence of a Randomized Clock

In this section we describe the methods we use to break the randomized clock countermeasure: oversampling, trace pre-processing, and CPA and DL-based side-channel analysis.

4.1 Oversampling

In signal processing, *oversampling* is the process of sampling a signal at a sampling frequency significantly higher than the Nyquist rate[4]. A signal is said to be oversampled by a factor of N if it is sampled at N times the Nyquist rate. It is known that oversampling can improve resolution and signal-to-noise ratio [19].

4.2 Pre-processing

Several pre-processing methods have been proposed to combat trace misalignment and re-enable a successful analysis. These methods include dynamic time wrapping (DTW)/elastic alignment [20], pattern matching [21], fast Fourier transform (FFT) [22], principal component analysis (PCA) [23], rapid alignment method (RAM) [24] and sliding window (SW) [25].

In this paper, we test two pre-processing methods: (1) sliding window [25] with a window size of 20 and (2) trace synchronisation based on deviation from the mean. We apply trace synchronisation on sufficiently oversampled power measurements using the following simple approach.

By setting a threshold based on the deviation from the mean of the value being more than 1.5σ, we identify peaks corresponding to the rising edge of the randomized clock which is used for encryption. As one can see from Fig. 4, traces captured with a high oversampling factor have distinct power peaks. These peaks can be used to synchronize traces for a specific round of the algorithm. The lower the oversampling factor is, the less distinct the peaks are. So, traces captured with a high oversampling factor are easier to synchronize. They are also more likely to accurately reflect the power consumption.

Using the threshold, we synchronize traces for the first round of AES by finding, for each trace, the first point where the trace crosses the threshold after setup instructions are completed. Selecting a window around this point yields a good synchronization as one can see in Fig. 5.

A similar synchronization strategy can be applied to the last round of AES by going backwards.

4.3 Correlation Power Analysis

We perform the CPA in a usual way [26], by assigning a power hypothesis to every trace in the data set, for every subkey guess, with the subkey size being

---

[4] The Nyquist rate is defined as twice the bandwidth of the signal.

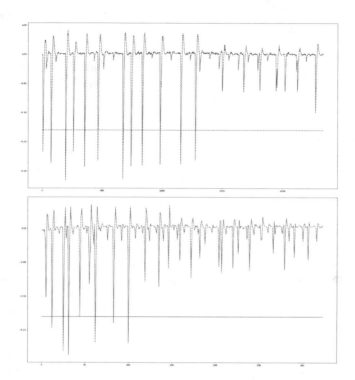

Fig. 4. Comparison of traces captured with 80× (top) and 8× (bottom) oversampling using the same threshold for identifying peaks. Insufficient oversampling may lead to an incorrect sampling/measurement of peak power consumption.

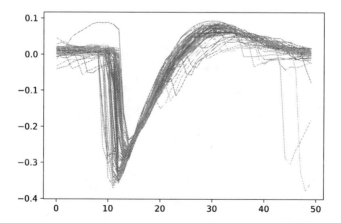

Fig. 5. A zoomed-in interval of traces from Fig. 3 representing the first round of AES after synchronization. This interval is given as input to MLPs.

a byte. The Hamming distance between the states of round 9 and round 10 is used as a power hypothesis:

$$P_i = HW(ShiftRows^{-1}(c_i) \oplus Sbox^{-1}(c_i \oplus RK10_i)),$$

where c_i is the ith byte of the ciphertext, $RK10_i$ is the guess for 10th round subkey i, and HW is the Hamming weight, for $i \in \{1, 2, \ldots, 16\}$.

To recover each subkey, we calculate the Pearson correlation coefficient for the corresponding power hypotheses and trace measurements and choose the subkey guess which maximizes the absolute value of the correlation coefficient.

4.4   Deep Learning-Based Analysis

It is known that deep learning-based side-channel analysis can handle trace misalignment caused by jitter without any pre-processing [27]. This makes it a good choice for dealing with temporal noise introduced by randomized clocks.

We use the profiling approach in which, at the profiling stage, a neural network model is trained to learn the power profile of the target algorithm implementation for all possible values of the subkey and, at the attack stage, the model is used to classify traces captured from the device under attack.

We train multilayer perceptron (MLP) neural networks of type $\mathcal{N}_i : \mathbb{R}^n \to \mathbb{I}^{256}$ for the subkey $i \in \{1, 2, \ldots, 16\}$, where n is the number of data points in traces, $\mathbb{R}$ is the set of real numbers, and $\mathbb{I} := \{x \in \mathbb{R} \mid 0 \leq x \leq 1\}$. The MLP architecture is listed in Table 1. *Sbox* output values in the first round were used as labels for traces.

For training, we use a set of 10M traces captured for random messages. From this set, 70% is used for training and 30% for validation. The training is carried out using *Nadam* optimizer with a learning rate of 0.002. The maximum number of epochs is set to 12 with a batch size of 1024. Only the model with the best validation accuracy is saved.

To test the models, we use two metrics:

1. Accuracy of subkey prediction from a single trace, and
2. Average number of traces required for the subkey recovery.

Note that the single-trace prediction accuracy metric is not applicable to CPA since single-trace CPA is impossible. The average number of required traces is defined as the average number of traces required to recover the subkey in the majority of tests performed on a randomly permuted test data set.

4.5   Importance of Using the First Round as the Attack Point

In previous work, the last round of AES is used as the attack point. This is because for a typical[5] FPGA implementation of AES, DPA/CPA attacks on the first round are not successful.

---

[5] Here by "typical" we mean the AES implementation in which one round is computed per clock cycle and the state is stored at the end of the round.

Table 1. MLP Architecture.

Layer (type)	Output Shape	Param #
batch_normalization_1	(None, 50)	200
dense_1 (Dense)	(None, 1024)	52224
batch_normalization_2	(None, 1024)	4096
relu_1 (ReLU)	(None, 1024)	0
dense_2 (Dense)	(None, 512)	524800
batch_normalization_3	(None, 512)	2048
relu_2 (ReLU)	(None, 512)	0
dense_3 (Dense)	(None, 256)	131328
batch_normalization_4	(None, 256)	1024
relu_3 (ReLU)	(None, 256)	0
dense_4 (Dense)	(None, 256)	65792
softmax_1 (Softmax)	(None, 256)	0
Total params:	781,512	
Trainable params:	777,828	
Non-trainable params:	3,684	

However, as our experiments show, the DL-based analysis can recover the key from the first round. Despite the weaker leakage of the first round as compared to the last, such an approach is preferable when a randomized clock is used as a countermeasure for the following reasons. In a first-round attack, the cumulative times to completion metric is reduced to the number of different frequencies. This considerably weakens any randomized clock countermeasure. For example, for a first round attack with $r = 1$ in [16], the number of different times to completion gets reduced from $67,584$ to $_{r+n-1}C_r \times m = 3 \times 1024 = 3,072$ and from $19,922,640$ to $_{r+n-1}C_r \times m = 8 \times 257 = 2,056$. Furthermore, when attacking the first round, the overall effect of randomness accumulated[6] over multiple encryption rounds is lost.

5 Experimental Results

This section presents the results of our experiments.

5.1 Equipment

The equipment used for our experiments is a CW1173 ChipWhisperer-Lite and a CW305 Artix 7 FPGA target board.

---

[6] The cumulative effect of randomness can be described by a random walk, and the variance of a random walk increases with the walk length. Thus, if the timing shifts are randomly distributed, the uncertainty in the first round is provably smaller than the uncertainty in the last.

ChipWhisperer [28] is a fully open-source, low-cost toolkit for hardware security evaluation. It handles power trace acquisition and communication of target devices with a computer, making side-channel attacks easier to perform. The power measurements are taken over a shunt resistor connected between the power supply and the target device. ChipWhisperer-Lite employs a synchronous capture method, which greatly improves trace synchronization while also lowering the required sample rate and data storage. ChipWhisperer-Lite has a buffer size of up to 24,400 samples that can be captured at a maximum sampling rate of 105 MS/s.

The CW305 target board used in our experiments is equipped with an Artix 7 XC7A35T-2FTG256 FPGA. The cryptographic algorithm implementation in which we integrated our randomized clock countermeasure is Google's AES-128 implementation which can be found in the Vault Project repository [29]. The AES core module is integrated into the ChipWhisperer interface [30]. The design synthesis and bitstream generation is performed with Vivado 2019.1.

5.2   Trace Acquisition with Oversampling

Side-channel analysis with a high oversampling rate requires the use of measuring equipment that allows high sampling frequencies. Our equipment, ChipWhisperer-Lite, can handle sampling rates of only up to 105 MS/s. Therefore, the FPGA must run at 1.3 MHz to approximate a 40× oversampling or at 0.65 MHz to approximate an 80× oversampling. This goes against the MMCM specification which requires an input frequency in the range of 10–800 MHz.

To overcome this limitation imposed by our equipment, we use a 10Mhz base frequency and add a clock divider after each frequency with the division parameter $d = 10$. The frequencies generated by the MMCM are: $f_1 = 11.9713$ MHz MHz, $f_2 = 7.7315$ MHz MHz, $f_3 = 9.2778$ MHz MHz, $f_4 = 12.6515$ MHz MHz, with an $f_{mean} = 10.408$ MHz. When oversampling, we assume an FPGA base frequency of 1 MHz, e.g. for 40× oversampling we sample at 80 MHz (taking into account the Nyquist rate).Since the frequency of the randomized clock is unknown, not all traces are oversampled by this nominal degree. Furthermore, the asynchronous frequency switching (discussed in Sect. 3) causes about 3% of ciphertexts to be incorrect. Incorrect encryptions are typically acceptable in applications in which re-encryption is possible, e.g. the encryption of a nonce for challenge-response authentication. To achieve an 80× oversampling, a sampling frequency of 160 Ms/s is required. This exceeds the maximum frequency of 105 Ms/s that is specified in the Chipwhisperer datasheet. However, we found out that the hardware can periodically capture traces at this requested frequency. Therefore, with the additional step of discarding the measurements where our equipment failed to meet the required sampling frequency, we were able to capture and analyse traces with 80× oversampling.

In a real attack, slowing down the clock of an FPGA implementation would require a different approach, especially if countermeasures to prevent it, e.g. the clock manipulation detector [10], are present. In our threat scenario, we do not consider such attacks. We assume that, to oversample, the adversary will use an

Table 2. Comparison of CPA results with previous work.

Method	# Traces to recover full key		Key Enumer	How Evaluated
	Unprotected	Protected		
RFTC [15]	<2K	>4M	No	not defined
DFR [16]	20-30K	>1-5M	$< 2^{25}$	avg of 20 tests
Presented	<1.1K	>10M*	No	avg. of 10 tests

*For 8× oversampling factor

oscilloscope that can capture traces at a much higher rate than the frequency of the clock used in the encryption core of the FPGA.

5.3   Overhead Evaluation

We compared our randomized clock implementation with two state-of-the-art architectures that offer the highest level of side-channel resistance: the Runtime Frequency Tuning Countermeasure (RFTC) [15] and the Dynamic Frequency Randomization (DFR) [16].

Table 3 lists the FPGA resources and timing overhead. One can see that the presented implementation has the smallest hardware and timing overhead.

5.4   Comparison Considerations

To compare countermeasures properly, one has to take into account the number of traces required to break the unprotected implementation, as well as the sampling and operating frequency of the implementations. The number of traces for CPA is shown in Table 2. When comparing these numbers it should be taken into account that [16] uses EM side-channels while [15] and the presented method use power. EM side-channels are usually noisier and attacks typically require an order of magnitude more traces.

Regarding sampling and operating frequencies, in [15], power measurements are collected using an oscilloscope with a 100 MHz bandwidth and a maximum sampling rate of 1 Gs/s. The randomized clock frequencies are in the range of 12–48 MHz.

In [16] an oscilloscope with a bandwidth of 500 MHz and maximum sampling rate of 5 Gs/s is used. The frequencies of the randomized clock are in the range of 17.5–213.3 MHz for the implementation based on four clocks, and 17.5–426.5 MHz for the one based on eight clocks.

No information about the sampling frequency is given in [15,16]. We can make a rough estimation as follows. Taking into account the maximum sampling frequency of their equipment, and considering the mean operating frequency as nominal, in [15] up to 17× oversampling can be achieved while in [16] up to 22× and 12× for the four and eight clock implementations, respectively. Since there is a big gap between their lowest and highest operating frequencies, these numbers are certainly not accurate. However, they are our best estimate.

Table 3. Overhead comparison with the state-of-the-art implementations of randomized clock.

Method	FPGA resources			Timing overhead
	# BRAM	# MMCM	# BUFG	
RFTC [15]	20	2	N/A	1.72×
DFR [16]	0	1	12-23	1.54-58.9×
Presented	0	1	5	1.27×

Table 4. CPA and MLP subkey recovery results for different oversampling factors on the proposed randomized clock implementation (average of 10 tests).

Over-sampling factor	Last round attack		First round attack	
	CPA-SYNC	SW-CPA	MLP	
	# Traces	# Traces	single-trace acc,%	# Traces
Unprotected 2×	400	1000	0.66	112
Protected 8×	>10M	>10M	0.39	>10M
Protected 20×	50k	>10M	0.49	582
Protected 40×	5k	>10M	0.51	319
Protected 80×	3k	5M	0.52	430

In our case, we sample $2n\times$ data points per clock cycle, for $n \in \{8, 20, 40, 80\}$. The frequencies of the randomized clock are in the range of 7.73–12.65 MHz.

5.5   Attack Results

Table 4 presents the results of our CPA and DL-based power analysis for different oversampling factors. In the table, we show results for the MLP networks only. We also performed experiments with Convolutional Neural Networks (CNN). The results were similar to the MLPs. This is probably because we synchronized traces at the pre-processing stage.

We can see that both methods fail for the 8× oversampling case. This is due to the poor synchronization and measurement quality caused by low oversampling. For 20× oversampling, we can see that both the CPA and DL-based attacks are able to recover the subkey and, as the oversampling factor grows, fewer traces are required.

Figure 6 shows the probability of recovering a subkey using the attack on the first round of AES after synchronizing the traces. The 8× oversampling case is omitted because the subkey cannot be recovered. Despite a slightly lower single-trace accuracy, the 40× model recovers subkeys faster than the 80× model. However, this may due to the fact that the number of tests was small.

The results of Table 4 highlight the importance of oversampling for side-channel analysis and show that ignoring oversampling may lead to an overestimation of the security of randomized clock countermeasures.

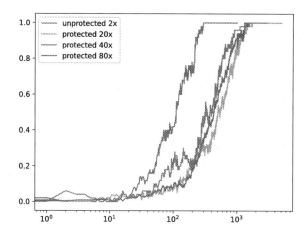

Fig. 6. MLP subkey recovery success rate.

5.6   Comparison to Previous DL-based Attacks

Next, we compare our results to [16] where a DL-based analysis based on MLP and CNN is also performed.

In one of their implementations, DFR-4-Ø, the MMCM has four output frequencies and a constant input frequency. This implementation does not have the best security/overhead trade-off, but it has a structure similar to ours. The only difference is that, in DFR-4-Ø, the switching between frequencies is done synchronously. Our implementation switches asynchronously to get a more unpredictable output clock.

According to [16], DFR-4-Ø can be attacked with 1M traces using FFT-CPA, 200K traces using FFT-MLP, and 20K traces using CNN. All attacks target the last round. Considering that EM-based attacks typically need an order of magnitude more traces compared to power analysis, these numbers translate to roughly 100K for the FFT-CPA, 20K for the FFT-MLP and 2K for the CNN. Also, considering that they need approximately twice as many traces as us to attack unprotected AES, these numbers are similar to the 10× oversampling case in Table 4. Their attack use key enumeration up to $3^{16} \approx 2^{25}$ (equivalent to key guessing entropy ≤ 2) while we do not use key enumeration.

6   Conclusion

We presented a powerful side-channel attack on an FPGA implementation of AES with a randomized clock targeting the first round as the attack point. Such an approach has a greater potential to break any randomized clock countermeasure than the attacks on the last round because the effect of randomness accumulated over the multiple rounds is lost. We also demonstrated the importance of high oversampling in the security analysis of randomized clock countermeasures. Our results show that these countermeasures have a fundamental flaw. Oversampling enabled us to synchronize power traces and this led to successful attacks.

All our scripts and the source code of the randomized clock implementation are publicly available at https://github.com/MichailM7/Do_not_rely_on_clock_randomization.

References

1. Kocher, P., Jaffe, J., Jun, B.: Differential power analysis. In: Wiener, M. (ed.) CRYPTO 1999. LNCS, vol. 1666, pp. 388–397. Springer, Heidelberg (1999). https://doi.org/10.1007/3-540-48405-1_25
2. Kocher, P.C., Jaffe, J., Jun, B.: Using unpredictable information to minimize leakage from smartcards and other cryptosystems. US Patent 6,327,661
3. Kocher, P.C., Jaffe, J., Jun, B., Rohatgi, P.: Introduction to differential power analysis. J. Cryptogr. Eng. 1, 5–27 (2011)
4. Bucci, M., Luzzi, R., Guglielmo, M., Trifiletti, A.: A countermeasure against differential power analysis based on random delay insertion. In: IEEE International Symposium on Circuits and Systems (ISCAS), vol. 4, pp. 3547–3550 (2005)
5. Lu, Y., O'Neill, M.P., McCanny, J.V.: FPGA implementation and analysis of random delay insertion countermeasure against DPA. In: 2008 International Conference on Field-Programmable Technology, pp. 201–208 (2008)
6. Zafar, Y., Har, D.: A novel countermeasure enhancing side channel immunity in FPGAs. In: 2008 International Conference on Advances in Electronics and Microelectronics, pp. 132–137 (2008)
7. Zafar, Y., Park, J., Har, D.: Random clocking induced DPA attack immunity in FPGAs. In: 2010 IEEE International Conference on Industrial Technology, pp. 1068–1070 (2010)
8. Boey, K.H., Hodgers, P., Lu, Y., O'Neill, M., Woods, R.: Security of AES Sbox designs to power analysis. In: 2010 17th IEEE International Conference on Electronics, Circuits and Systems, pp. 1232–1235 (2010)
9. Boey, K.H., Lu, Y., O'Neill, M., Woods, R.: Random clock against differential power analysis. In: 2010 IEEE Asia Pacific Conference on Circuits and Systems, pp. 756–759 (2010)
10. Güneysu, T., Moradi, A.: Generic side-channel countermeasures for reconfigurable devices. In: Preneel, B., Takagi, T. (eds.) CHES 2011. LNCS, vol. 6917, pp. 33–48. Springer, Heidelberg (2011). https://doi.org/10.1007/978-3-642-23951-9_3
11. Ravi, P., Bhasin, S., Breier, J., Chattopadhyay, A.: PPAP and iPPAP: PLL-based protection against physical attacks. In: 2018 IEEE Computer Society Annual Symposium on VLSI (ISVLSI), pp. 620–625. IEEE (2018)
12. Coron, J.-S., Kizhvatov, I.: An efficient method for random delay generation in embedded software. In: Clavier, C., Gaj, K. (eds.) CHES 2009. LNCS, vol. 5747, pp. 156–170. Springer, Heidelberg (2009). https://doi.org/10.1007/978-3-642-04138-9_12
13. Coron, J.-S., Kizhvatov, I.: Analysis and improvement of the random delay countermeasure of CHES 2009. In: Mangard, S., Standaert, F.-X. (eds.) CHES 2010. LNCS, vol. 6225, pp. 95–109. Springer, Heidelberg (2010). https://doi.org/10.1007/978-3-642-15031-9_7

14. Fritzke, A.W.: Obfuscating against side-channel power analysis using hiding techniques for AES (2012)
15. Jayasinghe, D., Ignjatovic, A., Parameswaran, S.: RFTC: runtime frequency tuning countermeasure using FPGA dynamic reconfiguration to mitigate power analysis attacks. In: 2019 56th ACM/IEEE Design Automation Conference (DAC), pp. 1–6. IEEE (2019)
16. Hettwer, B., Das, K., Leger, S., Gehrer, S., Güneysu, T.: Lightweight side-channel protection using dynamic clock randomization. In: 2020 30th International Conference on Field-Programmable Logic and Applications (FPL), pp. 200–207 (2020)
17. Jayasinghe, D., Ignjatovic, A., Parameswaran, S.: UCloD: small clock delays to mitigate remote power analysis attacks. IEEE Access **9**, 108411–108425 (2021)
18. Xilinx: Vivado Design Suite 7 Series FPGA and Zynq-7000 SoC Libraries Guide (UG953) (2022)
19. Schlichthärle, D.: Digital Filters. Editorial Springer (2000)
20. van Woudenberg, J.G.J., Witteman, M.F., Bakker, B.: Improving differential power analysis by elastic alignment. In: Kiayias, A. (ed.) CT-RSA 2011. LNCS, vol. 6558, pp. 104–119. Springer, Heidelberg (2011). https://doi.org/10.1007/978-3-642-19074-2_8
21. Abdellatif, K.M., Couroussé, D., Potin, O., Jaillon, P.: Filtering-based CPA: a successful side-channel attack against desynchronization countermeasures. In: Proceedings of the Fourth Workshop on Cryptography and Security in Computing Systems, pp. 29–32 (2017)
22. Schimmel, O., Duplys, P., Boehl, E., Hayek, J., Bosch, R., Rosenstiel, W.: Correlation power analysis in frequency domain. In: COSADE 2010 First International Workshop on Constructive SideChannel Analysis and Secure Design (2010)
23. Hogenboom, J., Batina, L.: Principal component analysis and side-channel attacks-master thesis. In: Principal Component Analysis and Side-Channel Attacks-Master Thesis, pp. 536–539 (2010)
24. Muijrers, R.A., van Woudenberg, J.G.J., Batina, L.: RAM: rapid alignment method. In: Prouff, E. (ed.) CARDIS 2011. LNCS, vol. 7079, pp. 266–282. Springer, Heidelberg (2011). https://doi.org/10.1007/978-3-642-27257-8_17
25. Fledel, D., Wool, A.: Sliding-window correlation attacks against encryption devices with an unstable clock. In: Cid, C., Jacobson, M., Jr. (eds.) SAC 2018. LNCS, vol. 11349, pp. 193–215. Springer, Cham (2019). https://doi.org/10.1007/978-3-030-10970-7_9
26. Brier, E., Clavier, C., Olivier, F.: Correlation power analysis with a leakage model. In: Joye, M., Quisquater, J.-J. (eds.) CHES 2004. LNCS, vol. 3156, pp. 16–29. Springer, Heidelberg (2004). https://doi.org/10.1007/978-3-540-28632-5_2
27. Robyns, P., Quax, P., Lamotte, W.: Improving CEMA using correlation optimization. IACR Trans. Cryptogr. Hardw. Embed. Syst. 1–24 (2019)
28. NewAE Technology Inc.: Chipwhisperer. https://newae.com/tools/chipwhisperer
29. ProjectVault: Verilog implementation of AES-128. https://github.com/ProjectVault/orp/tree/master/hardware/mselSoC/src/systems/geophyte/rtl/verilog/crypto_aes/rtl/verilog
30. NewAE Technology Inc.: CW305 Artix Target common sources. https://github.com/newaetech/chipwhisperer/tree/develop/hardware/victims/cw305_artixtarget/fpga/common

Post-quantum and UC-Secure Oblivious Transfer from SPHF with Grey Zone

Slim Bettaieb[1], Loïc Bidoux[2], Olivier Blazy[3], Baptiste Cottier[4(✉)], and David Pointcheval[4]

[1] Worldline, Seclin, France
[2] Technology Innovation Institute, Abu Dhabi, United Arab Emirates
[3] Ecole Polytechnique, IPP, Palaiseau, France
[4] DIENS, École normale supérieure, CNRS, Inria, PSL University, Paris, France
baptiste.cottier@ens.fr

Abstract. Oblivious Transfer (OT) is a major primitive for secure multi-party computation. Indeed, combined with symmetric primitives along with garbled circuits, it allows any secure function evaluation between two parties. In this paper, we propose a new approach to build OT protocols. Interestingly, our new paradigm features a security analysis in the Universal Composability (UC) framework and may be instantiated from post-quantum primitives. In order to do so, we define a new primitive named Smooth Projective Hash Function with Grey Zone (SPHFwGZ) which can be seen as a relaxation of the classical Smooth Projective Hash Functions, with a subset of the words for which one cannot claim correctness nor smoothness: the grey zone. As a concrete application, we provide two instantiations of SPHFwGZ respectively based on the Diffie-Hellman and the Learning With Errors (LWE) problems. Hence, we propose a quantum-resistant OT protocol with UC-security in the random oracle model.

1 Introduction

Smooth Projective Hash Function (SPHF), or Hash Proof System as introduced by Cramer and Shoup in [11], is a cryptographic primitive initially designed to provide IND-CCA encryption schemes. Over the years, SPHFs have been used for many applications such as Password-Authenticated Key Exchange [1, 2,14,18], Zero-Knowledge Proofs [3,16] or Witness Encryption [12]. Since their introduction, SPHFs have been developed over classical hard problems such as discrete logarithm or factorization. However, post-quantum cryptography does not seem to be as easily compliant with SPHF. In [17], Katz *et al.* introduced *Approximate Smooth Projective Hash Functions*. The correctness property of an SPHF claims that the hash value and the projective hash value are required to be equal on words in an NP-language, when knowing a witness, while the smoothness property expects them to be independent when no witness exists. Approximate SPHF uses an approximate correctness, that allows those values to be close, relatively to a given distance. Furthermore, languages relying on code-based or lattice-based ciphertexts result in a gap between the set of valid

G.-V. Jourdan et al. (Eds.): FPS 2022, LNCS 13877, pp. 54–70, 2023.
https://doi.org/10.1007/978-3-031-30122-3_4

ciphertexts of a given value μ, and the values that decrypt into μ. As mentioned in [5], an adversary could maliciously generate one of those ciphertexts and open the door for practical attacks. The presence of this gap can also be problematic when expecting to work in the Universal Composability framework [9].

Related Works. In this section, we focus on SPHF-related previous constructions. In code-based cryptography, the first proposition was made by Persichetti in [21]. The SPHF proposed there uses a weaker smoothness definition, called universality. Strictly speaking, this is not a drawback as we can transform an SPHF with universality property to a word-dependent SPHF with smoothness property. However, the main issue with this candidate is that the proof is done on random keys, rather than the whole keys. This has for consequence that an adversary can exploit some well-chosen keys resulting in a failure of the proof. A second construction was designed in [5]. As said before, when working with lattices and codes, languages based on ciphertexts present a grey zone. In this work, Bettaieb *et al.* withdraw this gap using a zero-knowledge proof asserting if two different ciphertexts of the same message are valid, reducing the SPHF on the set of valid ciphertexts, resulting in the first *gapless* post-quantum SPHF. A solution based on codes is also given in [24], but their solution offers an Approximate SPHF with computational smoothness, while real SPHF expects statistical/perfect smoothness. In lattice-based cryptography, the first construction was given in [17] where Katz *et al.* introduced the notion of Approximate SPHF. Their language not being exactly defined as the valid LWE-ciphertexts, decoding procedure was expensive, as detailed in [4]. This latter article, motivated by this issue, offers the first non-approximated SPHF based on lattices later used with the framework from [6] in [7] to build a Post-quantum UC-secure Oblivious transfer. Their construction, in the standard model, is UC-secure against adaptive corruptions but lacks of efficiency. While the two previous constructions of SPHF are in the standard model, Zha *et al.* [25] propose a SPHF requiring access to a random oracle. Indeed, their language relies on simulation-sound non-interactive zero-knowledge proofs, that we are not able to construct efficiently without random oracles.

Contribution. As mentioned above, a gap appears when working with cryptography based on lattices or codes. Rather than withdraw this gap as done in [5], we focus on the requirements needed in order to tame this gap, with an additional notion of *Decomposition Intractability* when trying to exploit this gap. Therefore, we introduce *Smooth Projective Hash Functions with Grey Zone* (SPHFwGZ) as an SPHF with the *Decomposition Intractability* property: we will require a language $\mathcal{L}$, hard to decide, as for any non-trivial SPHF, but also with additional intractability for finding two *complementary* words in $\mathcal{L}$ or the gap. As an application of SPHFwGZ, we show that one can design an Oblivious Transfer from any SPHF with Grey Zone on languages of ciphertexts for homomorphic encryption, where the security relies on the semantic security.

We provide two concrete instantiations of SPHFwGZ: the first one relies on the Diffie-Hellman Problem and the ElGamal cryptosystem. As no decryption failure occurs with the ElGamal cryptosystem, the grey zone is empty and the decomposition intractability is obvious. One can note that the resulting SPH-FwGZ is *de facto* an SPHF. The idea behind this instantiation is, on the one hand, to familiarise the reader with our construction, and on the other hand, to point out the fact that the construction is also available from any classical SPHF. A second instantiation is based on lattices and more precisely from the *Learning with Errors* problem. This allows to underline the genericity of our framework.

2   Preliminaries

Oblivious Transfer. Oblivious transfer, introduced by Rabin [22], involves a sender with input two messages m_0, m_1 and a receiver with input a selection bit b so that the latter receives m_b and nothing else, while the former does not learn anything. It provides sender-privacy (no information leakage about m_{1-b}) and receiver-privacy (no information leakage about b).

Universal Composability. Universal Composability is a security model introduced by Canetti [9] taking into account the whole environment (i.e. all exterior interactions) of the execution. Concretely, if a protocol is proven to be universally composable (or *UC-secure*), it can be used concurrently with other protocols without compromising the global protocol security. Proving universally composable security is done thanks to the real world/ideal world paradigm. In the ideal world, we consider an access to a trusted third party. A protocol Π is *UC-secure*, if, for all environment $\mathcal{E}$, there exists a simulator S such that the execution of the protocol Π with adversary $\mathcal{A}$ in the real world, is indistinguishable with the execution of the functionality $\mathcal{F}$ with simulator S in the ideal world.

Smooth Projective Hash Functions. Introduced in 2002 [11], Smooth Projective Hash Functions (SPHF), also known as Hash Proof System (HPS), initially aim to build the first public key encryption scheme secure against chosen ciphertext attacks. Nowadays, SPHF are mainly used for Honest Verifier Zero Knowledge Proofs or Witness Encryption. Such functions work on NP-languages $\mathcal{L} \subset \mathcal{X}$, defined by a binary relation $\mathcal{R}$ such that for any word $x \in \mathcal{X}$, $x \in \mathcal{L}$ if and only if there exists a witness w such that $\mathcal{R}(x, w) = 1$. Then, an SPHF defined on $\mathcal{L} \subset \mathcal{X}$ with values in $\mathcal{V}$ is defined by five algorithms:

- Setup(1^κ): Generates the parameters param from κ, the security parameter where param includes a description of $\mathcal{L}$, a language in $\mathcal{X}$;
- HashKG(param): Generates a random hash key hk;
- ProjKG(hk): Derives the projection key hp;
- Hash(hk, x): Returns the hash value $H_{hk} \in \mathcal{V}$ associated to the word x;
- ProjHash(hp, x, w): Returns $H_{hp} \in \mathcal{V}$ using a witness w linked to the word x.

Those algorithms should ensure two requirements:

- **Correctness:** For any $x \in \mathcal{L}$, with witness w, $H_{hk} = H_{hp}$ under the condition that $\mathcal{R}(x, w) = 1$;

- **Smoothness:** For any $x \in \mathcal{X} \backslash \mathcal{L}$, the distributions of $(\mathsf{hp}, H_{\mathsf{hk}})$ and $(\mathsf{hp}, v \leftarrow \mathcal{V})$ are indistinguishable.

The aforementioned definition of smoothness was introduced by Cramer and Shoup in [11]. Two variants of this definition have later been proposed: The first variation has been provided by Gennaro and Lindell in [14], leading to the notion of GL-SPHF. The only difference with the definition of Cramer and Shoup (recalled above) is that the projection key hp may depend on the word w of the language. The second variant, introduced by Katz and Vaikuntanathan in [17] considers the ability for an attacker to maliciously generate the word w after seeing the projection key hp. In KV-SPHF, the projection depends only on the hashing key and ensures the smoothness even if the word w is chosen after having seen the projection key. GL-SPHF will be enough for our applications, with word-dependent projection keys, as the word will be known beforehand.

3   Smooth Projective Hash Functions with Grey Zone

Our first contribution is the formalization of Smooth Projective Hash Functions with a Grey Zone (SPHFwGZ) which is a relaxation of the classical SPHF in which one cannot claim correctness nor smoothness for a subset of the words. Later, we will provide a quantum-resistant SPHFwGZ based on lattices. With this new definition, we will have two disjoint languages $\mathcal{L}, \mathcal{L}' \subset \mathcal{X}$ that will not necessarily partition the superset $\mathcal{X}$: the remaining subset $\mathcal{X} \backslash (\mathcal{L} \cup \mathcal{L}')$ will be the grey zone.

3.1   Basic Definitions

Let us describe our relaxation of *Smooth Projective Hash Function* from [10] to encompass a *Grey Zone*. An SPHFwGZ is defined with a tuple of algorithms:

- $\mathsf{Setup}(1^\kappa)$: Generate the parameters param from κ, the security parameter, or an explicit random tape (σ, ρ) in $\mathcal{S}_0 \times \mathcal{R}_0$. param includes a description of $\mathcal{L}, \mathcal{L}', \mathcal{X}$, where $\mathcal{L} \cup \mathcal{L}' \subset \mathcal{X}$ and $\mathcal{L} \cap \mathcal{L}' = \emptyset$, and $\mathcal{L}$ is a language hard to decide in $\mathcal{X}$;
- $\mathsf{HashKG}(\mathsf{param})$: Generates a random hash key hk;
- $\mathsf{ProjKG}(\mathsf{hk}, x)$: Derives the projection key hp (it may need x as input);
- $\mathsf{Hash}(\mathsf{hk}, x)$: Returns the hash value $H_{\mathsf{hk}} \in \mathcal{V}$, where $\mathcal{V}$ is the set of hash values, associated to the word x;
- $\mathsf{ProjHash}(\mathsf{hp}, x, w)$: Returns $H_{\mathsf{hp}} \in \mathcal{V}$ using a witness w linked to the word x.

As the classical SPHF, our SPHFwGZ verifies the following statistical properties, for any setup execution that provides param, defining $\mathcal{L}, \mathcal{L}', \mathcal{X}$:

- **Correctness:** For any $x \in \mathcal{L}$, $H_{\mathsf{hk}} = H_{\mathsf{hp}}$, where $\mathsf{hk} \leftarrow \mathsf{HashKG}(\mathsf{param})$, $\mathsf{hp} \leftarrow \mathsf{ProjKG}(\mathsf{hk}, x)$, $H_{\mathsf{hk}} \leftarrow \mathsf{Hash}(\mathsf{hk}, x)$, and $H_{\mathsf{hp}} \leftarrow \mathsf{ProjHash}(\mathsf{hp}, x, w)$ for the witness w of $x \in \mathcal{L}$;

– **Smoothness:** For any $x \in \mathcal{L}'$, the distributions of $(\mathsf{hp}, H_{\mathsf{hk}})$ and (hp, v) are indistinguishable, where $\mathsf{hk} \leftarrow \mathsf{HashKG}(\mathsf{param})$, $\mathsf{hp} \leftarrow \mathsf{ProjKG}(\mathsf{hk}, x)$, $H_{\mathsf{hk}} \leftarrow \mathsf{Hash}(\mathsf{hk}, x)$, and $v \xleftarrow{\$} \mathcal{V}$;

The algorithms and properties described above are the basic algorithms for SPH-FwGZ. For a later use, we need to define several additional properties.

3.2 Word Indistinguishability and Trapdoor

First, we assume languages $\mathcal{L}$ and $\mathcal{L}'$ in $\mathcal{X}$ are defined according to a random tape (σ, ρ) sampled in a set $\mathcal{S}_0 \times \mathcal{R}_0$ (i.e. from $\mathsf{param} \leftarrow \mathsf{Setup}(\sigma, \rho)$). The samplable set $\mathcal{S}_0$ is defined together with its twin set $\mathcal{S}_1$ such that when $\sigma \in \mathcal{S}_1$, and $\mathsf{param} \leftarrow \mathsf{Setup}(\sigma, \rho)$, there exists a trapdoor td_σ that allows to test if a given word $x \in \mathcal{X}$ is in $\mathcal{L}'$ or not. We then also need the following algorithms:

– $\mathsf{WordGen}\mathcal{L}(\mathsf{param})$: Samples and returns $x \xleftarrow{\$} \mathcal{L}$, together with its witness w;
– $\mathsf{WordTest}(\mathsf{td}_\sigma, x)$, using the trapdoor td_σ, tests if $x \in \mathcal{L}'$.

As we assumed $\mathcal{L}$ to be a hard subset of $\mathcal{X}$ when $\sigma \in \mathcal{S}_0$, we have the **Word-Indistinguishability Property**: An adversary can not distinguish between random words in $\mathcal{L}$ and random words in $\mathcal{X}$, for any $\sigma \in \mathcal{S}_0$, with more than a negligible advantage.

The string σ can be seen as a CRS, that admits a trapdoor when sampled from $\mathcal{S}_1$. The normal use is with $\sigma \xleftarrow{\$} \mathcal{S}_0$, which needs to be efficiently samplable. When $\sigma \in \mathcal{S}_1$, the trapdoor td_σ must be easy to compute from σ.

3.3 Decomposition Intractability and Trapdoor

We also define the alternate sets $\mathcal{R}_1$ and $\mathcal{R}'_1$ for $\mathcal{R}_0$. During normal use, ρ is sampled from $\mathcal{R}_0$, which needs to be efficiently samplable. When $\rho \in \mathcal{R}_1$, and $\mathsf{param} \leftarrow \mathsf{Setup}(\sigma, \rho)$, there exists a trapdoor $\mathsf{td}_\rho = (x, x', w, w')$, that must be easy to compute from ρ. When $\rho \in \mathcal{R}'_1$, and $\mathsf{param} \leftarrow \mathsf{Setup}(\sigma, \rho)$, there exists a trapdoor $\mathsf{td}_\rho = (x, x')$, that must be easy to compute from ρ. Let us define the complement algorithm, for any $\rho \in \mathcal{R}_0 \cup \mathcal{R}_1 \cup \mathcal{R}'_1$:

– $\mathsf{ComplementWord}(\mathsf{param}, \rho, x)$: from any word $x \in \mathcal{X}$, it outputs x';

From this complement algorithm, we expect the following statistical property, for any $\sigma \in \mathcal{S}_0 \cup \mathcal{S}_1$ but $\rho \in \mathcal{R}_0$:

– **Complement:** for any $x \in \mathcal{X}$, if $x' \leftarrow \mathsf{ComplementWord}(\mathsf{param}, \rho, x)$, then $x = \mathsf{ComplementWord}(\mathsf{param}, \rho, x')$;

But we also need a computational assumption: the **Decomposition Intractability**, which states that no adversary can generate, with non-negligible probability, for random $(\sigma, \rho) \xleftarrow{\$} \mathcal{S}_1 \times \mathcal{R}_0$, two words $x, y \notin \mathcal{L}'$ such that $y = \mathsf{ComplementWord}(\mathsf{param}, \rho, x)$, and so even with the trapdoor td_σ.

On the other hand, when $\rho \in \mathcal{R}_1$, the trapdoor $\mathsf{td}_\rho = (x, x', w, w')$ satisfies x and x' are uniformly random in $\mathcal{L}$ with witnesses w, w', and

$x' = \mathsf{ComplementWord}(\mathsf{param}, \rho, x)$. And when $\rho \in \mathcal{R}'_1$, the trapdoor $\mathsf{td}_\rho = (x, x')$ satisfies x and x' are uniformly random in $\mathcal{L}'$, and $x' = \mathsf{ComplementWord}(\mathsf{param}, \rho, x)$.

Again, the string ρ can be seen as a CRS, that admits a trapdoor when sampled from $\mathcal{R}_1$ or $\mathcal{R}'_1$. The normal use is with $\rho \xleftarrow{\$} \mathcal{R}_0$, which needs to be efficiently samplable. When $\rho \in \mathcal{R}_1$ or $\rho \in \mathcal{R}'_1$, the trapdoor td_ρ must be easy to compute from ρ.

Eventually, for the security proof to go through, we will make use of the **CRS Indistinguishability**: An adversary can not distinguish between $\mathcal{R}_0$, $\mathcal{R}_1$ and $\mathcal{R}'_1$, and between $\mathcal{S}_0$ and $\mathcal{S}_1$, with more than a negligible advantage.

Note that we independently consider the choices between $\mathcal{S}_0$ and $\mathcal{S}_1$ and between $\mathcal{R}_0$, $\mathcal{R}_1$ and $\mathcal{R}'_1$, but the latter choice could depend on the former choice. So the global CRS is the pair $\mathsf{crs} = (\sigma, \rho)$.

4 Oblivious Transfer from SPHFwGZ

In this section we first present our construction of Oblivious Transfers based on Smooth Projective Hash Functions with Grey Zone, and then provide a security proof of our Oblivious Transfer in the Universal Composability framework

4.1 Construction of Oblivious Transfer

Our Oblivious Transfer uses a $\mathsf{crs} = (\sigma, \rho) \in \mathcal{S}_0 \times \mathcal{R}_0$ as defined above, where we assume $\mathcal{S}_0 \times \mathcal{R}_0 \approx \mathcal{S}_1 \times \mathcal{R}_0 \approx \mathcal{S}_0 \times \mathcal{R}_1 \approx \mathcal{S}_0 \times \mathcal{R}'_1$. We describe in Fig. 1 the OT protocol $\Phi_{\mathsf{OT}}^{\mathsf{SPHFwGZ}}$.

Receiver		Sender
with input $b \in \{0, 1\}$		with input $m_0, m_1 \in \mathcal{M}$
for sid and $\mathsf{crs} = (\sigma, \rho)$ from $\mathcal{F}_{\mathsf{CRS}}$		for sid and $\mathsf{crs} = (\sigma, \rho)$ from $\mathcal{F}_{\mathsf{CRS}}$
$\mathsf{param} \leftarrow \mathsf{Setup}(\sigma, \rho)$		$\mathsf{param} \leftarrow \mathsf{Setup}(\sigma, \rho)$
$(x_b, w) \leftarrow \mathsf{WordGen}\mathcal{L}(\mathsf{param})$		
$x_{1-b} \leftarrow \mathsf{ComplementWord}(\rho, x_b)$	$\xrightarrow{\quad x_0 \quad}$	$x_1 \leftarrow \mathsf{ComplementWord}(\rho, x_0)$
		for i in $\{0, 1\}$:
		$\mathsf{hk}_i \leftarrow \mathsf{HashKG}(\mathsf{param})$
		$\mathsf{hp}_i \leftarrow \mathsf{ProjKG}(\mathsf{hk}_i, x_i)$
		$H_i \leftarrow \mathsf{Hash}(\mathsf{hk}_i, x_i)$
$H' \leftarrow \mathsf{ProjHash}(c_{b,1}, x_b, w)$	$\xleftarrow{\quad (c_0, c_1) \quad}$	$c_i = (H_i \oplus m_i, \mathsf{hp}_i)$
$m = H' \oplus c_{b,0}$		

Fig. 1. General description of the protocol $\Phi_{\mathsf{OT}}^{\mathsf{SPHFwGZ}}$

The protocol $\Phi_{\mathsf{OT}}^{\mathsf{SPHFwGZ}}$ provides **Correctness**. Indeed, with the honest generation $(x, w) \leftarrow \mathsf{WordGen}\mathcal{L}(\mathsf{param})$ we have $c = (H \oplus m, \mathsf{hp})$. Then, $m = H \oplus m \oplus \mathsf{ProjHash}(c_1, x, w)$ if and only if $H = \mathsf{ProjHash}(c_1, x, w)$ which is ensured due to the correctness property of the SPHFwGZ. Moreover, the **Complement** property ensures the value x_1 computed by the sender is always the same as the value x_1 computed by the receiver.

We now prove the privacy in the Universal Composability framework.

4.2   Security Analysis

Our Oblivious Transfer protocol will be proven in the CRS-hybrid model (as in [20]), with the functionality $\mathcal{F}_{\mathsf{CRS}}$, where the two players get the same random crs from the sid. In practice, as we assumed $\mathcal{S}_0$ and $\mathcal{R}_0$ efficiently samplable, (σ, ρ) can be derived from $\mathcal{H}(\mathsf{sid})$. As no rewind is required, the proof remains valid in case the CRS is generated using quantum-accessible random oracles [8]. Then, we recall below the ideal functionality $\mathcal{F}_{\mathsf{OT}}$ for a secure oblivious transfer, where there are two first messages from the sender with (m_0, m_1) and from the receiver with b, to initialize the process, and the final request message by the sender that decides when the receiver can get m_b:

$\mathcal{F}_{\mathsf{OT}}$ interacts with a sender S and a receiver R:

- Upon receiving a message $(\mathsf{sid}, \mathsf{sender}, m_0, m_1)$ from S, store (sid, m_0, m_1);
- Upon receiving a message $(\mathsf{sid}, \mathsf{receiver}, b)$ from R, store (sid, b);
- Upon receiving a message $(\mathsf{sid}, \mathsf{answer})$ from the adversary, check if both records (sid, m_0, m_1) and (sid, b) exist for sid. If yes, send (sid, m_b) to R, and sid to the adversary and halt. If not, send nothing but continue running.

Ideal Functionality $\mathcal{F}_{\mathsf{OT}}$

Theorem 1. *The protocol $\varPhi_{\mathsf{OT}}^{\mathsf{SPHFwGZ}}$ UC-realizes $\mathcal{F}_{\mathsf{OT}}$ in the $\mathcal{F}_{\mathsf{CRS}}$-hybrid model in the static-corruption setting, from any SPHFwGZ.*

We stress that we consider static corruptions only, where the corrupted players are known when each protocol execution starts.

Game G_0. This is the real game, where $\mathcal{F}_{\mathsf{CRS}}$ samples crs in $\mathcal{S}_0 \times \mathcal{R}_0$.

Game G_1. In this game, the simulator $\mathcal{S}$ simulates itself the sampling of crs $= (\sigma, \rho) \xleftarrow{\$} \mathcal{S}_0 \times \mathcal{R}_0$, and generates correctly every flow from the honest players, as they would do themselves, knowing the inputs (m_0, m_1) and b sent by the environment to the sender and the receiver, respectively.

Game G_2. In this game, we deal with **corrupted receivers**. Instead of sampling crs $= (\sigma, \rho) \xleftarrow{\$} \mathcal{S}_0 \times \mathcal{R}_0$, the simulator $\mathcal{S}$ samples crs $= (\sigma, \rho) \xleftarrow{\$} \mathcal{S}_1 \times \mathcal{R}_0$, and therefore with the trapdoor td_σ. This game is indistinguishable from the previous one due to the *CRS Indistinguishability*.

Game G_3. In this game, the simulator $\mathcal{S}$ uses the trapdoor td_σ to get $t_i = \mathsf{WordTest}(x_i, \mathsf{td}_\sigma)$ for $i \in \{0, 1\}$. If $t_0 = t_1 = 0$ (none of the words are in $\mathcal{L}'$), $\mathcal{S}$ aborts. This game is indistinguishable from the previous one, under the *Decomposition Intractability*, as $(\sigma, \rho) \in \mathcal{S}_1 \times \mathcal{R}_0$.

Game G_4. If $t_0 = t_1 = 0$, we still abort. If $t_0 = t_1 = 1$ we set $b = 0$, otherwise, we set b such that $t_b = 0$. Next, the simulator $\mathcal{S}$ proceeds on m_b with x_b and on a random message with x_{1-b}. Under the smoothness of the SPHFwGZ, as $x_{1-b} \in \mathcal{L}'$, and the *One-Time Pad Semantic Security*, this game is statistically indistinguishable from the previous one.

Game G_5. In this game, we deal with **corrupted senders**. Instead of sampling $\mathsf{crs} = (\sigma, \rho) \overset{\$}{\leftarrow} \mathcal{S}_0 \times \mathcal{R}_0$, the simulator $\mathcal{S}$ samples $\mathsf{crs} = (\sigma, \rho) \overset{\$}{\leftarrow} \mathcal{S}_0 \times \mathcal{R}_1$, and therefore with the trapdoor $\mathsf{td}_\rho = (x, x', w, w')$. This game is indistinguishable from the previous one due to the *CRS indistinguishability*.

Game G_6. In this game, the simulator $\mathcal{S}$ respectively sets (x_0, w_0, x_1, w_1) as (x, w, x', w') from td_ρ. It can then retrieve both m_0 and m_1. This game is indistinguishable from the previous one due to the *Word Indistinguishability*, and the uniform distribution of the trapdoor.

Game G_7. We now deal with **honest players**. Instead of sampling $\mathsf{crs} = (\sigma, \rho) \overset{\$}{\leftarrow} \mathcal{S}_0 \times \mathcal{R}_0$, the simulator $\mathcal{S}$ samples $\mathsf{crs} = (\sigma, \rho) \overset{\$}{\leftarrow} \mathcal{S}_0 \times \mathcal{R}_1'$, and therefore with the trapdoor $\mathsf{td}_\rho = (x, x')$, and simulates the flows with random $m_0, m_1 \overset{\$}{\leftarrow} \mathcal{M}$ and random $b \overset{\$}{\leftarrow} \{0, 1\}$. Under the *CRS Indistinguishability* and the smoothness of the SPHFwGZ, as both $x, x' \in \mathcal{L}'$, coupled with the *One-Time Pad Semantic Security*, this game is indistinguishable from the previous one.

Game G_8. This is the ideal game We can now make use of the functionality $\mathcal{F}_{\mathsf{OT}}$ which leads to the following simulator:
- If no participant is corrupted, one uses $\mathsf{crs} \overset{\$}{\leftarrow} \mathcal{S}_0 \times \mathcal{R}_1'$, and the simulator $\mathcal{S}$ simply uses random inputs for the sender and the receiver;
- If the receiver is corrupted, one uses $\mathsf{crs} \overset{\$}{\leftarrow} \mathcal{S}_1 \times \mathcal{R}_0$, and the simulator $\mathcal{S}$ extracts b using the trapdoor td_σ, and sends $(\mathsf{sid}, \mathsf{receiver}, b)$ to $\mathcal{F}_{\mathsf{OT}}$;
- If the sender is corrupted, one uses $\mathsf{crs} \overset{\$}{\leftarrow} \mathcal{S}_0 \times \mathcal{R}_1$, and the simulator $\mathcal{S}$ extracts m_0, m_1 using the trapdoor td_ρ, and sends $(\mathsf{sid}, \mathsf{sender}, m_0, m_1)$ to $\mathcal{F}_{\mathsf{OT}}$;
- The adversary sends $(\mathsf{sid}, \mathsf{answer})$ when it decides to deliver the result to the receiver.

4.3   Noisy Homomorphic Encryption Setup

We now define a general setup leading to an instantiation of our Oblivious Transfer from many (possibly with decryption failure and possibly amplified, as shown with our lattice-based instantiation) Homomorphic Encryption with group law $*$ on plaintexts and $\circledast$ on the ciphertexts.

We consider an encryption scheme $\Pi = (\mathsf{Setup}, \mathsf{KeyGen}, \mathsf{Encrypt}, \mathsf{Decrypt})$ with possible decryption failures. Thus, we set $\mathcal{X}$ as the ciphertext space of Π, and $\mathcal{L} = \{\mathsf{Encrypt}(\mathsf{pk}, 0; r)\} \subset \mathcal{X}$ and $\mathcal{L}' = \{c \in \mathcal{X}, \mathsf{Decrypt}(\mathsf{sk}, c) \neq 0\} \subset \mathcal{X}$.

Sets $\mathcal{S}_0$ and $\mathcal{S}_1$ can both be seen as public keys pk generated from $\mathsf{KeyGen}(1^\kappa)$ except that when $\sigma \in \mathcal{S}_1$, the secret key sk is known and defines the trapdoor td_σ. Hence, σ (which defines the public key pk) defines the sets $\mathcal{L}$ and $\mathcal{L}'$ in $\mathcal{X}$. On the other hand, we can define $\mathcal{R}_0 = \mathcal{X}$, the set of all the ciphertexts, or a superset, with uniform distribution; $\mathcal{R}_1 = \{c_0 \circledast c_1\}$, for two ciphertexts c_0, c_1 in $\mathcal{L}$, following the distribution of the encryption algorithm, on plaintext 0, and according the distribution of the randomness r_0, r_1, which allows to define the trapdoor td_ρ as (c_0, c_1, r_0, r_1); $\mathcal{R}'_1 = \{c_0 \circledast c_1\}$, for two ciphertexts c_0, c_1 in $\mathcal{L}'$, following the distribution of the encryption algorithm, on non-zero plaintexts, which allows to define the trapdoor td_ρ as (c_0, c_1). The setup defined above verifies both basic assumptions required to make the Oblivious Transfer Universally Composable:

- *CRS Indistinguishability*: Under the *semantic security* of the encryption scheme Π, $\mathcal{L}$, $\mathcal{L}'$, and $\mathcal{X}$ are indistinguishable. The homomorphic property implies that $\{x \circledast x' | (x, x') \in \mathcal{X}^2\} = \mathcal{X}$. As a consequence, we have indistinguishability between $\mathcal{R}_0 = \mathcal{X} = \{x \circledast x' | (x, x') \in \mathcal{X}^2\}$, $\mathcal{R}_1 = \{x \circledast x' | (x, x') \in \mathcal{L}^2\}$, and $\mathcal{R}'_1 = \{x \circledast x' | (x, x') \in \mathcal{L}'^2\}$. Furthermore, as $\mathcal{S}_0 = \mathcal{S}_1$, they are perfectly indistinguishable;
- *Word Indistinguishability*: Under the *semantic security* of the encryption scheme Π, one can not distinguish between $c_0 \in \mathcal{L}$, an encryption of 0 and $c_1 \in \mathcal{X}$, an encryption of a random value.
- **Complement:** for any $x \in \mathcal{X}$, $x' \leftarrow \mathsf{ComplementWord}(\mathsf{param}, \rho, x) = \rho \circledast x^{-1}$, hence $\mathsf{ComplementWord}(\mathsf{param}, \rho, x') = \rho \circledast (\rho \circledast x^{-1})^{-1} = x$;

Additional properties will depend on concrete instantiations.

5   Concrete Instantiations of SPHFwGZ

We now provide two concrete instantiations of SPHFwGZ based on the Diffie-Hellman and Learning With Errors problems. As both constructions rely on an Homomorphic Encryption scheme, we can already consider the basic properties shown in Sect. 4.3.

5.1   Instantiation from the Diffie-Hellman Problem

In this section, we focus on elliptic curve based cryptography, using the Decisional Diffie-Hellman assumption in a prime-order group.

Definition 2 (Decisional Diffie-Hellman (DDH)). *In a group $\mathbb{G}$ of prime order p, the Decisional Diffie-Hellman problem consists in, given g^a and g^b, distinguishing g^{ab} from g^c, for $a, b, c \xleftarrow{\$} \mathbb{Z}_p$.*

The Decisional Diffie-Hellman assumption states that the aforementioned Decision Diffie-Hellman problem is hard to solve, with non-negligible advantage in polynomial time.

ElGamal Encryption. As expected above, we need an IND-CPA (a.k.a. with semantic security) encryption scheme, with homomorphism. We use the ElGamal encryption scheme [13] in a group $\mathbb{G} = \langle g \rangle$ of prime order p, defined by the Setup algorithm:

- KeyGen(1^κ): picks $\beta \xleftarrow{\$} \mathbb{Z}_p$, and sets pk $= h = g^\beta$, sk $= \beta$.
- Encrypt(pk $= h = g^\beta$, $M \in \mathbb{G}$) encrypts the message M under the public key pk as follows: Pick $r \xleftarrow{\$} \mathbb{Z}_p$; Output the ciphertext: $c = (g^r, h^r \cdot M)$;
- Decrypt(sk, $c = (c_0, c_1)$) decrypts the ciphertext c using the decryption key sk as follows: $M = c_1 / c_0^{\mathsf{sk}}$.

Theorem 3. *The above ElGamal encryption scheme is IND-CPA under the Decisional Diffie-Hellman assumption.*

SPHFwGZ from ElGamal Encryption[1]. From the IND $-$ CPA ElGamal encryption scheme EG $=$ (Setup, KeyGen, Encrypt, Decrypt), in a group $\mathbb{G}$, denoted multiplicatively, of prime order p, with generator g.

We set $\mathcal{S}_0 = \mathcal{S}_1 = \{\sigma = h = g^{\mathsf{td}_\sigma}; \mathsf{td}_\sigma \xleftarrow{\$} \mathbb{Z}_p\}$. Then, $\mathcal{R}_0$ is defined as $\mathbb{G}^2 = \{\rho = (\hat{g}, \hat{h}) \xleftarrow{\$} \mathbb{G}^2\}$, $\mathcal{R}_1$ as $\{\rho = (\hat{g} \leftarrow g^{r_0} \cdot g^{r_1}, \hat{h} \leftarrow h^{r_0} \cdot h^{r_1}); (r_0, r_1) \leftarrow_\$ \mathbb{Z}_p\}$ and $\mathcal{R}_1'$ as $\{c_0 \circledast c_1; (c_0, c_1) \in \mathbb{G}^{2\times2}\}$. The crs is set as (σ, ρ). One can note that witnesses only exist when $\rho \in \mathcal{R}_1$ or $\rho \in \mathcal{R}_1'$, then $\mathsf{td}_\rho = (c_0 = (g^{r_0}, h^{r_0})$, $c_1 = (g^{r_1}, h^{r_1}), r_0, r_1)$ or $\mathsf{td}_\rho = (c_0, c_1)$ respectively. One can note c_0 and c_1 are encryptions of $M = g^0$, with respective randomness r_0 and r_1. Moreover, while td_σ always exists, it is not necessarily known.

From the above generic construction, we have $\mathcal{X} = \{(g^r, h^r \cdot M), M \in \mathbb{G}\} = \mathbb{G}^2$ and $\mathcal{L} = \{(g^r, h^r)\}$, which are indistinguishable under the Decisional Diffie-Hellman assumption. With param $= (g, \sigma = h)$, which determines all the sets (specified by the Setup algorithm), we can define:

- hk $=$ HashKG(param) $= (\alpha, \beta) \xleftarrow{\$} \mathbb{Z}_p^2$;
- hp $=$ ProjKG(hk) $= g^\alpha h^\beta$;
- $H =$ Hash(hk, $x = (u, v)) = u^\alpha v^\beta \in \mathbb{G}$;
- $H' =$ ProjHash(hp, x, $w = r$) $=$ hp^r, if $x = (g^r, h^r) \in \mathcal{L}$.
- $x' = (u', v') =$ ComplementWord($\rho = (\hat{g}, \hat{h})$, $x = (u, v)) = (\hat{g} \cdot u^{-1}, \hat{h} \cdot v^{-1})$

This is a word-independent SPHFwGZ. And we can show the expected properties:

- **Correctness:** When $x = (u, v) = (g^r, h^r) \in \mathcal{L}$, with witness r, $H = u^\alpha v^\beta = (g^\alpha h^\beta)^r =$ hp$^r = H'$;
- **Smoothness:** When $x = (u, v) = (g^r, h^{r'}) \notin \mathcal{L}$, then $r' = r + r''$ with $r'' \neq 0$: $H = u^\alpha v^\beta = (g^\alpha h^\beta)^r \times g^{r''\beta} =$ hp$^r \times g^{r''\beta} = H' \times g^{r''\beta}$. But β is perfectly hidden in hp, and $g^{r''\beta}$ is perfectly unpredictable;
- **Decomposition Intractability:** In ElGamal encryption there is no decryption failure: all the ciphertexts can be covered by the encryption algorithm, and the decryption perfectly inverts the encryption process. So we have $\mathcal{L}' = \mathcal{X} \backslash \mathcal{L}$. A random ciphertext ρ encrypts an $M \neq 1$ with overwhelming probability. Then, when it encrypts $M \neq 1$, from the homomorphic property, this is impossible to have two encryptions of 1 whose product is ρ. Hence, the *decomposition intractability* is statistical: the probability of existence of the decomposition is bounded by $1/p$, on ρ, even knowing the decryption key, and thus the trapdoor td_σ.

---

[1] Note that this construction exactly corresponds to the one from [10].

5.2   Instantiation from the Learning with Errors Problem

In this section, we focus on lattice-based cryptography. We are going to show how to instantiate the various required components from LWE:

Definition 4 (Shortest Independent Vectors Problem (SIVP$_\gamma$)). *The approximation version SIVP$_\gamma$ is the approximation version of SIVP with factor λ. Given a basis $\boldsymbol{B}$ of an n-dimensional lattice, find a set of n linearly independent vectors $v_1, \ldots, v_n \in \mathcal{L}(\boldsymbol{B})$ such that $\|v_i\| \leq \gamma(n) \cdot \lambda_n(\boldsymbol{B})$. for all $1 \leq i \leq n$. The approximation factor γ is typically a polynomial in n, the non approximated version assumes $\gamma = 1$.*

Definition 5 (Learning With Errors (LWE)). *Let $q \geq 2$, and χ be a distribution over $\mathbb{Z}$. The Learning With Errors problem LWE$_{\chi,q}$ consists in, given a polynomial number of samples, distinguishing the two following distributions:*

- *$(\mathbf{a}, \langle \mathbf{a}, \mathbf{s} \rangle + e)$, where $\mathbf{a}$ is uniform in $\mathbb{Z}_q^n$, $e \leftarrow \chi$, and $\mathbf{s} \in \mathbb{Z}_q^n$ is a fixed secret chosen uniformly, and where $\langle \mathbf{a}, \mathbf{s} \rangle$ denotes the standard inner product.*
- *$(\mathbf{a}, b)$, where $\mathbf{a}$ is uniform in $\mathbb{Z}_q^n$, and b is uniform in $\mathbb{Z}_q$.*

Regev Encryption. Regev [23] showed that for $\chi = D_{\mathbb{Z},\sigma}$, a Gaussian centered distribution in $\mathbb{Z}$ for any standard deviation $\sigma \geq 2\sqrt{n}$, and q such that $q/\sigma = \text{poly}(n)$, LWE$_{\chi,q}$ is at least as hard as solving worst-case SIVP for polynomial approximation factors, which is assumed to be hard to solve, even for quantum computers.

Trapdoor for LWE. Throughout this paper, we will use the trapdoors introduced in [19] to build our public matrix $\mathbf{A}$. Define $g_{\mathbf{A}}(\mathbf{s}, \mathbf{e}) = \mathbf{As} + \mathbf{e}$, the gadget matrix $\mathbf{G}$ as $\mathbf{G}^t = \mathbf{I}_n \otimes \mathbf{g}^t$, where $\mathbf{g}^t = [1, 2, \ldots, 2^k]$ and $k = \lceil \log q \rceil - 1$, and let $\mathbf{H} \in \mathbb{Z}_q^{n \times n}$ be invertible. The notation $[\mathbf{A} \,|\, \mathbf{B}]$ is for horizontal concatenation, while $[\mathbf{A} \,;\, \mathbf{B}]$ is for vertical concatenation.

Lemma 6 ([19, Theorems 5.1 and 5.4]). *There exist two PPT algorithms* TrapGen *and* $g_{(\cdot)}^{-1}$ *with the following properties assuming $q \geq 2$ and $m \geq \Theta(n \log q)$:*

- TrapGen$(1^n, 1^m, q)$ *outputs $(\mathbf{T}, \mathbf{A}_0)$, where the distribution of the matrix $\mathbf{A}_0$ is at negligible statistical distance from uniform in $\mathbb{Z}_q^{m \times n}$, and such that $\mathbf{TA}_0 = \mathbf{0}$, where $s_1(\mathbf{T}) \leq O(\sqrt{m})$ and where $s_1(\mathbf{T})$ is the operator norm of $\mathbf{T}$, which is defined as $\max_{\mathbf{x} \neq 0} \|\mathbf{Tx}\| / \|\mathbf{x}\|$.[2]*
- *Let $(\mathbf{T}, \mathbf{A}_0) \leftarrow$ TrapGen$(1^n, 1^m, q)$. Let $\mathbf{A_H} = \mathbf{A}_0 + [\mathbf{0} \,;\, \mathbf{GH}]$ for some invertible matrix $\mathbf{H}$ called a tag. Then, we have $\mathbf{TA_H} = \mathbf{GH}$. Furthermore, if $\mathbf{x} \in \mathbb{Z}_q^m$ can be written as $\mathbf{A_H s} + \mathbf{e}$, with $\mathbf{s} \in \mathbb{Z}_q^n$ and $\mathbf{e} \in \mathbb{Z}_q^m$ where $\|\mathbf{e}\| \leq B' := q/\Theta(\sqrt{m})$, then $g_{\mathbf{A_H}}^{-1}(\mathbf{T}, \mathbf{x}, \mathbf{H})$ outputs $(\mathbf{s}, \mathbf{e})$.*

---

[2] The bound on $s_1(\mathbf{T})$ holds except with probability at most 2^{-n} in the original construction, but we assume the algorithm restarts if it does not hold.

More precisely, to sample $(\mathbf{T}, \mathbf{A}_0)$ with TrapGen, we sample a uniform $\bar{\mathbf{A}} \in \mathbb{Z}_q^{\bar{m} \times n}$ where $\bar{m} = m - nk = \Theta(n \log q)$, and some $\mathbf{R} \leftarrow \mathcal{D}^{nk \times \bar{m}}$, where the distribution $\mathcal{D}^{nk \times \bar{m}}$ assigns probability $1/2$ to 0, and $1/4$ to ± 1. We output $\mathbf{T} = [-\mathbf{R} \,|\, \mathbf{I}_{nk}]$ along with $\mathbf{A}_0 = [\bar{\mathbf{A}} \,;\, \mathbf{R}\bar{\mathbf{A}}]$. Then, given a tag $\mathbf{H}$, with $\mathbf{A_H} = \mathbf{A}_0 + [\mathbf{0} \,;\, \mathbf{GH}]$, we have: $\mathbf{TA_H} = \mathbf{GH}$.

We will only consider a fixed tag $\mathbf{H} = \mathbf{I}$, for the Micciancio-Peikert encryption [19]. Our construction only requires CPA encryption so we don't need several tags, but we need to be able to reject improperly computed ciphertexts, and the gadget matrix is here, to allow this extra control during the decryption.

LWE Encryption à la Micciancio-Peikert. For this scheme, we assume q to be an odd prime. We set an encoding function for messages $\mathsf{Encode}(\mu \in \{0,1\}) = \mu \cdot (0, \ldots 0, \lceil q/2 \rceil)^t$. Note that $2 \cdot \mathsf{Encode}(\mu) = (0, \ldots, 0, \mu)^t \bmod q$, as $\lceil q/2 \rceil$ is the inverse of 2 mod q, for such an odd q.

Let $(\mathbf{T}, \mathbf{A}_0) \leftarrow \mathsf{TrapGen}(1^n, 1^m, q)$. The public encryption key is $\mathsf{pk} = \mathbf{A}_0$, and the secret decryption key is $\mathsf{sk} = \mathbf{T}$.

- $\mathsf{Encrypt}(\mathsf{pk} = \mathbf{A}_0, \mu \in \{0,1\})$ encrypts the message μ under the public key pk as follows: Let $\mathbf{A} = \mathbf{A}_0 + [\mathbf{0} \,;\, \mathbf{G}]$. Pick $\mathbf{s} \in \mathbb{Z}_q^n$, $\mathbf{e} \leftarrow D_{\mathbb{Z},t}^m$ where $t = \sigma\sqrt{m} \cdot \omega(\sqrt{\log n})$. Restart if $\|\mathbf{e}\| > B$, where $B := 2t\sqrt{m}$.[3] Output the ciphertext:
$$\mathbf{c} = \mathbf{As} + \mathbf{e} + \mathsf{Encode}(\mu) \bmod q \ .$$

- $\mathsf{Decrypt}(\mathsf{sk} = \mathbf{T}, \mathbf{c} \in \mathbb{Z}_q^m)$ decrypts the ciphertext $\mathbf{c}$ using the decryption key sk as follows: With $B'' := q/2\Theta(\sqrt{m})$, output
$$\begin{cases} \mu & \text{if } g_{\mathbf{A}}^{-1}(\mathbf{T}, 2\mathbf{c}, \mathbf{I}) = (2\mathbf{s}, 2\mathbf{e} + (0, \ldots, 0, \mu)) \\ & \qquad \text{where } \mathbf{s} \in \mathbb{Z}_q^n, \mathbf{e} \in \mathbb{Z}^m \text{ and } \|\mathbf{e}\| \leq B'' \ , \\ \bot & \text{otherwise.} \end{cases}$$

Noting $\Lambda(A) = \{\mathbf{As} | \mathbf{s} \in \mathbb{Z}_q^n\}$, honestly generated ciphertext $\mathbf{c}$ are such that $d(\mathbf{c} - \mathsf{Encode}(\mu), \Lambda(\mathbf{A})) \leq B$, while the decryption procedure is guaranteed not to return μ as soon as $d(\mathbf{c} - \mathsf{Encode}(\mu), \Lambda(\mathbf{A})) > B''$. (Note that the inversion algorithm $g_{(.)}^{-1}$ can succeed even if $\|\mathbf{e}\| > B''/2$, depending on the randomness of the trapdoor. It is crucial to reject decryption nevertheless when $\|\mathbf{e}\| > B''$ to ensure security).

From the decryption procedure, we have:
$$\mu' := \mathsf{Decrypt}(\mathbf{T}, \mathbf{c}) \neq \bot \iff d(\mathbf{c} - \mathsf{Encode}(\mu'), \Lambda(\mathbf{A})) < B'' \ .$$

Suppose that $m \geq \Theta(n \log q)$. The scheme is correct as long as $B \leq B''$, or equivalently $2\sigma m^{3/2} \cdot \omega(\sqrt{\log n}) \leq q$.

Theorem 7. *Assume $m \geq \Theta(n \log q)$. The above scheme is IND-CPA assuming the hardness of the $\mathsf{LWE}_{\chi,q}$ problem for $\chi = D_{\mathbb{Z},\sigma}$.*

Furthermore, this encryption scheme is homomorphic for plaintexts in $(\mathbb{Z}_2, +)$, and ciphertexts in $\mathbb{Z}_q^m$ with component-wise addition.

---

[3] This happens only with exponentially small probability $2^{-\Theta(n)}$.

Bit-SPHFwGZ from LWE Encryption Scheme. We consider, an LWE encryption scheme defined with a superpolynomial modulus. More precisely, we set $m = n\log(q), t = \sqrt{mn}.\omega(\sqrt{\log(n)})$, $k = \Theta(n), s \geq \Theta(\sqrt{n}) \wedge s/q = \mathsf{negl}(n), s = \Omega(mk^2q^{2/3})$. We also set R to be a *probabilistic* rounding function from $[0,1]$ to $\{0,1\}$, such that $R(x) = 1$ with probability $0.5 \cdot \cos(\frac{2\pi x}{q})$ and 0 otherwise.

We set $\mathcal{S}_0 = \mathcal{S}_1 = \{\sigma = \mathbf{A} = \mathbf{A}_0 + [\mathbf{0}\,;\,\mathbf{G}]|(\mathbf{T}, \mathbf{A}_0) \leftarrow \mathsf{TrapGen}(1^n, 1^m, q)\}$, td_σ being $\mathbf{T}$. Then, $\mathcal{R}_0$ is defined as $\{\rho = \mathbf{v} \in \mathbb{Z}_q^m\}$ and $\mathcal{R}_1$ is the set composed of all the sums of two honest encryptions of 0, in other words $\{\rho = \mathbf{A}(\mathbf{s} + \mathbf{s}') + \mathbf{e} + \mathbf{e}' \bmod q \mid \mathbf{s}, \mathbf{s}' \in \mathbb{Z}_q^n, \mathbf{e}, \mathbf{e}' \leftarrow D_{\mathbb{Z},t}^m \wedge \|\mathbf{e}\| \leq B \wedge \|\mathbf{e}'\| \leq B\}$ with $\mathsf{td}_\rho = (\mathbf{As} + \mathbf{e}, \mathbf{As}' + \mathbf{e}', (\mathbf{s}, \mathbf{e}), (\mathbf{s}', \mathbf{e}'))$.

With $\mathcal{X}_{bit} = \{\mathbf{c} \overset{\$}{\leftarrow} \mathbb{Z}_q^m\}$, $\mathcal{L}_{bit} = \{\mathbf{c}|\exists \mathbf{s}, \mathbf{e}, \mathbf{c} = \mathsf{Encrypt}(\mathbf{A}_0, 0; \mathbf{s}, \mathbf{e})\}$ defined following the description above, and $\mathcal{L}'_{bit} = \{\mathbf{c} \in \mathcal{X}_{bit}|\mathsf{Decrypt}(\mathbf{T}, \mathbf{c}) \neq 0\}$. Hence $\mathcal{R}'_1 = \{\mathbf{c}_1 + \mathbf{c}_2; (\mathbf{c}_1, \mathbf{c}_2) \in {\mathcal{L}'_{bit}}^2\}$ with $\mathsf{td}_\rho = (\mathbf{c}_1, \mathbf{c}_2)$. Note that $\mathbf{s}$ could be enough as a witness for $\mathbf{c} = \mathbf{As} + \mathbf{e} \in \mathcal{L}_{bit}$, as one can check $\mathbf{e} = \mathbf{c} - \mathbf{As}$ is small enough. This defines the Setup algorithm, and we have:

Definition 8 (Bit-SPHFwGZ over Micciancio-Peikert like Ciphertexts [4]). *For $k = \Theta(n)$, and picking $s \geq \Theta(\sqrt{n})$, and $s = \Omega(mk^2q^{2/3})$, we can define:*

- $\mathsf{HashKG}(\mathsf{param}) = hk = \mathbf{h} \overset{\$}{\leftarrow} D_{\mathbb{Z},s}^m$
- $\mathsf{ProjKG}(hk) = hp = \mathbf{A}^t\mathbf{h}$
- $\mathsf{Hash}(hk, \mathbf{c}) = R(\langle hk, \mathbf{c}\rangle) = R(\langle \mathbf{h}, \mathbf{c}\rangle) \in \{0, 1\}$
- $\mathsf{ProjHash}(hp, \mathbf{c}, w = \mathbf{s}) = R(\langle hp, \mathbf{s}\rangle) = R(\langle \mathbf{A}^t\mathbf{h}, \mathbf{s}\rangle)$

For a word $\mathbf{c} = \mathbf{As} + \mathbf{e}$ in the language $\mathcal{L}_{bit}$, $\langle \mathbf{h}, \mathbf{c}\rangle = \mathbf{h}^t\mathbf{As} + \mathbf{h}^t\mathbf{e} = \langle \mathbf{A}^t\mathbf{h}, \mathbf{s}\rangle + \mathbf{h}^t\mathbf{e}$. And by construction $\mathbf{h}^t\mathbf{e}$ is small. The choice of the rounding function $R(x)$, characterized by a coin flip where the outcome 1 is weighted by $0.5 \cdot \cos(\frac{2\pi x}{q})$, is such that it allows canceling out this small noise most of the time, while providing smoothness for words outside the language (ensuring that $R(\langle hk, \mathbf{c}\rangle)$ is random when given only hp)

It was shown in [4], that for this choice of random function, such bit-SPHFwGZ achieves negligible-universality, thanks to the rounding function, but $(3/4 + o(1))$-correctness for the chosen set of parameters.

Full-Fledged SPHFwGZ from LWE. The previous construction has limitations as it is neither perfectly correct, nor smooth, we need to apply a transformation to reach those goals. This transformation is explained below, first informally, then in more details:

- It is a bit-function meaning the final hash value lives in $\{0, 1\}$, while one needs a larger mask. To solve this issue, one has to run it in parallel a linear number of times, to have an output string long enough.
- The correctness is imperfect. The output bit only matches with probability $3/4 + o(1)$. As such, applications running $\mathsf{Encrypt}(pk, m; r)$ should encryption a redundant version of m, with an error-correcting code, $\mathsf{ECC}(m)$. Such

transformation makes the SPHF word-dependent (i.e. the projection key is dependent on the user/receiver input), however in our scenario, such a word-dependent function is enough.

More formally, given a word $\mathbf{c} \in \mathcal{X}_{bit}$, for any $\ell = \Omega(n)$ an error-correcting code ECC capable of correcting $\ell/4$ errors, then, we can define the SPHF as:

– SETUP(1^κ): Outputs the result from Setup(1^κ)
– HASHKG(param): Picks a random values $K \leftarrow \{0,1\}^\kappa$, and $\forall i \in [\ell]$, gets $\mathsf{hk}_i = \mathsf{HashKG}(\mathsf{param})$, and set $\mathsf{HK} = (\{\mathsf{hk}_i\}, K)$;
– ProjKG(HK, $\mathbf{c}$) : $\forall i \in [\ell]$, gets $\mathsf{hp}_i = \mathsf{ProjKG}(\mathsf{hk}_i)$, $H_i = \mathsf{Hash}(\mathsf{hk}_i, \mathbf{c})$. It then computes $T = \mathsf{ECC}(K) \oplus S$ where $S = (H_i)_{i \in [\ell]}$, and outputs $\mathsf{HP} = ((\mathsf{hp}_i)_{i \in [\ell]}, T)$;
– HASH(HK, $\mathbf{c}$): Returns K, from HK;
– PROJHASH(HP, $\mathbf{c}$, $w = \mathbf{s}$) : $\forall i \in [\ell]$, computes $H'_i = \mathsf{ProjHash}(\mathsf{hp}_i, \mathbf{c}, \mathbf{s})$. Then computes $S' = (H'_i)_{i \in [\ell]}$, and finally $K' = \mathsf{ECC}^{-1}(T \oplus S')$.

Such transformation allows to achieve *smoothness* which can be proven with an hybrid argument, handling intermediate distributions where the first H_i values are random. The *correctness* is simply inherited from the correcting-code capacity, while the number of errors to be corrected can be estimated thanks to the Hoeffding's bound [15]. We can guarantee the expected properties:

– **Correctness:** When $x = \mathbf{c} \in \mathcal{L}_{bit}$, with the above conversion, we have $K = K'$ with overwhelming probability, thanks to the error-correcting code;
– **Smoothness:** When $x = \mathbf{c} \notin \mathcal{L}_{bit}$, then the value K is random from an adversary point of view, as the parallelization technique allows to transform the negligible-universality to a classical smoothness (at the cost of a word-dependent SPHF);
– **Half Decomposition Intractability:** A random vector ρ should not be split into two ciphertexts that could be decrypted to 0, or at least not too often. We first deal with *half* decomposition intractability, when at most half of the random vectors can be split. To get a lower-bound on the number of vectors like such ρ, we can remark that a vector verifies this property as soon as $d(\rho, \Lambda(\mathbf{A}))$ is greater than 2 times the decryption bound.
    This is the reason, why we took a conservative value $B'' = B'/2$ in the encryption compared to classical Micciancio-Peikert encryption. By halving the decryption radius, we ensured that adding two elements that still decrypt within this bound will fall on classically decryptable ciphertexts. As such, at least half the elements cannot be reached (those that classically decrypted to 1). Hence, $\mathrm{Pr}_{\rho \in \mathbb{Z}_q^m}[\exists \mathbf{c}, \mathbf{d} | \rho = \mathbf{c} + \mathbf{d} \wedge \mathsf{Decrypt}(\mathsf{sk}, \mathbf{c}) = \mathsf{Decrypt}(\mathsf{sk}, \mathbf{d}) = 0] \leq 1/2$. This is a statistical bound, that holds even when knowing the decryption key.

Another amplification is required to make *full-fledged decomposition intractability*, by working on ciphertexts $(\mathbf{c}_j)_{j \in [k]}$, with k parallel executions of the SPH-FwGZ, with a final XOR of all the outputs, so that the smoothness for one word is enough to get the smoothness for the vector of words, but the correctness on all the words leads to the global correctness. With $\mathcal{X} = (\mathcal{X}_{bit})^k$, the acceptable languages, for correctness and smoothness respectively are then:

$$\mathcal{L} = (\mathcal{L}_{bit})^k = \{(\mathbf{c}_j)_{j \in [k]} | (\forall j \in [k]), \exists (\mathbf{s}_j, \mathbf{e}_j), \mathbf{c}_j = \mathsf{Encrypt}(\mathbf{A}_0, 0; \mathbf{s}_j, \mathbf{e_j})\} \subset \mathcal{X}$$

$$\mathcal{L}' = (\mathcal{L}'_{bit})^k = \{(\mathbf{c}_j)_{j \in [k]} | (\exists j \in [k]), \mathsf{Decrypt}(\mathbf{T}, \mathbf{c}_j) \neq 0\} \subset \mathcal{X}$$

Then, for random $(\rho_j)_{j \in [k]} \xleftarrow{\$} \mathcal{X}$, a decomposition would be a list of pairs $(\mathbf{c}_j, \mathbf{d}_j)_{j \in [k]} \in (\mathcal{X} \times \mathcal{X})$ such that for all j, $\rho_j = \mathbf{c}_j + \mathbf{d}_j$ and $\mathsf{Decrypt}(\mathbf{T}, \mathbf{c}_j) = \mathsf{Decrypt}(\mathbf{T}, \mathbf{d}_j) = 0$, which only exists with probability less than $1/2^k$. We thus have achieved all the security properties required for our applications.

6   Conclusion

In this paper, we introduced *Smooth Projective Hash Functions with Grey Zone*, that generalize SPHF to language subjected to gaps, thanks to the *Decomposition Intractability* property. This is enough to get Oblivious Transfer proven secure in the Universally Composable model. As such a primitive can be obtained from the LWE problem, we can then obtain a UC-secure post-quantum Oblivious Transfer.

Acknowledgments. This work was supported in part by the French ANR Project Crypto4Graph-AI.

References

1. Abdalla, M., Chevalier, C., Pointcheval, D.: Smooth projective hashing for conditionally extractable commitments. In: Halevi, S. (ed.) CRYPTO 2009. LNCS, vol. 5677, pp. 671–689. Springer, Heidelberg (2009). https://doi.org/10.1007/978-3-642-03356-8_39
2. Ben Hamouda, F., Blazy, O., Chevalier, C., Pointcheval, D., Vergnaud, D.: Efficient UC-secure authenticated key-exchange for algebraic languages. In: Kurosawa, K., Hanaoka, G. (eds.) PKC 2013. LNCS, vol. 7778, pp. 272–291. Springer, Heidelberg (2013). https://doi.org/10.1007/978-3-642-36362-7_18
3. Benhamouda, F., Blazy, O., Chevalier, C., Pointcheval, D., Vergnaud, D.: New techniques for SPHFs and efficient one-round PAKE protocols. In: Canetti, R., Garay, J.A. (eds.) CRYPTO 2013. LNCS, vol. 8042, pp. 449–475. Springer, Heidelberg (2013). https://doi.org/10.1007/978-3-642-40041-4_25
4. Benhamouda, F., Blazy, O., Ducas, L., Quach, W.: Hash proof systems over lattices revisited. In: Abdalla, M., Dahab, R. (eds.) PKC 2018. LNCS, vol. 10770, pp. 644–674. Springer, Cham (2018). https://doi.org/10.1007/978-3-319-76581-5_22
5. Bettaieb, S., Bidoux, L., Blazy, O., Connan, Y., Gaborit, P.: A gapless code-based hash proof system based on RQC and its applications. Des. Codes Cryptogr. **90**(12), 3011–3044 (2022). https://doi.org/10.1007/s10623-022-01075-7
6. Blazy, O., Chevalier, C.: Generic construction of UC-secure oblivious transfer. In: Malkin, T., Kolesnikov, V., Lewko, A.B., Polychronakis, M. (eds.) ACNS 2015. LNCS, vol. 9092, pp. 65–86. Springer, Cham (2015). https://doi.org/10.1007/978-3-319-28166-7_4

7. Blazy, O., Chevalier, C., Vu, Q.H.: Post-quantum UC-secure oblivious transfer in the standard model with adaptive corruptions. In: Proceedings of the 14th International Conference on Availability, Reliability and Security, ARES 2019. Association for Computing Machinery, New York (2019). https://doi.org/10.1145/3339252.3339280

8. Boneh, D., Dagdelen, Ö., Fischlin, M., Lehmann, A., Schaffner, C., Zhandry, M.: Random oracles in a quantum world. In: Lee, D.H., Wang, X. (eds.) ASIACRYPT 2011. LNCS, vol. 7073, pp. 41–69. Springer, Heidelberg (2011). https://doi.org/10.1007/978-3-642-25385-0_3

9. Canetti, R.: Universally composable security: a new paradigm for cryptographic protocols. In: 42nd FOCS, pp. 136–145. IEEE Computer Society Press (2001). https://doi.org/10.1109/SFCS.2001.959888

10. Cramer, R., Shoup, V.: A practical public key cryptosystem provably secure against adaptive chosen ciphertext attack. In: Krawczyk, H. (ed.) CRYPTO 1998. LNCS, vol. 1462, pp. 13–25. Springer, Heidelberg (1998). https://doi.org/10.1007/BFb0055717

11. Cramer, R., Shoup, V.: Universal hash proofs and a paradigm for adaptive chosen ciphertext secure public-key encryption. In: Knudsen, L.R. (ed.) EUROCRYPT 2002. LNCS, vol. 2332, pp. 45–64. Springer, Heidelberg (2002). https://doi.org/10.1007/3-540-46035-7_4

12. Derler, D., Slamanig, D.: Practical witness encryption for algebraic languages and how to reply an unknown whistleblower. Cryptology ePrint Archive, Report 2015/1073 (2015). https://eprint.iacr.org/2015/1073

13. ElGamal, T.: A public key cryptosystem and a signature scheme based on discrete logarithms. IEEE Trans. Inf. Theory **31**, 469–472 (1985)

14. Gennaro, R., Lindell, Y.: A framework for password-based authenticated key exchange. In: Biham, E. (ed.) EUROCRYPT 2003. LNCS, vol. 2656, pp. 524–543. Springer, Heidelberg (2003). https://doi.org/10.1007/3-540-39200-9_33. https://eprint.iacr.org/2003/032.ps.gz

15. Hoeffding, W.: Probability inequalities for sums of bounded random variables. J. Am. Stat. Assoc. **58**(301), 13–30 (1963). https://doi.org/10.1080/01621459.1963.10500830

16. Jutla, C., Roy, A.: Relatively-sound NIZKs and password-based key-exchange. In: Fischlin, M., Buchmann, J., Manulis, M. (eds.) PKC 2012. LNCS, vol. 7293, pp. 485–503. Springer, Heidelberg (2012). https://doi.org/10.1007/978-3-642-30057-8_29

17. Katz, J., Vaikuntanathan, V.: Smooth projective hashing and password-based authenticated key exchange from lattices. In: Matsui, M. (ed.) ASIACRYPT 2009. LNCS, vol. 5912, pp. 636–652. Springer, Heidelberg (2009). https://doi.org/10.1007/978-3-642-10366-7_37

18. Katz, J., Vaikuntanathan, V.: Round-optimal password-based authenticated key exchange. In: Ishai, Y. (ed.) TCC 2011. LNCS, vol. 6597, pp. 293–310. Springer, Heidelberg (2011). https://doi.org/10.1007/978-3-642-19571-6_18

19. Micciancio, D., Peikert, C.: Trapdoors for lattices: simpler, tighter, faster, smaller. In: Pointcheval, D., Johansson, T. (eds.) EUROCRYPT 2012. LNCS, vol. 7237, pp. 700–718. Springer, Heidelberg (2012). https://doi.org/10.1007/978-3-642-29011-4_41

20. Peikert, C., Vaikuntanathan, V., Waters, B.: A framework for efficient and composable oblivious transfer. In: Wagner, D. (ed.) CRYPTO 2008. LNCS, vol. 5157, pp. 554–571. Springer, Heidelberg (2008). https://doi.org/10.1007/978-3-540-85174-5_31

21. Persichetti, E.: Secure and anonymous hybrid encryption from coding theory. In: Gaborit, P. (ed.) PQCrypto 2013. LNCS, vol. 7932, pp. 174–187. Springer, Heidelberg (2013). https://doi.org/10.1007/978-3-642-38616-9_12

22. Rabin, M.O.: How to exchange secrets with oblivious transfer. Technical Report TR-81, Aiken Computation Laboratory, Harvard University (1981)

23. Regev, O.: On lattices, learning with errors, random linear codes, and cryptography. In: Gabow, H.N., Fagin, R. (eds.) 37th ACM STOC, pp. 84–93. ACM Press (2005). https://doi.org/10.1145/1060590.1060603

24. Shooshtari, M.K., Aref, M.R.: Smooth projective hash function from codes and its applications. IEEE Trans. Serv. Comput. 1 (2021). https://doi.org/10.1109/TSC.2021.3100323

25. Zhang, J., Yu, Yu.: Two-round PAKE from approximate SPH and instantiations from lattices. In: Takagi, T., Peyrin, T. (eds.) ASIACRYPT 2017. LNCS, vol. 10626, pp. 37–67. Springer, Cham (2017). https://doi.org/10.1007/978-3-319-70700-6_2

A New Class of Trapdoor Verifiable Delay Functions

Ahmed Zawia$^{(\boxtimes)}$ and M. Anwar Hasan

University of Waterloo, Waterloo, ON, Canada
{azawia,ahasan}@uwaterloo.ca

Abstract. A verifiable delay function (VDF) is a function whose evaluation involves lengthy sequential operations, yet its outcome is publicly verifiable. As an extension, a trapdoor-VDF is a VDF with a shortcut that speeds up the evaluation process. This paper presents a new class of trapdoor-VDFs featuring a large ensemble of trapdoors for each instantiation of the function. This way, a client can randomly choose a private trapdoor from the ensemble, thereby using it to encapsulate a secret to the future as a unique puzzle. To solve the puzzle, the server, which does not know the trapdoor, requires a prescribed number of sequential steps to evaluate the function. Any client can efficiently verify the correctness of the server's evaluation with zero knowledge of the trapdoor being used. We present an approach for constructing the proposed class of trapdoor-VDFs based on bilinear pairings and a long walk on supersingular isogeny graphs. Finally, we examine the security of our construction under trapdoor-VDF security notions.

Keywords: Delay primitives · verifiable delay functions · delay encryption · time-lock puzzle

1 Introduction

This work examines a remedy for the vulnerability that arises from knowing or predicting a protocol's outcome. The vulnerability stems from malicious participants influencing the outcome or gaining an advantage by knowing the outcome beforehand. One way to solve this problem is to impose a prescribed number of sequential steps to obtain the desired outcome. This solution has been introduced in the previous works such as time-lock puzzle (TLP) [29], proofs of sequential work (PoSW) [1, 15, 22, 26], and verifiable delay functions (VDFs) [6]. These primitives are all time-sensitive in that they only release the outcome after a prescribed delay (T). The outcome of VDF and PoSW is publicly verifiable, while that of TLP requires a secret. The public verification of the outcome's *uniqueness* is more efficient in VDF than in PoSW since the latter requires all T steps. The uniqueness property ensures that there are no multiple valid proofs for different outcome.

This work focuses more on the properties, specifically uniqueness and public verifiability, that make VDF stand out from others. Furthermore, we are interested in a VDF-like primitive that allows any participant (other than the trusted

G.-V. Jourdan et al. (Eds.): FPS 2022, LNCS 13877, pp. 71–87, 2023.
https://doi.org/10.1007/978-3-031-30122-3_5

setup) to predict the outcome in advance by knowing a secret trapdoor. In the absence of the secret trapdoor, participants obtain the desired outcome through a prescribed number of sequential evaluations. It is, however, possible to verify the result efficiently and publicly. We refer to primitives with such characteristics by trapdoor-VDF. Considering its importance, trapdoor-VDF is suitable for time-sensitive applications that require both public verification and timely release assurances. There are many possible applications, such as sealed-voting, delayed decapsulation [9,25], and front-running attack prevention [14].

Related Work. Since the work of Boneh et al. [6], several VDF constructions have been proposed based on Rivest, Shamir, and Wagner's time-lock assumption [29], including [5,17,24,28,30], and [34], which use different verification techniques, provide additional properties and offer enhancement. Several other constructions [12,18,31] are based on the difficulty of shortening the evaluation of isogeny with a large degree, which was first introduced by [18]. The verification proof of [18] is based on the bilinear pairing of the Boneh-Lynn-Shacham (BLS) signature scheme [8]. Similar to time-lock functions, Shani's [31] proof requires releasing a secret shortcut to the puzzle to recompute the puzzle's answer. In [12], Chavez-Saab et al. propose an inefficient verification method based upon succinct non-interactive arguments (SNARGs).

Later, a delay encryption scheme [9] was developed using Boneh and Franklin's identity based encryption (IBE) scheme [7] in conjunction with Feo et al.'s delay function [18]. The scheme in [9] can operate in batch mode so that the function can be evaluated once to perform many decryptions. However, the method requires a trusted, unpredictable seed, along with a considerable amount of storage to perform computations (e.g., 12 TB for 1 h delay [9]). Furthermore, their approach does not employ a trapdoor mechanism to predict the answer in advance. Hence, trapdoor-VDF is more comparable to TLP even though the former offers efficient public verification without revealing any secrets (i.e., the secret trapdoor). We note that recent work has extended the security of TLPs and discusses the notion of its public verifiability, some of which are [2,3,13,20].

In addition, the term "trapdoor-VDF" has been used previously in [34], though their approach differs from that presented in this paper. In [34], each participant constructs independent instances of trapdoor-VDF. Every instance has a secret trapdoor that shortens the long evaluation process. Therefore, an instance generator can answer any challenge faster as it has the secret trapdoor. Our work presents a new class of trapdoor-VDFs, where each instantiation includes a description of a finite trapdoor ensemble. Hence, any participant can generate a unique challenge, together with its answer, using a hidden trapdoor sampled at random from the ensemble.

Contributions. In this paper, we first formalize the security notions of trapdoor-VDF. We then introduce a novel approach to trapdoor-VDF; the proposed trapdoor-VDF is a VDF with a large ensemble of distinct efficient shortcuts called trapdoors. The delay function involves sequentially evaluating a large smooth degree supersingular isogeny, which was first proposed by Feo et al. [18]. The trapdoor ensemble is a set of isogenies of a smaller degree defined over $\mathbb{F}_p$, where p is a prime. In public verification, a bilinear pairing equality serves as proof of the correct evaluation of a secret trapdoor (i.e., a randomly sampled isogeny). Finally, we show that our proposal is secure under trapdoor-VDF security notions.

2 Preliminaries

General Notations. If n is a positive integer, the set $\{1, \ldots, n\}$ is denoted by $[n]$. In general, a finite set is denoted by calligraphic font (e.g., $\mathcal{S}$). The cardinality of a set $\mathcal{S}$ is denoted by $|\mathcal{S}|$. Let $e \leftarrow_R \mathcal{S}$ denote the process of uniformly sampling a random element e from $\mathcal{S}$. The deterministic selection of e from $\mathcal{S}$ is denoted by $e \leftarrow \mathcal{S}$. If Exe is an algorithm, $a \leftarrow_R \mathsf{Exe}$ denotes running Exe on fresh random coins and assigning the output to a. The deterministic execution of Exe, on the other hand, is denoted by $a \leftarrow \mathsf{Exe}$. The notation $\Pr[Evnt : P_1, P_2, \ldots, P_n]$ is used to represent the probability of an event $Evnt$ occurring after the ordered processes $P_1, P_2, \ldots, P_n$. We denote the composition of two functions by $\circ$ such that $\mathsf{f} \circ \mathsf{g}(x) = \mathsf{f}(\mathsf{g}(x))$ for some input x. Let $\boldsymbol{m} \leftarrow_R \mathcal{S}^n$ be the vector $(m_i)_{i \in [n]}$ of size n such that $m_i \leftarrow_R \mathcal{S}$ for all $i \in [n]$. The set of all odd prime numbers that are less than or equal to k is referred to as $\mathsf{Primes}(k)$. For an integer a and an odd prime b, the Legendre symbol is denoted by $\left(\frac{a}{b}\right)$.

Supersingular Elliptic Curve. Throughout this work, we consider a curve $E/\mathbb{F}_p$ to be a supersingular elliptic curve defined over a prime field $\mathbb{F}_p$ with a large prime p. A point P on $E/\mathbb{F}_p$ is the pair $(x, y) \in \mathbb{F}_p \times \mathbb{F}_p$. The set of $\mathbb{F}_p$-rational points on $E/\mathbb{F}_p$ is denoted as $E(\mathbb{F}_p)$ and the set size as $|E(\mathbb{F}_p)|$. Let ∞_E be the point at infinity on $E/\mathbb{F}_p$ and $\infty_E \in E(\mathbb{F}_p)$. The field $\overline{\mathbb{F}}_p$ is the algebraic closure of $\mathbb{F}_p$. The subgroup of points of order N is called the N-*torsion points* which is defined as $E[N] = \{P \in E(\overline{\mathbb{F}}_p) : [N]P = \infty_E\}$.

Definition 1 ([32]). *An elliptic curve $E/\mathbb{F}_p$ is supersingular if the following equivalent properties are true*

- *There is no $P \in E(\overline{\mathbb{F}}_p)$ with order p (i.e., $E[p] = \{\infty_E\}$).*
- *$|E(\mathbb{F}_p)| = p + 1 - t$ and $p|t$ (i.e., $\gcd(p, t) \neq 1$).*
- *The endomorphism ring of $E/\mathbb{F}_p$ is an order in a quaternion algebra.*

Otherwise, $E/\mathbb{F}_p$ is said to be an ordinary curve.

Isogenous Curves. An isogeny between curves $(\phi : E_1 \rightarrow E_2)$ is a surjective morphism that has a finite kernel such that $\phi(\infty_{E_1}) = \infty_{E_2}$. We say ϕ is defined over $\mathbb{F}_p$, if the non-constant rational map representing ϕ has coefficients in $\mathbb{F}_p$. Let $\langle S \rangle$ be a cyclic subgroup of $E(\overline{\mathbb{F}}_q)$ generated by S. In this work, we compute an isogeny ϕ with kernel $\langle S \rangle$ using Vélu's formulas [33]. Also, we will focus on separable isogenies where the isogeny degree is its kernel size (i.e., $\deg \phi = |\ker(\phi)|$). An isogeny of degree l is denoted by l-isogeny. Furthermore, an isogeny ϕ has a unique *dual* isogeny $\hat{\phi}$ with the same degree ($\deg \phi = \deg \hat{\phi}$) such that $\hat{\phi} : E_2 \rightarrow E_1$, and $\phi \circ \hat{\phi} = [\deg \phi]$ on E_2, where $[m]$ is multiplication-by m mapping (see [32, Theorem 6.1]). The non-backtracking walk is a sequence of isogenies that is not cyclic or followed by any dual isogeny(s).

The set of all group homomorphisms (i.e., isogenies) from E to itself is called the endomorphism ring of E (**End**(E)). The endomorphism ring defined over $\mathbb{F}_p$ is denoted as **End**$_{\mathbb{F}_p}(E)$. An isogeny is called *horizontal* isogeny if **End**$_{\mathbb{F}_p}(E_1) \cong$ **End**$_{\mathbb{F}_p}(E_2) \cong \mathcal{O}$ [21] where $\mathcal{O}$ is an order of an imaginary quadratic field. Furthermore, we donate the set of supersingular elliptic curves defined over $\mathbb{F}_p$ with $\mathcal{O}$ by $\mathcal{E}_{\mathbb{F}_p}(\mathcal{O})$. By definition, curves in $\mathcal{E}_{\mathbb{F}_p}(\mathcal{O})$ are connected by horizontal isogenies.

A Supersingular Isogeny Graph Over $\mathbb{F}_p$. The structure of a supersingular isogeny graph over $\mathbb{F}_p$ is studied by Delfs and Galbraith, which is described in [16, Theorem 2.7]. Let $\mathcal{L}$ be a set of distinct primes such that $p \notin \mathcal{L}$, $\left(\frac{-p}{l_i} \right) = 1$ for all $l_i \in \mathcal{L}$. For $p > 3$, the graph $\mathcal{G}(\mathbb{F}_p, l_i)$ is a directed supersingular isogeny graph where the vertices are a $\mathbb{F}_p$-isomorphism classes of supersingular elliptic curves represented by j-invariants with an extra information to classify them into their $\mathbb{F}_p$-isomorphism class (i.e., to differentiate between elliptic curve twists). The graph edges are equivalence classes of $\mathbb{F}_p$-rational isogenies of a degree l_i. In our work, we employ a graph that represents the union of all $\mathcal{G}(\mathbb{F}_p, l_i), \forall l_i \in \mathcal{L}$.

Isogeny and Pairing. Let N be a large prime such that $N \neq p$ and $N || E_1(\mathbb{F}_p)|$. Let μ_N be the group of Nth roots of unity in $\mathbb{F}_{p^u}^*$, where u is the smallest integer such that $N | p^u - 1$. The Weil pairing is the map $\hat{\mathsf{e}}_N^E : E[N] \times E[N] \to \mu_N$ that satisfies several properties. In particular, the Weil pairing has the property of being compatible with isogenies (see [32, Proposition 8.2]); and it is trivial to show that

$$\hat{\mathsf{e}}_N^{E_1}(P, [\deg \phi]Q) = \hat{\mathsf{e}}_N^{E_2}(\phi(P), \phi(Q)), \tag{1}$$

where $P \in E_1[N]$, $Q = \hat{\phi}(Q')$ for $Q' \in E_2[N]$, and $\phi \circ \hat{\phi} = [\deg \phi]$ on E_2.

3   Proposed Trapdoor-VDFs

By $\lambda \in \mathbb{N}$, we indicate the security level of a scheme. A function difficulty is denoted by T, which quantifies the amount of sequential work/steps necessary to produce/compute its output against any random input and with a polynomially large number of parallel processes. A function with a small T is identified as a short function, whereas one with a large T is called a long sequential function. Generally, we will denote the long sequential function by EVAL, with T being super-polynomial in λ.

An Informal Exposition. The proposed trapdoor-VDF is a VDF with a large ensemble of distinct shortcuts denoted by $\mathcal{F}$, called trapdoors. We say two trapdoors are equivalent if they produce the same output for the same inputs. The set of equivalent trapdoors is called a class. The class difficulty is the shortest trapdoor difficulty. Hence, the ensemble $\mathcal{F}$ is a collection of trapdoor classes.

Trapdoor-VDF Setup Agreement. Participants of a setup protocol agree on a long function EVAL with a difficulty T, a large ensemble of trapdoors $\mathcal{F}$, and possibly additional parameters for a security level λ.

Generation of a Challenge. In trapdoor-VDF, a Challenger can select a secret trapdoor tr_{sk} indexed (identified) in $\mathcal{F}$ by a random secret (sk). Using the trapdoor, the challenger can efficiently generate a challenge ($\mathbf{c}$) and its unique answer ($\mathbf{a}$). With the same parameters, distinct trapdoors produce different challenges (and accordingly different answers).

Obtaining the Answer. In the absence of sk, a Solver can only evaluate EVAL function in time no less than T to output the answer to $\mathbf{c}$ with a proof Π. Akin to VDF, the Solver gains no advantage from parallel computation. The Challenger can, however, get the answer $\mathbf{a}$ via the trapdoor tr_{sk} (i.e., in time less than T).

The Public Verification. The answer $\mathbf{a}$ is publically verifiable that is also in a zero knowledge of the secret sk. In a timeframe less than T, a **perfect** trapdoor-VDF is one in which the Challenger, who owns $\mathbf{c}$ and knows $\mathbf{a}$, cannot pass the public verification protocol. This is because the required proof cannot be fully computed before the specific time T.

A Formal Definition. We present our formal definition of trapdoor-VDF, which naturally overlaps with [6] and [34]'s VDF definition.

Definition 2. *Let $\mathcal{C}$, $\mathcal{S}$, $\mathcal{Y}$ be the challenge, secret, answer spaces, respectively. Our trapdoor-VDF is a tuple of algorithms (Setup, Challenger, Solver, Verify) defined below*

- *Setup: a randomized algorithm (runs in time $\text{Poly}(\lambda)$) that takes a security parameter λ and a difficulty T and outputs public parameter pk.*
- *Challenger: a randomized algorithm (runs in time $\text{Poly}(\log T, \lambda)$) that takes pk and selects a secret trapdoor tr_{sk} from the trapdoor ensemble $\mathcal{F}$ using a random secret sk (i.e., $\text{tr}_{sk} \leftarrow \mathcal{F}$ given $sk \leftarrow_R \mathcal{S}$); then, it generates a challenge $\mathbf{c} \in \mathcal{C}$.*
- *Solver: an algorithm that takes pk and a challenge $\mathbf{c} \in \mathcal{C}$ and outputs the answer $\mathbf{a} \in \mathcal{Y}$ and a "possibly empty" proof Π. This algorithm must at least run in time T with $\text{Poly}(\lambda)$ parallel processors.*
- *Verify: is a deterministic algorithm (runs in total time polynomial in $\log T$ and λ) takes a challenge $\mathbf{c}$, an answer $\mathbf{a}$, a proof Π, and pk; the algorithm outputs* ACCEPT *if $\mathbf{a}$ is indeed the corresponding answer to $\mathbf{c}$ under a given Π, otherwise* REJECT.

Trapdoor-VDF Properties. The following assumes that all statements are true for any λ, T and $pk \leftarrow_R \text{Setup}(1^\lambda, T)$. A trapdoor-VDF construction is well-defined if it is correct, unique, and efficient.

- *Correctness*: A trapdoor-VDF is correct only if the Verifier accepts, with probability one, an honest Solver's answer $\mathbf{a}$ for any honest challenge $\mathbf{c} \leftarrow_R$ Challenger(pk).
- *Uniqueness*: A trapdoor-VDF is unique only if there is only one valid answer $\mathbf{a}$, accepted by Verify, to every challenge $\mathbf{c} \leftarrow_R$ Challenger(pk) with a secret sk.
- *Efficiency*: A trapdoor-VDF is efficient if the Verify algorithm runs in a time $\text{Poly}(\log T, \lambda)$ that is significantly faster than the Solver algorithm, which has a

total running time polynomial in T and λ. Further, trapdoor-VDF must retain efficiency for any public parameters generated by Setup, runs in $\mathsf{Poly}(\log T, \lambda)$, and any challenge generated by Challenger, which runs in time $\mathsf{Poly}(\log T, \lambda)$.

Let $\mathcal{A}$ be a polynomially bounded adversary who has no knowledge of the secret sk. Let $\mathcal{A}_1$ be an algorithm that outputs pre-computation on pk. Let $\mathcal{A}_2$ be an online efficient evaluating algorithm that runs in parallel time with $\mathsf{Poly}(\lambda)$ processors and returns an answer $\mathbf{a'}$. Let $\mathcal{A}_3$ be an online forging algorithm that runs in time $\mathsf{Poly}(T, \lambda)$ and returns a malicious answer and proof $(\mathbf{a'} \neq \mathbf{a}, \Pi')$. To be secure, a well-defined trapdoor-VDF should satisfy two key properties: sequentiality and soundness.

- *Sequentiality:* A trapdoor-VDF is sequential only if there is no adversary $\mathcal{A} := (\mathcal{A}_1, \mathcal{A}_2)$ that has an online attack ($\mathcal{A}_2$) running in time less than T and has a probability of success

$$
\Pr \left[\mathbf{a'} = \mathbf{a} : \begin{array}{l} pk \leftarrow_R \mathsf{Setup}(1^\lambda, T), \\ \mathsf{pc} \leftarrow \mathcal{A}_1(pk), \\ \mathbf{c} \leftarrow_R \mathsf{Challenger}(pk), \\ (\mathbf{a'}, -) \leftarrow \mathcal{A}_2(pk, \mathbf{c}, \mathsf{pc}), \\ (\mathbf{a}, \Pi) \leftarrow \mathsf{Solver}(pk, \mathbf{c}). \end{array} \right]
$$

that is greater than a negligible function of λ.
- *Soundness:* A trapdoor-VDF is sound only if the Verifier rejects any proof Π' for any answer $\mathbf{a'}$ that is not an output from $\mathsf{Solver}(pk, \mathbf{c})$ on any $\mathbf{c} \leftarrow_R \mathsf{Challenger}(pk)$. The probability of success for the adversary $\mathcal{A} := (\mathcal{A}_1, \mathcal{A}_3)$ to output a proof Π' for an answer $(\mathbf{a'}, -) \neq \mathsf{Solver}(pk, \mathbf{c})$ is

$$
\Pr \left[\begin{array}{l} \mathrm{ACCEPT} \leftarrow \mathsf{Verify}(pk, \mathbf{c}, \mathbf{a'}, \Pi') \\ \text{and } \mathbf{a'} \neq \mathbf{a} \end{array} : \begin{array}{l} pk \leftarrow_R \mathsf{Setup}(1^\lambda, T), \\ \mathsf{pc} \leftarrow \mathcal{A}_1(pk), \\ \mathbf{c} \leftarrow_R \mathsf{Challenger}(pk), \\ (\mathbf{a}, \Pi) \leftarrow \mathsf{Solver}(pk, \mathbf{c}), \\ (\mathbf{a'}, \Pi') \leftarrow \mathcal{A}_3(pk, \mathbf{c}, \mathsf{pc}). \end{array} \right]
$$

that is a negligible function of λ.

Additionally, a well-defined trapdoor-VDF may comprise further properties, and one that is most relevant to our work is given below.

- *Perfectness:* The knowledge of tr_{sk} and the pair $(\mathbf{c}, \mathbf{a})$ solely does not provide an advantage in passing the public verification protocol. Let $\hat{\mathcal{A}}$ be an algorithm implementing Challenger, which outputs the pair $(\mathbf{c}, \mathbf{a})$ and an algorithm $\hat{\mathcal{A}}_2$. The probability of success for $\hat{\mathcal{A}}_2$ to output an acceptable proof Π', in time less than T, for any pair $(\mathbf{c}, \mathbf{a})$ is

$$
\Pr \left[\begin{array}{l} \mathrm{ACCEPT} \leftarrow \mathsf{Verify}(pk, \mathbf{c}, \mathbf{a}, \Pi') \\ \text{and } \mathrm{ACCEPT} \leftarrow \mathsf{Verify}(pk, \mathbf{c}, \mathbf{a}, \Pi) \end{array} : \begin{array}{l} pk \leftarrow_R \mathsf{Setup}(1^\lambda, T), \\ (\mathbf{c}, \mathbf{a}, \hat{\mathcal{A}}_2) \leftarrow \hat{\mathcal{A}}(\mathsf{Challenger}, pk), \\ (-, \Pi') \leftarrow \hat{\mathcal{A}}_2(pk, \mathbf{c}, \mathbf{a}), \\ (\mathbf{a}, \Pi) \leftarrow \mathsf{Solver}(pk, \mathbf{c}). \end{array} \right]
$$

that is a negligible function of λ.

Further on Trapdoor-VDF Properties. A secure well-defined trapdoor-VDF accounts also for the trapdoor properties and assumption(s). This is due to the fact that a secure well-defined Challenger requires a secure well-defined trapdoor. Formally, a trapdoor $\mathsf{tr}_{sk} \in \mathcal{F}$, associated with a domain $\mathcal{D}(\mathsf{tr}_{sk})$ and range $\mathcal{R}(\mathsf{tr}_{sk})$, is defined as follows

- tr_{sk}: a short function in $sk \leftarrow_R \mathcal{S}$, with evaluation time $\mathsf{Poly}(\log T, \lambda)$, that takes an input pk; the function evaluation returns a challenge and answer pair $(\mathbf{c}, \mathbf{a}) \in \mathcal{C} \times \mathcal{Y}$.

For any random secret $sk \leftarrow_R \mathcal{S}$ and $\mathsf{tr}_{sk} \leftarrow \mathcal{F}$, the trapdoors in trapdoor-VDF feature several properties.

- *Challenger correctness:* Let $(\mathbf{c}, \mathbf{a})$ be a challenge and its answer pair generated by tr_{sk}. The correctness property requires that the answer $(\mathbf{a}', -) \leftarrow$ $\mathsf{Solver}(pk, \mathbf{c})$ be equal to $\mathbf{a}$ with probability one (i.e., we must have $\mathbf{a}' = \mathbf{a}$ with probability one). There is, however, an extension to the previous statement. For instance, we can allow $\mathbf{a}' \neq \mathbf{a}$ only if there is a one-way public function (f) such that $\mathbf{a} \leftarrow \mathsf{f}(\mathbf{a}')$ and $\mathrm{ACCEPT} \leftarrow \mathsf{Verify}(pk, \mathbf{c}, \mathsf{f}(\mathbf{a}'), \Pi)$ is *true* for all $\mathbf{c} \in \mathcal{C}$ and all valid proofs Π. Having such an extension allows us to construct a **prefect** trapdoor-VDF in which the Challenger, who owns $\mathbf{c}$ and knows $\mathbf{a}$, cannot pass the public verification protocol before time T.
- *Challenger efficiency:* All trapdoors in a trapdoor-VDF must also be efficient. For any λ, T and $pk \leftarrow_R \mathsf{Setup}(1^\lambda, T)$, the efficiency implies that (as in [4]):
  - There is an algorithm that runs in time $\mathsf{Poly}(\log T, \lambda)$ and implements the process of sampling tr_{sk} from $\mathcal{F}$ for all $sk \in \mathcal{S}$.
  - There is an algorithm that runs in time $\mathsf{Poly}(\log T, \lambda)$ and implements the process of sampling an element from $\mathcal{D}(\mathsf{tr}_{sk})$ (and/or $\mathcal{R}(\mathsf{tr}_{sk})$).
  - There is an algorithm that evaluates tr_{sk} in time $\mathsf{Poly}(\log T, \lambda)$ for any element of $\mathcal{D}(\mathsf{tr}_{sk})$.
- *Challenger security:* To be secure, the following problems must be hard for any λ, T and $pk \leftarrow_R \mathsf{Setup}(1^\lambda, T)$.
  - Given any challenge $\mathbf{c} \in \mathcal{C}$ generated under the secret $\mathsf{tr}_{sk} \in \mathcal{F}$, find the challenge's answer $\mathbf{a} \in \mathcal{Y}$ in time less than T.
  - Given any challenge and answer pair $(\mathbf{c}, \mathbf{a}) \in \mathcal{C} \times \mathcal{Y}$ generated by $\mathsf{tr}_{sk} \in \mathcal{F}$, find $sk \in \mathcal{S}$.
  - Let $(\mathbf{c}', \mathbf{a}') \in \mathcal{C} \times \mathcal{Y}$ be any challenge and answer pair generated by $\mathsf{tr}_{sk'} \in \mathcal{F}$. Given a challenge $\mathbf{c} \in \mathcal{C}$ under $\mathsf{tr}_{sk} \in \mathcal{F}$, find its answer $\mathbf{a} \in \mathcal{Y}$.

Similar to VDF, the difficulty T is restricted to subexponential in λ. It is therefore cheaper to perform the T-sequential evaluation than to compromise the trapdoor-VDF security.

4   Design Rationale

This section discusses our approach to construct a proof-of-concept instance of trapdoor-VDF. To construct trapdoor-VDF, we begin by defining a long sequential public function $\mathsf{EVAL} : \mathcal{X} \to \mathcal{X}$ with a public challenge and answer (i.e., $x, y \in \mathcal{X}$ such that $y \leftarrow \mathsf{EVAL}(x)$). The secret is a random string ($sk \leftarrow_R \mathcal{S}$) that indexes a secret short map ($\mathsf{tr}_{sk} : \mathcal{X} \to \mathcal{X}$) in the ensemble $\mathcal{F}$. Using a random secret map, one may craft a trapdoor. A new challenge (x') can be obtained by masking x with tr_{sk} (i.e., $x' \leftarrow \mathsf{tr}_{sk}(x)$). The secret map tr_{sk}, which can also determine $y' \leftarrow \mathsf{tr}_{sk}(y)$, becomes the trapdoor. This statement is true assuming that the action $\mathsf{tr}_{sk} \circ \mathsf{EVAL}$ is equivalent to $\mathsf{EVAL} \circ \mathsf{tr}_{sk}$. In the absence of tr_{sk}, one can obtain y' by evaluating $y' \leftarrow \mathsf{EVAL}(x')$, which involves a large number of sequential steps.

Lastly, the verification procedure involves validating tr_{sk}'s correct computation statement with zero knowledge of tr_{sk}, where the Solver's answer (y'') serves as the statement witness. The validation arguments should be efficient, validating only the unique answer (i.e., a Verifier accepts only if $y'' = y'$).

In the following, we present a sketch construction of the proposed trapdoor-VDF. Essentially, the construction consists of evaluating a series of non back-tracking *horizontal* isogenies with a large degree (representing EVAL), whereas the secret trapdoor is a shorter *horizontal* isogeny walk in graphs over a finite field $\mathbb{F}_p$ (representing tr_{sk}). Our public verification protocol uses bilinear pairings similar to BLS signature scheme [8], which is also used in [9] and [18].

4.1   Construction Elements

First, we define the public parameters that we will use to construct our scheme. Following that, we will briefly describe the supersingular isogeny graph, upon which both the long evaluation function and short trapdoor operate. Lastly, we will discuss the scheme group structure and the scheme's public verification method.

Selection of the Scheme Parameters. The parameters for our scheme are generated with the help of the following algorithms.

- $(p, \mathcal{L}, N, \mathcal{S}, \boldsymbol{t}, E_0) \leftarrow \mathsf{GGen}(1^\lambda, T)$ is a public parameter generation algorithm that takes a security parameter λ and difficulty T as an input and outputs:
  - a large odd prime p such that $p = 7 \bmod 8$,
  - a set $\mathcal{L}$ of n small distinct primes defined as follow

  $$\mathcal{L} := \{2\} \cup \{l \in \mathsf{Primes}(6\log(p)^2) : (\frac{-p}{l}) = 1\},$$

  - a large prime N such that $N \notin \mathcal{L}$ and $N \mid p+1$,
  - the set $\mathcal{S} := \{-e, \ldots, e\}$ for a positive integer e where $|\mathcal{S}| = 2e + 1$,
  - the vector $\boldsymbol{t} \leftarrow \mathcal{T}^n$ of n elements, where $\mathcal{T} := \{-\lceil \frac{m_{\max}}{n} \rceil, \ldots, \lceil \frac{m_{\max}}{n} \rceil\}$, $\sum_{m \in \boldsymbol{t}} \mathsf{abs}(m) = T < 2^{o(\lambda)}$, and a positive integer $m_{\max} < 2^{o(\lambda)}$,

- a supersingular elliptic curve $E_0/\mathbb{F}_p$ on the surface of $\mathcal{G}(\mathbb{F}_p, 2)$, where $|E_0(\mathbb{F}_p)| = p + 1$ and possibly with j-invariant $\mathrm{j}(E_0) \in \{0, 1728\}$.
- $E \leftarrow_R \mathsf{Alg}(1^\lambda, E', \mathcal{L})$ is a randomized algorithm that takes an initial curve E', the set $\mathcal{L}$, and security parameter λ. The algorithm Alg outputs a random supersingular elliptic curve $E/\mathbb{F}_p$ on the graph surface. Basically, this algorithm involves taking a random horizontal isogeny walk (see [18]) of a length of at least $\mathsf{Poly}(\log p)$. It is required that the probability of finding isogeny (path) between the output curve E and an initial curve E' be a negligible function in λ.

4.2   The Graph in Use and the Single Step of Computation

The graph over $\mathbb{F}_p$ described in [16, Theorem 2.7] is the abstraction behind our scheme. In our scheme, the graph consists of two levels, namely a surface (i.e., $\mathcal{E}_{\mathbb{F}_p}(\mathbb{Z}[\frac{1+\sqrt{-p}}{2}]))$ and a floor (i.e., $\mathcal{E}_{\mathbb{F}_p}(\mathbb{Z}[\sqrt{-p}]))$. In this graph, surface and floor have one-to-one connection by 2-isogenies, and there are no odd-degree isogenies connecting them. On the graph surface, there are two horizontal isogenies of degree $l_i \in \mathcal{L}$ from each vertex, whereas the floor is connected by isogenies of degree $l_i \in \mathcal{L}/\{2\}$.

In our construction, a *sequential walk* on the graph is represented by the group action of the ideal class group $\mathbf{cl}(\mathcal{O})$ of an imaginary quadratic order $\mathcal{O} \cong \mathbb{Z}[\frac{1+\sqrt{-p}}{2}]$ on the set $\mathcal{E}_{\mathbb{F}_p}(\mathcal{O})$. Hence, both EVAL and tr_{sk} act on the set $\mathcal{E}_{\mathbb{F}_p}(\mathcal{O})$. The choice of $\mathcal{L}$'s elements enables us to represent the elements of $\mathbf{cl}(\mathcal{O})$ as a product of ideals of small norm $\mathsf{N}(\mathfrak{l})$ such that $\mathsf{N}(\mathfrak{l}) \in \mathcal{L}$. Thus, we represent a *single step* in the sequential walk by the group action of an ideal of a norm in $\mathcal{L}$ that acts on $\mathcal{E}_{\mathbb{F}_p}(\mathcal{O})$.

The elements of $\mathcal{L}$ are chosen to be Elkies primes. Hence, the ideal $l_i\mathcal{O}$ splits into $\mathfrak{l}_i = (l_i, \pi - 1)$ and $\hat{\mathfrak{l}}_i = (l_i, \pi + 1)$ for every $l_i \in \mathcal{L}$ (i.e., $l_i\mathcal{O} = \mathfrak{l}_i\hat{\mathfrak{l}}_i, \forall l_i \in \mathcal{L}$). This defines the direction of a *single step*. From every vertex in the graph surface, there are two actions of an ideal with norm l_i that can be applied, either $\mathfrak{l}_i$ or $\hat{\mathfrak{l}}_i$. Further, each direction can be computed via an isogeny using Vélu's formulas [33]. In other words, a single step in one direction, denoted by ϕ_{l_i}, is an isogeny of a kernel of order l_i intersecting with $\ker(\pi - [1])$. As for the step in the opposite direction, denoted by $\phi_{l_i}^{-1}$, represents an isogeny of a kernel of order l_i intersecting with $\ker(\pi + [1])$. Finally, for an integer m_i, we denote l_i-sequential walk by $\phi_{l_i}^{m_i}$, which represents m_i sequences of l_i-isogeny evaluation in the same direction.

The Long Evaluation Function. As with [18] and [31], the long evaluation is represented by an isogeny of large degree, exponential in T,

$$\mathsf{EVAL} := \phi_{\mathcal{L}}^t : E \to E_A$$

which is a composite of all $\phi_{l_i}^{m_i}$ for all $l_i \in \mathcal{L}$ and $m_i \in t$ (i.e., $\phi_{\mathcal{L}}^t := \phi_{l_n}^{m_n} \circ_n \cdots \circ_1 \phi_{l_1}^{m_1}$, where $m_i \in t$ and $|t| = n$). The degree of $\phi_{\mathcal{L}}^t$ is $\prod_{i=1}^n l_i^{\mathsf{abs}(m_i)}$ and it has a difficulty of $\sum_{i=1}^n \mathsf{abs}(m_i) = T$. The presumption is that to compute EVAL efficiently, all T composites of $\phi_{\mathcal{L}}^t$ must be evaluated sequentially.

The Secret Trapdoor and Secret Trapdoor Set. As with [11,31], we want to be able to efficiently sample a random trapdoor from their ensemble $\mathcal{F}$. We will therefore randomly sample $sk := s \leftarrow_R \mathcal{S}^n$ to represent the trapdoor as

$$\text{tr}_{sk} := \phi_{\mathcal{L}}^s : E \rightarrow E_B.$$

The set $\mathcal{S}$ is chosen so that the trapdoor $\phi_{\mathcal{L}}^s$ is much shorter than $\phi_{\mathcal{L}}^t$. However, the size of $\mathcal{S}$ must be large enough to ensure that there exist $|\mathcal{S}|^n \geq 2^{2\lambda}$ possible secrets.

4.3 The Scheme Group Structure and Its Public Verification

Let G_i^E be a subgroup of $E[N]$ where $E \in \mathcal{E}_{\mathbb{F}_p}(\mathcal{O})$ and $i \in [N]$. The trace-zero and the base-field subgroup of $E[N]$ are represented by subscripts 1 and 2, respectively[1]. Under the assumption that (i) N is coprime to $|\ker(\phi_{\mathcal{L}}^t)|$ and $N \neq p$, and (ii) E and E_A are isogenous (so that $|E[N]| = |E_A[N]|$), the surjective morphism $\phi_{\mathcal{L}}^t : E[N] \rightarrow E_A[N]$ must also be injective induced by the Lagrange's theorem; hence it is a bijective group homomorphism on the N-torsion subgroup (similar argument applies for $\phi_{\mathcal{L}}^s$). Let σ^{-1} be a *quadratic twist* defined as follows

$$\sigma^{-1} : E \rightarrow E^{(d)} \in \mathcal{E}_{\mathbb{F}_p}(\mathcal{O})$$

$$\sigma^{-1} : G_{i \in \{1,2\}}^E \rightarrow G_{2i \bmod 3}^{E^{(d)}}$$

where $E^{(d)}$ is a twist of the curve E. The inverse quadratic twist (i.e., $\sigma : E^{(d)} \rightarrow E$) is efficiently computable and it is defined as follows

$$\sigma : (x, y) \rightarrow (x/w^2, y/w^3)$$

where $w \in \mathbb{F}_{p^2}$, $w \notin \mathbb{F}_p$, and it has $w^2 \in \mathbb{F}_p$. In our configuration, it should be noted that $\sigma \circ \phi_{l_i}^{m_i}(E)$ and $\phi_{l_i}^{-m_i} \circ \sigma(E)$ are equivalent.

Pairing Based Public Verification in a Nutshell Let $\hat{e}_N^E : E[N] \times E[N] \rightarrow \mu_N$ be a non-degenerate Weil pairing map on E, where $\mu_N \subset \mathbb{F}_{p^2}^*$. A non-trivial bilinear Weil pairing can be defined as $\hat{e}_N^E : G_1^E \times G_2^E \rightarrow \mu_N$. This definition is equivalent to $\hat{e}_N^E : \sigma(G_2^{E^{(d)}}) \times G_2^E \rightarrow \mu_N$, which is efficiently computable with inputs of short representation. Let E, $E_A = \phi_{\mathcal{L}}^t(E)$, $E_B = \phi_{\mathcal{L}}^s(E)$, $E_{AB} = \phi_{\mathcal{L}}^s(E_A)$, and $E_{BA} = \phi_{\mathcal{L}}^t(E_B)$ be a set of isogenous supersingular elliptic curves. The public verification proceeds as follows:

– A Challenger, Verifier, and Solver all share as an input the description of the isogeny $\phi_{\mathcal{L}}^t : E \rightarrow E_A$ of difficulty T, and the point pair $(x^{G_1^E}, y^{G_1^{E_A}}) \in G_1^E \times G_1^{E_A}$ such that $y^{G_1^{E_A}} = \phi_{\mathcal{L}}^t(x^{G_1^E})$. All inputs are chosen for a security parameter λ.

---

[1] The subgroup G_1^E is defined as $G_1^E := E[N] \cap \ker(\pi + [1])$, whereas, $G_2^E := E[N] \cap \ker(\pi - [1])$.

- A Challenger selects $\boldsymbol{s} \leftarrow_R \mathcal{S}^n$ that defines the secret short isogeny $\phi_\mathcal{L}^s : E \to E_B$; then, it
  - randomly samples integers k_A, k_B, and k_{AB} such that $k_A k_B^{-1} k_{AB}^{-1} = \deg \phi_\mathcal{L}^s (\mathrm{mod}\, N)$,
  - computes and broadcasts the challenge $([k_A]Q^{G_2^{E_A}}, \hat{x}^{G_1^{E_B}}, Q^{G_2^{E_{AB}}}) \in G_2^{E_A} \times G_1^{E_B} \times G_2^{E_{AB}}$ such that $\hat{x}^{G_1^{E_B}} = [k_B]\phi_\mathcal{L}^s(x^{G_1^{E}})$, $Q^{G_2^{E_A}} \leftarrow_R G_2^{E_A}$, and $Q^{G_2^{E_{AB}}} = [k_{AB}]\phi_\mathcal{L}^s(Q^{G_2^{E_A}})$.
- A Solver computes the answer $\hat{y}^{G_1^{E_{BA}}} \leftarrow \phi_\mathcal{L}^t(\hat{x}^{G_1^{E_B}})$, which requires T sequential isogeny evaluations, and then broadcasts $\hat{y}^{G_1^{E_{BA}}}$.
- A Verifier outputs ACCEPT if $\hat{y}^{G_1^{E_{BA}}}$ satisfies the following equality

$$\hat{e}_N^{E_A}(y^{G_1^{E_A}}, [k_A]Q^{G_2^{E_A}}) = \hat{e}_N^{E_{AB}}(\hat{y}^{G_1^{E_{BA}}}, Q^{G_2^{E_{AB}}}), \qquad (2)$$

otherwise returns REJECT.

From Eq. (1), the above-mentioned verification is complete, as shown below.

$$\hat{e}_N^{E_A}(y^{G_1^{E_A}}, [k_A]Q^{G_2^{E_A}}) = \hat{e}_N^{E_{AB}}(\phi_\mathcal{L}^t \circ [k_B]\phi_\mathcal{L}^s(x^{G_1^{E}}), [k_{AB}]\phi_\mathcal{L}^s(Q^{G_2^{E_A}})),$$
$$\hat{e}_N^{E_A}(y^{G_1^{E_A}}, [\deg \phi_\mathcal{L}^s]Q^{G_2^{E_A}}) = \hat{e}_N^{E_{AB}}(\phi_\mathcal{L}^s(y^{G_1^{E_A}}), \phi_\mathcal{L}^s(Q^{G_2^{E_A}})).$$

Moreover, it is obvious that the correctness of the scheme depends on the terminal elliptic curves (i.e., E_{AB} and E_{BA}) being identical. To be consistent with previous work [18], Fig. 1 shows the proof system's structure.

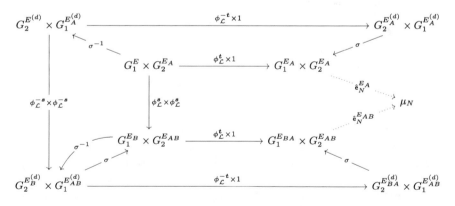

Fig. 1. The diagram illustrates the structure of the proposed trapdoor-VDF's proof system. The map $\phi_\mathcal{L}^{-t}$ is the $\mathcal{L}$-sequential walk $\phi_\mathcal{L}^t$ in the opposite direction (and similar for $\phi_\mathcal{L}^s$).

4.4   An Instance of the Trapdoor-VDF

The following is a formal description of a trapdoor-VDF instance constructed from the action of class groups on supersingular elliptic curves with bilinear pairings being used for public verification. They are all defined by the parameters chosen in the previous section.

Setup(1^λ, T):

1. $(\mathcal{L}, N, p, \mathcal{S}, \boldsymbol{t}, E_0) \leftarrow \mathsf{GGen}(1^\lambda, T)$
2. $E \leftarrow_R \mathsf{Alg}(1^\lambda, E_0, \mathcal{L})$
3. $x^{G_1^E} \leftarrow_R G_1^E$, s.t $\langle x^{G_1^E} \rangle = G_1^E$
4. $E_A \leftarrow \phi_{\mathcal{L}}^t(E)$
5. $y^{G_1^{E_A}} \leftarrow \phi_{\mathcal{L}}^t(x^{G_1^E})$
6. $pk \leftarrow$
   $\quad (\mathcal{L}, N, p, \mathcal{S}, \boldsymbol{t}, E, E_A, x^{G_1^E}, y^{G_1^{E_A}})$
7. **return** (pk)

Solver(pk, $\mathbf{c}$):

1. **if** $c.Q^{G_2^{E_A}} \notin G_2^{E_A}$ **then**
2. $\quad$ **return** REJECT
3. **if** $c.\hat{x}^{G_1^{E_B}} \notin G_1^{E_B}$ **then**
4. $\quad$ **return** REJECT
5. **if** $c.Q^{G_2^{E_{AB}}} \notin G_2^{E_{AB}}$ **then**
6. $\quad$ **return** REJECT
7. $E_{BA} \leftarrow \phi_{\mathcal{L}}^t(c.E_B)$
8. $\hat{y}^{G_1^{E_{BA}}} \leftarrow \phi_{\mathcal{L}}^t(c.\hat{x}^{G_1^{E_B}})$
9. $\mathbf{a} \leftarrow (E_{BA}, \hat{y}^{G_1^{E_{BA}}})$
10. **return** $(\mathbf{a})$

Challenger(pk):

1. $\boldsymbol{s} \leftarrow_R pk.\mathcal{S}^n$
2. $k_B^{-1}, k_{AB}^{-1} \leftarrow_R (\mathbb{Z}_N^*)^2$
3. $k_A = k_B k_{AB} \deg \phi_{\mathcal{L}}^s \bmod N$
4. $Q^{G_2^{E_A}} \leftarrow_R G_2^{E_A}$
5. $E_{AB} \leftarrow \phi_{\mathcal{L}}^s(pk.E_A)$
6. $Q^{G_2^{E_{AB}}} \leftarrow [k_{AB}]\phi_{\mathcal{L}}^s(Q^{G_2^{E_A}})$
7. $E_B \leftarrow \phi_{\mathcal{L}}^s(pk.E)$
8. $\hat{x}^{G_1^{E_B}} \leftarrow [k_B]\phi_{\mathcal{L}}^s(pk.x^{G_1^E})$
9. $Q^{G_2^{E_A}} \leftarrow [k_A]Q^{G_2^{E_A}}$
10. $\mathbf{c}_{\mathrm{EVAL}} \leftarrow (E_B, \hat{x}^{G_1^{E_B}})$
11. $\mathbf{c}_{\mathrm{verify}} \leftarrow$
    $\quad (E_{AB}, Q^{G_2^{E_A}}, Q^{G_2^{E_{AB}}})$
12. $\mathbf{c} \leftarrow (\mathbf{c}_{\mathrm{EVAL}}, \mathbf{c}_{\mathrm{verify}})$
13. **return** $(\mathbf{c})$

Verify(pk, $\mathbf{c}$, $\mathbf{a}$):

1. **if** $a.\hat{y}^{G_1^{E_{BA}}} \notin G_1^{E_{BA}}$ **then**
2. $\quad$ **return** REJECT
3. **if** $c.Q^{G_2^{E_{AB}}} \notin G_2^{E_{AB}}$ **then**
4. $\quad$ **return** REJECT
5. **if** $c.Q^{G_2^{E_A}} \notin G_2^{E_A}$ **then**
6. $\quad$ **return** REJECT
7. $l_{\mathrm{Side}} \leftarrow \hat{e}_N^{E_A}(pk.y^{G_1^{E_A}}, c.Q^{G_2^{E_A}})$
8. $r_{\mathrm{Side}} \leftarrow \hat{e}_N^{E_{BA}}(a.\hat{y}^{G_1^{E_{BA}}}, c.Q^{G_2^{E_{AB}}})$
9. **if** $l_{\mathrm{Side}} = r_{\mathrm{Side}}$ **&** $l_{\mathrm{Side}} \neq 1_{\mu_N}$ **then**
10. $\quad$ **return** ACCEPT
11. **return** REJECT

Fig. 2. The proposed trapdoor-VDF instance is defined by the four algorithms described above.

Discussion. It is imperative that a trusted process runs Setup due to an attack that exploits an elliptic curve with known endomorphism rings (see [18]). To generate the public parameters, the Setup must select E and then compute $\phi_{\mathcal{L}}^t$, which takes $O(T)$ steps. A Challenger must sample a one-time secret $\boldsymbol{s}$ to compute $\hat{x}^{G_1^{E_B}}$ and $Q^{G_2^{E_{AB}}}$, with the evaluation time being a polynomial function in λ. Essentially the challenge consists of three elliptic curve points. To obtain the answer, the Solver must compute $\phi_{\mathcal{L}}^t$, which is a separable isogeny of a degree exponential in T. Typically, the best approach for computing $\phi_{\mathcal{L}}^t$ is to sequentially compute each of its T compositions, of degrees $l_i \in \mathcal{L}$, using Vélu's formulas. A single point on the target curve E_{BA} serves as both the answer and the proof. The verification involves two bilinear pairings. It also involves determining whether all points are members of the appropriate group, a relatively trivial operation.

5   Security

We will show that the trapdoor-VDF proposed in Sect. 4.4 is secure well-defined with an honest challenge and the aforementioned setup that takes $O(T)$ steps.

Theorem 1. *The trapdoor-VDF instance in Sect. 4.4 is a secure well-defined trapdoor-VDF with a $O(T)$ steps long **Setup** and under the assumption of an honest Challenger.*

Correctness, and Uniqueness. The following assumes that all statements are true for any λ, T, $pk \leftarrow_R \mathsf{Setup}(1^\lambda, T)$. For all *honest* $\mathbf{c} \leftarrow_R \mathsf{Challenger}(pk)$, the correctness argument implies that any honest evaluator should be able to obtain the answer $\mathbf{a} \leftarrow \mathsf{Solver}(pk, \mathbf{c})$ which is Verify's acceptable answer.

However, the correctness argument is not complete yet. We also require that the $\mathsf{Challenger}$ and Solver must land on the same terminal elliptic curve and not only curves on the same isomorphism class. In other words, the evaluation output $(\phi_{\mathcal{L}}^t(\mathbf{c}.\hat{x}^{G_1^{E_B}}))$ and the challenge $(\mathbf{c}.Q_2^{G_2^{E_{AB}}})$ have to be on the same curve (i.e., $E_{BA} = E_{AB}$). This is required so that the Verifier can evaluate Eq. (2). The verification in Eq. (2) is likewise unique, as we employ a similar version of the [8]'s (and [18]) verifier.

Lemma 1. *Given any λ, T, and $pk \leftarrow_R \mathsf{Setup}(1^\lambda, T)$, a Solver's honest output $\mathbf{a}.\hat{y}^{G_1^{E_{BA}}}$ is indeed a point on the Challenger's terminal curve (E_{AB}) such that $\mathbf{a}.\hat{y}^{G_1^{E_{BA}}} = \hat{y}^{G_1^{E_{AB}}}$ and $\mathrm{ACCEPT} \leftarrow \mathsf{Verify}(pk, \mathbf{c}, \mathbf{a})$, for all honest $\mathbf{c} \leftarrow_R \mathsf{Challenger}(pk)$; further, there is no answer $\mathbf{a}'$ that is a valid answer (i.e., $\mathrm{ACCEPT} \leftarrow \mathsf{Verify}(pk, \mathbf{c}, \mathbf{a}'))$ unless $\mathbf{a}' = \mathbf{a} = \phi_{\mathcal{L}}^t(\mathbf{c}.\hat{x}^{G_1^{E_B}})$.*

Proof. The proof to the first part of the lemma follows from the result of Leonardi [23, Theorem 3.1]. Leonardi's result implies the equivalency between the action of $\phi_{\mathcal{L}}^s \circ \phi_{\mathcal{L}}^t$ and $\phi_{\mathcal{L}}^t \circ \phi_{\mathcal{L}}^s$ when all computed with Vélu's formulas. As for the uniqueness, we have set our parameters so that (i) as mentioned in Sect. 4.3, the surjective morphism $\phi_{\mathcal{L}}^t : E_B[N] \to E_{BA}[N]$ is a group isomorphism on the N-torsion subgroup and (ii) as discussed in [18], Eq. (2)'s right-hand side is a group isomorphism from $G_1^{E_{BA}}$ to μ_N for a given $\mathbf{c}.Q_2^{G_2^{E_{AB}}}$. Hence, $\mathsf{Verify}((pk, \mathbf{c}), \mathbf{a}')$ outputs ACCEPT if and only if $\mathbf{a}' = \mathbf{a} = \phi_{\mathcal{L}}^t(\mathbf{c}.\hat{x}^{G_1^{E_B}}) \in G_1^{E_{BA}}$.

Soundness. Since there is only one valid answer, the verification is unique, as is a property of [8]'s verifier. Thus, and similar to [18], our trapdoor-VDF is perfectly sound.

Sequentiality. In the following, we introduce the concept of sequentiality in our trapdoor-VDF by presenting the shortcut game.

Definition 3 (The shortcut game). *Let λ and T be a security and a difficulty parameters, respectively. Let $\mathcal{A} := (\mathcal{A}_1, \mathcal{A}_2)$ be a party that participates in the following game. (i) A trusted process computes and publishes $pk \leftarrow_R \mathsf{Setup}(1^\lambda, T)$,*

(ii) $\mathcal{A}$ preforms a pre-computation in time $\mathsf{Poly}(T, \lambda)$ and outputs $pc \leftarrow \mathcal{A}_1(pk)$, (iii) a trusted process then computes and publishes $\boldsymbol{c} \leftarrow_R \mathsf{Challenge}(pk)$, (iv) $\mathcal{A}$ computes and outputs $\hat{y}^{G_1^{E_{BA}}} \leftarrow \mathcal{A}_2(pk, \boldsymbol{c}, pc)$ in parallel time less than T, where $\hat{y}^{G_1^{E_{BA}}} \in G_1^{E_{BA}}$.

To win the game, $\mathcal{A}$'s output, $\hat{y}^{G_1^{E_{BA}}}$, is required to be the correct evaluation of $\phi_{pk.\mathcal{L}}^{pk.t}$ on $\boldsymbol{c}.\hat{x}^{G_1^{E_B}}$ (i.e., to be equal to $\boldsymbol{a} \leftarrow \mathsf{Solver}(pk, \boldsymbol{c})$).

The proposed trapdoor-VDF is sequential if there is no polynomially bounded player $\mathcal{A}$ with a non-negligible probability of winning the above shortcut game. A player $\mathcal{A}$ can win the game by finding (i) a shorter isogeny than $\phi_{\mathcal{L}}^t$, (ii) a faster method for computing $\phi_{\mathcal{L}}^t$, (iii) the inverse of pairing Eq. (2), or (iv) the secret isogeny $\phi_{\mathcal{L}}^s$ (or a short equivalent isogeny). The three former points have already been discussed in [18, Section 6]. With regards to the last point, the sequentiality is also determined by recovering the secret isogeny $\mathsf{tr}_{sk} := \phi_{\mathcal{L}}^s$ or obtaining a short equivalent isogeny. In other words, this is equivalent to recovering the ideal class $[\mathfrak{b}] \in \mathbf{cl}(\mathcal{O})$ that is computed via the secret isogeny $\phi_{\mathcal{L}}^s$.

Definition 4 (Key recovery [11]). *Given two supersingular elliptic curves E and E_B defined over $\mathbb{F}_p$ with the same $\mathbb{F}_p$-rational endomorphism ring $\mathcal{O}$, find an ideal $\mathfrak{b}$ such that $[\mathfrak{b}]E = E_B$ and $\mathfrak{b}$ is the product of ideals of small norm in $\mathcal{L}$.*

There are several possible attacks for recovering the secret, some of which are discussed in [11].

Brute-force Attack on the Secret Key. A basic attack searches over all potential keys. For a secret $\boldsymbol{s}$, its corresponding secret ideal class $[\mathfrak{b}]$ is represented as $[\mathfrak{l}_1^{m_1} \mathfrak{l}_2^{m_2} \cdots \mathfrak{l}_n^{m_n}] \in \mathbf{cl}(\mathcal{O})$ such that $\mathsf{N}(\mathfrak{l}_i) = l_i \in \mathcal{L}$ and $m_i \in \boldsymbol{s}$. Thus, it can be argued that $[\mathfrak{b}]$ has several representations (i.e., there are an equivalent $\hat{\boldsymbol{s}} \leftarrow \mathcal{S}^n$ that yields $[\mathfrak{b}] \in \mathbf{cl}(\mathcal{O})$), which is vulnerable to exhaustive search. Castryck et al. [11] show that the expected number of equivalent representations is $|\mathcal{S}|^n/\mathrm{ord}(G)$, assuming that $\mathbf{cl}(\mathcal{O})$ is almost cyclic with a very large cyclic component of order $\mathrm{ord}(G)$ close to $|\mathbf{cl}(\mathcal{O})|$. Therefore, it suffices to choose $n \log |\mathcal{S}| \approx \log(\sqrt{p})$, where $|\mathbf{cl}(\mathcal{O})| \approx \sqrt{p}$.

Pohlig-Hellman-style Attack. To our knowledge, the Pohlig-Hellman style attacks cannot be effectively applied to the construction in Sect. 4.4 to recover the secret degree ($\deg \phi_{\mathcal{L}}^s$) or the answer ($\hat{y}^{G_1^{E_{BA}}}$).

Castryck-Decru-style Attack [10]. As in [19], we mask the torsion points in pairing-based verification. Therefore, the point pairs $(y^{G_1^{E_A}}, [k_A]Q^{G_2^{E_A}})$ on E_A and $(\hat{y}^{G_1^{E_{AB}}}, Q^{G_2^{E_{AB}}})$ on E_{AB} are not images of the secret isogeny $\phi_{\mathcal{L}}^s$. In addition, the secret isogeny $\phi_{\mathcal{L}}^s$ has a hidden degree determined by $\boldsymbol{s}$, which is similar to the countermeasure suggested in [27]. Hence, to the best of our knowledge, our proposal is naturally resistant to a Castryck-Decru-style attack because we conceal torsion points' preimage and the secret isogeny degree.

Meet-in-the-middle Attack (MITM). To find the path $(\phi_{\mathcal{L}}^s : E_A \to E_{AB})$ in the isogeny graph $\bigcup_{l_i \in \mathcal{L}} \mathcal{G}(\mathbb{F}_p, l_i)$, MITH starts from E_A and E_{AB} to construct search trees. The attacker looks for the collision in the tree. The halfway point between E_A and E_{AB} is the isogeny evaluation of the halves of the set $\mathcal{L}$, $\mathcal{L}_{\mathbf{left}} := \{l_1, l_2, \ldots, l_{n/2}\}$, and $\mathcal{L}_{\mathbf{right}} := \{l_{\frac{n}{2}+1}, \ldots, l_n\}$ (for simplicity assume that n is even). Let $\mathcal{J}$ be the set size of all elliptic curves defined over $\mathbb{F}_p$ that are isogenous to E_A, constrained to $\mathcal{S}$, in the halfway to E_{AB}. We observe that the set size is $|\mathcal{J}| = |\mathcal{S}|^{n/2} - 1$; thus the attack average-case isogeny computation is about $\approx 2^{n \log(|\mathcal{S}|)/2}$. Setting $n \log(|\mathcal{S}|)$ to be $\approx \log(p)/2$, the attack's average-case complexity is $2^{\log(p)/4}$.

6   Conclusion

We have presented a new class of trapdoor-VDFs that have a large ensemble of trapdoors for each VDF instantiation. In the proposed scheme, a secret trapdoor, chosen randomly from the ensemble by Challenger, is used to generate a challenge. In a few steps, Challenger can obtain the answer to a challenge by using the secret trapdoor. Without knowing the secret trapdoor, a Solver on the other hand must perform the long sequential computations. We have also presented a trapdoor-VDF construction based on [11, 18, 31].

Our future work will focus on proving that the proposed construction eliminates computational advantage of the instance generator (i.e., not being able to obtain the trapdoor or break the scheme sequentiality). Further, the setup of the proposed instantiation requires evaluating the lengthy sequential computations, so it is beneficial to examine newer approaches to make the procedure efficient.

References

1. Abusalah, H., Kamath, C., Klein, K., Pietrzak, K., Walter, M.: Reversible proofs of sequential work. In: Ishai, Y., Rijmen, V. (eds.) EUROCRYPT 2019. LNCS, vol. 11477, pp. 277–291. Springer, Cham (2019). https://doi.org/10.1007/978-3-030-17656-3_10

2. Baum, C., David, B., Dowsley, R., Nielsen, J.B., Oechsner, S.: CRAFT: composable randomness and almost fairness from time. IACR Cryptology ePrint Archive, p. 784 (2020)

3. Baum, C., David, B., Dowsley, R., Nielsen, J.B., Oechsner, S.: TARDIS: a foundation of time-lock puzzles in UC. In: Canteaut, A., Standaert, F.-X. (eds.) EUROCRYPT 2021. LNCS, vol. 12698, pp. 429–459. Springer, Cham (2021). https://doi.org/10.1007/978-3-030-77883-5_15

4. Bellare, M., Halevi, S., Sahai, A., Vadhan, S.P.: Many-to-one trapdoor functions and their relation to public-key cryptosystems. IACR Cryptol., p. 19 (1998)

5. Block, A.R., Holmgren, J., Rosen, A., Rothblum, R.D., Soni, P.: Time- and space-efficient arguments from groups of unknown order. In: Malkin, T., Peikert, C. (eds.) CRYPTO 2021. LNCS, vol. 12828, pp. 123–152. Springer, Cham (2021). https://doi.org/10.1007/978-3-030-84259-8_5

6. Boneh, D., Bonneau, J., Bünz, B., Fisch, B.: Verifiable delay functions. In: Shacham, H., Boldyreva, A. (eds.) CRYPTO 2018. LNCS, vol. 10991, pp. 757–788. Springer, Cham (2018). https://doi.org/10.1007/978-3-319-96884-1_25

7. Boneh, D., Franklin, M.K.: Efficient generation of shared RSA keys. J. ACM **48**(4), 702–722 (2001)

8. Boneh, D., Lynn, B., Shacham, H.: Short signatures from the Weil pairing. In: Boyd, C. (ed.) ASIACRYPT 2001. LNCS, vol. 2248, pp. 514–532. Springer, Heidelberg (2001). https://doi.org/10.1007/3-540-45682-1_30

9. Burdges, J., De Feo, L.: Delay encryption. In: Canteaut, A., Standaert, F.-X. (eds.) EUROCRYPT 2021. LNCS, vol. 12696, pp. 302–326. Springer, Cham (2021). https://doi.org/10.1007/978-3-030-77870-5_11

10. Castryck, W., Decru, T.: An efficient key recovery attack on SIDH (preliminary version). Cryptology ePrint Archive, Paper 2022/975 (2022)

11. Castryck, W., Lange, T., Martindale, C., Panny, L., Renes, J.: CSIDH: an efficient post-quantum commutative group action. In: Peyrin, T., Galbraith, S. (eds.) ASIACRYPT 2018. LNCS, vol. 11274, pp. 395–427. Springer, Cham (2018). https://doi.org/10.1007/978-3-030-03332-3_15

12. Chavez-Saab, J., Rodríguez-Henríquez, F., Tibouchi, M.: Verifiable isogeny walks: towards an isogeny-based postquantum VDF. In: AlTawy, R., Hülsing, A. (eds.) SAC 2021. LNCS, vol. 13203, pp. 441–460. Springer, Cham (2022). https://doi.org/10.1007/978-3-030-99277-4_21

13. Chvojka, P., Jager, T., Slamanig, D., Striecks, C.: Versatile and sustainable timed-release encryption and sequential time-lock puzzles (extended abstract). In: Bertino, E., Shulman, H., Waidner, M. (eds.) ESORICS 2021. LNCS, vol. 12973, pp. 64–85. Springer, Cham (2021). https://doi.org/10.1007/978-3-030-88428-4_4

14. Cline, D., Dryja, T., Narula, N.: Clockwork: an exchange protocol for proofs of non front-running (2020). https://dci.mit.edu/clockwork, the Stanford Blockchain Conference

15. Cohen, B., Pietrzak, K.: Simple proofs of sequential work. In: Nielsen, J.B., Rijmen, V. (eds.) EUROCRYPT 2018. LNCS, vol. 10821, pp. 451–467. Springer, Cham (2018). https://doi.org/10.1007/978-3-319-78375-8_15

16. Delfs, C., Galbraith, S.D.: Computing isogenies between supersingular elliptic curves over $\mathbb{F}_p$. Des. Codes Cryptogr. **78**(2), 425–440 (2016)

17. Ephraim, N., Freitag, C., Komargodski, I., Pass, R.: Continuous verifiable delay functions. In: Canteaut, A., Ishai, Y. (eds.) EUROCRYPT 2020. LNCS, vol. 12107, pp. 125–154. Springer, Cham (2020). https://doi.org/10.1007/978-3-030-45727-3_5

18. De Feo, L., Masson, S., Petit, C., Sanso, A.: Verifiable delay functions from supersingular isogenies and pairings. In: Galbraith, S.D., Moriai, S. (eds.) ASIACRYPT 2019. LNCS, vol. 11921, pp. 248–277. Springer, Cham (2019). https://doi.org/10.1007/978-3-030-34578-5_10

19. Fouotsa, T.B.: SIDH with masked torsion point images. Cryptology ePrint Archive, Paper 2022/1054 (2022). https://eprint.iacr.org/2022/1054

20. Freitag, C., Komargodski, I., Pass, R., Sirkin, N.: Non-malleable time-lock puzzles and applications. In: Nissim, K., Waters, B. (eds.) TCC 2021. LNCS, vol. 13044, pp. 447–479. Springer, Cham (2021). https://doi.org/10.1007/978-3-030-90456-2_15

21. Kohel, D.R.: Endomorphism rings of elliptic curves over finite fields. Ph.D. thesis, University of California, Berkeley (1996)

22. Lenstra, A.K., Wesolowski, B.: A random zoo: sloth, unicorn, and trx. Cryptology ePrint Archive, Report 2015/366 (2015)

23. Leonardi, C.: A note on the ending elliptic curve in SIDH. IACR Cryptology ePrint Archive 2020, 262 (2020). https://eprint.iacr.org/2020/262
24. Loe, A.F., Medley, L., O'Connell, C., Quaglia, E.A.: A practical verifiable delay function and delay encryption scheme. IACR Cryptology ePrint Archive, p. 1293 (2021)
25. Loe, A.F., Medley, L., O'Connell, C., Quaglia, E.A.: Tide: A novel approach to constructing timed-release encryption. In: 27th Australasian Conference on Information Security and Privacy, 28–30 November 2022, Wollongong, Australia (2022)
26. Mahmoody, M., Moran, T., Vadhan, S.P.: Publicly verifiable proofs of sequential work. In: ITCS, pp. 373–388. ACM (2013)
27. Moriya, T.: Masked-degree SIDH. Cryptology ePrint Archive, Paper 2022/1019 (2022). https://eprint.iacr.org/2022/1019
28. Pietrzak, K.: Simple verifiable delay functions. In: ITCS. LIPIcs, vol. 124, pp. 60:1–60:15. Schloss Dagstuhl - Leibniz-Zentrum für Informatik (2019)
29. Rivest, R.L., Shamir, A., Wagner, D.A.: Time-lock puzzles and timed-release crypto (1996)
30. Rotem, L.: Simple and efficient batch verification techniques for verifiable delay functions. In: Nissim, K., Waters, B. (eds.) TCC 2021. LNCS, vol. 13044, pp. 382–414. Springer, Cham (2021). https://doi.org/10.1007/978-3-030-90456-2_13
31. Shani, B.: A note on isogeny-based hybrid verifiable delay functions. IACR Cryptology ePrint Archive, p. 205 (2019)
32. Silverman, J.H.: The Arithmetic of Elliptic Curves, Graduate Texts in Mathematics, vol. 106. Springer, New York (1986). https://doi.org/10.1007/978-1-4757-1920-8
33. Vélu, J.: Isogénies entre courbes elliptiques. CR Acad. Sci. Paris Sér. A **273**, 305–347 (1971)
34. Wesolowski, B.: Efficient verifiable delay functions. In: Ishai, Y., Rijmen, V. (eds.) EUROCRYPT 2019. LNCS, vol. 11478, pp. 379–407. Springer, Cham (2019). https://doi.org/10.1007/978-3-030-17659-4_13

Practical Homomorphic Evaluation
of Block-Cipher-Based Hash Functions
with Applications

Adda Akram Bendoukha[1(✉)], Oana Stan[1], Renaud Sirdey[1], Nicolas Quero[1,2], and Luciano Freitas[3]

[1] Université Paris-Saclay, CEA-List, 91120 Palaiseau, France
{adda.bendoukha,oana.stan,renaud.sirdey}@cea.fr
[2] Expleo, Saint-Quentin-en-Yvelines, Montigny-le-Bretonneux, France
nicolas.quero@expleogroup.com
[3] LTCI, Télécom Paris, Institut Polytechnique de Paris, Palaiseau, France
lfreitas@telecom-paris.fr

Abstract. Fully homomorphic encryption (FHE) is a powerful cryptographic technique allowing to perform computation directly over encrypted data. Motivated by the overhead induced by the homomorphic ciphertexts during encryption and transmission, the transciphering technique, consisting in switching from a symmetric encryption to FHE encrypted data was investigated in several papers. Different stream and block ciphers were evaluated in terms of their "FHE-friendliness", meaning practical implementations costs while maintaining sufficient security levels. In this work, we present a first evaluation of hash functions in the homomorphic domain, based on well-chosen block ciphers. More precisely, we investigate the cost of transforming PRINCE, SIMON, SPECK, and LowMC, a set of lightweight block-ciphers into secure hash primitives using well-established hash functions constructions based on block-ciphers, and provide evaluation under bootstrappable FHE schemes. We also motivate the necessity of practical homomorphic evaluation of hash functions by providing several use cases in which the integrity of private data is also required. In particular, our hash constructions can be of significant use in a threshold-homomorphic based protocol for the single secret leader election problem occurring in blockchains with Proof-of-stake consensus. Our experiments showed that using a TFHE implementation of a hash function, we are able to achieve practical runtime, and appropriate security levels (e.g., for PRINCE it takes 1.28 minutes to obtain a 128 bits of hash).

Keywords: FHE · Hash functions

1 Introduction

Fully homomorphic encryption (FHE) allows in theory to compute any function over an encrypted input. A plethora of works [5, 16, 20, 26] investigated the

---

N. Quero—This author contribution to this work was done while at CEA LIST.

G.-V. Jourdan et al. (Eds.): FPS 2022, LNCS 13877, pp. 88–103, 2023.
https://doi.org/10.1007/978-3-031-30122-3_6

evaluation of symmetric cryptographic primitives over FHE encrypted keys. The interest in this topic is mainly due to the advent of proxy-re-encryption or transciphering [12], which is a technique that partially solves transmission of massive FHE ciphertexts through limited bandwidth networks, by having the receiver computing an homomorphic decryption of a symmetric cryptosystem. Therefore, many stream and block-ciphers were designed to be efficiently evaluated using an FHE encryption of their key. All the above methods were designed mainly to protect data confidentiality, either through symmetric encryption (for the encryption step and the transmission), or through homomorphic encryption for their processing by an honest-but-curious entity. We argue that there are applications of FHE in which it is useful not only to have confidentiality guarantees but also an integrity check over homomorphically encrypted data. More precisely, in this work we discuss the evaluation of hash functions over an FHE encrypted message and provide several scenarios in which this application can be a solution to achieve integrity along with data privacy. Let us now present the major contributions of our paper.

1.1 Contribution and Motivation

In this paper, we present a set of FHE-friendly hash functions built on lightweight block-ciphers using provably-secure constructions, and with reasonable homomorphic execution times. Our choice for a block-cipher-based construction is well motivated and it is the result of investigating several other options, including the homomorphic execution of lightweight hash functions as well as the building of hash functions from FHE-friendly stream-ciphers. As discussed more in details in Sect. 1.2, the preliminary analysis of several lightweight hash functions candidate to the NIST competition on lightweight cryptography showed that they are not well suited for homomorphic execution. As for the second option, to the best of our knowledge, there is no known practical method to design a secure hash function directly from a stream-cipher (although universal constructions do exist based on Luby-Rackoff theory [31]). As such, we present here some hash function constructions from "FHE-friendly" block-ciphers such as PRINCE [11], LowMC [1] and SIMON [3]. These block-ciphers are interesting candidates to build hash functions, from the homomorphic evaluation point of view, since they have an appropriate design, and have already been implemented with second-generation homomorphic schemes in the context of transciphering.

First, we derive several constructions of hash functions from PRINCE by means of the double block length hash construction, which enables a 128-bits hash size taking into account that the original block size in the PRINCE design is only of 64 bits. We then look into more details and evaluate the performances of a TFHE [15] gate-bootstrapping implementation of these hash functions. Additionally, we leverage on SIMON and LowMC (in their 128-bits block size flavors) to obtain hash sizes of 256 bits via the same construction.

Finally, we describe several use-cases which may require to run our hash functions in the encrypted domain, including integrity checking of homomorphically encrypted data, oblivious authentication, homomorphic database querying, and a FHE-based protocol for single secret leader election.

1.2   Why Block Cipher-Based Constructions?

Beside security considerations, when constructing our hash functions, another criteria we looked at was to have a relatively fast evaluation in the homomorphic domain (e.g. less than one minute for a 256-size digest). A first idea for the construction of secure hashes suitable for homomorphic evaluation was to investigate three of the NIST lightweight competition finalists [17]: SPARKLE [4], XOODYAK [18] and Photon-Beetle [38]. We analysed them in function of the type of homomorphic bitwise operations one should execute: "free" operations such as permutations and concatenations, relatively easy operations such as the XOR and the AND (recall we use mainly TFHE in this work), and more difficult operations such as the modulo. We found out that their underlying primitives (e.g. S-boxes, modulo) and the number of rounds they require makes their homomorphic evaluation too expensive even with a bootstrapping-based homomorphic scheme, like TFHE. We also analyzed SPONGENT [8], another lightweight hash function, imposing to execute ≈30000 S-box in homomorphic domain (which corresponds to 68 S-boxes per round, 140 required rounds and 32 absorbing and squeezing steps) for 256-bits of output. Taking into account that the execution of the S-box used takes ≈0.6 s under TFHE, it follows that an homomorphic implementation of the SPONGENT hash function would be too slow to be of practical interest. Further details are available in [36].

Another appealing path was to explore hash-based constructions inspired from "FHE-friendly" stream ciphers. This option was tempting since nowadays there are several practical solutions implementing stream-ciphers into homomorphic domain (e.g. Kreyvium [12], Grain128 [5], PASTA [20]). However, even if it seems possible to obtain hash functions with very interesting homomorphic performances, their security seems difficult to assess and this, thus, remains an interesting open question. In essence, although theoretical constructions do exist, the symmetric cryptography community has, to the best of our knowledge, only marginally followed this path for building hash functions. Still, the possibility of achieving better FHE evaluation performances may be a new motivation for further investigations along this line.

As a consequence, we decided to consider block-cipher algorithms which have been already considered for homomorphic evaluations and turn them into secure hash functions using generic methods such the ones described in Sect. 2.3.

2   Background

2.1   Transciphering

Transciphering is a technique that allows offloading massive data from client to server with the aim to perform server-side homomorphic computations. Indeed, when a message m is encrypted under an FHE cryptosystem, the resulting size of the ciphertext $FHE.Enc_{FHE.pk}(m)$ is much larger than the size of the original message m, by an expansion factor which depends polynomially on the security parameter λ. In all modern FHE schemes for a λ large enough (in the 110–130 bits of security ranges) ciphertext sizes reach several kbytes or even megabytes (depending on the chosen cryptosystem and its security level). So, instead of encrypting m directly using an FHE scheme and sending $FHE.Enc_{FHE.pk}(m)$, a client will rather encrypt m using a symmetric cryptosystem and sends the encryption $SYM.Enc_{SYM.sk}(m)$ to the server along with $FHE.Enc_{FHE.pk}(SYM.sk)$, the FHE encryption of the symmetric key $SYM.sk$. The server then homomorphically runs $SYM.Dec_{FHE.Enc(SYM.sk)}(SYM.Enc(m))$ and recovers the message encrypted under the homomorphic public key $FHE.Enc_{FHE.pk}(m)$.

$SYM.Enc_{SYM.sk}(m)$ is roughly of the same size as m while $SYM.sk$, which is the only FHE encrypted and transmitted element, is of fixed size and often small enough to be homomorphically encrypted and sent (once and offline) through the network, whilst m can be arbitrarily large. Switching from a symmetric scheme to an FHE one allows a form of secure *compression* of the homomorphic ciphertexts. It requires however, the evaluation of $SYM.Enc$ homomorphically, which introduces a non-negligible additional computational overhead on the server-side. In [5, 12], it is argued that the use of a stream-cipher is more suitable for transciphering in the case of both 2nd generations FHE schemes (e.g., BGV, BFV) as well as TFHE. In [20] authors discuss the semantic security of transciphering seen as Key encapsulation/Data encapsulation mechanism (KEM-DEM) depending on the semantic security of both the symmetric and homomorphic schemes involved, and provide also an FHE-friendly stream-cipher named Pasta, suited for levelled FHE schemes.

2.2   Hash Functions and Security Properties

A general definition of a hash function is a mapping of messages of arbitrary length to a fixed size digest. Additionally, a *cryptographic* hash function requires the following security properties.

Pre-image Resistance. Given $h \in \{0,1\}^n$ the output of the hash function $H : \{0,1\}^* \to \{0,1\}^n$, it must be computationally hard to find $m \in \{0,1\}^*$ such that $H(m) = h$.

Collision Resistance. It must be computationally hard to find two distinct messages m_1 and m_2 such that $H(m_1) = H(m_2)$.

Second Pre-image Resistance. Given m and h such that $H(m) = h$, it must be computationally hard to find m' such that $m' \neq m$ and $H(m) = H(m')$.

Since we only consider cryptographic hash functions, for simplicity sake, in the remaining of the paper we will refer to a "cryptographic hash function" as "a hash function".

Black-Box Model. To prove the security of a block-cipher-based hash function independently of the underlying cipher's structure, it is used the black-box model, in which a block-cipher is modeled as an invertible random permutation defined by the key. An adversary is given access to encryption and decryption oracles, such that given m (resp. c) the encryption $E_k(m)$ (resp. the decryption $E_k^{-1}(c)$) is returned. The complexity of an attack is measured by the number of encryption and decryption queries that an optimal adversary performs. Since most attacks on block-cipher-based hash functions do not take advantage of the block-cipher's potential structural weaknesses or flaws, it is relevant to use a black-box model for security analysis.

2.3 Block-Cipher-Based Hash Functions

Among the most widely used constructions of hash functions are the iterated hash functions, in which a round function, also referred to as a compression function $F : \{0,1\}^n \cdot \{0,1\}^l \rightarrow \{0,1\}^n$ is iterated over every message block, taking as input the current message block of size n and the previous hash value[1]. The output of the final compression function call is the hash of the input message as shown in Algorithm 1. Due to its simplicity, this construction has been intensively studied in the state of the art [6,30], giving birth to many hashing standards such as SHA-0, SHA-1, and SHA-2. A large part of the security of these hash functions can be attributed to the underlying compression function[2]. In [19] authors demonstrate that the collision resistance of F implies collision resistance of the hash function built from F using the Merkle-Damgård construction.

These results raised interests in building secure compression functions from which it will be easy to build secure hash functions. A block-cipher is a primitive that already provides security properties by construction. Although the security requirements of an encryption algorithm are different by nature from those of a hash function, the question of how to build a secure compression function from a block-cipher quickly appeared and was intensively investigated, laying foundation for instance for the MDC family of hash functions [34] based on the block-cipher DES. The main motivation of this approach is to minimize design efforts, and use existing primitives. The task is to transform the security properties of a block-cipher into those of a cryptographic hash function, by carefully executing it over well-chosen linear combinations of the current message block, the chaining variable, or other conventional constants, taken as encryption keys or message blocks. This gave birth to a plethora of constructions, some of them were proven secure in the black-box model, others exhibited weaknesses regardless of the underlying block-cipher's potential weaknesses.

One important security element is the size of the digest. Due to the birthday paradox, collision security level of a hash function is upper-bounded by $O(2^{n/2})$, where n is the size of the hash. Thus, having a size for the hash equal to the size of the block for the cipher used to construct the compression function raised some

---

[1] A chaining value to provide dependency between successive hash values.

[2] The security under all aspects : Pre-image, second pre-image, and collision resistance.

issues. The size of some block-cipher's blocks can be too small to be considered as a secure hash size, and using a block-cipher with a large block length often results in higher execution times. Providing a secure construction that produces a hash twice larger than the block-cipher's block length was subject to several research efforts.

Algorithm 1. Merkle Damgård iterated hash function

input : $m = (m_0, m_1, \cdots, m_l)$
h_0 is set to an initialization vector
for i $= 0$ to l **do**
    $h_i = F(h_{i-1}, m_i)$
end for
return h_l

Single Block Length (SBL) Hash Functions. One of the very first constructions of single-block-length hash functions is the Davies-Meyer construction where $H_{i+1} = E_{M_i}(H_i) \oplus M_i$ and the Muguiyachi-Prennel's scheme with $H_{i+1} = E_{M_i}(H_i) \oplus M_i \oplus H_i$, where H_i is the previous hash value and each block of the message (M_i) is the key to a block cipher E.

Later, in [35], Prennel, Govaerts and Vandewalle (PGV) provided an exhaustive analysis of iterated hash functions defined over $\{0,1\}^* \to \{0,1\}^n$ and based on a block-cipher. The compression function is in the form $F(a,b) = E_a(b) \oplus c$ where a, b and c are in $\{m_i, h_{i-1}, IV, m_i \oplus h_{i-1}\}$, and E is $\{0,1\}^n \cdot \{0,1\}^n \to \{0,1\}^n$ block-cipher. There are $4^3 = 64$ such compression functions, among which 12 are presented as secure. Afterwards, Black, Rogaway and Shrimpton [7] provided formal security proofs in the black-box model of the 12 constructions analysed in [35]. They also demonstrated that among the remaining 52 constructions, 8 of them were actually secure with respect to collision and pre-image resistance. In this work we chose to evaluate Davies-Meyer's hash function under several block-ciphers, as it provides optimal security in the black-box model, and is equivalent in terms of computation complexity to other secure constructions from [7].

The security analysis and explicit constructions are provided in [7].

Double Block Length (DBL) Hash Functions. As mentioned before, constructions by PGV provide a hash of n-bits size when using a $\{0,1\}^n \cdot \{0,1\}^n \to \{0,1\}^n$ underlying block-cipher in the compression function. Due to the birthday paradox, these hash functions require block-ciphers with a large enough block length in order to provide security against collision attacks.

A measure of the efficiency of a hash function is its rate, that is, the inverse of the number of calls to the compression function per iteration.

In [33] Merkle presents three optimally collision resistant double block length hash functions, based on the block-cipher DES. However, their rates are low compared to the next generation of DBL constructions.

Lai and Massey proposed TANDEM-DM [28] for a rate 1/2 hash construction, using a $(n, 2n)$ block-cipher. It was proven optimally collision and pre-image secure in [21]. It makes however two non-independent calls[3] per iteration making it non-parallel. Abreast-DM [29] is another construction with a rate of 1/2 making two parallel calls to the block-cipher, and was proven to have optimal collision resistance in [22].

Lucks in [5] provides a first DBL construction of rate 1. Making a single block-cipher call per iteration comes at the cost of computing a heavy linear combination of the message block and the previous hash resulting in a significant overhead. Hirose in [25] provides a rate 1/2 construction with two distinct $(n, 2n)$ block-ciphers, then uses a tweak in order to use a single block-cipher. This construction provides optimal bounds for both collision and pre-image resistance in the black-box model, and is parallel. Indeed, the two calls to the compression function (and thus, to the block-cipher) are independent, making its performance comparable to rate 1 constructions.

Other works from [27,32] studied the possibility to build DBL hash functions from an (n, n)-block-cipher. MDC-2 fails to provide optimal security, while MDC-4 [32] is near optimal, but has a rate smaller than 1/2.

In this work, we homomorphically evaluate the constructions of Hirose and Tandem-DM. The goal is to provide an idea of the runtime of two optimally secure hash functions of rate 1/2 from both the parallel and non-parallel types on top of an FHE encryption layer.

3   Applications of Homomorphic Hash Functions

3.1   Homomorphic Data Integrity Check

As described in Sect. 2.1, transciphering allows to transfer symmetrically encrypted data instead of homomorphically encrypted and thus reduces the required bandwidth. However, transciphering while preserving data privacy does not ensure data integrity during transmission. In [5] authors describe how to include data integrity check within transciphering, but their approach required an AEAD encryption scheme (Authenticated Encryption with Associated Data).

Indeed, all stream-ciphers suffer from malleability, i.e., the possibility for an adversary to create an encryption of $m + k$ where k is some constant, from an encryption of m[4]. A malleable encryption scheme can be subject to man-in-the-middle attacks. Some modern stream-ciphers (e.g. [24]) come with the possibility to compute a MAC (Message Authentication Code) along with the encryption in an attempt to circumvent this issue. Another simple way to perform integrity check within transciphering when the chosen stream-cipher does not embed a MAC computation is to include a hash function. A client encrypts m concatenated to $H(m)$ using a symmetric encryption scheme. She then transmits these

---

[3] The output of the first block-cipher call is used to build the key of the second block-cipher call.

[4] $m \oplus keystream \oplus k = \mathsf{SYM.Enc}(m \oplus k)$.

elements to the server along with FHE.Enc(SYM.sk) (once and for all). Once the server has finished transciphering both the message and the hash, it recovers FHE.Enc(m') and FHE.Enc(h'), he computes $[h] = H(\text{FHE.Enc}(m'))$. If $m = m'$ then $h = h'$ (with overwhelming probability, of course). The server computes the homomorphically encrypted bit $[r]_{\text{FHE.pk}} = \prod_{i=0}^{n}(1 \oplus h_i \oplus h'_i)$ where n is the size of the hash. $[r]_{\text{FHE.pk}}$ is the output of the integrity check, such that :

$$[r] = \left[\begin{cases} \text{An encryption of 1 if } m = m' \\ \text{An encryption of 0 otherwise} \end{cases} \right], \tag{1}$$

This FHE encrypted bit could then be used in many ways. The server can simply transmit it to the client, in order to give him the ability to verify if his data was altered or corrupted during the transmission. Or the server could choose to reply with $[f(m)]$ or a NIL value outside of the range of f, according to the value of the bit r. In TFHE [15] for example, this can be realized using a homomorphic CMUX gate at roughly the cost of an extra homomorphic multiplication[5].

3.2 Single Secret Leader Election (SSLE)

The problem of securely electing a single leader in a distributed system was formally defined by Boneh et al. in [9]. For a committee of peers which collaboratively elect a node to complete a task, the problem consists in electing a node in a way that only this elected peer is able to know that he was elected and the others learn only that they were not elected. Also, the elected peer must be able to provide a proof of his election when he decides to reveal himself once his task is done. In [23] a solution to the SSLE problem is proposed based on Threshold Fully Homomorphic encryption [10] for partially-synchronous systems. A very high level description is the following. Every peer P_i wishing to register to the election at a given height and cycle (low and high level steps in the leader election protocol), provides an FHE encryption of $p_i = H(h||t_i||c)$ called the proof, where h is the height of the blockchain, c the current cycle of elections, and t_i a locally generated number belonging to process P_i. Every participating peer performs a sampling circuit following a weighted distribution over the FHE encrypted list of proofs and ids of all registered peers, using collaboratively generated randomness from [37]. Then, each peer homomorphically selects[6] a proof and the associated id from the set of all proofs. He then homomorphically hashes $(p_i||i)$ where i is the id of the elected peer, and p_i the corresponding proof. The next step is to broadcast a partial decryption of the voucher $v_{h,c,r} = H(p_i||i)$. Every honest peer samples the same p_i and i, and broadcasts his partial decryptions of $v_{h,c,r}$ using his secret key share. Assuming we have at least t honest peers in the system, where t is the decryption threshold, every peer must eventually receive enough partial decryptions and be able to perform a full decryption of $v_{h,c,r}$. The elected

---

[5] $\text{CMUX}([r], [f(m)], NIL) = [r] \cdot [f(m)] + (1 - [r]) \cdot NIL$

[6] I.e., homomorphically computes a one-hot encoding of an index in the proofs list and performs a dot-product to extract one such proof, thus without knowing which one.

peer recognizes his *voucher*, whereas other peers gain no information from plain $v_{h,c,r}$, nor can fake the election, since H is secure against pre-image and second pre-image attacks. Afterward, the leader is able to prove his election by submitting his plaintext proof $p_i = H(h||t_i||c)$. The verification is simply performed by running the test $H(p_i||i) == v_{h,c,r}$.

The homomorphically evaluated hash function plays a significant role in this protocol. It hides the sensitive elements from Byzantine peers providing the secrecy of the election and a simple proof mechanism, making the election easily verifiable, yet computationally hard to forge fake proofs.[7]

3.3 Homomorphic Database Querying

Suppose a server maintaining a database of elements DB such that query m has the answer A_m stored at index $H(m)$, where H is a hash function (with a small digest size w. r. t. to cryptographic standards). In this case H is not necessarily cryptographic. For instance pre-image resistance is not necessary since the query is already private under an FHE encryption layer. Nevertheless, we require from H to have balanced collisions[8] and, for this sake, one can use Luby-Rackoff's universal hash functions from [31]. In this setting, the server is able to homomorphically answer FHE encrypted queries.

A client homomorphically encrypts a query x and sends $[x]_{\text{FHE.pk}}$ to the server. The server computes $[i]_{\text{FHE.pk}} = H([x]_{\text{FHE.pk}})$, which is an FHE encryption of the index of A_x inside his database. The server then computes a vector V which contains FHE encryptions of 0 everywhere except at index i in which an encryption of 1 is stored. V is computed as follows : $V[k] = ([i]_{\text{FHE.pk}} == k)$ with $k \in [\![0, n-1]\!]$. Lastly, to extract an FHE encryption of A_x, the server performs a homomorphic dot product between the vector V and his database of elements $\sum_{i=0}^{n} DB[i] \cdot V[i]$, and sends back to the client the result of this final dot product, which will be $[A_x]_{\text{FHE.pk}}$.

One remaining problem of this use-case is to homomorphically resolve collisions of H. A first approach is to have the server creating lists of answers to different queries which hash to the same index at the position $H(x)$ in DB, and provide a second hash function H', whose output is smaller than the one of H, and which will compute the index of A_x inside the corresponding list. Thus, when an FHE encrypted query $[x]_{\text{FHE.pk}}$ is received, the position $(H([x]_{\text{FHE.pk}}), H'([x]_{\text{FHE.pk}}))$ provides an answer.

3.4 Oblivious Authenticated (Homomorphic) Calculations

It is well known that (keyed) hash functions are used in many authentication protocols where an entity (the user) can prove its knowledge of a secret (the key

---

[7] Secrecy is granted by the pre-image resistance of the hash function. Having a single verifiable leader is due to the second pre-image resistance of the hash function.

[8] $H : \{0,1\}^* \to \{0,1\}^n$ has balanced collisions if all elements in $\{0,1\}^n$ have the same number of pre-images under H.

of the hash function) to another entity (the server). To do so, the server sends a random challenge to the user which replies with the hash of the challenge. Since the server can also perform the same calculation, it can check the correctness of the client replies which proves the latter knowledge of the secret. With the ability of running hash functions in the homomorphic domain, we can now provide the server with an FHE encryption of the secret key and have the server performing the authentication in the encrypted domain i.e., the server generates a challenge in the clear domain, sends it to the user and get its (non encrypted) reply. The server can then run the (keyed) hash function homomorphically on its challenge, and homomorphically compare the obtained (encrypted) result with the reply received from the user. As the end of this process, the server possesses an encrypted boolean, say β, indicating whether or not the client has successfully authenticated (but has by construction no knowledge of whether or not that authentication was successful).

One way of using this consists in providing a valid calculation only to successfully authenticated users. In essence, rather than computing $f(x)$ in the homomorphic domain, the server can now compute $\beta f(x) + (1 - \beta)\bot$ (where $\bot$ denotes a constant value meaning, by convention, "not an answer"). As a consequence, (encrypted) valid calculation results are duly returned only to authenticated users, while other users receive only useless encryptions of $\bot$. This is then (nicely) done obliviously to the server, which cannot distinguish between ciphertexts of valid results and ciphertexts of $\bot$, and without revealing the secret hash function key (since it is only provided with an FHE-encryption of that secret key).

4 Adaptations of Block Ciphers for FHE-friendly Hashes

4.1 Block-Ciphers Considered

The Low-MC block-cipher [1] is part of a family of symmetric schemes designed for practical instantiations in homomorphic domain with the objectives of minimizing both the multiplicative complexity and the multiplicative depth, making it efficient for levelled homomorphic schemes. This design principle, had to be compensated with a large number of xor gates in order to ensure algebraic properties that provide an appropriate level of security. This latter fact makes it rather inefficient when ran under TFHE, since the cost of all Boolean homomorphic gates is the same within this FHE scheme (A bootstrapping operation is performed after every Boolean gate). It remains however a interesting candidate for hash constructions targeting efficient homomorphic evaluation in a levelled FHE setting. Even if the first variants of LowMC were successfully attacked, the subsequent proposed design is more secure and highly parametrizable. In particular, there is a closed-form formula to determine the minimal number of rounds to reach a given security target depending on the block size (128 or 256 bits), the key size, the number of S-boxes and the allowed data complexity.

PRINCE [11], SPECK and SIMON [3] are lightweight block-ciphers, with a relatively small block length. They were initially designed for constrained embedded execution environments. Their design approaches result in small gate counts[9] which results in high performances when ran under TFHE. Due to its small block length, PRINCE is better suited with double block length constructions, resulting in a hash function which provides $O(2^{64})$ collision resistance, and $O(2^{128})$ for pre-image resistance. SPECK and SIMON can be instantiated in both the DBL and SBL settings since they both provide a double-key-size variants.

4.2 FHE Schemes Considered

We chose to run our experiments under the TFHE cryptosystem since it provides the possibility to evaluate (multiplicatively) unbounded homomorphic circuits thanks to its fast bootstrapping operation. This scheme is more suited for protocols where scalability is a requirement. For example, the secret single leader election protocol [9] described in Sect. 3.2 requires flexibility regarding the number of peers being able to disconnect or join the committee at different times. These variations in the number of peers linearly increase the multiplicative depth of the sampling circuit, which would be difficult to manage if a levelled homomorphic scheme were to be used[10].

4.3 Tool: Cingulata Homomorphic Compiler

Cingulata, formerly known as Armadillo [14], is a toolchain and run-time environment (RTE) for implementing applications running over homomorphic encryption. Cingulata provides high-level abstractions and tools to facilitate the implementation and the execution of privacy-preserving applications.

Cingulata relies on instrumented C++ types to denote private variables, e.g., CiInt for integers and CiBit for Booleans. Integer variables are dynamically sized and are internally represented as arrays of CiBit objects. The Cingulata environment monitors/tracks each bit independently. Integer operations are performed using Boolean circuits, which are automatically generated by the toolchain. For example a full-adder circuit is employed to perform an integer addition. The Boolean circuit generation is configurable and two generators are available: focused on minimal circuit size or on small multiplicative-depth. More generally, it is possible to implement additional circuit generators or to combine them.

A CiBit object can be in either plain or encrypted state. Plain-plain and plain-encrypted bit operations are optimized out, in this way constant folding and propagation is automatically performed at the bit-level. Bit operations

---

[9] A round of encryption of a block-cipher often includes a multiplication of the internal state with an $\mathbb{F}^{k}$ matrix, this makes the number of operations quadratic with respect to its block size.

[10] In this category of homomorphic schemes, the multiplicative depth of the homomorphic circuit to be evaluated has to be known in advance in order to generate a parameter set which allows homomorphic computations up to this depth.

between encrypted values are performed by a "bit execution" object implementing the IBitExec interface. This object can either be a HE library wrapper, simply a bit-tracker object or even a plaint bit execution used for algorithm debugging purposes. When a HE library wrapper is used the Cingulata environment directly executes the application using the underlying HE library.

Another option is to use the bit-tracker in order to build a circuit representation of the application. This allows to use circuit optimization modules in order to further optimize the Boolean circuit representation. The hardware synthesis toolchain ABC[11] is used to minimize circuit size. It is an open-source environment providing implementations of state-of-the-art circuit optimization algorithms. These algorithms are mainly designed for minimizing circuit area or latency but, currently, none of them is designed for multiplicative depth minimization. In order to fill this gap, several heuristics for minimizing the multiplicative depth are available in Cingulata, refer to [2,13] for more details.

The optimized Boolean circuit is then executed using Cingulata's parallel run-time environment. The RTE is generic, meaning that it uses a HE library wrapper, i.e. a "bit execution" object as defined earlier, in order to execute the gates of the circuit. The scheduler of the run-time allows to fully take advantage of many-core processors. Besides, a set of utility applications are provided for parameter generation (given a target security level), key generation, encryption and decryption. These applications are also generic, in the same vein as the parallel RTE.

4.4   Experimental Results and Performances

We ran *multi core* performance tests on an Intel(R) Xeon(R) CPU E3-1240 v5 @ 3.50 GHz and 8 GB RAM using Cingulata in TFHE mode. We provide parallelism when possible using the OpenMP library.

For single block length construction, we implement Davies-Meyer's compression function which requires a (n, n)-block-cipher. Therefore, we instantiate this construction with SPECK, SIMON[12], and the (128, 128) variant of LowMC. In the double block length setting, since these constructions require an $(n, 2n)$-block-cipher, we instantiate Hirose's and Tandem-DM constructions with PRINCE, and the (128, 256) variants of LowMC, and SIMON. The results are shown in Table 1 with the execution times in minutes when the hash functions are instantiated, and an "-" symbol when the construction is not compatible with the sizes of the key and the block of the cipher.

The obtained performances are as expected: lightweight ciphers provide better runtimes compared to LowMC. PRINCE is the most efficient cipher for DBL

---

[11] http://people.eecs.berkeley.edu/alanmi/abc/.

[12] For SIMON, these are estimations based on the gate count from [3] and the gate-bootstrapping time of TFHE.

constructions as it has the lowest gate-count, and is also the most parallelizable cipher. The number of rounds performed in every construction to produce the hash of a 128-bits message is $\lceil \frac{128}{blocklength} \rceil$. Thus, in the first row, DBL-PRINCE performs two iterations and produces a 128-bits hash. All the remaining constructions perform a single iteration.

Table 1. Evaluation of hash functions over a 128-bits TFHE encrypted message in minutes

Instantiation	Davies-Meyer (SBL)	Hirose (DBL)	Tandem-DM (DBL)
(64, 128)-PRINCE	–	1.28	2.98
(128, 128)-SPECK	3.78	–	–
(128, 256)-SPECK	–	4.91	8.16
(128, 128)-SIMON	2.14	–	–
(128, 256)-SIMON	–	3.64	7.05
(128, 128)-LowMC	6.12	–	–
(128, 256)-LowMC	–	8.58	17.32

5 Conclusion and Perspectives

In this work, we have investigated scenarios in which the ability to (efficiently) evaluate hash functions in the homomorphic domain is an interesting building block. To the best of our knowledge, this work is one of the first to address this issue, at least for the TFHE cryptosystem. We also explored various provably-secure constructions of "(T)FHE friendly" hash functions based on respected block-ciphers in order to achieve several digest sizes. Fully homomorphic encryption on its own opens perspectives towards a new set of applications. Then, combining it with the execution of hash functions in the homomorphic domain provides it with additional versatility which can serve in various scenarios and protocols.

References

1. Albrecht, M., Rechberger, C., Schneider, T., Tiessen, T., Zohner, M.: Ciphers for MPC and FHE. Cryptology ePrint Archive, Paper 2016/687 (2016). https://eprint.iacr.org/2016/687
2. Aubry, P., Carpov, S., Sirdey, R.: Faster homomorphic encryption is not enough: improved heuristic for multiplicative depth minimization of Boolean circuits. In: Jarecki, S. (ed.) CT-RSA 2020. LNCS, vol. 12006, pp. 345–363. Springer, Cham (2020). https://doi.org/10.1007/978-3-030-40186-3_15
3. Beaulieu, R., Shors, D., Smith, J., Treatman-Clark, S., Weeks, B., Wingers, L.: The SIMON and SPECK families of lightweight block ciphers. Cryptology ePrint Archive, Paper 2013/404 (2013). https://eprint.iacr.org/2013/404
4. Beierle, C., et al.: Schwaemm and Esch: Lightweight authenticated encryption and hashing using the sparkle permutation family (2019)

5. Bendoukha, A.A., Boudguiga, A., Sirdey, R.: Revisiting stream-cipher-based homomorphic transciphering in the TFHE era. In: Aïmeur, E., Laurent, M., Yaich, R., Dupont, B., Garcia-Alfaro, J. (eds.) Foundations and Practice of Security. LNCS, vol. 13291, pp. 19–33. Springer, Cham (2022). https://doi.org/10.1007/978-3-031-08147-7_2

6. Biham, E., Dunkelman, O.: A framework for iterative hash functions - HAIFA. Cryptology ePrint Archive, Paper 2007/278 (2007). https://eprint.iacr.org/2007/278

7. Black, J., Rogaway, P., Shrimpton, T.: Black-box analysis of the block-cipher-based hash-function constructions from PGV. In: Yung, M. (ed.) CRYPTO 2002. LNCS, vol. 2442, pp. 320–335. Springer, Heidelberg (2002). https://doi.org/10.1007/3-540-45708-9_21

8. Bogdanov, A., Knežević, M., Leander, G., Toz, D., Varıcı, K., Verbauwhede, I.: SPONGENT: a lightweight hash function. In: Preneel, B., Takagi, T. (eds.) CHES 2011. LNCS, vol. 6917, pp. 312–325. Springer, Heidelberg (2011). https://doi.org/10.1007/978-3-642-23951-9_21

9. Boneh, D., Eskandarian, S., Hanzlik, L., Greco, N.: Single secret leader election. Cryptology ePrint Archive, Paper 2020/025 (2020). https://eprint.iacr.org/2020/025

10. Boneh, D., et al.: Threshold cryptosystems from threshold fully homomorphic encryption. Cryptology ePrint Archive, Paper 2017/956 (2017). https://eprint.iacr.org/2017/956

11. Borghoff, J., et al.: Prince - a low-latency block cipher for pervasive computing applications (full version). Cryptology ePrint Archive, Paper 2012/529 (2012). https://eprint.iacr.org/2012/529

12. Canteaut, A., et al.: Stream ciphers: a practical solution for efficient homomorphic-ciphertext compression. J. Cryptol. **31**(3), 885–916 (2018). https://doi.org/10.1007/s00145-017-9273-9

13. Carpov, S., Aubry, P., Sirdey, R.: A multi-start heuristic for multiplicative depth minimization of Boolean circuits. In: Brankovic, L., Ryan, J., Smyth, W.F. (eds.) IWOCA 2017. LNCS, vol. 10765, pp. 275–286. Springer, Cham (2018). https://doi.org/10.1007/978-3-319-78825-8_23

14. Carpov, S., Dubrulle, P., Sirdey, R.: Armadillo: a compilation chain for privacy preserving applications. In: Bao, F., Miller, S., Chow, S.S.M., Yao, D. (eds.) Proceedings of the 3rd International Workshop on Security in Cloud Computing, SCC@ASIACCS 2015, Singapore, Republic of Singapore, 14 April 2015, pp. 13–19. ACM (2015). https://doi.org/10.1145/2732516.2732520

15. Chillotti, I., Gama, N., Georgieva, M., Izabachène, M.: TFHE: fast fully homomorphic encryption over the torus. Cryptology ePrint Archive, Paper 2018/421 (2018). https://eprint.iacr.org/2018/421

16. Cho, J., et al.: Transciphering framework for approximate homomorphic encryption (full version). Cryptology ePrint Archive, Paper 2020/1335 (2020). https://eprint.iacr.org/2020/1335

17. Cryptography: NIST lightweight cryptography. https://csrc.nist.gov/Projects/Lightweight

18. Daemen, J., Hoffert, S., Peeters, M., Assche, G.V., Keer, R.V.: Xoodyak and a lightweight cryptographic scheme (2020)

19. Damgård, Ivan Bjerre: A design principle for hash functions. In: Brassard, Gilles (ed.) CRYPTO 1989. LNCS, vol. 435, pp. 416–427. Springer, New York (1990). https://doi.org/10.1007/0-387-34805-0_39

20. Dobraunig, C., Grassi, L., Helminger, L., Rechberger, C., Schofnegger, M., Walch, R.: Pasta: a case for hybrid homomorphic encryption. Cryptology ePrint Archive, Paper 2021/731 (2021). https://eprint.iacr.org/2021/731
21. Fleischmann, E., Gorski, M., Lucks, S.: On the security of TANDEM-DM. In: Dunkelman, O. (ed.) FSE 2009. LNCS, vol. 5665, pp. 84–103. Springer, Heidelberg (2009). https://doi.org/10.1007/978-3-642-03317-9_6
22. Fleischmann, E., Gorski, M., Lucks, S.: Security of cyclic double block length hash functions. In: Parker, M.G. (ed.) IMACC 2009. LNCS, vol. 5921, pp. 153–175. Springer, Heidelberg (2009). https://doi.org/10.1007/978-3-642-10868-6_10
23. Freitas, L., et al.: Homomorphic sortition - secret leader election for blockchain (2022). https://doi.org/10.48550/ARXIV.2206.11519, https://arxiv.org/abs/2206.11519
24. Hell, M., Johansson, T., Meier, W., Sönnerup, J., Yoshida, H.: An AEAD variant of the grain stream cipher. In: Carlet, C., Guilley, S., Nitaj, A., Souidi, E.M. (eds.) C2SI 2019. LNCS, vol. 11445, pp. 55–71. Springer, Cham (2019). https://doi.org/10.1007/978-3-030-16458-4_5
25. Hirose, S.: Provably secure double-block-length hash functions in a black-box model. In: Park, C., Chee, S. (eds.) ICISC 2004. LNCS, vol. 3506, pp. 330–342. Springer, Heidelberg (2005). https://doi.org/10.1007/11496618_24
26. Hoffmann, C., Méaux, P., Ricosset, T.: Transciphering, using FiLIP and TFHE for an efficient delegation of computation. In: Bhargavan, K., Oswald, E., Prabhakaran, M. (eds.) INDOCRYPT 2020. LNCS, vol. 12578, pp. 39–61. Springer, Cham (2020). https://doi.org/10.1007/978-3-030-65277-7_3
27. Jetchev, D., Özen, O., Stam, M.: Collisions are not incidental: a compression function exploiting discrete geometry. In: Cramer, R. (ed.) TCC 2012. LNCS, vol. 7194, pp. 303–320. Springer, Heidelberg (2012). https://doi.org/10.1007/978-3-642-28914-9_17
28. Lai, X., Massey, J.L.: Hash functions based on block ciphers. In: Rueppel, R.A. (ed.) EUROCRYPT 1992. LNCS, vol. 658, pp. 55–70. Springer, Heidelberg (1993). https://doi.org/10.1007/3-540-47555-9_5
29. Lee, J., Kwon, D.: The security of Abreast-DM in the ideal cipher model. Cryptology ePrint Archive, Paper 2009/225 (2009). https://eprint.iacr.org/2009/225
30. Lei, D., Lin, D., Chao, L., Feng, K., Qu, L.: The design principle of hash function with Merkle-Damgård construction. Cryptology ePrint Archive, Paper 2006/135 (2006). https://eprint.iacr.org/2006/135
31. Luby, M.: Pseudorandomness and Cryptographic Applications (1996). https://doi.org/10.2307/j.ctvs32rpn
32. Mennink, B.: On the collision and preimage security of MDC-4 in the ideal cipher model. Cryptology ePrint Archive, Paper 2012/113 (2012). https://eprint.iacr.org/2012/113
33. Merkle, R.C.: One way hash functions and DES. In: Brassard, G. (ed.) CRYPTO 1989. LNCS, vol. 435, pp. 428–446. Springer, New York (1990). https://doi.org/10.1007/0-387-34805-0_40
34. Preneel, B.: MDC-2 and MDC-4. In: van Tilborg, H.C.A., Jajodia, S. (eds.) Encyclopedia of Cryptography and Security, pp. 771–772. Springer, Boston, MA (2011). https://doi.org/10.1007/978-1-4419-5906-5_596
35. Preneel, B., Govaerts, R., Vandewalle, J.: Hash functions based on block ciphers: a synthetic approach. In: Stinson, D.R. (ed.) CRYPTO 1993. LNCS, vol. 773, pp. 368–378. Springer, Heidelberg (1994). https://doi.org/10.1007/3-540-48329-2_31

36. Quero, N.: Etude des fonctions de hachage homomorphes pour un protocole d'élection secrète pour la blockchain (2022). Internship report. REF: LIST/DSCIN/21-0189/NQ

37. de Souza, L.F., Tucci Piergiovanni, S., Sirdey, R., Stan, O., Quero, N., Kuznetsov, P.: Randsolomon: optimally resilient multi-party random number generation protocol. CoRR abs/2109.04911 (2021). https://arxiv.org/abs/2109.04911

38. Guo, J., Peyrin, T., Poschmann, A.: The PHOTON family of lightweight hash functions. In: Rogaway, P. (ed.) CRYPTO 2011. LNCS, vol. 6841, pp. 222–239. Springer, Heidelberg (2011). https://doi.org/10.1007/978-3-642-22792-9_13

Towards a Maturity Model
for Crypto-Agility Assessment

Julian Hohm, Andreas Heinemann[(✉)], and Alexander Wiesmaier

Hochschule Darmstadt, Darmstadt, Germany
andreas.heinemann@h-da.de

Abstract. Crypto-agility promises agile replacement of cryptographic building blocks and therewith supports context-aware and long-term security. To assess and evolve the degree of crypto-agility of one's IT system, a commonly agreed model is helpful, but, to the best of our knowledge, does not exist. This work proposes the Crypto-Agility Maturity Model (CAMM), a maturity model for determining the state of crypto-agility of a given software or IT landscape. CAMM consists of five levels, for each level a set of requirements have been formulated based on literature review. Initial feedback from field experts confirms that CAMM has a well-designed structure and is easy to comprehend. Based on our model, the cryptographic agility of an IT landscape can be systematically measured and improved step by step. We expect that this will enable companies and institutions to respond better and faster to threats resulting from broken cryptographic schemes. This work serves to promote CAMM and encourage others to apply it in practice and further develop it jointly.

Keywords: cryptographic agility · maturity model · CAMM

1 Introduction

Cryptographic primitives and protocols always have and will be subject to the threat of compromise, which implies the need to substitute endangered (or broken) cryptographic schemes with secure ones. In addition, different installation contexts (of the same application) may require the usage of different primitives and protocols, e.g. due to varying regulations within companies or countries, which implies the need to respectively adapt the choice of cryptographic schemes. The current efforts to standardize [9], disseminate [32], and integrate [3] post-quantum cryptography (PQC) are a contemporary example of changes in cryptography.

Among the latest and most prominent examples of past transitions of cryptographic primitives are the (not yet fully finalized) migration from SHA-2 to SHA-3 and from DES to AES, respectively. These have (again) shown that such migration is a time-consuming and resource-intensive process. Reasons for that are manifold, including the need to adapt depending standards and certifications, maintain interoperability with non-upgradable legacy systems, and plain

© The Author(s), under exclusive license to Springer Nature Switzerland AG 2023
G.-V. Jourdan et al. (Eds.): FPS 2022, LNCS 13877, pp. 104–119, 2023.
https://doi.org/10.1007/978-3-031-30122-3_7

and simply the necessary resources [3]. All of these concerns can be diminished by preparing systems for such changes beforehand by ensuring what is called cryptographic agility.

The notion of *cryptographic agility* (*crypto-agility* for short) is often associated with the ability to replace a cryptographic scheme in an agile manner with very little effort [2]. Following the view of Ott et al. [10], in our opinion, crypto-agility needs to be discussed and addressed in a broader sense. Ott et al. propose the concept of *modalities* for an expanded notion of crypto-agility. For example, context agility refers to a crypto-agile solution, where cryptographic algorithms and strength policies have the flexibility to be derived automatically from system attributes.

Amongst the first steps towards establishing crypto-agility is assessing the respective readiness of a particular software or IT system. With this knowledge, further development towards a crypto-agility solution can then take place. Our research on existing best practices for measuring and/or evolving crypto-agility shows that there is work on many aspects of crypto-agility in different contexts, but a holistic model that provides a systematic approach to assessing and evolving one's system in terms of crypto-agility seems to be missing.

To close this gap, in this work, we propose the *Crypto-Agility Maturity Model* (CAMM) to determine the crypto-agility level of a given software or IT System. CAMM comprises 5 maturity levels. For a system to reach a certain level, several given requirements must be met. We formulate these requirements based on an intensive literature review (see Sect. 3) and assign them to appropriate levels in our model. With CAMM at hand, IT managers can systematically assess their IT infrastructure and derive concrete measures to further develop their IT landscape in the direction of crypto-agility.

CAMM may be used for assessing one's crypto-agility without involving other guidelines. When not only assessing but also evolving one's crypto-agility, we strongly recommend an interplay of CAMM with established best practices for IT security management, such as defined in the ISO/IEC-27000 family.

We note that crypto-agility is associated with increased complexity compared to non-crypto-agile systems. IT management may also deliberately decide against this complexity and use technologies that require an update in the implementation if security problems are identified. One example is the Wireguard protocol, which deliberately omits crypto-agility by design [13].

The further text is structured as follows. Section 2 reviews related work on maturity models on which we build as well as crypto-agility in general and additionally with a focus on post-quantum cryptography. Section 3 identifies important requirements, aspects, and properties of crypto-agility derived from literature, which we integrate into our maturity model. This is followed by the methodology used to develop CAMM (Sect. 4). The model itself is described in Sect. 5. A brief preliminary evaluation of CAMM is provided in Sect. 6, followed by a short discussion and outlook in Sect. 7, where we point out issues we would like to address in the future.

2   Related Work

There is a whole range of maturity models, mainly from the field of information systems and business management, see [5,29]. The most popular Capability Maturity Model Integration (CMMI) family of maturity models focuses on processes and is thus not applicable for assessing the current maturity of a system's crypto-agility. Models more specialized in cybersecurity like the Cybersecurity Capability Maturity Model (C2M2) [12], the Cybersecurity Maturity Model Certification (CMMC) [33], the Systems Security Engineering - Capability Maturity Model (SSE-CMM) (ISO/IEC 21827:2008) [18], and the Information Security Management Maturity Model (O-ISM3) [1] focus mainly on improving processes and practices for cybersecurity and consider crypto-agility only briefly, if at all. The classification in the Post-Quantum Cryptography (PQC) Maturity Model [11] only focuses on measures against quantum computing threats. The Crypto Agility Risk Assessment Framework (CARAF) only provides a means to analyze and evaluate the risk that results from the lack of crypto-agility [26]. Cryptosense SA reduces its crypto-agility approach to technologies and practices provided by their proprietary Cryptography Lifecycle Management (CLM) [38]. To the best of our knowledge, none of the existing maturity models fits the purpose of being used as a holistic crypto-agility maturity model.

An IT landscape should be as crypto-agile as needed to be prepared for future threats, therefore a more general crypto-agility maturity model is needed. As there is no appropriate maturity model that supports all the requirements formulated for crypto-agility (see next section), we develop CAMM from scratch.

3   Cryptographic Agility: Definitions, Requirements, and Aspects

To the best of our knowledge, the notion of cryptographic agility was first mentioned around 2009/2010 by Bryan Sullivan [43,44] as a programming style for abstracting .NET code from hard-coded use of a concrete hash algorithm, in his case MD5. The term was also coined in 2011 in RFC 6421 [30] as a communication protocol property.

To systematically [6] identify cryptographic agility definitions, requirements, and aspects, we searched the online libraries IEEE Xplore, ACM Digital Library, Springer Link, Emerald Insight, the search engines Google Scholar and CiteSeerX using the following search strings: ("cryptographic agility" OR "crypto-agility") AND ("definition" OR "requirements")[1]. All returned articles (447 in total) were examined based on title, keywords, and abstract for their potential relevance. We sorted out 438 articles. Based on the remaining 9 articles, we carried out a backward and forward search [25], the results were again checked for relevance. In the end, we were able to identify the following 11 papers dealing with crypto-agility in general or certain requirements and aspects, which provide a basic understanding of crypto-agility:

---

[1] Please note that the actual query syntax used varies in the different online libraries.

According to McKay [20, page 9ff] crypto-agility includes (1) *the ability for machines to select their security algorithms in real-time and based on their combined security functions;* (2) *the ability to add new cryptographic features or algorithms to existing hardware or software, resulting in new, stronger security features;* and (3) *the ability to gracefully retire cryptographic systems that have become either vulnerable or obsolete.* Mehrez and el Omri [28] and Schneider [20, page 2] stress how easy the migration from one crypto scheme to another can take place with the help of crypto-agility. Schneider adds the aspect of remaining interoperability after a certain hard- or software has evolved. More recently, cryptographic agility has been mentioned in the context of PQC migration tasks [3,15,36].

In addition to the above understandings, at least the following requirements and aspects for cryptographic agility were requested: *IDs* (for algorithms or sets of algorithms), *transitioning, key management, interoperability (mandatory algorithms), balancing security strengths, opportunistic security, (effective) migration mechanism* [17]. *Measurability, interpretability, enforceability, security, performance* [10]. *Switch between crypto schemes in real-time, support for heterogenous environments, policy-aware access to crypto primitives, automatability (centralized), scalability* [27]. *Extensibility, removability, interoperability, flexibility, fungibility, reversibility, updateability, transition mechanism, backward compatibility* [28]. *Testable* [41], *usage of SDKs, crypto APIs* [31,45], and *preparing for failure* [20].

These requirements and aspects vary in granularity and are sometimes vague in their meaning, description, and implementation. Still, we managed to organize these requirements and address them at the different levels of CAMM. An accompanying website to this work lists the requirements and their source in a compact and tabular format (see Sect. 4.2).

4 Model Development

We now describe the development of CAMM. In general, there are two types of maturity models. First *focus area maturity models* [48] such as the Dynamic Architecture Maturity Matrix (DyAMM), the Test Process Improvement (TPI) model, and the Software Product Management (SPM) maturity matrix [21,46, 49]. Second, *fixed-level/staged maturity models* [4,5] such as CMM resp. CMMI [8,34]. We decided to aim for a fixed-level model because this type of models is far more widely used, easier to comprehend, and allows for more concrete and comparable statements [42,48]. In addition, focus area maturity models need more data and more experience in the crypto-agility domain in order to evaluate properly [48], and thus seemed inappropriate to us, as crypto-agility research is still in its infancy.

Lasrado et al. [24] identified three meta models [4,7,40], all describing a step by step iterative sequential approach for developing a maturity model. For CAMM, we followed Becker et al. [4] with 8 discrete phases (instead of 5 respectively 6) as we judge this approach as the most comprehensive and detailed methodology for the development of fixed-level models. We, therefore, used it as a starting point and adapted it for this work. As a result, our methodology uses the following top-down approach which consists of five phases/steps. We briefly describe each step on the basis of Fig. 1.

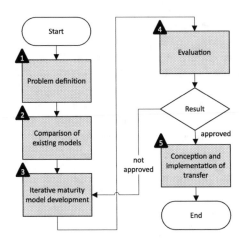

Fig. 1. Applied procedure model for developing CAMM, adapted from [4]

4.1   Methodology

Step 1: Problem Definition. The first step is to clarify whether and why the lack of a maturity model is currently a problem for crypto-agility and therefore whether it is worthwhile to develop a crypto-agility maturity model.

Step 2: Comparison of Existing Models. To solve the previously defined problem, it is researched whether existing models can be used, improved, or adapted in the given context or if an entirely new model has to be developed.

Step 3: Iterative Maturity Model Development. The main phase of the process is used to condense the existing crypto-agility literature requirements into specific dimensions. First, we determine the objectives and development areas of the iteration. These are the basis for the next iteration of a model. With an iterative process, the model is evaluated and evolves until all requirements fit into the various maturity levels and no inconsistencies exist. In the current state of CAMM, we have undergone 5 iterations. In the process of these iterations, we established a rough draft, removed duplication, improved comprehensibility, specified requirements, and later incorporated feedback from industry contacts.

Step 4: Evaluation. After the development of a maturity model, measures for evaluation, publication, and maintenance of the model need to be planned. Deviating from Becker et al. [4], we decided to conduct a first evaluation preceding the publication of the model to be able to implement potential improvements identified therein before gaining first publicity.

Step 5: Conception of Transfer and Implementation. Becker et al. [4] suggest publishing a maturity model and, in addition, establishing a website where the maturity level can be determined. Furthermore, the website should provide a survey of model acceptance, which may indicate the need for further development.

4.2 Outcome

Following the steps above, five maturity levels and corresponding requirements have been identified as the core of CAMM. More details are given in Sect. 5. A preliminary evaluation using expert interviews confirms a good structure and comprehensibility for CAMM (see Sect. 6). Following Becker et al. [4] we set up https://camm.h-da.io. This website is intended to serve as a central reference source for CAMM. In addition to a brief description of the model, it contains a list of all requirements, literature references, and publications.

5   The Crypto-Agility Maturity Model

The Crypto-Agility Maturity Model (CAMM) represents our understanding of the current state of research on crypto-agility. CAMM makes it possible to evaluate a given system according to its ability to implement crypto-agility requirements. At the same time, it forms a reference that encompasses the findings from both academia and practice and combines them into an understanding of the requirements of crypto-agile systems. CAMM's key components are the maturity levels and the requirements they contain at each level, along with their respective properties.

Since it is desirable to have the simplest possible classification while maintaining a high degree of precision, five maturity levels have emerged as an appropriate classification size for this model. This number also became a frequent standard value for maturity models due to the widespread adoption of CMM and CMMI [4,23] in other contexts. We introduce the CAMM maturity levels in the following. The dependencies between the requirements can be found on the accompanying website.

5.1   Maturity Levels

CAMM defines five maturity levels: 0 (INITIAL/NOT POSSIBLE), 1 (POSSIBLE), 2 (PREPARED), 3 (PRACTICED), and 4 (SOPHISTICATED), each representing a certain level of system maturity in terms of crypto-agility. Each level contains a certain number of requirements, all of which must be met in order to reach that level. In other words, as soon as a requirement of a given level X is violated, one falls back to level $X - 1$ with level 0 as the lowest possible level.

To make the individual maturity levels more tangible the respective motivation behind them is presented now. The requirements defined for a certain level are subsequently specified in Sect. 5.2.

0 Initial/Not Possible. This maturity level expresses the lowest maturity and is reached by default. The numbering explicitly begins at zero to illustrate the lack of evaluation or exclusion of crypto-agility. This maturity level implies that there is or might be at least one system or component that violates the requirements defined at level 1. Possible reasons for this may include hardware or software limitations that do not allow subsequent changes to the original design. Examples include devices in the IoT domain that are no longer supported by their manufacturer and platforms where cryptography is hard-coded to hardware features [10]. Another well-known scenario are embedded systems that are inaccessible to the end user, are built with extremely limited resources or ROM, or where the vendor is not interested in enabling updates.

1 Possible. This maturity level is reached by all systems that can be adapted so that their cryptography can respond dynamically to future cryptographic challenges. However, this does not require any specific activities to be carried out yet, but only the necessary primary conditions to be met. Many of the requirements of this level are typical for high-quality software or hardware design.

2 Prepared. Systems that already implement certain measures for crypto-agility, but are not yet fully ready to actively realize it, are assigned to this level. The actual change of cryptographic functions still requires some preparatory work and a particular effort, but crypto-agility is already seen as an implementable goal.

3 Practiced. Crypto-agility is practiced, i.e., migration between different cryptographic methods is demonstrably, effectively, and securely feasible. In this case, systems can be assigned to this maturity level. Therefore, several conditions must be met to ensure the necessary hardware and software requirements and migration mechanisms.

4 Sophisticated. The highest maturity level is attained by systems that implement advanced capabilities in terms of crypto-agility. They are particularly characterized by the fact that compatibility is not limited to a specific system but can be scaled across a broader infrastructure. Higher sophistication of the measures allows for a fast and automated migration between different cryptography schemes. This level of maturity should be strived for particularly by libraries and frameworks that are intended to be used in the context of crypto-agility.

5.2   Requirements

In the following, the requirements that are addressed at a certain level are presented. Please note, that there are no requirements associated with level 0 of CAMM. Each requirement is labeled with an 'R' followed by two numbers separated by a dot. The first number defines the corresponding maturity level, the second number defines a sequential ID. This ID does not necessarily imply any order of priority or dependency within a maturity level. Example: R3.4 labels requirement 4 of level 3. Within parentheses, each requirement is assigned to a certain category followed by a list of the requirements it directly depends on. These represent a brief description of all the attributes[2] we assigned to each requirement in the complete online version of CAMM, as is customary in requirements engineering, and are intended to improve the management and understandability of the model [35, 37, 47]. We have defined three different categories: *Knowledge (K)*, *Process (P)*, and *System property (S)*. Either new knowledge must be generated, processes must be adapted, or special system properties must be achieved through targeted adjustments to the system. We have assigned each requirement to the category that is most evident to us, although we do not want to rule out the possibility that a requirement may also be meaningful in the other two remaining categories.

The categorization allows the implementation of measures necessary to be grouped and addressed by a similar approach. For example, requirements from the category *Knowledge* often need the construction of a knowledge database.

In general, requirements should always be specified as SMART terms (Specific, Measurable, Achievable, Reasonable, Time-bound). However, our identified requirements – derived from literature – are on a rather abstract level and generic. Thus, we suggest looking at SMART as an assistance for the specific implementation in the respective concrete context. For example, requirement R3.3 *Testing* highly depends on the hard- or software specification and therefore needs to be specified in detail in a SMART manner for a given system context.

Level 1 – Possible: Requirements

R1.0: System Knowledge (K). An adequate evaluation of the requirements of crypto-agility demands detailed information about the corresponding system. System knowledge thus represents a requirement that must be met for a system to reach the first maturity level of crypto-agility. Without detailed knowledge of the system and its domain, a classification is not possible, and the crypto-agility goal of measurability identified by [10] cannot be met. Additionally, the ability to analyze the system is inevitable to assess the impact on a product or system of an intended change to one or more of its parts, to diagnose a product for deficiencies or causes of failures, or to identify parts to be modified [19].

R1.1: Updateability (P; R1.0). This property describes whether the system can be modified by those responsible and can be supplied with new software

---

[2] see https://camm.h-da.io/requirements/, last accessed 09.01.2023.

versions without the need to restrict its functionality [19]. The underlying motivation is the discovery of vulnerabilities in the system and its cryptography, which need to be fixed after detection. As initially described in [28], a system must therefore provide the ability to perform updates. A prerequisite for the development of such updates is system knowledge.

R1.2: Extensibility (S; R1.1). Extensibility can be understood as the process of introducing new cryptographic algorithms and parameters. In the case of a new attack vector affecting previous algorithms, new, more secure alternatives can thus be retrofitted. The ability to add further cryptography methods, variants, and protocols to a system can be understood as an acceptance criterion. This requirement originates from the crypto-agility properties of [28] and requires updateability of the software.

R1.3: Reversibility (P; R1.0). In addition to updates, the reversibility of systems is also an important factor for crypto-agility. The goal of this requirement is to allow a system to be reset to a previous state. However, unlike the therefore required updateability, this is not a property of the system but requires an organizational process, which keeps the previous version states for recovery. As described by [28] a system needs to be able to return to the previous version if the update does not operate as expected.

R1.4: Cryptography Inventory (K; R1.0). A cryptography inventory is the documentation of the cryptography used in a system. In addition to simply documenting the algorithms and parameters used, it is also important to understand their level of security. Thus, this requirement is an aspect that presupposes a certain knowledge about the system and the current state of cryptographic security. The rationale for this requirement is the need to assess a system's security. The authors of [22,41] demand a cryptography inventory to enable a fast evaluation of whether a system is affected by certain vulnerabilities, so countermeasures can be initiated if necessary.

Level 2 – Prepared: Requirements

R2.0: Cryptographic Modularity (S; R1.0, R1.1). In the context of crypto-agility, cryptographic modularity is understood as a system design that enables changes to the cryptographic components without affecting the functionality of the other system components. In the event of a vulnerability, the implementation of cryptographic functions, their parameters and primitives can be replaced without affecting the system logic. System knowledge is required to evaluate this property. The necessity of this property is already confirmed by a large number of experts in this regard [17,22,27,28,36].

R2.1: Algorithm IDs (K; R1.4). Cryptographic procedures cannot be negotiated between two subsystems without a convention denoting algorithms and parameters. Thus, common knowledge is essential to uniquely associate algorithms with their specific parameters for building agile encrypted communication channels. For IETF protocols, a mechanism for identification is already mandatory and [17] also lists it as a requirement for crypto-agility.

R2.2: Algorithm Intersection (S; R2.1). This requirement implies that all subsystems support a common set of cryptographic algorithms. Without this intersection of algorithms, secure communication cannot be established and therefore, at least one algorithm must be defined that all subsystems mandatorily support. This principle is also prescribed for IETF protocols and highlighted in RFC 7696 [17] for cryptographic algorithms agility.

R2.3: Algorithm Exclusion (S; R1.1, R2.1). As a counterpart to mandatory algorithms, this property requires a way to exclude supported algorithms from use. The reason for this is that algorithms known to be vulnerable should not be used to maintain the security of the system. However, as originally stated in [17,28], the exclusion of algorithms simultaneously affects the interoperability of subsystems.

R2.4: Opportunistic Security (S; R1.1, R2.1, R2.2, R2.3). This requirement pursues the goal of always using the strongest algorithm supported by the respective communication partners, and that is appropriate in the respective application context, e.g., resource requirements or performance issues. If a particular algorithm cannot be used for some reason, it is better to use a less secure one than to communicate without cryptography altogether [14]. Even with weak cryptography, resilience to attacks is increased, albeit minimally in the worst case. This property requires an intersection of multiple algorithms, assignable by their ID, which are ranked by their security in the crypto inventory. However, this property may be constrained by policies that, for example, mandate a certain level of security. This concept is described in [14] and proposed by [17] for the crypto-agility of IETF protocols.

R2.5: Usability (S; R1.0, R1.2, R1.3, R2.1). Insofar as cryptographic aspects and properties make their way through to the user interface, care must be taken to ensure that a changeover does not lead to a deterioration in usability. For example, if keys are printed out onto QR codes, newer algorithms may require longer keys and thus a greater information density on the QR codes, which in turn can make the QR codes more error-prone and thus less usable [10,20].

Level 3 – Practiced: Requirements

R3.0: Policies (P; R2.2, R2.3, R2.4, R3.5). Policies serve to constrain the algorithms that are allowed and their parameters [27]. Without them, insecure algorithms or algorithms inappropriate for the context could be used. As an essential factor for the security of systems, they are an essential step in the system design process and ongoing management. Their specification can constrain the algorithm intersection, result in algorithm exclusion, and hinder opportunistic security.

R3.1: Performance Awareness (K; R1.0). Performance awareness describes that the additional overhead for crypto-agility is known and accepted [10,17]. If the additional effort of adaptations and deployment for crypto-agility is not known and accounted for, it may result in unexpected performance degradation and cost, which could cause the system to fail to meet specific requirements. To understand the impact of crypto-agility on the specific circumstances of the system, a deep knowledge of the system is essential.

R3.2: Hardware Modularity (S; R1.1). In addition to the cryptographic modularity, a loose binding between hardware and software is another critical property to support crypto-agility [10,28,36]. It represents the possibility of further additions or replacements to both hardware and software independently and their compatibility with each other.

R3.3: Testing (P; R1.0). If requirements are not tested, no conclusions can be drawn about their compliance and the quality of the system. A crucial part of the process towards crypto-agility is regularly testing the system for compliance with crypto-agile requirements [10,39,41]. Therefore, test criteria must exist to determine which properties the system must meet. The crypto-agility requirements defined here should be part of the testing.

R3.4: Enforceability (P; R1.0, R3.0). Appropriate measures to achieve crypto-agility must be taken for all system areas. When the required techniques are carefully specified, a crypto-agile design can be effectively mandated and enforced [10]. The work at hand contributes to increasing the enforceability of crypto-agility by providing the requirements from which actions for systems can be derived and subsequently implemented.

R3.5: Security (K; R2.3, R3.0, R3.3). Maintaining security is another integral factor when implementing crypto-agility [10]. This requires ensuring that the system is not vulnerable to the threats of various attacks. If this and the maintenance of the overall security objectives cannot be ensured by the particular implementation of the cryptographic techniques, they do not fulfill the expected benefits. To obtain knowledge about the security state of a given system at this level, regular checks must confirm a healthy security state of the used cryptography and transition mechanisms.

R3.6: Backwards Compatibility (S; R1.1, R2.2, R3.7). This property refers to the time-limited phase during which new versions are compatible with older states of the system [28]. This transition period is necessary because the overall system will not be functional if different concurrently used version states of the subsystems cannot interact. To ensure that the system does not remain permanently endangered due to security vulnerabilities in old versions, backward compatibility must only exist respectively be applied within a limited period.

R3.7: Transition Mechanism (P; R1.1, R2.1, R2.2, R2.3, R3.6). The process with which it is possible to migrate between cryptographic methods is mainly responsible for the dynamics of crypto-agility. Here, the transition mechanism constitutes the strategy that ensures the operability of the overall system for the transition period of performing an update [17,22,28,41]. Without a regulated and secure process, the compatible transition to the compatible transition to the new version is highly error-prone. Therefore, in crypto-agile systems, a methodology must exist that regulates compatibility and secure communication between subsystems in different version states for the time-limited duration of the transition and results in all subsystems being in the new version state afterwards.

R3.8: Effectiveness (P; R1.4, R3.3, R3.7). The effectiveness of crypto-agility expresses that the process of migrating between cryptographic algorithms must be feasible in a reasonable amount of time [10]. The rationale behind this requirement is to ensure security. If the migration takes longer than the security of the algorithms can be guaranteed, the whole system is vulnerable.

Level 4 – Sophisticated: Requirements

R4.0: Automation (P; R3.7, R3.8). This is a more advanced measure of crypto-agility, used primarily when a wide range of platforms should be made crypto-agile. Through automation, customizations to crypto-agile modules require no, or very little user interaction and must be able to be performed automatically based on predefined attributes such as time and context, without human interaction with the system [27]. Thus, the effort for processes within crypto-agility is minimized by reducing the manual interactions required for it to a minimum.

R4.1: Context Independence (S; R2.0, R3.2). This property requires that requirements and techniques are portable such that they can be used for other cryptographic scenarios. Also known as interpretability and flexibility [10,28]. This property circumvents the problem that the approaches used for crypto-agility are each applicable only in their specific context, and thus a separate solution must be found for each domain.

R4.2: Scalability (P; R2.0, R3.2, R4.1, R4.4). To avoid repeating the process of developing a system module for crypto-agility for all systems, the crypto module must be deployable on other systems without substantial adjustments. Otherwise, the implementation would always be tied to specific platforms, and each additional system to be made crypto-agile would again require a considerable development effort [27].

R4.3: Real-Time (P; R3.7, R4.0, R4.2). Another challenge for crypto agility processes is the time required to run them. In this context, real-time systems assure that adaptations to crypto functions become active in the production system within a defined period. The goal here is to ensure that adaptations to the cryptography do not require re-coding and/or re-booting of the system [27].

R4.4: Cross-System Interoperability (S; R2.2, R2.3). A necessary consideration for crypto-agility is communication beyond the context of a single system. Here the property of cross-system interoperability expresses that different crypto-agile systems are compatible with each other [17,28]. The challenge is that connected systems might not always be in one's own administrative domain and therefore cannot be influenced directly. Nevertheless, the global IT infrastructure should be compatible with all approaches to crypto-agility. To achieve this, crypto-agile systems must enable information exchange with all foreseen communication partners based on their respective specifications.

6   Evaluation

To the best of our knowledge, there is no (other) existing maturity model tailored to crypto-agility to which we could compare CAMM. As argued in Sect. 2, existing maturity models in the broader field do not address all major requirements for crypto-agility that we extracted from literature (cf. Sect. 3). CAMM is the first of breed and needs to undergo expert reviews and field tests. While the latter is pending, we have taken a first step towards the former by conducting an initial expert review of CAMM together with a partner company as part of a master's thesis [16]. There, semi-structured interviews were conducted with two inhouse-experts (one Security Officer and one Software Architect) with regard to the comprehensibility of CAMM. In addition, the relevance of crypto-agility in the context of post-quantum cryptography (PQC) within the company was assessed. While PQC is not yet seen as relevant, they acknowledge the benefit of the more general crypto-agility concept. Both experts confirmed the comprehensibility of CAMM and appreciated the sound structure. On the other hand, both assume that CAMM must be brought into use so that more experience can be gained with the model. They assume that especially level 4 SOPHISTICATED may be extended or modified.

7   Conclusion and Outlook

Starting from our observation that there is no maturity model available that addresses all aspects of cryptographic agility, we collected all requirements and aspects found in literature on crypto-agility and used them as a foundation for CAMM. We were able to arrange all requirements into five maturity levels in a consistent and sound manner, as confirmed to us by initial interviews with domain experts.

We have shown that it is feasible to unite the various, only partly overlapping, crypto-agility requirements from different literature sources into a consolidated maturity model. The major challenges thereby were, apart from identifying relevant literature, dealing with the different terminology and levels of detail throughout literature and sorting the requirements into a hierarchical structure.

Now, a broad application of CAMM has to take place to verify the validity and usefulness of our model and, if necessary, an adjustment of the requirements of respective levels. Based on feedback from the industry, a first, minor revision of CAMM has already been made with the addition of requirement R2.5.

Accompanying, we want to develop a toolbox that helps to verify individual requirements at a certain level with as little effort as possible. CAMM is currently labeled with *Version 1.1*. Further developments can then be tagged with higher version numbers. Additionally, the description of case studies that use CAMM in practice is planned.

Acknowledgment. Funded by the German Federal Ministry of Education and Research and the Hessian Ministry of Higher Education, Research, Science and the Arts within the National Research Center for Applied Cybersecurity ATHENE.

References

1. Aceituno, V.: Open information security management maturity model. Open group standard, The Open Group (2017). https://www.ism3.com/node/39
2. Alnahawi, N., Schmitt, N., Wiesmaier, A., Heinemann, A., Graßmeyer, T.: On the state of crypto agility. In: 18. Dt. IT-Sicherheitskongress. SecuMedia (2022)
3. Alnahawi, N., et al.: On the state of post-quantum cryptography migration. In: INFORMATIK 2021—PQKP-Workshop. LNI, vol. 308 (2021)
4. Becker, J., Knackstedt, R., Pöppelbuß, J.: Developing maturity models for IT management. Bus. Inf. Syst. Eng. **1**(3), 213–222 (2009). https://doi.org/10.1007/s12599-009-0044-5
5. Becker, J., Niehaves, B., Pöppelbuß, J., Simons, A.: Maturity models in is research. In: ECIS 2010 Proceedings. AISeL (2010)
6. Brocke, J.v., Simons, A., Niehaves, B., Reimer, K., Plattfaut, R., Cleven, A.: Reconstructing the giant: on the importance of Rigour in documenting the literature search process. In: European Conference on Information Systems (2009)
7. Bruin, T.D., Rosemann, M., Freeze, R., Kaulkarni, U.: Understanding the main phases of developing a maturity assessment model. In: Australasian Conference on Information Systems (ACIS), pp. 8–19. Australasian Chapter of the Association for Information Systems (2005)
8. CMMI Product Team: Cmmi® for development, version 1.3. Technical report, Software Engineering Institute, Hanscom AFB (2010)
9. Computer Security Division, ITL: NIST. PQC Standardization Project (2017). https://csrc.nist.gov/projects/post-quantum-cryptography
10. Computing Community Consortium (CCC): Identifying Research Challenges in Post Quantum Cryptography Migration and Cryptographic Agility (2019)
11. DigiCert: Post-quantum cryptography (PQC) maturity model. Technical report, DigiCert, Inc. (2020). https://www.digicert.com/content/dam/digicert/pdfs/post-quantum-cryptography-maturity-model-whitepaper-en.pdf

12. DOE: Cybersecurity capability maturity model (C2M2) (2021). https://www.energy.gov/sites/default/files/2021-07/C2M2%20Version%202.0%20July%202021_508.pdf, version 2.0
13. Donenfeld, J.A.: WireGuard: next generation kernel network tunnel. In: NDSS Symposium (2017)
14. Dukhovni, V.: Opportunistic Security: Some Protection Most of the Time. RFC 7435 (2014). https://rfc-editor.org/rfc/rfc7435.txt
15. Grote, O., Ahrens, A., Benavente-Peces, C.: A review of post-quantum cryptography and crypto-agility strategies. In: 2019 International Interdisciplinary PhD Workshop, pp. 115–120. IEEE (2019)
16. Hohm, J.: Reifegradmodell für die Krypto-Agilität. Master's thesis, Hochschule Darmstadt, Darmstadt, Germany (2021)
17. Housley, R.: Guidelines for Cryptographic Algorithm Agility and Selecting Mandatory-to-Implement Algorithms. RFC 7696 (2015)
18. ISO/IEC: Information technology - Security techniques - Systems Security Engineering - Capability Maturity Model® (SSE-CMM®). Standard ISO/IEC 21827:2008, International Organization for Standardization, Geneva, CH (2008)
19. ISO/IEC: Systems and software engineering - systems and software quality requirements and evaluation (square) - system and software quality models. Standard ISO/IEC 25010:2011(E), International Organization for Standardization (2011)
20. Johnson, A.F., Millett, L.I. (eds.): Cryptographic agility and interoperability. Proceedings of a Workshop. The National Academies Press, Washington, DC (2017). https://doi.org/10.17226/24636
21. Koomen, T., Pol, M.: Test Process Improvement: A Practical Step-by-Step Guide to Structured Testing. Addison-Wesley Longman Publishing Co. Inc, USA (1999)
22. Kreutzer, M., Niederhagen, R., Waidner, M. (eds.): Eberbacher Gespräch on Next Generation Crypto. Fraunhofer SIT (2018)
23. Lahrmann, G., Marx, F., Mettler, T., Winter, R., Wortmann, F.: Inductive design of maturity models: applying the Rasch algorithm for design science research. In: Jain, H., Sinha, A.P., Vitharana, P. (eds.) DESRIST 2011. LNCS, vol. 6629, pp. 176–191. Springer, Heidelberg (2011). https://doi.org/10.1007/978-3-642-20633-7_13
24. Lasrado, L.A., Vatrapu, R., Andersen, K.N.: Maturity models development in is research: a literature review. In: IRIS Selected Papers of the Information Systems Research Seminar in Scandinavia. vol. 6. IRIS, New York (2015)
25. Levy, Y., Ellis, T.J.: A systems approach to conduct an effective literature review in support of information systems research. Informing Sci. J. 9, 181–212 (2006)
26. Ma, C., Colon, L., Dera, J., Rashidi, B., Garg, V.: CARAF: crypto agility risk assessment framework. J. Cybersecurity 7(1), tyab013 (2021)
27. Macaulay, T., Henderson, R.: Cryptographic agility in practice: emerging use-cases. Infosec Global
28. Mehrez, H.A., El Omri, O.: The crypto-agility properties. In: Callaos, N.C. (ed.) The 12th International Conference on Society, Cybernetics and Informatics, pp. 99–103. IIIS (2018). https://www.iiis.org/cds2018/cd2018summer/papers/ha536vg.pdf
29. Mettler, T., Rohner, P., Winter, R.: Towards a classification of maturity models in information systems. In: D'Atri, A., De Marco, M., Braccini, A.M., Cabiddu, F. (eds.) Management of the Interconnected World. pp. 333–340. Physica-Verlag HD (2010). https://doi.org/10.1007/978-3-7908-2404-9_39
30. Nelson, D.B.: Crypto-Agility Requirements for Remote Authentication Dial-In User Service (RADIUS). RFC 6421 (2011)

31. Niederhagen, R., Waidner, M.: Practical post-quantum cryptography. white paper. Technical report, Fraunhofer SIT, Darmstadt (2017)
32. NSA: Commercial National Security Algorithms Suite 2.0 (2022)
33. OUSD(A&S): Cybersecurity maturity model certification (2020). https://www.acq.osd.mil/cmmc/docs/CMMC_ModelMain_V1.02_20200318.pdf
34. Paulk, M.C., Curtis, B., Chrissis, M.B., Weber, C.V.: Capability maturity model, version 1.1. IEEE Softw. **10**(4), 18–27 (1993)
35. Pohl, K.: Requirements Engineering Fundamentals: A Study Guide for the Certified Professional for Requirements Engineering Exam-foundation Level-IREB Compliant. Rocky Nook Inc., San Rafael (2016)
36. Richter, S., et al.: Agile and versatile quantum communication: signatures and secrets. Phys. Rev. X **11**(1), 011038 (2021)
37. Robertson, S., Robertson, J.: Mastering the Requirements Process: Getting Requirements Right. Addison-Wesley/Pearson, Upper Saddle River (2013)
38. Ross-Gower, S.: What is cryptography lifecycle management and why do i need it? Cryptosense (2021). https://cryptosense.com/blog/what-is-cryptography-lifecycle-management-and-why-do-i-need-it
39. Salem, M.B., McCarty, B.: The race to crypto-agility. Technical report. Accenture (2021)
40. Solli-Sæther, H., Gottschalk, P.: The modeling process for stage models. J. Org. Comput. Electron. Commer. **20**, 279–293 (2010)
41. Steel, G.: Achieving 'crypto agility'. Cryptosense (2019). https://cryptosense.com/blog/achieving-crypto-agility
42. van Steenbergen, M., van den Berg, M., Brinkkemper, S.: A balanced approach to developing the enterprise architecture practice. In: Filipe, J., Cordeiro, J., Cardoso, J. (eds.) ICEIS 2007. LNBIP, vol. 12, pp. 240–253. Springer, Heidelberg (2008). https://doi.org/10.1007/978-3-540-88710-2_19
43. Sullivan, B.: Cryptographic agility. MSDN Mag. **24**(8) (2009). https://docs.microsoft.com/en-us/archive/msdn-magazine/2009/august/cryptographic-agility
44. Sullivan, B.: Cryptographic Agility: Defending Against the Sneakers Scenario (2010). https://infocondb.org/con/black-hat/black-hat-usa-2010/cryptographic-agility-defending-against-the-sneakers-scenario. Talk at BLACK HAT 2010, USA
45. Utimaco: Post-quantum cryptography: Secure encryption for the quantum age (2018). White Paper
46. Van Den Berg, M., Van Steenbergen, M.: Building an Enterprise Architecture Practice: Tools, Tips, Best Practices, Ready-to-Use Insights. Springer, Berlin (2007)
47. van Lamsweerde, A.: Requirements Engineering: From System Goals to UML Models to Software Specifications. Wiley, Chichester (2009)
48. van Steenbergen, M., Bos, R., Brinkkemper, S., van de Weerd, I., Bekkers, W.: The design of focus area maturity models. In: Winter, R., Zhao, J.L., Aier, S. (eds.) DESRIST 2010. LNCS, vol. 6105, pp. 317–332. Springer, Heidelberg (2010). https://doi.org/10.1007/978-3-642-13335-0_22
49. van de Weerd, I., Bekkers, W., Brinkkemper, S.: Developing a maturity matrix for software product management. In: Tyrväinen, P., Jansen, S., Cusumano, M.A. (eds.) ICSOB 2010. LNBIP, vol. 51, pp. 76–89. Springer, Heidelberg (2010). https://doi.org/10.1007/978-3-642-13633-7_7

Machine Learning

Reducing the Cost of Machine Learning Differential Attacks Using Bit Selection and a Partial ML-Distinguisher

Amirhossein Ebrahimi[1]([✉]) [iD], Francesco Regazzoni[2,3] [iD], and Paolo Palmieri[1] [iD]

[1] School of Computer Science and IT, University College Cork, Cork, Ireland
{a.ebrahimimodhaddam,p.palmieri}@cs.ucc.ie
[2] University of Amsterdam, Amsterdam, The Netherlands
f.regazzoni@uva.nl
[3] Università della Svizzera italiana, Lugano, Switzerland
regazzoni@alari.ch

Abstract. In a differential cryptanalysis attack, the attacker tries to observe a block cipher's behavior under an input difference: if the system's resulting output differences show any non-random behavior, a differential distinguisher is obtained. While differential cryptanlysis has been known for several decades, Gohr was the first to propose in 2019 the use of machine learning (ML) to build a distinguisher.

In this paper, we present the first Partial Differential (PD) ML distinguisher, and demonstrate its effectiveness on cipher SPECK32/64. As a PD-ML-distinguisher is based on a selection of bits rather than all bits in a block, we also study if different selections of bits have different impact in the accuracy of the distinguisher, and we find that to be the case. More importantly, we also establish that certain bits have reliably higher effectiveness than others, through a series of independent experiments on different datasets, and we propose an algorithm for assigning an effectiveness score to each bit in the block. By selecting the highest scoring bits, we are able to train a partial ML-distinguisher over 8-bits that is almost as accurate as an equivalent ML-distinguisher over the entire 32 bits (68.8% against 72%), for six rounds of SPECK32/64. Furthermore, we demonstrate that our obtained machine can reduce the time complexity of the key-averaging algorithm for training a 7-round distinguisher by a factor of 2^5 at a cost of only 3% in the resulting machine's accuracy. These results may therefore open the way to the application of (partial) ML-based distinguishers to ciphers whose block size has so far been considered too large.

Keywords: Differential cryptanalysis · Machine Learning based cryptanalysis · Partial ML-distinguisher

1 Introduction

Block ciphers are cryptographic algorithms that provide confidentiality by encrypting data using a symmetric key. Block ciphers operate on fixed-length

This publication has emanated from research supported in part by a Grant from Science Foundation Ireland under Grant number 18/CRT/6222.

G.-V. Jourdan et al. (Eds.): FPS 2022, LNCS 13877, pp. 123–141, 2023.
https://doi.org/10.1007/978-3-031-30122-3_8

groups of bits, called blocks; rather than encrypting one bit at a time as in stream ciphers. Block ciphers are fundamental components in the design of many cryptographic protocols and are widely used to encrypt large amounts of data, either locally or over network communication. Recently, the cryptographic community has focused on the design of lightweight cryptographic (LWC) schemes, which are suitable for resource-constrained devices that are commonplace in settings such as the Internet of Things, healthcare, and sensor networks. The need for dedicated ciphers rises from the fact that the majority of current cryptographic algorithms were designed having desktop and server environments in mind, and due to this many of these algorithms are too computationally heavy to operate onto constrained devices. The US National Institute of Standards and Technology, who has a prominent role in the standardization of cryptogrphic algorithms recognized worldwide, has recently launched an initiative to solicit, evaluate, and standardize lightweight cryptographic algorithms [1], with the objective to achieve a set of standards for lightweight cryptographic algorithms by 2022.

Given their pervasive use, it is vital to evaluate the security of block ciphers, and especially those in the LWC domain, who have appeared more recently and have therefore been less studied than standard block ciphers such as the Advanced Encryption Standard (AES) [2]. In the research domain of cryptanalysis, which studies ciphers to find weaknesses and potential attacks, there are many generic and robust statistical techniques that can be used to attack algorithms and therefore help assess their security. The two most famous examples are *differential* [3] and *linear* [4] cryptanalysis. The main idea behind these attacks is to find a statistical pattern introduced by the cipher: this is achieved by looking at the ciphertexts produced by the algorithm, and by trying to distinguish between a random permutation and a block cipher. In a simple differential attack, which is usually a chosen plaintext attack, pairs of plaintext related by a constant difference (e.g. a logical XOR operation) are used. The attacker encrypts the plaintexts and computes the differences of the corresponding ciphertexts, in order to detect statistical patterns in their distribution. This pattern, whose statistical properties depend upon the nature of the S-boxes[1] used for encryption, is called a *differential*. On the basis of the differential, the cipher can be distinguished from random, obtaining what is called a *distinguisher*.

Traditionally however, the implementation of differential cryptanalysis techniques requires a massive amount of data and memory, and the time complexity of finding a good distinguisher could be infeasible in most cases. Consequently, there is an active line of research aimed at automating these cryptanalysis methods. Until recently, the main focus was to transform the problem of finding a good distinguisher into an optimization problem [5,6], which can then be solved more efficiently with optimization solvers like Gurobi [7]. While this approach is more practical, the process is still time-consuming, and the attacker still needs a good knowledge about the block cipher under attack.

---

[1] In symmetric key algorithms, the S-box (substitution-box) is a fundamental building block that is responsible for carrying out the substitution of bits.

For many years, it was believed that Machine Learning (ML) and cryptography could not work well together due to the random behavior of block ciphers and other cryptosystems [8,9]. However, in a seminal paper in 2019 Gohr presented an ML-based cryptanalysis of the SPECK32/64 cipher that was better than previous attacks [10]. In that paper, it was illustrated that by using deep learning, a differential distinguisher could be achieved in an automated way and with less time complexity than other attacks, to the point where the cryptanalysis process can be implemented on a personal computer.

Using artificial intelligence (AI) techniques such as machine learning for the cryptanalysis of block ciphers can open many exciting opportunities. For instance, with the help of AI, it is possible to extend the known differential distinguishers for block ciphers [11]. In this paper, we focus on reducing the memory and computation costs of differential ML attacks by proposing the first partial differential ML-based distinguisher. In doing so, we also establish the first experimental differential evaluation of the role of each bit of the input and output of a cipher in its security.

1.1 Related Work

In 2019, Aron Gohr introduced an 8-round differential distinguisher for the SPECK32/64 cipher with the help of machine learning [10], and based on that, an 11-round attack was established, which was better than previous classic attacks. Gohr's central idea was using distinguishing attacks with the help of AI. He trained a neural classifier that can classify between a block cipher and a random permutation by looking at the output differences of the ciphertexts for a specific plaintext difference in SPECK32/64. He then compared this neural distinguisher with the traditional *all-in-one* differential distribution table of SPECK32/64, which was commutable due to cipher's small block size, and noticed ML-distinguishers could be a good model of it. Furthermore, he presented a method to find a good input difference for distinguishing attacks with the help of ML without any prior knowledge.

Following Gohr's intuition, a subsequent study was published by Baksi et al. [12] which used deep learning differential to train distinguishers for non-Markov ciphers, and on that basis could simulate non-Markov cipher's all-in-one differential distribution table. This was modeled successfully for ciphers with big state sizes such as Gimli. Moreover, the paper studied other architectures of deep learning networks, including Long Short-Term Memory (LSTM) and Multilayer Perceptron (MLP). Their results indicate that an MLP network with three hidden layers can be efficient enough to train a distinguisher.

Linear cryptanalysis has also been recently attempted using machine learning. Hou et al. applied machine learning on DES cipher to achieve a linear attack [13], using known plaintext and their corresponding ciphertexts. The results show that a neural network can recognize the XOR distribution of a linear expression in DES cipher. Other attacks such as integral have also been investigated in conjunction with machine learning [14].

Recent research in this direction is not limited to block ciphers: Liu et al. in [15] analyze the security of variants of Xoodyak hash mode against preimage attack utilizing deep learning. They trained a model for one round of permutation to predict the message of a hash function and discover that the accuracy is high. However, as the number of rounds is increased, the deep learning preimage attack diminishes in effectiveness.

Benamira et al. contributed a more in-depth analysis of the functioning of ML-based distinguishers, and focused in particular on what information they use [16]. Their results indicate that these machines not only use the differential distribution on ciphertext pairs, but the distinguisher depends on the penultimate or antepenultimate rounds. Based on these findings, they propose a new pure cryptanalysis distinguisher with the same accuracy as Gohr's neural distinguisher.

Due to the fact that the majority of the literature review on differential machine learning analysis focuses on the Speck cipher, such as the aforementioned [10,16], and [17], our primary emphasis in this paper is also on this cipher.

An important limitation of current attacks relates to their complexity. To attack $n + 1$ rounds of a block cipher using n-round of Gohr's neural distinguisher, we need to guess all the possible last-round subkeys. Although this approach works well on SPECK32/64, whose length of subkeys is 16 bits, it may not work efficiently for many other ciphers. For example, in AES-128 [2] the size of subkeys (round keys) and the main secret key is equal to 128 bits, so the complexity of trying all last-round subkeys is equivalent to a brute force attack.

Furthermore, the block size of ciphers can affect the training phase of ML-distinguishers because each bit in the training stage acts as a feature for the machine. SPECK32/64 has a 32 bits block size, but usually, ciphers have a block size higher than that. As a result, training ML-distinguishers could be harder for other block ciphers, especially ones with a Substitution-Permutation Network (SPN)[2] structure.

1.2   Contribution

In this paper, we present novel results that advance the efficiency, and reduce the cost of ML-based distinguishers. In particular, we show experimentally that not all the bits in a block are necessary as features to have an adequate neural distinguisher. We also find that different selections of bits (features) in the ML-distinguisher lead to vastly different accuracy results, and that certain bits are consistently better than others for this purpose. On this basis, we propose a new feature selection method for partial differential ML-based distinguishers. We use the selection method to obtain a much more compact partial differential ML-based distinguisher.

---

[2] Given a plaintext block and a key, the substitution-permutation network (SPN) generates the ciphertext block through a series of rounds or layers of substitution boxes (S-boxes) and permutation boxes (P-boxes).

In particular, we first present a novel method aimed at training a neural distinguisher more efficiently than in current literature. We do so by introducing the first partial differential machine learning based distinguisher (PD-ML-distinguisher). The idea behind a partial differential ML distinguisher is that it is not necessary to train the ML model on all the bit differences of ciphertext pairs in order to achieve a distinguisher. Consequently, if we have an ML-distinguisher that can tell, without knowing all bits, whether some difference in ciphertext pairs $\delta = C_0 \oplus C_1$ is generated as random or as the result of the encryption of the plaintext pairs, then we do not need to guess all the subkeys in the last round to recover the secret key.

Secondly, we implement the PD-ML-distinguisher for SPECK32/64 (the reference cipher in related works in the literature [10,16,17]) and we measure the effectiveness of each bit of δ in the training of ML-distinguishers. Through an extensive series of experiments we find that different bits have a different impact in the training of the distinguisher. This characteristic can be reliably observed in separate, independent experiments. Based on our measurements, we assign a score to each bit with the help of the PD-ML-distinguishers. The bits with higher scores are more important for the training of the models, as they lead to machines that are significantly more effective (68.8% for 8 bits) than those trained on the lowest scoring bits (52% for 8 bits). On this basis, we can therefore select only the most effective bits when training PD-ML-distinguishers, achieving better time efficiency in training the distinguisher. This is evidenced by the training of a 6-round distinguisher for SPECK32/64 with just 8 bits achieving an accuracy of 68.8%, against an accuracy of 72% for an equivalent ML distinguisher trained on the full 32 bits.

In order to demonstrate how our proposed model can be put to use in practice, we also train a distinguisher for 7-round SPECK32/64 using a 6-round distinguisher utilizing the key-averaging algorithm proposed by [10]. The experiment shows that our proposed model can reduce the time complexity of this algorithm from 2^{16} to 2^{11}, with the cost of just 3% in accuracy of resultant distinguisher (from 61% to 58%).

1.3   Outline

The structure of this paper is as follows. Section 2 gives an overview of the SPECK32/64 block cipher, and a brief description of Gohr's neural distinguisher is explained. In Sect. 3, PD-ML-distinguishers are introduced, and they are examined on the SPECK32/64 cipher. In Sect. 4, an experiment is presented to measure effectiveness of each bit for training ML-distinguishers, and extensive experimental evidence is discussed.

2   Preliminaries

2.1   The SPECK Cipher

SPECK is a family of lightweight block ciphers designed by the NSA in 2013 [18]. These ciphers have many different block sizes and key sizes, but in this paper, SPECK with 32 bits block size and 64 bits key size is evaluated, and it is specified by SPECK32/64. Like many other block ciphers, it is an iterative cipher, which means it has a function that iterates for many rounds until the ciphertext is generated. The number of rounds for SPECK32/64 is 22.

SPECK is a Feistel cipher. Accordingly, the plaintext is divided into two equal parts (R, L), and in the case of 32 bits block size $R, L \in \{0, 1\}^{16}$, then the below function applies to inputs at each round:

$$SPECK32/64 : \begin{array}{l} L_{r+1} = ((L_r >> 7) \boxplus R_r) \oplus k_r \\ R_{r+1} = (R_r << 2) \oplus L_{r+1} \end{array} \tag{1}$$

In Eq. (1) $<<$ and $>>$ are cyclic left and right shift, respectively, $\boxplus$ is modular addition, and $\oplus$ is an exclusive OR (XOR).

2.2   ML-Based Differential Distinguishers

To analyze the security of a block cipher with block size of n against differential attack, cryptographers study the statistical behavior of a *difference* through a block cipher. For this, they choose an input difference and encrypt it for a specific number of rounds and, lastly, try to find non-randomness in corresponding output differences. Throughout this paper, the input difference is represented by Δ, and it is defined as a XOR of two plaintexts; additionally, P_i and C_i stand for the plaintexts and ciphertexts, respectively. The output difference is specified by $\delta = E(P_0) \oplus E(P_1 = P_0 \oplus \Delta)$ and $(\Delta \rightarrow \delta)$ is called a *differential*. The occurrence probability of a differential can be shown by $Pr(\Delta \rightarrow \delta)$. In a random permutation with block size of n, the average probability of a differential is:

$$\forall \Delta, \delta : Pr(\Delta \rightarrow \delta) = 2^{-n}$$

If an attacker can find a differential such that $Pr(\Delta \rightarrow \delta) > 2^{-n}$ for a block cipher, a differential distinguisher is achieved.

In Gohr's attack [10], an ML-based distinguisher is trained with the aid of ciphertext pairs. These pairs are generated in two ways: in the first group, they are real ciphertexts (C_0, C_1) of a block cipher for a specific plaintext pairs (P_0, P_1), where $P_0 \oplus P_1 = \Delta$; in the second group they are selected randomly (noted by $\in_r$) where $C_0, C_1 \in_r \{0, 1\}^n \times \{0, 1\}^n$. Then, the accuracy of this distinguisher is evaluated, and if this accuracy is more than 50%, a distinguisher is obtained. selection It is important to note that the power and efficacy of this ML-based differential attack compares positively with the All-in-One attack [19] for SPECK32/64. The All-in-One attack is a powerful differential analysis that considers a set of all output differences for a fixed given input difference Δ instead of one specific differential trail $\Delta \rightarrow \delta$.

$$All - in - one = \{\delta | \delta = E(P_0) \oplus E(P_0 \oplus \Delta)\}$$

The steps of finding an ML-based differential distinguisher for r round of SPECK32/64 cipher are as follows. Considering the feistel structure of SPECK32/64, every plaintext can be represented like $P = (L, R)$ that $L \in \{0,1\}^{16}$ and $R \in \{0,1\}^{16}$ are left and right part of plaintext, respectively. Furthermore, the 32-bit values for plaintexts, ciphertexts, and differences are represented in hexadecimal form, for e.g., $6659 = 0x1a03$.

1. First, 10^7 plaintext pairs $(P0, P1)$ are randomly generated in a way that $\Delta = (L_0 \oplus L_1, R_0 \oplus R_1) = (0x0040, 0x0000)$. Meanwhile, 10^7 labels $Y \in_r \{0,1\}^1$ are randomly generated and allocated to the pairs.
2. if $Y = 0$ the $P1$ is randomly changed to $P_1 \in_r \{0,1\}^{32}$ then all these pairs are encrypted with r rounds of SPECK32/64, and all the ciphertext pairs $(C0, C1)$ are stored with their corresponding labels in a dataset.
3. An AI machine is trained with the help of these ciphertext pairs. In this training phase, zero label $Y = 0$ means it is a datum from a random permutation, while $Y = 1$ demonstrates a ciphertext for a fixed input difference $\Delta = (0x0040, 0x0000)$.
4. In testing stage, steps (1) and (2) are repeated for another 10^6 pairs, and the accuracy of the machine is measured. If accuracy is more than 50%, then the machine is a differential distinguisher.

As discussed in Sect. 1.1, following Gohr's seminal work several papers have investigated the use of ML in cryptanalysis [11,12,20]. Some of these works changed certain steps of the original attack as mentioned above. For instance, in [12] there are two major changes. Firstly, it is shown that using a multilayer perceptron (MLP) for training the ML-distinguisher can achieve better results than CNN network as used in [10]; and secondly, the training dataset containing $C0 \oplus C1$ instead of $(C0, C1)$ is more useful for increasing the accuracy of ML-distinguisher.

The final goal of having a distinguisher is to attack the cipher. By having a r-round ML-based distinguisher, a trivial attack on $r + 1$ rounds of SPECK32/64 cipher can be implemented as follows.

1. For a fixed input difference $\Delta = (0x0040, 0000)$, n pairs of $(P0, P1)$ is formed and their corresponding ciphertext $(C0, C1)_{r+1}$ after $r + 1$ rounds is obtained by asking from an oracle.
2. For all possible subkeys in round $r + 1$, (k_{r+1}), ciphertexts are partially decrypted for one round and $(C0, C1)_r$ saved in a dataset.
3. given each $(C0, C1)_r$ to r round ML-based distinguisher in the test phase, a score is attained for every ciphertext pair.
4. Average all the scores to have a final score for each subkey k_{r+1}.
5. Rank the subkeys based on their score. The subkey with the highest score has the most probability to be the correct subkey.

3   Partial Differential ML-Distinguisher

In this section, we show that it is possible to train an adequate neural distinguisher based on a subset of bits in a block, rather than the entire block as in previous literature. As a result, we introduce the first Partial Differential ML-distinguisher.

To analyze the security of a cipher, the complexity of the attack algorithm should be less than brute force. The brute force attack complexity for a block cipher is $2^{\min(|k|,|n|)}$, where $|k|$ and $|n|$ are key and block size, respectively. As shown in Sect. 2.2, in order to find the key of a cipher with the help of a ML-distinguisher, all the subkeys in the last round need to be guessed. Therefore, to attack r rounds of SPECK32/64 cipher, the attacker has to guess all bits of subkey k_r, which has 16 bits length. As a result, the complexity of the attack is 2^{16} which is less than brute force attack 2^{32}, and it is a successful cryptanalysis for SPECK32/64.

On the other hand, in many ciphers, especially those with SPN structures like AES, the complexity of guessing the last round subkey is equal to brute force attack. In this paper, we train partial differential distinguishers (PD-ML-distinguishers) and compare their accuracy to a full state differential distinguisher for 6-round SPECK32/64. We show that PD-ML-distinguishers can still distinguish output differences that are generated by SPECK32/64 from a random output. The proposed classifiers also reduce the complexity of further cryptanalysis, as there is no need to guess all the subkeys in the last round.

3.1   Methodology

In order to show the feasibility of training a ML-based distinguisher by using partial differences of (P_0, P_1) and (C_0, C_1), we set up an experiment where many PD-ML-distinguishers are trained for six rounds of SPECK32/64, and their accuracy is recorded. We chose Speck as this has emerged as the reference cipher in related works on ML distinguishers (such as [10,16] and [17]) and therefore allows for better and more significant comparison of our results.

The number of rounds for encrypting plaintext pairs is set to six rounds: this is consistent with current literature, as in [10], which shows that reasonably strong distinguishers against up to six rounds of Speck can be trained by using ten-layer residual networks. On the other hand, extending distinguishers to 7 and 8 rounds requires the use of more sophisticated algorithms like *Key Averaging* [10] for the additional rounds. As our objective is to demonstrate the feasibility and greater efficiency of a partial differential ML-distinguisher attack compared to a simple ML-distinguisher, in this work we focus on the first 6 rounds, as it is done in the previous ML-distinguishers in the literature we are comparing too. However, for completeness, we discuss extending the proposed distinguisher using Key Averaging in Sect. 4.2, and we find that our technique results in a significant reduction in complexity of key averaging as well.

Each bit of the output difference acts as a feature for the machine learning based distinguishers. Consequently, to achieve a partial ML-distinguisher for SPECK32/64, the machine is trained by subset bits of the ciphertext difference, δ, rather than all 32 bits. To experimentally verify to what extent we can trim the output difference, δ, without significantly reducing the effectiveness and robustness of the PD-ML-distinguisher, we conduct an experiment as follows. We first train our distinguisher with just one feature, the least significant bit (LSB) of δ, and record its accuracy. Next, we again train another partial distinguisher, but this time we increase the number of features by one, where the feature is the second least significant bit of δ. This process is repeated until we have 32 different distinguishers. Algorithm 1 gives details on the experiment. The plaintext difference Δ to generate ciphertexts difference is $\Delta = (0x0040, 0x0000)$, and the dataset is 32 bits differences $\delta = [\delta_0, \ldots, \delta_{31}]$. In order to demonstrate the repeatability of the results, we repeat the above process 3 times, each time using a different pairs of (P_0, C_0) and (P_1, C_1) to create new δs, while maintaining $P_0 \oplus P_1 = \Delta = (0x0040, 0x0000)$.

Baski et al. showed in [3] that the Multilayer Perceptron (MLP) architectures are more efficient than Convolutional neural networks (CNN), including Residual networks, or Long Short-Term Memory (LSTM) for training an ML-based differential distinguisher. As a result, in this paper, a Multilayer Perceptron (MLP) machine with three dense layers and a sigmoid activation function is used for training. The number of neurons for dense layers is 32, 64 and 32, respectively. These have been selected though a standard fine-tuning process. For each number of input bits, a new machine was trained for ten epochs on 10^7 different $C_0 \oplus C_1 = \delta$. Also, another 10^6 sample was generated for validation. The loss function for optimization was binary cross-entropy plus L2 weights regularization with parameter $c = 10^{-5}$ using Adam algorithm [21]. The learning schedule applied in these ML-distinguishers is the cyclic learning rate used in [10]. All other parameters are the default parameters in Keras [22].

In each iteration of Algorithm 1, we concatenate difference bits based on their position. If we assume that the accuracy of the machines entirely depends on the number of bits, rather than which bits are selected, then a different selection method should produce comparable results, accounting for statistical differences. In order to verify this hypothesis, we repeat the above process using Algorithm 1; however, this time, instead of starting from the least significant bit δ_{31}, we start from the most significant bit (MSB) δ_0, and then we concatenate the next MSB to our feature space for the next iteration of the while loop and trained our machine.

The results of the experiment for SPECK32/64 are shown in Figs. 1 (LSB→MSB) and 2 (MSB→LSB), and are discussed in the following. The results clearly indicate that a partial differential ML-distinguisher is effective, as a distinguisher can be obtained for a reduced number of bits. However, by looking at the figures, it is also immediately evident that the accuracy changes if we change

---

Algorithm 1: Training PD-ML differential distinguishers

---

1 10 **Input:** Data set for training the machines: $\delta = [\delta_0, \ldots, \delta_{31}]$
   Output: Accuracy of machines: A
2 $i = 31, j = 0$;
3 Initialize an empty array X_{temp} ;
4 Initialize array A with size 32;
5 **while** $i \geq 0$ **do**
6 $X_{temp} = \delta[i] || X_{temp}$;
7 $D \longleftarrow$ TrainMachine(X_{temp}) ;
8 $A[j] =$ AccuracyTest(D);
9 $j = j + 1$, $i = i - 1$

---

the selection of bits. These initial experimental results indicate that different bits have a different impact on the machine accuracy. We build on these findings in Sect. 4, where we analyse in detail the impact each bit has in the effectiveness of the partial differential ML-distinguisher.

3.2   Results and Discussion

By looking at Figs. 1 and 2, it can be seen that we can achieve a distinguisher without giving all bits of output difference to the machine. For instance, in Fig. 1, we can have a suitable machine with just the first 20 bits of output difference. However, in Fig. 2, we train the machines by concatenating the output differences from the opposite MSB to LSB direction. In that case, the number of bits that we need to achieve almost the same accuracy is 28, as shown in Fig. 2. From this, we can conclude that the bits position chosen for the PD-ML-distinguisher training can be effective in its accuracy.

We repeat this experiment three times for each direction (LSB to MSB and MSB to LSB) to see how the machines' behavior changes for different datasets. Each color in Figs. 1 and 2 represents one run of Algorithm 1. By looking at the figures, it is clear that the results achieved in the experiment can be reliably repeated in different experimental instances. We also note that increasing the number of features (bits) makes the accuracy of PD-ML-distinguishers fluctuate slightly between experiments (for a number of bits >28). The reason for this is that the number of epochs is set to 10 due to reducing training time, so it is harder for machines to converge when the number of features is higher. Nevertheless, this is not true when the number of bits is lesser than 22 for both directions. Therefore, we can conclude that using PD-ML-distinguishers can reduce feature size, resulting in faster convergence of the machines.

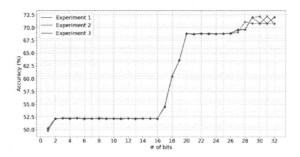

Fig. 1. Accuracy of ML-distinguishers according to number of bits in LSB→MSB direction for 6 round of SPECK32/64

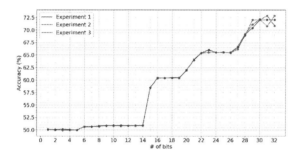

Fig. 2. Accuracy of ML-distinguishers according to number of bits in MSB→LSB direction for 6 round of SPECK32/64

4 Measuring Bit Effectiveness for ML-distinguishers

The results presented in Sect. 3 show that we do not need all bits of the δ to obtain a ML-based distinguisher. In fact, we were able to train a partial differential ML distinguisher with fewer training bits and achieve results comparable to distinguishers learned on full data. In this section, we aim to identify the best strategy for finding the best machine, trained with the least number of bits. Since the desire of block cipher designers is that the output bits of the encrypted message have the most negligible correlation to each other, there is no trivial or pre-defined way to determine which bits are the best for training the partial distinguisher. Hence, we introduce a new experimental method to find the bits of output difference δ for 6-round of SPECK32/64, which have the most impact on the effectiveness of a partial differential ML-distinguisher. The main goal of this experiment is to assign a score to each bit of δ, so that with the help of these scores we can find the most effective bits for training a PD-ML-distinguisher.

4.1 Methodology

The experiment setup is as follows. Given the set of bit positions in a block $B = \{b_0, \ldots, b_{31}\}$, where 0 indicates the position of the most significant bit, we select a subset $\mathcal{C}_B^{16} = \{\mathcal{C}_0, \ldots, \mathcal{C}_{99}\}$ of the all the possible 16-combinations of B (that is, the subsets of 16 distinct elements of B), in a way that the distribution of each $b_i \in B$, in $\mathcal{C}_i$s be uniform, where $0 \leq i \leq 99$. Each of these 100 16-combinations represents a selection of 16 bits out of the 32 total bits in a SPECK32/64 block to be used in the training of a PD-ML-distinguisher.

We use the following procedure in the experiment (Algorithm 2). For each combination, $\mathcal{C}_i \in \mathcal{C}_B^{16}$ we train a PD-ML-distinguisher, and we record its accuracy in an array $A = [a_0, \ldots, a_{99}]$. In the next step, we construct a matrix $M_{32 \times 100}$ in which every row and column correspond to b_is and $\mathcal{C}_j$s, respectively. Equation 2 represents the M matrix, and how to construct it.

$$M_{32 \times 100} = \begin{bmatrix} m_{0,0} & \cdots & m_{0,99} \\ \vdots & \ddots & \vdots \\ m_{31,0} & \cdots & m_{31,99} \end{bmatrix} \quad \text{and} \quad m_{ij} = \begin{cases} 0 & b_j \notin \mathcal{C}_i \\ 1 & b_j \in \mathcal{C}_i \end{cases} \tag{2}$$

This matrix tells us which bits are chosen for every $\mathcal{C}_i$s. For example, if MSB bit is in combination set $\mathcal{C}_0$ then $m_{00} = 0$ otherwise, $m_{00} = 1$. Then, considering the matrix M, we can compute a score for each bit, $S = \{s_0, \ldots, s_{31}\}$, as follows:

$$s_i = \frac{\sum_{j=0}^{99} m_{ij} * a_j}{\sum_{j=0}^{99} m_{ij}}. \tag{3}$$

This score s_i is calculated as the average accuracy of all the PD-ML distinguishers built on combinations where the ith bit is included. A bit with a higher score means that the combinations with that bit in their set lead to a PD-ML-distinguisher with a higher accuracy on average. As a result, with the help of this score, we can select the most effective bits for training a PD-ML-distinguisher.

4.2   Results and Discussion

By having all the scores from each combination set, we can select the most effective bits for training a PD-ML-distinguisher with the minimum number of features. If the scores shown in each set, $\mathcal{C}_i \in \mathcal{C}_B^{16}$, were almost similar for all the bits, then we could conclude that all the bits of δs have equal effect on training a PD-ML-distinguisher. However, in our experiment we observed that there are bits, like 12th, 14th and 29th, with higher scores. As a result, we can confirm this hypothesis that the position of δ bits used for training PD-ML distinguisher affects its accuracy.

Algorithm 2: Scores of effectiveness

---

1 10 **Input**: Sequence set of combinations: $\mathcal{C}_B^{16} = [\mathcal{C}_0, \ldots, \mathcal{C}_{99}]$
    Output: Sequence set of scores: $S = [s_0, \ldots, s_{31}]$
    Training Data: differences of ciphertext pairs of 6-round SPECK32/64 : $\delta = [\delta_0, \ldots, \delta_{31}]$
2 Initialize Sequence set A with size 100
3 Initialize $M_{32 \times 100}$ Matrix
4 Initialize Sequence set S with size 32
5 **for** $\mathcal{C}_i \in \mathcal{C}_B^{16}$ **do**
    /* Training PD-ML distinguishers   */
6      $D \longleftarrow$ TrainMachine$(\mathcal{C}_i)$
7      $A[i] =$ AccuracyTest(D)
    /* Making M matrix   */
8   **for** δ_j *in* δ **do**
9 | **if** $\delta_j \in \mathcal{C}_i$ **then** $M[j][i] = 1$ **else** $M[j][i] = 0$
    /* Computing the score   */
10 **for** $0 <= i <= 31$ **do** $S[i] = \dfrac{\sum\limits_{j=0}^{99} m_{ij} * a_j}{\sum\limits_{j=0}^{99} m_{ij}}$

In order to demonstrate the repeatability of these results, and since $\mathcal{C}_B^{16}$ is chosen randomly, we repeat the Algorithm 2 three more times and obtain 4 different scores for each bit. Then, we normalize all the scores based on the average for each experiment. Figure 3 shows the result. Also, Table 1 indicates the average score and standard deviation for each bit of δ, considering all scores in the four experiments.

As can be seen, the scores for some bits are always above average. By looking at Fig. 3 and Table 1, we choose 8 bits with the best score. We propose two selection of bits for 6-round PD-ML distinguisher of SPECK32/64: $\delta^T = [\delta_{29}, \delta_{28}, \delta_{22}, \delta_{15}, \delta_{14}, \delta_{13}, \delta_{12}, \delta_5]$ and $\delta^{T'} = [\delta_{29}, \delta_{28}, \delta_{21}, \delta_{15}, \delta_{14}, \delta_{13}, \delta_{12}, \delta_5]$. The rationale for choosing these bits is that except bit $\delta_{22} \in \delta^T$ and $\delta_{21} \in \delta^{T'}$ other

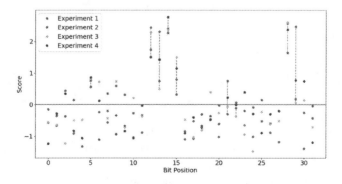

Fig. 3. Normalized Scores for 4 different combination sets. The bits with vertical lines are the ones that are chosen as the most effective bits for training a PD-ML-distinguisher for six rounds of SPECK32/64.

Table 1. The average score (s_i) and standard deviation (SD_i) of each bit of δ in the experiments.

i	0	1	2	3	4	5	6	7	8	9	10	11	12	13	14	15
s_i	-0.62	-0.48	-0.19	-0.51	-0.83	0.75	-0.12	-0.20	0.01	-0.47	-0.53	-0.40	1.99	1.25	2.45	0.94
SD_i	0.38	0.16	0.66	0.41	0.36	0.11	0.66	0.35	0.68	0.46	0.53	0.30	0.38	0.69	0.18	0.43

i	16	17	18	19	20	21	22	23	24	25	26	27	28	29	30	31
s_i	-0.82	-0.75	-0.62	-0.22	-0.47	0.15	-0.10	-0.34	-0.71	-0.36	-0.59	-0.52	2.29	0.87	-0.18	-0.59
SD_i	0.22	0.29	0.19	0.36	0.37	0.39	0.16	0.50	0.55	0.38	0.20	0.39	0.39	0.96	0.78	0.41

bits always have a score above average, zero. In the case of δ_{22}, it has a very low standard deviation while its average score is near the total average (zero), while δ_{21} has the next-highest average score across experiments, despite scoring lower than δ_{22} in some instances.

Finally, we train a new distinguisher with just these eight bits to verify if they are sufficient for training a neural distinguisher, and we obtain a PD-ML-distinguisher with an accuracy of 68.7% for δ^T and 68.8% for $\delta^{T'}$. For comparison, we train a comparable non-partial differential ML-distinguisher, using all 32 bits, and we obtain an accuracy of 72%. For further comparison and verification, we also train a PD-ML-distinguisher on the lowest scoring 8 bits. This time, we obtain an accuracy of 52%, only slightly above the 50% threshold, at which the ML model is not able to distinguish from random, and therefore a distinguisher is not obtained. Figure 4 illustrates the process of the training PD-ML-distinguishers.

The above results clearly indicate the validity and effectiveness of the novel partial differential ML-based distinguisher approach we propose in this paper. The proposed bit selection mechanism further improves the results, and makes it possible to train a PD-ML-distinguisher using a fraction (25%) of the bits, and therefore leading to a reduction in the time and space complexity of training the model, as well as a reduced size for the neural network. This reduced size means we will have a lesser number of neurons in the input layer. Therefore, it decreases the time complexity of the training phase because we can train the machine with a lower number of input features compared to when we increase the feature space of the dataset.

Although in Sects. 3 and 4 we use the same input difference as Gohr's paper, this bit selection can be used in a black-box method. In [12], a procedure was introduced to find the best input difference Δ for the All-in-One differential attack without any prior knowledge by ML-based distinguishers. So, for having a black-box bit selection, we can use the ML-distinguisher for finding the best possible Δ and then use the bit selection of this section.

In the following, when discussing the differences between our machine and Gohr's results, it is important to consider an important distinction. According to [16], the Gohr machine understands information better than the pure differential distribution of outputs. In fact, if we give the ML-distinguisher $(C_0||C_1)$ as input instead of $C_0 \oplus C_1$, the machine understands the differential distribution

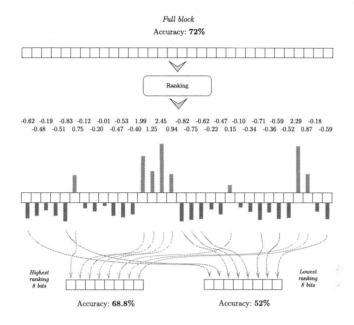

Fig. 4. The Training Process of PD-ML-distinguishers. Rank values are as per Table 1. Plotted bars are approximation of the values (due to graphical constraints).

in the penultimate and antepenultimate rounds as well. To prove this assumption, Bnamira et al. [16] used the Gohr ML-distinguisher in one experiment, but instead of ciphertext pairs, they used $C_0 \oplus C_1 = \delta$ as an input of the distinguisher and observed that the machine's accuracy decreased from 78.8% to 75.4%. So, they conclude that Gohr's machine can extract more information than just the differential distribution of outputs. Hence, throughout this paper, we aim to assess how each bit of the output difference, δ, affects the training of the distinguisher. When comparing our results to the accuracy of other machines, we do so referring to pure differential inputs, which in the case of Speck32/64 is 75.4% [16].

The details of the ML models used are summarised in Table 2, showing that our Partial ML-distinguisher machine is significantly smaller in terms of depth, number of epochs and number of features than the comparable Gohr's machine [10].

4.3   Reducing the Time Complexity of *key Averaging*

While the this work focuses on the ML-distinguisher, and therefore on the first six rounds of the SPECK32/64, as per the relevant literature, the proposed partial differential ML-distinguisher can also reduce the complexity of algorithms targeting subsequent rounds, and in particular the *key averaging* algorithm, which is described in [10]. By employing an r-round differential ML-distinguisher, the key averaging method is utilized to raise the number of rounds for a differential

Table 2. Comparison of different machine learning based differential distinguishers. The training time refers to the networks running on the Google Colab platform [23]

Reference	Network	Number of input features	Depth	Epochs	Input of the Machine	Training time per epoch	Accuracy
[10]	CNN	32 (bits)	10	200	$C_0 \| C_1$	$\approx 7\,\mathrm{min}$	%78.8
[16]	CNN	32 (bits)	10	200	$C_0 \oplus C_1$	$\approx 7\,\mathrm{min}$	%75.4
[17]	MLP	32 (bits)	6	10	$C_0 \oplus C_1$	$\approx 2.5\,\mathrm{min}$	%7.5[a]
This work	MLP	32 (bits)	3	10	$C_0 \oplus C_1$	$\approx 1\,\mathrm{min}$	%72
This work	MLP	8 (bits)	3	10	$C_0 \oplus C_1$	$\approx 30\,\mathrm{sec}$	%68.8

[a]This machine is not a binary classifier; rather, the training set includes 32 distinct classes. More information can be found at [17].

ML-distinguisher to $r + 1$ rounds. [10] employed a six-round neural distinguisher to assess the one round partial decryption of each ciphertext pair in the test set, and the aggregated results were used to compute a score for each pair by average across them. The complexity of this approach for Gohr's distinguisher is 2^{16}, and he was able to create a 7-round distinguisher with a 61% accuracy. Using the proposed PD-ML-distinguisher, however, we can execute this method with a complexity of 2^{11} and obtain a 7-round distinguisher with a 58% accuracy. The complexity is therefore significantly reduced, as we do not need to know all of the bit differences in the ciphertext pairings, at a small cost in the accuracy. While extending to further rounds is outside of the scope of this work, the application and improvement of key averaging and other techniques to the PD-ML-distinguisher represent an interesting future research direction, as discussed in the Conclusion. The time complexity and accuracy of the 7-round ML-distinguisher produced by our proposed model, based on the key averaging algorithm, are compared to those of Gohr's model in the Table 3.

Table 3. Evaluation of the performance of ML-distinguishers in executing the key averaging algorithm.

Reference	Time Complexity	Accuracy of resultant distinguisher
[10]	2^{16}	%61
This work	2^{11}	%58

The same is true if an attacker wishes to apply the key ranking to the final round of the cipher. In this type of attack, the attacker employs a r-round ML-distinguisher to attack the $r + 1$-round of the block cipher by guessing all of the required subkeys from the previous round. Again, if we use the Gohr's ML-distinguisher to perform the key ranking attack, we must guess 2^{16} subkeys; however, with the help of our proposed model, this time complexity can be reduced to 2^{11}, because we only need to partially decrypt 8-bits of the previous round, which we can do by guessing 11 bit keys.

Furthermore, our model allows attackers to find a trade-off between time complexity and distinguisher accuracy. To accomplish this, the attacker simply needs to increase the number of inputs for the machine based on their score and then have a higher accuracy. This flexibility is useful in SPN-like ciphers, where the length of the subkey is typically the same as the length of the block, and guessing all of the keys from the last round makes the attack infeasible due to time complexity.

5   Conclusion

In this paper, we investigated the applicability of partial differences in training neural distinguishers, and we proposed the first partial differential Machine Learning (ML) distinguisher. As a partial differential ML-distinguisher is trained on a selection of bits rather than all bits in a block, we also studied the impact of the selection of bits in the accuracy of the distinguisher, and we established that certain bits have reliably higher effectiveness than others, through a series of independent experiments on different inputs. On this basis, we proposed an algorithm for assigning an effectiveness score to each bit in the block.

In applying a differential attack, our goal was to find non-random behavior in a block cipher when we do not have all bits of difference in ciphertext pairs, δ. To achieve this purpose, we trained a ML-based differential distinguisher for 6-rounds of SPECK32/64 by using just some parts of δ, and we studied the effectiveness of such a partial ML-based differential distinguisher, which we call PD-ML-distinguisher. Our experiments indicate that it is possible to achieve PD-ML-distinguishers with high accuracy, that is comparable to that of a ML-distinguisher trained on the full 32-bits of the block. We also observe that increasing the number of bits does not necessarily lead to an increase in the machine accuracy; but it can reduce the converging speed.

Based on these results, we then experimentally examined if all bits have an equal impact on the training stage by creating new PD-ML-distinguishers. We detect that the accuracy changes when we alter the bits. We conclude that some bits are more critical for ML-distinguishers.

To find the most effective bits in the training phase, we proposed an algorithm to allocate a score to each bit of δ for 6-round SPECK32/64. With the help of this score, we could select the eight most effective bits and construct a 6-round PD-ML-distinguisher for SPECK32/64 achieving an accuracy of 68.8%. This is comparable, and only slightly lower than the 72% accuracy of a ML-distinguisher trained on the full 32-bits, which implies a significantly higher cost in terms of computational and space complexity.

The reduced input also leads to a significant reduction in the complexity of a potential subsequent key recovery attack, as we would not need to guess all the possible subkeys, but rather just 8 bits of them. As an example, we compared our model's performance to that of Gohr's when both were used to execute the key-averaging algorithm on SPECK32/64 and found that our model improved runtime (reducing complexity from 2^{16} to 2^{11}), while sacrificing just a small amount of the resulting ML-distinguisher's accuracy ($\sim 3\%$).

While our experiments are obtained on lightweight cipher SPECK32/64 (the most widely used cipher in the ML-distinguishers literature), the proposed techniques are generic and can be applied on other ciphers. These results are in fact likely to open the way to efficient ML-based differential cryptanalysis of ciphers with larger block sizes, placing standard block ciphers potentially within reach.

As a future research direction, further analysis of the PD-ML-distinguishers may determine the factors that influence the effectiveness of particular bits and, based on that, establish precise criteria concerning the round functions of a cipher. Also, additional insight into the connection between the features (bits) and the prediction may be gleaned from comparing our proposed algorithm with machine learning model interpretations like SHAP or LIME. Another direction may be to use r round distinguishers to create new distinguishers for $r + 1$ or higher number of rounds. For instance, as briefly discussed in Sect. 4.2, the key averaging algorithm can produce a 7-round distinguisher by using 6-round distinguisher without training a new machine. In this scenario, utilizing PD-ML distinguishers may reduce the complexity of the algorithms used to do this.

References

1. Bassham, L., Çalık, Ç., McKay, K., Turan, M.S.: Submission requirements and evaluation criteria for the lightweight cryptography standardization process. US National Institute of Standards and Technology (2018)
2. Daemen, J., Rijmen, V.: AES proposal: Rijndael (1999)
3. Biham, E., Shamir, A.: Differential cryptanalysis of the full 16-round DES. In: Brickell, E.F. (ed.) CRYPTO 1992. LNCS, vol. 740, pp. 487–496. Springer, Heidelberg (1993). https://doi.org/10.1007/3-540-48071-4_34
4. Matsui, M.: Linear cryptanalysis method for DES cipher. In: Helleseth, T. (ed.) EUROCRYPT 1993. LNCS, vol. 765, pp. 386–397. Springer, Heidelberg (1994). https://doi.org/10.1007/3-540-48285-7_33
5. Fu, K., Wang, M., Guo, Y., Sun, S., Hu, L.: MILP-based automatic search algorithms for differential and linear trails for speck. In: Peyrin, T. (ed.) FSE 2016. LNCS, vol. 9783, pp. 268–288. Springer, Heidelberg (2016). https://doi.org/10.1007/978-3-662-52993-5_14
6. Mironov, I., Zhang, L.: Applications of SAT solvers to cryptanalysis of hash functions. In: Biere, A., Gomes, C.P. (eds.) SAT 2006. LNCS, vol. 4121, pp. 102–115. Springer, Heidelberg (2006). https://doi.org/10.1007/11814948_13
7. Gurobi Optimization, L.: Gurobi optimizer reference manual (2021). https://www.gurobi.com
8. Schneier, B.: Applied Cryptography: Protocols, Algorithms, and Source Code in C, 20th edn. Wiley, Hoboken (2015)
9. Abadi, M., Andersen, D.G.: Learning to protect communications with adversarial neural cryptography. arXiv preprint arXiv:1610.06918 (2016)
10. Gohr, A.: Improving attacks on round-reduced SPECK32/64 using deep learning. In: Boldyreva, A., Micciancio, D. (eds.) CRYPTO 2019. LNCS, vol. 11693, pp. 150–179. Springer, Cham (2019). https://doi.org/10.1007/978-3-030-26951-7_6

11. Yadav, T., Kumar, M.: Differential-ML distinguisher: machine learning based generic extension for differential cryptanalysis. In: Longa, P., Ràfols, C. (eds.) LAT-INCRYPT 2021. LNCS, vol. 12912, pp. 191–212. Springer, Cham (2021). https://doi.org/10.1007/978-3-030-88238-9_10

12. Baksi, A., Breier, J., Chen, Y., Dong, X.: Machine learning assisted differential distinguishers for lightweight ciphers. In: 2021 Design, Automation & Test in Europe Conference & Exhibition (DATE), pp. 176–181. IEEE (2021)

13. Hou, B., Li, Y., Zhao, H., Wu, B.: Linear attack on round-reduced DES using deep learning. In: Chen, L., Li, N., Liang, K., Schneider, S. (eds.) ESORICS 2020. LNCS, vol. 12309, pp. 131–145. Springer, Cham (2020). https://doi.org/10.1007/978-3-030-59013-0_7

14. Zahednejad, B., Li, J.: An improved integral distinguisher scheme based on deep learning. EasyChair, Technical report (2020)

15. Liu, G., Lu, J., Li, H., Tang, P., Qiu, W.: Preimage attacks against lightweight scheme Xoodyak based on deep learning. In: Arai, K. (ed.) FICC 2021. AISC, vol. 1364, pp. 637–648. Springer, Cham (2021). https://doi.org/10.1007/978-3-030-73103-8_45

16. Benamira, A., Gerault, D., Peyrin, T., Tan, Q.Q.: A deeper look at machine learning-based cryptanalysis. IACR Cryptol. ePrint Arch **287**, 2021 (2021)

17. Baksi, A., Breier, J., Dasu, V.A., Hou, X.: Machine learning attacks on speck. In: Security and Implementation of Lightweight Cryptography (SILC), pp. 1–6 (2021)

18. Beaulieu, R., Shors, D., Smith, J., Treatman-Clark, S., Weeks, B., Wingers, L.: The SIMON and SPECK lightweight block ciphers. In: Proceedings of the 52nd Annual Design Automation Conference, pp. 1–6 (2015)

19. Albrecht, M.R., Leander, G.: An all-in-one approach to differential cryptanalysis for small block ciphers. In: Knudsen, L.R., Wu, H. (eds.) SAC 2012. LNCS, vol. 7707, pp. 1–15. Springer, Heidelberg (2013). https://doi.org/10.1007/978-3-642-35999-6_1

20. Bellini, E., Rossi, M.: Performance comparison between deep learning-based and conventional cryptographic distinguishers. IACR Cryptol. ePrint Arch. **2020**, 953 (2020). https://eprint.iacr.org/2020/953

21. Kingma, D.P., Ba, J.: Adam: a method for stochastic optimization. arXiv preprint arXiv:1412.6980 (2014)

22. Chollet, F., et al.: Keras (2015). https://github.com/fchollet/keras

23. Bisong, E.: Building Machine Learning and Deep Learning Models on Google Cloud Platform: A Comprehensive Guide for Beginners. Apress (2019)

Data-Driven Evaluation of Intrusion Detectors: A Methodological Framework

Solayman Ayoubi[1]([✉])(iD), Gregory Blanc[2](iD), Houda Jmila[2](iD),
Thomas Silverston[1](iD), and Sébastien Tixeuil[3](iD)

[1] LORIA, Universite de Lorraine, Vandœuvre-lès-Nancy, France
solayman.ayoubi@loria.fr
[2] SAMOVAR, Télécom SudParis, Institut Polytechnique de Paris, Palaiseau, France
[3] Sorbonne Université, CNRS, LIP6, Institut Universitaire de France, Paris, France

Abstract. Intrusion detection systems are an important domain in cybersecurity research. Countless solutions have been proposed, continuously improving upon one another. Yet, and despite the introduction of distinct approaches, including machine-learning methods, the evaluation methodology has barely evolved.

In this paper, we design a comprehensive evaluation framework for Machine Learning (ML)-based intrusion detection systems (IDS) and take into account the unique aspects of ML algorithms, their strengths and weaknesses. The framework design is inspired by both i) traditional IDS evaluation methods and ii) recommendations for evaluating ML algorithms in diverse application areas. Data quality being the key to machine learning, we focus on data-driven evaluation by exploring data-related issues. Our approach goes beyond evaluating intrusion detection performance (also known as *effectiveness*) and aims at proposing standard data manipulation methods to tackle robustness and stability. Finally, we evaluate our framework through a qualitative comparison with other IDS evaluation approaches from the state of the art.

Keywords: Intrusion Detection System · Machine learning · Data-driven Evaluation · Evaluation Framework

1 Introduction

It has been almost twenty years since the publication of the NIST internal report on testing intrusion detection systems [29]. The NIST report identified 10 measurable characteristics, and 4 challenges (incl. how to use background traffic to test IDS), and presented recommendations to improve both datasets and metrics. While some of these characteristics and challenges remain relevant, they also highlight the need to update and improve our IDS evaluation approaches.

Although new techniques like artificial intelligence were introduced to intrusion detection systems, researchers still use outdated evaluation methodologies and datasets. Since 2006, the article by Bermúdez-Edo et al. [8] revealed that

G.-V. Jourdan et al. (Eds.): FPS 2022, LNCS 13877, pp. 142–157, 2023.
https://doi.org/10.1007/978-3-031-30122-3_9

the databases used for IDS evaluation are obsolete, however, they are still used today. According to Tavallaee et al. [37], in 2010, almost 28% (resp. 24%) of research papers used the obsolete KDD99 (resp. DARPA) datasets.

Milenkoski et al. [30] proposed an evaluation technique based on a design space comprised of a workload (dataset property), customized metrics, and a measurement methodology. In their publications, Milenkoski et al. suggest a number of measurement methodologies that correlate to the potential property (Attack detection accuracy, Resistance to evasion techniques...) for evaluation.

In the literature related to ML-based IDS, which generally focuses on the property *Attack detection accuracy*, which is essentially a measurement methodology as described by Milenkoski et al.and is defined as the accuracy of an IDS in the presence of mixed workloads (benign and malicious traffic), *Resistance to evasion methods* or *Resource consumption* are rarely covered. However, additional ML-related issues, such as the bias from the data, also affect the generalization or stability of the ML-based IDS.

Furthermore, despite the datasets' obvious quality problems, they are nonetheless used without any oversight. Therefore, in order to enhance the overall quality of the evaluation, we propose a generic and general approach to evaluate machine learning-based IDS from multiple perspectives: we go beyond the classical quantitative evaluation methods, that solely focus on measuring effectiveness using fundamental metrics, and considers data-driven evaluations by focusing on the data used for the assessment. In the IDS context, we analyze machine-learning concerns like explainability and robustness to adversarial examples. To do so, we examine (i) IDS-specific assessment methods, (ii) AI-specific evaluation methods that can be applied to IDS, and (iii) relevant recommendations from the state of the art [5] and the standards [29].

This article is structured as follows: Sect. 2 presents some related works, Sect. 3 analyses a number of IDS solutions with a focus on evaluation methods. Then, we present our proposal in Sect. 4 as well as a generic evaluation framework. Finally, we conclude in Sect. 5.

2   Related Work

Throughout the years, researchers have presented numerous IDS evaluation approaches. In this part, we introduce some of them. All of the methodologies make an effort to give researchers resources to assess IDS.

Milenkoski et al. [30] identify the most common practices to evaluate different types of intrusion detection systems. To do so, they define a three-part design space including (i) workloads, which are testing sets of data, and their means of production; (ii) metrics, which quantify performance-related properties (non-functional with respect to IDS), or security-related ones; (iii) measurement methodology, which specifies the evaluation properties along with its associated workloads and metrics.

Indeed, they include methods and tools to generate workloads and focus on metrics that quantify the accuracy of the detection. Our proposed framework is inspired by the measurement methodology proposed by Milenkoski et al. but shifts its initial paradigm towards machine-learning-based IDS, i.e., it relies on the evaluation of best practices from the field of machine learning, in particular with respect to data-related issues.

Magán-Carrión et al. [26] examine Network IDS (NIDS) solutions and point out the lack of a standardized method for evaluating machine learning-based NIDS. According to the authors, it is challenging to compare various NIDS because the state of the art does not provide enough information on the evaluation methods. Hence, their methodology specifies the best practices for pre-processing the dataset, training, and assessing the model. In the end, their approach focuses on standardizing model preparation rather than introducing any new evaluation techniques, they clearly present the different training stages of a model: Feature Engineering, Feature Selection, Data Pre-processing, Hyper-parameters Selection, and Performance Metrics.

Bermúdez-Edo et al. [8] suggest requirements for implementing standardized IDS evaluation framework. The authors present a new method for evaluating anomaly-based IDS with a focus on data-partitioning approaches. The authors then offer a technique to get the databases ready for model training, testing, and evaluation. They outline 3 steps: 1. they separate the attacks in one set and the normal in another set, 2. they split the two datasets between a training set, a test set, and a validation set, and 3. they combine some parts to produce three final datasets (train, test, validation). In this method, the authors concentrate on dataset partitioning.

Cardenas et al. [10] presents an IDS evaluation framework that allows for a consistent comparison of the most used metrics in the literature. The authors present a graphical method for comparing the different metrics for a wide range of parameters. They provide a new metric that plots all variables influencing an IDS performance. According to the authors, it is more interesting to determine the IDS that performs best against the most severe attacks than on average. The proposed metric is beneficial for our approach since it enables the results of other domain-specific metrics to be summarized.

3   Analysis of Evaluation Approaches in ML-Based IDS

In this section, we review evaluation methods employed in recent ML-based IDS publications in order to identify common practices that help create a generic evaluation approach. We selected the publications from recent surveys [2, 11] which respectively presented articles from 2019–2021 and 2015–2018 and updated the list with new papers. Following many searches using terms such as "intrusion detection" or "ML-based intrusion detection", we retained the most recent publications (2020–2022) that fell under the scope.

Table 1 highlights a few components of the evaluation method employed in these publications, namely the dataset and the metrics used, as well as some specific evaluation measures beyond what could be described as a common evaluation approach. The remainder of this section details the various evaluation measures that we have noticed in this corpus of publications, both common (*classical measures*) and specific to each publication.

Classical Measures. From our survey of the state of the art in machine-learning-based (network) IDS, the evaluation measures employed by the researchers rarely differ. Although we did find more peculiar measures (as detailed in the last columns of Table 1), a common, allegedly conventional, methodology stood out. This classical evaluation can be defined using the methods introduced by Magán-Carrión et al. [26].

Some examined publications [13,22,35,38] that fall into this category solely advocate for obtaining and contrasting the outcomes of basic metrics (accuracy, precision, and recall) on various model architectures. For instance, in order to enhance the performance of their deep neural networks, the writers of these publications compared several architectures by varying some parameters such as the size of the hidden layers for Gao et al. [13], the neural network activation functions for Thing [38], the number of memory blocks and cells in LSTM for Staudemeyer [35], and finally, the learning rate and the size of the hidden layers for Kim et al. [22].

Data-Related Measures. Data-related measures encompass any evaluation techniques dealing with data-related manipulation, e.g., augmenting the dataset, reducing its dimensionality, generating data with a specific environment, and random resampling. We are primarily interested in these methods given that we wish to evaluate ML-based IDS.

Zhang et al. [44] leverage SMOTE to create the missing data in the unbalanced NSL-KDD dataset. This results in increasing the detection performance of their CNN-based IDS on previously under-represented classes. Tang et al. [36] heavily reduced the data representation of the NSL-KDD dataset from 41 features to 6. This makes their DNN-based flow anomaly detector more efficient. Zolotukhin et al. [46] used the Realistic Global Cyber Environment (RGCE) to run their simulation, RGCE is a closed environment that replicates the user traffic and organizational structures of the real Internet. This article is included in our survey's environment category since it makes use of a simulated environment. Al-Qatf et al. [3] suggest combining SVM and Sparse Autoencoder. The following two methods are used to assess the effectiveness of their method using the NSL-KDD dataset, for this purpose a ten-fold cross-validation is carried out for both training and testing. Random resampling can be done using the k-fold cross-validation method.

Multi-label Measures. ML-based IDS are often termed behavioral IDS or anomaly-based IDS[1], that is, binary classifiers attempting to distinguish malicious traffic from a normal one. But some datasets offer more depth in exhibiting several classes of attacks, which could be interesting for IDS to discriminate with respect to producing a specific intrusion response. To that end, multi-label classi-

---

[1] We believe however that the term "anomaly-based IDS" should solely apply to IDS trained on normal traffic only.

Table 1. Comparison of the surveyed publications. Most IDS evaluations employ a subset of the above datasets and metrics with little to no variation. Additional measures deal with varying model architectures (§), multi-label classification (♦) or data-related manipulations (□)

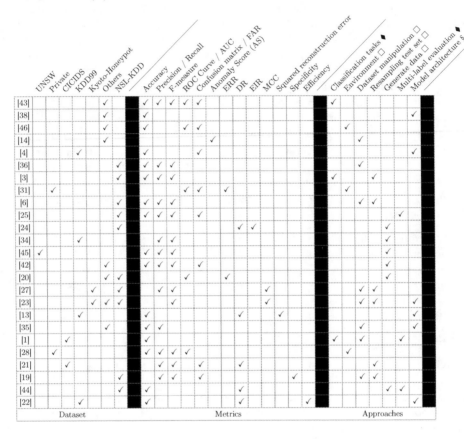

fication is employed. We have found some works measuring its advantage, either in comparison with binary classification or in evaluating per-class performance.

For example, Yu et al. [43] propose a novel network intrusion model by stacking dilated convolutional autoencoders and they evaluate their method on two new intrusion detection datasets. Several experiments were carried out to check the effectiveness of their approach. They used two different datasets: CTU-UNB & Contagio-CTU-UNB and six classical evaluation metrics. To evaluate they perform 3 types of classification tasks: 6-class classification using the Contagio-CTU-UNB dataset and 2-class and 8-class classification using the CTU-UNB dataset.

Moreover, Abbas et al. [1] proposed an ensemble model combining Naive Bayes, Logistic Regression, and a Decision Tree. In order to assess the performance of their suggestion they determine the accuracy of their model for each label. They end up with a total of 15 different accuracies, each of which represents the detection performance for this label.

Table 1 compares ML-based IDS proposals with respect to their evaluation methodology. What can be observed is that they often share the same evaluation approach. Many evaluations were replicating approaches previously seen in the state of the art, and the trend has been shifting over the years, for example from computing accuracy only to computing both precision and recall instead. It is still the case today although intrusion detection-specific metrics were proposed [10,17,18,39]. Another worrying aspect is the choice of the dataset. Although NSL-KDD has been perused for many years, many datasets were created and shared in the last 10 years. It affects evaluation in its timeliness as the attacks it contains are outdated and far from the sophistication of modern attacks. Often, other simple data-related issues, e.g., unbalance, are addressed using evaluation measures such as augmenting the dataset or reducing its dimensionality.

Finally, additional measures that we have observed with respect to multi-label classification, dataset construction, or model architectures are seldom used in combination, reducing the quality of the models trained and tested. This advocates for the definition and formalization of a holistic framework enabling researchers of the domain in mastering the ML pipeline and adapting it to the task of evaluating ML-based IDS with respect to a wide range of properties including detection performance and resource consumption, of course, but also generalization, robustness, and so on.

4   Proposal of an Evaluation Framework

One of the objectives of this framework is to bring together the different evaluation methods found in the literature, in particular those that propose to evaluate aspects specific to the use of machine learning such as robustness and generalization, and to suggest a method for researchers to properly assess their models. Our research is inspired by Milenkoski et al. [30], who define the measurement methodology of an evaluation property as the selection of appropriate workload (dataset) and metrics.

Our proposal adapts this approach to ML-based IDS and embeds it into a framework that generalizes the evaluation of several properties beyond detection performance (also known as *effectiveness*). In particular, it focuses on a dataset construction component as a generalization of the workload concept and extends it to accommodate feedback from the evaluation analysis, ultimately providing continuous improvement to both the ML models used by the IDS and the data representation they use. Not only does the property have an impact on the metrics that evaluate it, but the dataset may embed some challenges that the metrics should account for (*e.g.*, when using unbalanced datasets).

We also want to add some aspects not yet studied enough in the application of machine learning to IDS such as explainability. The complete framework can be found in Fig. 1. The framework is divided into several modules that contribute to the complete evaluation process. The first module focuses on the property that we want to examine. From the selected properties, the *metrics module* will output a set of relevant metrics, and the *dataset module* will construct the appropriate dataset to assess them. Both outputs form the *experiment setting* that will configure the *evaluation module* which will perform the training and testing of one or several models to be assessed by the evaluator. We further detail each module in the ensuing subsections.

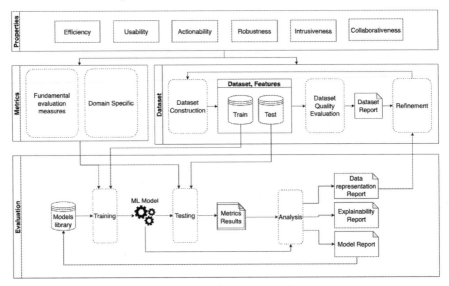

Fig. 1. Data-driven Evaluation framework for ML-based IDS

4.1   Properties

This module allows an evaluator to select a set of properties that the target IDS (system under test) is assessed against.

Effectiveness is the usual property for assessing the detection performance of an IDS. However, relying solely on performance evaluation is one of the major issues in the evaluation of ML-based IDS since other crucial characteristics, such as the ML algorithm's robustness or generalizability must be considered.

Besides *effectiveness*, the properties we propose in our framework are influenced by both works in the domain of intrusion detection, such as Axelsson's [5], and data-related problems in ML:

i) *efficiency* measures how many computing resources the IDS requires; ii) *usability* measures how easy it is for a non-security expert to use the IDS; iii) *actionability* measures how useful are the alerts for a security operator; iv) *robustness* measures how well the IDS resists incidents or attacks directed against it (e.g., adversarial examples, concept drift); v) *intrusiveness* measures the privacy risks on the data manipulated by the IDS; vi) *collaborativeness* measures how well the system collaborates with other security mechanisms.

4.2   Datasets

As the main focus of our approach, the dataset module is central in our framework, deriving the datasets appropriate to evaluate a property and feeding them to the evaluation module. Indeed, the kind of dataset to be utilized is determined by the requirement to evaluate a specific property. This module has 3 main processes: *construction*, *evaluation*, and *refinement*.

Dataset Construction. This process produces one or several datasets (each of them later split into a training set and a test set) that may be represented according to various subsets of features. Similar to Milenkoski et al. [30], we consider various sources of the data, ranging from raw traffic captures to extracted flows to packet traces to feature vectors that have been generated from a broad set of environments including production environments (rare!), emulation/simulation testbeds, or legitimate and attack traffic generation tools. Generation tools also encompass generative methods that output synthetic feature vectors. These sources also come as readily exploitable datasets, some of them have been shared among the IDS research community. A comprehensive list of the publicly available datasets that are commonly used is presented by Ring et al.in their survey [32].

Dataset construction outputs datasets that fit the measurement methodology as expressed by Milenkoski et al. [30], that is it enables the evaluation of a given property. A dataset may actually enable the evaluation of more than one property.

For example, Bermúdez-Edo et al. [8] propose steps to acquire and partition a network traffic dataset for evaluating the effectiveness of anomaly-based IDS, among others. Some generation criteria are as follows: i) both *normal* and attack traffic should be present, and the dataset should be partitioned between training (only normal), validation, and test (both types of traffic) sets with realistic proportions; ii) the dataset should be sufficiently voluminous as to be representative of most traffic behaviors. They also described approaches to tackle a number of issues: i) generating *anomalous* traffic (i.e., new attacks in a hybrid setting) by using two filters (one obsolete and one up-to-date), ii) improving the *robustness* of the dataset (increase the effective size of the data available for training and testing) when its size is modest by resampling training and test sets, and averaging the performance results, and iii) updating models by shifting the datasets: the up-to-date rules become the out-of-date rules and the new rules become the up-to-date rules.

Combining datasets can help to fill in any gaps that may exist in the chosen or generated datasets, eventually creating more *representative* datasets. To be representative the dataset needs samples large enough to adequately reflect the general community's norms, including both permitted and prohibited behaviors.

Regardless of the sources of data, a dataset $D^p_{F_j}$ is an instance of a dataset D^p constructed so as to contain diverse samples allowing the evaluation of a property p, and in which each sample is represented by the set of features F_j. Its split between the training set $Tr(D^i_{F_j})$ and the test set $Tt(D^i_{F_j})$ is conditioned by both the property to be evaluated and the type of IDS (binary classifier, multi-classifier, anomaly detector).

Dataset Evaluation. We suggest evaluating the dataset upstream so that it might potentially be improved through a refinement stage in order to get the best evaluation possible.

For example, Gharib et al. [15] have proposed a weighted score on 11 criteria to evaluate the quality of an intrusion detection dataset. The 11 criteria are attack diversity, anonymity, available protocols, complete capture, complete interaction, complete network configuration, complete traffic, feature set, heterogeneity, labeled dataset, and metadata. Practitioners are invited to define weights themselves, that best suit their requirements.

Viegas et al. [40] tackled the issue of realistic network conditions for the evaluation of intrusion detectors by generating datasets using a honeypot with a client-server approach. The generated datasets should satisfy a number of expected properties [40]: i) realism: the produced network traffic can be observed in production environments; ii) validity: packets are well-formed and follow the client-server communication paradigm; iii) prior labeling: samples are correctly labeled to enable correct classification; iv) high variability (diversity): the dataset should present a diverse set of services, client behaviors, and attacks; v) correct implementation: attacks follow a well-known or *de facto* standard; vi) ease of updating: the dataset should incorporate new services and attacks; vii) reproducibility: experts should be able to compare datasets; viii) without sensitive data: the dataset should not contain or reveal sensitive information, so as to be shared among researchers.

Additionally, one might desire more focused techniques, such as evaluating datasets produced by a Generative Adversarial Network. Early works in other fields have emerged, such as the one from Gonçalves et al. [16] that proposed a method for the generation and evaluation of synthetic patient data. Using a set of complementary metrics, they evaluated the quality of the synthetic data generators. These metrics can be divided into 2 groups, the *data utility* and the *information disclosure*. The *data utility* metrics measure how well the synthetic dataset incorporates the statistical characteristics of the original data, and the *information disclosure* metrics quantify to which extent the synthetic data may reveal the real data. They proposed 5 data utility metrics (Kullback- Leibler (KL) divergence, pairwise correlation difference, log-cluster, support coverage, and cross-classification) and 2 information disclosure metrics (membership disclosure, attribute disclosure).

Although the work is not in the field of intrusion detection, it shows promises for evaluating synthetic discrete tabular data that appears frequently in network traffic datasets.

Finally, Wasielewska et al. [41] propose to experimentally investigate the limits of detection by using their dataset quality assessment method (PerQoDA). This method makes it simple to determine whether the dataset's information is comprehensive enough to reliably classify observations. In multidimensional datasets, it can spot irregularities in the connections between observations and labels. An efficient method for evaluating dataset quality aids in understanding how performance outcomes are affected by dataset quality and can be useful in resolving issues relating to the deterioration of model performance. Prior to any ML application, they recommend, assessing the dataset quality.

Dataset Refinement. The dataset refinement process describes the step where we use all the observations made to improve the dataset. The goal is to use the various reports from the model evaluation as well as the dataset evaluation to raise the dataset's quality.

Initially, we can easily address the many issues brought up by the assessment using Gharib's method: for instance, if we discover a deficit in the proportion of attacks, we can try to add the missing traffic.

However, after receiving feedback from a first training session, particularly from the *data representation report*, one could wish to make adjustments. In this scenario, a variety of strategies can be used to change the dataset's feature set. For example, Bronzino et al. [9] propose a complete method named *Traffic Refinery*. This approach aims to transform the traffic in real-time to produce a variety of feature representations for machine learning models. With this tool, we can explore and evaluate which representations work best for the property to be evaluated.

Indeed, there is no standard set of features for Network Intrusion Detection Datasets. Different representations may actually yield different performances for the same model. To prove this, Sarhan et al. [33] proposes to evaluate and compare two different sets of features, the Netflow-based features, and the CICFlowMeter features. The evaluation has been conducted on three datasets and using two machine learning classifiers. The results show a constant superiority of the NetFlow features. In addition to this, the authors used SHAP to explain the prediction results of the ML models to identify the key features for each dataset. With this approach, we can choose the best data representation methods.

4.3 Metrics

In this section, we detail the families of metrics that are needed to produce an accurate and customized evaluation, it's essential to pick the appropriate metrics in order to properly analyze a property. Although the metrics described in this part are primarily concerned with detection performance, choosing a dataset and metric based on the evaluation of a property allows for the study of more properties with the same metrics than only effectiveness.

Bekkar et al. [7] expressly identify three groups: *fundamental evaluation measures*, *combined evaluation measures*, and *graphical performance evaluation*. The authors apply these metrics to compute the effectiveness of an IDS in the presence of unbalanced datasets. They remark that accuracy places more weight on the most common classes than on the rare ones so using metrics like accuracy completely skews the results. It appears therefore that one should carefully choose metrics that compensate for a dataset's shortcomings. Even though the authors, in this case, are interested in unbalanced datasets, we recommend using at least the categories of metrics established by Bekkar et al.in order to account for the various defaults of the datasets. The metrics categories that we advise are the following.

Fundamental Evaluation Measures. This class of metrics relates to the metrics that can be calculated using the confusion matrix's results. Identified fundamental measures include *accuracy, precision,* and *recall.*

Combined Evaluation Measures. The metrics derived from fundamental measures are included in this category. The following metrics can be found: G-means, the likelihood ratios, Discriminant power, F-Measure, Balanced Accuracy, Youden index, and finally the Matthews correlation coefficient (MCC). These metrics combine the fundamental measures in a way that they are less susceptible to potential class imbalance.

Graphical Performance Evaluation. In this category the metrics are based on the ROC curve: the true positive rate (TPR) and false positive rate (FPR) are plotted against one another at different threshold values.

The AUC, which is defined as a summary indication of the ROC curve performance, is used to indicate the performance of a classifier into a single measure. But there are also several other metrics such as Weighted AUC, Cumulative Gains Curve and lift chart and Area Under Lift. These metrics provide a concise summary of the fundamental evaluation measures and enable the selection of potentially optimal models while disqualifying subpar ones regardless of the cost context or class distribution.

Domain Specific. As early as 2006, Gu et al. [17] employed information theory to model the capability of an IDS to correctly classify normal and intrusive traffic. Their objective was to incorporate existing metrics while not relying on subjective measures and reduce the *uncertainty* about the input given the IDS output. The proposed metric called the *Intrusion Detection Capability,* or C_{ID}, is the ratio of the mutual information between the IDS input and output to the entropy of the input. Mutual information measures the amount of uncertainty of the input resolved by knowing the IDS output. Later, Imoize et al. [18] extended C_{ID} to select an optimal operating point, calculate the expected cost and compare intrusion detectors. To that end, they incorporated a decision-tree-based analysis to determine the optimal operating point, as done by Ulvila and Gaffney [39].

These metrics are some examples of what we can find in the literature to specifically evaluate IDS.

4.4   Evaluation

This module performs the evaluation of a system under test (an IDS) for a given set of properties, and their appropriately derived datasets and metrics. Aside from model training and testing, the subsequent results are analyzed to refine both the model fueling the ML-based IDS and the dataset.

Training and Testing. These processes in the evaluation module are the most simple and common ones, yet mandatory.

The result of the training process is the trained model and validated model. This model is then used in the testing process (also known as *inference*) to output the *metrics results*, which include the outcomes of the selected metrics computed using the test set. These reports are often found in other publications evaluating IDS proposals using the classical methodology and contain different values of the fundamental metrics for a set of model architectures.

Analysis. The incorporation of an analysis process is the real improvement we advocate for model evaluation. Through this process, we are able to acquire a number of reports that are highly helpful for both the IDS's improvement and its comprehensive evaluation.

The *data representation report* helps determine whether or not our dataset is suitable for the model. Although the initial assessment of the dataset during the construction phase gives us a general quality measure, the evaluation following the test phase enables us to evaluate, using performance metrics, its suitability for our purposes. We obviously want to determine whether a set of features is appropriate for our models. The findings in this report can then be applied to the refinement process in a subsequent iteration of the evaluation.

Since some ML (rather Deep Learning) models are regarded as black boxes that do not allow for a straightforward explanation of their decisions, it impairs the user's ability to interpret the findings. A growing number of techniques known as XAI that enable an explanation of the outcomes have been developed in response to this issue, Charmet et al. [12] conduct a thorough literature review on the connection between cybersecurity and XAI. The *explainability report* details the application of such methods to the evaluation of IDS models.

The *model report* clarifies whether the chosen model is suitable for the desired task. In fact, we may want to assess a number of models for which we derive the various performance measures. From these outcomes, we produce this report with the aim of demonstrating the effectiveness of the employed algorithms. This report allows us to modify the model library's list of models so that we only keep the most effective ones in an evolutionary approach.

In conclusion, the framework provides instructions for developing the assessment environment and procedure. Some of the activities are loops that enable the improvement of various evaluation components, such as the dataset and model selection, at each iteration.

4.5   Qualitative Assessment of the Proposed Framework

Table 2. Comparison of our framework with other evaluation methods

Reference	Properties	Dataset Construction	Dataset Evaluation	Refinement	Domain Specific Metrics	Analysis
Our proposal	✓	✓	✓	✓	✓	✓
[30]	✓	✓			✓	
[26]	Partially	Partially				
[8]	Partially	Partially				
[10]	Partially				✓	

We outlined current issues with IDS assessment in Sect. 1 in addition to the fact that many relatively recent works still use outdated evaluation environments. The approaches are obsolete and not designed for the assessment of ML models. In Sect. 3, we looked for some unique assessment techniques in various intrusion detection proposals. In this section, we offer a qualitative assessment of our suggested framework by contrasting our procedures with those used by other researchers in the literature.

Here, we contrast our suggestion with the articles listed in the Sect. 2. The discrepancies between our proposal and the current methodologies are clearly shown in Table 2, where many of the elements in our framework are either partially or missing. Indeed, the various evaluation techniques do only consider one aspect at a time. For instance, Cardenas et al. [10], and Milenkoski [30] recommend using domain-specific metrics, yet do not recommend studying the model explicability, or evaluating the dataset itself, two features we include in our framework.

5   Conclusion

We observed that relatively few evaluation techniques in the literature include all required elements for a thorough evaluation of ML-based intrusion detection systems, including in particular: dataset evaluation, explainability, etc. As a result, we propose a methodological framework to assess ML-based IDS in a systematic manner. Our framework is constructed as follows: The framework's first module outlines the various properties that we wish to assess, and it links to the metrics and datasets modules. In our framework, we take into account that the metrics and dataset are defined depending on the property to be evaluated. Given that both components are crucial to the assessment process, the metrics module and the dataset module are connected to the last module, the evaluation module. Some of our modules include loops that can be used for fine-tuning specific assessment processes in future iterations of the evaluation.

Our framework paves the way for future research developments, including 1. actually implementing the framework, 2. formalizing the evaluation part of the framework, and 3. construct a benchmark to evaluate and compare various ML-based intrusion detection systems.

Acknowledgements. This work is funded by the GRIFIN project (ANR-20-CE39-0011).

References

1. Abbas, A., Khan, M.A., Latif, S., Ajaz, M., Shah, A.A., Ahmad, J.: A new ensemble-based intrusion detection system for internet of things. Arab. J. Sci. Eng. **47**(2), 1805–1819 (2022). https://doi.org/10.1007/s13369-021-06086-5
2. Abdelmoumin, G., Whitaker, J., Rawat, D.B., Rahman, A.: A survey on data-driven learning for intelligent network intrusion detection systems. Electronics **11**(2), 213 (2022)
3. Al-Qatf, M., Lasheng, Y., Al-Habib, M., Al-Sabahi, K.: Deep learning approach combining sparse autoencoder with SVM for network intrusion detection. IEEE Access **6**, 52843–52856 (2018)
4. Alrawashdeh, K., Purdy, C.: Toward an online anomaly intrusion detection system based on deep learning. In: 2016 15th IEEE International Conference on Machine Learning and Applications (ICMLA), pp. 195–200 (2016)
5. Axelsson, S.: The base-rate fallacy and the difficulty of intrusion detection. ACM Trans. Inf. Syst. Secur. (TISSEC) **3**(3), 186–205 (2000)
6. Aygun, R.C., Yavuz, A.G.: Network anomaly detection with stochastically improved autoencoder based models. In: 2017 IEEE 4th International Conference on Cyber Security and Cloud Computing (CSCloud), pp. 193–198 (2017)
7. Bekkar, M., Djemaa, H.K., Alitouche, T.A.: Evaluation measures for models assessment over imbalanced data sets. J. Inf. Eng. Appl. **3**(10), 27–38 (2013)
8. Bermúdez-Edo, M., Salazar-Hernández, R., Díaz-Verdejo, J., García-Teodoro, P.: Proposals on assessment environments for anomaly-based network intrusion detection systems. In: Lopez, J. (ed.) CRITIS 2006. LNCS, vol. 4347, pp. 210–221. Springer, Heidelberg (2006). https://doi.org/10.1007/11962977_17
9. Bronzino, F., Schmitt, P., Ayoubi, S., Kim, H., Teixeira, R.C., Feamster, N.: Traffic refinery. Proc. ACM Meas. Anal. Comput. Syst. **5**, 1–24 (2021)
10. Cárdenas, A., Baras, J., Seamon, K.: A framework for the evaluation of intrusion detection systems. In: 2006 IEEE Symposium on Security and Privacy (S&P'06), pp. 15–77 (2006)
11. Chalapathy, R., Chawla, S.: Deep learning for anomaly detection: a survey (2019)
12. Charmet, F., et al.: Explainable artificial intelligence for cybersecurity: a literature survey. Ann. Telecommun. **77**, 789–812 (2022). https://doi.org/10.1007/s12243-022-00926-7
13. Gao, N., Gao, L., Gao, Q., Wang, H.: An intrusion detection model based on deep belief networks. In: 2014 Second International Conference on Advanced Cloud and Big Data, pp. 247–252 (2014)
14. García Cordero, C., Hauke, S., Mühlhäuser, M., Fischer, M.: Analyzing flow-based anomaly intrusion detection using replicator neural networks. In: 2016 14th Annual Conference on Privacy, Security and Trust (PST), pp. 317–324 (2016)
15. Gharib, A., Sharafaldin, I., Lashkari, A.H., Ghorbani, A.A.: An evaluation framework for intrusion detection dataset. In: 2016 International Conference on Information Science and Security (ICISS), pp. 1–6. IEEE (2016)
16. Goncalves, A., Ray, P., Soper, B., Stevens, J., Coyle, L., Sales, A.P.: Generation and evaluation of synthetic patient data. BMC Med. Res. Methodol. **20**(1), 108 (2020)
17. Gu, G., Fogla, P., Dagon, D., Lee, W., Skorić, B.: Measuring intrusion detection capability: an information-theoretic approach. In: Proceedings of the 2006 ACM Symposium on Information, Computer and Communications Security, pp. 90–101 (2006)

18. Imoize, A.L., Oyedare, T., Otuokere, M.E., Shetty, S.: Software intrusion detection evaluation system: a cost-based evaluation of intrusion detection capability. Commun. Netw. **10**(4), 211–229 (2018)
19. Imrana, Y., et al.: χ^2-BidlSTM: a feature driven intrusion detection system based on χ^2 statistical model and bidirectional LSTM. Sensors **22**(5), 2018 (2022)
20. Intrator, Y., Katz, G., Shabtai, A.: MDGAN: boosting anomaly detection using multi-discriminator generative adversarial networks. ArXiv abs/1810.05221 (2018)
21. Khan, M.A.: HCRNNIDS: hybrid convolutional recurrent neural network-based network intrusion detection system. Processes **9**(5), 834 (2021)
22. Kim, J., Kim, J., Thu, H.L.T., Kim, H.: Long short term memory recurrent neural network classifier for intrusion detection. In: 2016 International Conference on Platform Technology and Service (PlatCon), pp. 1–5 (2016)
23. Kwon, D., Natarajan, K., Suh, S.C., Kim, H., Kim, J.: An empirical study on network anomaly detection using convolutional neural networks. In: 2018 IEEE 38th International Conference on Distributed Computing Systems (ICDCS), pp. 1595–1598 (2018)
24. Lin, Z., Shi, Y., Xue, Z.: IDSGAN: generative adversarial networks for attack generation against intrusion detection. ArXiv abs/1809.02077 (2018)
25. Lopez-Martin, M., Carro, B., Sanchez-Esguevillas, A., Lloret, J.: Conditional variational autoencoder for prediction and feature recovery applied to intrusion detection in IoT. Sensors **17**(9), 1967 (2017)
26. Magán-Carrión, R., Urda, D., Díaz-Cano, I., Dorronsoro, B.: Towards a reliable comparison and evaluation of network intrusion detection systems based on machine learning approaches. Appl. Sci. **10**(5), 1775 (2020)
27. Malaiya, R.K., Kwon, D., Kim, J., Suh, S.C., Kim, H., Kim, I.: An empirical evaluation of deep learning for network anomaly detection. In: 2018 International Conference on Computing, Networking and Communications (ICNC), pp. 893–898 (2018)
28. Mehedi, S.T., Anwar, A., Rahman, Z., Ahmed, K., Rafiqul, I.: Dependable intrusion detection system for IoT: a deep transfer learning-based approach. IEEE Trans. Ind. Inform. **19**(1), 1006–1017 (2022)
29. Mell, P., Lippmann, R., Chung, Haines, J., Zissman, M.: An overview of issues in testing intrusion detection systems (2003)
30. Milenkoski, A., Vieira, M., Kounev, S., Avritzer, A., Payne, B.D.: Evaluating computer intrusion detection systems: a survey of common practices. ACM Comput. Surv. (CSUR) **48**(1), 1–41 (2015)
31. Mirsky, Y.: Autoencoders for online network intrusion detection. ArXiv abs/1802.09089 (2018)
32. Ring, M., Wunderlich, S., Scheuring, D., Landes, D., Hotho, A.: A survey of network-based intrusion detection data sets. Comput. Secur. **86**, 147–167 (2019)
33. Sarhan, M., Layeghy, S., Portmann, M.: Evaluating standard feature sets towards increased generalisability and explainability of ML-based network intrusion detection (2021)
34. Shahriar, M.H., Haque, N.I., Rahman, M.A., Alonso, M.: G-IDS: generative adversarial networks assisted intrusion detection system. In: 2020 IEEE 44th Annual Computers, Software, and Applications Conference (COMPSAC), pp. 376–385 (2020)
35. Staudemeyer, R.C.: Applying long short-term memory recurrent neural networks to intrusion detection. S. Afr. Comput. J. **56**, 136–154 (2015)

36. Tang, T.A., Mhamdi, L., McLernon, D., Zaidi, S.A.R., Ghogho, M.: Deep learning approach for network intrusion detection in software defined networking. In: 2016 International Conference on Wireless Networks and Mobile Communications (WINCOM), pp. 258–263 (2016)
37. Tavallaee, M., Stakhanova, N., Ghorbani, A.A.: Toward credible evaluation of anomaly-based intrusion-detection methods. IEEE Trans. Syst. Man Cybern. Part C (Appl. Rev.) **40**(5), 516–524 (2010)
38. Thing, V.L.L.: IEEE 802.11 network anomaly detection and attack classification: a deep learning approach. In: 2017 IEEE Wireless Communications and Networking Conference (WCNC), pp. 1–6 (2017)
39. Ulvila, J.W., Gaffney, J.E., Jr.: Evaluation of intrusion detection systems. J. Res. Nat. Inst. Stand. Technol. **108**(6), 453 (2003)
40. Viegas, E.K., Santin, A.O., Oliveira, L.S.: Toward a reliable anomaly-based intrusion detection in real-world environments. Comput. Netw. **127**, 200–216 (2017)
41. Wasielewska, K., Soukup, D., Čejka, T., Camacho, J.: Evaluation of detection limit in network dataset quality assessment with permutation testing. In: 4th Workshop on Machine Learning for Cybersecurity (MLCS) (2022)
42. Yin, C., Zhu, Y., Liu, S., Fei, J., Zhang, H.: An enhancing framework for botnet detection using generative adversarial networks. In: 2018 International Conference on Artificial Intelligence and Big Data (ICAIBD), pp. 228–234 (2018)
43. Yu, Y., Long, J., Cai, Z.: Network intrusion detection through stacking dilated convolutional autoencoders. Secur. Commun. Netw. **2017**, 4184196 (2017)
44. Zhang, X., Ran, J., Mi, J.: An intrusion detection system based on convolutional neural network for imbalanced network traffic. In: 2019 IEEE 7th International Conference on Computer Science and Network Technology (ICCSNT), pp. 456–460 (2019)
45. Zixu, T., Liyanage, K.S.K., Gurusamy, M.: Generative adversarial network and auto encoder based anomaly detection in distributed IoT networks. In: GLOBECOM 2020–2020 IEEE Global Communications Conference, pp. 1–7 (2020)
46. Zolotukhin, M., Hämäläinen, T., Kokkonen, T., Siltanen, J.: Increasing web service availability by detecting application-layer DDoS attacks in encrypted traffic. In: 2016 23rd International Conference on Telecommunications (ICT), pp. 1–6 (2016)

CHIEFS: Corneal-Specular Highlights Imaging for Enhancing Fake-Face Spotter

Muhammad Mohzary[1,2]([✉]), Khalid Almalki[3], Baek-Young Choi[1], and Sejun Song[1]

[1] School of Science and Engineering, University of Missouri-Kansas City, Kansas City, MO, USA
{mm3qz,choiby,songsej}@umsystem.edu
[2] Department of Computer Science, Jazan University, Jazan, Saudi Arabia
mmohzary@jazanu.edu.sa
[3] College of Computing and Informatics, Saudi Electronic University, Riyadh, Saudi Arabia
k.almalki@seu.edu.sa

Abstract. This paper presents a novel Machine Learning (ML)-based DeepFake detection technology named CHIEFS (Corneal-Specular Highlights Imaging for Enhancing Fake-Face Spotter). We focus on the most reflective area of a human face, the eyes, upon the hypothesis that the existing DeepFake creation methods fail to coordinate their counterfeits with the reflective components. In addition to the traditional checking of the reflection shape similarity (RSS), we detect various corneal-specular highlights features, such as color components and textures, to find corneal-specular highlights consistency (CHC). Furthermore, we inspect the ensemble of the highlights with the surrounding environmental factors (SEF), including the light settings, directions, and strength. We designed and built them as modular features and have conducted extensive experiments with different combinations of the components using various input parameters and Deep Neural Network (DNN) architectures on Generative Adversarial Network (GAN)-based Deep-Fake datasets. The empirical results show that CHIEFS with three modules improves the accuracy from 86.05% (with the RSS alone) to 99.00% with the ResNet-50-V2 architecture.

Keywords: DeepFake · DeepFake Detection · Media Manipulation · Digital Media Forensics · Corneal-Specular Highlights

1 Introduction

The AI-fueled production and manipulation techniques of fictitious human facial images, DeepFake, have accomplished notable advancement. Due to the sophisticated DeepFake generation technologies [15,16,26], it is getting harder to distinguish the forged images by eye. Despite many benign applications such as fun memes, visual effects, and realistic avatars, the generated fake media can be

© The Author(s), under exclusive license to Springer Nature Switzerland AG 2023
G.-V. Jourdan et al. (Eds.): FPS 2022, LNCS 13877, pp. 158–172, 2023.
https://doi.org/10.1007/978-3-031-30122-3_10

malignantly used by spreading misinformation on social media, creating deception for identity theft, and causing manipulation on election security. Hence, DeepFake has become a pandemic risk to authenticity, privacy, and security for our society. DeepFake detection technologies have become essential vaccines to mitigate the possible malignant risks.

There has been a large number of research works to detect DeepFakes. For example, [33] proposed an attention-based DeepFake detection distiller by applying frequency domain learning and optimal transport theory in knowledge distillation to improve the detection of low-quality DeepFake images. Le et al. [17] explored the asynchronous frequency spectra of color channels to train unsupervised and supervised learning models to identify GAN-based synthetic facial images. [31] extracted deep features from facial images using a Convolutional Neural Network (CNN). Another technique [19] checked eye blinking motions, which tended to be missing in DeepFake videos using the Long-Term Recurrent Convolutional Network (LRCN). Sun et al. [30] also detected DeepFake using facial geometric characteristics. However, previous methods lacked detection generalization on unseen data because they were trained on datasets containing few low-quality video frames generated with a single model and fewer subjects. In addition, eye-based DeepFake detection techniques in [7,9,19], and [22] only focused on a single artifact of eyes, either iris color, blinks, or similarity of corneal reflections on both eyes. Hence, they failed to detect sophisticated DeepFake media.

This paper presents a novel ML-based DeepFake detection technology named **CHIEFS** (**C**orneal-Specular **H**ighlights **I**maging for **E**nhancing **F**ake-Face **S**potter). As shown in Fig. 1, we focus on the most reflective area of a human face, eyes, upon the hypothesis that DeepFake technologies, such as replacement and synthesis, are hard to coordinate their counterfeits with the reflective components. We seek similarity and consistency of corneal-specular highlights (CSH) with multiple surrounding semantics, such as illumination and environmental conditions that are hard to forge. Thus, instead of checking a single aspect of the eyes, we extract multiple features, including *CSH*s' color components, shapes, and textures. In addition, we extract facial images surrounding environmental factors (SEF) to check the ensemble of the reflectance with the *SEF* such as indoor/outdoor, bright/dark, backgrounds, and light strength. CHIEFS embeds the *SEF* into the feature extraction and classification process to detect the symmetricity and consistency in both eyes' color components and reflection patterns.

As illustrated in Fig. 2, CHIEFS consists of a couple of ML components, including Training Data Collection and Annotation (TDCA), Highlights and Environmental Factors Detection (HEFD), and Feature Extraction, Embedding, and Classification (FEEC). The TDCA involves creating and annotating a new dataset named CHIEFS DeepFake Detection (CHIEFS-DFD). The CHIEFS-DFD dataset includes real and GAN-generated DeepFake facial images annotated with various *CSH* and environmental information. The HEFD detects right and left *CSH*, as well as identifies the *SEF* features. The FEEC extracts features

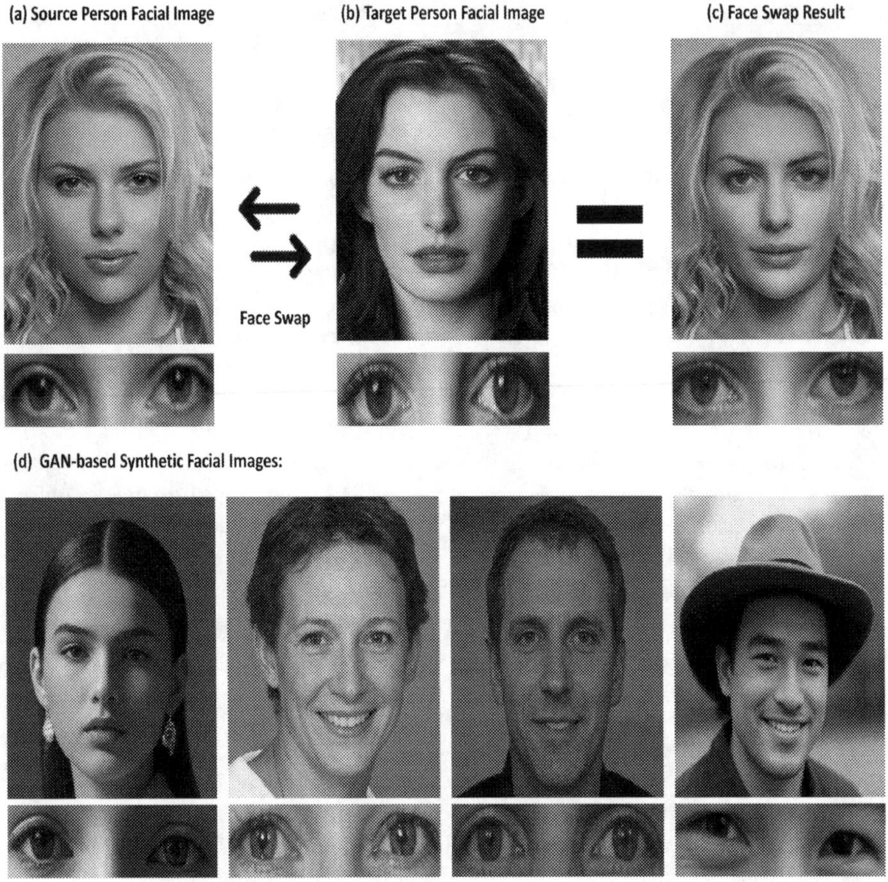

Fig. 1. Samples of Real and DeepFake Facial Images with their Reflective Elements. (a) and (b) are both Real, (c) is a DeepFake Face Generated Using the Face Swapper Online Tool [11], and Facial Images in (d) are GAN-based Synthetic Faces From [2,15].

from the *CSH* images, measures the right and left corneal highlights consistency (CHC), embeds additional *SEF* features, and classifies the input facial images as fake or real. We use Siamese Convolutional Neural Networks (SCNN) with various configurable neural network backbones, including ResNet-50-V2 [8], VGG-16 [29], Xception [3], and DenseNet-201 [10], for the feature extraction. We have conducted experiments with various GAN-generated DeepFake datasets to validate the accuracy of CHIEFS. The results show that CHIEFS achieves 99.00% accuracy in detecting highly realistic DeepFake facial images. Further, the modular design of CHIEFS renders itself as a complementary DeepFake detection module for any existing tools to limit the potential harm from DeepFake.

The main contributions of this work include:

- A new facial images dataset is collected and annotated for corneal reflection segmentation and DeepFake detection applications.
- A ML method is proposed to build an ensemble with various facial reflection features instead of a single feature.
- We study the impact of environmental factors on reflectance by collecting various parameters such as color and illumination conditions.
- We made modular designs for feature extraction and embedding to make it portable to other existing tools as a complementary solution module.

The remainder of this paper is organized as follows. Section 2 describes the existing DeepFake detection methods. Section 3 explains the design of CHIEFS. Section 4 discusses the experiment setups and results. Section 5 concludes the paper.

2   Related Work

This section discusses the current GAN-generated DeepFake detection methods and their limitations. Recently, several works have been proposed for DeepFake images detection. For instance, [21] presented a shallow learning method that fused spatial and spectrum features from an image to capture the up-sampling artifacts of DeepFake faces. [21] achieved 87% average accuracy on the Face-Forensics++ dataset and AUC rates of 76.88% and 66.16% on the Celeb-DF and DFDC datasets, respectively. Mo et al. [23] proposed a CNN-based Deep-Fake images detection method that transformed the input image into residuals and fed the resulting residuals into three-layer groups where each group was composed of a convolutional layer with rectified linear activation function and a max-pooling layer. Next, the last group's output feature maps were aggregated and fed into two fully connected layers. Finally, the softmax layer was used to produce the output probability. The proposed method achieved 99.4% accuracy in detecting real facial images from CELEBA- HQ dataset [12], and DeepFake images from the fake face images database generated by [12]. Nguyen et al. [24] also developed a multi-task DeepFake images detection approach which performed classification and segmentation using an autoencoder model containing an encoder and a Y-shaped decoder. The activation of the encoded features was used for classification. The output of one branch of the decoder was used for segmentation, and the output of the second branch was used to reconstruct the input data. Their model achieved 92.60% average accuracy on the FaceForensics dataset and 68% average accuracy on the FaceForensics++ dataset.

Furthermore, several methods have exploited the eyes' visual features for DeepFake image detection. For example, [22] identified GAN-synthesised faces through the eyes' inconsistent iris colors or missing corneal specular reflections. However, such artifacts have been improved in the recent DeepFake generation models. Similarly, Hu et al. [9] also proposed a GAN-synthesized faces detection method that used the inconsistency of the corneal specular highlights between the two synthesized eyes, assuming that two eyes looking at the same scene, their corneal specular highlights should show high similarities. This method can distinguish between the real and GAN-synthesized faces when light sources are visible to both eyes, and the eyes are distant from the light source. However, when these two conditions are defied, [9] will raise many false positives. [7] presented a DeepFake detection method based on irregular pupil shapes. This method can be effective on a specific dataset, but it will result in wrong predictions when the pupil shapes are non-elliptical in the real faces or there are occlusions on the pupil.

CHIEFS is designed to efficiently detect sophisticated DeepFakes using similarity and consistency of corneal-specular reflections with multiple surrounding semantics, such as illumination and environmental conditions, that are hard to counterfeit. It also coordinates various features (e.g., colors, edge, textures, etc.) of *CSH* images. It embeds surrounding environmental factors, such as indoor/outdoor, bright/dark, and light strength, and checks the ensemble with the reflectance.

3   CHIEFS Architecture

CHIEFS is an ML-based DeepFake detection technology that analyzes facial images' corneal-specular highlights consistency (CHC) and checks the ensemble of the highlights with multiple surrounding environmental factors (SEF). CHIEFS is designed in a hierarchical structure, and its components are separated into three modules. Training Data Collection and Annotation (TDCA), Highlights and Environmental Factors Detection (HEFD), and Feature Extraction, Embedding, and Classification (FEEC) modules in Fig. 2. The modular structure of CHIEFS allows agile updates of every module, like adding new features and enhancements according to specific use cases, as well as making CHIEFS available as a complementary DeepFake detection module for other existing tools.

3.1   Training Data Collection and Annotation (TDCA)

Current DeepFake detection datasets, such as UADFV [34], FaceForensics++ [27], Celeb-DF [20], and DFDC [5] do not contain the *CSH* annotation or facial image environmental factors information. Therefore, the main responsibility of *the TDCA module in Fig.* 2(a) is to create CHIEFS-DFD dataset [1] by collecting and annotating real and GAN-generated DeepFake facial images. We manually label the right and left *CSH* and provide the facial image-specific *SEF* information using the VGG Image Annotator (VIA) software [6]. The CHIEFS-DFD dataset contains 1,285 facial images in high resolution. 716 real facial images were collected from different datasets, including Flickr Faces HQ (FFHQ) dataset [14], Celeb-DF dataset, FaceForensics++ dataset, and DFDC dataset. Additionally, 569 GAN-generated DeepFake facial images were acquired

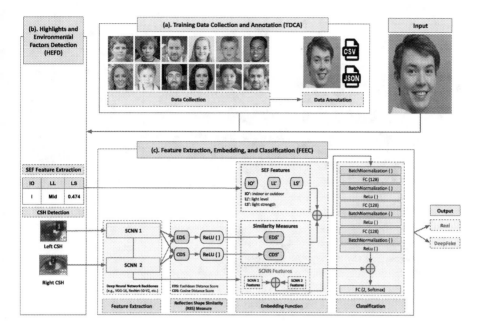

Fig. 2. The CHIEFS Architecture Block-diagram.

from various DeepFake detection datasets and human visual DeepFake generation tools, such as StyleGAN2 [15], StyleGAN3 [13], FSGAN [25], DeepFaceLab
[26], and FaceShifter [18].

As illustrated in Fig. 3 (a), the CHIEFS-DFD dataset contains DeepFake and
real facial images in high resolutions with different environmental parameters,
including illumination conditions, background colors, indoor or outdoor settings,
face pose orientations, age, ethnicity, and appearances (e.g., wearing makeup
and accessories). As demonstrated in Fig. 3 (b) and Fig. 3 (c), the CHIEFS-
DFD-dataset contains two types of annotations. The *CSH* region annotation
in Fig. 3 (b) defines the shapes and locations of *CSH* and classifies them into
right-reflection and left-reflection classes. The *Image Annotation* in Fig. 3 (c)
identifies the image label (either Real or DeepFake), along with *SEF*, including
indoor or outdoor (IO), light level (LL), and light strength (LS). The CHIEFS-
DFD dataset contains the 2,570 annotated *CSH* segmentation masks for 1,285
facial images (two eyes per facial image). In addition, 959 images (74.63%) are
labeled as indoor, and 362 images (28.17%) are labeled as outdoor. Furthermore,
collecting and analyzing the distribution of CHIEFS-DFD dataset facial images'
LS values (explained in Subsect. 3.2) results in different LL classes (806 mid
images (62.72%), 258 low images (20.07%), and 221 high images (17.19%)).

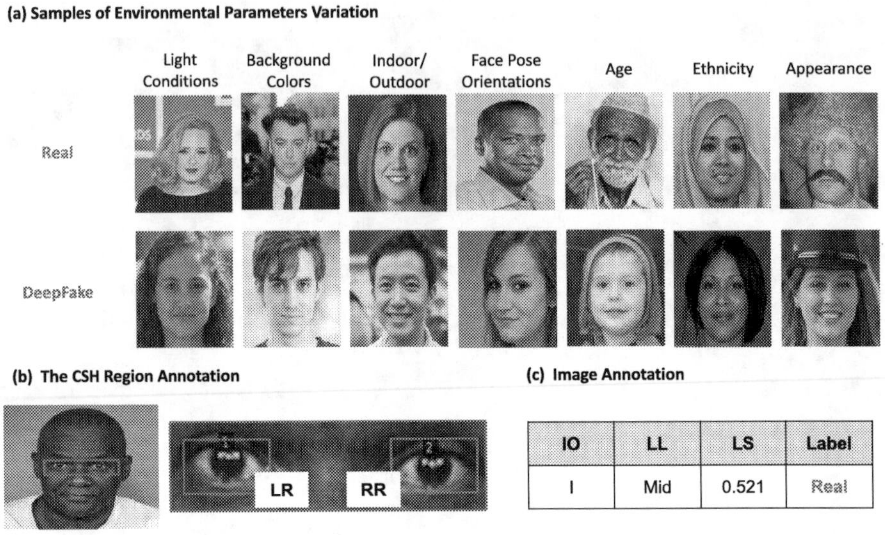

(a) Samples of Environmental Parameters Variation

(b) The CSH Region Annotation   **(c) Image Annotation**

IO	LL	LS	Label
I	Mid	0.521	Real

Fig. 3. Environmental Parameter Samples and Annotations in CHIEFS-DFD Dataset.

3.2 Highlights and Environmental Factors Detection (HEFD)

The HEFD module in Fig. 2*(b)* performs two major tasks, including *SEF* feature extraction and *CSH* detection. The *SEF* parameters include *IO*, *LS*, and *LL*. We train a MobileNet-V2 model on the Dense Indoor and Outdoor Depth (DIODE) dataset [32] and labeled facial images from the CHIEFS-DFD dataset (total 20,420 images) to classify the *IO* of an input image. To calculate the *LS*, we convert the input image's color space into a LAB format. The *L* channel is independent of color information in the LAB color space and only encodes intensity. The other two channels *A* and *B* encode color. Then, we extract the *L* channel and normalize it by dividing all pixel values by the maximum pixel value to have an *LS* value of the input image. Using the *LS* value, we identify an *LL* into the low, mid, and high classes (e.g., according to the *LS* distribution, the *LL* is a low if *LS* is less than 0.419, high if *LS* is greater than 0.637, and a mid if it is in between). To detect the right and left reflections, we train the *CSH* detection model using the MobileNetV2-SSDLite [28] to detect the bounding boxes of right and left *CSH* regions and class labels.

3.3 Feature Extraction, Embedding, and Classification (FEEC)

Using the right and left *CSH* images and the *SEF* extracted from the HEFD module Sect. (3.2), ***the FEEC module in Fig.*** 2*(c)* performs four primary functions, including deep hierarchical feature extraction using Siamese Convolutional Neural Network (SCNN) model with configurable neural network backbones, reflection shape similarity (RSS) measure, similarity measures (*RSS*), environmental factors (*SEF*), and CSH features embedding, and classification.

Feature Extraction: As shown in Fig. 2 (c), two SCNN models with the same weights and network architecture receive the right and left *CSH* images in parallel. Various configurable neural network backbones can be used for feature extraction, including VGG-16, Xception, ResNet-50-V2, and DenseNet-201. The two SCNN models use feedforwards to extract features using a global max-pooling layer by removing the fully-connected layer at the top of every network ($include_top$ = False). We do not need activation and classes because we only use the backbone models for feature extraction. Then, we use the right and left *CSH* features to measure *RSS* using euclidean and cosine distance scores.

Reflection Shape Similarity (RSS) Measure: *CSH* can be detected in various shapes, which can be deformed in different colors according to illumination conditions and blended into the background. Furthermore, *CSH* can be occluded by glasses, eyelids, or eyelashes, and only a tiny portion of the reflection can be visible. Hence, the similarity measures of a single factor, such as the shape or color of the *CSH* alone, cannot be a strong indicator for classifying DeepFake or real images. We measure the similarity scores using the extracted feature vectors, which contain multiple features, including color, edge, and the texture of the *CSH* images. We measure both Euclidean distance scores (EDS) and cosine distance scores (CDS) to statistically compare the similarity between two extracted feature vectors and find the geometric differences between right and left *CSH* images. The EDS is defined as:

$$d\left(A, B\right) = \sqrt{\sum_{i=1}^{n} \left(A_i - B_i\right)^2} \tag{1}$$

where n is the number of elements of the feature vectors, A and B are the corresponding *CSH* image vectors. d is a numerical value representing the Euclidean distance between A and B. The more similar *CSH* images, the EDS converges to 0. We also compute CDS, which is defined as:

$$\cos(A, B) = \frac{\sum_{i=1}^{n} A_i B_i}{\sqrt{\sum_{i=1}^{n} \left(A_i\right)^2} \sqrt{\sum_{i=1}^{n} \left(B_i\right)^2}} \tag{2}$$

If A and B are identical, the $\cos(A, B) = 1$. Otherwise, if they are completely different $\cos(A, B) = -1$. Thus, numbers between 0 and 1 indicate a similarity score, and numbers between -1 and 0 indicate a dissimilarity score. We applied the ReLU activation function to the EDS and CDS to avoid vanishing gradient problems while training our classifiers. The output [CDS, EDS] represents the semantic similarity between the projected representations of the two input *CSH* images.

Embedding Similarity Measures and Environmental Factors: In addition to the reflection shape similarity (RSS) measure, we have designed similarity measures and environmental factors embedding function, which takes similarity measures [CDS, EDS], *SEF* features, and extracted (right and left) CSH features. Taking [IO, LL, LS] values from the input and annotated *SEF* values from the TDCA during training or from HEFD during testing, the similarity measures and environmental factors embedding function creates adjusted *SEF* values such as [IO', LL', LS']. Merging them with the similarity measures [CDS', EDS'] creates a row of mixed values [CDS', EDS', IO', LL', LS'] as an output. Finally, it takes vectors of (right and left) *CSH* images features and combines them in a vector for classification.

Classification: As illustrated in Fig. 2, the classification module classifies the input image, either real or DeepFake, by taking features from the embedding facility. We defined the classification network with a sequence of five blocks. The first block consists of a single BatchNormalization layer that normalizes its inputs ([CDS', EDS', IO', LL', LS']) by applying a transformation that maintains the mean output close to 0 and the output standard deviation close to 1. The following three blocks are similar. Every block consists of a sequence of a fully connected (*fc*) layer with 128 nodes, a single BatchNormalization layer followed by a ReLU activation function. The BatchNormalization layer centers the learned features from the fully connected layer on 0, while the ReLU activation uses 0 as a pivot to keep or drop the activated channels [4]. The fifth block consists of a concatenate layer and a fully connected layer. The concatenate layer merges the fourth block's output tensor with the CSH features vector. The fully connected layer (predication layer) returns a probability distribution with two nodes and a softmax activation function for binary classification. A binary cross-entropy probabilistic loss function was used to compute the cross-entropy loss between actual and predicted labels and to measure the model's accuracy during training and testing. Eventually, it creates a binary classification result (either real or DeepFake).

4   Evaluations

We conducted extensive experiments using CHIEFS-DFD datasets to evaluate the performance under real-world scenarios and compare the accuracy with current state-of-the-art (SOTA) DeepFake detection methods. We demonstrate one of the environmental parameter classification results (indoor or outdoor (IO)) and evaluate *CSH* regions detection. Finally, we present the classification performances with the CHIEFS-DFD datasets using different feature extraction backbone models and various similarity measures and environmental factors.

4.1   Evaluation of Indoor/Outdoor Classification

The primary purpose of this experiment is to assess the CHIEFS accuracy in classifying input facial images to either indoor or outdoor environments. We combined the CHIEFS and DIODE datasets with training the indoor/outdoor classifier. Among the 20,420 images, we labeled indoor (50%) and outdoor (50%) images equally and divided 16,336 images (80%) for the training set and 4,084 images (20%) for validation and testing sets. We used MobileNetV2 inverted residuals and linear bottlenecks neural network with binary cross-entropy loss function, dense layer of two nodes, and softmax activation at the top of the network to train the indoor/outdoor classifier. All images were pre-processed and scaled between -1 and 1. We used the Glorot normal initializer from the Keras library for the default weight initialization. We trained the model on the GPU environment for 18 h using the Google Colab Compute Engine (GCE) VM backend with (NVIDIA Tesla-P100-PCIE-16 GB) model for 512 iterations with an RMSprop optimizer, batch size of 32, and learning rate of 0.001. The early stopping criterion was used with patience set to 32 to stop training when a monitored metric (validation loss) stopped improving. The indoor/outdoor classifier achieves a 94.00% success rate in predicting indoor and outdoor images. The result indicates that CHIEFS can efficiently classify input facial images into indoor or outdoor categories.

4.2   Evaluation of CSH Regions Detection

We evaluated the CHIEFS accuracy in detecting *CSH* regions from the facial images. We split the CHIEFS dataset (1,285 facial images containing 2,570 annotated *CSH* segmentation masks) into 1,028 images (80%) for the training set and 257 images (20%) for validation and testing sets. We used the MobileNet-V2 feature extractor model and the Single Shot Detector (SSD) to detect and return the bounding boxes of right and left *CSH* regions and class labels. We trained the *CSH* detection model on the GPU environment for 6 h using the Google Colab Compute Engine (GCE) VM backend with (NVIDIA Tesla-P100-PCIE-16GB) model for 1,028 iterations. We use the standard RMSprop optimizer by configuring decay and momentum to 0.9, the standard weight decay to 0.00004, an initial learning rate of 0.045, a learning rate of 0.98 per epoch, and a batch size of 32. The result demonstrates that the overall mean average precision (mAP) of detecting right and left *CSH* regions is 90.53%, the right-reflection average precision (AP) is (90.81%), and the left-reflection AP is (90.26%), both are high enough for the *CSH* detection task.

Fig. 4. Sample of the CHIEFS-DFD Testing Dataset Classification Result.

Table 1. Classification Performance Comparison on CHIEFS-DFD Dataset with Different Backbone Models for Feature Extraction.

Backbone	Accuracy	Loss
CHIEFS (DenseNet-201)	96.00%	0.592
CHIEFS (Xception)	98.00%	0.242
CHIEFS (VGG-16)	98.75%	0.203
CHIEFS (ResNet-50-V2)	**99.00%**	**0.160**

4.3   Classification Using Different Backbone Models for Feature Extraction

We evaluated the CHIEFS method with four different neural network backbones for feature extraction, including ResNet-50-V2, VGG-16, Xception, and DenseNet-201, using the CHIEFS-DFD dataset. After splitting the dataset with an 80:20 (training vs. validation) ratio. We trained the models on the GPU environment using the Google Colab Compute Engine (GCE) VM backend with (NVIDIA Tesla-P100-PCIE-16GB) model for 1,024 iterations with RMSprop optimizer, batch size of 8, and a learning rate of 1e−5. The early stopping criterion was used with patience set to 64 epochs to stop training when a monitored metric (validation loss) stopped improving. The results in Table 1 show the classification accuracy and loss of the CHIEFS method with different backbone models for feature extraction on the CHIEFS-DFD testing datasets. Overall, CHIEFS performs well with different feature extractors. For example, CHIEFS (ResNet-50-V2) is the best in both accuracy (99.00%) and loss (0.160). CHIEFS (VGG-16) is the second-best in both accuracy (98.75%) and loss (0.203). CHIEFS (Xception) is the third-best with accuracy (98.00%) and loss (0.242). Finally, CHIEFS (DenseNet-201)'s accuracy is the least (96.00%), and its loss is the highest (0.592). Figure 4 presents samples of the CHIEFS-DFD testing dataset classification results. CHIEFS detects DeepFake images with various face pose orientations, age, ethnicity, and appearances, such as makeup and accessories. Results indicate that CHIEFS performs well on realistic human visual DeepFake images.

4.4   Classification Using Different Feature Classifiers

Using the CHIEFS-DFD dataset, we assess different feature classifiers for CHIEFS (ResNet-50-V2). Table 2 shows that using all features, including right and left *CSH*, *RSS* ([CDS', EDS']), and *SEF* ([IO', LL', LS']) for classification achieves the best performance for CHIEFS (ResNet-50-V2) (99.00%) in accuracy. However, using a single *RSS* feature alone, such as [CDS'] or [EDS'], results in low accuracy (around 89.92%) with [CDS'] and (86.05%) with [EDS']. It also demonstrates that using right and left *CSH* features achieves high accuracy (93.00%) compared with other single components such as [CDS'] and [EDS']. When *SEF* features are used with the *CSH* features, the accuracy improves to (97.00%). Similarly, when *SEF* features are used with [CDS'] and [EDS'], the accuracy also improves to (94.00%) and (96.00%), respectively. The results indicate that using a single feature alone is not a good idea, and combining various features can improve performance greatly. In addition, the *SEF* features significantly impact accuracy improvement.

Table 2. Classification Performance Comparison with CHIEFS-DFD Dataset Using Different Feature Classifiers (i.e., CSH, CDS', EDS', IO', LL', LS') for CHIEFS (ResNet-50-V2).

Feature Classifiers	Accuracy
[CDS']	89.92%
[CDS', IO', LL', LS']	94.00%
[EDS']	86.05%
[EDS', IO', LL', LS']	96.00%
[CDS', EDS']	91.47%
[CSH]	93.00%
[CSH, IO', LL', LS']	97.00%
[CSH, CDS', EDS', IO', LL', LS']	**99.00%**

5   Conclusions

We proposed a novel ML-based DeepFake detection technology named CHIEFS (Corneal-Specular Highlights Imaging for Enhancing Fake-Face Spotter). We focus on the most reflective area of a human face, eyes, using *CSH* images. We verified the hypothesis that DeepFake technologies struggle to fake reflective components in their counterfeits by using various classifiers with environmental factors embedding. We designed and implemented feature extractors, classifiers, and embedding functions using advanced DNN architectures and tested them with different GAN-generated DeepFake datasets. The experimental results show that CHIEFS achieved high accuracy 99.00% in detecting sophisticated GAN-generated DeepFake images. Note that the modular design of CHIEFS renders itself as a complementary DeepFake detection module for any existing tools.

References

1. Chiefs-DFD dataset (2022). https://github.com/READFake/CHIEFS-DFD-Dataset. Accessed 26 Nov 2022
2. Lexica stable diffusion search engine (2022). https://lexica.art/. Accessed 24 Nov 2022
3. Chollet, F.: Xception: deep learning with depthwise separable convolutions. In: Proceedings of the IEEE Conference on Computer Vision and Pattern Recognition, pp. 1251–1258 (2017)
4. Chollet, F.: Deep Learning with Python. Simon and Schuster, New York (2021)
5. Dolhansky, B., et al.: The DeepFake detection challenge (DFDC) dataset. arXiv preprint arXiv:2006.07397 (2020)
6. Dutta, A., Zisserman, A.: The VIA annotation software for images, audio and video. In: Proceedings of the 27th ACM International Conference on Multimedia. MM 2019, ACM, New York, NY, USA (2019). https://doi.org/10.1145/3343031.3350535

7. Guo, H., Hu, S., Wang, X., Chang, M.C., Lyu, S.: Eyes tell all: irregular pupil shapes reveal GAN-generated faces (2021)
8. He, K., Zhang, X., Ren, S., Sun, J.: Identity mappings in deep residual networks. In: Leibe, B., Matas, J., Sebe, N., Welling, M. (eds.) ECCV 2016. LNCS, vol. 9908, pp. 630–645. Springer, Cham (2016). https://doi.org/10.1007/978-3-319-46493-0_38
9. Hu, S., Li, Y., Lyu, S.: Exposing GAN-generated faces using inconsistent corneal specular highlights. arXiv preprint arXiv:2009.11924 (2020)
10. Huang, G., Liu, Z., van der Maaten, L., Weinberger, K.Q.: Densely connected convolutional networks (2016). https://doi.org/10.48550/ARXIV.1608.06993, https://arxiv.org/abs/1608.06993
11. Icons8: Face Swapper (2022). https://icons8.com/swapper
12. Karras, T., Aila, T., Laine, S., Lehtinen, J.: Progressive growing of GANs for improved quality, stability, and variation. CoRR abs/1710.10196 (2017). http://arxiv.org/abs/1710.10196
13. Karras, T., et al.: Alias-free generative adversarial networks. In: Proceedings of the NeurIPS (2021)
14. Karras, T., Laine, S., Aila, T.: A style-based generator architecture for generative adversarial networks. In: Proceedings of the IEEE/CVF Conference on Computer Vision and Pattern Recognition, pp. 4401–4410 (2019)
15. Karras, T., Laine, S., Aittala, M., Hellsten, J., Lehtinen, J., Aila, T.: Analyzing and improving the image quality of StyleGAN. In: Proceedings of the CVPR (2020)
16. Korshunova, I., Shi, W., Dambre, J., Theis, L.: Fast face-swap using convolutional neural networks. In: Proceedings of the IEEE International Conference on Computer Vision, pp. 3677–3685 (2017)
17. Le, B.M., Woo, S.S.: Exploring the asynchronous of the frequency spectra of GAN-generated facial images. CoRR abs/2112.08050 (2021). https://arxiv.org/abs/2112.08050
18. Li, L., Bao, J., Yang, H., Chen, D., Wen, F.: FaceShifter: towards high fidelity and occlusion aware face swapping (2020)
19. Li, Y., Chang, M.C., Lyu, S.: In Ictu oculi: Exposing AI generated fake face videos by detecting eye blinking. arXiv preprint arXiv:1806.02877 (2018)
20. Li, Y., Yang, X., Sun, P., Qi, H., Lyu, S.: Celeb-DF: A large-scale challenging dataset for DeepFake forensics. In: 2020 IEEE/CVF Conference on Computer Vision and Pattern Recognition (CVPR), pp. 3204–3213 (2020). https://doi.org/10.1109/CVPR42600.2020.00327
21. Liu, H., et al.: Spatial-phase shallow learning: Rethinking face forgery detection in frequency domain (2021)
22. Matern, F., Riess, C., Stamminger, M.: Exploiting visual artifacts to expose Deep-Fakes and face manipulations. In: 2019 IEEE Winter Applications of Computer Vision Workshops (WACVW), pp. 83–92. IEEE (2019)
23. Mo, H., Chen, B., Luo, W.: Fake faces identification via convolutional neural network. In: Proceedings of the 6th ACM Workshop on Information Hiding and Multimedia Security, p. 43–47. IH& MMSec 2018, Association for Computing Machinery, New York, NY, USA (2018). https://doi.org/10.1145/3206004.3206009
24. Nguyen, H.H., Fang, F., Yamagishi, J., Echizen, I.: Multi-task learning for detecting and segmenting manipulated facial images and videos. In: 2019 IEEE 10th International Conference on Biometrics Theory, Applications and Systems (BTAS), pp. 1–8 (2019). https://doi.org/10.1109/BTAS46853.2019.9185974
25. Nirkin, Y., Keller, Y., Hassner, T.: FSGAN: subject agnostic face swapping and reenactment. In: Proceedings of the IEEE International Conference on Computer Vision, pp. 7184–7193 (2019)

26. Petrov, I., et al.: DeepFaceLab: a simple, flexible and extensible face swapping framework. arXiv preprint arXiv:2005.05535 (2020)
27. Rossler, A., Cozzolino, D., Verdoliva, L., Riess, C., Thies, J., Nießner, M.: Face-Forensics++: learning to detect manipulated facial images. In: Proceedings of the IEEE/CVF International Conference on Computer Vision, pp. 1–11 (2019)
28. Sandler, M., Howard, A., Zhu, M., Zhmoginov, A., Chen, L.C.: MobileNetV2: inverted residuals and linear bottlenecks. In: Proceedings of the IEEE Conference on Computer Vision and Pattern Recognition, pp. 4510–4520 (2018)
29. Simonyan, K., Zisserman, A.: Very deep convolutional networks for large-scale image recognition. arXiv preprint arXiv:1409.1556 (2014)
30. Sun, Z., Han, Y., Hua, Z., Ruan, N., Jia, W.: Improving the efficiency and robustness of DeepFakes detection through precise geometric features (2021)
31. Tariq, S., Lee, S., Kim, H., Shin, Y., Woo, S.S.: Detecting both machine and human created fake face images in the wild. In: Proceedings of the 2nd International Workshop on Multimedia Privacy and Security, pp. 81–87 (2018)
32. Vasiljevic, I., et al.: DIODE: a dense indoor and outdoor depth dataset. CoRR abs/1908.00463 (2019). http://arxiv.org/abs/1908.00463
33. Woo, S., et al.: Add: frequency attention and multi-view based knowledge distillation to detect low-quality compressed DeepFake images. In: Proceedings of the AAAI Conference on Artificial Intelligence, vol. 36, pp. 122–130 (2022)
34. Yang, X., Li, Y., Lyu, S.: Exposing deep fakes using inconsistent head poses. In: 2019 IEEE International Conference on Acoustics, Speech and Signal Processing (ICASSP). ICASSP 2019, pp. 8261–8265. IEEE (2019)

Cybercrime and Privacy

Where is the Virtual Machine Within CPYTHON?

Guillaume Bonfante and Anuyan Ithayakumar[(✉)]

Carbone Team, Lorraine University - CNRS - LORIA, Nancy, France
anuyan.ithayakumar@depinfonancy.net

Abstract. It is known that code interpreters (also known as Virtual Machine (VM)) may be used for binary code obfuscation. For instance, this is the underlying technique on which the packer VMProtect is based. Our long-term objective is to attack such obfuscations. Here, we concentrate on the identification of the implementation of the VM. It is quite standard to consider that a VM is implemented through a single fetch and a single dispatch mechanism, see for instance [SBP18]. But in practice, such a hypothesis is very restrictive. For instance, the standard implementation of PYTHON does not fulfill it. We give a generic model of virtual machine implementation with an experimental validation.

1 Introduction

This work finds its origin in a paper by Salwan, Bardin and Potet [SBP18] dealing with virtual machine based code obfuscations. We recall that a virtual machine, also known as an interpreter, is a program that runs a program written for a guest processor on a host processor. In the sequel, as Jones does [Jon97], we use the words "processor" and "machine" as synonyms.

When a program is run through a virtual machine, what we may see is actually an interpreter running. Without further analysis, that means we observe a big non informative loop. That is the key idea behind obfuscation by virtualization, a method used by several packers among which we mention VMProtect addressed in [SBP18].

What happens for a program such as cpython[1]? Roughly speaking, when running a program written in PYTHON, say hello.py, cpython will compile it into a bytecode program (potentially as a hello.pyc file) and then run an interpreter on the produced bytecode. In other words, cpython involves an interpreter. Accordingly, we tried to apply naively the method mentioned above, but could not manage to extract correctly the behavior of the code. Why does a basic, non obfuscated program resists to the analysis? The answer lies in the shape of the interpreter that is far more complex than supposed. Our main contribution is a more generic model of interpreters together with its associated tool.

---

[1] the standard application to run PYTHON programs. Those can be run via other programs such as pypy, but that latter one is not based on an interpreter.

G.-V. Jourdan et al. (Eds.): FPS 2022, LNCS 13877, pp. 175–191, 2023.
https://doi.org/10.1007/978-3-031-30122-3_11

So, the general question can be reformulated as follows. Given a program, does it contain a virtual machine? Actually, we will ask for some evidences in case of a positive answer. More precisely, interpreters involve the presence of a fetch mechanism (the operation that reads the bytecode) and a dispatch one (the one that switches to the correct handler). Our method provides both.

We made the largest part of our experiments on cpython. We chose it for two main reasons. First, given that its source code is available, it is possible to extract a clean ground truth compared to obfuscated binaries/malwares for which that is not easy. We think it is an important feature for the evaluation. Second, as we will show in Sect. 6, cpython exists in very different forms running different bytecodes. There are several implementations such as python2.7, python3.8, etc. and each implementation can be compiled with different options. To conclude, cpython offers an interesting variety of interpreters.

Nevertheless, we do not use[2] any PYTHON's specific features. Our aim is to have a generic model of an interpreter. Actually, we made successful preliminary tests of our tool on "JerryScript" that is a lightweight javascript interpreter intended to run on constrained devices. However, we consider our verifications are not mature enough to be fully reported. Thus we stick here on PYTHON.

Finally, our ultimate goal being a fast virtual machine identification analyzer that would allow its usage in a Security Operation Center (SOC), we restricted ourselves to efficient algorithms. We only "allow" lightweight methods with linear time complexity as horizon.

Searching for a virtual machine has already been addressed in the past as we have mentioned at the beginning of our introduction [SBP18]. The main differences with previous works is that we are not on the same playing field. For instance, the closest to our approach are Sharif, Lanzi, Giffin and Lee in [SLGL09]. Their analysis is based on a purely dynamic tool. Their target is clearly the identification of the instruction pointer. For that, their idea is to identify the variables in the program containing the interpreter and extract the variables having a behaviour characteristic of the instruction pointer of an interpreter.

Let us also mention the work by Liang, Li, Zeng and Fang in [LLZF18]. They use a method targeting the dispatch instruction as we do. However, their approach is restricted to the one-dispatch model that is clearly insufficient[3].

Finally, in [KGM17], Kalysch, Götzfriedand, Müller present an other interesting tool: Vmattack that is however limited to stack-based virtual machines. Vmattack relies on different modules to filter out instructions belonging solely to the interpreter. Among these modules, clustering analysis, via a dynamic analysis, allows to build groups of repeating instructions and to infer their roles in the program. Again, the approach, though interesting, is not as general as the one we propose.

---

[2] at least intentionally.
[3] For threaded interpreters, such as cpython when compiled with --with-computed-gotos flag.

After the introductory Sect. 2, we present our general model in Sect. 3. Then, in Sect. 4, we give an explicit model for the X86 host processor. Section 5 presents our implementation and Sect. 6 describes result we got for cpython.

2 Machines, Programs and Control Flow Graphs

We present briefly the general notions that are used all along the contribution. We choose on purpose a lightweight description, in other words, at some points, we skip some technical details. We refer the reader to the book by Jones [Jon97] for a deeper presentation of the notion of machines and to reverse-engineering books (such as [DGBJ14]) for control flow graphs.

A *machine* is characterized by a set of instructions together with their semantics. Next to that, we suppose that the machine works as follows: at each step, the machine reads the current instruction via an *instruction pointer*, then modify *data* according to the semantics of the instruction, and ends updating the instruction pointer. The state of the machine is the datum composed of the data and the instruction pointer.

In what follows, we are mainly concerned by two machines, the X86's one and the machine that lies behind CPYTHON. The X86 family of processors enter the above mentioned model. The instruction pointer is rip and the data is the virtual memory.

One of the implementations for the evaluation of PYTHON based programs is the CPYTHON interpreter (which itself can be compiled on different processor architectures and in particular on the X86's one). The interpreter CPYTHON defines a notion of *bytecode* that is a concrete[4] set of instructions. At each step, the current instruction is executed as presented above. The structure of the data is too complex to be presented here. Just keep in mind that it lies in the host processsor's memory.

One should take care that the bytecode is specific to CPYTHON and that it changes along the different versions of PYTHON (See the online documentation https://docs.python.org/3/library/dis.html, "No guarantees are made that bytecode will not be added, removed, or changed between versions of Python."). For that reason, we worked with quite different versions of PYTHON, namely 2.7, 3.8 and 3.11.

Instructions may have an internal structure. We suppose that they are decomposed in opcodes (the action to be performed: "mov", "push", "load", etc.) and arguments (the part of the data to be read/written: "rax", "1234", "[0x12]"). Both X86 and cpython instruction sets follow that schema.

A *program* is two fold. The source program is a human readable object that is *compiled* into its binary counterpart that relies on the instruction set of some given machine M. The (binary) program is *launched* on the machine, meaning the state of the machine is initialized according to some *specific*[5] rules. Then,

---

[4] Here meaning that there is a syntax.

[5] Actually given by the Operating System.

the machine is run according to its own semantics. Globally speaking a program will read inputs $\vec{x}$ and output a result denoted $[\![P]\!]_M(\vec{x})$ depending on $\vec{x}$.

Running a program leads to the notion of *trace*. It is the sequence of instructions that have been executed after the initialization of the program. More precisely, it is the sequence of values of the instruction pointer met during execution.

From a trace, one defines a dynamic control flow graph as follows: nodes are addresses (or identifiers for a bytecode) identifying the instructions and we set an edge between node a and node b if b has been executed just after a in the trace.

One should be aware that a trace depends on the input. More generally speaking, the control flow graph unifies all the graphs obtained via traces.

Actually, we will group together any node a and b such that b is the unique son of a and a is the unique father of b. This will group instructions into what is known as *basic block*.

3   The Heart of a Virtual Machine

Definition 1. *Given two machines M_1 and M_2, a virtual machine of M_2 is a program I running on the host M_1 that outputs the same result as one would get running directly on M_2: in other words, for any program P for M_2 and any input $\vec{x}$, we have $[\![I]\!]_{M_1}(P, \vec{x}) = [\![P]\!]_{M_2}(\vec{x})$.*

In other words, the program P meant for M_2 can be run on M_1 via I, also called an interpreter in the literature.

Let us see in more details how and interpreter can be implemented. Naturally, there is not one solution, but let us look at the way it can be done in practice. Roughly speaking, the following shows a general pattern (that is the one within [SLGL09]).

```
while (!interrupt) {
    inst = code[vip];                   (1)
    opcode = extract_opcode(inst);      (2)
    switch (opcode){                    (3)
      case OP1: function1(inst);        (4...)
      case OP2: function2(inst);
      ...
    }
}
```

In other words, at each step, (1) the instruction is *fetched* within data, then, (2) is decomposed (opcode on one side, arguments on the other one) and then, depending on the instruction (3), the data is modified (4) via some specific functions, next called handlers. Figure 1 presents the *control flow graph* that one may get after compilation of the preceding interpreter.

A *fetch* is the (not unique in the following) instruction block corresponding to (1), that is where the virtual instruction is read. The dispatch is the one corresponding to (3), that is the instruction in charge of running the right handler.

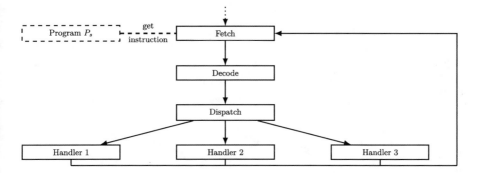

Fig. 1. 1-fetch/1-dispatch VM example.

Actually, in the following, we will be even more precise. Fetches and dispatches are identified to some specific instructions within their block.

Definition 2 (1-fetch/1-dispatch). *We say that a virtual machine follows the 1-fetch/1-dispatch pattern whenever it contains exactly one fetch block and one dispatch block.*

This is typically the case of the interpreter of Fig. 1. However, such a model is clearly insufficient in practice. Indeed, this model does not allow to describe threaded interpreters which are omnipresent in most modern virtual machines (CPython, Google V8...). Indeed, threaded interpreters, as opposed to switch-based interpreters, allow a performance gain by eliminating the jump to the switch instruction and by taking better advantage of the branch prediction at the processor level. So, we propose a more general pattern, next called N fetch/M dispatch whose source code may follow the following pattern:

```
void interpreter(){
inst = code[vip]; // vip: virtual intruction pointer
opcode = extract_opcode(inst);
void* routine = dispatch[opcode]; //dispatch is the Direct
    Threading Table that maps an opcode to &&handler1, &&
    handler2, ...
goto *routine;

handler1:
...
... // VM state update
if (interrupt) goto exit;
inst = code[vip];
opcode = extract_opcode(inst);
routine = dispatch[opcode];
goto *routine;

handler2:
...
```

```
... // VM state update
if (interrupt) goto exit;
inst = code[vip];
opcode = extract_opcode(inst);
routine = dispatch[opcode];
goto *routine;
}
```

The entry point of the interpreter is the `interpreter` function. As above, it reads the current instruction and depending on its opcode compute its corresponding handler (`routine = ...`). Then, it gives the hand to the handler. However, compared to the previous interpreter, the handler will itself read the next instruction and compute the next handler. Thus, fetches and dispatches are duplicated. Actually, we will be a little bit more general. Handlers may contain more than one fetch and more than one dispatch.

Definition 3. *The N-fetch/M-dispatch is any interpreter whose control flow graph has the shape presented in Fig. 2.*

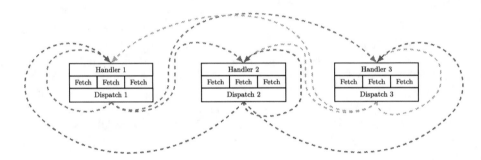

Fig. 2. N-fetches/M-dispatches VM example. Decodes are not represented. The dotted lines represent the possible jumps from each dispatch.

Concerning CPython, the compilation option `--without-computed -gotos` allows to compile the CPython interpreter as a switch-based interpreter (1-fech/1-dispatch model). The `--with-computed-gotos` compiler option allows to compile CPython as a threaded interpreter (N fetch/M dispatch)[6].

---

[6] In practice, the source code of CPython, implements both forms of interpreters: https://github.com/python/cpython/blob/main/Python/ceval.c.

Remark 1. Not all implementations enter this shape of course. For instance, one may think of duplicating dispatches for each handler. We let it for further extensions of this work.

3.1   Obfuscation via Virtualization

As mentioned in introduction, virtualization is a well known technique for program obfuscation. Indeed, a priori, the analyst will see only the interpreter running without direct access to the internal logics of the virtualized program.

To sum up, given a program P, obfuscation via virtualization consists in writing it (or to compile it) for a machine M_1. And then, to encompass P's binary form within an interpreter I for some target machine M_2, in other words, the operation consists in specializing I on P resulting in a program I_P that will essentially start the interpreter on P (see for instance [Bla] for a definition of specialization).

4   The VM Model

Targeting N fetch/M dispatch interpreters, we provide in this section a more concrete description of our model. That will cover some hypotheses on the machine, on the shape of dispatches and on the shape of fetches.

4.1   General Assumptions

First, we make the hypothesis that the size of the encoding of virtual instructions is bounded by some constant Δ. In other words, virtual instructions cannot have an arbitrary length. This seems to be a very light limitation. In the experiments, we took $\Delta = 8$ or $\Delta = 16$ bytes, knowing that 15 bytes is the maximal size of an X86 instruction.

Second, we suppose that the virtualized instructions are stored in a small number of chunks within memory. In other words, the virtual program is not split *façon puzzle*.

Third, we make the hypothesis that the control flow graph follow the shape of Fig. 2. More concretely, we suppose that dispatches and fetches are interleaved.

Fourth, to render the fact that the interpreter introduce a global loop—at each step, ...—, we suppose that it is implemented within a function. As a consequence, dispatches and fetches occur in a common function frame. This assumption will allow us to reduce the complexity of the problem. Indeed, let us suppose that we have a set of candidate dispatches. Therefore, a subset of this set is the largest group of dispatches. However, it is not realistic to study all these groups, since the number of groups evolves exponentially with the size of the set of candidate dispatches.

About Dispatches. According to what precedes, a dispatch is an instruction that performs the switch between handlers given the opcode of the instruction. We suppose that such a switch is dynamically computed. Such a switch is in general implemented with a dynamic jump (or a dynamic call). For instance, on the x86 processor, that corresponds to an instruction of the shape `jmp [rax+4*rcx]` where `rax` corresponds to the begining of a table and `rcx` to the index of the handler.

Moreover, since the dynamic jump is supposed to perform a switch, we suppose that it is followed by at least two different instructions. As a matter of facts, that prevents calls to dynamic libraries, sometimes implemented via dynamic jumps (for instance on WINDOWS), to be considered as dispatchers.

About Fetches. The fetch is supposed to extract the virtual instruction. Since, the virtual program lies in memory, that means the fetch must evaluate the value of some pointer. Technically, we suppose that the virtual instruction is stored in memory at some address E where E is an expression depending on register values and immediates. Thus, a typical fetch has the shape `mov rax, [rbx+4*rcx+0x1234]`.

This value will be used by a dispatch instruction. Let us enumerate some consequences.

First, dispatch and fetches are closely related. Actually, they form a bipartite graph: each fetch correspond to some dispatch and vice versa.

Second, fetches and dispatches are interleaved. Dispatch necessarily follows a fetch. And a fetch only occurs after the handler that itself necessarily follows dispatch. Thus,

- third, there must be a path within the control flow graph between a fetch and its corresponding dispatch(es) and vice versa and
- fourth, a path between the fetch and the dispatch cannot cross an other fetch.

Fifth, we mentioned that dispatches are in charge of the switch depending on the opcode of the virtual instruction that is read by the fetch. Thus, the semantics of a dispatch must depend on the value of its corresponding fetch(es).

Finally, we will make the hypothesis that a fetch is closely related to its corresponding dispatch. Thus, we suppose that the size of the path from a fetch to its dispatch is limited to $d_{F \to D}$ instruction blocks, where $d_{F \to D}$ is a parameter left to the algorithm.

4.2   The Machine Spectrum

We suppose we are given a program P containing a virtual machine and an associated trace $T = t_1, \ldots, t_k$. Let I_D be the set of indexes in T corresponding to dispatches and I_F be the corresponding set for fetches. Then, let $D = \{t_i \mid i \in I_D\}$ and $F = \{t_i \mid i \in I_F\}$ respectively the set of dispatches and the set of fetches. Given $i \in I_F$, let $E(t_i)$ be the value of the virtual instruction pointer used by the associated fetch. From T, we extract the sub-sequence $U = u_{i_1}, \ldots, u_{i_n}$ made only of fetches and dispatches. This sub-sequence is an alternation of fetches and dispatches (and the first element is a fetch!).

Now, given $(f, f') \in F \times F$, let us consider $\Theta(f, f') = \{i \in \mathbb{N} : u_i = f, u_{i+2} = f'\}$, that is the set of successive transitions from f to f'. Let $\sigma(f, f') = (E(u_i) - E(u_{i+2}) \mid i \in \Theta(f, f'))$ the sequence of variations of the virtual pointer. Now, we introduce the spectrum $S : F \times F \to \mathcal{F}(\mathbb{Z}, \mathbb{N})$ as follows:

$$(f, f') \mapsto (\delta \in \mathbb{Z} \mapsto \#\{i \mid \sigma(f, f')(i) = \delta\})$$

where $\#$ is the cardinal function. The spectrum is an abstract device describing the way the virtual pointer jumps within memory. We expect these jumps to be small. For instance, let the following trace (only showing fetches and dispatches)

$$U = f_1 \ d_1 \ f_2 \ d_1 \ f_1 \ d_2 \ f_1 \ d_1 \ f_2 \ d_2 \ f1 \ d_3 \ f_2 \ d_1$$
$$E = 22 \quad 24 \quad 22 \quad 28 \quad 24 \quad 26 \quad 28$$

Then, $\sigma(f_1, f_2) = (22 - 24, 28 - 24, 26 - 28)$ and thus $S(f_1, f_2) = \{-2 \to 2, +4 \to 1\}$.

Given a maximal instruction size Δ, we define the spectral matrix $\Sigma_\Delta : F \times F \to \mathbb{R}$ with

$$\Sigma_\Delta[f, f'] = \begin{cases} \dfrac{\sum_{\delta \in [-\Delta, \Delta] \setminus [0]} S(f, f')(\delta)}{\sum_{\delta \in \mathbb{Z}} S(f, f')(\delta)}, & \text{if defined} \\ 0, & \text{otherwise} \end{cases} \quad (1)$$

Thus, with the previous trace, if we consider that $\Delta = 2$, we get the following spectral matrix:

$$\Sigma_{\Delta=2} = \begin{array}{c} \\ f_1 \\ f_2 \end{array} \begin{array}{c} f_1 \ f_2 \\ \begin{pmatrix} 0 & \frac{2}{3} \\ 1 & 0 \end{pmatrix} \end{array}$$

Given two fetches f and f', the term $\Sigma_\Delta[f, f']$ of the spectral matrix compares the number of "differences between the addresses successively read by f and f' that are lower than Δ" to the "total number of executions of f followed by f'".

Therefore, for a virtual program that is contiguous in memory, without control flow instructions[7] and such that its execution trace includes all possible combinations of fetches, we can expect its spectral matrix to be the matrix with only ones.

---

[7] For instance a virtual program such that for all instruction, the next instruction to be executed is positioned at the address of the current virtual instruction $+ \Delta$.

5   VM Identification

Now we come to the operational aspects of the solution. Recall that our system is supposed to take as input a program P and to return the list of fetches/dispatches that can be extracted within P whenever they exist. To do that, we proceed in two main steps, first, we compute an (approximated) control flow graph, from which we extract fetches and dispatches.

5.1   Extraction of the CFG

The input program is run–within a sandbox if necessary–under the supervision of a `Pintool`, see Intel's documentation[8] about it. The `Pintool` outputs an execution trace, to each instruction along the computation. We register T_n:

- the current address of the (host machine) instruction,
- the opcode, source operands and target operands of the current instruction,
- addresses of memory access if any.

After that step, we get a sequence $\vec{T} = T_1, T_2, T_3, \ldots$. The program is interrupted after a while if necessary.

From the addresses recorded along $\vec{T}$, we build a (approximated) control flow graph. We then regroup nodes into instruction blocks.

5.2   Dispatch and Fetch Candidates

In a first step, since it is a necessary condition for dispatches, we extract all dynamic jumps from the CFG. We keep only dynamic jumps that are followed by at least two distinct instructions in the trace[9]. Indeed, a dispatch is supposed to perform a switch. Let us call $\mathcal{D}$ this set. For cpython, the first step leads typically to hundreds of instructions.

In a second step, we regroup candidates in $\mathcal{D}$ sharing the same function frame. Thus, that leads to a partition of $\mathcal{D} = \bigcup_{i \in C} \mathcal{D}_i$ where C denotes the set of function calls. All coming operations will be done on each of the $\mathcal{D}_i$ independently with $i \in C$, but to keep notations simple, we will write $\mathcal{D}$ for $\mathcal{D}_i$.

Fetch Mapping. For each dispatch d, we compute a set F_d of corresponding fetch candidates as follows.

First, we select all instructions that read some bytes at some non fixed address within memory.

Second, from those, we select those instructions f for which there is a path of length at most $d_{F \to D}$ within the control flow graph from f to d. By path, we

---

[8] https://www.intel.com/content/www/us/en/developer/articles/tool/pin-a-dynamic-binary-instrumentation-tool.html.

[9] In practice, once a first group of dispatches has been extracted using the following method, we use the assumption that the interpreter is within a function in order to add the dispatches that are followed by only one instruction.

mean a sequence of instructions without: calls, return instruction and dynamic jumps.

Third, to account of the dependency of the behavior of the dispatch regarding the address read by the fetch, we proceed by (reverse) tainting analysis. For that sake, for each instruction on the path between the fetch and the dispatch, we taint registers and virtual memory. A fetch is kept only if its color taints the dispatch.

Alternation Verification. So far, we got a set D of potential dispatches together with sets of potential fetches F_d for each $d \in D$. Let $F = \cup_d F_d$. Actually, a fetch may correspond to several dispatches. Thus, fetches and dispatches form a bipartite graph associating fetches to dispatches.

We have seen above, dispatches and fetches must alternate along the execution. From the candidates we got above, we must extract those for which that criterion is fulfilled. Actually, this problem has more than one solution in general (for instance, two empty sets is a solution). Thus, we turn it into an optimisation problem: we maximize the number of fetches. For efficiency reasons, this is solved via a SAT solver.

First, we define the alternation matrix $A : F \times F \to \{0, 1\}$ with $A[f_1, f_2] = 1$ if there is a path from f_1 to f_2 that does not cross some dispatch instruction (again, a path without calls, return instructions nor dynamic jumps) and 0 otherwise. In that case, to keep alternation, either f_1 or f_2 must be rejected. Given $f \in F$, $A[\_, f]$ denotes the column within A corresponding to f's line and $A[f, \_]$ the line corresponding to f's column.

In the matrix A, let us write

$$F_{\mathrm{ok}} = \{f \in F \mid A[f, \_] = (0) \text{ and } A[\_, f] = (0)\}$$

where (0) denotes the null vector. Elements $f \in F_{\mathrm{ok}}$ are only reachable from other fetches via a dispatch and conversely. Such fetches can be kept as is. As a logical formula, that means:

$$\Phi_{\mathrm{ok}} = \bigwedge_{f \in F_{\mathrm{ok}}} x_f$$

where x_f is a boolean variable meaning "f is a fetch". So, we restrict our attention to fetches $F_{\mathrm{dontknow}} = F \backslash F_{\mathrm{ok}}$:

$$F_{\mathrm{dontknow}} = \{f \in F \mid A[\_, f] \neq (0) \vee A[f, \_] \neq (0)\}.$$

Now, set:

$$\Phi_{\mathrm{dontknow}} = \bigwedge_{f, f' \in F_{\mathrm{dontknow}} \times F_{\mathrm{dontknow}}} (A[f, f'] = 1) \Rightarrow (\neg x_f \bigvee \neg x_{f'}).$$

In ambiguous cases, at most one of the candidates is a fetch. Any solution to

$$\Phi = \Phi_{\mathrm{ok}} \wedge \Phi_{\mathrm{dontknow}}$$

is a solution to the initial problem. We search for solutions with a maximal number of fetches. For that, we use the library PYSAT (see [IMM18]).

5.3 Spectrum Criterion

For each dispatch candidates group (recall we group dispatches by function frame), we build the spectrum S of fetches candidates. A fetch f such that $\Sigma_M[f, \_] = 0$ or $\Sigma_M[\_, f] = 0$ is a fetch that is not reached, nor followed by a sequential instruction. Such fetches are rejected from the candidates.

5.4 Selecting Dispatches

At this point, we make a last observation. Whenever the set of dispatches and fetches is not empty, we output the group of dispatches that occurs the most within the execution trace. In other words, we account for the fact that the virtual program being interpreted, there is an underlying loop within the interpreter.

6 Experiments

6.1 Configuration of the Benchmark

Selected Interpreters. The benchmark is composed of six binaries obtained by compiling three versions (2.7, 3.8 and 3.11) of the cpython interpreter with respectively the two compilation options --with-computed-gotos and --without-computed-gotos. The choice of these versions of python and compilation options are based on the difference in functionality and implementation of their underlying instruction set but also on differences of the interpreter structure. This allows us to test our implementation on relatively different interpreter architectures.

Moreover, python interpreters have been included in some malicious programs such as Trilog[10].

Extraction of the Ground Truth. In order to evaluate the performance of the algorithm, the true fetches and dispatches of the interpreter must be extracted for each binary of the benchmark. The extraction of these instructions was done manually using the python source code to locate the interpreter within the binary.

Program Execution. Benchmark binaries can run virtual programs in two ways.

- The program is written in the Python high-level language (prog.py) and is presented directly to the binary. Thus, the transformation to the Python bytecode and the interpretation are done in the same x86 binary. This procedure approximates the behaviour of a partially virtualised x86 program.

---

[10] See for instance https://www.mcafee.com/blogs/other-blogs/mcafee-labs/triton-malware-spearheads-latest-generation-of-attacks-on-industrial-systems/.

- The program is first compiled into its Python bytecode form (prog.pyc). Then it is presented to the X86 binary interpreter.

To avoid a bias due to the nature of the guest code, we used two Python programs,

- fibonnaci that implements and call the fibonacci function with different arguments.
- binary tree that implements a binary tree class, initiates an object and inserts numbers.

Given a python interpreter and a python program, we collect only a single execution trace and perform only a single program execution from which we determine the fetches and dispatches.

As far as we could see, the interpreted programs do not play an important role in the evaluation of the method. Nevertheless, generally speaking, when a program is bigger and its execution lasts longer, the dynamic trace contains more informations. For instance, the approximation of the static control flow graph by the trace will be better.

6.2   Results

In the following, the results are presented in table form with the columns:

- "Dynamically detectable" which indicates the real number of distinct dispatches or fetches that are present in the dynamic trace of the program.
- "Total detected" which indicates the number of dispatches or fetches output by the algorithm.
- "Correctly detected" which indicates the number of true positives.
- "Undetected" which indicates the total number of undetected dispatches or fetches within the static program.
- "SAT estimate" indicates the estimate by our algorithm of the number of false fetches by SAT resolution.

Table 1. Results for python 2.7 - --without-computed-gotos.

	without computed-gotos	Dynamically detectable	Total detected	Correctly detected	Undetected	SAT estimate
Fibonacci	Dispatches	1	1	1	0	■■■
	Fetches	1	2	1	1	1
Binary tree	Dispatches	1	1	1	0	■■■
	Fetches	1	2	1	1	1

Table 2. Results for python 2.7 - --with-computed-gotos.

	with computed-gotos	Dynamically detectable	Total detected	Correctly detected	Undetected	SAT estimate
Fibonacci	Dispatches	23	23	23	74	
	Fetches	23	36	23	73	13
Binary tree	Dispatches	20	20	20	77	
	Fetches	19	31	19	77	12

Table 3. Results for python 3.8 - --without-computed-gotos.

	without computed-gotos	Dynamically detectable	Total detected	Correctly detected	Undetected	SAT estimate
Fibonacci	Dispatches	1	1	1	0	
	Fetches	2	3	2	0	1
Binary tree	Dispatches	1	1	1	0	
	Fetches	2	3	2	0	1

Table 4. Results for python 3.8 - --with-computed-gotos.

	with computed-gotos	Dynamically detectable	Total detected	Correctly detected	Undetected	SAT estimate
Fibonacci	Dispatches	39	28	28	100	
	Fetches	40	30	29	99	1
Binary tree	Dispatches	38	28	28	100	
	Fetches	38	29	29	99	0

Table 5. Results for python 3.11 - --without-computed-gotos- fibonacci.py for $\Delta = 16$ and $\Delta = 8$.

	without computed-gotos	Dynamically detectable	Total detected	Correctly detected	Undetected	SAT estimate
$\Delta = 16$	Dispatches	1	1	1	0	
	Fetches	52	54	51	138	4
$\Delta = 8$	Dispatches	1	1	1	0	
	Fetches	52	48	47	142	2

6.3   Analysis

Compliance with the Model. As far as the model is globally respected by the interpreter, the algorithm correctly detects the dispatches occuring in the dynamic trace. We essentially miss dispatches that were not executed. True fetches are also detected but accompanied by false positives. However, the estimation obtained by SAT problem solving is able to correctly estimate the number of false positives[11] as shown in the Tables 1 and 2 for Python 2.7 and Tables 3 and for Python 3.8.

---

[11] Total detected - Correctly detected.

However, we can observe for python 3.8 `--with-computed-gotos` in Table 4 that some detectable dispatches are not detected. This is due to the fact that multiple calls to the interpreter can be made and the concatenation of the different groups of dispatches is not systematic. Indeed, in these conditions, two groups of dispatches are concatenated only if they have a dispatch in common.

Finally, as expected, some dispatches and fetches are not detected because our approach relies on dynamic analysis.

Non-compliance with the Model. The condition for picking the true group of dispatches out of all the groups of candidate dispatches gives good results as seen above. However, when the real dispatch group is less executed than another dispatch candidate group, the criterion may be insufficient. For example, it has been found that the compilation process to the Python bytecode can sometimes be confused with the dispatch group.

However, we can claim that the proposed "quick and dirty" approach allows an analyst to narrow the focus of his work by reducing the number of groups to be studied. At that point, it is time to reuse the deep analysis we mentioned in introduction.

We notice for Python 3.11, in Table 5 that the SAT estimate is incorrect. This discrepancy is again due to a non-exhaustiveness of the dynamic analysis. We miss some part of the control flow graph. Therefore, there is a special pattern in the graph with two fetches. In that case, our procedure removes one of the two.

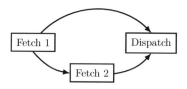

Finally, we observed for python 3.11 for $\Delta = 8$ (Table 5) that among the dynamically detectable fetches, 5 fetches are not detected. However, by changing the value of Δ to 16 (Table 5), among the dynamically detectable fetches, only one fetch is not detected. Indeed, since Python 3.11, the notion of "inline caching" has been introduced, which allows to insert data directly into the virtual program in the form of a cache instruction in order to save the cost of some calculations.

7   Conclusion

So, we get an effective procedure catching dispatches and fetches within a binary code. On that, one may describe in more details the behavior of the virtual machine. First, one should determine two remarkable virtual pointers:

the instruction pointer and the stack pointer whenever it exists. In his master thesis, Mathis Bouverot showed how to get those for a 1-fetch/1-dispatch interpreter [Bou].

Second, the SAT solver appeared to be remarkably efficient. It is not surprising since we formalized the problem as a 2-SAT formula. It is clear that we could go further on that way with a complete formalization of the problem in logical terms. Notice also that we solve an optimization problem. For those, the computation time depends heavily on the formulation of the problem. Extensions may be quite tricky.

There are quite simple extensions of the model. For instance, we could generalize a little bit the shape of dynamic jumps. For instance, we could think of `calls` or `ret`. Since these cannot occur as a result of a standard compilation procedure, we just skipped them. But for obfuscated code, we should take them into account.

Here, we formalized the relationship between the fetch and its dispatch via a tainting analysis. One could take some finer approach using the spectral analysis. The behavior of the virtual pointer is close to the behavior of the host pointer. It does a lot of small jumps corresponding to sequential virtual instructions. However, this approach leads to some algorithmic issues that we left for further work.

Final point, we will publish our tool at the time of the conference.

Acknowledgments. The authors would like to thank the ORION program for its contribution to the funding of A. Ithayakumar's research internship. This work has benefited from a government grant managed by the Agence Nationale de la Recherche with the reference ANR-20-SFRI-0009.

References

[Bla]   Blazytko, T.: Analysis of virtualization-based obfuscation. In: r2con2021, editor, r2con2021 - witchcraft edition (2021)

[Bou]   Bouverot, M.: Shallow description of the python virtual machine

[DGBJ14]   Dang, B., Gazet, A., Bachaalany, E., Josse, S.: Practical Reverse Engineering: x86, x64, ARM, Windows Kernel, Reversing Tools, and Obfuscation. Wiley, Hoboken (2014)

[IMM18]   Ignatiev, A., Morgado, A., Marques-Silva, J.: PySAT: a python toolkit for prototyping with SAT oracles. In: Beyersdorff, O., Wintersteiger, C.M. (eds.) SAT 2018. LNCS, vol. 10929, pp. 428–437. Springer, Cham (2018). https://doi.org/10.1007/978-3-319-94144-8_26

[Jon97]   Jones, N.: Computability and Complexity: From a Programming Perspective. The MIT Press, Cambridge (1997)

[KGM17]   Kalysch, A., Götzfried, J., Müller, T.: VMAttack: deobfuscating virtualization-based packed binaries. In: Proceedings of the 12th International Conference on Availability, Reliability and Security, ARES 2017, New York, NY, USA. Association for Computing Machinery (2017)

[LLZF18] Liang, M., Li, Z., Zeng, Q., Fang, Z.: Deobfuscation of virtualization-obfuscated code through symbolic execution and compilation optimization. In: Qing, S., Mitchell, C., Chen, L., Liu, D. (eds.) ICICS 2017. LNCS, vol. 10631, pp. 313–324. Springer, Cham (2018). https://doi.org/10.1007/978-3-319-89500-0_28

[SBP18] Salwan, J., Bardin, S., Potet, M.-L.: Symbolic deobfuscation: from virtualized code back to the original. In: Giuffrida, C., Bardin, S., Blanc, G. (eds.) DIMVA 2018. LNCS, vol. 10885, pp. 372–392. Springer, Cham (2018). https://doi.org/10.1007/978-3-319-93411-2_17

[SLGL09] Sharif, M., Lanzi, A., Giffin, J., Lee, W.: Automatic reverse engineering of malware emulators. In: 2009 30th IEEE Symposium on Security and Privacy, pp. 94–109 (2009)

Automating Device Fingerprinting Attacks in 4G and 5G NSA Mobile Networks

Daniel Fraunholz[✉], Dominik Brunke, Lorenz Dumanski, and Hartmut Koenig

Communications Department, ZITiS, München, Germany
daniel.fraunholz@zitis.bund.de

Abstract. Mobile networks are essential for modern societies. High bandwidth and low latency communications for massive numbers of subscribers have enabled various applications with much impact on life quality. However, the widespread of mobile network communications has also increased the interest in security and privacy issues. In this work, a known 4G and 5G NSA vulnerability, attach request fingerprinting, is examined in detail and a novel classification method for attach request fingerprinting is proposed and extensively evaluated. The novel method significantly increases the severity of the privacy attack.

Keywords: Device fingerprinting · Privacy violation · 5G · 4G · Mobile networks · Information security

1 Introduction

Long Term Evolution (LTE) and 5G are modern and dynamically growing technologies. Not least because its use is widespread all over the world and radio-capable terminals are now used in many areas of everyday life. Such radio-capable terminals, User Equipment (UE)s, can represent a router, embedded hardware or cell phones. Since 2007, annual sales of cell phones to end users have increased more than tenfold per year [5]. Wireless technologies that enable faster download and upload rates have steadily advanced. It is hardly surprising that the protocols used in the 4G and 5G network are among the most complex in the networking domain. Because UEs and often network offer backward compatibility, problems from previous technologies prevail for multiple decades, even if more recent technologies would provide countermeasures to mitigate known vulnerabilities. Such a vulnerability, the attach request Fingerprinting, is the focus in this work.

The attach request is the initial request from a UE to connect to the radio cell for further communication. As at this point in the communication, the UE and the network do not know which security algorithms are supported and the network also doesn't know which key material to use, the request has to be transmitted unencrypted. However, as the request does contain an abundance of additional information, this can be abused to derive information on the UE.

G.-V. Jourdan et al. (Eds.): FPS 2022, LNCS 13877, pp. 192–207, 2023.
https://doi.org/10.1007/978-3-031-30122-3_12

In this work, an in-depth investigation on the possibilities in terms of information that can be deducted is performed in experiments with a large number of real UEs. Various cell phones but also other devices such as routers and Internet of Things (IoT) devices were tested. Furthermore, a novel classification method for attach request-based fingerprinting is introduced. This method uses machine learning to optimize itself based on the available data for classification. Current state of the art relies on expert knowledge to build classifiers for this attack [4,11,11]. On the other hand, our method is scalable and required minimal knowledge on each parameter that is used for classification. We evaluated our method against the state of the art and found that our method significantly outperforms current classification methods. We also investigated several advanced classification objectives, such as to derive the UE vendor or the software versions. The following research questions (RQs) are answered in this work:

1. How well do machine learning (ML)-based classifiers perform compared to state of the art expert classifiers?
2. Can a distinction be made between chipset vendors based on the attach request?
3. Can Android devices be distinguished from Apple devices based on the attach request?
4. Does the operating system version have an influence on the attach request?
5. Can the device type, i.e. cell phone, router, IoT be distinguished based on the attach request?
6. Can manufacturers of cell phones be distinguished based on the attach request?

The remainder of this work is structured as follows: In Sect. 2, an overview of related mobile security topics is provided. Our experimental setup is described in Sect. 3, followed by the description of our experimental procedure in Sect. 3.2. Based on the conducted experiments, our novel classification approach is introduced in Sect. 3.3. The results are extensively presented and discussed in Sect. 4. Section 5 concludes the work.

2   4G and 5G NSA Mobile Networks and Security

Mobile networks are organized in two domains, the Radio Access Network (RAN) and the core network. UE initially establish a connection with the base station, which is part of the RAN. After the radio link, also called Access Stratum (AS), is established, a Non Access Stratum (NAS) link between UE and core network can be used. This basic architecture is the same for all mobile network generations. However, to facilitate a smooth transition from 4G to 5G a in-between solution, called 5G Non-Stand Alone, was introduced. This means that the RAN from 5G and the core network from 4G is used to establish AS and NAS connectivity. Therefore, NAS security mechanisms for 4G and 5G NSA are similar.

In general, essential parts of the mobile network cryptography rely on symmetric keys stored on the Universal integrated circuit Card (UICC) and in the

Table 1. Mandatory parameters of the attach Request, excerpt from 3GPP TS 24.008 V17.6.0 [1]. M: Mandatory, O: Optional

Information Element	Presence
Protocol Discriminator	M
Skip indicator	M
Attach request message identity	M
MS network capability	M
Attach type	M
GPRS ciphering key sequence number	M
DRX parameter	M
Mobile identity	M
Old routing area identification	M
MS Radio Access capability	M
...	O

mobile network core network, e.g. the Home Subscriber Server (HSS) in 4G. Initially, cell phones establish an unprotected AS link to base stations nearby based on cell selection, handover or cell re-selection mechanisms. Afterwards, an attach request is send via the NAS link to the core network. This requests contains the International Mobile Subscriber Identity (IMSI) and several more parameters. As the network cannot know the identity of a subscriber before the IMSI is available, no key can be selected from the key database (e.g. HSS in 4G) and thus, no encryption or other protection can be applied to this message. After the attach request is received, the network selects the relevant key for the subscriber based on the received IMSI. Based on this key, an authentication request is created and send to the UE. The UE responds with the authentication result. If the result is correct, the network considers the authentication successful. The network as well as the UE derive sessions keys from the stored keys and begin to encrypt the subsequent communication.

Many vulnerabilities are associated with this procedure, which is called Authentication and Key Agreement (AKA) since 2G. The reader is referred to Rupprecht et al. [10] for a general introduction in mobile network vulnerabilities from 2G to 4G and to Kahn and Martin [8] for recent vulnerabilities in 5G.

In 2019, Shaik et al. [11] presented the attach request-based fingerprinting attack. Their method is to derive information about the UE from the parameters transmitted encrypted over the air within the attach request. They derive information on the baseband vendor and the device type from the network capabilities included in the attach request. The network capabilities are parameters, e.g. supported security algorithms, that the network can use to provide early optimizations or that are needed to establish the connection. Capabilities are organized in so-called information elements. Each of these elements serves as a domain for the specific parameters. Of these information elements, 10 out of 30 are mandatory, and the remaining 20 are optional [1]. The mandatory elements can be found in the Table 1. A complete list can be found in the 3GPP specification TS 24.008.

The number of parameters transmitted in an attach request cannot be known before as most parameters are optional. However, a recent work found the numbers to be between 100 and 220 for mobile phones [4]. Shaik et al. used a small number of about 10 parameters for classification.

3   Experimental Setup

In order to assess the accuracy of the classifier of Shaik et al. and to develop improved algorithms, a test bed was developed, which features the following components: Mobile network (RAN and core), capability database and classifier. Commercial devices, e.g. mobile phones, were used as UEs. An overview of the experimental setup is given in Fig. 1.

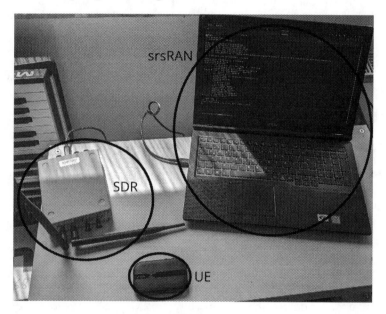

Fig. 1. Test setup, from left to right: URSP B210 (SDR), D-Link 4G Portable Router (UE), Fujitsu Lifebook with srsRAN

3.1   Mobile Network Components

Mobile network RAN and core build on the open source software srsRAN, running on a Fujitsu notebook with Manjaro Linux and the kernel 5.15.28-1-MANJARO as operating system. The Fujitsu Lifebook has a Intel i3 processor of the 8th generation and 16GB RAM. As radio front-end a USRP B210 with two VERT900 antennas is used. For the interaction with the card reader the pySim software is used. A SCR3310 is used to read and write the Universal Integrated Circuit Card (UICC)s (sysmoISIM-SJA2).

The capabilities are transmitted in the attach request, which is part of the NAS protocol. We monitored and captured all NAS communication between RAN and core network (*s1ap* protocol) with Wireshark. Since this method results in many packets that are irrelevant to this work, the relevant packet must be extracted from the captures. An attach request is identified in NAS via *message type 0x41*. The filter *nas_eps.nas_msg_emm_type == 0x41* will thus only include the attach request. Using the tshark application, a Command Line Interface (CLI) implementation of Wireshark, it is possible to parameterize this filter for generating a JavaScript Object Notation (Json) file, which includes all attach requests received by the mobile network.

To further process the Json formatted attach request, a parser was implemented in Python that iterates over files and pulls the nested Json structure to one level. The flattened capabilities are then stored in a SQLite database. From the generated list of all capabilities present at the UEs, a database schema is generated. The columns carry the names as specified in the Wireshark Dissector. If a capability does not exist, it takes the value NULL on initialization. Tables including information on the device type, baseband manufacturer and the captured capabilities are linked to the main table, which includes all UEs used in the experiment. The database is designed to be able to represent other device types as well.

Based on the capabilities and further information, e.g. manufacturer etc., a classifier is trained and used to derive information about a particular UE from the capabilities captured. So that the attach requests can be analyzed, the Evolved Packet System (EPS) is simulated first. For the classifier and visualization the following Python libraries were used: scikit-learn, matplotlib, pandas, numPy, pySimpleGUI and graphviz.

3.2 Attach Request Capturing Procedure

As a manual recording of a large number of devices is time-consuming and error prone, a Python script was implemented to automate the control of srsRAN, the capture of attach requests and the capability extraction and storage.

Each run involves manually entering the UEs metadata and automatically extracting the attach request. Once the device has connected to the cell, the network record is stored with a name generated from the metadata. The metadata, whose schema is tied to the UE database model, is retrieved manually via the CLI.

All captured capabilities are transformed into a json file. However, the capabilities are also filtered to remove unnecessary capabilities. Unnecessary capabilities are capabilities that have no value to derive information about UEs. Particularly, capabilities that have always the same value for each UE or that are set randomly, e.g. the Global Unique Temporary Identifier (GUTI), are removed from the set of capabilities to build a classifier. A status flag initialized with *0* or *1*, which is assigned to each capability, determines whether the parameter is included in the classification procedure. The list resulting from this pre-

Table 2. Example transformation for one-hot encoding using the example capability exmplPrmtr. Left: Input data, right: One-Hot encoded data. *NULL* Values can be normalized.

UE	Capability	Value
UE 1	exmplPrmtr	0xFF
UE 2	exmplPrmtr	0x0F
UE 3	exmplPrmtr	0xF1
UE 4	exmplPrmtr	NULL

$\rightarrow$

UE	Capability	Value
UE 1	exmplPrmtr_CON_0xFF	1
UE 1	exmplPrmtr_CON_0x0F	0
UE 1	exmplPrmtr_CON_0xF1	0
UE 2	exmplPrmtr_CON_0x0F	1
UE 2	exmplPrmtr_CON_0xFF	0
UE 2	exmplPrmtr_CON_0xF1	0
UE 3	exmplPrmtr_CON_0xF1	1
UE 3	exmplPrmtr_CON_0xFF	0
UE 3	exmplPrmtr_CON_0x0F	0
UE 4	exmplPrmtr_CON_0xF1	NULL
UE 4	exmplPrmtr_CON_0xFF	NULL
UE 4	exmplPrmtr_CON_0x0F	NULL

processing is then provided to a data extraction application for further consideration.

In cases were UEs do not transmit a particular capability, the database field is initialized with the default value NULL. This also applies to One-Hot encoded parameters.

Since decision trees are used as classifier, it is required to process only binary capabilities, i.e. capabilities that have one out of two possible values (typically 0 and 1). However, the transferred value of a capability does not necessarily take either *0* or *1*. For example, a hexadecimal or decimal value is often associated with the capability. Such parameters must be binarized. The One-Hot Encoding scheme is used for this purpose. An example transformation is shown in Table 2.

3.3   Classification of Device Fingerprints

Decision trees are a classification and regression method. An algorithm is trained so that a classification is possible on the basis of different, successively queried attributes. Attributes are the capabilities transmitted in the attach request. Which attributes are relevant for classification is calculated by the algorithm itself, reducing the required expert knowledge and also the manual effort significantly.

Two well-known calculation methods can be used to select the attributes with the most significance - entropy-based calculation and Gini index-based calculation. In our initial testing, both calculation methods provide almost similar results with a slight accuracy advantage when using entropy. However, the calculation of entropy is more complex than for Gini index [3]. As in our scenario the calculation is part of the offline phase of the attack, meaning that computational resources and time consumption is less significant for the attack to succeed, the entropy-based calculation method was used for best results.

One advantage of decision trees is their comprehensible representation. The capabilities used for the decision can be easily extracted and verified from a generated tree diagram.

There are several parameters that need to be provided for configuration of decision trees, such as the maximum number of attributes in combination that may be decisive for the classification (depth), how many terminal nodes there may be, or the minimum number of objects assigned to a class. If not specified otherwise in this work, the default settings from scikit-learn were used.

4   Performance of Decision Tree-Based Classifiers

After the data is pre-processed and stored in the database, scikit-learn was used to define the decision tree classifiers. Proprietary classifiers are based on decision trees.

We used the classifier from Shaik et al. as a reference to evaluate the performance of our proposed classifier. However, several System On Chip (SoC) manufacturers such as Samsung, Huawei, Apple and also Google build modems into their solutions that are not manufactured or designed by themselves. An example of this is the Google Pixel 6, which implements an in-house chip called Tensor, but uses a modem from Samsung [7]. In some cases, across different product lines, the suppliers of the modems have been diversified. For example, Apple uses modems from Intel and Qualcomm and states that it is already on its way to developing its own solution [9]. Since the chipset manufacturer is always specified for cell phones and it can be assumed that the hardware used does not vary for a given SoC solution, our classifier distinguishes by chipset manufacturer.

4.1   Reference Classifier

A partial result of the work of Shaik et al. [11] was that manufacturers of the baseband modem are recognized based on a combination of four different capabilities. These are the following parameters: EIA0 - EPS Integrity Algorithm, CM Service Prompt, CSFB - Circuit Switch Fallback, Extended Measurements. These take either the value 0, meaning disabled, or the value 1, meaning enabled. UEs that cannot be classified using the parameter combination, are assigned the characteristic Non-Classifiable (NC). The result is shown in Fig. 2 (a).

As it can be seen, Qualcomm chipsets in particular are less likely to be classified incorrectly (F1 score = 0.92). On the other hand, the classification of other chipsets are less accurate. Mediatek chipset are also classified as Qualcomm, Exynos, Intel and non-classifiable. About 50% of the UEs with Kirin chipsets are classified as UEs with Intel chipsets.

Overall, nine devices are non-classifiable, meaning that the classification method from Shaik et al. provides no conclusive result on the chipset of the

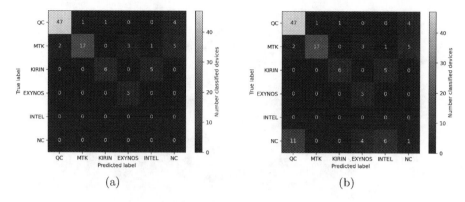

Fig. 2. (a): Performance of the Shaik et al. classifier. [11] on classifiable data, NC = Non-Classifiable. F(QC)=0.92, F(MTK)=0.74, F(KIRIN)=0.67, F(EXYNOS)=0.77, F(INTEL)=0, F(NC)=0. (b): Performance of the Altaf Shaik classifier to our complete data set. F(QC): 0.83, F(MTK): 0.74, F(Kirin): 0.67, F(Exynos): 0.59, F(Intel): 0.0, F(NC): 0.06

UE. An in-depth analysis found that some of the tested UEs do not transmit all capabilities required for the Shaik et al. classifier. A concrete example of this is the Samsung Galaxy S6, which is interestingly among the devices used in their original work [11, attachment]. In our experiment, the Extended Measurement Capability was missing.

In a next step, the UE with chipsets from Apple, Spreadtrum and Unisoc are included. However, as previously discussed it is unknown which modems the chipsets include, therefore the added UEs are in the NC class. The results are shown in Fig. 2 (b).

As expected, non-classifiable UEs are assigned to either Exynos or Intel. This means that non-classifiable UEs transmit a capability combination that can be associated with manufacturers.

According to Shaik et al. [11, appendix], two capabilities are crucial when classifying operating systems into Apple's iOS and Google's Android. These are the parameters VoiceOverPS-HS-UTRA-FDD and MS-Assisted GPS. Each of them can be used as a stand alone classification parameter, i.e. if set to 1 the UE is an Android device, else an Apple device. Testing with both parameters revealed no difference in the quality of the result. Thus, it can be concluded that each of them can be used interchangeably. The resulting confusion matrix is given in Fig. 3.

The classification shows that all iOS devices are also classified as such. However, overall there are 55 correctly classified UEs (40 Android, 15 Apple) and 59 UEs that are Android devices but were classified as Apple devices. The F1 scores for the Operating System (OS) classifier from Shaik et al. are therefore rather low (Android: 0.56, Apple: 0.35).

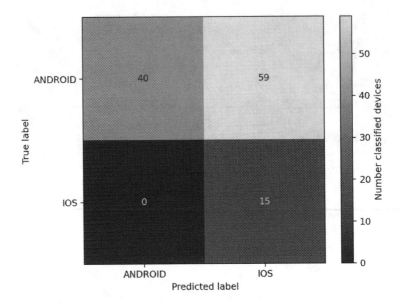

Fig. 3. Operating systems according to classifier of Shaik et al. [11] F(Android)=0.56, F(IOS)=0.34

4.2   UE Modem Classification

To train the decision tree, a part of the complete data available is split. The split can be defined by the user. The best results were obtained with a 40 % training data and 60 % test data split. Other parameters are set as follows: Maximum number leaves := 8 and maximum tree depth := 6.

Accordingly, a maximum of 5 parameters may be used for classification and the tree has 8 terminal nodes. This prevents overfitting of the tree so that it does not make single case decisions, i.e. decisions which are only used for one UE within the dataset, as much as possible. The results are visualized in Fig. 4.

Since the dataset is not considered as a whole to train the decision tree, there may be too few devices from certain chipset manufacturers. Unisoc and Spreadtrum belong to these manufacturers and are therefore not included in the classification procedure. Apple as a chipset manufacturer is, as previously discussed, not a modem manufacturer, however, since the objective is to investigate to what extent chipset manufacturers can be predicted based on capabilities, Apple is defined as class. Despite an under-representation of other classes in the test set compared to Qualcomm, the devices are mostly classified correctly. This indicates that chipset manufacturers have a strong influence on the capabilities.

With respect to RQ01 (Comparing the ML-based approach to Shaik et al. expert approach), it can be stated that the classifier of Shaik et al. works well for distinguishing the modems. However, we found that the trained decision tree achieved significantly higher F1 scores. As the dataset used by Shaik et al. was significantly smaller, the result is not surprising, however, it points out that large

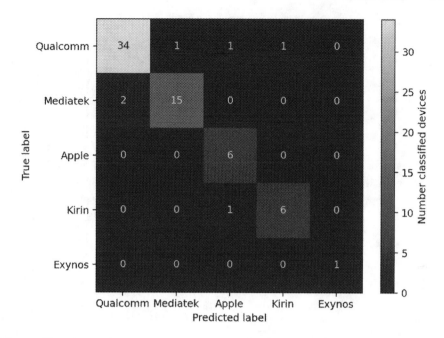

Fig. 4. Classifier with trained decision tree, F(QC): 0.93, F(MTK): 0.91, F(Apple): 0.86, F(Kirin): 0.86, F(Exynos): 1

datasets are required for high quality classification and that manual derivation of decision rules by experts is not feasible for large datasets. Having the same scope for each chipset manufacturer as for Qualcomm makes the procedure even more accurate. The results favor the possibility that the chipset manufacturer has significant impact on the network capabilities and therefore can often be inferred (RQ02). To provide a more apt comparison between classifiers, one would need to classify the manufacturer of the modem as well.

4.3 UE Operating System Classification

After training the decision tree with the corresponding split (40% training data, 60% test data), it can be assumed that a distinction can be made based on the capabilities. Only two Apple devices are wrongly classified as Android, as can be seen in Fig. 5.

It is also noticeable that decisions are only made on the basis of two capabilities. This can be seen from the exemplary decision tree in Fig. 6.

For Apple, Idle Mode Signaling Reduction (isr) is mostly disabled. This does not apply to the iPhone 12, which is equipped with an A14 Bionic chipset. However, the capability is disabled on the chipset-equivalent iPhone 12-Pro. Since it was shown in the differentiation between chipset manufacturers that Apple can be distinguished from others in most cases, it would make sense to combine the chipset and OS classifiers to increase their overall accuracy.

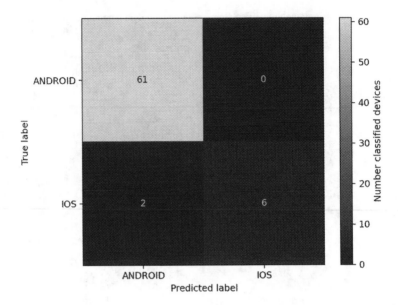

Fig. 5. Operating systems according to own classifier, F(Android)=0.98, F(iOS)=0.88

With respect to RQ03, it can be stated that even after little optimization on the training process for the decision tree, it can be said that a distinction between Apple and Android is reliably possible. To further optimize the classifier, one could evaluate even more Apple devices.

4.4   Influence of the Operating System Version

In order to verify whether the OS version has an influence on the transferred capabilities (RQ04), two older devices with long-term update capabilities were analyzed in-depth. These are the LG V30, which was updated from Android 7 to 9, and the Apple iPhone 6s. Especially Apple devices have rather long-term update support. The iPhone 6s can be upgraded from iOS version 9 to 15. This corresponds to a period from 2015 to 2021, and for LG from 2016 to 2018. After both devices were resumed with the updated OS, no difference in the essential parameters of the attach request could be detected.

If the capabilities were easy to extend by the OS, it stands to reason that this would be practiced. However, the version of the OS does not seem to have any effect on the attach request for the same device. Among other things, energy-saving measures are defined in the capabilities, which is why especially older devices could benefit greatly. Just because Apple consistently provides its devices with updates over a long period of time, it would have an even stronger sales argument. It might not be profitable to optimize in this respect. However, it should be noted that only two devices were examined. This is too small for a test volume to make a sound statement.

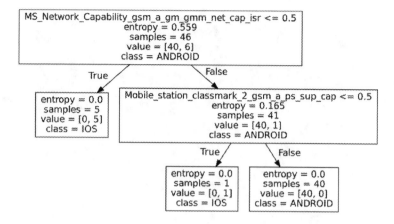

Fig. 6. Decision tree operating system according to own classifier

4.5   UE Type Classification

A different approach is taken for differentiation of device types, as amount of test data is rather limited in our experiments to sufficiently evaluate a potential classifier. Four LTE routers, three LTE cameras, and one stick are available to train the decision tree. The result of the training shows that 101 of the phones have two parameters in common and can thus be distinguished from the rest of the devices. The result would be even clearer if one of the cameras did not have ue usage setting-capability in common with the phones. This parameter determines whether the UE Prefers data- or voice-based communications [2,6]. If only phones and non-phones were considered, the resulting tree in this example would have only five leaves. A maximum of three parameters are decisive for the classification into cell phones or other devices. This indicates that cell phones can easily be distinguished from other devices.

With respect to RQ05, it can be stated that it is reliably possible to distinguish device types. How granular this is practicable would have to be investigated with a database expanded to include routers, sticks, cameras, and other UEs.

4.6   UE Manufacturer Classification

For the UE manufacturer classification, several manufacturers were excluded in the training procedure because, only one phone per manufacturer was included in the overall data set. These are the following manufacturers: Ulefone, Reolink, Fairphone and Archos. The split of the training data had a significant influence on the quality of the results. If a training data ratio larger than 40% was chosen, more devices are predicted incorrectly, hinting to over-fitting of the decision tree. The same was observed for a training data ratio below 30%, which is typical in the case of under-fitting. The best results were achieved with a split of 35% training data and 65% test data and the resulting confusion matrix is given in Fig. 7.

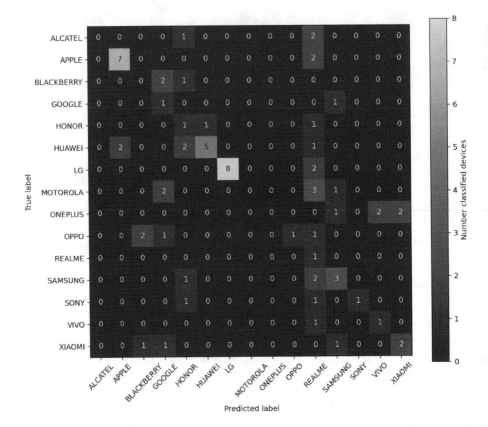

Fig. 7. Confusion matrix for differentiation by device manufacturer. F(ALCATEL) =0, F(APPLE)=0.78, F(BLACKBERRY)= 0, F(GOOGLE)=0.22, F(HONOR)=0.2, F(HUAWEI)=0.63, F(LG)=0.89, F(MOTOROLA)=0, F(ONEPLUS)=0, F(OPPO) =0.33, F(REALME)=0.11, F(SAMSUNG)=0.46. F(SONY)=0.5, F(VIVO)=0.4, F(XIAOMI)=0.44

It is noticeable that a particularly large number of devices from several vendors are wrongly considered as Realme. Motorola, Oneplus and Blackberry were not even once classified correctly. The fact that so many devices are classified as Realme could be due to the fact that this manufacturer implements three different chipset manufacturers (Mediatek, Qualcom, Unisoc). As already expected, this indicates that the chipset has a significant influence on the attach request.

With respect to RQ06, it can be stated that the classifier trained for the mobile phone manufacturers gives by far the worst results. Most likely, this is because of the distribution of chipset manufacturers among smartphone manufacturers. However, even UE manufacturers such as Apple and Huawei have reasonable F1 scores, in comparison to other UE manufacturers the results of the chipset classifier are significantly better, indicating that the chipset is more relevant for the attach request capabilities than the UE manufacturer. Therefore, it can be stated that some manufacturers might be distinguished, however

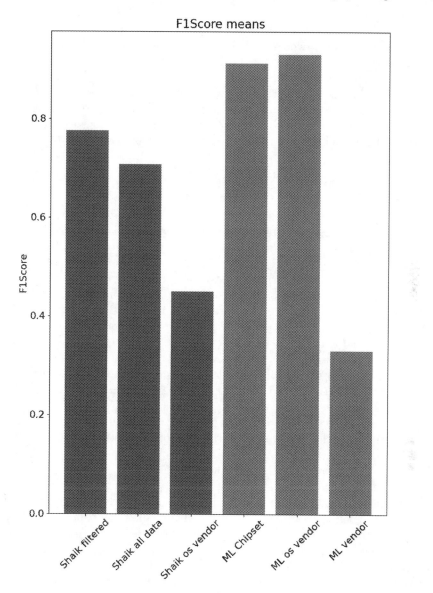

Fig. 8. Comparison of the F1 score of the Shaik et al. classifiers and the proposed classifier.

it is not clear to which degree this classification correlates with the distribution of chipsets used by a particular UUE manufacturer.

4.7   Overall Classifier Performance

The performance of the F1 scores of each classifier previously discussed is visualized in Fig. 8. The outliers in the Shaik et al. procedure [11], which are attributable to the Intel and non-classifiable classes, are not considered. The columns represent the average F1 score of each class. Even without in-depth optimization, the Machine-Learning (ML)-based method produced better results, with the exception of the device manufacturer.

The results after evaluation and analysis of the classifiers based on attach requests support the hypothesis that manual expert-based classifier construction can be automated with ML-based decision trees and also that the performance of these classifiers is significantly better than the baseline classifier.

5   Conclusion and Discussion

In this work, the attach request-based device fingerprinting was analyzed in-depth. Attach request-based device fingerprinting allows an attacker to actively (i.e. interacting with the target UE) or passively (monitoring the radio channel without any interaction) derive information on a device or even to track users based on a particular fingerprint that can be derived from the attach request [4]. This attack is possible in 2G, 3G, 4G and 5G NSA networks, while 5G SA networks introduced a countermeasure that limits the severity of the attack by minimizing the number of parameters that are allowed to be transferred in the attach request (3GPP TS 33.501).

Two major contributions were provided. First, a series of research questions regarding the general possibilities and limitations of attach request-based device fingerprinting were evaluated. The findings can be summarized as follows: 1. ML-based classifiers (in our case decision trees) archive an overall high performance in the classification 2. The chipset vendor can be distinguished based on the attach request with a high probability (F1 score = 95%) 3. Android devices can be distinguished from Apple devices with a high probability (F1 score = 97%) 4. The operating system version does most likely not have a significant impact on the attach request. 5. The device types of mobile network devices, e.g. cell phones, routers, IoT, can be distinguished based on certain parameters (as already postulated by Shaik et al.) 6. The manufacturer of cell phones can only be distinguished with a low probability (F1 score = 35%) Second, a method was introduced, implemented and evaluated against state of the art classifiers for decision tree-based classification of attach requests. The main advantage of our method is that it does not require any expert knowledge for training and also that it does not require any manual effort in analyzing the attach requests. Therefore even large data sets can easily be used to further optimize the classifiers and archive an even higher F1 score.

References

1. 3GPP: Ts 24.008 mobile radio interface layer 3 specification; core network protocols; stage 3 (2022)
2. 4Gmobiletech: LTE basics (2022). https://www.4gmobiletech.com/basics

3. Aznar, P.: Decision trees: Gini vs entropy (2020). https://quantdare.com/decision-trees-gini-vs-entropy/
4. Fraunholz, D., Schoerghofer-Vrinssen, R., Konig, H., Zahoransky, R.: Show me your attach request and ill tell you who you are: Practical finterprinting attacks in 4G and 5G mobile networks (2022)
5. Department, S.R.: Number of smartphones sold to end users worldwide from 2007 to 2021 – statista (2022). https://www.statista.com/statistics/263437/global-smartphone-sales-to-end-users-since-2007/. Accessed 16 May 2022
6. ETSI TS 124 301 v9.7.0 124, 301. https://www.etsi.org/deliver/etsi_ts/124300_124399/124301/09.07.00_60/ts_124301v090700p.pdf
7. INFO I: Pixel 6 und pixel 6 pro verwenden ein 5G-modem von samsung und umgehen qualcomm (2021). https://br.atsit.in/de/?p=136873
8. Khan, H., Martin, K.: A survey of subscription privacy on the 5G radio interface - the past, present and future. WiSec (2020)
9. Quandt, R.: Nach intel fällt bald qualcomm: Apple baut eigene smartphone-modems (2020). https://winfuture.de/news,119991.html
10. Rupprecht, D., Dabrowski, A., Holz, T., Weippl, E.R., Pöpper, C.: On security research towards future mobile network generations. CoRR abs/1710.08932 (2017). http://arxiv.org/abs/1710.08932
11. Shaik, A., Borgaonkar, R., Park, S., Seifert, J.P.: New vulnerabilities in 4G and 5G cellular access network protocols: exposing device capabilities. In: Proceedings of the 12th Conference on Security and Privacy in Wireless and Mobile Networks, pp. 221–231. WiSec 2019, Association for Computing Machinery, New York (2019). https://doi.org/10.1145/3317549.3319728

Malicious Human Behaviour in Information System Security: Contribution to a Threat Model for Event Detection Algorithms

Olivier de Casanove[1,2(✉)] and Florence Sèdes[1,2]

[1] Université Toulouse III - Paul Sabatier, 118 route de Narbonnes,
31062 CEDEX 9 Toulouse, France
[2] Institut de Recherche en Informatique de Toulouse (IRIT), Toulouse, France
{olivier.decasanove,florence.sedes}@irit.fr

Abstract. Among the issues the information system security community has to fix, the security of both data and algorithms is a concern. The security of algorithms is dependent on the reliability of the input data. This reliability is questioned, especially when the data is generated by humans (or bots operated by humans), such as in online social networks. Event detection algorithms are an example of technology using this type of data, but the question of the security is not systematically considered in this literature. We propose in this paper a first contribution to a threat model to overcome this problem. This threat model is composed of a description of the subject we are modelling, assumptions made, potential threats and defence strategies. This threat model includes an attack classification and defensive strategies which can be useful for anyone who wants to create a resilient event detection algorithm using online social networks.

Keywords: Threat model · Adversarial Learning · Online Social Network · Event Detection · Security

1 Introduction

The reliability of the output data of a machine learning algorithm is determined, among other factors, by the reliability of the input data. A small perturbation in the input can result in a misleading output [25]. This perturbation may be due to either data gathering or malicious behaviour. When the input data are generated by human, perturbations due to malicious behaviour cannot be disregarded. Data from online social networks is an example of data generated by human or prone to malicious perturbation.

Online Social Networks (OSN) allow users to exchange short messages and media. From these data published in real time, information can be extracted on events. Atefeh and Khreich [5], in their review on event detection on OSN, stated that "in general, events can be defined as real-world occurrences that unfold over space and time". To detect these events, event detection algorithms can be used. They take as an input the OSN stream of messages and give as an output clusters of messages, where each cluster defines an event. There are many applications, ranging from earthquake detection to musical event detection [5]. The literature on the subject focuses on how to improve the performances of the detection and the question of the detection's security is neglected. Yet, when the input data is made up of messages crafted by unknown users, this subject becomes a concern. If the implicit hypothesis: "Input data are absent from malicious messages crafted in order to disrupt the event detection" may hold in specific contexts, it does not in others. For example, when detecting events related to cybersecurity, the adversaries want their attacks to stay undetected. In this field, it's easy to find papers which do not take into account a potential threat to their detection [14,21]. When this hypothesis is false, we find ourselves in an adversarial learning context and event detection is under many threats.

This paper is a first contribution to a threat model for event detection algorithms on Twitter, but the same threat model could be used for other OSN. According to OWASP (Open Web Application Security Project) [19], a threat model is "a structured representation of all the information that affects the security of an application. In essence, it is a view of the application and its environment through the lens of security. [...] A threat model typically includes:

- Description of the subject to be modelled.
- Assumptions that can be checked or challenged in the future as the threat landscape changes
- Potential threats to the system
- Actions that can be taken to mitigate each threat
- A way of validating the model and threat and verification of success of actions taken."

Our contribution addresses all the points of this definition except for the fifth one, which will be addressed in future works. We believe that this threat model can be used to develop more resilient event detection algorithms and therefore, develop a technology more suited for real-life applications.

In the next section, we briefly discuss the related work. We will use the previous definition of a threat model to structure the rest of our paper. In Sect. 3, we describe the subject we model. In Sect. 4 we provide the assumptions on which our model is based. In Sect. 5 we describe the threats. In Sect. 6 we present defence strategies. In Sect. 7 we present future works and possible extensions to our threat model. Finally, we conclude in Sect. 8.

2   Related Work

Adversarial learning is a recent field, yet there is already a good literature on it [25]. Current threat models for machine learning focus on three aspects: attack direction (does the attack happen during the learning phase or the classification phase?), security violation (which kind of security concept the attack violates, traditionally confidentiality, integrity and availability) and attack specification (is it a targeted attack or not). We will see in Subsect. 5.2 why this threat model is not useful for us, as it is. Adversarial learning specifically applied to OSN has been studied in three different ways. The first one focuses on text processing applications, which is what event detection algorithms are. Alsmadi et. al. [3] review the literature to categorise attacks against text processing applications. All the attacks identified are message-level attacks, while event detection algorithms could also be attacked at the event-level (set of messages); therefore attacks against event detection algorithms are not fully covered in [3]. The second one is more specific, it is about evading spam detection [10]. Cleaning the input data with spam detection is a common and useful preprocessing step for text processing applications, but once again these attacks focus on message-level. For the same reason as in the previous point, this does not fully cover attacks against event detection algorithms. The third one consists in listing the adversaries and threats which can be faced in OSN. For example, Sabottke et al. [22] proposed an event detection algorithm with a list of actors willing to disrupt their algorithm. This is a first step, we used this list as a basis to construct the list of profiles in Subsect. 5.1, but this work needs to be extended into a complete threat model. Finally, the subject of fake news is out of scope because they impact the users. They are not meant to disrupt the operation of a machine learning algorithm.

3   Modelling Event Detection Algorithms

Atefeh and Khreich [5] as well as Hasan et. al. [11] reviewed the literature to list the techniques used to detect events on social media. Regardless of the technique used, an event can be formalised with the following definition:

Definition 1 (Event). *An event is defined by a tuple of messages related one to another and which are in the same spatial or time window. We note an event e_k, where $e_k \in \mathbb{E}$ and $\mathbb{E}$ is the set of all events possible and $k \in \mathbb{N}$ is the unique identifier of the event.*

We define the function F, the function which associates to a tuple of messages the corresponding event if the messages actually form an event and e_0 otherwise. Here, e_0 symbolise the null event, which means that the messages are not related. The set of all messages possible (or in our case all tweets possible) is noted $\mathbb{T}$.

Definition 2 (Event Detection function).

$$F \colon \mathbb{T}_1 \times \ldots \times \mathbb{T}_n \to \mathbb{E}$$

$$(t_1, \ldots, t_n) \mapsto \begin{cases} e_k & \text{if } t_1, \ldots, t_n \text{ form an event} \\ e_0 & \text{else} \end{cases}$$

An attacker can create fake messages thanks to techniques such as Markov Chain or Neural Network. When executed, these algorithms will produce a new fake message contained in a set of messages the algorithm is able to generate. Therefore we can represent the fake message by a random variable.

Definition 3 (Fake message random variable). *Let X be a random variable following an unknown distribution over the set $\mathbb{T}$.*

We define a false positive event (FP event), in the adversarial context, as an event which is composed of both legitimate and crafted tweets, but if the legitimate tweets were to be considered alone, no event would be triggered.

Definition 4 (False Positive Event).

Let $(X_i)_{i \in \mathbb{N}^*}$ be independent and identically distributed variables following the same law as X, $\forall (t_j)_{j \in \mathbb{N}^*} \in \mathbb{T}$ and $\forall k \neq 0$ if $F(t_1, ..., t_n) = e_0$ and $F(X_1, ..., X_m, t_1, ..., t_n) = e_k$ then e_k is a false positive

In opposition, we define a true positive event (TP event), in the adversarial context, as a set of messages mainly composed of legitimate messages and recognised as an event.

Definition 5 (True Positive Event).

Let $(X_i)_{i \in \mathbb{N}^*}$ be independent and identically distributed variables following the same law as X, $\forall (t_j)_{j \in \mathbb{N}^*} \in \mathbb{T}$ and $\forall k \neq 0$ if $F(t_1, ..., t_n) \neq e_0$ and $F(X_1, ..., X_m, t_1, ..., t_n) = e_k$ then e_k is a true positive

4 Assumptions

As previously said in Sect. 1, a threat model needs assumptions. We identify three assumptions for this threat model to make sense.

Assumption 1. *Input data from Twitter, and more generally social networks, contain messages written by malicious users with the objective to deceive event detection algorithms taking this data as input.*

We know that extracted data from Twitter contain spams and other malicious messages like phishing, for example. Those messages have an influence on the quality of the detection of our algorithms. Working in an adversarial context means taking the idea one step further and supposing that malicious users craft messages just to disrupt event detection algorithms.

Assumption 2. *Attackers have access to the algorithms, training and test dataset and any other relevant information.*

The datasets used to compare event detection algorithms are public, papers describing how event detection works are also easily accessible; therefore it is safe to assume that the attackers have access to any information related to event detection. It also means that the system is a "grey box" for the attackers, they have at least partial knowledge of how it works. Security by obscurity is not an option here.

Assumption 3. *The benefit of disrupting the detection for the attacker is equal to the cost for the defender to see its detection disrupted.*

We make this assumption to model the adversarial context as a zero-sum game. A zero-sum game, in game theory, is a situation where the benefit of a player (i.e. the attacker) is exactly equal to the cost of the other player (i.e. the defender). Interesting properties could be derived from zero-sum game, we will use them in a future work to validate the model. This is a common assumption in adversarial problems [24,28] and in information system security in general [26,27].

5   Threats to the System

In our context, a threat is defined as the combination of a malicious actor (the attacker) and a means to disrupt the event detection (the attack). We will detail both the attacker and the attack in the next two subsections.

5.1   Attacker Profiles

In a previous paper, we reviewed other contributions [8] and identified three profiles in the literature: trolls, spammers and adversaries. We will summarise these three profiles except for the troll where we can give a better definition than the one originally given. This gives us the following attacker classification:

- Trolls: their objective is to create rumors or make disappear subjects and therefore, events. They target both humans and automatic tools which analyse the news. In the second case, their objective is to create FP events and make TP events disappear.
- Spammers: they publish a lot of messages serving their own interests. They can use buzzwords, keywords or tag people to improve the efficiency of the spamming activity. They do not target our algorithm directly, but their activity creates a lot of noise in the Twitter stream.
- Adversaries: their objective is specifically to attack the event detection algorithm, in every way possible. Their means are diverse, but we can suppose that they have at least partial knowledge of the technology behind event detection since they are directly targeting it.

The definitions of the attackers are centred around the impact he could have. These profiles could be refined with two additional criteria: 1) is the attacker ignorant or knowledgeable of the system? And 2) is the attacker constrained or free of any constraints? Indeed the attacker could have multiple types of constraints, economic or political, for example. Now that we discussed about the profiles of the attackers, let's continue with the type of attacks they can use.

5.2 Attacks

In information system security, the CIA model (Confidentiality, Integrity and Availability) is often used [23]. However, this model does not suit our needs well in our adversarial learning context. For example, it does not make sense to defend the confidentiality of the detected events when all of the message composing it are public and messages. We propose instead to use the reliability and validity, which are measurement properties. "A measurement property is a quality aspect of an instrument" [1], i.e. event detection algorithms. "Each measurement property requires its own type of study to assess it" [1].

Reliability. The reliability of a test is its ability to stay consistent. In other words, a same input should always give the same output. In our adversarial context, the reliability becomes 1) the ability of the event detection algorithm to detect a same event, both when the input data are not corrupted and when a malicious actor is tampering with the input messages, with no less messages in it and 2) the ability to detect an event, with no more messages in it, when a malicious actor is tampering our data. To measure the impact on consistency, we need to first run our algorithm on a dataset without fake messages and label the messages associated to an event. We run again our algorithm, this time with the fake messages in the dataset and we compare the new clusters to the initial labels. This is a clustering problem, therefore a relevant metric for clustering tasks should be used. Traditional metrics such as recall or precision are not the best option for that. According to their review of different metrics for clustering tasks, Amigo et. al. [4] conclude that the best metrics, in regard of the properties they defined in their paper, are the BCubed recall and the BCubed precision combine into the BCubed F1-Score; therefore we choose these metrics for our problem. They define BCubed recall as "how many items from its category appear in its cluster" [4], which match our first objective for reliability and the define BCubed precision as "how many items in the same cluster belong to its category" [4], which match our second objective. The BCubed precision and the BCubed recall are calculated for every cluster, then "The overall BCubed recall [respectively the BCubed precision] is the averaged BCubed recall [respectively BCubed precision] of all items in the distribution" [4]. These two metrics are then combined to create the BCubed F1-score in the same way that traditional precision and recall are combined to create the F1-score. In conclusion, we will use the BCubed F1-score to measure the reliability.

$$\text{Reliability} = \text{BCubed F1-Score}$$

The exact formula of the BCubed F1-score is complex and would require the introduction of multiple notions. We encourage the interested readers to go read Amigo et. al. [4] if they want to go into BCubed metrics in depth.

Validity. The validity of a test is its ability to detect what it pretends to detect. In our case, is the event detection algorithm detecting events and not just give a random output? The objective of the event detection algorithm is therefore to maximise TP events and minimise FP events. The precision metric increases when the number of TP increases and decreases when the number of FP increases; therefore we will use the precision to measure the validity.

$$\text{Validity} = \text{Precision} = \frac{TP}{TP + FP}$$

Attacks Classification. After studying event detection algorithms, we identify eight attacks. These attacks are described in terms of their impacts on the reliability and the validity of the detection. They are classified in three categories: event creation, event dispersion and event modification. These categories gather the attacks which use the same means, but they don't always have the same goal. We summarise the attacks in Table 1.

Event creation. The attacker triggers an event detection, which increases the FP events and therefore impact the validity. The attacker uses a tool to procedurally generate fake tweets. Those messages are then injected in the Twitter stream. We identify three attacks in this category:

- Craft: fake tweets are created. Those messages are close enough for the event detection algorithm to consider them as related but does not necessarily make sense for a human. Those messages trigger a detection.
- Message expansion: real tweets, not related to any event, in association with malicious tweets trigger an event. This attack also impacts the reliability since a legitimate message, not related to any event, becomes related to an event.
- Replay: A TP event is replayed, entirely or partially, at a time where the event doesn't make sense.

Event dispersion. The objective is to inject enough malicious messages during a small lapse of time so the legitimate tweets appear too far from one another in the Twitter stream for the event to be detected. Three attacks exist in this category:

- Fragmentation: an event is split in two or more subgroups of tweets, resulting in detection of multiple events when they are the same. One TP events become many TP events under attack; therefore the reliability is impacted.
- Cancellation: an event doesn't trigger a detection when it should. The tweets are so split by the malicious messages that they aren't recognised as an event anymore. This attack decreases the number of TP events and transforms a TP event in nothing, therefore both the validity and the reliability are impacted.
- Deterioration: the number of tweets in an event decreases when under attack. This is a mix case between fragmentation and cancellation. The first or last messages are too far to be associated with the event, but they are still enough messages to trigger a detection. This is an inconsistency under attack; therefore it impacts reliability.

Table 1. Attacks against event detection algorithms

Name	Description	Impact on Reliability	Impact on validity
Event Creation			
Craft	A collection of fake tweets triggered an event	NO	YES
Message Expansion	A collection of fake and real tweets, which wouldn't have triggered an event otherwise, triggered an event	YES	YES
Replay	A true event is replayed a second time by the attacker	NO	YES
Event Dispersion			
Fragmentation	An event triggered multiple detection due to spam activities	YES	NO
Cancellation	An event doesn't trigger detection due to spam activities	YES	YES
Deterioration	The number of tweets related to an event is less than expected due to spam activities	YES	NO
Event Modification			
Drift	The attacker change the event keywords or event	YES	NO
Merge	Messages from an event start to aggregate to another event	YES	NO

Event modification. The attacker generates malicious tweets which seem related to one another by the event detection algorithm. As for event creation, the messages are generated procedurally.

– Drift: the attacker creates malicious tweets which aggregate on a TP event. The objective is to change the event keywords or subject. It creates an inconsistency; therefore the reliability is impacted.
– Merge: the attacker changes the event keywords or subject so another event messages start to aggregate on the first event. For this attack to be successful, the attacker needs to know the subject of two different events. It is safe to assume that if the attacker knows this, then both events already have been detected by our algorithm. Therefore it only creates an inconsistency on the number of messages aggregated to each event, and not in the number of TP events detected. The reliability is impacted.

6   Defence Strategies

The defender can protect the detection by adding filters at two different levels. The first one is at the level of the tweets, where tweets which seem malicious are filtered. The second level is at the level of the cluster, where TP events are distinguished from FP events. We define the filter function h, the function which associates, to each set of messages recognised as an event, 0 if the set of messages does not satisfy the constraints or a unique value otherwise.

Definition 6. (Filter Function).

$$h \colon \mathbb{E} \to \mathbb{E}$$

$$e_k \mapsto \begin{cases} e_k & \text{if } e_k \text{ satisfies the filters} \\ e_0 & \text{else} \end{cases}$$

With this new element in mind, we redefined TP and FP event as follows:

Definition 7. (True Positive Event).

Let $(X_i)_{i \in \mathbb{N}^*}$ be independent and identically distributed variables following the same law as X, $\forall (t_j)_{j \in \mathbb{N}^*} \in \mathbb{T}$ and $\forall k \neq 0$ if $F(t_1, ..., t_n) \neq e_0$ and $(h \circ F)(X_1, ..., X_m, t_1, ..., t_n) = e_k$ then e_k is a true positive

Definition 8. (False Positive Event).

Let $(X_i)_{i \in \mathbb{N}^*}$ be independent and identically distributed variables following the same law as X, $\forall (t_j)_{j \in \mathbb{N}^*} \in \mathbb{T}$ and $\forall k \neq 0$ if $F(t_1, ..., t_n) = e_0$ and $(h \circ F)(X_1, ..., X_m, t_1, ..., t_n) = e_k$ then e_k is a false positive

We will now discuss what the defence strategies are. Table 2 summarises which defence strategies mitigate which attacks.

6.1 Filtering Messages

The objective of a spam filter is to distinguish fake users, spams and spammers from legitimate tweets and users [2]. A spam filter can be made on the content of the tweets, the characteristics of the tweets, the users behind the tweets or the relationships in the OSN of the users behind the tweets [2]. All these solutions are machine learning solutions; therefore we introduce a new level of adversarial learning. However, the problem of adversarial learning for spam detection has already been discussed by [6,7,9,13]. Generating fake messages that can fool the spam filter increases the cost of the attack. Therefore, this strategy is effective against every attack which needs to create fake tweets. It is especially effective against dispersion attacks since those attacks are based on flooding and flooding are easily detected by spam filters. Finally, spam detection based on user features is effective against replay attacks because it means that the accounts replaying the events should avoid spam detection; therefore it increases the cost of the attack.

6.2 Filtering Clusters

TP and FP events have different characteristics. Setting thresholds for these characteristics is a way to differentiate TP from FP events. These thresholds are used as filters to discard FP events. We identified five metrics in the literature on which events can be filtered:

- Word entropy: The entropy of a cluster was introduced by [20]. The formula (1) is used where X is a random variable and $P(X_i)$ is the probability to draw a specific word out of all the words of the cluster. A cluster with a very low word entropy is probably composed of very similar crafted messages.
- User diversity: The formula (1) is applied but instead of applying it to words, it is applied to users in the cluster. We have X a random variable and $P(X_i)$ the probability to draw a specific user out of all the users of a cluster. *User diversity* in a cluster was introduced by [15]. This metric is particularly interesting because accounts are the most difficult thing to fake as an attacker. *User diversity* is one of the rare defence measures against event replay. The attacker can replay the exact same tweets but not the exact same author.
- Least Common Subsequence (LCS): Hasan et al. in [12] use a filtering method based on the LCS at word-level. The idea, based on empirical evidence they found, is that cluster of newsworthy events will have a higher LCS than non-newsworthy events. In their paper, the authors fixed an LCS threshold under which an event is discarded. It may help to identify drifted and merged events since the first and last messages of these events are likely to be very different.
- Named entity recognition: This technique is introduced by [18] as a way to pre-select tweets with significant improvement in the final result. The argument behind this constraint is that a tweet without a named entity does not provide any information and is therefore useless.
- Event size: Intuitively a cluster of fewer than 3 tweets cannot be considered as an event. However, finding an exact event size threshold separating meaningful events from similar but not related messages is impossible. Event size should be considered as a hyperparameter of our model to help us drop FP events.

$$H(X) = -\sum_i^n P(X_i)log_b P(X_i) \tag{1}$$

Some of the filter proposed are easy to bypass. For example, attackers can automatically add a random named entity in their fake tweets. We should keep in mind that, for the attacker, every attack is a trade-off between the costs and benefits of the attacks. Therefore, every defence strategy increasing the cost of the attack is worthwhile.

6.3 Other Strategy

Defragmentation is a process where events are reviewed to check if two detected events are in fact only one. Some event detection algorithms are prone to fragmentation [5]. Our context adds another interest to defragmentation: the resilience to the event splitting attack. We found one utilisation of defragmentation in [12].

Table 2. Defence strategies

Attack	Defence strategy
Tweets Expansion	Spam filters, Cluster filters
Event Crafting	Spam filters, Cluster filters
Event Replay	Spam filters, User diversity filter
Event Fragmentation	Spam filters, Defragmentation
Event Cancellation	Spam filters
Event Deterioration	Spam filters
Event Drifting	Spam filters, LCS filter
Event Merging	Spam filters, LCS filter

7   Future Works

We seek in future works to validate the model with a mathematical proof of how this formalisation is relevant. Thanks to our definition of TP and FP events, the hypothesis 3 and game theory theorems, we can prove that it exists a point where neither the attacker nor the defender will have interest into changing their strategies; therefore we avoid the pitfall of the Red Queen hypothesis [17]. The Red Queen hypothesis, in cybersecurity, is the hypothesis that there is a form of coevolution between attackers and defenders. Attackers develop their offensive strategies and the defenders develop countermeasures, which will lead to the attackers to change their strategies and so on.

On another note, we would like to develop a solution which could emulate the attacks in 1. We will need for that a public dataset for event detection [16] and a text generator able to generate credible messages and credible set of messages to form an event. The solution would automatically insert the fake messages in the dataset and the event detection algorithms would be tested on this new dataset. The resilience of the event detection algorithms would be measured thanks to reliability and validity. This future work can help to test the resilience of event detection algorithms.

8   Conclusion

In this paper we proposed a first contribution to a threat model for event detection. We define the situation we are modelling, assumptions that were made, the attackers' profile, possible attacks and defence strategies. In future works we will propose a way to validate our model. This threat model includes an attack classification and defensive strategies. This work is dedicated to help future event detection algorithms to be more resilient against adversarial attacks and therefore, develop a technology more suited for real-life applications. This threat model is especially useful when the event detection algorithms detect events related to any subject where an adversary can be found.

References

1. COSMIN Taxonomy of Measurement Properties • COSMIN. https://www.cosmin. nl/tools/cosmin-taxonomy-measurement-properties/
2. Abkenar, S.B., Kashani, M.H., Akbari, M., Mahdipour, E.: Twitter Spam Detection: A Systematic Review. arXiv:2011.14754 [cs] (2020). version: 2
3. Alsmadi, I., et al.: Adversarial Attacks and Defenses for Social Network Text Processing Applications: Techniques, Challenges and Future Research Directions. arXiv:2110.13980 [cs] (2021). http://arxiv.org/abs/2110.13980
4. Amigó, E., Gonzalo, J., Artiles, J., Verdejo, F.: A comparison of extrinsic clustering evaluation metrics based on formal constraints. Inf. Retr. **12**(4), 461–486 (2009). https://doi.org/10.1007/s10791-008-9066-8
5. Atefeh, F., Khreich, W.: A Survey of techniques for event detection in Twitter. Comput. Intell. **31**(1), 132–164 (2015). https://doi.org/10.1111/coin.12017
6. Biggio, B., Fumera, G., Roli, F.: Design of robust classifiers for adversarial environments. In: 2011 IEEE International Conference on Systems, Man, and Cybernetics, pp. 977–982 (2011). https://doi.org/10.1109/ICSMC.2011.6083796, ISSN: 1062-922X
7. Brückner, M., Kanzow, C., Scheffer, T.: Static prediction games for adversarial learning problems. J. Mach. Lear. Res. **13**(1), 2617–2654 (2012)
8. de Casanove, O., Sèdes, F.: Apprentissage adverse et algorithmes de détection d'évènements : une première typologie. In: Rendez-vous de la Recherche et de l'Enseignement de la Sécurité des Systèmes d'Information (RESSI 2022) (2022). https://hal.archives-ouvertes.fr/hal-03668829, poster
9. Chan, P.P.K., Yang, C., Yeung, D.S., Ng, W.W.Y.: Spam filtering for short messages in adversarial environment. Neurocomputing **155**, 167–176 (2015). https://doi.org/10.1016/j.neucom.2014.12.034
10. Duddu, V.: A survey of adversarial machine learning in cyber warfare. Def. Sci. J. **68**(4), 356 (2018)
11. Hasan, M., Orgun, M.A., Schwitter, R.: A survey on real-time event detection from the Twitter data stream. J. Inf. Sci. **44**(4), 443–463 (2018). https://doi.org/10.1177/0165551517698564
12. Hasan, M., Orgun, M.A., Schwitter, R.: Real-time event detection from the Twitter data stream using the TwitterNews+ Framework. Inf. Process. Manage. **56**(3), 1146–1165 (2019). https://doi.org/10.1016/j.ipm.2018.03.001
13. Imam, N.H., Vassilakis, V.G.: A survey of attacks against Twitter spam detectors in an adversarial environment. Robotics **8**(3), 50 (2019). https://doi.org/10.3390/robotics8030050
14. Khandpur, R.P., Ji, T., Jan, S., Wang, G., Lu, C.T., Ramakrishnan, N.: Crowdsourcing cybersecurity: cyber attack detection using social media. In: Proceedings of the 2017 ACM on Conference on Information and Knowledge Management, pp. 1049–1057 (2017)

15. Kumar, S., Liu, H., Mehta, S., Subramaniam, L.V.: From Tweets to Events: Exploring a Scalable Solution for Twitter Streams. arXiv:1405.1392 [cs] (2014)

16. Mazoyer, B., Cagé, J., Hervé, N., Hudelot, C.: A French corpus for event detection on Twitter. In: Proceedings of the 12th Language Resources and Evaluation Conference, pp. 6220–6227. European Language Resources Association, Marseille, France (2020)

17. Mazurczyk, W., Drobniak, S., Moore, S.: Towards a systematic view on cybersecurity ecology. In: Akhgar, B., Brewster, B. (eds.) Combatting Cybercrime and Cyberterrorism. ASTSA, pp. 17–37. Springer, Cham (2016). https://doi.org/10.1007/978-3-319-38930-1_2

18. McMinn, A.J., Jose, J.M.: Real-time entity-based event detection for Twitter. In: Mothe, J., et al. (eds.) CLEF 2015. LNCS, vol. 9283, pp. 65–77. Springer, Cham (2015). https://doi.org/10.1007/978-3-319-24027-5_6

19. OWASP: Threat modeling (2022). https://owasp.org/www-community/Threat_Modeling

20. Petrović, S., Osborne, M., Lavrenko, V.: Streaming first story detection with application to Twitter. In: Human Language Technologies: The 2010 Annual Conference of the north American Chapter of the Association For Computational Linguistics, pp. 181–189 (2010)

21. Ritter, A., Wright, E., Casey, W., Mitchell, T.: Weakly supervised extraction of computer security events from Twitter. In: Proceedings of the 24th International Conference on World Wide Web, pp. 896–905. WWW 2015, International World Wide Web Conferences Steering Committee, Republic and Canton of Geneva, CHE (2015). https://doi.org/10.1145/2736277.2741083

22. Sabottke, C., Suciu, O., Dumitras, T.: Vulnerability disclosure in the age of social media: exploiting twitter for predicting real-world exploits. In: 24th USENIX Security Symposium (USENIX Security 15), pp. 1041–1056. USENIX Association, Washington, D.C. (2015), https://www.usenix.org/conference/usenixsecurity15/technical-sessions/presentation/sabottke

23. Samonas, S., Coss, D.: The CIA strikes back: redefining confidentiality, integrity and availability in security. J. Inf. Syst. Sec. **10**(3), 1–25 (2014)

24. Vamvoudakis, K.G., Hespanha, J.P., Sinopoli, B., Mo, Y.: Adversarial detection as a zero-sum game. In: 2012 IEEE 51st IEEE Conference on Decision and Control (CDC), pp. 7133–7138 (2012). https://doi.org/10.1109/CDC.2012.6426383

25. Wang, X., Li, J., Kuang, X., Tan, Y.A., Li, J.: The security of machine learning in an adversarial setting: a survey. J. Parallel Distrib. Comput. **130**, 12–23 (2019). https://doi.org/10.1016/j.jpdc.2019.03.003, https://www.sciencedirect.com/science/article/pii/S0743731518309183

26. Wu, C., Li, X., Pan, W., Liu, J., Wu, L.: Zero-sum game-based optimal secure control under actuator attacks. IEEE Trans. Autom. Control **66**(8), 3773–3780 (2021). https://doi.org/10.1109/TAC.2020.3029342

27. Zhou, R., Lin, J., Liu, L., Ye, M., Wei, S.: Analysis of SDN attack and defense strategy based on zero-sum game. In: Ren, J., et al. (eds.) BICS 2019. LNCS (LNAI), vol. 11691, pp. 479–485. Springer, Cham (2020). https://doi.org/10.1007/978-3-030-39431-8_46

28. Zhou, Y., Kantarcioglu, M., Xi, B.: A game theoretic perspective on adversarial machine learning and related cybersecurity applications. In: Game Theory and Machine Learning for Cyber Security, Chapter 13, pp. 231–269. John Wiley & Sons, Ltd (2021). https://onlinelibrary.wiley.com/doi/abs/10.1002/9781119723950.ch13

A Taxonomy and Gap-Analysis in Digital Privacy Education

Sumit Kumar Paul[1]([✉]) and D. A. Knox[2]

[1] Department of Electrical and Computer Engineering, University of Ottawa, Ottawa, Canada
spaul058@uottawa.ca
[2] School of Engineering Design and Teaching Innovation (and School of Electrical Engineering and Computer Science), University of Ottawa, Ottawa, Canada
dknox@uottawa.ca

Abstract. Computers of different types and portable devices like: mobile phones, smartwatches and an increasing number of IoT devices, collect and use our personal data, to improve and simplify our daily lives in new and unexpected ways. So, the awareness and safety measurements in this area are pretty important. Computer and networking security (e.g. attacks on confidentiality, integrity and availability) are subjects in undergraduate and graduate curriculums. Security awareness training has become a ubiquitous requirement for employees in industrial settings. However, privacy-related education has not advanced as quickly as security-related education. As the value of our private information and the possibilities for its misuse increase, we must develop and learn more about privacy-enhancing technologies and the role that they can play in our digital lives. Therefore, appropriate privacy education is required at different levels in the education system. This paper reviews and analyzes the digital privacy education research literature and identifies potential future research areas, based on coverage gaps that are detected using a taxonomy of the surveyed academic literature on privacy-based education. This taxonomy is based on: a classification decision about the subject of the data as personal or for a third party, the application domain, the specific teaching delivery method, and the teaching modality (e.g. collaborative, synchronous, asynchronous online, experiential, etc.).

Keywords: Privacy · Education · Survey · Taxonomy · Teaching-methods

1 Introduction

Private information leakage has become more of a problem, with the increased use of digital devices and the rapid growth in AI and Machine Learning. This has motivated efforts to improve privacy protection [28]. Data stored via the internet can be used for different purposes and can persist for long periods of time, without the owner's awareness or the owner's control or both. Although these points should be clearly mentioned in the privacy policy, very few users verify such policies completely or at all. Even if a privacy policy is read and understood by a user, the remote entity may or may not be auditable against that policy, presuming legislation exists to require compliance. Moreover, privacy

© The Author(s), under exclusive license to Springer Nature Switzerland AG 2023
G.-V. Jourdan et al. (Eds.): FPS 2022, LNCS 13877, pp. 221–235, 2023.
https://doi.org/10.1007/978-3-031-30122-3_14

also means different things to different people [1]. Research has started in the areas of privacy-enhancing technologies and related data handling laws and related software behavior is evolving quickly.

Therefore, currently, privacy education might be more important than law enforcement [9]. In Europe, GDPR legislation was enacted in 2018 to protect all digital data. NIST has also proposed a framework [31] for privacy improvement. People can understand the importance of privacy and may even want to protect their personal information when and if explicitly informed [44]. While privacy-related laws might exist [46], privacy education seems to be relatively absent [45].

Privacy education programs for younger children [51] have been created and education material has been tailored specifically for small children [42, 50]. However, very few technical undergraduate and graduate-level privacy programs and courses are available in universities and colleges, worldwide. Most of these are being offered by faculties of law [22]. Moreover, nothing like the European GDPR legislation [55] exists yet in North America, although the U.S. state of California has pioneered legislation [56].

In this paper, we analyze the different privacy education initiatives that have been proposed in the literature for privacy education. We categorize what is being taught, to whom, and the methods that are being used to teach privacy-related material at all educational levels. We exclude education that is based on law or focused on privacy policy, focusing instead on technology-based research. We create a taxonomy, based on this categorization, and use it to analyze current trends and identify possible education gaps. Finally, we suggest future development areas and approaches for teaching privacy, especially at the post-secondary level.

Our paper should be valuable to researchers in privacy technology education, but should also assist educators who want to teach technical aspects related to privacy (e.g. to help them design their curricula). Our work should provide researchers or educators in non-technical fields with a view of the current state of the art in privacy technology education.

In general, we would like to have more research in privacy technology education and increase the amount of privacy technology education that takes place at all levels, including in university undergraduate education. Privacy technologies will shape our future society in significant and fundamental ways, which can be both exciting and concerning, depending on their design and implementation.

Privacy legislation can constrain and limit technological development in certain ways. By understanding privacy technologies, exciting new possibilities can also be considered that might otherwise be overlooked in a "privacy environment of constraint" alone. Equilibrium is required between the design of new privacy-impacting technologies and the privacy laws that are designed to protect us, as we use those technologies. Education is required on both sides of this privacy technology equation. We limit our study to technical privacy education, rather than focusing on broader analysis in a social or legal context, although both of these are also clearly very important.

2 Research Method

We are mainly interested in how the non-legal, academic world has responded to the specialized need for digital privacy education learning material in the last decade. Not only is privacy now emerging as an independent research area, even a secure system can still leak private information [64]. In keeping with our objective of stimulating privacy technology-related education, we have chosen to exclude research papers that discuss privacy education as a side-topic to a more central cybersecurity education main topic.

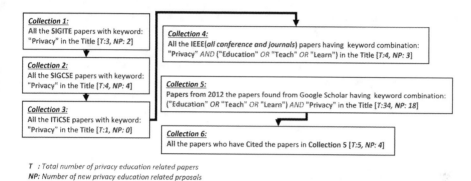

Collection 1:
All the SIGITE papers with keyword: "Privacy" in the Title [*T:3, NP: 2*]

Collection 2:
All the SIGCSE papers with keyword: "Privacy" in the Title [*T:4, NP: 4*]

Collection 3:
All the ITiCSE papers with keyword: "Privacy" in the Title [*T:1, NP: 0*]

Collection 4:
All the IEEE{*all conference and journals*} papers having keyword combination: "Privacy" *AND* {"Education" *OR* "Teach" *OR* "Learn"} in the Title [*T:4, NP: 3*]

Collection 5:
Papers from 2012 the papers found from Google Scholar having keyword combination: {"Education" *OR* "Teach" *OR* "Learn"} *AND* "Privacy" in the Title [*T:34, NP: 18*]

Collection 6:
All the papers who have Cited the papers in Collection 5 [*T:5, NP: 4*]

T : Total number of privacy education related papers
NP: *Number of new privacy education related prposals*

Fig. 1. Privacy education research related data gathering process

To review the "state-of-the-art" of privacy education, we decided to findout what research happened in the last ten years around the world. We first looked at specialized journals and conference proceedings for education in information technology and computer science like SIGITE, SIGCSE, and ITiCSE. Then we used some keyword combinations in Google Scholar. After filtering out the papers, we read the *Title, Abstract* and *Conclusion* sections to determine the related papers.

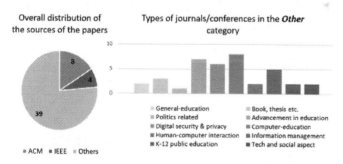

Overall distribution of the sources of the papers

Types of journals/conferences in the *Other* category

⊛ General-education   ⊛ Book, thesis etc.
⊛ Politics related   ⊛ Advancement in education
⊛ Digital security & privacy   ⊛ Computer-education
⊛ Human-computer interaction   ⊛ Information management
⊛ K-12 public education   ⊛ Tech and social aspect

⊛ ACM ⊛ IEEE ⊛ Others

Fig. 2. Distribution of the sources of the collected papers

Figure 1 illustrates the entire search process. In total, 51 articles were found that related to digital privacy education, including 31 papers that suggested different kinds of teaching proposals. The rest of the papers used human participants to determine the importance of different types of learning material or methods. We found one unique and interesting older paper that proposes privacy education, specifically for the marketing domain.

We have considered all the papers having "Privacy" in the title in SIGITE, SIGCSE, and ITiCSE. However, our search strategy might not be exhaustive in the case of IEEE and Google Scholar, due to the use of keyword combination search. While searching in Google Scholar, we found a few duplications which were already covered in the previous search categories, and we discarded those. To make sure that no important related paper is missed, we have gone through the "Title", "Abstract", and "Conclusion" sections of all the filtered papers, before discarding any unrelated paper. Figure 2 also demonstrate the diversity of the sources of the collected papers, which suggests this survey provides a solid attempt at summarizing the "state-of-the-art" in digital privacy education.

Interestingly, privacy-related course listings in universities around the globe were reviewed recently [22], and found that undergraduate level offerings in privacy are scarce. Also, the authors have shown how privacy education varies with geographic location and disciplines. We have not duplicated this work. There might also be recent training or awareness programs, from commercial or private organizations. Our focus in this work is on the public, academic literature.

3 Taxonomy of Privacy Education

We now define and justify each of the four descriptors for our classification. Most reviewed articles talk about a specific target audience in a specific context. The specific details for the privacy education that is being described usually depends on this audience and context heavily.

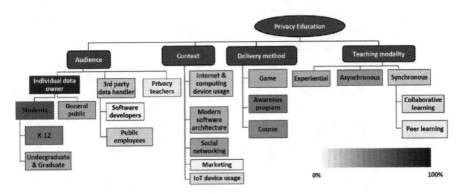

Fig. 3. Taxonomy of Privacy Technology Education Research

We have attempted to cluster or categorize these audiences or contexts in our work and also to cluster the education methods being used or studied. We believe that newer papers should be classifiable with our taxonomy, but are not claiming that this is the only possible taxonomy.

Besides the different audience and contexts, all reviewed papers discuss one of three basic education delivery methods (Fig. 3). Researchers tried to attract learners toward privacy education by using games and awareness programs along with formal courses. Education researchers continue to investigate personalized teaching modalities or are studying ways to improve overall teaching effectiveness, also making this a useful ontological classifier.

The figure shows a taxonomy of existing privacy technology education-related academic articles. Each category is further broken down into multiple subcategories. Not all papers have all of the main categories defined (e.g. delivery method might not be specified, while audience is always specified).

The level of opacity of the grey color in the background of the boxes of the figure represent the percentage of articles in the specific category or subcategory, relative to the total number of surveyed papers. The darker the background color of the box (i.e. the larger the percentage of the total number of academic papers) and the 'hotter" the research area. Details for each of these categories are given in the subsequent chapters.

4 Target Audience

Studies have shown that privacy education impacts privacy-protective behavior [14]. However, the same kind of privacy education is neither effective nor required for all [6]. Most of the existing teaching methods are targeted toward a specific audience.

Broadly speaking, privacy education initiatives are usually aimed at the owner of the information, which we term "Individual data owner". Within this category, students of various ages or education levels are specified. If not, the audience defaults to a "general public" category.

Students at undergraduate and graduate levels are more mature and might be more capable of understanding newer privacy-enhancing technologies (PETs). This includes non-technology students who might not be expected to be computer systems or security experts (e.g., medical students) [47]. Despite this, very few privacy -related courses are analyzed in the literature at the undergraduate or graduate level and most that do address the subject from a legal perspective [22]. In the last five years, a few initiatives in the technology domain have been presented [7, 20, 54], along with a few earlier studies [12, 18, 19].

Maintaining the privacy of others is more critical, based on the number of people that are potentially affected. Software developers often play a crucial role in maintaining the privacy of others but seldom receive formal or even informal education in this area. Designing software to preserve the privacy of others relates to basic questions about the storage and usage of the data of those third parties. However, designers have been criticized for having a lower sense of privacy than their users [21].

Public employees deal with the private information of others regularly. Therefore, they need to know the value of that information and how to deal with it safely. For this reason, the education of specific public sector employees, notably health informatics workers [3, 4] and librarians [36, 52], has been evaluated.

Although organization-specific training programs for software developers related to privacy might be common in industry and there are several websites that talk about the legislative requirements, especially in Europe, only a single academic research paper has been found in this category [54]. However, software developers are a critical audience, especially when handling personal information for large numbers of end users. There are now examples of courses that focus on privacy, specifically, often as part of a software requirements research framework [65].

Teachers are needed at different levels who can teach privacy-related issues and technology to others. Therefore, "privacy teachers" themselves are an important potential audience. Lesson planning and learning material design are discussed in [50]. High-school level teaching of different aspects of privacy has also been studied [10].

5 Application Context

Many teaching initiatives start from basic requirements of personal privacy protection, such as understanding the careful usage of computing devices with internet connections and awareness of the associated privacy implications. Making people aware of what information is private and how such data may be leaked while interacting via public websites has been studied [5, 13, 24]. Precautionary measures when using common personal devices (e.g. disabling the GPS, lowering the brightness on a smartphone) can be taught early in the education cycle [20, 40].

Privacy awareness is required in the context of system development as well. Learners should understand the basic components of modern software architectures and how attackers may target them to gain private information. Teaching initiatives have been taken to make learners more aware of the privacy implications of using data mining, big-data etc., [37, 38], which may be used to analyze a large amount of personal information.

Privacy concerns when using Single Sign On (SSO) authentication systems have been analyzed for education purposes [19]. Privacy implications of mouse-keyboard, malicious use of cookies etc., can be considered [12, 18, 19]. Developers can be taught to consider obfuscation techniques, while dealing with user location information, to enhance the privacy of the resulting applications [54]. The idea of blurring images or videos to enhance privacy is also explored in an educational context [53].

Sensitive and non-sensitive personal information is often shared on different social media platforms. Default security configurations are often used, without full understanding of the corresponding privacy implications. Adopting the persona of a hacker is one teaching method used to make learners aware of the methods that can be used to extract lucrative information from social media postings [33]. Other education approaches like gamification [2] or novel visual methods [32] have been used to educate students about the flow of private information and to encourage proper configuration of privacy settings (e.g. in profiles for web applications).

IoT devices continue to proliferate and permeate different areas of our lives (e.g., smart meters and thermostats, home security systems, vehicles, and many more). IoT devices will account for over half of the world's internet traffic by 2023 [60]. Sophisticated personal devices like fitness trackers and smartwatches can monitor and record our activity levels using heart rate measurement sensors and step counters, as well as our movement levels and location information [26]. While IoT security education seems to be increasing, privacy education is lagging.

Information can be recorded locally on devices or transferred to remote servers for storage and analysis. However, few people read the privacy policies and waivers associated with such data logging. Several initiatives have been taken in the IoT domain, like the OWASP Internet of Things Project [34], to help people better understand the security and privacy issues associated with their IoT devices.

An interesting, recent educational toolkit [23] has been developed to educate people about potential privacy-related issues associated with their personal and IoT devices.

The challenge for such education aids is to keep them up to date with new software applications.

The marketing industry has taken advantage of progress in machine learning and artificial intelligence. However, this can come at the expense of client privacy. Privacy and ethical aspects for information protection should be taught carefully in modern business and management courses and this has been proposed for teachers creating marketing courses [17].

6 Education Delivery Method

Different delivery methods have been adapted to suit specific audiences and contexts. As already mentioned, using games in privacy education has become more popular [48]. Research on the use of interactive elements, different intrinsic motivation factors, and other modern pedagogical research areas are now being considered in the context of privacy-related education.

While games are the primary focus in several papers [25, 26], researchers may only use gamification as a sub-module for the primary privacy-related learning material [2]. This depends on the context for the learning, which has already been discussed. Students can learn through playing games using web-based simulations [11] or can participate on their mobile devices [13]. Besides digital games, physical games (e.g., Card-based games) have also resulted in good educational outcomes [5, 15].

Privacy-awareness initiatives and campaigns [8, 24] often use websites, YouTube content, etc., to teach privacy, combined with "in person" delivery methods. Using more traditional approaches, privacy experts provide live lectures to specific sets of learners [36]. Push notifications in digital media [3, 27] or hands-on activities with audiences are also used. These activities vary from experiments in controlled lab-like environments [12, 18] to gathering data from more "authentic" learning environments [4], including outdoor activities [40].

While advanced digital privacy courses are scarce [22], countries like Canada are adding introductory-level concepts and countermeasures to the curriculum of younger students [42]. Resources to make privacy teachers more knowledgeable are also in the development phase [10]. Many market research and advertising methods can conflict with basic requirements for customer information privacy too. As already mentioned, privacy education needs to be incorporated into the business curriculum for this reason [17]. Historically, few advanced-level, structured courses are available for STEM students [19, 37], but this seems to be changing. A common body of knowledge has been identified recently [16], identifying productive areas for course development.

7 Teaching Modality

Several teaching modalities can be used to improve the privacy education process. "Hands-on" experiments can enhance learning and are becoming more common in the privacy education literature. Students perform supplementary experiments in combination with preliminary reading activities [2, 12, 18, 19].

Experiments can be the main focus of the training. For example, a hands-on learning approach based on the RapidMiner data analysis tool [61] was designed to teach privacy related to Big-data and data mining, etc. [38]. Other researchers used experiments with pictures to show students how even simple images can leak critical private information [40].

Clearly, other theoretical and practical pedagogical advancements could inform the teaching of privacy-related material too. Reviewing these advances is not feasible here, but we note a significant focus of the privacy technology education literature on asynchronous learning methods. It is not clear whether this focus is related to the recent global pandemic or pedagogical experiment, rather than on established pedagogical principles or based on the subject topic of privacy education itself, which is often closely linked with digital forms of personal information in the literature.

Health informatics students were asked to collect information from different stakeholders of a drug supply chain [4] to illustrate privacy-related issues. Privacy leakage via shoulder surfing might be classified as security-related, but researchers in [39] identified this as more of a privacy-related issue almost two decades ago. Recent work with a simulated social networking platform ("Fakesbook") allows students to see a graph-based visualization of their social networking profile data, as it proliferates between simulated platform users [32].

Along with traditional textual information, using audio-visual elements in an offline/asynchronous learning method has been shown to improve student learning. As an example, adding movie themes provided good results in privacy education for middle-school students [38]. Personalized "nudging", in a peer-based teaching modality, was shown to be reasonably effective in [27].

As already stated, non-digital, physical teaching modalities can also be used [5]. The effectiveness of using interactive elements to teach abstract concepts like privacy has also been shown to vary with different age groups [41]. To address this, pedagogical methods that emphasize motivation, like the ARCS model [43], have been applied to improve learning, especially in the earlier age groups [13]. These methods are probably applicable to other learning settings, as already mentioned.

We define "peer learning", as situations where learners interact with other learners of potentially different abilities to learn material. This is usually done while being taught in other ways or by other people (i.e. instructors). While potentially applicable anywhere, using group work in privacy education has had promising results. For example, in a collaborative learning setting, where students formed groups to achieve a common goal, privacy education worked very well with younger students [30].

However, the effectiveness of peer learning can depend on different social aspects. The sense of community for group members and even the group formation process, itself, can be critical to learning outcomes. This has been seen in the context of teaching privacy-related material [29, 35].

Learners can role-play as a "teacher" but also learn in parallel with the "student". Non-experts can benefit from this approach, while creating privacy teaching materials in the context of social media [25]. Similarly, researchers have studied the effectiveness of a teaching initiative, where undergraduate students led a privacy education campaign to teach middle school-aged students [24].

8   Gap Analysis and Recommendations

In contrast to the privacy education papers in the technology domain, we attempted to quantify concurrent security education activity using similar search methods. Specifically, we used a similar keyword search *("Education" OR "Teach" OR "Learn") AND "Security"* in Google Scholar using only their Title, Abstract, and Conclusion sections. We also tried to capture the state of research regarding privacy in the legal domain in the last ten years by simple keyword search *("Privacy" AND "Law")* in the title (Fig. 4).

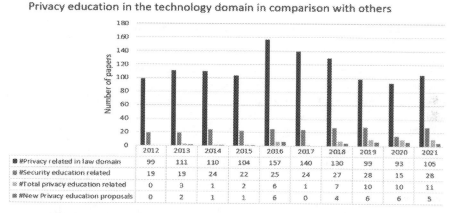

Privacy education in the technology domain in comparison with others

	2012	2013	2014	2015	2016	2017	2018	2019	2020	2021
▣ #Privacy related in law domain	99	111	110	104	157	140	130	99	93	105
▣ #Security education related	19	19	24	22	25	24	27	28	15	28
▨ #Total privacy education related	0	3	1	2	6	1	7	10	10	11
▣ #New Privacy education proposals	0	2	1	1	6	0	4	6	6	5

Fig. 4. Privacy education in the technology domain in comparison to others

Among the reviewed papers, we have found some common key findings. The main obstacle against privacy education is the lack of awareness of the audience regarding the concept of privacy and why it is important. In fact, even if they are made aware, the ease of using digital platforms and sometimes the notation of a false trust on the used platform restrain them from following privacy-preserving behaviour [14]. Among the applied different approaches, the inclusion of interactive activities like hands-on activities, games (especially with multiple participants) etc., are most common. In contrast, detailed and complicated approaches did not work well [5]. However, regarding multi-party games, researchers put a lot of emphasis on effective partner matching. The need for customized privacy teaching is identified, even among people from the same audience class [27].

Lack of diversity among the researchers is noted in (Fig. 5), and it raises a lot of concerns. In today's world, everyone uses technology and may be a victim of privacy-related attacks. However, the privacy problems, solutions, teaching methods, etc., vary depending on the person's culture, background, local law, etc. So, diversity among researchers is an essential criterion for making privacy education effective.

Very little technical research has been done to educate students about third-party privacy and data handling (e.g. for software developers). Among the 31 novel methods, only four of them relate to this area. Many workplace environments require this kind of understanding, (e.g. software developers, system adtministrators) and not just those in the public sector, like healthcare workers, and librarians.

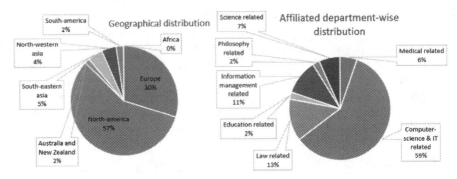

Fig. 5. Geographical and affiliated department-wise distribution of the researchers

Software users can require education, themselves, making the software developer's education even more important. Indeed, the number of available privacy experts or technical workers is smaller than required by the software industry [57]. Privacy (and security) can be viewed as more than just "another" functional requirement and perhaps more of a mandatory area of study for STEM students.

Equally, more researchers and teachers are required with this technical privacy expertise, so that this is possible. In general, both cybersecurity and privacy education professionals are currently scarce, which might explain the observed research focus on asynchronous online methods for teaching privacy-related concepts.

Encouragingly, there are now a few examples of universities and colleges that include privacy-related material in their security curriculum at the graduate level. However, this is less common at the undergraduate level. Some elementary privacy-related topics are usually covered inside secondary school security-related courses, usually when access control is being discussed.

For computer science or software undergraduate students in secondary education settings, privacy courses might be focused on: available Privacy-Enhancing Technologies (PETs), common PET usage as well as their relative advantages and disadvantages. Applicable legal requirements might also be extracted and interpreted.

In undergraduate medical programs, students need to be aware of standards like HIPPA [62]. In experiential learning contexts, understanding and then interpreting such standards in practical situations would be useful. Besides understanding the legal constraints, medical students also need a basic understanding of the capabilities of the technology, as the amount of personal data, collected by personal and non-personal digital devices, increases.

The marketing industry has always embraced the use of data. However, business students would benefit from reconciling modern marketing methods, that rely on data mining techniques at different levels of granularity, with privacy preservation legislation (e.g. European GDPR). For successful marketing campaigns, an understanding of technology and its capabilities and required restrictions is also useful [58]. This remains the least populated education area in our research taxonomy (Fig. 3).

In a recent comparison of the effectiveness of different methods for teaching privacy-related material, a combination of classroom training and gamification was proposed as being the most effective [49]. Practice and rehearsal were shown to aid retention in learners and this may not be specific to privacy-related education. Similarly, gamification, for privacy-related training, will be constrained by the difficulty of designing good educational games [59].

Much of the existing pedagogical research needs to be applied and adapted for privacy-related education. As can be seen from our taxonomy, privacy education varies with the age of the students and applies to personal data as well as the treatment of the personal data of others, resulting in different learning objectives in each situation.

Formal courses to teach privacy as a stand-alone subject are required. Developing (or developed) legislation needs to be compared with the capabilities of available technology and the control mechanisms that are provided or that need to be provided with that technology. Understanding of and practice using PETs is required and must be taught. It is possible for our own privacy rights or those of others to conflict with the desires of governments to observe our activities or control those rights, so learning privacy technology "on the job" might be dangerous or just inefficient.

Synchronous learning activities seem to help students learn complex topics like privacy [63]. Moreover 75% of the experiential learning activities reviewed take place in a synchronous setting, although this value cannot be discerned directly from Fig. 1. Privacy (and security) instructors are scarce and the industry demand for privacy and security professionals currently exceeds supply, which might explain researcher interest in minimizing the role of the instructor in asynchronous teaching modalities.

The research trends might then also make sense in the context of the recent restrictions that have been imposed by the current global pandemic. Synchronous teaching of privacy-related material, while now recognized as being important, is harder to implement. Perhaps, novel teaching modalities that combine online learning with peer-based learning somehow (and yet remain "experiential") are the most promising and practical approaches to privacy-related education or perhaps online learning will diminish as the memory of the global pandemic recedes. The privacy technologies themselves are evolving, and privacy education needs to track these changes.

9 Conclusions

We have reviewed the literature related to digital privacy education. We used this to produce a taxonomy and identified several gaps. These gaps could help guide future research on how to educate people about digital privacy more effectively. Our research has shown the need for related undergraduate curriculum changes in privacy education.

New graduates from STEM programs will need to understand privacy-related issues from personal and third-party perspectives. Indeed, privacy awareness among IT employees has become more critical in North America, which lags Europe in privacy-related legislation. Indeed, the research on how to teach privacy-related information management, especially for third parties, seems inadequate, especially when compared with security-related education activities.

This might be because the cost models of security-related attacks are clearer and more tangible. Various teaching modalities (e.g., experiments, interactive elements, and interpersonal activities) seem to be effective in creating new courses for privacy-related education, and it is encouraging to see them being studied in the context of privacy-related education. Novel education methods are worthwhile considering, to compensate for instructor shortages.

Acknowledgements. We thank the anonymous reviewers for their comments and ideas for improvements.

References

1. Adams, C.: Introduction to Privacy Enhancing Technologies: A Classification-Based Approach to Understanding PETs. Springer, Cham (2021). https://doi.org/10.1007/978-3-030-81043-6
2. Alemany, J., Del Val, E., Garcia-Fornes, A.: Assessing the effectiveness of a gamified social network for applying privacy concepts: an empirical study with teens. IEEE Trans. Learn. Technol. **13**(4), 777–789 (2020)
3. Amiri, F., Neshati, A., Hannani, S., Azadi, N.: Effect of mobile-based education of patient's privacy protection principles on the knowledge, attitude and performance of operating room staff. Ann. Roman. Soc. Cell Biol. **25**(6), 6876–6882 (2021)
4. Amro, B.M., Al-Jabari, M.O., Jabareen, H.M., Khader, Y.S., Taweel, A.: Design and development of case studies in security and privacy for health informatics education. In: 2018 IEEE/ACS 15th International Conference on Computer Systems and Applications (AICCSA), pp. 1–6. IEEE (2018)
5. Barnard-Wills, D., Ashenden, D.: Playing with privacy: games for education and communication in the politics of online privacy. Polit. Stud. **63**(1), 142–160 (2015)
6. Büchi, M., Festic, N., Just, N., Latzer, M.: Digital inequalities in online privacy protection: effects of age, education and gender. In: Handbook of Digital Inequality. Edward Elgar Publishing (2021)
7. Burd, B., et al.: Courses, content, and tools for internet of things in computer science education. In: Proceedings of the 2017 ITiCSE Conference on Working Group Reports, pp. 125–139 (2018)
8. Chattopadhyay, A., Christian, D., Ulman, A., Petty, S.: Towards a novel visual privacy themed educational tool for cybersecurity awareness and K-12 outreach. In: Proceedings of the 19th Annual SIG Conference on Information Technology Education, p. 159 (2018)
9. Cvetkovski, A.: Data protection and the right to privacy in the computer age–through law enforcement or through education? IJAEDU-Int. E-J. Adv. Educ. **7**(21), 207–211 (2021)
10. Egelman, S., Bernd, J., Friedland, G., Garcia, D.: The teaching privacy curriculum. In: Proceedings of the 47th ACM Technical Symposium on Computing Science Education, pp. 591–596 (2016)
11. Ghazinour, K., Messner, K., Scarnecchia, S., Selinger, D.: Digital-PASS: a simulation-based approach to privacy education. In: Proceedings of the 18th ACM Workshop on Privacy in the Electronic Society, pp. 162–174 (2019)
12. Ghiglieri, M., Stopczynski, M.: Seclab: an innovative approach to learn and understand current security and privacy issues. In: Proceedings of the 17th Annual Conference on Information Technology Education, pp. 67–72 (2016)
13. Giannakas, F., Gritzalis, S.: Raising internet security and privacy awareness in primary and early secondary education via mobile gamification. Ph.D. Dissertation (2018). Πανεπιστη΄μιο Αιγαι΄ου. Σχολη΄ Πολυτε χνικη΄. Τμη΄μα Μηχανικω΄ ν Πληροφοριακω΄ ν και . . .

14. Heinrich, M.: Does education impact the use of privacy enhancing behavior? A longitudinal study. Ph.D. Dissertation. Creighton University (2021)
15. Jost, P., Divitini, M.: From paper to online: digitizing card based co-creation of games for privacy education. In: De Laet, T., Klemke, R., Alario-Hoyos, C., Hilliger, I., Ortega-Arranz, A. (eds.) EC-TEL 2021. LNCS, vol. 12884, pp. 178–192. Springer, Cham (2021). https://doi.org/10.1007/978-3-030-86436-1_14
16. Lavranou, R., Tsohou, A.: Developing and validating a common body of knowledge for information privacy. Inf. Comput. Secur. **27**, 668–686 (2019)
17. Peltier, J.W., Milne, G.R., Phelps, J.E., Barrett, J.T.: Teaching information privacy in marketing courses: Key educational issues for principles of marketing and elective marketing courses. J. Mark. Educ. **32**(2), 224–246 (2010)
18. Peltsverger, S., Zheng, G.: Hands-on privacy labs. In: Proceedings of the 14th Annual ACM SIGITE Conference on Information Technology Education, pp. 137–138 (2013)
19. Peltsverger, S., Zheng, G.: Enhancing privacy education with a technical emphasis in IT curriculum. J. Inf. Technol. Educ. Innov. Pract. **15**, 1 (2016)
20. Rege, A., Mendlein, A., Williams, K.: Security and privacy education for STEM undergraduates: a shoulder surfing course project. In: 2019 IEEE Frontiers in Education Conference (FIE), pp. 1–7. IEEE (2019)
21. Senarath, A.R., Arachchilage, N.A.G.: Understanding user privacy expectations: a software developer's perspective. Telemat. Inform. **35**(7), 1845–1862 (2018)
22. Steinhagen, D., Lucas, C., Francis, M., Lawrence, M., Streff, K.: An Inventory of Privacy Curricula Offerings in Higher Education. Inf. Syst. Educ. J. **19**(3), 21–30 (2021)
23. Visoottiviseth, V., Khengthong, T., Kesorn, K., Patcharadechathorn, J.: ASPAHI: application for security and privacy awareness education for home IoT devices. In: 2021 25th International Computer Science and Engineering Conference (ICSEC), pp. 388–393. IEEE (2021)
24. Walker, K.L., Kiesler, T., Malone, S.: Youth-driven information privacy education campaign 2015–16: digital trust foundation final grant report. Online Submission (2016)
25. Wang, W., Tao, Y., Wang, K., Jedruszczak, D., Knutson, B.: Leveraging crowd for game-based learning: a case study of privacy education game design and evaluation by crowdsourcing. arXiv preprint arXiv:1603.02766 (2016)
26. Williams, M., Nurse, J.R.C., Creese, S.: (Smart) watch out! Encouraging privacy-protective behavior through interactive games. Int. J. Hum. Comput. Stud. **132**(2019), 121–137 (2019)
27. Wisniewski, P.J., Knijnenburg, B.P., Lipford, H.R.: Making privacy personal: profiling social network users to inform privacy education and nudging. Int. J. Hum. Comput. Stud. **98**(2017), 95–108 (2017)
28. Wu, Y.: The spread of artificial intelligence technology challenges the bottom line of privacy protection. In: 2022 7th International Conference on Cloud Computing and Big Data Analytics (ICCCBDA), pp. 407–411 (2022). https://doi.org/10.1109/ICCCBDA55098.2022.9778934
29. Yusri, R.: A game theoretical model for a collaborative e-learning platform on privacy awareness (2020)
30. Yusri, R., Abusitta, A., Aïmeur, E.: Teens-online: a game theory-based collaborative platform for privacy education. Int. J. Artif. Intell. Educ. **31**(4), 726–768 (2021)
31. NIST Privacy Framework: A Tool for Improving Privacy through. https://nvlpubs.nist.gov/nistpubs/CSWP/NIST.CSWP.01162020.pdf. Accessed 17 Junw 2022
32. Zinkus, M., Curry, O., Moore, M., Peterson, Z., Wood, Z.J.: Fakesbook. In: Proceedings of the 50th ACM Technical Symposium on Computer Science Education, pp. 892–989 (2019). https://doi.org/10.1145/3287324.3287486
33. Ghazinour, K., Scarnecchia, S., Rabideau, J., Pecore, B.: A novel approach to social media privacy education through simulated role reversal. Proc. Comput. Sci. **177**(2020), 112–119 (2020). https://doi.org/10.1016/j.procs.2020.10.018

34. OWASP Internet of Things | OWASP Foundation. https://owasp.org/www-project-internet-of-things/. Accessed 19 June 2022

35. Girard, E., Yusri, R., Abusitta, A., Aïmeur, E.: An automated stable personalised partner selection for collaborative privacy education. Int. J. Integr. Technol. Educ. **10**(2), 9–22 (2021). https://doi.org/10.5121/ijite.2021.10202

36. Noh, Y.: Digital library user privacy: changing librarian viewpoints through education. Libr. Hi Tech **32**(2), 300–317 (2014). https://doi.org/10.1108/lht-08-2013-0103

37. Knorr, E.M., Riva, G.V.D., Vakarelov, O.: Anatomy of a new data science course in privacy, ethics, and security. In: Proceedings of the 23rd Western Canadian Conference on Computing Education (2018). https://doi.org/10.1145/3209635.3209640

38. Dryer, A., Walia, N., Chattopadhyay, A.: A middle-school module for introducing data-mining, big-data, ethics and privacy using RapidMiner and a hollywood theme. In: Proceedings of the 49th ACM Technical Symposium on Computer Science Education (2018). https://doi.org/10.1145/3159450.3159553

39. Orgill, G.L., Romney, G.W., Bailey, M.G., Orgill, P.M.: The urgency for effective user privacy-education to counter social engineering attacks on secure computer systems. In: Proceedings of the 5th Conference on Information Technology Education - CITC5 (2004). https://doi.org/10.1145/1029533.1029577

40. Schulz, S.: Teaching privacy outdoors – first approaches in the field in connection with STEM education. Research on outdoor STEM education in the digital Age. In: Proceedings of the ROSETA Online Conference in June 2020, pp. 163–170 (2020). https://doi.org/10.37626/ga9783959871440.0.20

41. McDonald, A.M., Reeder, R.W., Kelley, P.G., Cranor, L.F.: A comparative study of online privacy policies and formats. In: Proceedings of the 5th Symposium on Usable Privacy and Security - SOUPS (2009). https://doi.org/10.1145/1572532.1572586

42. Dyszlewski, A.: The landscape of digital citizenship education in Canada from grades K-12: online privacy education. https://knowledgecommons.lakeheadu.ca/handle/2453/4269. Accessed 21 June 2022

43. Keller, J.M.: Development and use of the ARCS model of instructional design. J. Instruct. Dev. **10**(3), 2–10 (1987). https://doi.org/10.1007/bf02905780

44. Bross, T., Camp, L.: I just want your anonymized contacts! Benefits and education in security & privacy research. In: 2013 IEEE Security and Privacy Workshops (2013). https://doi.org/10.1109/spw.2013.6915057

45. Romney, V.W., Romney, G.W.: Neglect of information privacy instruction. In: Proceedings of the 5th conference on Information technology education - CITC5 (2004). https://doi.org/10.1145/1029533.1029553

46. Rutherfoord, R.H., Rutherfoord, J.K.: Privacy and ethical concerns in internet security. In: Proceedings of the 2010 ACM Conference on Information Technology Education - SIGITE (2010). https://doi.org/10.1145/1867651.1867686

47. Olaza-Maguiña, A.F., De La Cruz-Ramirez, Y.M.: Information security education and self-perception of privacy protection risk in mobile web in obstetrics students from Peru. In: Bentahar, J., Awan, I., Younas, M., Grønli, T.-M. (eds.) MobiWIS 2021. LNCS, vol. 12814, pp. 32–43. Springer, Cham (2021). https://doi.org/10.1007/978-3-030-83164-6_3

48. Karagiannis, S., Papaioannou, T., Magkos, E., Tsohou, A.: Game-based information security/privacy education and awareness: theory and practice. In: Themistocleous, M., Papadaki, M., Kamal, M.M. (eds.) EMCIS 2020. LNBIP, vol. 402, pp. 509–525. Springer, Cham (2020). https://doi.org/10.1007/978-3-030-63396-7_34

49. Dupuis, M.J., Gordon, C.: Evaluating Prevalence, perceptions, and effectiveness of cyber security and privacy education, training, and awareness programs (unpublished)

50. Fuster, G.G., Kloza, D.: The European handbook for teaching privacy and data protection at schools (2016)

51. Fuster, G.G., De Hert, P., Kloza, D.: State-of-the-art report on teaching privacy and personal data protection at schools in the European Union (2015)
52. Snowman, A.M.: Privacy and confidentiality: using scenarios to teach your staff about patron. J. Access Serv. **10**(2), 120–132 (2013). https://doi.org/10.1080/15367967.2012.762267
53. Chattopadhyay, A., Christian, D., Ulman, A., Sawyer, C.: A middle-school case study: piloting a novel visual privacy themed module for teaching societal and human security topics using social media apps. In: 2018 IEEE Frontiers in Education Conference (FIE) (2018). https://doi.org/10.1109/fie.2018.8659278
54. Florea, I.M., Vornicu, D., Văduva, J.A. Rughiniș, R.: Teaching privacy through the development and testing of a location obfuscation solution. eLearn. Softw. Educ. **2** (2020)
55. REGULATION (EU) 2016/ 679 General Data Protection Regulation. https://eur-lex.europa.eu/legal-content/EN/TXT/PDF/?uri=CELEX:32016R0679. Accessed 30 June 2022
56. California Consumer Privacy Act. California Legislative Information. https://leginfo.legislature.ca.gov/faces/billTextClient.xhtml?bill_id=201720180AB375&search_keywords=privacy. Accessed 30 June 2022
57. Data Privacy Jobs Report Shows Demand. https://www.cpomagazine.com/data-privacy/data-privacy-jobs-report-shows-demand-for-privacy-pros-at-record-high-thanks-to-complex-regulatory-requirements-mass-migration-to-cloud-services/. Accessed 30 June 2022
58. Foxman, E.R., Kilcoyne, P.: Information technology, marketing practice, and consumer privacy: ethical issues. J. Public Policy Mark. **12**(1), 106–119 (1993). https://doi.org/10.1177/074391569501200111
59. Law, E.-C., Kickmeier-Rust, M.D., Albert, D., Holzinger, A.: Challenges in the development and evaluation of immersive digital educational games. In: Holzinger, A. (ed.) USAB 2008. LNCS, vol. 5298, pp. 19–30. Springer, Heidelberg (2008). https://doi.org/10.1007/978-3-540-89350-9_2
60. Office of the Privacy Commissioner of Canada. A Framework for the Government of Canada to Assess Privacy-Impactful Initiatives in Response to COVID-19; Office of the Privacy Commissioner of Canada: Ottawa, QC, Canada (2020)
61. Cisco Annual Internet Report (2018–2023) White Paper. https://www.cisco.com/c/en/us/solutions/collateral/executive-perspectives/annual-internet-report/white-paper-c11-741490.html. Accessed 1 July 2022
62. RapidMiner for Academics - RapidMiner. https://rapidminer.com/platform/educational/. Accessed 1 July 2022
63. HIPAA Home | HHS.gov. https://www.hhs.gov/hipaa/index.html. Accessed 14 Aug 2022
64. Burgess, A., Van Diggele, C., Roberts, C., Mellis, C.: Team-based learning: design, facilitation and participation. BMC Med. Educ. **20** (2020). https://doi.org/10.1186/s12909-020-02287-y
65. Peixoto, M.M.: Privacy requirements engineering in agile software development: a specification method. In: REFSQ Workshops 2020 (2020)
66. Obar, J.A., Oeldorf-Hirsch, A.: The biggest lie on the internet: ignoring the privacy policies and terms of service policies of social networking services. Inf. Commun. Soc. **23**(1), 128–147 (2020)

Differentially Private Friends Recommendation

Kamalkumar Macwan, Abdessamad Imine, and Michael Rusinowitch[✉]

Université de Lorraine, CNRS, Inria, Loria, 54000 Nancy, France
{kamalkumar.macwan,abdessamad.imine,michael.rusinowitch}@loria.fr

Abstract. Most recommendation systems in social networks provide
users with relevant new friend suggestions by processing their personal
information or their current friends lists. However, providing such recommendations may leak users' private information. We present a new differentially private recommendation algorithm that preserves the privacy
of both attribute values and friend links. The algorithm mainly proceeds
by adding calibrated noise to an adequate matrix representation of the
social network. To get a good trade-off between privacy and accuracy,
the required amount of noise should be limited and therefore we need
to mitigate the prohibitive sensitivity of the matrix representation. For
that, we apply a graph projection technique to control the size of friends
lists. The effectiveness of our approach is demonstrated by experiments
on real-world datasets and comparisons with existing methods.

Keywords: Social Networks · Recommendation · Link Privacy ·
Differential Privacy

1 Introduction

Online social networks (OSN) have been widely used by people to get connected
with other users. Users choose to create profiles by setting some personal details
like gender, age, hobbies, etc. OSN also allows users to create different groups,
or pages to have a connection with other users of similar interests.

Suggesting suitable candidates for friendship to a target user is a challenging
task for a recommendation system. In the existing literature, different approaches
have been proposed to solve this problem. Recommendation methods are classified into different categories: relationship-based recommendations, interest-based
recommendation, location-based recommendation, etc. [2]. In general, OSN users
receive recommendations from their platforms based on their profiles and their
behavior. Due to privacy concerns, users hide their sensitive information from
other users but this information can be leveraged by the service provider to
generate more accurate recommendations.

Current recommendation systems (RS) apply artificial intelligence techniques
to predict users' behavior or users' preferences. As each user of an OSN is connected with friends, some RS exploits information provided by the user's friends

Funded by LUE DigiTrust (http://lue.univ-lorraine.fr/fr/article/digitrust/).

G.-V. Jourdan et al. (Eds.): FPS 2022, LNCS 13877, pp. 236–251, 2023.
https://doi.org/10.1007/978-3-031-30122-3_15

to generate recommendations [3]. Matrix factorization is considered as an efficient approach to generate recommendations by identifying latent factors that characterize users or items [4]. Without private user information, a recommendation result may be less accurate and even fail to generate personalized service. Hence, RS inputs should include such information, possibly in noisy form.

Differential privacy (DP) considers the leakage prevention of private data by adding calibrated noise to query results [5]. DP has been widely adopted to implement effective privacy-preserving recommendations where a Service Provider (SP) collects user information and generates recommendations. Existing literature [6] has also introduced Local Differential Privacy (LDP), a decentralized version of DP where every user injects noise locally. LDP is particularly interesting to ensure privacy in a setting where the SP is not trustworthy.

To illustrate privacy issues with social recommendations let us consider an OSN that allows the user to specify a friend-list and values for some attributes. Assume User u has 40% friends who have declared "football" as their favorite sport. The remaining 60% have opted to keep it hidden. Now, if the recommendation model suggests some pages/videos related to "basketball" to User u then u can make a guess that a majority of those 60% friends have declared "basketball" for sport. Assume another situation where User u has 65% friends that are male (private attribute value) and have chosen "soccer" as a sport (public attribute value), then u will probably get "soccer" as a recommendation. Now, if another User v has the same friends as u but gets a different recommendation such as "badminton", then u and v can infer each other's gender. In another case where User u keeps their friend-list hidden and User u is recommended to User v (e.g., because they are sharing many friends) then v can make a guess about u's friends. These scenarios show privacy problems while generating recommendation results. *This motivates us to design a recommendation system that takes advantage of both user's friends and attribute values for a more accurate friend recommendation, while mitigating the risk of leaking attribute values or friendship links.*

In this paper, we model an OSN by a labeled graph and propose a *privacy-preserving friend recommendation system* for OSN users. A service provider extracts the social network data and applies it to a recommendation algorithm. We assume that recommendations are generated by a fully trusted service provider (TSP). TSP has access to public and private information of every user to generate a recommendation result. This operation is based on computing the number of connections attached to every user for every attribute value. This approach allows one to refine standard binary approaches that only record whether a user has some attribute value or not: in our proposal, we record the proportion of friends that have some attribute value and this allows one to measure the interest of a user for some value. The recommendation results may be shared publicly for further usage by any third party, e.g., it can be used to target users for advertisement.

For the social graph setting, we assume that attribute values and friend links (or connections) are hidden from other users. Obviously, there is an exception when user u is a friend with user v since in that case, v knows one link from u. The concept of DP is enforced by TSP on the connection counting matrix to make the recommendation results implausible to reveal the user's private attributes. For a given social graph, we aim to generate the recommendation results while ensuring that any malicious attacker cannot accurately infer a user's private information.

The main contributions of this paper are: 1) a recommendation system for OSN users that leverages both friends and attributes information 2) a differential privacy setting that ensures that recommendations preserve OSN users' privacy 3) experiments on real social graphs to evaluate the proposed approach and compare it with existing ones. From the experimental analysis, we can tune parameters to get a good trade-off between privacy and utility.

The paper is organized as follows. In Sect. 2, we summarize existing methods of DP models. Section 3 contains the explanation of some fundamental definitions and terms related to a social network. The proposed approaches are briefly described in Sect. 4. In Sect. 5, we perform an experimental analysis of our proposed approach. We conclude and define future scope in Sect. 6.

2   Related Work

Privacy of recommendation systems for OSN can be ensured with cryptographic protocols as in [7,20] but with significant computational cost and high key update management due to the size and dynamics of OSN. The privacy-preserving friend recommendation system proposed in [8] considers anonymized social graph structure. However, the approach does not provide a formal analysis of the privacy risks that we can benefit from differential privacy.

In [9], the authors present a differentially private system for recommending friends in social networks while preserving the privacy of links. Their system is based on metrics between nodes such as Common Neighbours, Katz Centrality, and Graph Distance. Therefore the system ignores attribute information and admits a cold-start problem when some user joining the network does not have any friends yet. Instead, our recommendation system relies on collaborative filtering through matrix factorization. As a result, our friend recommendations also take into account user attributes and this leads to more accurate suggestions. Unlike other perturbation methods, DP-based recommendation systems quantify formally the amount of privacy leakage in order to ensure some recommendation accuracy [5]. Indeed, DP injects noise that depends on the sensitivity of the data queries and the level of privacy offered to the user. In [3], DP is applied to recommendation systems by injecting Laplace noise to the covariance matrix for the prediction of missing ratings. The same concept has also been applied to the recommendation in OSN platforms [10] but disregarding the recommendation of friends.

The privacy-preserving friend recommendation system in [15] focuses on protection against fake accounts attacks by building a *friends candidate graph* from the user's phonebook. The authors do not evaluate the privacy level offered by their solution. In [11], the authors present an item recommendation system based on graph embedding and neural network approaches that prevent inference attacks on user profile sensitive data, through the combination of several differential privacy techniques. They do not consider friend recommendations. In our case, we rely on matrix factorization and besides attributes, we also take advantage of friends links and OSN homophily properties to perform friend recommendations.

Based on a latent factor model for recommendations, [6] shows that adding noise to inputs gives the best accuracy while ensuring robust protection against attacks aimed at gaining knowledge about user ratings. We will adopt here a similar input perturbation approach. Moreover, we consider both the friend-list and attributes attached to each user. This allows one to generate more accurate recommendations and also to provide useful results even if the user has only a profile with attributes but no friend-list or vice versa.

3   Preliminaries

In this section, we give the notation and concepts used throughout the paper.

3.1   Labeled Social Graphs

A labeled social graph is defined as $G = (V, E, L)$, where V is the set of users, E is the set of undirected edges representing relationships or connections between nodes and L is the labeling of nodes by attributes values defined as follows. Consider A is a set of attributes where each attribute $a \in A$ has a set of values $\bar{a}$.

We assume that for any two distinct attributes $a, b \in A$, their set of values $\bar{a}$ and $\bar{b}$ are disjoint, and the set of all attribute values $\bar{A} = \bigcup_{a \in A} \bar{a}$ is ordered as $z_1, z_2, \ldots, z_k$. The labeling function L assigns to every node u a set of attribute values. The label or attribute-value for user u is defined by:

$$L(u) = \bigcup_{a \in A} l(u, a) \tag{1}$$

where $l(u, a)$ is a subset of $\bar{a}$ for all u, a.

Definition 1 (Attributed Connections (AC)). *For a labeled social graph $G = (V, E, L)$, user $u \in V$ and attribute value $z \in \bar{a}$ where $a \in A$, the set of attributed connections is $AC_G(u, z) = \{v \mid (u, v) \in E$ and $z \in l(v, a)\}$. If there is no confusion we write $AC(u, z)$ instead of $AC_G(u, z)$.*

Given a labeled social graph $G = (V, E, L)$ and user $u \in V$, $N(G)$ represents the adjacency matrix of G and $d_G(u)$ represents the degree of u in G. We use simply N and $d(u)$ when G is clear from context. Given two matrices C and D with the same number of rows, $C\|D$ represents the matrix obtained by concatenating their corresponding rows.

3.2 Differential Privacy

DP [5] provides formal guarantees of individual privacy against adversaries with background knowledge. DP effectively perturbates computations by injecting noise to ensure that the output is not significantly affected by a single change in the inputs. Initially defined for tabular data, DP has been extended to graph data, e.g., to protect a node or an edge.

Given a query f on a social dataset D, we look for an algorithm A which returns a noised result obtained from D, that is sufficiently close to $f(D)$ to be useful. DP ensures privacy for participating users in the social dataset while minimizing the difference between $A(D)$ and $f(D)$, by adding a controlled amount of noise. The ϵ-differential privacy property (ϵ-DP) [5] is satisfied for a positive real number ϵ if:

$$Pr[A(D_1) \in S] \leq e^{\epsilon} Pr[A(D_2) \in S] \tag{2}$$

for all subsets S of the set of outputs and for all neighbour datasets D_1 and D_2, where the neighbouring definition is specific to the dataset and the data to be protected. For a social network dataset, the neighboring datasets can be defined with reference to nodes, edges or labels (attribute values) attached to nodes. Existing literature [12] has introduced node-neighbor graphs and edge-neighbor graphs and the related differential privacy notions: Node-DP and Edge-DP, respectively. In this work, we consider neighbour graphs to be pairs of graphs that differ either by one edge or by the presence of one label in a single node. This two part definition is a variant of the one in [13]. We recall our assumption that for any two distinct attributes their set of values are disjoint.

Definition 2 (Neighbor Graphs). *Two labeled social graphs $G_1 = (V, E_1, L_1)$ and $G_2 = (V, E_2, L_2)$ are neighbors if either i) there is a node v such that the symmetric difference of $L_1(v)$ and $L_2(v)$ is a singleton and for all nodes $u \neq v$, $L_1(u) = L_2(u)$, or ii) they differ by a single edge.*

In order to evaluate the magnitude of noise to be injected into the query result, one has to compute the maximum variation of the query result on neighbor graphs, which is known as *Global Sensitivity*.

Definition 3 (Global Sensitivity). *For a numeric function $f : G \rightarrow \mathbb{R}$, the global sensitivity GS_f of f for neighbor graphs G_1 and G_2 is defined as:*

$$GS_f = \max_{G_1, G_2} |f(G_1) - f(G_2)| \tag{3}$$

This definition is extended to function returning vectors (or matrices) by interpreting the notation $|.|$ as the L_1-norm.

A well-known technique to achieve DP is to apply Laplace mechanism [5].

Definition 4 (Laplace Distribution). *The Laplace distribution centered at 0 and with scale parameter b has for density function:*

$$Lap(x|b) = \frac{1}{2b} exp(-\frac{|x|}{b}) \tag{4}$$

The Laplace mechanism injects noise into the result of function f. The noise is drawn from Laplace distribution $Lap(x|b)$ where the scale coefficient b is the quotient of the global sensitivity of f by the privacy parameter ϵ.

Proposition 1. *[14] Given a function f with value in $\mathbb{R}^k$, $f_{DP}(x) = f(x) + (Y_1, \ldots, Y_k)$ satisfies ϵ-differential privacy when the Y_i are independent, identically distributed random variables sampled from distribution $Lap(x|GS_f/\epsilon)$.*

To simplify notations, the noised version of $f(x)$ above will be denoted by $f_{DP}(x) = f(x) + Lap(GS_f/\epsilon)$.

3.3   Social Recommendations

Matrix Factorization Approach. Matrix factorization (MF) is a popular approach of recommendation systems because of its prominent predictive accuracy and computational scalability. Given m users and n items, we consider a matrix R of size $m \times n$ where each of the entries r_{ij} represents the rating of User i for Item j whenever $(i, j) \in \mathcal{E}$ ($\mathcal{E}$ the set of couples for which the rating is available) and a default value $\perp$ otherwise. In order to predict the rating r_{ij} for a pair $(i, j) \notin \mathcal{E}$ an SP can apply MF to compute an approximate factorization of R into matrices U and V of dimensions $m \times d$ and $d \times n$, respectively, are called user latent factor matrix and item latent factor matrix respectively. We assume that d is small w.r.t. m, n. Row u_i of U represents the weights for user i of d user latent factors. Likewise, column v_j represents the weights for item j of d item latent factors. Then, the service can recommend Item j to User i according to the value of $u_i \cdot v_j$, where $a \cdot b = \sum_{s=1}^{d} a_s b_s$ is the usual inner product in $\mathbb{R}^d$.

The (approximate) factorization can be obtained by the following least-square estimation:

$$\min_{\{u_i\}_1^m, \{v_j\}_1^n} \sum_{(i,j) \in \mathcal{E}} |r_{ij} - u_i \cdot v_j|^2 \tag{5}$$

The minimization in Expression 5 can be achieved by stochastic gradient descent or alternating least squares method [16]. Once the latent matrices are generated, the prediction of the missing rating can be done by doing the dot product of the corresponding user and item latent factors vectors:

$$\widehat{r_{ij}} = u_i.v_j \tag{6}$$

If $r_{ij} = \perp$ and $\widehat{r_{ij}} > T$ for some fixed threshold T determined experimentally then the system will recommend j to i.

Application to Friends Recommendation. To recommend friends in OSN, the approach is the same as above, except we replace the set of items with the union of the set of users and the set of attribute values. Then the rating matrix r is defined as follows:

- if j is the column index of a user then $r_{ij} = 1$ if users i and j are friends and 0 otherwise;

– if j is the column index of an attribute value then r_{ij} records the importance of this attribute value for User i. For instance $r_{ij} = 1$ if attribute value j is in the profile of i. Otherwise, r_{ij} is the proportion of friends of User i who have attribute value j.

To get an idea of our friend recommendation approach, note that if users i and j have many mutual friends and common attribute values, their vectors will be close to each other. Matrix factorization will tend to complement the vectors so that they get even closer together. In our proposed approach, the attributes are included in columns along with the users for factorization. As a result, the recommendation not only depends on friends but also on attributes. Thus, our approach outperforms standard recommendation methods where a new connection is suggested to users when they have a certain number of mutual friends. In addition to the graph structure, our approach exploits attribute information to improve the recommendation as detailed below.

4   Differentially Private Recommendations for Social Networks

In this section, we consider a scenario where user information including sensitive one can be shared with the TSP in charge of providing recommendations.

4.1   Overview of Social Networking Scenario

We consider a TSP that collects information from all OSN users and provides useful recommendations to each of the users. Given a set S we denote the number of elements in S by $|S|$.

To generate the recommendation, the TSP builds the adjacency matrix $N(G)$ (of dimension $|V| \times |V|$) and an auxiliary matrix $M(G)$ (of dimensions $|V| \times |\bar{A}|$) where V is the set of users and $\bar{A} = \bigcup_{a \in A} \bar{a}$. A matrix entry $M(G)(u, z)$ stores 1 if User u has attribute value z, otherwise it stores $\frac{AC_G(u,z)}{d(u)}$, i.e., the number of connections of $u \in V$ that are labelled with attribute value $z \in \bar{A}$ divided by the number of friends of u (i.e., the proportion of u's friends with label z). We recall our assumption that different attributes have disjoint sets of values.

The attribute value $z \in \bar{A}$ can be either public or private. Information in matrix $M(G)$ records the number of user friends labeled by a specific attribute value and thus allows one to infer user preferences by appealing to a *homophily principle*: the likelihood that a node has some given label increases with the ratio of its connections with the same label. Therefore this matrix will be applied as an input to the recommendation module. Now, as we want to generate the recommendation using private information too, processing directly raw information may violate the user's privacy. Thus, the attributed connection count in the matrix should be differentially private before it is transferred to the recommendation module.

To do that, we devise an algorithm that generates a matrix $M_{\epsilon_1}(G)$ by adding noise to $M(G)$ such that for two label-neighboring graphs G_1 and G_2:

$$\forall S, Pr(M_{\epsilon_1}(G_1) \in S) \leq e^{\epsilon_1} Pr(M_{\epsilon_1}(G_2) \in S) \qquad (7)$$

As a consequence, the algorithm satisfies ϵ_1-DP and any label of any user in G will be protected (i.e., plausibly deniable) if we can take ϵ_1 sufficiently small. In the same way, we consider the adjacency matrix $N(G)$ of G and we generate a matrix $N_{\epsilon_2}(G)$ by adding noise to $N(G)$ in such a way that it satisfies ϵ_2-DP.

4.2 Differential Privacy with a Trusted Service Provider

We present here a differentially private recommendation model for a TSP. Figure 1 shows the system architecture for the proposed approach. The TSP collects attributes (i.e., attributes of user profile such as gender, age, occupation, etc.) related to each user and connections among users from the social platform. Each user can opt to hide some of their attributes or their friend-list considered to be private. So, every user can view the public information of other users but cannot access their private (hidden) information. However the TSP collects both public and private information.

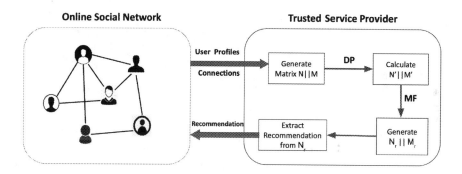

Fig. 1. Differentially Private Social Network Recommendation Scenario

The TSP receives the structural information of a graph and the profile of each user. Based on this information, a matrix M is generated. The matrix M represents connections among every node pair and the impact of all attribute values for each user. Since this matrix records AC count for sensitive attributes too, the TSP should keep the matrix entries secret to prevent an attacker to predict a specific user attribute value. Therefore some noise is added by the TSP to the matrix M to obtain matrix M'. Next, M' is combined with N' a noisy version of adjacency matrix N. Finally, the recommendation is computed by factorization of the combined matrix. Every user can see the recommendations made by the TSP for all users of the social network.

Although the recommendation results are public, an attacker cannot derive other users' private information with full confidence since the combined matrix computation satisfies DP which is preserved by post-processing [5]. Here, the post-processing mainly consists of Matrix Factorization (explained in Subsect. 3.3).

The different steps of the approach are detailed below.

Reducing Sensitivity by Graph Projection. We plan to compute a matrix $M(G)$ whose entries record the proportion of friends (connections) of a given user u that have a given attribute-value z_1. We can show that the global sensitivity GS for $M(G)$

$$GS_{M(G)} \leq Max(d_{max}, 2|\bar{A}|) \tag{8}$$

where d_{max} is the largest degree (or friend list size) of a node in the social graph. Since the number of connections for any attribute value may be very large (up to the number of social network users), this leads to a large value for global sensitivity GS. As a consequence, without further operations, a reasonable trade-off between privacy and utility is not possible since a high Laplace noise would be required for preserving privacy. To solve this issue, we appeal to the graph projection technique [13] which permits to get a lower sensitivity by truncating high-degree nodes. For a given value of $\lambda < d_{max}$, the projection technique deletes some edges from G in order to obtain a new graph $\mu(G, \lambda)$ with the same set of nodes but such that $d_{\mu(G,\lambda)}(u) \leq \lambda$ for all nodes u. We recall the result from [13] and [17] (Definition 2 page 110) that we adapt to our framework:

Definition 5 (Edge Truncation Algorithm [13,17]). *Given a graph $G = (V, E, L)$, a truncation parameter $\lambda > 0$ and a canonical ordering on E, the truncation algorithm $\mu(G, \lambda)$ is defined by iterating on E and deleting every edge (u, v) such that either $degree(u) > \lambda$ or $degree(v) > \lambda$*

The following lemma and its proof are adapted from Proposition 1 in [17]. Our bounds are not the same since the queries we consider are different from [17].

Lemma 1. *Given two neighbor graphs G and G', we have $|M(\mu(G, \lambda)) - M(\mu(G', \lambda))|_1 \leq Max(\lambda, 4|\bar{A}|)$.*

Proof. Let us consider label neighbor graphs $G = (V, E, L)$ and $G' = (V, E, L')$. Let us assume there is a node u and an attribute value z such that $L'(u) = L(u) \setminus \{z\}$. Since the labels have no effect on the projection, the same edges are deleted in G and G': $\mu(G, \lambda)$ and $\mu(G', \lambda)$ are equal up to the label z of u. Therefore for all v, and for all $t \neq z$, $AC(v, t)$ is identical for $\mu(G, \lambda)$ and $\mu(G', \lambda)$. Since the attribute value z is removed from u'label set in $\mu(G', \lambda)$, for all w connected to u in $\mu(G, \lambda)$ (or $\mu(G', \lambda)$), $AC(w, z)$ differs by 1 whether computed in $\mu(G, \lambda)$ or in $\mu(G', \lambda)$). As there are at most λ nodes w connected to u, at most λ entries are different in $M(\mu(G', \lambda))$ from the respective ones in $M(\mu(G', \lambda))$. Therefore, $|M(\mu(G, \lambda)) - M(\mu(G', \lambda))|_1 \leq \lambda$.

Now let us assume $E' = E \setminus \{(u, v)\}$. The projection operation deletes k edges incident to u if u has $k + \lambda$ incident edges. Since u has only $k - 1 + \lambda$ incident edges in G' the projection will delete $k - 1$ edges incident to u in G'. If u has less than λ incident edges in G then none is deleted in G or G'. We can reason in the same way for v. As a consequence $\mu(G, \lambda)$ and $\mu(G', \lambda)$ differ by at most 3 edges [17] namely (u, v), one edge incident to u and one edge incident to v. Therefore only values $AC(c, a_1)$ where c is one of the 4 extremities of the differing edges are modified. Hence $|M(\mu(G, \lambda)) - M(\mu(G', \lambda))|_1 \leq 4|\bar{A}|$.

We can also determine easily the sensitivity for adjacency matrix N:

Lemma 2. *Given two neighbor graphs G and G', we have $|N(G) - N(G')|_1 \leq 1$.*

Proof. Changing node labels does not change the matrix N. Changing one edge impacts only one entry by 1 above the diagonal of N and since N is symmetric the result follows.

Since the sensitivity of N is small, the projection was not required for that case.

Generating the Recommendation Matrix. The next step after graph projection is to compute matrix M to store the number of connections (friends) linked to each node for all possible values of attributes in the projected graph. To do that, we introduce a connection matrix M of dimension $|V| \times |\bar{A}|$, where V is the set of users and $\bar{A}$ is the set of all possible values of all attributes. For instance, if user u is "Male" then $M(u, Male) = 1$. Otherwise, if u has no explicit gender value we resort to their connections. In this case, if u has no connections with gender value "Female" and m connections with gender value "Male" then $M(v, Female) = 0$ and $M(v, Male) = m/d_{\mu(G,\lambda)(u)}$. Note that every entry of M has value in $[0, 1]$.

In the following, two parameters are to be tuned, namely (i) λ for balancing utility and privacy, and (ii) threshold T for recommendation accuracy.

1. TSP collects the attribute values and connections attached to every user to build a social graph G and its adjacency matrix N. Data are sent directly to the TSP by users.
2. TSP computes $\mu(G, \lambda)$.
3. TSP computes matrix M such that for all u, z_1:
   $M(u, z_1) = AC_{\mu(G,\lambda)}(u, z_1))/d_{\mu(G,\lambda)}(u)$.
4. TSP adds independent Laplace noises to M's entries to generate:
   $M'(u, z_1) = M(u, z_1) + Lap(\Delta f/\epsilon_1)$ where $\Delta f = Max(\lambda, 4|\bar{A}|)$.
5. TSP adds independent Laplace noises to N's entries above the diagonal to derive N' as follows:
   For $u < v$, let $P(u, v) = N(u, v) + Lap(1/\epsilon_2)$. Then we define
   $$N'(u, v) = \begin{cases} P(u, v) & \text{if } P(u, v) \in [0, 1] \\ 0 & \text{if } P(u, v) < 0 \\ 1 & \text{if } P(u, v) > 1. \end{cases}$$
   For $u > v$, define $N'(u, v) = N'(v, u)$ and
   For $u = v$, define $N'(u, v) = 0$.

6. TSP applies MF to $N'||M'$ and generates $N_r||M_r$, where N_r has dimension $|V| \times |V|$.
7. TSP recommends to every user u the users v such that $N_r(u,v) > T$ and v is not already a friend of u (in G).

We can deduce:

Theorem 1. *The procedure to derive the recommendation matrix N_r satisfies $\epsilon_1 + \epsilon_2$-DP.*

Proof. Laplace noise added to M (resp., N) has been chosen in order to get matrix M' (resp., N') satisfying ϵ_1-DP (resp., ϵ_2-DP) (see also Proposition 1). By applying the *sequential composition* property of DP [5], the result follows.

5   Experimental Evaluation

We have implemented the proposed approach in Python and experimented on social datasets. In this section, we describe the evaluation metrics and the results of our experiments.

5.1   Datasets

Our experiments have been performed on publicly available OSN data collected from Facebook with a Python crawler. We are committed to keep them in secure storage and only use for the time necessary to achieve our work. We have then extracted connections and attributes attached to the collected profiles.

The extracted dataset contains 2262 connections among 487 users. We have also extracted 626 pages and the sensitive gender and marital status attributes from user profiles. Then we have selected the top 100 pages that are the most liked/followed by the users.

5.2   Evaluation Metrics

Since the recommendation results from the differentially private inputs generally differ from the original one (without noise) we need to evaluate the accuracy loss. The following metrics are used to assess the deviation in the recommendation result due to injected noise:

1. Root Mean Square Error (RMSE). The utility of our approach is defined by comparing scores generated for each pair of nodes. For node-pair $v_i, v_j \in V$, let $R1(i,j)$ and $R2(i,j)$ be the results of matrix factorization derived without and with differential privacy, respectively, then RMSE is defined as:

$$\text{RMSE} = \sqrt{\frac{\Sigma_{i=0}^{|V|-1} \Sigma_{j=0}^{|V|-1} (R1(i,j) - R2(i,j))^2}{|V|^2}} \tag{9}$$

2. F-score. The F-score parameter measures the accuracy of the proposed model. The value of true positive, false positive and false negative are computed by comparing the attribute suggestions obtained from the original and from the noised matrix. We compute the F-score over all users of the social network as follows:

$$\text{F-Score} = \frac{2 \times \texttt{True Positive}}{2 \times \texttt{True Positive} + \texttt{False Positive} + \texttt{False Negative}} \quad (10)$$

5.3   Experimental Results

Experiments are performed on the dataset of Sect. 5.1. First, we evaluate the effectiveness of the recommendation model without noise (Table 1). In that model User $u_j \in V$ is recommended to User $u_i \in V$ if $N_r(i,j)$ is greater than the predefined threshold T. In the following, we always take $T = 0.5$.

In order to verify our recommendation model, we randomly removed some connections and tried to recover them from existing connections and attributes. We have varied the percentage of removed connections. Table 1 shows that the proposed recommendation model can recover 50%–65% of missing connections.

Table 1. Recommendation results for $|V| = 487, |E| = 2262$

No. of missing connections	Recovered connections	Total no. of recommendations
5	2	376
10	5	436
25	15	462
50	33	483
75	56	510
100	67	439

Second, we compare the recommendation results generated from matrices without noise and with noise for different values of ϵ and λ. We compute F-score and RMSE parameters for different levels of privacy. We report below the average obtained from executing the same experiments 10 times. First, we set the value of λ to 10 since the average node degree is 9.28 in our dataset (i.e., $|V|=487$ and $|E| = 2262$). When ϵ_1 and ϵ_2 are assigned the same value we write it ϵ.

Figures 2 and 3 show F-score and RMSE respectively for different ϵ values. We observe how the F-score increases with the privacy budget ϵ. But, RMSE decreases from 0.35 to 0.10 when ϵ increases since less noise is injected. We note a generally good accuracy (from 0.60 to 0.75) for different ϵ (0.8 to 2).

The projected graph for various values of λ differs in terms of the number of edges. To represent the impact of λ on F-score and RMSE, we have experimented

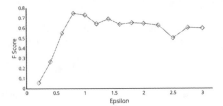

Fig. 2. F-Score for various ϵ values

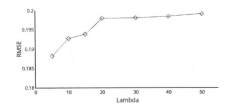

Fig. 3. RMSE for various ϵ values

with a fixed $\epsilon = 1$ and various values of λ in the range from 5 to 50 as shown in Figs. 4 and 5. F-score value is around 0.70 for large λs (i.e., 50). As the sensitivity depends on λ (see Lemma 1), a larger λ means that more noise has to be injected. The utility parameter RMSE increases with λ as shown in Fig. 5.

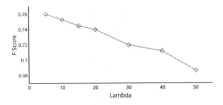

Fig. 4. F-Score for various λ values

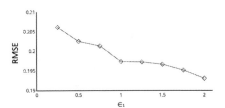

Fig. 5. RMSE for various λ values

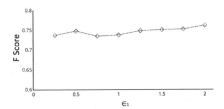

Fig. 6. F-Score for various ϵ_1 values

Fig. 7. RMSE for various ϵ_1 values

Next, we perform experiments to observe the results by considering different values of ϵ_1 and ϵ_2. The parameter ϵ_1 (resp. ϵ_2) controls the noise added to matrix M (resp. N). Figures 6 and 7 show the recommendation results in terms of F-score and RMSE for various values of ϵ_1 while keeping $\epsilon_2 = 1$. As ϵ_1 is used exclusively for attribute count, the recommendation result is not highly sensitive to variations of ϵ_1: there is only a minor change in F-score and RMSE values with increasing ϵ_1. Now, in Figs. 8 and 9 we analyze the impact of ϵ_2 on evaluation metrics for various values, while keeping $\epsilon_1 = 1$. As the injected noise in N depends on ϵ_2, considerable deviations in F-score and RMSE values

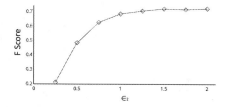
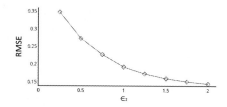

Fig. 8. F-Score for various ϵ_2 values   **Fig. 9.** RMSE for various ϵ_2 values

can be noticed. An increase of ϵ_2, induces an increase of F-score and a decrease of RMSE. For ϵ_2 in interval [0.75–1.25], F-score is about 0.7 while RMSE lays between 0.22 to 0.18. Consequently, this range of ϵ_2 offers a good trade-off for privacy and utility.

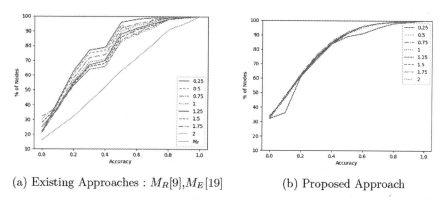

(a) Existing Approaches : M_R[9],M_E[19]   (b) Proposed Approach

Fig. 10. Comparison with [9] and [19] using our dataset

We have performed additional experiments to compare our approach with existing ones, M_R [9] and M_E [19]. These two differentially private recommendation approaches consider only the structure of the graph (i.e., friendship links) and generate noise with an exponential mechanism. We have applied M_R and M_E to our dataset. To compare the results, we have also considered the accuracy metrics (defined in Sect. 5.1.4 in [9]). These metrics are based on common neighbours and cumulative distribution function (CDF). Figure 10 shows, for a given accuracy δ on the x-axis, the percentage of users that obtain recommendations with accuracy $\leq \delta$ on the y-axis.

We observe that for different values of ϵ, M_R has major deviations in the accuracy whereas M_E has minor deviations. So, the results of M_R for different values of ϵ are presented in the graph. Figure 10 shows that our approach provides better accuracy than M_R and M_E (w.r.t. the number of users), irrespective of the privacy parameter ϵ. Next, we consider Facebook dataset from [18]. Results obtained with M_R, M_E are shown in Fig. 11a and with our approach in Fig. 11b.

Compared to M_R and M_E, our approach provides better accuracy. In particular, unlike M_R and M_E, our approach can suggest friends to non-connected users even if they do not have any common friend.

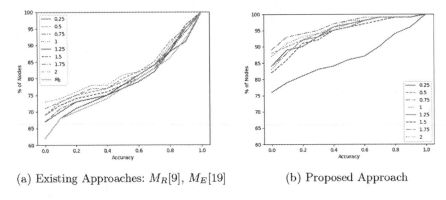

(a) Existing Approaches: M_R[9], M_E[19]   (b) Proposed Approach

Fig. 11. Comparison with [9] and [19] using Facebook dataset [18]

6   Conclusion

We have presented a privacy-preserving friend recommendation system for OSN users that leverages their friend lists and attribute values. To reduce the sensitivity of the information provided by users we have selected a subset of friend links and attribute values. Matrix factorization is applied to generate the final recommendation result. By experimenting with various values of ϵ and λ parameters, we have observed that we can get a good accuracy (F-score = 0.70) of the proposed approach and therefore good utility. Moreover, the experimental results are helpful to choose a proper value for privacy parameters ϵ_1 and ϵ_2.

In future work, we will show how to preserve privacy with an untrusted service provider by implementing a perturbation method based on Local Differential Privacy (see e.g., [1]). We will investigate sensitivity reduction by random selection of attribute values in order to decrease their number. We also plan to experiment with the recent optimizations of matrix factorization algorithms.

References

1. Arcolezi, H.H.: Jean-François Couchot, Sébastien Gambs, Catuscia Palamidessi, Majid Zolfaghari: Multi-Freq-LDPy: Multiple Frequency Estimation Under Local Differential Privacy in Python. ESORICS **3**(2022), 770–775 (2022)
2. Cheng, H., Qian, M., Li, Q., Zhou, Y., Chen, T.: An efficient privacy-preserving friend recommendation scheme for social network. IEEE Access **6**, 56018–56028 (2018)

3. McSherry, F., Mironov, I.: Differentially private recommender systems: building privacy into the Netflix prize contenders. In: Proceedings of the 15th ACM SIGKDD International Conference on Knowledge Discovery and Data Mining, pp. 627–636 (2009)
4. Barathy, R., Chitra, P.: Applying matrix factorization in collaborative filtering recommender systems. In: 2020 6th International Conference on Advanced Computing and Communication Systems (ICACCS), pp. 635–639 (2020)
5. Dwork, C., Roth, A.: others, the algorithmic foundations of differential privacy. Found. Trends Theor. Comput. Sci. **9**, 211–407 (2014)
6. Berlioz, A., Friedman, A., Kaafar, M., Boreli, R., Berkovsky, S.: Applying differential privacy to matrix factorization. In: Proceedings of the 9th ACM Conference on Recommender Systems, pp. 107–114 (2015)
7. Nikolaenko, V., Ioannidis, S., Weinsberg, U., Joye, M., Taft, N.: Privacy-preserving matrix factorization, pp. 801–812. CCS, Dan Boneh (2013)
8. Zhang, S., Li, X., Liu, H., Lin, Y., Sangaiah, A.K.: A privacy-preserving friend recommendation scheme in online social networks. Sustain. Cities Soc. **38**, 275–285 (2018)
9. Guo, T., Luo, J., Dong, K., Yang, M.: Differentially private graph-link analysis based social recommendation. Inf. Sci. **463–464**, 214–226 (2018)
10. Liu, Z., Wang, Y., Smola, A.: Fast differentially private matrix factorization. In: Proceedings of the 9th ACM Conference on Recommender Systems, pp. 171–178 (2015)
11. Zhang, S., Yin, H., Chen, T., Huang, Z., Lizhen, C., Zhang, X.: Graph embedding for recommendation against attribute inference attacks. In: WWW, pp. 3002–3014 (2021)
12. Day, W., Li, N., Lyu, M.: Publishing graph degree distribution with node differential privacy. In: Proceedings of the 2016 International Conference on Management of Data, pp. 123–138 (2016)
13. Blocki, J., Blum, A., Datta, A., Sheffet, O.: Differentially private data analysis of social networks via restricted sensitivity. In: Proceedings of the 4th Conference on Innovations in Theoretical Computer Science, pp. 87–96 (2013)
14. Dwork, C., McSherry, F., Nissim, K., Smith, A.: Calibrating noise to sensitivity in private data analysis. In: Halevi, S., Rabin, T. (eds.) TCC 2006. LNCS, vol. 3876, pp. 265–284. Springer, Heidelberg (2006). https://doi.org/10.1007/11681878_14
15. Brendel, W., Han, F., Marujo, L., Jie, L., Korolova, A.: Practical privacy-preserving friend recommendations on social networks. In: Companion Proceedings of the Web Conference 2018, pp. 111–112 (2018)
16. Smith, S., Park, J., Karypis, G.: An exploration of optimization algorithms for high performance tensor completion. In: SC2016: Proceedings of the International Conference for High Performance Computing, Networking, Storage And Analysis, pp. 359–371 (2016)
17. Jorgensen, Z., Yu, T., Cormode, G.: Publishing attributed social graphs with formal privacy guarantees. In: Proceedings of the 2016 International Conference on Management of Data, pp. 107–122 (2016)
18. Leskovec, J., Mcauley, J.: Learning to discover social circles in ego networks. In: Advances in Neural Information Processing Systems, vol. 25 (2012)
19. Machanavajjhala, A., Korolova, A., Sarma, A.: Personalized social recommendations-accurate or private? ArXiv Preprint: ArXiv:1105.4254 (2011)
20. Samanthula, B., Cen, L., Jiang, W., Si, L.: Privacy-preserving and efficient friend recommendation in online social networks. Trans. Data Priv. **8**, 141–171 (2015)

Physical-Layer Security

Underwater Confidential Communications in JANUS

Yannick Beaupré[1]([✉]) [iD], Michel Barbeau[1] [iD], and Stéphane Blouin[2] [iD]

[1] School of Computer Science, Carleton University, Ottawa, Canada
yannick-beaupre@outlook.com,
barbeau@scs.carleton.ca
[2] Defence R&D Canada Atlantic Research Centre, Dartmouth, Canada
Stephane.Blouin2@forces.gc.ca
https://carleton.ca/scs/

Abstract. JANUS is a NATO underwater communications standard. In this paper, confidential communications for JANUS are explored. The focus is on work published in 2021, Venilia and Tiny Underwater Block cipher (TUBcipher). Venilia consists of protocol elements that had been developed to provide confidential JANUS underwater communications. It leverages TUBcipher, a symmetric cryptography scheme. Some important details were not considered in this original work, including the security analysis of TUBcipher and key establishment and distribution. Intending to improve Venilia, these two points are addressed in the current paper. A security analysis is conducted for TUBcipher. TUBcipher has been implemented. Entropy data of ciphertexts have been collected with the ENT tool. Our results show that TUBcipher achieves close to the theoretical maximum entropy value. Two key establishment/distribution solutions are introduced. They provide methods of practically implementing Venilia within underwater communication networks.

Keywords: Underwater communications · confidential communications · security protocol · JANUS · Venilia · TUBcipher

1 Introduction

In contrast to classical networks, underwater communication networks present unique challenges. They involve sending messages through multitudes of nodes within large bodies of water. It is a harsh environment for communications [17]. Electromagnetic waves do not propagate well through bodies of water [4]. Acoustic waves are used to send messages. While they propagate in water, bandwidth is narrow, and packets that can be sent are limited in size. Furthermore, acoustic waves travel at a much slower speed than electromagnetic waves. It is an environment where packet processing performance is not critical due to the relatively low achievable data rates, particularly for long distances. However, the optimal use of a small packet size is a critical aspect.

© Crown 2023
G.-V. Jourdan et al. (Eds.): FPS 2022, LNCS 13877, pp. 255–270, 2023.
https://doi.org/10.1007/978-3-031-30122-3_16

JANUS, the Roman God of openings and gateways, is the name of an underwater communication standard developed and tested by the North Atlantic Treaty Organization (NATO)'s members. It specifies a means of encoding data within acoustic waves [15]. The packet size is 64 bits. Such a small packet size is not adapted to modern cryptographic methods that require a relatively large block size. For example, the Advanced Encryption Standard (AES) [12] requires a minimum block size of 128 bits. Thus, a small block cipher, called TUBcipher, has been created to work alongside a new JANUS data block class called Venilia [8].

The Venilia protocol is one of a kind. It aims to achieve confidential underwater communications. However, there are important aspects of it that deserve further investigation, such as the security analysis of TUBcipher. In this paper, the security of Venilia is analyzed. Concrete measurements of security metrics on TUBcipher are presented. They enable making statements about the security provided by TUBcipher, in comparison to other small block ciphers. It is concluded that TUBcipher does not achieve perfect indistinguisability, but does reach near maximum entropy. Ideas to improve the current Venilia solution are developed. A problem complementary to confidentiality is dynamic key distribution. Two key distribution protocols to be used with Venilia are created, a simple approach and a more complex one.

Related work is reviewed in Sect. 2. Section 3 describes the security analysis conducted for TUBcipher. The two key distribution solutions are discussed in Sect. 4. Section 5 concludes.

2 Background Work

JANUS, the Venilia class, and TUBcipher are briefly introduced.

2.1 JANUS

JANUS is a NATO communication protocol for underwater assets [15]. It aims at manufacturer independence and interoperability within networks containing assets of different suppliers. It was developed to become an underwater communications standard.

JANUS packets are smaller than typical network packets because of the harsh underwater propagation environment. The tiny sizes of packets make traditional cryptographic schemes unfeasible for use with JANUS. For reference, a typical UDP or TCP packet has a size of 1,500 bytes, that is, 12,000 bits [6]. Thus, the 128-bit block size of AES, a popular and strong cryptographic scheme, does not cause any problems for typical internet communications. However, JANUS packets have a size of 64 bits. Every packer comprises a 34-bit data block, over three times smaller than the required block size of AES. Given this limitation, a user class named Venilia, was developed for confidential JANUS communications [8]. A user class designates the purpose of the communication. Different user classes handle the 34-bit data blocks of packets differently. Venilia is proposed as user class id 17 for confidential JANUS communications. The Venilia class is described in more detail in the upcoming section.

2.2   Venilia and TUBcipher

A solution to JANUS' lack of security has been proposed as a new class named Venilia [8] and a small block cipher called TUBcipher [9].

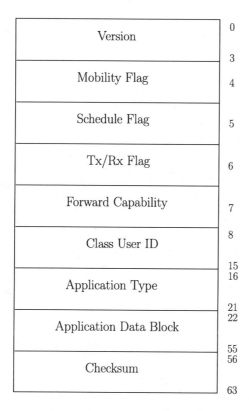

Fig. 1. 64-bit JANUS packet.

A JANUS packet has 64 bits, of which only 34 bits are utilized for a data block, while the rest is overhead, see Fig. 1. According to the suggested behavior of the Venilia class, there is an eight-bit Pre-Canned Message field, which contains an index for one of 256 unique messages predefined in the Venilia code book [8].

It is followed by the fields Destination ID (7 bits), Source ID (7 bits), and Inner Cyclic Redundancy Check (CRC) (5 bits), see Fig. 2.

Venilia adopted a code book approach to message content coding [8]. Given that only eight bits are used for the message in a packet, an integer from zero

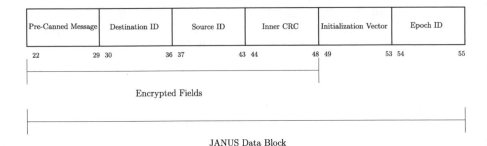

Fig. 2. JANUS class 17: Venilia data block.

to 255 is sent. This integer corresponds to a message for command and control or status communications.

Confidentiality is achieved through partial content encryption. Only the first 27 bits of the data block are encrypted using TUBcipher, i.e., the fields Pre-Canned Message, Destination ID, Source ID, and Inner CRC. Hence, encryption requires a block size of only 27 bits [9]. TUBcipher is a deterministic cryptosystem. The remaining seven bits of the 34-bit data block comprise a nonce made of an Initialization Vector (IV) (5 bits) and an Epoch ID (2 bits). The nonce is part of a mechanism for replay attack detection [19].

TUBcipher is a symmetric small block cipher based on PRINTcipher, originally developed for integrated circuit printing [11]. TUBcipher is a substitution-permutation network that encrypts a 27-bit block with a 2560-bit key over 56 rounds [9]. The 2560-bit key is generated using a concatenation of an epoch ID, a 256-bit key, an IV, and an eight-bit counter. This concatenation is hashed with SHA512. This process is repeated five times, every time incrementing the counter. All five hashes are then concatenated to form the 2560-bit key used in the cipher. The first 2520 bits of the key are partitioned into 45-bit subkeys. Every subkey is used in one round. Each round starts with keyed XOR, using the first 27 bits of the current round subkey, followed by a fixed permutation, a keyed permutation using the last 18 bits of the round subkey, and a fixed substitution. The process is reversed for decryption.

TUBcipher solves the problem of encrypting a small amount of data. However, open problems remain. One of them is key distribution. It is important to note that since the cryptography scheme is symmetric, the 2560-bit encryption key is the same 2560-bit decryption key used. Thus, two parties communicating using Venilia/TUBcipher must have a secure channel to establish this shared key. Another open area is the security analysis of the TUBcipher. The analysis is required to achieve confidence in the security provided by the TUBcipher.

3   TUBcipher Security Analysis

A security analysis aims at demonstrating a cryptography scheme's security. It can provide confidence in the scheme. In this case, security analysis can assist in deciding if Venilia can become a standard or if there are better alternatives. There is no security analysis of TUBcipher. Besides, TUBcipher is based on PRINTcipher, an already established small block cipher whose security has been analyzed in the paper that introduced it [11]. However, we cannot assume that the results of this security analysis also apply to TUBcipher, as both differ in certain areas. Namely, block size, key size, number of rounds, and handling of the key in every round. PRINTcipher keeps the same key between rounds but updates it with a round-dependent value determined via a shift register-based counter. TUBcipher uses a different segment of the 2560-bit key every round, effectively using a different key every round. TUBcipher has been implemented and a security analysis has been conducted.

3.1   Implementation

The implementation of the cipher was done in Python 3 [2]. This language was chosen to keep the implementation to be as simple and straightforward as possible. To verify its correctness, we first check that given a key, an epoch, an IV, and a plaintext, the correct ciphertext is generated. The paper originally describing TUBcipher does include sample inputs and outputs [9]. Using the paper's sample key, epoch, IV, and plaintext, our implementation does generate the same ciphertext. The implementation has also been submitted 100 different randomly generated plaintexts and 100 randomly generated 2560-bit keys, allowing the test of 10,000 encryption and decryption operations. Every random plaintext was encrypted and decrypted with every random key. The plaintext before encryption and the plaintext after decryption were compared. When they were the same, the test was deemed successful. All encryption and decryption combinations were successful. The random plaintexts and random keys were generated with a random data generation procedure that is described in the sequel.

Given that several keys were needed to analyze the security of TUBcipher properly, we developed a key generation procedure to create 2560-bit keys. The procedure takes a 32-bit epoch, a 256-bit key, a 32-bit IV and creates five concatenations with the following general form:

$$Concatenation_i = (epoch||key||IV||i)$$

for $i = 0, \ldots, 4$, left padded with zeros to eight bits. Every concatenation is hashed with SHA512 and concatenated together as follows:

$$Hash_0||Hash_1||...||Hash_4.$$

This concatenation of five hashes forms the 2560-bit key. It is important to note that some parts of the key generation procedure are not addressed in the original description of Venilia/TUBciper, such as the generation of the epoch, 256-bit key, and IV. Thus, for the 256-bit key, we generate a random 256-bit string. The epoch and IV do not need to be random as long as their combination is only used once. A counter is used that is incremented after every key generation. Given that the counter is used to generate 64-bit of data, no duplicate epoch and IV combination is generated until 1.8×10^{19} keys are produced. Hence, no duplicate epoch and IV combination has been used during the analysis of TUBcipher.

The 2560-bit keys were used to create several ciphertexts for the security analysis. Every ciphertext was created using a 2560-bit key and a 27-bit plaintext. Thus, we required a procedure to generate random plaintexts. The Java `SecureRandom` class is used. It has been well analyzed and tested [10].

3.2   Indistinguishability

The indistinguishability property for a cryptographic scheme is nice to have [3]. Indistinguishability means that for any plaintext, given the ciphertext produced by the cryptographic scheme and a random string, an adversary cannot determine which is the ciphertext with odds significantly better than 50%. In other words, no information can be gained from analyzing the ciphertext alone [14]. This property is investigated theoretically and empirically.

Definition 1 (Birthday attack). *The goal of the birthday attack is to find two plaintexts x_1 and x_2 that are encrypted with the same nonce and produce ciphertexts x_1' and x_2' such that $x_1' = x_2'$. The pair x_1, x_2 is called a collision.*

Proposition 2. *Let us consider the TUBcipher used to encrypt m one-block messages. An adversary perpetrating the birthday attack has the probability of success at most $1 - \left(\frac{2^{37}-1}{2^{37}} \right)^m$.*

Proof. Given that the IV is five bits and Epoch ID is thirty-two bits, there is a thirty-seven-bit nonce associated with every message. There are $2^{37} \cdot 2^{37} = 2^{74}$ unique nonce pairs while there are $2^{37} \cdot \left(2^{37} - 1 \right)$ pairs of nonces, where the coupled nonces are different. Hence, the non-collision probability for two random one-block messages is

$$\frac{2^{37} \cdot \left(2^{37} - 1 \right)}{2^{74}} = \frac{2^{37} - 1}{2^{37}}.$$

For m one-block messages, the non-collision probability is

$$\left(\frac{2^{37} - 1}{2^{37}} \right)^m.$$

Hence, the collision probability is at most

$$1 - \left(\frac{2^{37} - 1}{2^{37}} \right)^m.$$

Table 1 provides the probabilities of collision as a function of m, in logarithmic form. TUBcipher does not achieve perfect indistinguishability due to a non-negligible collision probability. But let us also investigate that empirically.

To investigate empirically, we need a metric of randomness. Entropy provides this metric. In information theory, the entropy of a random variable is the amount of information, or uncertainty, that a variable contains based on its possible

Table 1. Probability of collision versus the number of messages, in logarithmic form $(\log_2 m)$.

$\log_2 m$	Collision Probability $(\times 10^{-9})$
1	0.0146
2	0.0291
3	0.0582
4	0.116
5	0.233
6	0.466
7	0.931
8	1.86

outcomes [16]. If all outcomes have the same probability, the variable's entropy equals the theoretical maximum value, which is one. This value signifies that the outcome of the event is uncertain. The outcome is effectively random. Such a variable contains the maximum amount of information. If some outcomes are more likely than others, the value of the variable's entropy is between zero and one, but not zero or one. These values signify that the outcome of the event is not completely uncertain. The outcome is not completely random. This variable would contain less information than the theoretical maximum. The following equation defines the computation of entropy:

$$H(X) = -\sum_{i=1}^{n} P(x_i) log P(x_i) \tag{1}$$

The concept of entropy is used to measure the randomness of TUBcipher. TUBcipher encryption is the random variable X. The ciphertexts produced are possible outcomes $x_1, \ldots, x_n$, with respective probabilities $P(x_1), \ldots, P(x_n)$. When entropy $H(X)$ has the value of one or very close to one, it signifies that the ciphertexts are effectively random. In other words, such a value signifies that the ciphertexts are indistinguishable from a random string. It is demonstrated empirically that TUBcipher possesses the indistinguishability property.

To measure the entropy of generated ciphertexts, we used the pseudorandom number sequence test tool ENT authored by Walker [18]. This tool can measure the entropy of a bit string at the bit level, producing a value between zero and one. Twelve data points of 5,000 ciphertexts each were collected for five distinct data sets. The first three sets measure the entropy value of ciphertexts from the TUBcipher, while the last two sets measure the entropy of other random sources for comparison. The first set, 1PXK, measured the entropy of ciphertexts generated from the same plaintext and 5,000 different keys. The second set, XP1K, measured the entropy of ciphertexts generated from 5,000 different plaintexts and the same key. The third set, XPXK, measured the entropy of ciphertexts generated from 71 different plaintexts and 71 different keys for a total of 5,041 ciphertexts. The fourth set measured the entropy of 5,000 random 27-bit strings generated from Java's SecureRandom class. The final set measured the entropy of 5,000 random 27-bit strings generated from the Windows `CryptGenRandom` function, being called via Python's `os.urandom()` function. Statistical measurements were made from those 12 data points, including the mean, range, variance, standard deviation, and standard error. A high entropy mean value was expected from the set of data generated from Java's `SecureRandom`. A lower entropy mean value was expected from the set of data generated from Windows `CryptGenRandom`.

Table 2. Statistical measurements of entropy from five sets of 12 data points. Each data point consists of ∼132KB of 27-bit strings.

	Mean	Range	Variance	Standard Deviation	Standard Error
		$(\times 10^{-5})$	$(\times 10^{-10})$	$(\times 10^{-5})$	$(\times 10^{-6})$
1PXK	0.9999	1.1	0.103	0.321	0.926
XP1K	0.9999	2.2	0.515	0.718	2.07
XPXK	0.9999	1.9	0.684	0.827	2.39
SecureRandom	0.9991	46.1	145	12	34.8
CryptGenRandom	0.9999	1.7	0.342	0.585	16.9

A summary of the statistical measurements calculated from the gathered data of all five sets is displayed in Table 2. The range, variance, standard deviation, and standard error of the sets 1PXK, XP1K, XPXK, and CryptGenRandom are low, indicating that the size of the data sets is sufficiently big. As expected, the mean entropy value of Java's SecureRandom is close to the theoretical best value of one, with a difference of 0.000922. This is consistent with previous research [10]. Unexpectedly, the mean entropy value of Windows' CryptGenRandom is higher than that of Java's SecureRandom, with a difference of 0.000918. This could reflect changes that have been made to Windows' CryptGenRandom algorithm since 2009, which is when the cryptanalysis was performed, or it is possible that given a larger data set, the mean entropy value of Java's SecureRandom would have been higher than CryptGenRandom's. However, the mean eFor example, withpy values for each set of TUBcipher ciphertexts 1PXK, XP1K, and XPXK, are close to the theoretical maximum, with the highest difference being 0.000008.

Given that the entropy measured from ciphertexts is equivalent to or better than the entropy measured from randomly generated strings with SecureRandom and CryptGenRandom, we can be confident that an adversary would not be able to distinguish the ciphertexts from random strings with odds better than 50%. Thus, we can conclude that TUBcipher ciphertexts look nearly perfectly random

4   Venilia Key Distribution

Augmenting Venilia with key distribution is discussed. A symmetric cryptography scheme such as the TUBcipher encrypts and decrypts data with the same key. This is a secret shared by both the sending and receiving parties. Typically, symmetric keys are generated and transmitted through a secure channel before the data payload is sent. With Transport Layer Security (TLS), asymmetric cryptography schemes, such as Rivest, Shamir and Ademan (RSA), are used to securely share symmetric session keys, which are then utilized to encrypt and decrypt the data payload of the session [5]. Asymmetric ciphers make great candidates for symmetric key distribution as they use two separate keys for encryption and decryption. The key used for encryption, the public key, can be shared in open channels, while the key used for decryption, the private key, is not shared. This provides a secure channel to share secrets with the private key holder. This method works well for typical Internet applications, as an entire symmetric key can be shared within one packet. However, underwater networks have unique constraints. One is the amount of data that can be sent with one packet. Sending a 256-bit symmetric key in the clear or encrypted with an asymmetric cipher is not feasible. Given the largest data payload possible with JANUS, 34 bits, eight packets would need to be transmitted to send a 256-bit key. As such, Internet key distribution solutions are not applicable for JANUS. A new solution must be created with the underwater medium in mind. Two approaches are explored: key pre-configuration and dynamic key distribution. In the sequel, we assume the principle of confidentiality states that only the sender and receiver of a message should be able to access the information it contains [13].

4.1   Key Pre-configuration

One simple solution is configuring nodes with 256-bit symmetric encryption keys before deploying them underwater. Nodes can send encrypted Venilia packets to other nodes, given that they have their symmetric keys. However, simplicity comes with flexibility constraints. Once a network of nodes is configured and deployed, no new nodes can be added. Let us assume that we have n nodes to be deployed. Before deployment, each node is configured with its key and the other's 256-bit key. As such, every node has n keys: $\{k_1, k_2, ..., k_n\}$. To deploy a new node into the network, node $n + 1$, the node would have to be configured with the keys of every other node in the network. This new node would need $n + 1$ keys $\{k_1, k_2, ..., k_n, k_{n+1}\}$. Since each node currently in the network was not configured with the key for node $n + 1$, no other node could communicate confidentially with it.

No new keys can be distributed to the nodes already deployed without a dynamic method for key distribution. Therefore, no further nodes can be added to the network for confidential communications. To circumvent this problem, every node could be configured with the same network key before deployment. Using a single network key allows for new nodes to be added to the confidential network since the number of keys a node must be configured with no longer increases with the addition of nodes within the network. Suppose all confidential communications within the network are encrypted with the same key. Without confidential node-to-node communications, any network node can decrypt encrypted messages.

4.2 Dynamic Key Distribution

An alternative solution is proposed, more flexible than the solution of Sect. 4.1, at the expense of simplicity. This solution involves four components: a specific network topology, node pre-configuration, session key generation, and a session protocol.

Network Topology. Underwater networks are divided into subnetworks. Each subnetwork node shares one 256-bit master key. Each subnetwork contains regular nodes but may also have border nodes. Border nodes can communicate confidentially to at least one other node from another subnetwork. Subnetworks may also contain mobile nodes. The nodes that communicate on several subnetworks simultaneously are defined as mobile. Figure 3 pictures an example of this topology. It is important to note that this approach avoids key desynchronization issues since the master key never changes. To deal with border node failures, backup border nodes can be included to take over when they have heard the border nodes for a certain delay.

Pre-configuration. All underwater nodes must be preconfigured with the 256-bit master key of the subnetwork they belong to. Since non-border and non-mobile nodes only require a 256-bit master key, the number of keys that these nodes must know never changes and always remains at one. This allows newly deployed nodes to communicate confidentially with any other subnetwork node. In other words, new nodes can be deployed within these subnetworks without concern. Border nodes must also be preconfigured with the master keys of other subnetworks they connect to. Border nodes allow newly deployed subnetworks to communicate confidentially with other subnetworks. Already deployed border nodes within the existing subnetworks do not need to be modified, as the one deployed in the new subnetwork can be preconfigured with the required master keys instead. Mobile nodes must be preconfigured with the master keys of the subnetworks they use.

Session Key Generation. All network nodes using the same key violates the confidentiality principle. To circumvent this issue, the master key can be used to send an encrypted session key instead of the data itself. The session key, specific to a session between two nodes, can then be used to send confidential data. Since the sender and recipient only know this session key, data can only be decrypted by those two nodes, and thus, this approach provides better confidentiality than the simple solution. However, an entire 256-bit key is infeasible to send with

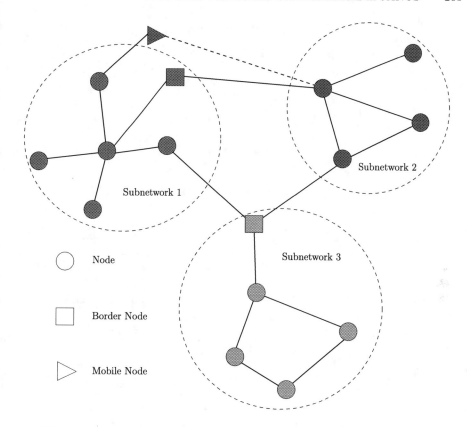

Fig. 3. Example of network topology for Venilia key distribution solution.

Venilia. Thus, a session key must instead be generated from some known secret and information that can be sent with Venilia and JANUS packets. Session keys are thus generated from the 256-bit master key, a 26-bit random number, and an 8-bit random number. Each session key is compromised of 230 bits from the master key and 26 random bits such that the session key is identical to the master key up to bit i, where bit i to bit $i+25$ are random, followed by the same bits as the master key from bit $i+26$ to bit 255. The eight-bit random number denotes the bit location to replace the master key bits with the 26 random bits. In other words, the session keys are the master key with 26 consecutive bits replaced with 26 random bits at location i to location $i+25$ where i is random. The procedure for key generation is displayed in Fig. 4.

This approach allows an entire session key to be generated from two packets; one encrypted Venilia packet sending the eight-bit random location and one clear JANUS packet sending the 26 random bits. This method is inspired by the export cipher schemes seen in the SSLv2 protocol, where a 40-bit of a 128-bit symmetric key was sent in the clear [7]. This method does indeed reduce the effective key size. However, in our case, 230 bits remain secret, and these session

Let x_i, y_i denote bit at position i:

$$Master\ Key = K_m = x_0 x_1 ... x_{254} x_{255}$$

$$Key\ Piece\ = K_p = y_0 y_1 ... y_{24} y_{25}$$

$$Secret = j$$

$$\downarrow$$

$$Session\ Key = \underbrace{x_0 x_1 ... x_{j-1}}_{K_m}\ \underbrace{y_0 ... y_{25}}_{K_p}\ \underbrace{x_{j+26} ... x_{254} x_{255}}_{K_m}$$

Fig. 4. Session key generation

keys are not vulnerable to brute force attacks from outside the subnetwork. It is important to note that an attack can be perpetrated inside a subnetwork. Given that the 26-bit key piece is sent in clear and that the master key is known within the subnetwork, an eavesdropper could decrypt the eight-bit secret and build the session key. From there, they could decrypt confidential data encrypted with the session key. An eavesdropping attack would, however, have to be carried out at the start of a session to capture the important key generation information. Of course, with the assumption that legitimate nodes only share the master key, this vulnerability is no longer present. However, this solution provides a more complex system to attack than the solution where all nodes already possess the key to decrypt confidential data. As such, this solution offers better confidentiality than the solution of Sect. 4.1.

This approach is also safe from session key collisions. If the same session key is generated for two or more sessions, nodes other than the intended recipient could decrypt and read confidential data. However, given that there are 2^{26} possible random 26-bit sequences and 2^8 possible locations for these sequences, there are effective 2^{34} possible session keys. Even with a network that is compromised of one million nodes, an extreme number of nodes for an underwater network, the probability of having two nodes generate the same session key is around 0.005%.

Plaintexts encrypted with the 2560-bit extended keys generated from these session keys must also have similar entropy as plaintexts encrypted with 2560-bit extended keys generated from an entirely different 256-bit key. If the entropy of these plaintexts is not high, there might be patterns to them. Such patterns yield valuable information for malicious actors. Given that in the worst-case scenario (where the random eight-bit number is the same for two session keys), only 26 bits differ from one session key to the next, this is an important metric to verify. Following the same method described in Sect. 3.2, ciphertexts were generated from a set of random plaintexts and 256-bit keys. For our base case, these 256-bit keys were randomly generated. For our session keys, the same base 256-bit key was modified with 26 random bits at all the 256 possible locations to create the encryption session keys. In each case, 71 plaintexts were encrypted with 71 keys, generating 5,041 ciphertexts. The entropy of the 5,041 ciphertexts was then calculated with the ENT tool. This process was completed for 12 sets of

5041 ciphertexts. The results are displayed in Table 3. The entropy of plaintexts encrypted with the session keys is comparable to that of plaintexts encrypted with entirely different 256-bit keys. Given this result, it follows that the TUB-Cipher achieves indistinguishability with the session keys.

Table 3. Statistical measurements of entropy from the base case and session key ciphertexts. Measurements were taken from 12 data points, each consisting of $\sim$132 KB of 27-bit strings.

	Mean	Range	Variance	Standard Deviation	Standard Error
		$(\times 10^{-5})$	$(\times 10^{-10})$	$(\times 10^{-5})$	$(\times 10^{-6})$
Base Case	0.9999	2.1	0.512	0.715	2.06
Session key	0.9999	1.7	0.737	0.859	2.48

Session Protocol. A protocol is defined for creating and maintaining a session between two underwater nodes. It is inspired by TLS [5]. It includes session establishment, session key generation and distribution, the transmission of confidential data, and session closure. The protocol is illustrated in Fig. 5. A node first sends an acknowledgment to another node to establish a session. The receiving node must then respond to this acknowledgment. These packets can be sent in the clear with a standard JANUS packet. The session is established once both nodes have received an acknowledgment. Once a session is established, the sending node generates the 26-bit key piece (KP) and the eight-bit secret described in the previous section. The key piece is then sent to the receiving node in the clear with a JANUS packet. The eight-bit secret is sent in a Venilia packet encrypted with the master key (MK). Using the key piece and secret; both nodes generate the session key (S_k) following the method described in the key generation section. To transmit confidential data, the sending node encrypts the data with the session key and sends the encrypted data in a Venilia packet. The receiving node decrypts the data with the same key. Confidential data is transmitted following this method until no more data needs to be sent. The session is then closed, and the session key is discarded. When confidential data needs to be transmitted again, a new session is established, and a new session key is generated.

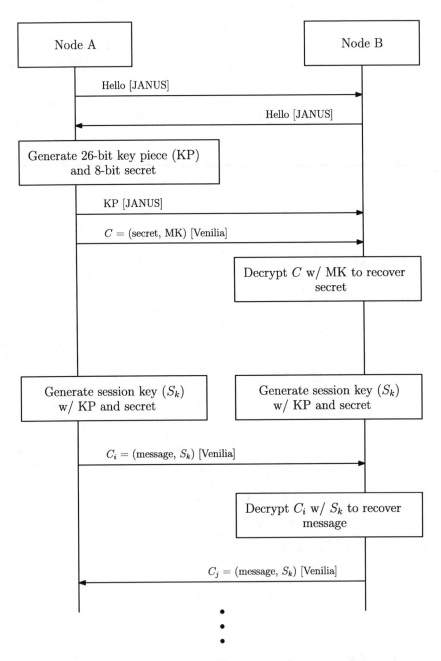

Fig. 5. Venilia key distribution and session protocol. x[JANUS] denotes message x is sent with JANUS, and x[Venilia] denotes message x is sent with Venilia.

5   Conclusion

The goal was to conduct further research for secure underwater communications. The efforts focused on developing solutions that are compatible with JANUS. As of the writing of this paper, the only solution that has been proposed to secure JANUS communications is Venilia. Efforts were devoted to improving this solution.

Areas of the Venilia class that can be improved have been highlighted. Firstly, no security analysis of the TUBcipher has been published. Without such an analysis, it is difficult to trust the security provided by the cipher. A security analysis of the cipher has been performed. The entropy of ciphertexts produced with the TUBcipher was measured. The results were very close to the highest theoretical value of one, at an average of 0.9999. It can be concluded that the TUBcipher, and by extension Venilia, provides near perfectly random ciphertexts for JANUS communications.

There was also no key distribution solution for Venilia. The eight-bit message size maximum makes key distribution challenging. However, such a solution provides important practicality. Key distribution solutions were developed for Venilia. The solutions explore practical approaches to the implementation of Venilia for underwater communications. The small message size of Venilia communications has also been considered. A codebook approach for these eight-bit messages allows 255 different messages. This could be a beneficial area of improvement. A small message size limits the flexibility of communications by only allowing predefined messages and limits potential key distribution solutions and other potentially useful security mechanisms such as cryptographic signatures. A cryptography scheme with less overhead would remedy this issue. However, such a scheme would have to be developed considering the constraints of the JANUS standard. Another way to improve message size could be to create secure communications for another underwater protocol together [1].

Acknowledgments. This work was supported by the Public Works and Government Services Canada under Contract No. W7707-227202/001/HAL through the Defence Research and Development Canada.

References

1. Barbeau, M., Blouin, S., Traboulsi, A.: Adaptable design for long range underwater communications. Wirel. Netw. 1–17 (2022). https://doi.org/10.1007/s11276-022-03027-4
2. Beaupré, Y.: TUBCipher Python Implementation. https://github.com/YBeaupre/TUBCipher.git
3. Bellare, M., Rogaway, P.: Introduction to modern cryptography (2005). https://web.cs.ucdavis.edu/rogaway/classes/227/spring05/book/main.pdf. Accessed 11 July 2022

4. Blouin, S., Lucas, C.: Early results and description of an underwater electric-field sensing and communication experiment in Bedford Basin. In: Proceedings of the 35th Canadian Conference on Electrical and Computer Engineering (CCECE2022), pp. 1–4. IEEE, September 2022

5. Dierks, T., Rescorla, E.: The transport layer security (TLS) protocol version 1.2. RFC 5246, RFC Editor, October 2008. https://www.rfc-editor.org/rfc/rfc5246

6. Gass, R., Scott, J., Diot, C.: Measurements of in-motion 802.11 networking. In: Seventh IEEE Workshop on Mobile Computing Systems & Applications (WMCSA'06 Supplement), pp. 69–74. IEEE (2005)

7. Hickman, K.: The SSL protocol. Technical report, Netscape Communications Corp (1995)

8. Hobbs A, H.S.: JANUS class 17 Venilia: secure pre-canned messaging. DSTL Cyber and Information Systems, pp. 1–22 (2021)

9. Hobbs A, H.S.: Tiny underwater block cipher (TUBcipher): 27-bit encryption scheme for JANUS class 17. DSTL Cyber and Information Systems, pp. 1–22 (2021)

10. Kenan, İ.: Security analysis of Java SecureRandom library. Eur. J. Sci. Technol. 157–160 (2021)

11. Knudsen, L., Leander, G., Poschmann, A., Robshaw, M.J.B.: PRINTcipher: a block cipher for IC-printing. In: Mangard, S., Standaert, F.-X. (eds.) CHES 2010. LNCS, vol. 6225, pp. 16–32. Springer, Heidelberg (2010). https://doi.org/10.1007/978-3-642-15031-9_2

12. National Institute of Standards and Technology: Advanced Encryption Standard (AES). https://csrc.nist.gov/publications/detail/fips/197/final. Accessed 29 June 2022

13. van Oorschot, P.C.: Computer Security and the Internet. Springer, Cham (2020). https://doi.org/10.1007/978-3-030-83411-1

14. Phan, D.H., Pointcheval, D.: About the security of ciphers (semantic security and pseudo-random permutations). In: Handschuh, H., Hasan, M.A. (eds.) SAC 2004. LNCS, vol. 3357, pp. 182–197. Springer, Heidelberg (2004). https://doi.org/10.1007/978-3-540-30564-4_13

15. Potter, J., Alves, J., Green, D., Zappa, G., Nissen, I., McCoy, K.: The JANUS underwater communications standard. In: 2014 Underwater Communications and Networking (UComms), pp. 1–4. IEEE (2014)

16. Rényi, A.: On measures of entropy and information. In: Proceedings of the Fourth Berkeley Symposium on Mathematical Statistics and Probability, Volume 1: Contributions to the Theory of Statistics, vol. 4, pp. 547–562. University of California Press (1961)

17. Van Walree, P.A.: Propagation and scattering effects in underwater acoustic communication channels. IEEE J. Oceanic Eng. **38**(4), 614–631 (2013)

18. Walker, J.: ENT: A pseudorandom number sequence test program (2008). https://www.fourmilab.ch/random/. Accessed 10 Dec 2021

19. Wikipedia: Replay attack. https://en.wikipedia.org/wiki/Replay_attack. Accessed 06 Oct 2022

Defense Models for Data Recovery in Industrial Control Systems

Alvi Jawad$^{(\boxtimes)}$ and Jason Jaskolka

Systems and Computer Engineering, Carleton University, Ottawa, ON, Canada
{alvi.jawad,jason.jaskolka}@carleton.ca

Abstract. Industrial control systems (ICS) have become a focal point for cyberattacks due to the shift from trusted proprietary environments. The now exposed attack surface mandates that ICS be equipped with defenses to prevent or mitigate the impact of potential attacks. Consequently, along with exploring the impact on system mission objectives, impact analysis studies need to consider implementable defenses that may reduce such impact. In this work, we equip a manufacturing ICS with three system defenses, modeled using timed automata in UPPAAL, that can perform data recovery against data corruption attacks. Additionally, we compare and contrast how capable each model is in mitigating the impact caused by data corruption attacks. The analysis provides insight into different defensive behaviors and their effectiveness, how they can be affected by attacker behaviors, and suggests some recommendations for developing future ICS defensive strategies.

Keywords: Impact Analysis · Industrial Control Systems · Data Recovery · Data Corruption · Timed Automata · Statistical Model Checking

1 Introduction

Industrial control systems (ICS) were once thought to be immune to cyberattacks due to their proprietary nature and reliance on "security by obscurity." With the emergence of ransomware attacks and other forms of cyber incidents [8], this outdated viewpoint has proven to be nothing but a simple myth [4]. Modern ICS that connect to the internet typically have some form of defensive mechanism against common attacks such as firewalls and intrusion detection systems. Consequently, studies that analyze the impact of attacks on ICS should also consider how the impact of different attacks changes based on the existence and capability of such defenses.

Impact analysis studies on ICS tend to focus primarily on the delayed, disrupted, or halted ICS processes caused by various cyberattacks [13]. However, often the solutions to such a problem, i.e., how to mitigate such impact using defensive mechanisms, are not considered. We assert that it is equally important for such studies to examine how implementing targeted countermeasures in ICS

© The Author(s), under exclusive license to Springer Nature Switzerland AG 2023
G.-V. Jourdan et al. (Eds.): FPS 2022, LNCS 13877, pp. 271–286, 2023.
https://doi.org/10.1007/978-3-031-30122-3_17

can reduce the expected impact. This undertaking will allow incorporating hypothetical defenses into existing impact analysis approaches and assess whether the time and resources spent on implementation would be worth the investment.

In our previous work on impact analysis [12], examining the impact of data tampering and spoofing attacks allowed us to observe compromised ICS behavior and operations. In this work, we emphasize examining defenses, leading to our two main contributions:

1. Modeling three different system defense behaviors for data recovery (instant recovery, delayed recovery, delayed recovery in safe mode) against data corruption attacks on an ICS case study using timed automata in UPPAAL, and
2. Characterizing the effectiveness of the different data recovery mechanisms in impact reduction using statistical model checking (SMC).

The analysis results provide insight into different interactions between the defenses, the system, and the attacker, potential undesirable consequences, and important considerations to guide the development of ICS defensive solutions.

The rest of the paper is organized as follows. Section 2 provides an overview of the proposed approach. Section 3 introduces the ICS case study. Sections 4–6 detail the activities involved in the various stages of the proposed approach. Section 7 discusses related works. Lastly, Sect. 8 concludes the work.

2   Overview of the Approach

In this section, we provide an overview of our impact analysis approach and show where defense modeling fits in the process. The approach involves modeling the target system of analysis and possible attackers that can perform attacks on the system model using timed automata [1] in UPPAAL [7].

Timed automata is a hybrid mathematical modeling formalism that uses a finite set of real-valued clocks to represent continuous time in a discrete-event system [1]. A timed automaton is a tuple (L, l_0, C, A, E, I) [2], where L is a set of locations, $l_0 \in L$ is the initial location, C is the set of clocks, A is a set of actions, co-actions, and the internal τ-action, $E \subseteq L \times A \times B(C) \times 2^C \times L$ is a set of edges between locations with an action, a Boolean guard, a set of clocks to be reset, and $I : L \to B(C)$ assigns invariants to locations. Selecting a timed modeling formalism is critical to model deviations in ICS processes, varying attacker behaviors, and the speed and efficacy of various system defenses.

UPPAAL is an integrated tool environment that supports the modeling and verification of real-time systems as networks of timed automata [2]. The UPPAAL modeling language extends timed automata with additional capabilities, allowing one to model real-time networked processes with bounded delays. The advantages of UPPAAL are clear from applications in several time-critical case studies such as bounded transmission protocols [6], remote control of industrial processes [12], and timed botnet behavior [14]. We use UPPAAL-SMC

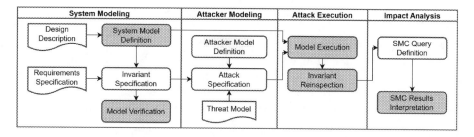

Fig. 1. Four-stage impact analysis approach and the associated activities.

(v4.1.26-1) available under a free academic license[1]. Details on the notations used to create timed automata models in UPPAAL can be found in [2].

2.1   Impact Analysis Approach

We take a four-stage systematic approach (as shown in Fig. 1) to identify and analyze the impact of attacks on ICS. Activities are depicted as rounded rectangles (in blue), and inputs to activities are depicted as documents (in red). In this work, our focus is on the activities depicted in green fill, indicating that they are related to defense modeling (see Sect. 2.2). As such, we only briefly discuss the other activities in the original approach below, a detailed demonstration of which can be found in [12].

System Modeling. In the first stage, a system model is built by leveraging information from the system design description. A set of system invariants are specified using temporal logic based on the system requirement specifications. To verify that the system model represents the expected behavior and satisfies the specified invariants, classical model checking is used for model verification.

Attacker Modeling. The second stage focuses on modeling different types of attackers and their expected behavior using timed automata. From system threat model information, potential attacks on the system are identified and used to form and specify attack strategies for each attacker model.

Attack Execution. In the third stage, the system and attacker models are executed in parallel to visualize the impact of attacks on system behavior. System simulations are studied, and the specified system invariants are reinspected to identify requirement violations due to attacks. Attacks that lead to a violation or negatively impact the system's objectives are selected for further analysis.

Impact Analysis. In the final stage, a suitable set of statistical model checking (SMC) [7] queries are defined to quantify the impact of the attacks selected in the third stage and gain further insight into the impacted system objectives.

---

[1]   https://uppaal.org/downloads/#academic-licenses/.

2.2 Role of Defense Modeling

Defense modeling involves identifying potential defenses to the attacks modeled in the second stage of our impact analysis approach. The behavior of the defenses is then modeled to assess their effectiveness in reducing the impact of attacks. Activities in our original impact analysis approach that need to be redone for the analysis of defenses are depicted in green fill as shown in Fig. 1.

Modeling. First, in the *System Modeling* stage, the system defenses are modeled as an extension (separate processes) to the originally defenseless system model. This is followed by a model verification with the previously specified invariants to ensure the expected system behavior. Notably, none of the activities in the *Attacker Modeling* stage is affected, as the attacker models are modular, and their behavior is separate from that of the system or the defenses.

Analysis. Next, we execute the attacker models in parallel with the augmented system model with defenses in the *Attack Execution* stage to visualize how the defenses mitigate the impact of attacks. Additionally, we reinspect our system invariants to identify whether attacks can still impact the system operations. Finally, we move to the *Impact Analysis* stage to obtain statistical data on the potential impact and compare them with the defenseless case.

A detailed demonstration of these activities can be found in Sects. 4–6.

3 Case Study: Manufacturing Cell Control System

We will use a manufacturing cell control system (MCCS) as a case study to illustrate the different steps of our approach related to defense modeling. The MCCS is illustrative of a small ICS consisting of four primary system agents, each of which consists of one or more components and an internal control system. The expected operation of the MCCS is shown in Fig. 2 where solid and dashed lines represent message-passing and shared-variable communications, respectively.

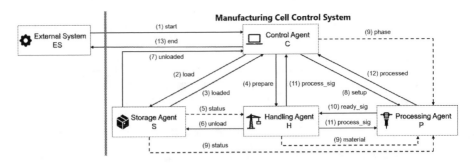

Fig. 2. Collaboration diagram depicting the expected operation of the MCCS

The *Control Agent* C is the central control system that manages the manufacturing phases and coordinates the activities of other system agents. The

Storage Agent S keeps track of whether the raw material inventory is full, and performs loading and unloading of materials. The *Handling Agent* H is responsible for moving materials from the storage to the *Processing Agent* P, allowing P to process (e.g., drill) the material. The MCCS continues operating until it has reached its mission objective of *processing the required (M) units of material within strict time constraints.*

The simulations in this work will assume that a successful sequence of loading-unloading-moving(handling)-working(processing), as shown in Fig. 6, will lead to a single unit of material being produced within 10 time units. Uninterrupted MCCS operations will thus lead to a production of 3 material units within 30 simulated time units. More details on the MCCS operations and its networked timed automata model can be found in [12].

4   System Modeling with Defenses

In this section, we explain the concept behind modeling defenses for a system and demonstrate the process through different abstract system agents. In essence, this is an extension of the *System Modeling* stage of our impact analysis approach where we extend the system model capabilities with defensive mechanisms.

4.1   Defense Modeling

There are two important parts to modeling defenses: (1) *the detection process (DP)* and (2) *the defensive action (DA).* The behavior and efficacy of the system defenses modeled in this work will be demonstrated using data corruption attacks on the MCCS. Consequently, the DP and DA, respectively, would entail detecting data corruption attempts and performing a *corruption recovery* for data restoration. In this work, we focus on three types of defenses:

1. **Instant Defense:** The DP and the DA are both instantaneous, essentially resulting in the prevention of an attack before it can cause an impact.
2. **Delayed Defense:** Both the DP and the DA take some amount of time to complete, constituting a more realistic defensive mechanism. This is similar to mitigating an attack since the attack may have already caused an impact by the time the DA has finished.
3. **Delayed Defense in Safe Mode:** A special case of the delayed defense where the system is taken to a safe mode during the DA. In the safe mode, system processes are temporarily halted so that a race condition or fault does not occur, and attackers are prevented from affecting the system processes.

Modeling Instant Defenses. To model a system with instant defenses, we need to add a DP and a DA capability to the system that can be performed instantaneously. To prevent data corruption attacks on the MCCS, we can do this by extending the system model with two new agents focused on data recovery.

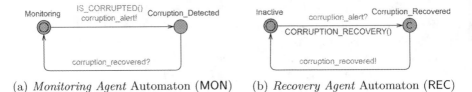

(a) *Monitoring Agent* Automaton (MON)   (b) *Recovery Agent* Automaton (REC)

Fig. 3. Modeling instant detection and recovery

The first agent (shown in Fig. 3a) is a *Monitoring Agent* (MON) that can monitor the shared system variables and raise an alert (corruption_alert!) whenever there is a corruption of such variables. The behavior is similar to file system integrity checking tools like Tripwire [15]. The corruption can be detected by continuous monitoring of the shared variables (e.g., through an IS_CORRUPTED() Boolean function) and detecting whether any variable is assigned a value outside its allowed value range. For example, in case of the phase variable, the allowed values are 0, 1, 2, and 3, representing the four system phases. Therefore, at any point during the system operations, assigning any values other than these four allowed values would make MON send out a corruption_alert!.

The corruption_alert? is received by the second agent (shown in Fig. 3b), named *Recovery Agent* (REC), that can take an instantaneous DA by performing an immediate corruption recovery. The recovery action (CORRUPTION_RECOVERY()) can be performed by determining the ideal state of the corrupted variable based on the current overall system state and reassigning to it the ideal value. Once the corruption is recovered, REC can send a corruption_recovered! message to MON, informing that the effect of the corruption has been removed and that MON can start monitoring the system again. The use of *urgent synchronization channels* allows both the detection and recovery action to be instantaneous, thus resulting in immediate recovery from any corruptions.

This duo of a monitoring and recovery agent will be used in our impact analysis approach to constitute a data recovery defensive mechanism and demonstrate its effectiveness against data corruption attacks. Furthermore, extensions to these models will allow us to model other defensive behaviors.

Modeling Delayed Defenses. While the capability to instantaneously detect and recover from any attempted corruption seems great on paper, in reality, this is hardly feasible. There may always be delays due to various reasons in both the detection and recovery process. For example, some attacks may be harder to detect than others, and the time to perform the recovery may include the recovery of system data and parameters and resetting the system data to their original state [5]. To model this varying delay, we extend the *Monitoring Agent* and the *Recovery Agent* models discussed before, as shown in Fig. 4a and Fig. 4b.

Two additional clocks (mon_clk and rec_clk) and a set of four new parameters (min_detection_time, max_detection_time, min_recovery_time,

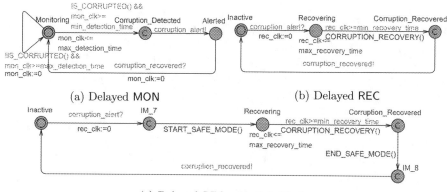

(a) Delayed MON   (b) Delayed REC

(c) Delayed REC with Safe Mode

Fig. 4. Modeling Delayed Detection and Recovery

max_recovery_time) allow one to control the detection and recovery time for data corruption. Once assigned, the DP or the DA will take a uniform random time between the minimum and maximum allowed values. In our simulations, we will assume that both the DP and the DA take at least one time unit to complete to see the delayed behavior.

Modeling Delayed Defenses with Safe Mode. When multiple entities can modify a shared variable, there are always chances of encountering a race condition. With the inclusion of the *Recovery Agent* for defensive purposes, there are now three different entities (i.e., system agents, an attacker, and a defense agent) that can modify a shared system variable. For example, the status variable can be assigned by the *Storage Agent* during normal system operations, by the *Attacker Automaton* to cause data corruption, and by the *Recovery Agent* to recover from corruption simultaneously. Therefore, the existence of multiple actors leads to a few different problems and escalates when delays are involved.

For one, when we consider delayed defenses, the detection and defensive action decisions are made before the delay is applied. This means that if an attacker attacks and causes another compromise (e.g., data corruption) between the time the recovery decision was made and the actual recovery is done, it can lead to impacted system behavior despite a successful recovery action. Additionally, the system itself may complete a process (e.g., processing), leading to a system assignment of different variables while the detection and recovery are being done. When the recovery finally finishes, the system will be in a completely different state than when the recovery started, and as a result, the recovery may be done incorrectly. Thus, a delayed defense must consider the various race conditions and the potentially undesirable consequences.

To augment the system model with delayed defenses with a safe mode, we use the same *Monitoring Agent* shown in Fig. 4a while extending the capabilities of the *Recovery Agent*. REC is extended (Fig. 4c) with two intermediate committed states [12] IM_7 and IM_8 that start (START_SAFE_MODE()) and end (END_SAFE_MODE()) the safe mode, respectively. The safe mode spans the duration of the recovery action.

The goal of the safe mode is twofold: (1) the system may not complete any processes, i.e., may not assign to any shared variables, and (2) an attacker may not attack the system during the safe mode, i.e., may not tamper with any shared variable. The first goal is reflective of pausing the ongoing system processes and putting a lock on shared variables until DAs are completed. The second goal is the equivalent of putting the system in a state where attacks cannot happen (e.g., by closing certain ports to prevent malicious remote connections from external entities). While the DA will inevitably slow down the system processes, they will allow the recovery to be done correctly without the possibility of being affected by concurrent compromises by an attack and/or system process assignments.

4.2   Verification with Modeled Defenses

An ICS must always (1) *reach its mission objectives (e.g., production end) in time*, and (2) *reach the mission objectives uninterrupted*. Thus, for the MCCS, we specify two corresponding system invariants for the MCCS using temporal logic in UPPAAL's verifier[2], details of which can be found in [12].

Invariant 1: $ES.Begin \rightsquigarrow (ES.End \wedge total\_time \leq M * 10)$

Invariant 2: $A \square (\neg H.WFM \wedge \neg P.WFI \wedge \neg P.WFR)$.

Any time a new defensive mechanism (e.g., a defense agent) is added to a system, it is important to recheck the system invariants (specified based on system requirements) in the *Invariant Specification* activity. This check ensures that the system retains its former capabilities, and that adding new defensive functions does not inhibit it from reaching its mission objectives. For the MCCS, adding the *Monitoring Agent* and the *Recovery Agent* should not prevent it from reaching its mission objective of producing M materials within the specified time. By rechecking the system invariants in UPPAAL, we confirm that *all system invariants are still satisfied* even after the addition of the two defense agents.

Overall, the defense models presented in this section are reusable for any ICS as long as the detection (i.e., IS_CORRUPTED()) and recovery (i.e., CORRUPTION_RECOVERY()) functions are adapted to meet the defensive needs of the system in question. The base defense model shown in Fig. 3 is extensible, as shown in Fig. 4 with the addition of clocks, parameters, and additional states.

5   Attack Execution

To execute attacks on various system defense configurations, we will follow the impact analysis approach activities outlined in Sect. 2. As part of the *Attack Modeling* stage of our impact analysis approach, we first execute data corruption attacks in the *Model Execution* activity by a *random* attacker and then

---

[2] The syntax and semantics of the query language used by UPPAAL is a subset of timed computation tree logic (TCTL) and can be found in [2].

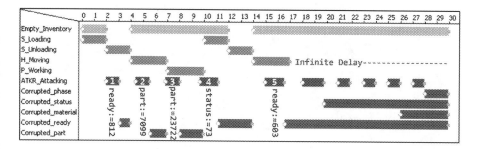

Fig. 5. Data corruption attacks on a defenseless system by a *random* attacker

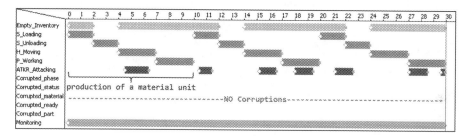

Fig. 6. Effect of instant recovery against data corruption by a *random* attacker

perform *Invariant Reinspection* to quickly check for system invariant violations. The *random* attacker has randomized behavior, and for simulation purposes, it will prepare for a uniform random time between one and five time units before each attack and take one to two time units to perform each attack. Details on the attacker model and its behavior can be found in [12].

5.1 Model Execution

To compare with the case where data corruption attacks are performed by a *random* attacker on a defenseless system model, we can look at the simulation run in Fig. 5) generated by UPPAAL. The attacks, performed in random intervals, end up corrupting random shared variables with garbage values when successful (see the corruption of variables ready, part, and status by attempts 1 through 5). The attacks can ultimately lead to a *time deadlock* [12], which is equivalent to an infinite delay for a system that has no way to recover from data corruption. Now, we examine attacks by the same attacker but with the system model being equipped with three different defenses to compare their effectiveness.

Instant Recovery. We start by looking at the MCCS system model equipped with an instant recovery mechanism (refer to Sect. 4.1). Figure 6 shows an example simulation run of a *random* attacker attempting to corrupt the data within the system. The *Monitoring Agent* can be seen to constantly monitor the system (depicted in green) for any data corruption. Any attempted corruption by

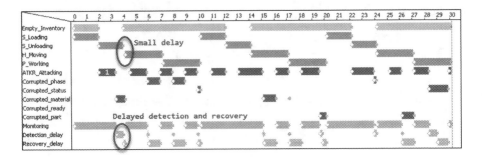

Fig. 7. Effect of delayed recovery against data corruption by a *random* attacker

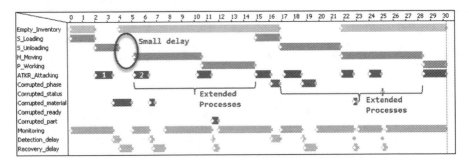

Fig. 8. Effect of recovery in safe mode against corruption by a *random* attacker

the attacker was immediately found, and the *Recovery Agent* was alerted, which recovered from the corruption immediately. This is an ideal case scenario where both detection and recovery are instantaneous and can be seen by the system remaining free of any corruption even after multiple attempts by the attacker. While not exactly prevention (since the recovery is done on the already corrupted data), this is a close equivalent for harder-to-prevent attacks since the effects of the attacks are still prevented from impacting the system.

Delayed Recovery. Next, we look at data corruption attacks on a more realistic MCCS model equipped with a detection and recovery mechanism with some delays (Fig. 7). We can see the first data corruption attempt of the attacker succeeding slightly after three time units. The corruption was present in the system for a short while as the detection and recovery mechanism both required some time to complete. This led to a small impact on the system processes as the moving action was delayed due to unreadable corrupted values. The system resumed its moving action after the corruption was recovered and all three material units were produced, albeit taking slightly longer than 30 time units. Although not shown in this particular simulation, if the simulations are run long enough, race conditions would occur for the delayed recovery case for the reasons identified in Sect. 4.1. This is especially apparent when system processes and delays between consecutive attacks are relatively shorter, and the recovery process takes longer. To deal with such a situation, we make the delayed recovery action more robust with a safe mode for the third system defense.

Delayed Recovery with Safe Mode. Finally, we examine data corruption attacks on the MCCS model that has delayed recovery capabilities with safe mode (Fig. 8). The simulated detection and recovery times are the same as the delayed recovery case, however, the safe mode prevents the system agents and the attacker from taking any action during the recovery process. The first attempt of the attacker leads to a corruption slightly after three time units which result in a small delay before the data recovery is done in the safe mode. The drawback of stopping the system processes, however, can be seen from the second attempt by the attacker. The safe mode pauses the system processes during the recovery, and as a result, the moving process is extended beyond the expected duration of three time units. Similar extensions can be seen in the case of processing (about four time units) in the same production cycle and in the case of the unloading and moving processes (combined duration of about 11 time units) in the second production cycle. The MCCS could not even produce two units of material within 30 time units due to both delays due to corruption and process extensions caused by the safe recovery action.

5.2 Invariant Reinspection

Once the system model is executed in parallel with attacker models, it is important to re-examine which system invariants (specified in the *Invariant Specification* activity of Sect. 4.2) are violated and identify the reason behind it. In our earlier work [12], we found the data corruption attack by *random* attackers to lead to violations of both system invariants, but not to a system *deadlock*. Additionally, we found the attacks to lead to a *time deadlock* and enter three stalled states [12], where the system operations are endlessly waiting for correct values of shared variables before they can proceed.

In this work, even with the system augmented with three different defenses against data corruption attacks, we reached the same results through a reinspection of the invariants. However, the biggest difference is that the states of *time deadlock* do not lead to an infinite delay. Rather, the system leaves the undesirable stalled states after a successful corruption recovery. While it may seem that instant detection and recovery should be able to avoid a *time deadlock* altogether, we did not find that to be the case. Part of the reason is that UPPAAL cannot model "true concurrency." At the same simulation time, both a system agent, the DA, and the DP may be scheduled to act. Depending on which transition fires first, the system invariants may be violated, and stalled states may be briefly encountered. The persisting violations indicate that regardless of the defense type, there is some amount of impact involved. For a more detailed measure of the impact and how much of that is reduced by each of the three defenses, we move to the final stage of our impact analysis approach.

Table 1. Impact analysis results for different defenses against data corruption attacks by a *random* attacker

Defense type	Probability of producing 864 material units (%)		Average units of material produced (no. of materials)		Average total production delay (minutes)		Production delay (%)
	within 1 d	within 23 h	within 1 h	within 1 d	within 1 h	within 1 d	within 1 d
Defenseless	0	0	2.27	2.13	55.74	1435.89	99.71
Instant recovery	59.1	0	35.99	863.60	0.06	3.02	0.21
Delayed recovery	0	0	13.59	14.3	36.50	1413.65	98.17
Delayed recovery with safe mode	0	0	19.59	475.61	0	7.37	0.51

6   Impact Analysis

In this section, we analyze the impact of attacks in the *SMC Results Interpretation* activity. Statistical model checking (SMC) is used to verify a formal model based on whether it satisfies a property with a certain confidence level δ and maximum error limit ϵ by monitoring stochastic simulations and leveraging results from the statistics area [7]. The use of SMC enables us to gain further insight into the impact of data corruption for the worst-case scenario (defenseless system) and how effectively each defense model can reduce the impact.

Using SMC, we gather results from three queries in the *SMC Query Definition* activity: (1) The probability of reaching system mission objectives (manufacturing M units), (2) The expected level of mission completion (average units of material produced), and (3) The average expected delay in system operation (delayed production) in a timespan of t time units. The corresponding SMC queries are specified as follows, details of which can be found in [12].

SMC Q 1: $\Pr[total\_time \leq sim\_time; sim\_runs]$ $(\Diamond\ processed\_mat == M)$
SMC Q 2: $\mathrm{E}[total\_time \leq sim\_time; sim\_runs]$ $(max : processed\_mat)$

SMC Q 3: $\mathrm{E}[total\_time \leq sim\_time; sim\_runs]$ $(max : total\_delay)$

6.1   Impact of Attacks by a *Random* Attacker

The SMC query results, each with 1000 sample simulation runs, are shown in Table 1. Each simulated time unit is assumed to represent ten seconds, mandating 100 s to produce a material unit. In the ideal scenario, the MCCS would reach an hourly production of 36 and a daily production of 864 material units. Undesirable results are depicted in red, whereas results considered to be a significant improvement over the defenseless case are depicted in green. A detailed discussion of the results for the *defenseless system* can be found in [12].

The results from *SMC Q 1* (columns 2–3) allow us to quickly see how likely the system is to reach its daily production goal. Only the *instant recovery* case improves the odds of reaching the goal with a probability of 59.1%. Although instant, this recovery mechanism is still not able to reach the ideal value of 100% due to modeling artifacts (refer to Sect. 5.2). The two other defenses produce results similar to the defenseless system, indicating that some system process

Table 2. Impact analysis results for different defenses against accelerated data corruption attacks by a *random* attacker

Defense type	Probability of producing 864 material units (%)		Average units of material produced (no. of materials)		Average total production delay (minutes)		Production delay (%)
	within 1 d	within 23 h	within 1 h	within 1 d	within 1 h	within 1 d	within 1 d
Defenseless	0	0	0.17	0.26	58.95	1438.97	99.93
Instant recovery	41.9	0	35.86	857.12	0.15	39.47	2.74
Delayed recovery	0	0	2.29	2.20	55.89	1436.29	99.74
Delayed recovery with safe mode	0	0	0	0	2.32	85.86	5.96

delays are inevitable even when these defenses are active. This happens due to these two defenses having delays in both their DP and DA. Furthermore, the *delayed recovery* mechanism is affected by race conditions, and the *delayed recovery with safe mode* itself delays system processes to perform a safer DA.

In terms of the average production, i.e., *SMC Q 2* (columns 4–5), we see significant improvements in the *instant recovery* case. The production is nearly identical to the ideal scenario of 36 and 864 material units produced hourly and daily, respectively, despite the occasional delays identified by the results from *SMC Q 1*. The results from the *delayed recovery* case are the worst, reaching an irreversible state within the first few minutes of simulation start due to race conditions. This is exemplified by similar average production both in the daily and the hourly case. While the *delayed recovery in safe mode* halts system processes during the recovery process, the benefits are evident; the MCCS is able to produce many more materials (about 50% of the ideal case) despite the DP taking the same, and the DA taking longer than the delayed recovery case.

Results from *SMC Q 3* (columns 6–8) show a similar trend as *SMC Q 2* for the first two defense types. The *instant recovery* mechanism is able to prevent nearly all production delays, whereas the *delayed recovery* case is not very effective at doing the same as the results are similar to the defenseless case with 98.17% daily production delay. The *delayed recovery with safe mode* is more interesting; even though fewer materials are produced, we can only see less than 1% production delay. In this case, the production is less not because of delays caused by data corruption but due to deliberately pausing the system processes during the recovery operation to prevent any race conditions.

6.2 Impact of *Accelerated* Attacks by a *Random* Attacker

To get a different view of the effectiveness of the defensive mechanisms, we now configure the *random* attacker model [12] to perform *accelerated* attacks. The goal is to see whether attacks performed in quick succession, e.g., attacks from a script, differ in the caused impact. For simulation purposes, a *random* attacker will both prepare and perform each *accelerated* attack within one time unit.

Table 2 summarizes the SMC query results for *accelerated* attacks performed by a *random* attacker. For a *defenseless* system, the impact is much higher, as shown by the MCCS not producing even one unit of material on average, as it is spending almost all of its time (99.93%) in stalled states waiting for a corruption recovery. There is barely any impact when the MCCS is equipped with the *instant recovery* mechanism; the delays caused by the *accelerated* attacks are minimal (2.74%), and the MCCS consistently reaches very close to its hourly and daily production goals, with 41.9% chance of reaching its daily objectives.

More significant impacts can be observed for the other two, arguably more realistic, defenses with delays. For the *delayed recovery* case, the overall impact is close to that of a *defenseless* system. The *accelerated* attacks cause more frequent race conditions, especially as during the DP and the DA, the *random* attacker may perform more than one *accelerated* attack. The impact is amplified with the inherent properties of the *delayed recovery with safe mode*. Even though there is less delay caused by corruption, the MCCS can never produce any material unit. The safe mode forces the system processes to be halted during the recovery action, which is extended indefinitely if further attacks are performed before the recovery action and subsequent system process can finish.

In summary, compared to the *delayed recovery*, the *delayed recovery in safe mode* allows producing more materials when attacks are not highly frequent or when the system process duration is short enough to not be paused indefinitely. Our study shows how the same defensive mechanism (e.g., corruption recovery) can exhibit different behaviors and how the characteristics of a defensive mechanism can prove to be a bad match-up or be targeted by certain types of attackers. Such efforts can lead to an enhanced understanding of potential trade-offs and aid decision-making when implementing defensive mechanisms with privileges.

7   Related Work

Hou et al. [11] proposed an event-triggered cyber defense strategy that can correct frequency deviations caused by non-simultaneous cyberattack events on energy systems. Hong et al. [9] proposed a power system domain principle that involves a collaborative defensive scheme using intelligent electronic devices (IEDs) to detect and block potential impacts caused by cyberattacks and human errors. Kiss et al. [16] presented a framework to assess the awareness of anomaly-based intrusion detection systems (IDS) against stealthy attacks in power grids. Cam et al. [5] established attackability conditions to bypass the detection of an anomaly-based IDS for distributed control systems. Some game-theoretic approaches that analyze cyber defense strategies include using discrete-event simulations to analyze how a combination of controllable defense policies and uncontrollable security-based parameters can reduce performance impact caused by attacks [3], reinforcing system infrastructure parts or components to defend against incidental degradation [18], identifying that several attack factors and defensive countermeasures play influential roles in a system's resiliency against attacks [17], work on a multi-defender model responsible for CPS components and sharing management of nodes [10], suggesting a systematic ICS patch prioritization method to reduce the impact of potential attacks [19], among others.

In contrast, our work incorporates modeling and analysis of different defensive behaviors in an existing systematic impact analysis approach [12]. We used simulations to perform a timed analysis of the defensive behavior in parallel with system and attacker activities to observe mitigated and unmitigated impacts and other potentially undesirable situations, such as race conditions.

8   Conclusions

Impact analysis approaches for ICS need to involve potential defenses when considering the impact on system mission objectives. In this work, we focused on reducing the impact of data corruption attacks on ICS operations by modeling three different defensive behaviors related to data recovery. The defenses were modeled as extensions to an manufacturing cell control system model using timed automata in UPPAAL. Statistical model checking was used to analyze the impact of data corruption attacks on the system equipped with each defense at a time, allowing us to assess the effectiveness of each defense in reducing the impact.

Throughout the process, the timed analysis of the concurrent behavior of the system, defenses, and attackers proved to be effective in identifying potential race conditions and undesirable impacts such as process delays. Additionally, using SMC, we characterized the residual impact of attacks when defenses were active and observed how defenses vulnerable to a particular type of attacker behavior could compound the impact. The analysis is helpful when designing defensive behaviors to understand the many different and often unseen interactions and to assign appropriate privileges to defenses by considering the trade-offs on the system's mission objectives.

Our priority in future work is to examine the impact with more comprehensive defensive actions, such as recovery with patching [19], along with defenses against more challenging attacks, such as data modification and spoofing [12].

References

1. Alur, R., Dill, D.L.: A theory of timed automata. Theoret. Comput. Sci. **126**(2), 183–235 (1994)
2. Behrmann, G., David, A., Larsen, K.G.: A tutorial on Uppaal. In: Bernardo, M., Corradini, F. (eds.) Formal Methods for the Design of Real-Time Systems: International School on Formal Methods for the Design of Computer, Communication, and Software Systems, Bertinora, Italy, September 13–18, 2004, Revised Lectures, pp. 200–236. Lecture Notes in Computer Science, Springer, Berlin, Heidelberg (2004)
3. Bracho, A., Saygin, C., Wan, H., Lee, Y., Zarreh, A.: A simulation-based platform for assessing the impact of cyber-threats on smart manufacturing systems. Procedia Manuf. **26**, 1116–1127 (2018)
4. Byres, E., Dr, P.E., Hoffman, D.: The myths and facts behind cyber security risks for industrial control systems. In: Proceedings of VDE Kongress (2004)
5. Cam, H., Mouallem, P., Mo, Y., Sinopoli, B., Nkrumah, B.: Modeling impact of attacks, recovery, and attackability conditions for situational awareness. In: 2014 IEEE International Inter-Disciplinary Conference on Cognitive Methods in Situation Awareness and Decision Support (CogSIMA), pp. 181–187, March 2014

6. D'Argenio, P.R., Katoen, J.-P., Ruys, T.C., Tretmans, J.: The bounded retransmission protocol must be on time! In: Brinksma, E. (ed.) TACAS 1997. LNCS, vol. 1217, pp. 416–431. Springer, Heidelberg (1997). https://doi.org/10.1007/BFb0035403

7. David, A., Larsen, K.G., Legay, A., Mikučionis, M., Poulsen, D.B.: Uppaal SMC tutorial. Int. J. Softw. Tools Technol. Transfer **17**(4), 397–415 (2015)

8. Hemsley, K., Fisher, R.: A history of cyber incidents and threats involving industrial control systems. In: ICCIP 2018. IAICT, vol. 542, pp. 215–242. Springer, Cham (2018). https://doi.org/10.1007/978-3-030-04537-1_12

9. Hong, J., Nuqui, R.F., Kondabathini, A., Ishchenko, D., Martin, A.: Cyber attack resilient distance protection and circuit breaker control for digital substations. IEEE Transactions on Industrial Informatics **15**(7), 4332–4341, July 2019

10. Hota, A.R., Clements, A.A., Sundaram, S., Bagchi, S.: Optimal and game-theoretic deployment of security investments in interdependent assets. In: Zhu, Q., Alpcan, T., Panaousis, E., Tambe, M., Casey, W. (eds.) GameSec 2016. LNCS, vol. 9996, pp. 101–113. Springer, Cham (2016). https://doi.org/10.1007/978-3-319-47413-7_6

11. Hou, J., Lei, S., Yin, W., Sun, W., Hou, Y.: Cybersecurity enhancement for multi-infeed high-voltage dc systems. IEEE Trans. Smart Grid **13**(4), 3227–3240, July 2022

12. Jawad, A., Jaskolka, J.: Analyzing the impact of cyberattacks on industrial control systems using timed automata. In: 2021 IEEE 21st International Conference on Software Quality, Reliability and Security (QRS), pp. 966–977, December 2021

13. Jawad, A., Jaskolka, J.: Modeling and simulation approaches for cybersecurity impact analysis: state-of-the-art. In: 2021 Annual Modeling and Simulation Conference (ANNSIM), pp. 1–12, July 2021

14. Jawad, A., Newton, L., Matrawy, A., Jaskolka, J.: A formal analysis of the efficacy of rebooting as a countermeasure against IoT botnets. In: ICC 2022 - IEEE International Conference on Communications, pp. 2206–2211, May 2022

15. Kim, G.H., Spafford, E.H.: The design and implementation of tripwire: a file system integrity checker. In: Proceedings of the 2nd ACM Conference on Computer and Communications Security, pp. 18–29. CCS 1994, November 1994

16. Kiss, I., Genge, B., Haller, P., Sebestyén, G.: A framework for testing stealthy attacks in energy grids. In: 2015 IEEE International Conference on Intelligent Computer Communication and Processing (ICCP), pp. 553–560, September 2015

17. Orojloo, H., Azgomi, M.A.: A stochastic game model for evaluating the impacts of security attacks against cyber-physical systems. J. Netw. Syst. Manage. **26**(4), 929–965 (2018)

18. Rao, N.S.V., Poole, S.W., Ma, C.Y.T., He, F., Zhuang, J., Yau, D.K.Y.: Defense of cyber infrastructures against cyber-physical attacks using game-theoretic models. Risk Anal. **36**(4), 694–710 (2016)

19. Yadav, G., Gauravaram, P., Jindal, A.K., Paul, K.: SmartPatch: a patch prioritization framework. Comput. Ind. **137**, 103595 (2022)

SCADA Radio Blackbox Reverse Engineering

Jean-Benoit Larouche[1]([⊠]), Sébastien Roy[1], Frédéric Mailhot[1],
Pierre-Martin Tardif[2], and Marc Frappier[3]

[1] Electrical and Computer Engineering Department, Université de Sherbrooke,
Sherbrooke, QC, Canada
djibylarouche@hotmail.com
[2] Management School, Université de Sherbrooke, Sherbrooke, QC, Canada
[3] Computer Science Department, Université de Sherbrooke, Sherbrooke, QC, Canada

Abstract. Supervisory control and data acquisition (SCADA) systems
were designed to be open, robust, and easy to operate and repair, but
not necessarily secure. In recent years, there have been multiple successful attacks targeting SCADA systems. Most of them have been caused
by deploying malware on a supervisory computer in order to control
and manage programmable logic controllers (PLCs) and remote terminal units (RTUs). This work investigates a different potential way to
control PLCs or RTUs in a plant which consists in inflitrating over-the-
air (OTA) links based on SCADA wireless modems. Indeed, PLCs and
RTUs are often linked to a supervisory computer wirelessly using outdated radios, with low security at the physical-layer level. An example of
such a radio is the CalAmp Guardian-400 wireless modem. A blackbox
reverse engineering of the physical layer of the latter is performed, which
leads to complete signal demodulation and decoding. Our results demonstrate that any electronic equipment connected serially to the radio is
vulnerable to wireless packet injection.

Keywords: SCADA · software defined radio · scrambling · NRZI ·
digital phase locked loops · FSK

1 Introduction

Radio waves can transfer information between two or more points quite effectively, over large distances, at the speed of light. However, anyone with the adequate equipment can act as a valid receiver and intercept those electromagnetic
waves, or interfere with the signal by transmitting on the same time/frequency
resource, commonly known as *jamming*. With the ubiquitous presence of radios
in many essential aspects of our day-to-day life (such as Wi-Fi, cellphones, cars,
computers, TVs, etc.), wireless security is of utmost importance. The same degree
of care should be applied to any wireless device required in industrial processes
and critical infrastructures underlying our modern society.

© The Author(s), under exclusive license to Springer Nature Switzerland AG 2023
G.-V. Jourdan et al. (Eds.): FPS 2022, LNCS 13877, pp. 287–302, 2023.
https://doi.org/10.1007/978-3-031-30122-3_18

SCADA stands for Supervisory Control and Data Acquisition. A SCADA system is a combination of hardware and software that enables the automation of industrial processes by capturing Operational Technology (OT) data. Hardware such as Remote Terminal Units (RTUs) and Programmable Logic Controllers (PLCs) serve as local collection points for acquiring this OT data. This information can be acted upon directly using programmed logic or gathered by a computer commonly known as a gateway.

Gateways can come in various forms such as edge computers, Human Machine Interfaces (HMI) or a central server. One advantage of such an architecture resides in the ability to monitor and control systems from multiple locations. In the past, it has often been common practice to air gap such control system networks as they typically didn't need to interact with other corporate systems or the Internet. In theory, having this disconnection has been a sufficient security measure, however this is often no longer operationally feasible in today's connected world.

IBM Managed Security Services (MSS) data reveals there has been a 110% increase in attacks on industrial control systems since 2016 - a threat landscape that is predicted to grow at a phenomenal rate in the upcoming years [7]. A second report from Raytheon [8] mentions that 80% of companies expect an increase in cyber risk over the coming years. This is to be expected since OT systems constitute easy targets. Communication protocols designed without stringent security measures (ModBus, DNP3 [2]), corporate environments running outdated software and default passwords on embedded accounts and/or personal devices are all common security vulnerabilities which can cause a lot of damage on many different fronts (loss of operations and revenue, infrastructure shutdown, loss of physical well-being, etc.). Additionally, updating and/or replacing industrial devices can prove to be quite expensive and complicated. This directly leads to a large quantity of obsolete legacy equipment still in operation and involved in critical tasks. The present paper exposes a cyber risk linked to the usage of outdated hardware designed without stringent security measures, in an industrial power plant. More specifically, the vulnerability resides in the radios used to establish wireless links between PLCs and supervisory computers.

The popular malware attacks on SCADA systems drove a lot of research in the field of cybersecurity, but most of it focuses on potential network breaches or possible software exploits. There is very little research on the potential risks involved when using legacy RF equipment with an unsecured physical layer. The only relevant work found on this topic is presented in [4]. Therein, the reverse-engineering of a widely deployed GE MDS-9710 radio is performed. The physical layer of the latter frequency-modulates a scrambled, duo-binary coded signal as a means to transfer information OTA. Using GNU radio, successful demodulation of the MDS-9710 radio signals was achieved, thanks to their access to the theory of operation document (filed with the FCC by the manufacturer) and the digital signal processor (DSP) firmware. In a similar fashion, our work presents a step-by-step blackbox reverse engineering of the Guardian-400 wireless modem physical layer, using only an ADALM-PLUTO SDR [9] platform and

MATLAB software. No firmware access or technical document was available, besides the user manual. Still, even with very limited knowledge, our work shows how an unsecured physical layer can be simple to analyze, using widely accessible and inexpensive tools.

The CalAmp Guardian-400 commercial radio is conveniently interoperable with multiple discontinued radios such as the CalAmp DL-3400 analog transceiver, the DL-3282 analog radio, and the T-96SR wireless modem. The latter has the most interesting mode of operation since it is capable of telemetry transmission at a rate of 9600 bps and thus, is more relevant in the context of today's SCADA systems.

The T-96SR radio was developed many years ago, circa 1999 [5], when wireless data transmission was very niche. Thus, little effort was made to protect the equipment from potential wireless attacks and as a consequence, the radio consists of a simple and unsecured physical layer. From [1], it is found that the T-96SR physical layer implements differential raised-cosine minimum shift keying (DRCMSK) modulation. Before modulation, the payload bits are scrambled using a 7-bits scrambler, then differentially encoded using NRZI (Non-Return-to-Zero Inverted). No forward error correction (FEC) and packet structure is defined. Thus, it is assumed that the Guardian-400 radio behaves in the same manner when in compatibility mode with the T-96SR. This constitutes the starting point of our reverse-engineering process.

2   Previous Results

This paper is based on an in-depth signal analysis of OTA recordings, obtained by standing at a 1 km radius from a power plant with an ADALM-PLUTO SDR platform. In order to extract the transmitted bits, an FSK demodulator is required. The block diagram in Fig. 1 shows the developed FSK demodulator.

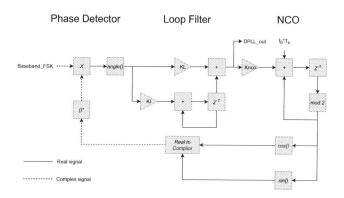

Fig. 1. FSK demodulator block diagram.

The demodulated bits are extracted from the *DPLL_out* signal. This signal follows the ADALM-PLUTO SDR sampling rate of 528 KHz and is affected by multiple RF impairments. In order to extract the bits, a bit extractor, based on the digital phase-locked loop (DPLL) presented in Fig. 1, is used. The phase detector is replaced by an inductive minimum mean-square error (MMSE) timing error estimator, which samples the *DPLL_out* input at twice the expected symbol rate of 9600 bps, then calculates the discrete-time derivative. Figure 2 illustrates this concept.

Fig. 2. Correct sampling phase vs. late sampling phase at twice the symbol rate.

The timing error estimation is calculated using the following formula:

$$\tau_{k+1} = \tau_k - (Q_k - A_k)(Q_{k+1} - Q_{k-1})$$

where $A_k = \pm 1$, following the polarity of Q_k. A NCO (Numerically Controlled Oscillator) is used to generate the sampling instants 19200 Hz, with its phase being controlled by the filtered timing error estimate. The complete block diagram, including the MMSE timing error estimator, a loop filter and the NCO is illustrated in Fig. 3.

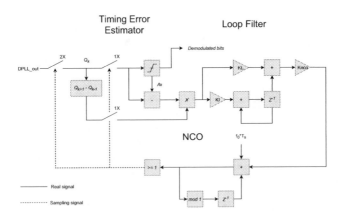

Fig. 3. Symbol extractor block diagram.

The first phase concludes with the fact that by using a signal processing software such as MATLAB, one can use DPLLs to demodulate a Guardian-400 signal down to its transmitted bits. These bits however, are assumed to be encoded and scrambled at the physical layer and thus, no direct extraction of payload bits can be performed.

The present paper goes deeper into the physical layer analysis of the radio, thanks to its commercial availability. It is shown that one could potentially recover transmitted payload bits from OTA recordings but more importantly, could inject its own message at the output of the radio's serial port. Thus, any piece of software or hardware connected to the Guardian-400 is exposed to potential security threats.

2.1 Hardware Description

The two main pieces of hardware and their relevant settings are presented in Table 1.

Table 1. Hardware configuration

	GUARDIAN-400	*ADALM-PLUTO SDR*
Tx frequency (MHz)	450	425.5
Rx frequency (MHz)	425.5	450
Data rate (bps)	9600	9600
Bandwidth (kHz)	25	25
Sampling rate (kHz)	N.A	528

Both devices can be connected to a Windows 10 laptop using USB cables. The Guardian-400's software is used to configure and communicate with the Guardian-400 radio through a USB-to-serial cable and MATLAB is used to configure and communicate with the ADALM-PLUTO SDR.

3   Tests Description

3.1   Loopback Test

As mentioned in Sect. 2, one can demodulate the transmitted bits using DPLLs but not unravel their encoding, thus leaving one unknown layer to traverse to get to the payload. In order to investigate these unknowns, the following test plan was enacted:

1. Configure the Guardian-400 to transmit a known test vector;
2. Perform an OTA recording using the ADALM-PLUTO SDR;
3. Perform FSK demodulation and symbol clock recovery on the recording using DPLLs;
4. Using the recovered encoded bits, draw conclusions regarding the physical layer processing blocks.

In order to transmit a known test vector, the Guardian-400 is configured in transmit mode with a 1-second interval ASCII pattern. The pattern used to build the packets has the following format (55 ASCII characters):

000ABCDEFGHIJKLMNOPQRSTUVWXYZabcdefghijklmnopqrstuvwxyz
001ABCDEFGHIJKLMNOPQRSTUVWXYZabcdefghijklmnopqrstuvwxyz

- - -

998ABCDEFGHIJKLMNOPQRSTUVWXYZabcdefghijklmnopqrstuvwxyz
999ABCDEFGHIJKLMNOPQRSTUVWXYZabcdefghijklmnopqrstuvwxyz
000ABCDEFGHIJKLMNOPQRSTUVWXYZabcdefghijklmnopqrstuvwxyz
001ABCDEFGHIJKLMNOPQRSTUVWXYZabcdefghijklmnopqrstuvwxyz

The second step towards this goal is to perform a recording using the ADALM-PLUTO SDR. This is easily achieved in MATLAB using the ADALM-PLUTO SDR FM receiver example from Mathworks as a starting point. The real portion of a 2-seconds recording is shown in Fig. 4.

From Fig. 4, it can be observed that the Guardian seems to transmit data continuously once in transmit mode. The ASCII pattern is only 55 characters in length. Short transmit bursts were expected every second, in an otherwise unbroken silence. At this point, the actual position of the payload within this recording is unknown. Nevertheless, the DPLLs developed in the first phase can be used in order to demodulate the bits. As a reminder, the demodulated bits are (theorically) differentially coded using NRZI and scrambled using a 7-bits scrambler. The details about both processes were still unknown at this point in our investigation.

In order to ensure that our recording included the known test vector, the recording can be transmitted back to the Guardian-400 for demodulation. To do so, a 2-FSK modulator was developed. There are multiple ways to implement such a modulator, but an approach which uses the NCO in Fig. 1 seemed the most logical.

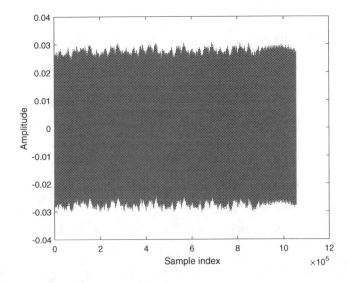

Fig. 4. Recording of the Guardian-400 ASCII pattern transmission.

Generating the 2-FSK waveform using the demodulated bits and transmitting them OTA using the ADALM-PLUTO SDR yielded the following results on the Guardian-400 software ASCII terminal.

$$\text{FGHIJKLMNOPQRSTUVWXYZabcdefghijklmnopqrstuvwxyz} \qquad (1)$$

A portion of the expected ASCII pattern was correctly received, but it is important to point out that a total of 19200 bits (2-second recording at 9600bps) were sent by the ADALM-PLUTO in order to achieve this result, which is much more than the 47 received ASCII characters in output (1) (which gives 376 bits assuming an 8-bits ASCII representation). At that point, it is obvious that the pattern of interest is somewhere in the recorded file. However, it is not clear where and it is also not clear why there is so much overhead.

3.2   Payload Analysis

Following the loopback test, it is now of interest to dig deeper into the received payload bits and try to reverse-engineer the modulation process (from ASCII characters to differentially-coded and scrambled bits). As a first step, the bits of interest need to be isolated from the overhead bits in order to perform further processing. By visual inspection of the demodulated bits in Fig. 5, one can identify surprisingly long series of 1's or 0's at many points in the bit stream.

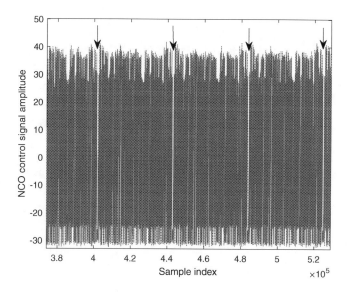

Fig. 5. Sequences of same polarity bits from the demodulated bit stream.

It is surprising since the bits are supposed to be scrambled, which should remove such scenarios. This could indicate the presence of some kind of preamble or synchronization pattern. Secondly, these series of bits also seem to appear periodically. In order to check for the periodicity, convolution is performed using the following coefficients, taken from the demodulated bits:

$$coeff = \begin{bmatrix} 1 & -1 & -1 & -1 & -1 & -1 & -1 & -1 & -1 & -1 & -1 & -1 & -1 & -1 & -1 & 1 \end{bmatrix}$$

Plotting the result of the convolution operation gives the output shown in Fig. 6.

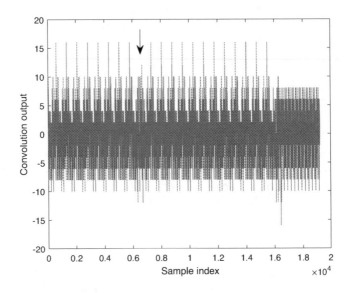

Fig. 6. Convolution output using *coeff*.

From Fig. 6, it can be observed that a good portion of the demodulated bits seems to be filled with a repetitive pattern. It also shows two other locations of interest, which are right after the first eight peaks and at the tail portion of the recording. Using the convolution peaks as delimiters, the 19200 bits can be divided into multiples blocks of bits which enables us to iteratively test for the location of our ASCII bits, by simply sending these chunks of bits, one at a time, to the Guardian-400. Using that process enables us to locate the bits of interest which are between the eight and ninth convolution peaks, inside a block of 1504 bits. This is definitely a step forward but the block still contains more than the expected 376 bits.

3.3 NRZI and Scrambler Decoding

At this point, the exact location of the payload bits is unknown. We began the analysis of the NRZI decoding and scrambling processes, which prevented us from relating the demodulated bits at the output of the DPLLs to the ASCII characters being sent. Figure 7 illustrates an initial hypothetical block diagram of the expected ASCII characters encoding/decoding process.

Fig. 7. Hypothetical Guardian-400 encoding/decoding process.

It is also important to mention that the block diagram in Fig. 7 acts as a starting point, extrapolated from the information in [1] and only from that source. Therefore, at this point, it is possible that additional blocks are present and/or that some information may be false, such as the length of the scrambler for example.

Compared to NRZ (Non-Return-to-Zero), NRZI is a differential encoding technique which distinguishes data bits by the presence or absence of a bit polarity transition at clock edges. Two NRZI scenarios are thus possible: a transition from one polarity to the opposite polarity could either represents a 1 or a 0.

Regarding the scrambler, a 7-bits scrambler is expected from the data in [1]. However, the architecture of the scrambler and the scrambler polynomial are unknown and thus, represent the main challenge to overcome. One popular and well known 7-bits scrambler is the 802.11 (WiFi) scrambler shown in Fig. 8.

Fig. 8. 802.11 7-bits synchronous scrambler.

This is a synchronous scrambler with polynomial $1 + x^4 + x^7$. One important point to note is the fact that the input bits are not influencing the states of the registers in such architecture. As a consequence, for correct descrambling, the descrambler needs to be put into a specific state, at input bit b, usually using a preamble detection mechanism which could be possible in our case, since there are multiple overhead bits. Both the scrambler and the descrambler are identical in such an architecture.

A second possible architecture, which is simpler implementation-wise but prone to error propagation, could also be used: a self-synchronous architecture. The scrambler/descrambler of the latter is shown in Fig. 9.

These are 7-bits self-synchronous scrambler/descrambler of polynomial $1 + x^6 + x^7$. Compared to the synchronous architecture, the register states are

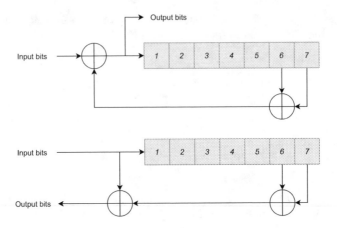

Fig. 9. 7-bits self-synchronous scrambler(top) and descrambler(bottom).

affected by the input bits and thus, a detection error at the receiver will tend to propagate through the descrambler. However, a preamble detection mechanism is not required, which reduces the required hardware resource and computing power. This architecture is definitely a possibility since there is hypothetically no packet structure defined (so no specific preamble section defined). Furthermore, its low resource usage is a good fit to the limited processing capability of an old T-96SR radio.

That being said, there remains numerous possibilities which need to be investigated. As a first investigative step, one can try to take the FSK demodulated bits from the DPLLs and decode them in MATLAB into the expected ASCII characters, using a brute-force approach, by testing all possible configurations. The 7-bits synchronous architecture is analysed first.

3.4 Synchronous Architecture

As mentioned above, synchronous scramblers/descramblers require a specific state reset mechanism for correct descrambling. In other words, at a specific bit b, the scrambler/descrambler needs to be in a specific state. This means that there is a total of four variables to test in order to cover all possible scenarios:

1. NRZI transitions either represent a 0 or a 1;
2. The starting bit b of our encoded ASCII sequence which is somewhere in the 1504 bits block;
3. The state of the descrambler at bit b;
4. The descrambler polynomial.

This looks intimidating at first but this can be coded using multiple *for* loops rather easily, it simply takes a significant amount of processing time. The output of the descrambling process is validated using a convolution operation with the 8-bits representation of the following ASCII sequence: *JKLM*.

After multiple iterations of the current approach, the expected convolution result of 32 never occurred. Descrambler sizes of 6-bits and 8-bits were also tried but didn't give the expected results.

3.5 Self-synchronous Architecture

Following the results in the previous section, the code was slightly modified in order to implement a 7-bits self-synchronous architecture. The same four variables are tested but again, the approach never gave a convolution result of 32.

4 Single Error Injection Approach

After the unsatisfactory results of the brute force approach, it is clear that some form of understanding is missing. Another approach to resolution is therefore proposed: the error injection approach. This approach consists of transmitting the 1504-bits block, which contains the ASCII characters bits, to the Guardian-400 but with the insertion of a single bit error beforehand. The goal of such a test is to study how the received ASCII characters are affected by this error and try to draw some conclusions about the unknown variables. Through trial and error, flipping the 554th bit gave the result on the Guardian-400 ASCII terminal shown below (2).

$$\text{FGH}^{a}\text{KKLMNOPQRSTUVWXYZabcdefghijklmnopqrstuvwxyz} \qquad (2)$$

By careful observation, one can see that the I and J ASCII characters were affected by the single bit flip, which already gives a good hint regarding the descrambler architecture. In a synchronous architecture, a single bit error at the input gives a single bit error at the output, but it is not the case in a self-synchronous architecture. The error will affect the state of the descrambler and thus, multiple bits at the descrambler output. A closer look at the IJ ASCII characters and their error-injected version is presented in Table 2.

Table 2. I and J with error injection

I	J
01001001	01001010
a	K
10101010	01001011

From Table 2, it is clear that multiple bits were affected by our single error injection. It is also clear that the 554th bit corresponds to the I character LSB (rightmost bit). The same single error injection test was repeated by flipping the 555th, 556th, 557th, 558th, 559th bits. By checking the 8-bits representation of the decoded ASCII characters, two interesting observations are obtained. First, the ASCII characters are definitely 8 bits long and second, the bits of each ASCII character are sent OTA to the Guardian-400, LSB first. This is an important point, since, in the brute-force approach, it was assumed that the *JKLM* sequence used for the convolution operation was simply the direct 8-bits representation of each character taken from the 8-bits ASCII table. So, instead of testing for the bit sequence in Table 3, one should have checked for the sequence in Table 4.

Table 3. MSB first "IJKL" bit sequence

I	J	K	L
01001001	01001010	01001011	01001100

Table 4. LSB first "IJKL" bit sequence

I	J	K	L
10010010	01010010	11010010	00110010

4.1 Multiple Bits Injection Approach

At this point, a self-synchronous scrambler is supposed, and another test comes to mind, which exploits the fact that the input bits of the descrambler can affect the register's state. The second test consists of inserting a long string of NRZI modulated ones or zeros. The following NRZI sequence is inserted in the 1504-bits block, at bit position 554:

1111 1111 1111 1111

The Guardian-400 ASCII terminal gives the result below (3).

FGHNÿøoLMNOPQRSTUVWXYZabcdefghijklmnopqrstuvwxyz   (3)

New characters appear on the screen, more importantly the ÿ character at the expected location. The 8-bits ASCII representation of the ÿ character is 11111111, which tells us about the NRZI encoding. The ability to fill the descrambler registers with 1's by using an NRZI sequence which contains no polarity transition, means that a binary 1 is encoded by the absence of a transition and thus, a 0 is encoded by the presence of a polarity transition. It is now known how to communicate a 1 and a 0 to the Guardian-400 and control the state of the descrambler.

4.2   Descrambler Impulse Response

Following the results from the previous test, it is now time to test for the impulse response of the descrambler by first, feeding the descrambler with a series of 1's to put the descrambler in a known state and secondly, injecting a single 0, followed again by multiple 1's. The used NRZI coded sequence is as follows:

1111 1111 1111 1111 -1-1-1-1 -1-1-1-1 -1-1-1-1 -1-1-1-1

Transmission OTA to the Guardian-400 gives the output below (4) on the ASCII terminal.

$$FGHNÿ^ÿYJKLMNOPQRSTUVWXYZabcdefghijklmnopqrstuvwxyz \qquad (4)$$

The characters of interest are $ÿ^ÿ$ which is illuminating with regards to the number of registers of the descrambler and its polynomial. It is clear from the ASCII characters that the descrambler is in an all-ones state, then a zero is fed, which goes through all the registers, creating a sequence of multiple states before going back to the all-ones state. The 8-bits representation of the ASCII characters (left to right = MSB to LSB) is shown in Table 5.

Table 5. $ÿ$ and $^$ 8-bits representation

$ÿ$	$^$	$ÿ$
11111111	01011110	11111111

Simply by looking at the $^$ character from LSB to MSB, some hypothesis can be made regarding the descrambler. First and foremost, it is indeed a 7-bits descrambler and secondly, the polynomial is $1 + x^5 + x^7$, which is not an optimal choice since it is not a primitive one. One can validate these assumptions by performing the descrambling process, by hand. The proposed descrambler architecture from the all-ones initial state is shown in Fig. 10.

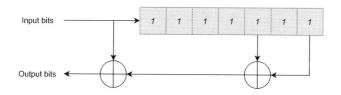

Fig. 10. Proposed self-synchronous descrambler architecture.

From Table 6, it is clear that the register length and the polynomial seem to be correct.

Table 6. Proposed descrambler impulse response

Inputs bits	Register states	Descrambled bits
0	1111111	0
1	0111111	1
1	1011111	1
1	1101111	1
1	1110111	1
1	1111011	0
1	1111101	1
1	1111110	0

4.3   Hello World! Test

With all this new information in hand regarding the encoding and decoding process, one could be tempted to send his own message to the Guardian-400, using the ADALM-PLUTO SDR. To perform this test, a modulator now needs to be developed. The modulator needs to perform the following tasks:

1. Convert the *ÿÿHello World!* ASCII message to 8-bits representation (*ÿ* is used to put the descrambler in a known state);
2. Perform a bit flip from left to right for each ASCII character, in order to feed the bits LSB first;
3. Scramble the bit sequence using a self-synchronous scrambler of polynomial $1 + x^5 + x^7$, with initial state 1111111;
4. Encode the scrambled bits differentially using NRZI, where $1 =$ No transition and $0 =$ Transition.

The test is successful if the *Hello World!* message is correctly decoded by the Guardian-400 ASCII terminal. Using MATLAB, the *Hello World!* message is encoded and sent to the FSK modulator, for transmission to the Guardian-400. The output of the ASCII terminal, by inserting our encoded bits at position 554 in the 1504 bits chunk, is shown below (5).

$$\text{FGH/ÿHello World!]JKLMNOPQRSTUVWXYZabcdefghijklmnopqrstuvwxyz} \quad (5)$$

The test is conclusive and validates our assumptions regarding the encoding and decoding process of the Guardian-400.

4.4   Updated Brute-Force Approach

Having successfully transmitted the *Hello World!* message, it could now be interesting to go back to the brute-force approach and validate if the approach was legitimate after all. Performing the brute-force approach, with the correct descrambler polynomial and architecture, with the proposed LSB first *JKLM* convolution sequence still did not yield the expected result of 32.

However, performing the same approach with another sequence, *GHIJ*, did give the expected convolution result of 32. The brute-force approach also gave some interesting information regarding the location of the sequence and the state of the descrambler. It actually gave multiple locations, which comes from the fact that the polynomial is not primitive.

From these results, the longer sequence *GHIJK* was tried but did not give the expected convolution results. Inspection of the descrambled data shows the presence of the following ASCII character, which follows the *GHIJ* sequence: ~ or *0x7E*. This character appears periodically in the descrambled sequence (for each 3 or 4 ASCII characters) and also appears to be added to the sequence, since now, if the test sequence becomes *GHIJ~K*, the convolution results gives the expected result.

Bottom line, going back to the brute-force approach gave an additional piece of information, the presence of a ~ character, probably used for synchronisation purposes since it never appeared on the ASCII terminal in our tests. This is validated easily by performing the *Hello World!* test with the following message:

$$\sim\sim\sim\sim\sim\sim H \sim el \sim lo \sim \ Wo \sim r \sim ld \sim\sim\sim\sim\sim\sim !$$

Multiple tests were performed with multiple different numbers of sync characters and insertion locations and the result on the ASCII terminal is still simply *Hello World!.*

4.5   Preamble Detection

From the results of the previous tests, it is now easy to find and remove the excess bits from the 1504 bits chunk, simply through trial and error. But simply sending our NRZI encoded and scrambled *Hello World!* message without any of the previous bits of the 1504 bits does not work. There is definitely some kind of preamble which is used to trigger the radio's decoding process. Through trial and error, it is found within a few minutes that bits 334 to 513 seem to include that preamble. Creating an NRZI message with these bits, followed by the scrambled and encoded $\sim\sim\sim\sim\sim\sim H \sim el \sim lo \sim \ Wo \sim r \sim ld \sim\sim\sim\sim\sim\sim !$ message, gives the output on the ASCII terminal, shown below (6).

$$\text{Hello World!} \tag{6}$$

This additional piece of information is definitely useful. This preamble can now be used to trigger the radio demodulation mechanism but this preamble could also be used in order to intercept actual OTA signals from Guardian-400/T-96SR radios and potentially extract sensitive information, since the payload bits follow the preamble.

5 Conclusion

In this report, a thorough analysis of the Guardian-400 physical layer is achieved. As presented in Fig. 7, a 7-bits scrambler and an NRZI encoder are the only processing blocks which manipulate the payload bits before FSK modulation. Additionally, the existence of a synchronisation character and a preamble is observed. In order to perform these tests, one simply needs a Guardian-400, an off-the-shelf SDR platform and a laptop. The absence of any packet structure, authentication process and forward error correction mechanism makes the Guardian-400 physical layer unsecure and easy to investigate. This work illustrates the necessity to add additional security layers to any equipment connected to a Guardian-400. This recommendation can confidently be extended to any SCADA system which includes radios which are interoperable with the latter, such as the T-96SR, the DL-3400 and the DL-3282. Finally, using the acquired knowledge from the present work, one can look back at Appendix A in [1] and identify other radios which could be potentially reverse-engineered, which is worrisome. Most of them are using FSK modulation but integrate additional signal processing techniques, such as Hamming Code FEC and Cyclic Redundancy Checks (CRCs). The capability to reverse-engineer such radios would be very interesting to investigate in the future. Our work demonstrates that the underlying assumption when those SCADA radios were designed—that usage of an obscure and secret modulation format was secure enough—no longer holds given the widespread availability of low-cost SDR hardware and associated knowledge.

References

1. Roark, R.C., Van Wie, D.G.: Feasibility Study of a New Air Interface and Physical Layer Packet Definition for the ALERT User Community (2003)
2. Boyes, W.: Instrumentation Reference Book, 4th edn, p. 27. Butterworth-Heinemann (2011). ISBN 978-0-7506-8308-1
3. Siggins, M.: 14 Major SCADA Attacks and What You Can Learn From Them. DPS Telecom. Accessed 26 Apr 2021
4. Reverse-Engineering Wireless SCADA Systems. https://shmoo.gitbook.io/2016-shmoocon-proceedings/build_it/10_reverse-engineering-wireless-scada-systems. Accessed 14 Dec 2020
5. FCC Id NP42424016-001 - CalAmp Wireless Networks Corporation T-96SR Telemetry Transceiver/Modem. https://fccid.io/NP42424016-001. Accessed 16 July 2022
6. Blossom, E.: GNU radio: tools for exploring the radio frequency spectrum. Linux J. (2004)
7. Attacks targeting industrial control systems is up 110 percent. https://securityintelligence.com/attacks-targeting-industrial-control-systems-ics-up-110-percent/. Accessed 29 Aug 2022
8. Global Cyber Megatrends. https://www.raytheon.com/sites/default/files/2018-02/2018_Global_Cyber_Megatrends.pdf. Accessed 29 Aug 2022
9. ADALM-PLUTO Software-Defined Radio Active Learning Module. https://www.analog.com/en/design-center/evaluation-hardware-and-software/evaluation-boards-kits/adalm-pluto.html. Accessed 23 Nov 2022

Blockchain

Finding Unchecked Low-Level Calls
with Zero False Positives and Negatives
in Ethereum Smart Contracts

Puneet Gill, Indrani Ray, Alireza Lotfi Takami, and Mahesh Tripunitara[✉]

Electrical and Computer Engineering, University of Waterloo, Waterloo, Canada
{p24gill,iray,alotfitakami,tripunit}@uwaterloo.ca

Abstract. Smart contracts are a relatively new class of computer programs that are intended to run on a blockchain. Checking a smart contract for security vulnerabilities is recognized as an important problem in both research and practice. Motivated by recent empirical work that suggests that existing tools suffer high numbers of false positives and negatives for vulnerabilities that belong to commonly-occurring classes, we ask: for even one such class of vulnerabilities, can there exist a tool that is highly effective? We answer in the affirmative by construction: for the class of unchecked low-level calls, checking for which is undecidable in general and **PSPACE**-complete under finitizing assumptions we adopt, we propose an approach for Ethereum smart contracts that comprises a reduction to model-checking, encoding the property in Linear Temporal Logic (LTL) and use of an off-the-shelf model checker. We find that across almost 200 smart contracts drawn from curated and "wild" datasets from the publicly available benchmark that underlies the prior empirical work that points out that existing tools suffer high numbers of false positives and negatives, our approach is highly effective in that we see zero false positives and negatives.

Keywords: Smart contract · Security vulnerability · Unchecked low-level calls · Model checking · Linear Temporal Logic (LTL)

1 Introduction

A smart contract is a computer program written with an intent of running it on a blockchain [15]. A blockchain, as a substrate of running a smart contract, offers certain guarantees when events occur in the running of that smart contract; for example, when the smart contract transmits digital currency to another smart contract and the latter accepts it, both the sender and the receiver can be assured that these events have indeed occurred, and that this fact is recorded immutably.

We focus on smart contracts written for the Ethereum blockchain [11]. Ethereum provides a so-called Ethereum Virtual Machine (EVM) within which a smart contract runs. The language an EVM understands and executes is called

G.-V. Jourdan et al. (Eds.): FPS 2022, LNCS 13877, pp. 305–321, 2023.
https://doi.org/10.1007/978-3-031-30122-3_19

EVM code [33]. EVM code is a somewhat low-level language, with instructions similar to those we find in an assembly language. From the standpoint of expressive power, EVM has been called quasi-Turing-complete; the rationale from Wood [33] is: "the *quasi* qualification comes from the fact that the computation is intrinsically bounded through a parameter, *gas*, which limits the total amount of computation done". (In Sect. 4, we address the computational complexity of verification problems of interest to us more clearly). Typically, a programmer writes a smart contract in a higher-level language such as Solidity [10], which is then compiled to EVM code for deployment in Ethereum.

```
pragma solidity ^0.4.18;
contract Lotto {
    bool public payedOut = false;
    address public winner;
    uint public winAmount;

    function sendToWinner() public {
        require(!payedOut);
        winner.send(winAmount);
        payedOut = true;
    }
    function withdrawLeftOver() public {
        require(payedOut);
        msg.sender.send(this.balance);
    }
}
```

```
...63ffffffff1680631846f51a146100725780...

         :
         :

[48] PUSH4 0xffffffff
[53] AND
[54] DUP1
[55] PUSH4 0x1846f51a
[60] EQ
[61] PUSH2 0x0072
[64] JUMPI
[65] DUP1

         :
         :
```

Fig. 1. The Solidity code for `Lotto.sol` from the curated dataset of Durieux et al. [8] is to the left. To the right is a portion of its complied EVM code as bytecode to the top, and the bytecode written as human-recognizable instructions and their arguments below it. A number in square brackets, e.g., "[48]", is the byte number within the bytecode, starting at 0, of the particular instruction + arguments.

Figure 1 shows a smart contract written in Solidity and a portion of its encoding as EVM code. As the Solidity code suggests, there is the notion of a contract, within which one can specify functions. The `address` data type identifies a publicly visible contract that resides on the Ethereum blockchain. A function in a contract may be invoked from another contract, sometimes with arguments. A function may invoke another contract, for example, via a `send()` call as shown in the example code. EVM code, as we show to the right of the figure, is a string of bytes. Each byte is either an instruction, e.g., `PUSH4`, or an argument to an instruction, e.g., `0x0072`.

Our Work. Verification as to whether a smart contract contains security vulnerabilities is a well-recognized problem in both research and practice. There are a number of software tools that address this; we present some of the most closely related to our work in Sect. 2. Our work is motivated by a recent empirical assessment of several such tools [8], which points out that they suffer high numbers of false positives and false negatives when they check for vulnerabilities from common occurring classes [23] in real-world smart contracts. (A false positive is a tool reporting a vulnerability where there is none. A false negative is a vulnerability that goes undetected by the tool). We think that the underlying reason is that existing tools "try to do everything, none of them well." Said differently, the poor performance of existing tools leads us to ask: if we were to focus on even one class of vulnerabilities only, can there exist a tool that for real-world smart contracts, is highly effective? Lest one mistakenly think that checking for only one class is somehow "easy", as we discuss in Sect. 3, even a basic verification problem, such as whether a contract is guaranteed to halt when run on some input, is intractable for Ethereum smart contracts.

In this work, we answer the above question in the affirmative. Our proof is by construction—we discuss our reduction to model-checking, the use of Linear Temporal Logic (LTL) to meaningfully encode the property to be checked for, and the use of the off-the-shelf model checker nuXmv [3]. Our choice of the class of vulnerabilities is unchecked low-level calls. An unchecked low-level call is an invocation to another contract whose return value is not checked. As we establish in Sect. 3, this problem is undecidable in general, and **PSPACE**-complete under the finitizing assumptions we adopt. Our empirical results on almost 200 contracts from the benchmark of Durieux et al. [8] suggest that our approach is highly effective—we see zero false positives and negatives.

The remainder of this paper is organized as follows. In the next section, we discuss related work. In Sect. 3 we address the computational complexity of the problem. In Sect. 4, we present our reduction to model-checking and encoding in SMV. In Sect. 5, we discuss our empirical validation. We conclude with Sect. 6 in which we discuss also future work.

2   Related Work

Our work addresses checking a smart contract for security vulnerabilities that belong to commonly occurring classes of such vulnerabilities. As such, our work is related to work that proposes classifications of security vulnerabilities in smart contracts, and tools and techniques for detecting vulnerabilities. From the standpoint of tools, we focus on one class of vulnerabilities only, but are highly effective for that class. That is the key distinction between our work and all prior work on tools. We leverage a particular classification [23], but otherwise make no contributions to that aspect.

From the standpoint of classifications, several exist—Rameder [27] and Tolmach et al. [31] provide comprehensive surveys. We adopt the classification and taxonomy of DASP [23], which in turn is adopted by the empirical work of Durieux et al. [8]. The work of Durieux et al. [8] proposes two datasets of smart contracts which they have made available publicly [9], and using which they have assessed several existing tools and demonstrated that those tools suffer from too many false negatives. One of these is a curated set, with several smart contracts in each of the categories of DASP. Their other dataset is a "wild" dataset of several thousand smart contracts. We rely on their datasets for our empirical assessment. There have been other datasets that have been proposed, such as that of Ghaleb and Pattabiraman [13].

As the surveys of Rameder [27] and Tolmach et al. [31] express, there are several tools which analyze smart contracts for security vulnerabilities; a comprehensive discussion is beyond the scope of this work. In the remainder of this section, we survey several of the prior tools. We emphasize that none, to our knowledge, claims to suffer zero false positives and negatives for even one class of security vulnerabilities. That is the main difference between our work and prior approaches.

A piece of work that is closest to ours is that of Nehai et al. [24]. That work proposes applying model checking, and specifically the use of nuSmv, to "capture the behaviour of the Ethereum blockchain, the smart contracts themselves and the execution framework". Many of the other tools are based on verification techniques that check for security assurance and correctness of smart contracts. For example, Bhargavan et al. [2] create a framework that compiles contracts written in Solidity to F* and checks for, e.g., safety with respect to runtime errors; and decompiles EVM bytecode into F* code to check for low-level properties such as bounds on the amount of gas required for a transaction. Other tools, such as the one created by Amani et al. [1] extend formalisations of the Ethereum Virtual Machine and use theorem provers such as Isabelle or Coq to check for reachability properties in smart contracts, such as termination. There are symbolic execution frameworks, such as Manticore [21], which implement state exploration, but do not target smart contract vulnerabilities that can be exploited by attacks.

Oyente [19], however, does so. This symbolic execution tool uses the Z3 solver to determine the feasibility of execution traces of smart contracts (input as bytecode) to detect given vulnerabilities such as transaction-order dependence. Kalra et al. [16] argue that Oyente is neither sound nor complete and propose a symbolic model checker, Zeus, for Solidity-based smart contracts which categorizes them into incorrect and unfair groups, and further detects vulnerabilities such as re-entrancy in the former and 'incorrect logic' in the latter. Zeus inserts assertions based on vulnerabilities into smart contract code and, after translation to LLVM bitcode, uses the SeaHorn verifier to determine assertion violations. Zeus' soundness claims are refuted by the creators of eThor [30]: a sound and static analyzer for bytecode. This tool creates semantic abstractions based off of the blockchain environment, gas modelling, the memory model, and the callstack and scans for reachability properties to search for re-entrancy bugs.

Several other symbolic execution tools exist. MadMax [14] uses another tool, Vandal [4] to translate EVM bytecode to an intermediate representation and then detects out-of-gas exceptions. Maian [25] (based on Oyente) detects three types of vulnerable contracts: suicidal (can be killed by anyone), prodigal (can send Ether to anyone), and greedy (cannot have Ether extracted from). Mythril [22] uses a symbolic interpreter for EVM bytecode known as LASER to find abstract program states and reason about their reachability (using a Z3 solver) given certain conditions to determine vulnerabilities (such as integer overflow); then uses concolic testing to deign whether the vulnerabilities are exploitable. Securify [32] is a security analyzer for smart contracts that takes as input the bytecode of a contract and checks for compliance and violation security patterns such as locked Ether.

teEther [18] is an automated framework which scans bytecode for instructions (such as CALL) that can be used to extract Ether, and then creates exploits. Another tool (which focuses on instructions related to inter-contract reasoning, memory, and hash functions) is the bounded model checker EthBMC [12]. The creators of the tool test it against others upon toy smart contract examples before conducting a large-scale analysis and comparing their results with those received from their experiments using teEther and Maian. That work has since been followed-up by those of Perez et al. [26] Zhang et al. [35], Rodler et al. [28], Chinen et al. [7], Cecchetti et al. [5] and Chen et al. [6]. All these pieces of work except those of Rodler et al. [28] and Cecchetti et al. [5] address detection of exploits and vulnerabilities; those two pieces of work propose defenses, the former via patching and the latter via a new type system.

Finally, specifically as it pertains to unchecked low-level calls, there is work on simply replacing such calls entirely in the source-code [34]. However, that work has its own set of limitations, such as the inability to identify all low-level calls, and whether the replacement indeed results in a contract that is equivalent to the original.

3   Computational Complexity

Our approach, which we discuss in the next section, is based on model-checking. In this section, we articulate the underlying foundations in computational complexity. We have two sets of results: that in general, checking for unchecked low-level calls in Ethereum smart contracts is undecidable, and that under finitizing assumptions we make, it is **PSPACE**-complete. To establish these results, we appeal to the halting problem for smart contracts. We omit full proofs on account of lack of space, and provide sketches only.

As we mention in Sect. 1, EVM has been called quasi-Turing-complete, with the quasi- being attributed to the fact that a sequence of computations is bounded by a parameter called gas, and every computation consumes some gas. Therefore, assuming that the value for gas is bounded by a constant, EVM is not Turing-complete. However, in our observation, gas is not the only limiting factor in this regard. The only storage offered in EVM are: (i) a *program counter*, which is 256 bits, (ii) a *stack*, which has a maximum size of 1024, each entry 256 bits, (iii) *memory*, addressed by 256 bits, each entry 8 bits, and, (iv) *storage*, addressed by 256 bits, each entry 256 bits. As all of these are bounded by constants, we do not have the unboundedness required to encode an arbitrary Turing machine. However, as the number 2^{256} is large, certainly from the standpoint of verification in practice, we may assume that any value whose upper-bound is 2^{256} is unbounded.

Theorem 1. *If we assume that any value bounded by 2^{256} only is unbounded, and gas is unbounded, then whether a run of a contract encoded in EVM halts on some input is undecidable.*

Our proof is by construction—we have an encoding of a Turing machine in Solidity, which then compiles to EVM. Our Solidity code uses the `uint` data type which is 256 bits for anything that may be unbounded, for example, the number of states, the size of the alphabet and the tape.

Corollary 1. *Detecting unchecked low-level calls in EVM is undecidable.*

We can reduce the halting problem that underlies the proof for Theorem 1 to the complement of the problem of finding unchecked low-level calls, and then appeal to the fact that a problem is undecidable if and only if its complement is undecidable. We wrap every instruction that causes a smart contract in EVM to stop running with a `CALL` instruction and a check of its return value. Thus, the contract halts if and only if the return value from the `CALL` is checked. There are only a few instructions in EVM that cause a contract to stop running, e.g., `STOP` and `REVERT`.

Theorem 2. *Suppose the number of memory and storage locations allocated and accessed by a smart contract C is at worst polynomial in the size of C and in $\log g$ where g is the value of the gas parameter. Then the problem of determining whether C terminates on some input is **PSPACE**-complete.*

The proof for **PSPACE**-hardness follows from an encoding of a Linear-Bounded Automaton (LBA) using our construction for a Turing machine to which we refer in the Proof for Theorem 1, and the fact that the halting problem for LBAs is **PSPACE**-hard. To prove that the problem is in **PSPACE**, we can construct a non-deterministic algorithm, denote it $\mathcal{A}$, to decide the problem such that $\mathcal{A}$ allocates at worst polynomial space only. We then appeal to Savitch's theorem that **NPSPACE = PSPACE** [29]. $\mathcal{A}$ simply allocates the maximum space that may be needed and runs the smart contract on the input. For any uninitialized or unknown value, e.g., the return from a `CALL` to an external contract, $\mathcal{A}$ chooses a return value non-deterministically. We know, from our assumptions, that the space $\mathcal{A}$ must allocate is at worst polynomial in the size of the input.

We need the "log" qualification for the input gas g for the reason that g may be encoded, for example, in binary, in which case, under the assumption that each instruction consumes constant gas, the contract C may run, on some input, for time $\Theta(g)$, and therefore may allocate space as much as $\Theta(g)$, where $\Theta(\cdot)$ represents a tight asymptotic bound.

Corollary 2. *Determining whether an EVM contract has an unchecked low-level call under the finitizing assumptions of Theorem 2 is **PSPACE**-complete.*

Similar to the proof for Corollary 1, we appeal to the fact that a problem is **PSPACE**-complete if and only if its complement is **PSPACE**-complete.

4   Reduction

From Corollary 2 in the previous section, we have a sufficient condition for our problem to be **PSPACE**-complete, and therefore, reduction to model checking that is complete for **PSPACE** is an appropriate approach. This is exactly what we do. Our implementation encodes the model checking problem in SMV [3], but more abstractly, the output of our reduction is a Kripke structure [17]. To us, a state is uniquely determined by the value of several variables that we associate with a state. We then define state-transitions between those states, some of which are non-deterministic. The variables are for the basic components of the state of an EVM: (1) The stack, memory and storage of the EVM, (2) the current stack-head, (3) the next instruction to be executed, and, (4) the gas remaining.

Program Counter. To keep track of the instructions, we have a variable which we call operationName, which is an enumeration of every instruction that appears in the EVM code that is input, annotated with its byte location. For example, suppose we have the EVM code 6005600401. This corresponds to:

```
[0]  PUSH1  0x05
[2]  PUSH1  0x04
[4]  ADD
```

Then, our reduction would introduce:

```
operationName : {begin, PUSH1_0, PUSH1_2, ADD_4, end};
```

The begin and end are keywords we introduce to delimit the sequence of instructions. The state-transitions of the instructions would be the following (in SMV syntax, the value of the variable in the next state is shown after the colon, ":"):

```
next(operationName) :=   case
    operationName = begin : PUSH1_0;
    operationName = PUSH1_0 : PUSH1_2;
    operationName = PUSH1_2 : ADD_4;
    operationName = ADD_4 : end;
    TRUE : operationName;
esac;
```

Unless we have a JUMP or JUMPI instruction, our program counter increments sequentially, i.e., by the number of bytes the previous instruction + operands consume. We maintain also an operationArray[ ], which identifies an operand, if any, in the EVM code for any operation. In the above example of two pushes and then an add, the argument to each of the two pushes is in the EVM code, and the argument to the add is not. Consequently, we would initialize and never change our operationArray[ ] as follows (0ud$x$... is the SMV syntax for an unsigned x-bit value):

```
operationArray[0]  :=  0ud8_5;
operationArray[2]  :=  0ud8_4;
```

Stack, Memory and Storage. For each of the stack, memory and storage, we maintain arrays. For the stack we maintain also a stack_head. We also exercise a design choice on the size of each entry in the stack. While we can certainly set those to 256-bit, for most smart contracts we observe in the benchmarks, this is too large. We can estimate the size we need via a simple static analysis for the PUSH instructions, and other instructions such as ADD and MUL that increase the size of a stack-entry. In EVM code, the push instructions are PUSH1,...,PUSH32, where PUSHx means x bytes are pushed. For memory and storage, the situation is different. There are two memory-store instructions, MSTORE, which stores 256 bits, and MSTORE8, which stores 1 byte—we find only the former in the datasets we have adopted [9]. There is only one storage-store instruction, SSTORE, which stores 256 bits. However, the value stored in memory and storage comes from the stack. Therefore, we again rely on our estimate of the maximum size stored on the stack for the sizes to be stored in memory and storage. Also, with the stack, in EVM, the maximum number of entries is 1024. However, this is again an upper-bound that is often loose. A count of the number of PUSH instructions gives us a tighter upper-bound on the number of possible entries in the stack. We may need to account for the possibility that the same PUSH instruction may be executed more than once. This depends on the specific property we are checking for. For unchecked low-level calls, we know that we need to account for at most a constant number of executions of a PUSH instruction.

```
stack : array 0 .. 9 of unsigned word[16];
stack_head : 0 .. 9;
memory : array 0 .. 3 of unsigned word[16];
memory_offsets : array 0 .. 3 of unsigned word[16];
storage : array 0 .. 4 of unsigned word[16];
storage_keys : array 0 .. 4 of unsigned word[16];
```

The memory_offsets and storage_keys are needed to identify to exactly which memory and storage locations a corresponding instruction refers. Consider, as an example, the following EVM code.

```
[0]  PUSH1 0x80
[2]  PUSH1 0x40
[4]  MSTORE
```

The MSTORE instruction takes two arguments, both off the stack: an offset or location within memory, and the value to be stored. In the above example, the offset is 0x40 and the value to be stored is 0x80. We would store the offset in some index, call it i, of memory_offsets[ ], and ensure that the value in memory[i] is the value stored at that offset. We discuss below under "Instructions that need more than one transition" as to the manner in which we handle the MSTORE, SSTORE and their corresponding load instructions via state-transitions in our model.

The `stack[ ]` array changes based on (i) the particular instruction, and (ii) the current value of the `stack_head`. Given the quirks of the SMV syntax, we need to enumerate every possible next-state value of each entry of the stack. Thus, if our `stack[ ]` was specified to be of 10 entries, indexed $0 \ldots 9$ as we show above, then, we would have a `next(stack[i])` case statement for every $i = 0, \ldots, 9$. For example:

```
next ( stack [6] )  :=  case
    ...
    operationName  =  PUSH1_2 & stack_head  =  6  :  operationArray [2];
    operationName  =  DUP2_4 & stack_head  =  6  :  stack [4];
    ...
```

To explain the above, we first clarify that our stack grows downwards, i.e., as we push more items onto the stack, the value of `stack_head` increases. Also, the value of `stack_head` is the next entry in the stack; thus, for example, if `stack_head` is 6, then the top of at the stack is at 5, and we initialize `stack_head` to 0. Thus, in the above snippet, the only way the value in `stack[6]` can change in a state-transition is if the current value of `stack_head` is 6. If the instruction is `PUSH1`, then we get the value to be stored in `stack[6]` from our EVM code, which in turn is in our `operationArray[ ]` (see above for a discussion of this variable). If the instruction is `DUP2`, we need to make a copy of the value from one below the current head of the stack, i.e., `stack[4]`, and store that in `stack[6]`—DUPx pushes a copy of the value that is at depth x in the stack, where $x = 1$ refers to the top of the stack, $x = 2$ one below the top and so on.

The `stack_head` also changes based on the instruction and the current value of `stack_head`. As we say above, the stack grows downwards, i.e., we increment the `stack_head` as items are added to the stack and decrement it as items are popped. The only other detail is that in our implementation, our stack is circular, and every change to the `stack_head` is performed modulo its maximum size. This has enabled us to quickly experiment with small stack-sizes albeit while risking correctness, specifically, false negatives.

```
next ( stack_head )  :=  case
    operationName  =  CALL_0  :  max (0, stack_head + 4) mod 10;
    operationName  =  SWAP4_1  :  stack_head;
    operationName  =  POP_2  :  max (0, stack_head + 9) mod 10;
    ...
```

In the above example, the maximum size of the stack has been set to 10, with the items indexed $0, \ldots, 9$. The `CALL` instruction pops 7 items off the stack and pushes 1, for a net of 6 items popped. Consequently, we update the stack head to `stack_head` + 4 mod 10. The `SWAP`x instruction swaps item at depth $x + 1$ on the stack with the item at the top; it does not change `stack_head`. The `POP` instruction decrements `stack_head` by 1.

Instructions that Need One Transition Only. We observe that for most instructions in EVM, we require one state-transition in our model only. The simplest examples are those involving basic arithmetic, such as ADD and MUL which are supported directly in SMV. For example:

```
next ( stack [ 2 ] )  :=  case
       ...
       operationName = MUL_28 & stack_head = 4 :  ( stack [ 2 ]  *  stack [ 3 ] ) ;
       ...
next ( stack_head )  :=  case
       ...
       operationName = MUL_28 :  max ( 0 ,  stack_head + 9 )  mod  1 0 ;
       ...
```

The above shows that if our instruction is MUL, then our stack decreases by a net of 1—MUL pops two items off the stack, multiplies them and pushes the result. Thus, if our current stack_head is 4, we multiply stack_head[2] and stack_head[3] and store the result in stack[2].

There are also numerous other examples of instructions that require one state-transition only in our model. For example, the CALL instruction is crucial for us in our empirical validation on unchecked low-level calls (see Sect. 5). For our purposes, modeling CALL is somewhat surprisingly straightforward. The instruction causes another contract to be called with optional arguments. If we return from the other contract, we get a return value. From our standpoint, CALL causes a net decrement of 6 to the stack, and the return value that is stored on the top of stack is chosen non-deterministically, because we do not know what value will be returned. In the example above, we have shown the manner in which stack_head changes with a CALL. The following shows the change to an entry in the stack.

```
next ( stack [ 1 ] )  :=  case
       operationName = CALL_23 & stack_head = 8 :  CALL_23_return_value ;
       ...
```

The variable CALL_23_return_value is declared but never assigned a value; the model checker non-deterministically chooses a value for it.

Instructions that Need More than One Transition. For the other instructions, we require more than one transition in our model. Consequently, we need to be careful that any termination condition we specify to the model checker does not match an "intermediate" state because such as state would not exist in the EVM. Two examples of such instructions are JUMP (unconditional jump) and JUMPI (conditional jump). We adopt the mnemonic "_DUMMY_" to refer to the intermediate state. Below, we discuss JUMP; JUMPI is realized similarly. The only valid destination for a jump instruction is a byte that has the opcode JUMPDEST. Consequently, in our reduction, we only need to check to which JUMPDEST a particular JUMP or JUMPI seeks to jump in a particular instance. Suppose we have a JUMP instruction in the EVM code at byte #7, and a JUMPDEST at byte #12. Then, our operationName would be declared as:

```
operationName :  { ... ,  JUMP_7 ,  JUMP_7_DUMMY ,  ... ,  JUMPDEST_12 ,  ... } ;
```

For each JUMPDEST_x, we introduce a boolean variable jump_destination_is_x. Its value is initialized and changes as follows (as before, we assume that our stack has maximum size 10, indexed $0, \ldots, 9$):

```
init ( jump_destination_is_12 )  :=  FALSE ;
...
next ( jump_destination_is_12 )  :=  case
  ...
  operationName = JUMP_7 & stack_head = 6 & stack [5] = 0ud16_12 : ↵
      TRUE ;
  ...
```

That is, we set the value of jump_destination_is_12 to true if and only if the current operationName is a JUMP, and the value at the head of the stack is the same as the byte number of this JUMPDEST. The reason is that in EVM, JUMP's operand, which is the destination of the jump, is the value at the top of the stack. Note also that no two jump_destination_is_x variables can be simultaneously true. If the instruction is JUMPI instead, we would check also whether the value immediately below the top of stack, i.e., stack[4] in our above example, is > 0, because that is exactly where the condition for the JUMPI resides. We can then carry out the state-transition that effects the changes to operationName to the appropriate JUMPDEST. That is, we effect one state-transition to setup the correct destination for the jump (and check the condition, in the case of JUMPI), and a next state-transition to correctly update the operationName, i.e., our version of the program counter.

```
next ( operationName )  :=   case
  ...
  operationName = JUMP_7 : JUMP_7_DUMMY ;
  operationName = JUMP_7_DUMMY & jump_destination_is_12 : JUMPDEST_12 ;
  operationName = JUMP_7_DUMMY & jump_destination_is_317 : JUMPDEST_317 ;
  ...
```

For MSTORE and SSTORE, we use "_DUMMY_" variables for a similar reason that we need to setup the location at which we store. The only difference between MSTORE and SSTORE is that the former stores a value at at offset within memory while the latter's storage space is indexed by a key, often computed by exercising a cryptographic hash function, Keccak-256 or SHA-3. Corresponding to the hash function, EVM has an instruction, byte value 0x20, opcode KECCAK256 [33]. The computation of this hash value has itself been identified in some prior work as a source of difficulty in verifying smart contracts [12]—owever, we observe that while we could certainly implement either of those hash functions in SMV, we have simplified the work by realizing the Adler-32 checksum instead [20]. From our standpoint, there is no consequence except ease of implementation.

Gas. We capture gas in a variable, and use the various values on consumption of gas that are specified for EVM [33].

4.1 Unchecked Low-Level Calls

An unchecked low-level call is an invocation of a function of another contract from this contract. If and when that call eventually returns, a return value is pushed onto the stack of this contract. A contract is vulnerable if and only if there exists an instance of execution in which that return value is not checked. In Solidity, there are a number of ways to call another contract, e.g., call(), send() and staticcall(). In EVM code, there is one way only: the CALL instruction. Also, in Solidity, there are several different ways of checking the return value from such a call; e.g., using an if statement or by invoking the require() convenience function. In EVM code, the check is achieved using the ISZERO instruction. We adopt the algorithm in Fig. 2 to find unchecked low-level calls.

---

1 $S \leftarrow$ trim_contract()
2 **foreach** *contract snippet* $s \in S$ **do**
3   Statically check whether the initial CALL is followed by an ISZERO
4   If no, halt and report "is vulnerable"
5   If yes, reduce s to a model-checking instance
6   Add an LTLSPEC (see below)
7   Invoke the model checker; if it does not return a counterexample, report "is vulnerable"

Fig. 2. Our algorithm for finding unchecked low-level calls.

In trim_contract(), we first find each instance of the CALL instruction. We then scan forward in the EVM code from that instruction till we hit an instruction that we consider terminating from the standpoint of our trimming: JUMP, JUMPI, STOP, RETURN, REVERT or another CALL. We expect there to be at least one ISZERO before we hit one of these instructions; if not, we report that the contract is vulnerable in Line (4) of the above algorithm. If we proceed past Line (4) for a particular snippet s, we know that in s, the CALL is followed by at least one ISZERO. Corresponding to each ISZERO in a snippet s, we ask whether it checks the return value from the CALL. Assume that we have an ISZERO in byte # 12 and another in byte # 35 of the snippet. We first generate a random value, 59061 in the example below. We then ask whether there exists a reachable state in which the top of the stack contains that value when we hit any ISZERO instruction that follows the CALL in the snippet. In the example below, the maximum stack-size is 10, with the entries indexed $0, \ldots, 9$.

```
LTLSPEC G !(
(CALL_0_return_value = 0ud16_59061 & stack_head = 1 & stack[0] = ↵
    CALL_0_return_value & operationName = ISZERO_12) |
(CALL_0_return_value = 0ud16_59061 & stack_head = 1 & stack[0] = ↵
    CALL_0_return_value & operationName = ISZERO_35) |
(CALL_0_return_value = 0ud16_59061 & stack_head = 2 & stack[1] = ↵
    CALL_0_return_value & operationName = ISZERO_12) |
 ...
```

CALL_x_return_value is a variable we declare and allow the model checker to assign non-deterministically. If the model checker finds a counter example to the above LTLSPEC, then that is evidence that some instance of ISZERO that follows the CALL in the snippet s checks the return value from the CALL, and therefore no vulnerability exists. Otherwise, we know and report that a vulnerability exists. We recognize that there is a small probability of a false negative here because it is possible that the top of the stack takes the random value we generate, 59061 in the above example, not because it corresponds to the return value from the CALL, but on account of some other computations. We can simply repeat to exponentially decrease this probability.

5   Empirical Validation

A model-checker that can take specifications in SMV as input is nuXmv [3], and that is indeed what we have used. We have employed it in bounded model-checking more, where we infer the bound from the size of each contract snippet we check. For our empirical validation, we use the curated and "wild" datasets of Durieux et al. [8]. Their curated dataset comprises smart contracts written in Solidity classified into the 10 categories of DASP [23]. One of these classes is unchecked low-level calls. Each contract in the curated set is labelled where the vulnerability exists. For example, the contract in Fig. 1 from Sect. 1 suffers from an unchecked low-level call in the line winner.send(winAmount).

When one considers the smart contracts from the entire curated set, we know that at least one contract in every file within the unchecked_low_level_calls subset contains the vulnerability. But, there may also be contracts in the curated set outside of that subset that suffer from the unchecked low-level calls vulnerability. Consequently, we organize our discussions below as follows. We first focus on files in the unchecked_low_level_calls subset of the curated set. As every one of those files contains the vulnerability, we cannot report any false positives. The question is whether we report any false negatives. We then consider the remainder of the files from the entire curated set. We report the manner in which our approach performs on them; in this case, both false positives and negatives are possible. Finally, we discuss our assessment on the "wild" dataset.

	Curated, unchecked low-level calls subset	Curated, all others	Wild
# files	52	91	47,581
# files we assessed	52	91	100
# contracts in files we assessed	84	129	664
# instances of CALL	269	160	805
# we determine are vulnerable	87	23	5
# false positives	0	0	0
# false negatives	0	0	0

Fig. 3. Table with statistics and our empirical results.

The table in Fig. 3 reports statistics on the datasets and our results. The first row of the table reports the number of smart contract files in each of the three datasets. The second row reports the number of files we assessed empirically against our implementation: it was all the files from the curated set, and 100 files chosen randomly from the "wild" set. The third row reports the total number of contracts in the Solidity code in each dataset, and the fourth row reports the total number of CALL instructions in the EVM code across all the contracts in the files we assessed. Thus, as we say in the table in the fourth row, we assessed more than 1000 contract snippets in the algorithm we discuss above. The fifth row, "# we determine vulnerable", is the number of those instances of the CALL instruction that we deem to be vulnerable. The final two rows reports the number of false positives and negatives, which are both zero. Our unit of measurement for the number of false positives and negatives is at the granularity of a file.

Comparison to Other Tools. The work of Durieux et al. [8] allows us to compare our results with prior tools. Their work reports "Vulnerabilities identified per category by each tool," (Table 5 in that work) from which we get a lower-bound on the number of false negatives for those tools. We observe that for unchecked low-level calls, every tool they studied suffers from a high number of false negatives—the best performer, Mythril [22], was able to detect only 5 of the total 12 instances of vulnerabilities. Our work is on a later, larger version of the dataset used in Durieux et al. [8] and we achieve zero false positives and negatives on the larger dataset.

Other Vulnerabilities. While the above results suggest that for unchecked low-level calls, our approach is highly effective, a natural question is whether we can extend it to address other commonly occurring classes of vulnerabilities in smart contracts. We think that the answer to this question is 'yes'. For example, it is possible for us to adopt the reduction from Sect. 4 with a different algorithm and LTL property than the ones from Sect. 4.1 to address reentrancy [23]. We leave this for future work.

6   Conclusions and Future Work

We have taken a different mindset than existing work towards checking for security vulnerabilities in smart contracts. Rather than trying to check for several different kinds of such vulnerabilities and as a consequence, building a tool that suffers high numbers of false positive and negatives as has been observed for such tools, we validate the hypothesis that if we focus on a class of commonly occurring vulnerabilities only, we can build a tool that suffers zero false positives and negatives for real-world smart contracts. The class which is our focus is as computationally hard as any other class we may want to check for. Our empirical results on a publicly available benchmark are highly promising—our tool suffers zero false positives and negatives.

Some future work is to extend our reduction to be able to detect other classes of vulnerabilities that are of particular interest in the context of smart contracts, such as reentrancy and front-running [23]. There is also the question as to whether we can detect new classes of vulnerabilities that are not members of known, commonly occurring classes. More broadly, there is the question of identifying characteristics unique to smart contracts from the standpoint of security vulnerabilities in them.

References

1. Amani, S., Begel, M., Bortin, M., Staples, M.: Towards verifying Ethereum smart contract bytecode in Isabelle/HOL. In: Proceedings of the 7th ACM SIGPLAN International Conference on Certified Programs and Proofs, CPP 2018, New York, NY, USA, pp. 66–67 (2018). https://doi.org/10.1145/3167084
2. Bhargavan, K., et al.: Formal verification of smart contracts: short paper. In: Proceedings of the 2016 ACM Workshop on Programming Languages and Analysis for Security, PLAS 2016, New York, NY, USA, pp. 91–96 (2016). https://doi.org/10.1145/2993600.2993611
3. Bozzano, M., et al.: nuxmv 2.0.0 user manual (2019). https://es.fbk.eu/tools/nuxmv/downloads/nuxmv-user-manual.pdf
4. Brent, L., et al.: Vandal: a scalable security analysis framework for smart contracts (2018). https://doi.org/10.48550/ARXIV.1809.03981
5. Cecchetti, E., Yao, S., Ni, H., Myers, A.C.: Compositional security for reentrant applications. In: 2021 IEEE Symposium on Security and Privacy (SP), pp. 1249–1267 (2021). https://doi.org/10.1109/SP40001.2021.00084
6. Chen, W., et al.: SADPonzi: detecting and characterizing Ponzi schemes in Ethereum smart contracts. Proc. ACM Meas. Anal. Comput. Syst. 5(2), 1–30 (2021). https://doi.org/10.1145/3460093
7. Chinen, Y., Yanai, N., Cruz, J.P., Okamura, S.: RA: hunting for re-entrancy attacks in Ethereum smart contracts via static analysis. In: 2020 IEEE International Conference on Blockchain (Blockchain), pp. 327–336 (2020). https://doi.org/10.1109/Blockchain50366.2020.00048
8. Durieux, T., Ferreira, J.F., Abreu, R., Cruz, P.: Empirical review of automated analysis tools on 47,587 Ethereum smart contracts. In: Proceedings of the ACM/IEEE 42nd International Conference on Software Engineering, ICSE 2020, New York, NY, USA, pp. 530–541 (2020)
9. Durieux, T., Ferreira, J.F., Abreu, R., Cruz, P.: Smartbugs repository. https://github.com/smartbugs/smartbugs. Accessed July 2022
10. Ethereum: Solidity. https://docs.soliditylang.org/. Accessed July 2022
11. ethereum.org: Welcome to ethereum. https://ethereum.org/. Accessed July 2022
12. Frank, J., Aschermann, C., Holz, T.: ETHBMC: a bounded model checker for smart contracts. In: USENIX Security Symposium, USENIX 2020, pp. 2757–2774 (2020)
13. Ghaleb, A., Pattabiraman, K.: How effective are smart contract analysis tools? evaluating smart contract static analysis tools using bug injection. In: Proceedings of the 29th ACM SIGSOFT International Symposium on Software Testing and Analysis, ISSTA 2020, pp. 415–427. Association for Computing Machinery, New York (2020)

14. Grech, N., Kong, M., Jurisevic, A., Brent, L., Scholz, B., Smaragdakis, Y.: Mad-Max: surviving out-of-gas conditions in ethereum smart contracts. In: Proceedings of the ACM on Programming Languages. OOPSLA, vol. 2, pp. 1–27. New York (2018)

15. IBM: What is blockchain technology? https://www.ibm.com/topics/what-is-blockchain. Accessed July 2022

16. Kalra, S., Goel, S., Dhawan, M., Sharma, S.: ZEUS: analyzing safety of smart contracts. In: Network and Distributed Systems Security (NDSS) Symposium, NDSS 2018, pp. 18–21 (2018). https://doi.org/10.14722/ndss.2018.23082, http://pages.cpsc.ucalgary.ca/~joel.reardon/blockchain/readings/ndss2018_09-1_Kalra_paper.pdf

17. Kripke, S.: Semantical considerations on modal logic. Acta Philos. Fennica 83–94 (1963)

18. Krupp, J., Rossow, C.: teEther: gnawing at Ethereum to automatically exploit smart contracts. In: USENIX Security Symposium, USENIX 2018, pp. 1317–1333 (2018)

19. Luu, L., Chu, D.H., Olickel, H., Saxena, P., Hobor, A.: Making smart contracts smarter. In: CCS, CCS 2016, New York, NY, USA, pp. 254–269 (2016)

20. Maxino, T.: Revisiting Fletcher and Adler Checksums. DSN 2006 Student Forum (2006). https://doi.org/10.1184/R1/6625619.v1, https://kilthub.cmu.edu/articles/journal_contribution/Revisiting_Fletcher_and_Adler_Checksums/6625619

21. Mossberg, M., et al.: Manticore: a user-friendly symbolic execution framework for binaries and smart contracts. In: IEEE/ACM International Conference on Automated Software Engineering (ASE), ASE 2019, pp. 1186–1189 (2019). https://doi.org/10.1109/ASE.2019.00133

22. Mueller, B.: Smashing Ethereum smart contracts for fun and real profit. In: 9th Annual HITB Security Conference (HITBSecConf) (2018)

23. NCC Group: Decentralized security project (2022). https://dasp.co

24. Nehai, Z., Piriou, P.Y., Daumas, F.: Model-checking of smart contracts. In: 2018 IEEE International Conference on Internet of Things (iThings) and IEEE Green Computing and Communications (GreenCom) and IEEE Cyber, Physical and Social Computing (CPSCom) and IEEE Smart Data (SmartData), pp. 980–987 (2018). https://doi.org/10.1109/Cybermatics_2018.2018.00185

25. Nikolic, I., Kolluri, A., Sergey, I., Saxena, P., Hobor, A.: Finding the greedy, prodigal, and suicidal contracts at scale. In: Proceedings of the 34th Annual Computer Security Applications Conference, ACSAC 2018, New York, NY, USA, pp. 653–663 (D2018). https://doi.org/10.1145/3274694.3274743

26. Perez, D., Livshits, B.: Smart contract vulnerabilities: vulnerable does not imply exploited. In: USENIX Security Symposium, pp. 1325–1341 (2021)

27. Rameder, H.: Systematic review of Ethereum smart contract security vulnerabilities, analysis methods and tools. Diploma thesis (2021). https://doi.org/10.34726/hss.2021.86784

28. Rodler, M., Li, W., Karame, G.O., Davi, L.: EVMPatch: timely and automated patching of ethereum smart contracts. In: USENIX Security Symposium, pp. 1289–1306 (2021)

29. Savitch, W.J.: Relationships between nondeterministic and deterministic tape complexities. J. Comput. Syst. Sci. 4(2), 177–192 (1970). https://doi.org/10.1016/S0022-0000(70)80006-X

30. Schneidewind, C., Grishchenko, I., Scherer, M., Maffe, M.: eThor: practical and provably sound static analysis of Ethereum smart contracts. In: CCS, CCS 2020, New York, NY, USA, pp. 621–640 (2020). https://doi.org/10.1145/3372297.3417250

31. Tolmach, P., Li, Y., Lin, S.W., Liu, Y., Li, Z.: A survey of smart contract formal specification and verification. ACM Comput. Surv. **54**(7), 1–38 (2021)

32. Tsankov, P., Dan, A., Cohen, D.D., Gervais, A., Buenzli, F., Vechev, M.: Securify: practical security analysis of smart contracts. In: CCS, CCS 2018, New York, NY, USA, pp. 67–82 (2018). https://doi.org/10.1145/3243734.3243780

33. Wood, G.: Ethereum: a secure decentralised generalised transaction ledger. Technical report Version 3078285, Ethereum & Parity (2022). https://ethereum.github.io/yellowpaper/paper.pdf

34. Xi, R., Pattabiraman, K.: When they go low: Automated replacement of low-level functions in Ethereum smart contracts. In: 2022 IEEE International Conference on Software Analysis, Evolution and Reengineering (SANER), pp. 995–1005 (2022)

35. Zhang, M., Zhang, X., Zhang, Y., Lin, Z.: TXSPECTOR: uncovering attacks in Ethereum from transactions. In: USENIX Security Symposium, pp. 2775–2792 (2020)

Decentralized Vision-Based Byzantine Agent Detection in Multi-robot Systems with IOTA Smart Contracts

Sahar Salimpour$^{(\boxtimes)}$, Farhad Keramat, Jorge Peña Queralta,
and Tomi Westerlund

Turku Intelligent Embedded and Robotic Systems, University of Turku,
Turku, Finland
{sahars,fakera,jopequ,tovewe}@utu.fi
https://tiers.utu.fi

Abstract. Multiple opportunities lie at the intersection of multi-robot systems and distributed ledger technologies (DLTs). In this work, we investigate the potential of new DLT solutions such as IOTA, for detecting anomalies and byzantine agents in multi-robot systems in a decentralized manner. Traditional blockchain approaches are not applicable to real-world networked and decentralized robotic systems where connectivity conditions are not ideal. To address this, we leverage recent advances in partition-tolerant and byzantine-tolerant collaborative decision-making processes with IOTA smart contracts. We show how our work in vision-based anomaly and change detection can be applied to detecting byzantine agents within multiple robots operating in the same environment. We show that IOTA smart contracts add a low computational overhead while allowing to build trust within the multi-robot system. The proposed approach effectively enables byzantine robot detection based on the comparison of images submitted by the different robots and detection of anomalies and changes between them.

Keywords: Distributed ledger technologies · Blockchain · Deep learning · Anomaly detection · Change detection · Multi-robot systems · Computer vision · IOTA · Smart Contracts · Distributed Robotic Systems

1 Introduction

In recent years, byzantine agent detection has become an important aspect of distributed autonomous systems [6,10,29]. Indeed, with the growth and increasing ubiquity of autonomous robots, security and safety issues for systems deployed in the real world have attracted an ever-growing attention in both industrial and academic areas [18,19]. As robotic systems are deployed in larger numbers, single autonomous robots have been replaced by fleets of multi-robot systems that need to coordinate and collaborate. Many multi-robot applications, including security monitoring, public safety [32], industrial applications [23,24], and

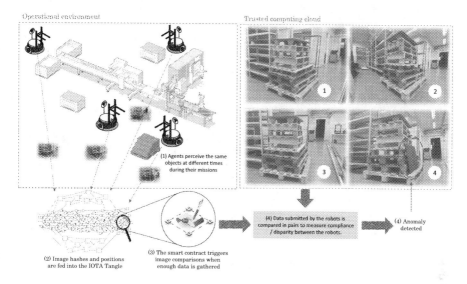

Fig. 1. Conceptual illustration of the proposed vision-based byzantine agent detection approach with IOTA smart contracts.

Internet of Things (IoT) systems [16], are at risk of being manipulated through the injection of fabricated or noisy data, or the performance of a large system might significantly decrease because of a single malicious or byzantine actor. Consequently, byzantine robots could potentially lead to a failure of the entire multi-robot operation. Therefore, it is important to be able to detect and neutralize the actions of byzantine agents, particularly if operating in environments together with humans.

In multi-robot systems, vision-based perception often plays a major role in use cases involving safety, surveillance, and environment monitoring. Vision-based approaches to detect changes or anomalies in the environment can potentially be used to also detect differences between sensing data gathered by different robots operating in a common environment. A majority of visual anomaly detection problems are focused on a specific class of images and attempt to identify pixel-level anomalies in them. They mostly require training their deep learning (DL)-based models using large amount of *normal* data [5,30,31]. However, the detection of anomalies based on visual data in more general and potentially unknown environments easily becomes a challenging task, especially in the context of mobile robotic applications.

Novel approaches in the literature with potential to address the identification of byzantine robots in multi-robot systems are blockchain-based solutions through smart contracts. Blockchain technology was originally developed for the purposes of financial transactions [17], but it has also been utilized as a distributed computing framework for applications in general, e.g., within the Internet of Things (IoT) domain, as well as in multi-robot systems. A distributed system integrating blockchain technology is a priori capable of delivering a trusted and decentralized system between independent and untrusted agents. In the case of autonomous robots, this allows for decentralized collaborative decision making without the need for a third-party central organization. By doing so, a consistent global state makes the whole system resilient and fault-tolerant against byzantine robots.

IOTA smart contracts, designed for IoT devices, are one of the promising distributed ledger technology (DLT) solutions that can be used in multi-robot systems. In our previous work [10], we have presented a general partition-tolerant and byzantine-tolerant framework built on top of IOTA smart contracts and integrated to ROS 2. By leveraging this framework, all non-byzantine robots could reach a consensus about which robot is byzantine in a decentralized manner.

Blockchains or other distributed ledger technologies (DLTs) have potential to be an innovative solution to vision applications. However, to the best of our knowledge, no studies have been conducted on this topic within the context of multi-robot systems. In this study, we present a framework to detect byzantine robot(s) in a secure network and operating in a common environment by analyzing the RGB images which are captured by each robot. In the proposed method we use our previous study [25], presenting a general framework to detect anomalies and changes between images, to compare in pairs images gathered by different robots. In this case, an anomaly could be something that has been moved or removed from the environment or something that does not belong there, as well as potentially altered or fabricated data.

Our objective is to study what are the implications of integrating more complex byzantine agent detection approaches (e.g., based on vision data) with blockchain smart contracts, from the perspective of usability, computational requirements and other potential system-level aspects to consider. This paper therefore integrates a vision-based approach for anomaly and change detection in autonomous inspection robots together with IOTA smart contracts, as illustrated by Fig. 1. The result is a decentralized solution to anomaly detection that can be applied to byzantine agent detection within multi-robot systems. The blockchain serves as a tool for storing agent locations and image hashes, while smart contracts calculate where and when to perform the anomaly and change detection once enough data has been acquired. The DL model itself runs on a trusted server, owing to the impossibility of integrating such complex computation (deep neural networks) within a smart contract, and therefore limiting the decentralization of the solution. However, this is a first step towards a fully distributed implementation where multiple nodes will be able to validate the output of the DL models. In summary, the main contributions of this work are the following:

i) The design and implementation of a blockchain-based approach to byzantine agent detection using IOTA smart contract and vision sensors;

ii) the extension of our previous work in anomaly and change detection for autonomous inspection robots to comparing data from multiple robots operating in the same environment towards byzantine agent detection; and

iii) the integration of the DL models with IOTA smart contracts that trigger data comparisons after tracking the position of robots and the location of gathered data.

The rest of the manuscript is structured as follows. Section 2 discusses related research on blockchain technology in robotic systems, and the problem of anomaly detection in multi-robot systems. A general introduction on the background is given in Sect. 3, and a description of our methodological approach is provided in Sect. 4. Section 5 presents the results, and Sect. 6 summarizes the work and points to future directions.

2   Related Work

Generally, byzantine and fault detection in robotics can be divided into two major groups: self-monitoring and group-monitoring anomaly detection. Several studies proposed the self-monitoring approach, in which each robot detects anomalies independently. A framework for detecting mechanical faults and sensor faults in wheeled robots was presented in [33]. Tingting et al [3]. Proposed an unsupervised anomaly detection model using a sliding-window convolutional variational autoencoder in terms of time series effect. However, swarm-level anomaly detection methods analyze the collaboration between robots and the data collected from the entire swarm [15].

Many studies have addressed byzantine robot detection in multi-robot missions using blockchain technology. In [28] a blockchain-based approach was explored for swarm robotics systems with byzantine robots. The authors utilized Ethereum-based decentralized smart contracts to detect and remove the byzentine swarm members. Their approach was evaluated using a collective decision-making scenario in which robots must agree on the most frequent tile color in an environment. In another work [6], a blockchain was used as a secure communication tool in Byzantine Follow The Leader (BFTL) missions. Through their approach, leader robots guide follower robots to specific destinations under the threat of Byzantine robots misdirecting them. In addition, some research conducted to implement blockchain protocols into secure communication multi-agent systems with unmanned aerial vehicles [1,9].

The immutability of blockchain makes it a secure solution for detecting anomalous behaviors and attacks in various systems with chains of information blocks, such as industrial control systems [8], electricity consumption [11], and health systems [2]. The authors in [12] implemented smart contracts to store robot information and compute them to detect anomalies, which were simulated internal failure, in machinery and register them in the blockchain. Golomb et al. [7] introduced a collaborative anomaly detection model for a large network of IoT devices by leveraging blockchain technology in conjunction with extensible Markov model.

A number of recent studies have focused on detecting visual anomalies within specific image classes, such as railway images [31], road datasets [26], and industrial production images [22]. In a recent visual-based blockchain task [21], the technology of blockchain was used to provide decentralized communication between robots so they could find their way back home using common visual landmarks. In [13], external parties, Oracle, analyze captured images to determine how many balls need to be picked by UR3 arm. With this information, smart contracts can securely control robots, ensuring that no one can change the logic once it is on the blockchain. In another study [14], the authors proposed an approach for securing the robot's workspace and controlling its action using smart contracts and 3D image analysis.

3   Background

Through this section, we provide a general overview of our previous works about the proposed visual anomaly detection framework and the distributed ledger technology solution for multi-agent systems.

3.1   Deep Feature Extraction and Matching

Matching and extracting feature points are critical steps when a different environmental condition, such as lighting and viewpoints, affects image comparison and matching. SuperPoint is a fully convolutional neural network self-supervised feature point extraction. It uses a basic detector called MagicPoint that is pretrained on a synthetically generated dataset consisting of simple shapes, along with homographic adaptation for more training samples from each image. Therefore, it can detect interest points more sensitively than traditional corner detectors [4].

After the feature extraction process, various methods can be used to take key points and their descriptors in image pairs and match them with corresponding points. SuperGlue is a feature point matching method based on graph neural networks that show better performance for points extracted by the SuperPoint model. The method is based on two layers, a graph neural network, and an optimal matching layer [27]. Using a differentiable Sinkhorn algorithm, matchable points are efficiently paired, and non-matchable points are rejected.

3.2   IOTA Smart Contracts

As a subset of the wider DLT domain, blockchain systems have grown in popularity in a variety of use cases. Through smart contracts, specific tasks can be executed when certain conditions are met in distributed applications. The most commonly used blockchain platform for swarm robotics is Ethereum, which uses Turing-complete smart contracts written in Solidity [29]. Ethereum's intrinsic scalability is the main limitation due to its classical single-chain structure. The Tangle [20], a directed acyclic graph (DAG)-based DLT, was introduced to solve some of the fundamental weaknesses in classic blockchain systems. IOTA DLT uses the Tangle as its underlying structure, where transactions are the primary data structures. A graph-based ledger rather than a linear chain, which is the

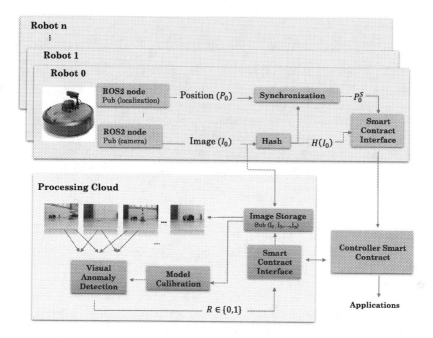

Fig. 2. High-level overview of the proposed system architecture. In the current implementation, a trusted processing cloud performs the vision-based anomaly detection. In the future, this workload can be distributed and validated through the smart contracts, but will still run off-chain.

concept behind Tangles, would make it more flexible in terms of network partitioning. Multi-robot systems relying on IOTA are therefore unique from a DLT perspective.

As part of ensuring the Tangle's robustness and security, the IOTA foundation has a centralized coordinator that confirms valid transactions. The second version of IOTA, Shimmer, was launched in order to achieve full decentralization. In this work, we use the Go implementation of Shimmer called GoShimmer. As the data structure in the Tangle is graph-based, the implementation of IOTA's smart contract mechanism was challenging. As a solution, the IOTA foundation introduces the IOTA Smart Contract Platform (ISCP) as a second layer on top of the Tangle. In this second layer, Wasp, which is the implementation of ISCP in Go, creates a chain.

4 Methodology

Based on the proposed framework for using IOTA smart contracts with ROS 2 in [10] for a multi-robot system, we propose the system depicted in Fig. 2. Every robot in this system and the processing cloud runs an instance of GoShimmer and Wasp nodes to form the IOTA network and enable running smart contracts.

For simplicity in this proof of concept, the proposed system is not supporting partition tolerance, but according to our earlier framework this can be done easily. All the Wasp nodes create a single chain and deploy the smart contract on it. The smart contract's scheme is shown in 1.1. The processing cloud is a trusted server to perform the operations which needs high computation power that can not be deployed on the smart contract.

Every robot in the system publishes its position and images captured by the camera. Since the publishing rate of the position and images are different we use a synchronization node in ROS 2 which checks the timestamp of images and positions and associates a position for each image because the positions are published at a higher rate. Every image is sent to the storage unit of the processing cloud. Then the hash of the image, and the position are submitted to the *submitPair* function of the smart contract.

The smart contract is mainly responsible to find the pairs of images to be compared and determining which robot is behaving maliciously based on the comparison results. We define intersections for data comparison as the locations where at least $3f + 1$ robot have visited and where images are available with at least a certain overlapping viewpoint (calculated based on position and orientation of the robots). The value f is the number of byzantine robots that our method can tolerate. The schema of the smart contract for IOTA is show in the Listing 1.1. The *Pair* is a struct defined to store the hash of an image, its position, and orientation. Every robot uses the *submitPair* method to store the images. This function then calls the *findIntersections* function.

To find the intersections, the *findIntersections* function divides the map into overlapping $2d \times 2d$ cells. The amount of overlap is d among the adjacent cells. In this way every image will be assigned to four adjacent cells based on the location of image. After associating every image to the cells, inside each cell an exhaustive search is performed to find a set of $3f + 1$ images each from different robot that has each pair of them has maximum distance of d and maximum orientation difference of δ. By using this method we can make sure that any set of images that have maximum distance of d and maximum orientation difference of δ will not be missed and it is computationally faster than searching over all the locations since it is related to number of cells instead of number of locations. In each cell, at most one intersection is selected. This also prevents the byzantine robot to compromise from submitting several correct images and one altered image with same position.

The set of images found by *findIntersections* function is stored in the *sets* state variable of the smart contract. On the other hand, the processing cloud polls the smart contract by *getIntersection* functions. The cloud retrieves the set. Based on the hash of images in the set, corresponding images are extracted from the storage unit. Then every two pair of the images are passed to Visual Anomaly Detection module. The result of this module is a binary value indicating if the two images have any difference of not. The cloud submits this results by *submitComparison* function to the smart contract.

Listing 1.1. Smart Contract Schema.

```
name:  VisionByzContract
description:  Vision  based  byzantine  detection  smart  contract
events:  {}
structs:
  Pair:
    // Hash  of  the  image  and  its  position
  CompResult:
    // Includes  two  robot  IDs  and  their  score
typedefs:  {}
state:
  scores:  Int8 []        // Score  of  each  robot
  state:  Bool []         // Indicates  if  every  robot  is
    byzantine  or  not
  intersections:  Pair []
  cells:  Position []
funcs:
  init:
    params:
      f:  Int32
      n:  Int32
  submitPair:
    params:
      pair:  Pair
  submitComparison:
    params:
      res:  CompResult
  findIntersections:
    access:  self
    params:  {}
views:
  getIntersection:
    results:
      pairs:  Pair []
  getRobotState:
    results:
      state:  Bool
```

The smart contract keeps a score for each robot based on the results of comparisons. A robot's score is incremented by one if the cloud finds a difference in the comparison. If we suppose that robots pass by sufficient amount of intersections, the smart contract can detect the byzantine robot based on the scores. If the robot's score is bigger than the average of scores by a certain threshold, the robot can be marked as byzantine. This decision also stored in the smart contract and can be used for further applications.

4.1   Visual Anomaly Detection Module

In our last study [25], we proposed a general framework to detect regions that have changed in pair images as pixel-based visual anomalies. To detect anomalies in an unknown environment without training, we applied pre-trained deep learning models for extraction, matching, and segmentation. The performance and final results of SuperPoint and SuperGlue are influenced by confidence parameters such as keypoint detection and matching confidence thresholds. We applied a few-shot calibration procedure based on the coefficient of variation of matched keypoints to find the optimum matching and extracting thresholds.

In order to find overlap areas, we apply masks to both images based on matched interest points. Then, we segment not matched points using the Mask-RCNN instance segmentation method. As the segmentation model is not trained for all objects, we use DBSCAN clustering algorithm to group the remaining not-matched points belonging to new foreign objects. The proposed system architecture for visual anomaly processing is illustrated in Fig. 2 in the processing cloud unit. When a change is detected in either image of an image pair, the processing cloud returns True for both suspicious images, otherwise it returns False. With this, we measure compliance or disparity between pairs of images, and allows us to build a measure of trust within the system.

5   Experimental Results

This section discusses the results of the byzantine robot detection experiment with ground robots that was conducted to evaluate the functionality and effectiveness of the proposed framework.

5.1   Experiment Setup

Hardware. The employed multi-robot system in this paper consists of four ground TurtleBot4 Lite robots built on top of the iRobot Create 3 mobile base with a Luxonis OAK-D-Lite stereo camera. For localization, we utilize an external motion capture system with four Optitrack PrimeX 22 cameras and robots move in the area defined by the motion capture system forming a square of approximately $48\,m^2$. In this study, we placed several objects from a variety of classes of the COCO dataset in the environment, along with some unknown objects and some with unclear textures.

Software. The Turtlebot4 robots run ROS 2 Galactic under Ubuntu 20.04 and publish camera images at 1 Hz. Localization is running in ROS 1 Noetic with a 120 Hz publishing rate. Data is forwarded from ROS 1 to ROS 2 with a the ros1_bridge package and the data from the two topics synchronized for saving image locations. Each robot explores the environment following a predefined trajectory and publishes its topics to the trusted storage unit and through the smart contract interface. Figure 3 illustrates the trajectory of the robots during the experiment.

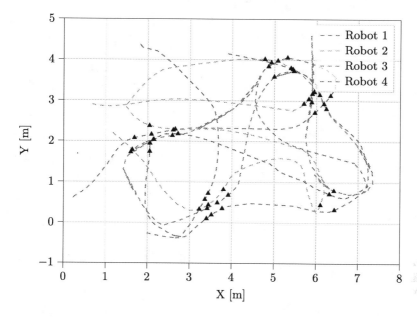

Fig. 3. Trajectories of the different robots during the experiments. The yellow circles show the locations that the smart contract computes for data comparisons. (Color figure online)

The trusted processing cloud is represented in the experiments by a computer with an Intel Core i7-11800H processor and 64 GB of memory. Robots and the processing unit are running Wasp v0.2.5 and GoShimmer v0.7.4 nodes and they are all connected to the same wireless network. The smart contract schema illustrated in Listing 1.1 is implemented in the Go programming language.

5.2   Smart Contract

In this experiment, we choose $f = 1$ to tolerate at most one byzantine robot. To find an intersection $3f + 1 = 4$ robot should therefore visit the same location with similar orientation to allow for enough overlapping pixel area in the images. In the smart contract we set $d = 0.5$ m and $\delta = 0.4$ rad to define an intersection. In Fig. 3, we illustrate the path traversed by each robot. The smart contract outputs 17 intersection sets. All points in these sets are marked by black triangles in the figure. The CPU utilization time is illustrated in Fig. 4, measured by the Linux perf tool.

Calibration. The image storage section chooses a few image pairs of the operational environment with the linear shift to calculate matching and extracting thresholds in order to calibrate the SuperPoint + SuperGlue model. The optimum matching threshold is $\Delta = 0.35$, and the best keypoint extracting threshold is $\lambda = 0.001$. In both cases the selected value differs from the default value of $\Delta = 0.2$ and $\lambda = 0.005$.

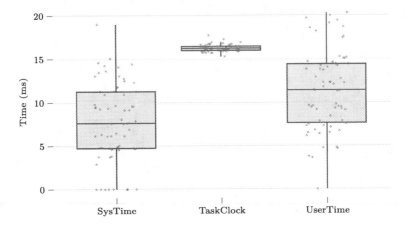

Fig. 4. Analysis of the CPU utilization time of the *submitPair* method measured with the Linux perf tool. The graph demonstrates a low performance impact induced by the blockchain integration.

Anomalous Object Identification. We now describe experiments we conducted with the ground robots to demonstrate the effectiveness of the proposed byzantine agent detection process based on the results of visual anomaly detection.

Figure 5 illustrates the result of processing a set of images meeting the requirements in terms of relative position and orientation. These comparisons are requested by the smart contract. A two-by-two analysis is conducted for images from the four robots. As can be seen in the figure, the proposed model identifies three anomalies related to robot number 1, and one related to robot number 4, over a total of six comparisons.

Figure 6 shows a series of images received from a byzantine robot and a *normal* robot in different places. In inspection or monitoring applications, the anomaly detected during the visual processing stage could be an object which is removed or added in the time elapsing between the visits of the different robots to that location. Alternatively, the same approach serves to identify altered or manipulated data from potentially malicious agents. Our method is robust to different classes, so it is capable of clustering non-matched points when they cannot be segmented by the Mask-RCNN model based on the predefined set of known objects. There main limitations are, however, with some new texture-less objects that cannot be detected because of the lack of enough interest points to match.

In Fig. 6 Robot 1 is the byzantine robot. The graph $G = (V, E)$ in each row illustrates the comparisons between each pair of images. Vertices of the graph represents each robot, and edges represents the result of the comparison between the images from the corresponding vertices. Red edges indicate that there is an anomaly detected in the comparisons. For every set score of a robot is calculated by summing the number of red edges connected to its vertex. For example in the first row, the score of Robot 1 is 3 and the score of Robot 3 is 1. Figure 7

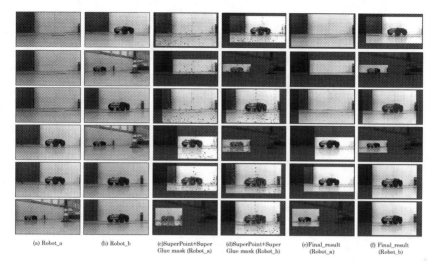

| (a) Robot_a | (b) Robot_b | (c)SuperPoint+Super Glue mask (Robot_a) | (d)SuperPoint+Super Glue mask (Robot_b) | (e)Final_result (Robot_a) | (f) Final_result (Robot_b) |

Fig. 5. Comparison of pair images related to the required locations by IOTA smart contract. The first two columns represent images submitted by robots. After feature extraction and clustering, the final results represent different robot pairs.

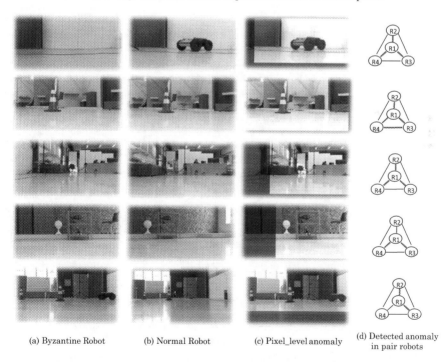

| (a) Byzantine Robot | (b) Normal Robot | (c) Pixel_level anomaly | (d) Detected anomaly in pair robots |

Fig. 6. The image submitted by the byzantine robot (a) and the image submitted by a honest robot (b). In column (c) the anomalies detected by the visual anomaly detection module are marked in red. And column (d) illustrates how this comparisons effect the score of each robot. (Color figure online)

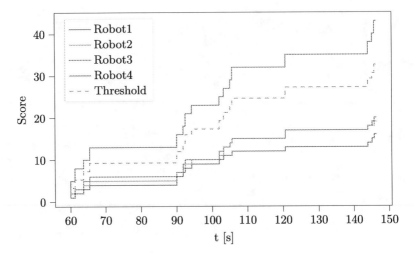

Fig. 7. Accumulated score of each robot over time and the threshold determining the byzantine robot. Through the mission, Robot 1 is deemed byzantine having too high disparity score.

illustrates the accumulated score of each robot over the time. The threshold is defined 30% bigger than the average of all scores.

In summary, our method is able to effectively identify anomalies or changes and build a measure of trust (through measuring similarities and disparities between images submitted by different robots) within the system. Even though this proof of concept relies on a central trusted server for the actual data comparisons, the smart contracts deciding what data is to be compared run in a decentralized manner, and the results are available through the system with the smart contract interface. The types of anomalies or changes identified do not necessarily imply malicious or byzantine behaviour, but rather flag robots that gather data that differs more from the rest of the fleet. In a practical scenario, a human operator would analyze the data whenever a robot is flagged as potentially byzantine.

6   Conclusion

This paper presents a solution to byzantine agent detection using IOTA smart contracts. In comparison with the state-of-the-art, with solutions that are mostly based on the Ethereum blockchain, the IOTA-based approach presented is theoretically more scalable, has lower computational impact and can be implemented to be partition tolerant. Additionally, we show the integration of more complex data comparison using deep learning and a vision-based approach to byzantine agent detection. Our results show that the blockchain layer adds negligible computational overhead, while the anomaly detection algorithm allows for building a measure of trust among the robots in the system. Our system effectively detects a potentially byzantine robot based on the disparity of its data when compared to the data gathered by other robots. In future works, we aim at fully decentralizing the proposed system by adding incentives for robots or other nodes in the blockchain to run the deep learning inference models, so that their result can also be validated even when part of the data processing occurs off-chain.

Acknowledgment. This research work is supported by the R3Swarms project funded by the Secure Systems Research Center (SSRC), Technology Innovation Institute (TII).

References

1. Santos de Campos, M.G., Chanel, C.P., Chauffaut, C., Lacan, J.: Towards a blockchain-based multi-uav surveillance system. Front. Robot. AI, 90 (2021)
2. Castaldo, L., Cinque, V.: Blockchain-based logging for the cross-border exchange of ehealth data in europe. In: Gelenbe, E., et al. (eds.) Euro-CYBERSEC 2018. CCIS, vol. 821, pp. 46–56. Springer, Cham (2018). https://doi.org/10.1007/978-3-319-95189-8_5
3. Chen, T., Liu, X., Xia, B., Wang, W., Lai, Y.: Unsupervised anomaly detection of industrial robots using sliding-window convolutional variational autoencoder. IEEE Access **8**, 47072–47081 (2020)
4. DeTone, D., Malisiewicz, T., Rabinovich, A.: Superpoint: self-supervised interest point detection and description. In: Proceedings of the IEEE Conference on Computer Vision and Pattern Recognition Workshops, pp. 224–236 (2018)
5. Di Biase, G., Blum, H., Siegwart, R., Cadena, C.: Pixel-wise anomaly detection in complex driving scenes. In: Proceedings of the IEEE/CVF Conference on Computer Vision and Pattern Recognition, pp. 16918–16927 (2021)
6. Ferrer, E.C., Jiménez, E., Lopez-Presa, J.L., Martín-Rueda, J.: Following leaders in byzantine multirobot systems by using blockchain technology. IEEE Trans. Rob. **38**(2), 1101–1117 (2021)
7. Golomb, T., Mirsky, Y., Elovici, Y.: Ciota: Collaborative IoT anomaly detection via blockchain. arXiv preprint arXiv:1803.03807 (2018)
8. Jadidi, Z., Dorri, A., Jurdak, R., Fidge, C.: Securing manufacturing using blockchain. In: 2020 IEEE 19th International Conference on Trust, Security and Privacy in Computing and Communications (TrustCom), pp. 1920–1925. IEEE (2020)
9. Kapitonov, A., Lonshakov, S., Krupenkin, A., Berman, I.: Blockchain-based protocol of autonomous business activity for multi-agent systems consisting of UAVs. In: 2017 Workshop on Research, Education and Development of Unmanned Aerial Systems (RED-UAS), pp. 84–89. IEEE (2017)
10. Keramat, F., Peña Queralta, J., Westerlund, T.: Partition-tolerant and byzantine-tolerant decision-making for distributed robotic systems with iota and ROS 2. arXiv:2208.13467 (2022)
11. Li, M., Zhang, K., Liu, J., Gong, H., Zhang, Z.: Blockchain-based anomaly detection of electricity consumption in smart grids. Pattern Recogn. Lett. **138**, 476–482 (2020)
12. Lopes, V., Alexandre, L.A.: Detecting robotic anomalies using robotchain. In: 2019 IEEE International Conference on Autonomous Robot Systems and Competitions (ICARSC), pp. 1–6. IEEE (2019)

13. Lopes, V., Alexandre, L.A., Pereira, N.: Controlling robots using artificial intelligence and a consortium blockchain. arXiv preprint arXiv:1903.00660 (2019)
14. Lopes, V., Pereira, N., Alexandre, L.A.: Robot workspace monitoring using a blockchain-based 3d vision approach. In: Proceedings of the IEEE/CVF Conference on Computer Vision and Pattern Recognition Workshops (2019)
15. Miller, O.G., Gandhi, V.: A survey of modern exogenous fault detection and diagnosis methods for swarm robotics. J. King Saud Univ. Eng. Sci. **33**(1), 43–53 (2021)
16. Mohanta, B.K., Jena, D., Satapathy, U., Patnaik, S.: Survey on IoT security: Challenges and solution using machine learning, artificial intelligence and blockchain technology. Internet Things **11**, 100227 (2020)
17. Nakamoto, S.: Bitcoin: a peer-to-peer electronic cash system. Decentralized Bus. Rev. 21260 (2008)
18. Peña Queralta, J., Qingqing, L., Ferrer, E.C., Westerlund, T.: Secure encoded instruction graphs for end-to-end data validation in autonomous robots. IEEE Internet Things J. **9**(18), 18028–18040 (2022)
19. Peña Queralta, J., Qingqing, L., Zou, Z., Westerlund, T.: Enhancing autonomy with blockchain and multi-access edge computing in distributed robotic systems. In: The 5th International Conference on Fog and Mobile Edge Computing (2020). IEEE (2020)
20. Popov, S.: The tangle. White Pap. **1**(3), 30 (2018)
21. Rahouti, M., Lyons, D., Santana, L.: Vrchain: A blockchain-enabled framework for visual homing and navigation robots. arXiv preprint arXiv:2206.11223 (2022)
22. Roth, K., Pemula, L., Zepeda, J., Schölkopf, B., Brox, T., Gehler, P.: Towards total recall in industrial anomaly detection. In: Proceedings of the IEEE/CVF Conference on Computer Vision and Pattern Recognition, pp. 14318–14328 (2022)
23. Salimi, S., Morón, P.T., Peña Queralta, J., Westerlund, T.: Secure heterogeneous multi-robot collaboration and docking with hyperledger fabric blockchain. arXiv preprint (2022)
24. Salimi, S., Queralta, J.P., Westerlund, T.: Towards managing industrial robot fleets with hyperledger fabric blockchain and ros 2. arXiv e-prints, pp. arXiv-2203 (2022)
25. Salimpour, S., Queralta, J.P., Westerlund, T.: Self-calibrating anomaly and change detection for autonomous inspection robots. arXiv preprint arXiv:2209.02379 (2022)
26. Santhosh, K.K., Dogra, D.P., Roy, P.P.: Anomaly detection in road traffic using visual surveillance: a survey. ACM Comput. Surv. (CSUR) **53**(6), 1–26 (2020)
27. Sarlin, P.E., DeTone, D., Malisiewicz, T., Rabinovich, A.: Superglue: learning feature matching with graph neural networks. In: Proceedings of the IEEE/CVF Conference on Computer Vision and Pattern Recognition, pp. 4938–4947 (2020)
28. Strobel, V., Castelló Ferrer, E., Dorigo, M.: Managing byzantine robots via blockchain technology in a swarm robotics collective decision making scenario (2018)
29. Strobel, V., Castelló Ferrer, E., Dorigo, M.: Blockchain technology secures robot swarms: a comparison of consensus protocols and their resilience to byzantine robots. Front. Robot. AI **7**, 54 (2020)
30. Wang, T., Xu, X., Shen, F., Yang, Y.: A cognitive memory-augmented network for visual anomaly detection. IEEE/CAA J. Automatica Sinica **8**(7), 1296–1307 (2021)
31. Wang, T., Zhang, Z., Tsui, K.L.: A deep generative approach for rail foreign object detections via semi-supervised learning. IEEE Trans. Ind. Inf. **19**(1), 459–468 (2022)

32. Xiao, W., Li, M., Alzahrani, B., Alotaibi, R., Barnawi, A., Ai, Q.: A blockchain-based secure crowd monitoring system using UAV swarm. IEEE Netw. **35**(1), 108–115 (2021)
33. Yuan, X., Song, M., Zhou, F., Chen, Z., Li, Y.: A novel mittag-leffler kernel based hybrid fault diagnosis method for wheeled robot driving system. Comput. Intell. Neurosci. **2015**, 65 (2015)

Money Transfer on Transaction Signature-Based Ledger

Momoko Shiraishi[✉] and Hitoshi Aida

The University of Tokyo, Tokyo, Japan
shiraishi@os.ecc.u-tokyo.ac.jp

Abstract. Money transfer is indispensable in our daily lives. For providing the services, financial institutions bear great costs for verifying customers' identity and behaviors, so called KYC (Know Your Customer) costs. This paper proposes a comprehensive transaction scheme to reduce the KYC costs, by sharing customers' information among multiple financial service providers. Once a trusted service provider identifies a user using an image of his/her physical ID such as passports and residence certificates, the provider issues a digital certificate of the user's public key. When the user opens another account at different providers, the providers can identify the user with the certificate without proceeding the KYC step. The security analysis shows that the proposed transaction scheme is resistant even to harsh attacks in a network represented by Man-in-the-Middle (MITM) attacks, as long as the user's physical ID is tied to his/her public key appropriately. The performance analysis shows that the proposed scheme is applicable in terms of computation time and storage space.

Keywords: Public key infrastructure · Transaction signature · Digital identity

1 Introduction

Money transfer service is indispensable in our daily lives and also for economic growth. Meanwhile, for providing secure transfer services, financial institutions must meet the high-level security requirements. KYC (Know Your Customer) is the mandatory process of verifying the customer's identity at opening an account and during the service use over time, while the cost is high. According to a Thomson Reuters survey [24], the average cost for a bank to meet the KYC compliance is 60 million U.S. dollars a year, and some banks spend up to 500 million U.S. dollars annually.

This paper then proposes a comprehensive transaction scheme to reduce the KYC costs. Under the proposed scheme, service providers can share the users' identity information with stronger security and also verify the traceability of the transaction data in the long run. The underlying idea of the proposed scheme is that a provider issues a digital certificate of a user's public key. Different providers can confirm the user's identity, only by verifying the validity of the

G.-V. Jourdan et al. (Eds.): FPS 2022, LNCS 13877, pp. 338–354, 2023.
https://doi.org/10.1007/978-3-031-30122-3_21

certificate. Also, the traceability of a transaction data can be attained by its multi-signature between a sender and a receiver. As a result, it leads for providers to reduce their KYC costs.

The contribution of this paper is summarized as follows:

- We newly provide a transaction scheme, sharing individuals' public key as their identity information. A trusted host service provider issues each user's public key certificate after confirming his/her physical ID. When the user opens another account, providers only need to verify the certificate issued by the host provider. This mechanism reduces KYC costs for each provider, possibly resulting in low transaction fee.
- Under the proposed scheme, a transaction is multi-signed by the sender and the receiver, and stored in the host provider's database with the multi-signature. The signed ledger is called as Transaction Signature-based Ledger (TS-L). As a result, the traceability of the transaction data can be assured by its signature verification.
- The security analysis shows that the proposed mechanism is resistant to attacks in a network communication such as Man-in-the-Middle (MITM) attacks, as long as the user's physical ID is tied to his/her generated key pair appropriately. Particularly in remittance, under satisfying the condition, even if losing a secret key, unintended transactions due to its leakage can be traced and canceled with a rationale.
- The performance analysis shows that the scheme is easily applicable in terms of signing and verifying time.

The next section describes the architecture of the proposed scheme. After Sect. 3 presents its security analysis, Sect. 4 offers the performance analysis. Section then 5 provides related works. Lastly, Sect. 6 provides a conclusion.

2   System Architecture

This section describes the transaction scheme on the Transaction Signature-based Ledger (TS-L). A transaction indicates a money transfer between accounts. Also, as a premise, when each user digitally signs, it is assumed that the user possesses a secret key and a public key. The proposed scheme relies on FIDO2 (Fast Identity Online) protocol [1] for creating keys and signing in the user's device.

2.1   Related Parties

As shown in Fig. 1, exhibiting the transaction execution process, there are seven roles: a sender, a receiver, a trusted service provider, an inquirer, a conventional bank, a Time Stamping Authority (TSA), and a Certificate Authority (CA). Hereafter, "a user" indicates an entity who registers for the service, including the sender, the receiver and the inquirer. The user can represent either one individual or one organization. The following describe the parties respectively.

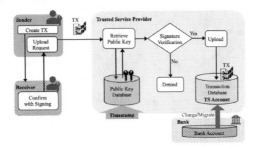

Fig. 1. Overview of the transaction execution process

Sender: An entity who registers for the transaction service, opens the Transaction Signature-based account (TS account), and sends money to a receiver.

Receiver: An entity who registers for the service, opens the TS account, and receives some money from the sender.

Trusted Service Provider: An entity who provides the transaction service, and manages the users' TS accounts. The trusted service provider generates a pair of secret and public keys, and the certificate of the provider's public key is issued by a CA. The provider is "trusted" in terms of verifying transaction signatures and managing databases appropriately. Specifically, the provider notifies administrative authorities of the money transfer business and establishes his/her trust. In a case that the sender and the receiver have opened their accounts under different providers, multiple providers will be involved in the transaction. Here, all of the providers are assumed to be trusted, for example, without considering a case of a collusion with unauthorized recipients to take money from a legitimate sender.

Inquirer: An entity who registers for the service and refers to a user's transaction records. It can be the data owner himself/herself or someone authorized by the data owner.

Conventional Bank: An entity who manages some users' deposits, when this transaction service is about to start. The first step to initiate the transaction service is to inflow money, from existing bank accounts to TS accounts. For this transfer operation, the conventional bank also registers for the service, generating a pair of secret and public keys. Then, the bank as a sender and a user who migrates his/her bank account into his/her TS account, as a receiver, conduct the transaction procedure in the same as a transaction between individual users. When the conventional bank switches to a TS account-based system, the trusted service provider is identical to this conventional bank.

Time Stamping Authority (TSA): An entity who issues timestamps to the users' public keys. A time information affixed to each transaction is also assumed to be conveyed from the TSA to the provider.

Certificate Authority (CA): A trusted party who issues digital certificates for public keys.

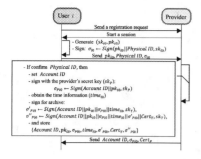

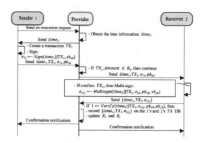

Fig. 2. Service registration protocol

Fig. 3. Transaction execution protocol under identical provider

2.2 Protocol Design

Under the transaction service based on the TS-L, the six operations are prepared. The following subsections explain them.

1) Service Registration: First of all, a provider is assumed to hold a pair of secret and public keys (sk_P, pk_P). A certificate for the provider's public key $(Cert_P)$ is issued by a CA. Also, assume that a channel between the provider and a user is based on a Transport Layer Security (TSL) communication. Any certificate used for the communication is separated from the provider' certificate $(Cert_P)$ and the user's certificate created in the following registration process. As shown in Fig. 2, at the beginning, user i generates a pair of secret and public keys (sk_{i0}, pk_{i0}). The secret key is stored in a secure area in the user's device. The user then prepares his/her physical ID information and takes its photo, converting the physical ID into the digital information. The user also takes his/her profile photo. These digital information for the identity proofing are denoted as $Physical\,ID$ in this model. The method to obtain the $Physical\,ID$ relies on the digital identity guidelines by NIST [11]. For an individual, the $Physical\,ID$ is for example, passport, residence certificate and driver's license. For an organization as the user, it will be some legal documents. One novelty in the proposed scheme is that the user here creates a signature (σ_{i0}) for the $Physical\,ID$ and his/her public key (pk_{i0}). The signing process is based on the FIDO protocol, and assumes that a credential such as biometric information is input to the device. The matching of the credential is confirmed in the device, and the signature is created. The signing on the image of the physical IDs is possible because the image information and the signing process can be handled simultaneously on a device. Note that since the current FIDO protocol does not cover this scheme, for more specific mechanism for signing the image in the device, further analysis is expected. These information $(pk_{i0}, Physical\,ID, \sigma_{i0})$ are then sent to the provider. If the provider confirms the $Physical\,ID$ by image verification processing, first creates the user's account ID $(Account\,ID)$. Specifically, the provider here stores the user's personal information such as his/her address and birthday from the physical ID information, linking them to the $Account\,ID$.

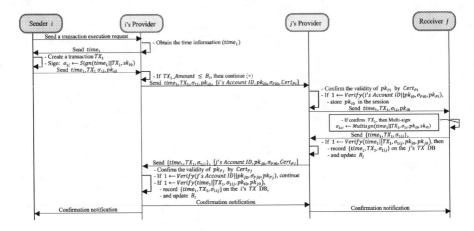

Fig. 4. Transaction execution protocol under different providers

Afterwards, the provider signs the user's public key (pk_{i0}) with the provider's secret key (sk_P), outputting the signature (σ_{Pi0}). This signature is the certificate of the user's public key (pk_{i0}) issued by the provider. The provider then asks its long-time signature to the TSA. The process relies on the long-term signature standard offered by ISO (International Organization for Standardization) [16]. The long-term signature (σ''_{Pi0}) is obtained using the TSA's secret key (sk_T). As a result, the provider stores $\{Account\,ID, pk_{i0}, \sigma_{Pi0}\}$ with its long-term signature in the user's public key database, and notifies the user of $Account\,ID$, σ_{Pi0} and $Cert_P$. Here, the user's public key registration is completed and the TS account is opened. The set of $\{Account\,ID, pk_{i0}, \sigma_{Pi0}, Cert_P\}$ can be used for identity proofing for different providers from this time on. Hereafter, "a host provider" for a user indicates the provider who issues the certificate for the user and records the user's public key updates.

2) Transaction Execution: As a premise, the proposed system does not provide operation of deleting or modifying once recorded transaction data, but only appending operation. The deletion or modification purpose is achieved in cancelling operation described in the following (2.2.3.Transaction Cancellation).

As shown in Fig. 3, consider a case where a sender i transfers money to a receiver j. Both of them are assumed to have opened the TS account under the same provider. After the provider receives a transaction request from the sender i, the provider obtains the time information ($time_1$) from the TSA and sends it to the sender. The sender then creates a transaction, i.e., $TX_1 = \{i'\,Account\,ID, j'\,Account\,ID, Amount\}$. The sender signs the TX_1 using his/her secret key (sk_{i0}), outputting the signature (σ_{1i}). After the provider receives the information ($time_1, TX_1, \sigma_{1i}, pk_{i0}$), first the provider confirms whether the transfer amount (TX_1_Amount) is less than the balance of the i's TS account (B_i). If it is satisfied, the provider sends the information to the receiver. The receiver confirms the content of the transaction and signs

TX_1 with his/her secret key (sk_{j0}), creating the multi-signature (σ_{1ij}). The provider verifies the multi-signature with the sender's and receiver's public keys (pk_{i0}, pk_{j0}), referring their account IDs. If it is successful, the transaction record $\{time_1, TX_1, \sigma_{1ij}\}$ is uploaded on the transaction database of the sender's and the receiver's account. At this time, their balance (B_i, B_j) are also updated. This is the whole process for transaction execution under one provider.

On the other hand, when the sender and receiver have opened the TS account under different providers, additional steps are required. Assume that a channel between the providers relies on a TSL communication. The server certificates used for the communication are separated from the providers' certificates for signing users' public key $(Cert_{Pi}, Cert_{Pj})$. As shown in Fig. 4, after the sender i's provider receives the transaction information from the sender i ((*) in Fig. 4), this time the provider sends the information $(time_1, TX_1, \sigma_{1i}, pk_{i0})$ to the receiver j's provider, adding the validity information about the sender's public key $\{i's\ Account\ ID, pk_{i0}, \sigma_{Pi0}, Cert_{Pi}\}$. The j's provider then confirms the validity of the i's provider's public key (pk_{Pi}) by using its certificate $(Cert_{Pi})$. If it is successful, next the j's provider verifies the signature (σ_{Pi0}) with that i's provider's public key (pk_{Pi}). If it is also successful, the j's provider stores the i's public key (pk_{i0}) during this session. The receiver then confirms the transaction TX_1, and creates the multi-signature (σ_{1ij}). The j's provider verifies it using the sender's and receiver's public key (pk_{i0}, pk_{j0}). The sender's public key is the one stored in the previous step. If it is successful, the j's provider inserts the transaction data $\{time_1, TX_1, \sigma_{1ij}\}$ on the j's transaction database. Afterwards, the i's provider conducts the same procedure as the j's provider did. When all the verification are completed, the transaction data $\{time_1, TX_1, \sigma_{1ij}\}$ is recorded on the i's transaction database Here, the execution process is completed. Although we have shown the two cases regarding whether the sender's and receiver's providers are identical or not, the mechanism does not vary. The transaction is signed with the sender's and receiver's secret keys, and the provider verifies and records it. Under the different providers' case, the additional step is only for the provider to confirm the validity of the user's public key by using the valid host provider's public key.

In the practical use, the first step to activate this system is to transfer money from the conventional bank account to the TS account. The conventional bank is now assumed to be different from the provider, therefore the bank registers for the service and generates the bank's secret and public key. When user i transfers money from the user's bank account to the user's TS account, he/she sends a transfer request to the bank via the provider. According to the request, the bank creates the transaction $TX_B = \{i's\ bank\ Account\ ID, i's\ TS\ Account\ ID, Amount\}$. The bank signs the TX_B with its secret key, creating the signature. When confirming the transfer (TX_B), the user signs with his/her secret key, creating the multi-signature. The multi-signature is verified with the bank's key and user's public key by the provider. If it is successful, the money transfer (TX_B) is executed. The money $Amount$ is subtracted from the i's bank account in the conventional bank system, and the $Amount$ is added to the TS account,

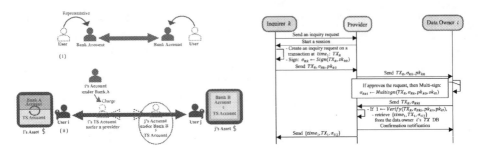

Fig. 5. Implementations of the TS account   **Fig. 6.** Inquiry protocol

with the balance updated. Even when the provider is the conventional bank itself, and the bank migrates the existing system to the TS accounts-based system, the same procedure is conducted. In that case, the bank verifies the transaction which is multi-signed by the bank itself and the user. Figure 5 illustrates example cases to implement the TS accounts. Under (i), the conventional banks take the money transfer service. Under (ii), user i opens a TS account under a provider, totally holding two accounts, an account under the bank A and the TS account. On the other hand, the bank B migrates to the TS-based system, and the user j remains his/her asset under the bank B, while all of the records are stored with the transaction signatures.

3) Transaction Cancellation: If, for some reason, unintended transactions are executed, cancellation is possible by newly creating offset transactions. For example, when cancelling the transaction $TX_1 = \{i's\ Account\ ID, j's\ Account\ ID, \$10\}$, the offset transaction $TX_1' = \{j's\ Account\ ID, i's\ Account\ ID, \$10\}$ is executed. Although the execution procedure is completely identical between the TX_1 and the TX_1', when cancelling related to past transaction records, evidence is required. It is that the past transaction (TX_1) was definitely executed at a certain point.

The provider saves the transaction in the form of $\{time_1, TX_1, \sigma_{1ij}\}$, including the time information $(time_1)$. Additionally, the provider records the history of the user's public keys. From the sender's (receiver's) account ID and the transaction time $(time_1)$, the provider identifies the i's public key at that time as a certain public key (pk_{i0}). The validity of the user's public key is assured by the provider's signature (σ_{Pi0}). Here, the signature is supported by the validity of the provider's public key (pk_P), while the provider's public key is supported by the certificate issued by the CA $(Cert_P)$. Furthermore, since all the users' public keys are stored with archive-stamps and the long-term signatures are updated by the TSA, it is possible to prove the existence of the user's public key for a long time into the future. As a result, using the pointed valid user's public key (pk_{i0}), the fact of the transaction (TX_1) is confirmed, which is described as $(1/\bot) \leftarrow$ **Verify**$(time_1 \| TX_1, \sigma_{1ij}, pk_{i0})$. If it is successful, then the fact is presented that the sender was consent to the transaction (TX_1) at the time $(time_1)$.

The link between the TS account ID and the person in real is tied in the registration process using the physical ID, therefore, the individual's commitment for transactions can be investigated. Moreover, even if the sender's balance at the cancellation time is not enough, the offset amount can be charged with the rationale. In this way, it is shown that the proposed scheme satisfies traceability, accountability and non-repudiation.

4) Records Inquiry: Two types of users can refer the records in the database: the data owner himself/herself, or someone else authorized by the data owner. Referring to Fig. 6, consider that an inquirer k, different from the data owner i, inquires about the i's records. The inquirer request for the transaction of the data owner at a certain time $(time_1)$ is described as $TX_R = \{k's\ Account\ ID, i's\ Account\ ID, time_1\}$. The inquirer signs the request with the inquirer's secret key (sk_{k0}), creating the signature (σ_{Rk}). The information $(TX_R, \sigma_{Rk}, pk_{k0})$ is sent to the data owner via the provider. When confirming the request, the data owner creates the multi-signature (σ_{Rki}). The provider verifies it with the inquirer's and data owner's public key (pk_{k0}, pk_{i0}). If it is successful, the provider retrieves the requested record $\{time_1, TX_1, \sigma_{1ij}\}$ from the data owner's transaction database, and sends it to the inquirer.

Under the case that the inquirer and the data owner are not identical, registering under different providers, then the providers exchange information about the validity of the inquirer's and data owner's public key one another. This is completely the same as it in the transaction execution process in Sect. 2.2. Moreover, when the inquirer is identical to the data owner, a single-signature with the inquirer's secret key is created, instead of a multi-signature.

5) User Side's Key Refreshing: The critical issue of the TS-L scheme is that an attacker obtains a legitimate user's secret key and uploads a false transaction. Note that there is a recovery option by cancellation in case of the leak as described in 2.2.3. When the user notices his/her secret key leakage, he/she conducts this refreshing process at first, and then cancels the unintended transactions. Moreover, as a precaution, it is recommended for each user to refresh the key pair periodically. Here, also in terms of compliance, it is desirable that customer information be kept inspected periodically in addition to the moment of opening accounts. This key exchange is assumed to be done with strict verification of identity, thereby, it is considered that continuous monitoring can be conducted with this. Furthermore, particularly if the user is a company rather than an individual and some periodic legal documents are additionally required, then the submissions can be signed by the host provider and shared with different providers. As for the process, based on Fig. 2 in the registration phase in Sect. 2.2.1, the user generates a new key pair (sk_{i1}, pk_{i1}), and creates a signature (σ_{i1}), given by $\sigma_{i1} \leftarrow \mathbf{Sign}(pk_{i1} || Account\ ID || Physical\ ID, sk_{i1})$. Here, also the user's account ID $(Account\ ID)$ is added in signing. After the set of the information $(pk_{i1}, Account\ ID, Physical\ ID, \sigma_{i1})$ is sent to the provider, the same procedure as the registration phase is conducted. Finally, the user's new public key (pk_{i1}) is registered and the set of its certificate and the provider's public key certificate $(\sigma_{Pi1}, Cert_P)$ is sent to the user. The updated public key (pk_{i1})

is also delivered from the host provider or the user himself/herself to different providers.

6) Provider Side's Public Key Database Validating: The host provider stores the history of the users' public keys with the long-term signatures, so that the transaction traceability, accountability and non-repudiation are satisfied, as described in cancellation process in 2.2.3. Here, the certificates in the archive timestamps attached to all public keys expire at some point in time, requiring to update them. The providers then ask the TSA to renew all the certificates at the expiration time. A new certificate is attached and a new signature is created, and they are stored affixed to each public key information. The storage size for the public key updates is provided in Sect. 4.

2.3 Identity Proof Sharing and Paths for Reducing KYC Costs

In addition to the purpose of ensuring the transaction traceability, the user's public key information dedicates to share his/her identity information among different service providers. Once a trusted host provider confirms user i's identity using his/her physical ID, then the information $\{Account\,ID, pk_i, \sigma_{Pi0}, Cert_P\}$ can be shared. When the user opens another TS account under a different provider, the provider first checks the validity of the host provider's public key (pk_P) using its certificate ($Cert_P$). Afterwards, the provider verifies the signature (σ_{Pi0}) using the confirmed host provider's public key (pk_P), described as $(1/\bot) \leftarrow$ **Verify**($Account\,ID\|pk_{i0}, \sigma_{Pi0}, pk_P$). Note that the validity period of the provider's public key (pk_P) is longer than the validity period of the user's public key (pk_{i0}), recommending each user to refresh his/her key as a precaution for its loss and also for periodical monitoring checks. In this way, the user's public key information can be shared among different providers based on the trust to the host provider. This leads to save the different providers' KYC costs. When the different provider from the host provider starts the service, the legitimacy of the registration request is verified, only by verifying the user's public key and an affixed signature on the request. Unlike the other conventional authentication methods such as passwords, the different providers can verify requests directly with a public key as a credential.

3 Security Analysis

The security goal of the TS-L is to achieve data integrity in the sense that the transaction is intended for the sender and the receiver of the money. This section describes the possible vulnerabilities to break the integrity and the corresponding countermeasure. We consider four places: a channel between a user and a provider, the user side, the provider side, and a channel between the providers.

1) Channel between the User and the Service Provider: While the channel between the user and the provider implements the TSL communication, there is a possibility of MITM (Man-in-the-Middle) attacks, in which an attacker positioned between two communicating parties intercepts or alters data traveling between them [6,11]. The attacker replaces an original server certificate with a modified certificate. If the user neglects a warning notification from a browser and inputs the required information for remittances, then the attacker can execute fraudulent money transfers using the legitimate user's account. Under the proposed scheme, transaction signatures are created in the user's device. Therefore, even if the attacker rewrites the transaction contents on the communication channel, the provider can detect the tampering in verifying the signature. This is the primary advantage of using transaction signatures. The signing is completed in the user's device with a credential such as biometric information and the credential is kept in the device, enabling to be resistant to the attacks arising in a network. Multi-signatures are used not only in transaction execution but also in inquiry. This is for the purpose of maintaining the message integrity of all the requests in the network. Since all networks are insecure, regardless of whether it is inside or outside an organization network, data is signed within individual devices and sent to a recipient. In other words, the zero trust [25] is assumed here. Since the transaction signatures inherently contributes to security in these attacks in the network, some methods were proposed. For example, IBM Zurich Research Laboratory invented a token-based transaction signature for online banking [34]. However, as a whole, these specialized devices take costs to prepare, becoming an obstacle to implement them [9]. A feature of the proposed method is that it assumes authentication with familiar devices such as smartphones and PCs, without preparing additional devices, dedicating for the provider's efficiency.

2) User Side: In the current FIDO authentication scheme, a mis-binding attack has been pointed out [12,14]. In a registration phase, attackers register their own device linking a legitimate user name, indicating that the attackers' public key is registered to the application provider. Communication within modules in a device is not authenticated for one another, allowing malware to perform unauthorized operations. For this attack, the proposed method requires the signature information of the physical ID at the registration. Therefore, unless the attacker obtains the image of the legitimate physical ID, the provider detects the fraud, and the attacker fails to register by impersonating the legitimate user. Ultimately, under the assumption that providers are trusted, the most serious problem is that the image of the physical ID is forged by the attacker. If the image of the digitized physical ID of the sender is forged and the receiver's physical ID is correctly submitted, it can be canceled by the cancellation process. However, if the digitized physical IDs for both the sender and the receiver are forged and the attacker's public keys are registered to the host provider, then the fraudulent transaction cannot be canceled, although it would be difficult for the attacker to succeed it. When the fraudulent transaction amount is converted to cash, the legitimate sender would lose the money. In order to prevent this physical ID forgery attack, it is recommended, for example, to improve the accuracy of image verification.

The following attacks might be successful. However, ultimately cancellations work for the attacks, as long as the linkage between a physical ID and a public key for the receiver is appropriately tied. A straightforward attack is that credentials used for signing such as biometric information and PIN codes, are stolen. However, even if these credentials are forged, fraudulent requests can be cancelled if the linkage between a public key and a physical ID is properly linked. Under MITB (Man-in-the-Browser) attacks, a malware infects the web browser. An attacker eavesdrops and alters the transaction content between the web browser and the web server, and executes unintended requests. Zbot is a representative malware, first identified in 2007 [33]. While the MITB attack is basically difficult to be observed and unsolvable, the proposed transaction scheme is resistant to this MITB attack. The current FIDO protocol defines the software module to create the signature called authenticator. The transaction signature is created in that authenticator, then the required signed information is passed from it to the browser. Therefore, even if a fraudulent transaction is created in a malicious browser, the legitimate signature cannot be created in the legitimate authenticator, enabling to be detected in the provider's signature verification. However, once if several parts in the device are infected with malware, unintended transactions can be successfully verified by providers. Under a clickjacking attack, a malicious software presents a false display and executes unintended transaction operation [13,15,23]. In this case, the legitimate user signs the fraudulent transaction with his/her own secret key, without being aware of it. The provider then approves the transaction. Note that the false transaction can be cancelled later. Specifically, a parallel session attack in software modules within a device supports the successful attack. Under the parallel session attack, a malicious software module exists between legitimate modules [12,14]. The attacker sends a request again and obtains random values generated for each session, leading the successful attack. A DoS (Denial of Service attack) attack is another possible attack [12]. A malicious software present in the device can halt transaction executions. Although these malware are difficult to be implemented, improvements in the protocol are expected. For example, it is recommended to authenticate each software module in the user's device for each session.

3) Provider Side: For appropriate transaction executions, the provider has mainly four roles under assuming that the provider is trusted. First, the provider surely confirms the authenticity of a person in real with his/her physical ID in the registration phase. The requirement of the physical ID in the account opening process will determine the level of security of the service. Second, when executing transactions, the provider properly verifies the transaction signature sent by the user and records it on the database. The provider prepares the control devices in a secure place, as well as appropriate allocation of its security managers within an organization. Third, the provider properly manages databases, i.e., the account information database, the transaction database, and the public key database. Against malfunction, cyber attacks, and natural disaster, the databases are located in multiple places, and hold both online and offline back-up options for one another. Note that it does not imply that each user has the

Table 1. Parameters for Performance Analysis

Notation	Description	Benchmark
T_R	The average period for refreshing a user's key pair	-
T_E	The average validity period of certificates for long-term signatures ($Cert_T$)	10 [years] [10]
T_{TX}	The average frequency for executing a transaction	-
T	Arbitrary time	-
n_{pk}	The number of bits for a public key (pk)	96 [bytes] [4]
n_{sig}	The number of bits for a signature (σ)	48 [bytes] [4]
n_{id}	The number of bits for an account ID	80 [bits] [32]
n_{time}	The number of bits for a time information ($time$)	48 [bits] [2]
n_{TX}	The number of bits for a transaction (TX)	-
n_{cer}	The number of bits for a certificate ($Cert$)	1500 [bytes] [19]

databases, rather each host provider is responsible for the users in charge. For efficient resource management, the provider can deposit all of the data to a cloud, by encrypting with the provider's encryption key if it needs. Current cloud services have these security options [18]. Lastly, the provider keeps the provider's secret key securely. The secret key is used for signing the user's public key information. Originally, public key certificates are issued by CAs under strict security, while in the proposed framework, each provider takes its role for the users. The provider is therefore, assumed to own a HSM (Hardware Security Module). It is a hardware that securely stores keys and computes digital signatures. Similar to the conventional requirements for financial industries and government agencies, it is assumed to satisfy the requirements of FIPS 140-3 level 3, defined by FIPS (Federal Information Processing Standard) [8].

4) Channel between the Providers: The communication between the trusted providers is based on the TLS communication. They confirm the trust by verifying the public key certificates for one another. Furthermore, the host provider's registration requirements reflect to the following provider's trust, when the providers share the identity proofing with the user's public key. Therefore, each provider checks the other provider's requirements, so that they can attain their desired security level.

4 Performance Analysis

This section presents a computational evaluation for the TS-L. As a multi-signature schemes, BLS signature [3,5] is implemented. Its signature size is 48 bytes, indicating the BLS signature attains smaller in size [35]. Under the proposed scheme, all of the data is signed and stored with the signature. Prioritizing the storage size of the provider to manage the information, the BLS signature is here adopted. The public key size is 96 bytes referred to [4]. SHA-256 is assumed for the hash function. The execution time is measured on Apple M1 CPU with

Table 2. storage size of the transaction database for a user

Frequency	Data Size	Time-span		
T_{TX}	n_{TX}	10 years	50 years	90 years
5 times per a day	128 [B]	4 [MB]	18 [MB]	32 [MB]
	1 [MB]	18 [GB]	91 [GB]	164 [GB]
once per a month	128 [B]	23 [KB]	115 [KB]	207 [KB]
	1 [MB]	120 [MB]	600 [MB]	1080 [MB]

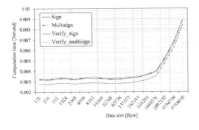

Fig. 7. Computation time for signing and verifying [second]

Fig. 8. Storage size of a user's public key database at time T [byte]

8 GB memory, and PBC library is used. The results are the average of the 100 times simulations. Table 1 summarizes the parameters for the model.

The user side's cost is considered as the signing time in uploading transactions (data items) or in requesting an inquiry. Figure 7 shows the computation time for them given a data size. Since it does not take much time to create an aggregate signature, the difference between **Sign** and **Multisign** is small. In executing a transaction, the transaction data size can be around 128 or 256 bytes, implying to take approximately 0.003 s. The result shows that the signing operation of each user is light for regular data size.

For the service provider, we analyze the verification time for signatures, the storage size of transactions (data items), and the storage size of users' public keys. Figure 7 shows the computation time for the verifying operation for a single-signature and for a multi-signature. Similar to the signing cost, the verification time is around 0.003 s and starts increasing from approximately 2 MB. For more frequent transaction operations, the verification time is simply increasing. However, the goal of the TS-L is to share KYC information, and it is assumed that there exist multiple providers. Consequently, the transaction verification will not be concentrated on one provider, resulting in a feasible verification time for a provider.

The storage size of the transaction database at time T for a user is defined as $S_{(TX,T)} = \frac{T}{T_{TX}} \cdot (n_{\mathrm{id}} + n_{\mathrm{time}} + n_{TX} + n_{\mathrm{sig}})$. Table 2 describes the examples of the storage size for a user. Even if frequent transactions are stored for a long time, the storage size is feasible.

The storage size of a user's public keys managed by the provider at time T is describes as $S_{(pk,T)} = \frac{T_E}{T_R} \cdot \left(\frac{T}{T_E} \cdot (n_{id} + n_{time} + n_{pk} + 2n_{sig} + n_{cer}) + \left(\sum_{i=1}^{\frac{T}{T_E}} i \right) \cdot (n_{cer} + n_{sig}) \right)$. The number of renewal time is simply determined by the average validity period of certificates for long-term signatures (T_E). At a renewal time, the storage size for a new certificate and a signature is added by $(n_{cer} + n_{sig})$ bits. Figure 8 describes the required size given a time. For example, when the user refreshes his/her key once per a year, it takes approximately 300 KB in 50 years. Even if it is 100 years, the size is around 1 MB. In the case of less frequent refreshing such as once per 2 years or 3 years, it requires much smaller. Note that as for the computation time for validating the certificates on the user's public key, the TSA needs to update certificates on long-term signature with signing by 10 years. Overall, the result shows that the public key updating mechanism is easily applicable to the providers.

5 Related Literature

Role-based access control using digital certificates was described in multiple works [7,29,30]. Digital certificates link to device IDs and they are used for controlling access to network resources. Comparing with them, the proposed scheme directly ties the digital certificate and the individuals' identity.

Regarding signed data, some literature proposed methods to deposit signed data in the cloud [17,28,32]. They assumed that the cloud is an untrustworthy entity, therefore the data owners check its integrity by verifying the digital signature on the retrieved data by themselves. In particular, [32] assumed financial and medical database, and adopts multi-signatures by multiple data owners. Since the proposed method assumes the trusted provider, the signature is used only to verify the validity of the data. As an extension, these methods will be incorporated if individuals desire to verify the integrity by themselves. In the other direction, under assuming a trusted verifier, the importance of determining database access policies based on signature verification was mentioned in [31], while any specific method was not provided.

Transaction signatures have been implemented in a wide variety of blockchain-based transaction schemes [21,22,27]. Particularly, Bitcoin [22] is a well-know payment scheme. While both the TS-L and the blockchain-based upload data after verifying the transaction signature, these systems do not assume a trusted central administrator of the system. Since the proposed scheme prioritizes the user authenticity tied to the physical person, over the other information security properties such as confidentiality and privacy, the trusted provider is assumed. For the other directions of blockchain, a permissioned scheme with trusted participants was suggested [26]. As for database resources, under the system, the database is shared among multiple network participants in an attempt to prevent a single point of failure. On the other hand, under the proposed scheme, the host provider who manages the user's public key information and issues certificates, is responsible for managing the databases, holding backup functions. If it is inefficient to prepare the database resources on-premise, a cloud database can be chosen. The current cloud services can meet appropriate security standards, taking measures to prevent failures. For data privacy, the host provider can encrypt data and deposit it in the cloud. Regarding the integrity of the database, it is an extension of the proposed scheme to detect anomalies using a Merkle tree [20], as the blockchain scheme implements. However, the computational complexity needs to be examined. Overall, the proposed method focuses more on the message integrity of transmission channels in a network space, rather than the database integrity of start and end-points of the communications.

6   Conclusion

This paper proposes a comprehensive transaction scheme to reduce the KYC costs, by sharing customers' information among multiple providers. For further research, for example, improvements in detailed signature schemes to attain lighter computation complexity or additional verification features are expected. In addition, since the linkage between physical IDs and public keys is critical under this scheme, further analysis on that point is necessary.

References

1. World Wide Web Consortium, Web authentication: An API for accessing public key credentials level 2. https://www.w3.org/tr/webauthn/ (2021)
2. Adams, C., Cain, P., Pinkas, D., Zuccherato, R.: Rfc 3161: Internet x. 509 public key infrastructure time-stamp protocol (tsp) (2001)
3. Boneh, D., Drijvers, M., Neven, G.: Compact multi-signatures for smaller blockchains. In: Peyrin, T., Galbraith, S. (eds.) ASIACRYPT 2018. LNCS, vol. 11273, pp. 435–464. Springer, Cham (2018). https://doi.org/10.1007/978-3-030-03329-3_15
4. Boneh, D., Gorbunov, S., Wahby, R.S., Wee, H., Zhang, Z.: BLS Signatures. Internet-Draft draft-irtf-cfrg-bls-signature-04, Internet Engineering Task Force (2020). https://datatracker.ietf.org/doc/html/draft-irtf-cfrg-bls-signature-04
5. Boneh, D., Lynn, B., Shacham, H.: Short signatures from the weil pairing. In: Boyd, C. (ed.) ASIACRYPT 2001. LNCS, vol. 2248, pp. 514–532. Springer, Heidelberg (2001). https://doi.org/10.1007/3-540-45682-1_30
6. Callegati, F., Cerroni, W., Ramilli, M.: Man-in-the-middle attack to the https protocol. IEEE Secur. Priv. **7**(1), 78–81 (2009)
7. Chadwick, D., Otenko, A., Ball, E.: Role-based access control with x. 509 attribute certificates. IEEE Internet Comput. **7**(2), 62–69 (2003)
8. Cooper, M.J., Schaffer, K.B., et al.: Security requirements for cryptographic modules (2019)
9. Delgado, O., Fúster Sabater, A., Sierra, J.: Analysis of new threats to online banking authentication schemes (2008)
10. DigiCert, I.: Certificate policy version 5.5 (2011)
11. DRAFT NIST: Special publication 800–63-3. Digital Identity Guidelines (2017)
12. Feng, H., Li, H., Pan, X., Zhao, Z.: A formal analysis of the FIDO UAF protocol. In: Proceedings of 28th Network and Distributed System Security Symposium (NDSS) (2021)

13. Fratantonio, Y., Qian, C., Chung, S.P., Lee, W.: Cloak and dagger: from two permissions to complete control of the UI feedback loop. In: 2017 IEEE Symposium on Security and Privacy (SP), pp. 1041–1057. IEEE (2017)

14. Hu, K., Zhang, Z.: Security analysis of an attractive online authentication standard: FIDO UAF protocol. China Commun. **13**(12), 189–198 (2016)

15. Huang, L.S., Moshchuk, A., Wang, H.J., Schecter, S., Jackson, C.: Clickjacking: Attacks and defenses. In: 21st {USENIX} Security Symposium ({USENIX} Security 12), pp. 413–428 (2012)

16. ISO: ISO 14533–2:2021 processes, data elements and documents in commerce, industry and administration - long term signature - part 2: Profiles for xml advanced electronic signatures (xades) (2021)

17. Juels, A., Kaliski Jr, B.S.: Pors: proofs of retrievability for large files. In: Proceedings of the 14th ACM Conference on Computer and Communications Security, pp. 584–597 (2007)

18. Mathew, S.: Overview of amazon web services: AWS whitepaper. Amazon Web Services, Seattle, WA, USA, White Paper (2020)

19. McGrew, D., Pritikin. M.: The compressed x.509 certificate format draft-pritikin-comp-x509-00 (2010)

20. Merkle, R.C.: A certified digital signature. In: Brassard, G. (ed.) CRYPTO 1989. LNCS, vol. 435, pp. 218–238. Springer, New York (1990). https://doi.org/10.1007/0-387-34805-0_21

21. Miller, A., Juels, A., Shi, E., Parno, B., Katz, J.: Permacoin: repurposing bitcoin work for data preservation. In: 2014 IEEE Symposium on Security and Privacy, pp. 475–490. IEEE (2014)

22. Nakamoto, S.: Bitcoin: a peer-to-peer electronic cash system. Decentralized Bus. Rev. 21260 (2008)

23. Niemietz, M., Schwenk, J.: Ui redressing attacks on android devices. Black Hat Abu Dhabi (2012)

24. Reuters, T.: Thomson reuters 2016 know your customer surveys reveal escalating costs and complexity. Thomson Reuters **9**, 06–20 (2016)

25. Rose, S., Borchert, O., Mitchell, S., Connelly, S.: Zero trust architecture (2nd draft). Technical report, National Institute of Standards and Technology (2020)

26. Sajana, P., Sindhu, M., Sethumadhavan, M.: On blockchain applications: hyperledger fabric and ethereum. Int. J. Pure Appl. Math. **118**(18), 2965–2970 (2018)

27. Sasson, E.B., et al.: Zerocash: decentralized anonymous payments from bitcoin. In: 2014 IEEE Symposium on Security and Privacy, pp. 459–474. IEEE (2014)

28. Shacham, H., Waters, B.: Compact proofs of retrievability. In: Pieprzyk, J. (ed.) ASIACRYPT 2008. LNCS, vol. 5350, pp. 90–107. Springer, Heidelberg (2008). https://doi.org/10.1007/978-3-540-89255-7_7

29. Silva, E.F., Muchaluat-Saade, D.C., Fernandes, N.C.: Across: a generic framework for attribute-based access control with distributed policies for virtual organizations. Futur. Gener. Comput. Syst. **78**, 1–17 (2018)

30. Thompson, M., Johnston, W., Mudumbai, S., Hoo, G., Jackson, K., Essiari, A.: Certificate-basedaccesscontrol forwidelydistributedr esources. In: Proceedings 8th UsenixSecurity Symposium (1999)

31. Vegh, L., Miclea, L.: Access control in cyber-physical systems using steganography and digital signatures. In: 2015 IEEE International Conference on Industrial Technology (ICIT), pp. 1504–1509. IEEE (2015)

32. Wang, B., Li, H., Liu, X., Li, F., Li, X.: Efficient public verification on the integrity of multi-owner data in the cloud. J. Commun. Netw. **16**(6), 592–599 (2014)

33. Wazid, M., Zeadally, S., Das, A.K.: Mobile banking: evolution and threats: malware threats and security solutions. IEEE Consum. Electron. Mag. **8**(2), 56–60 (2019)

34. Weigold, T., Kramp, T., Hermann, R., Höring, F., Buhler, P., Baentsch, M.: The zurich trusted information channel – an efficient defence against man-in-the-middle and malicious software attacks. In: Lipp, P., Sadeghi, A.-R., Koch, K.-M. (eds.) Trust 2008. LNCS, vol. 4968, pp. 75–91. Springer, Heidelberg (2008). https://doi. org/10.1007/978-3-540-68979-9_6

35. Xiao, Y., Zhang, P., Liu, Y.: Secure and efficient multi-signature schemes for fabric: an enterprise blockchain platform. IEEE Trans. Inf. Forensics Secur. **16**, 1782–1794 (2020)

A Decentralized Mnemonic Backup System for Non-custodial Cryptocurrency Wallets

Thierry Sans[1,2]([envelope]), Ziming Liu[2], and Kevin Oh[2]

[1] University of Toronto Scarborough, Toronto, Canada
thierry.sans@utoronto.ca
[2] PriFi Labs Inc., Toronto, Canada
{david.liu,kevin.oh}@prifilabs.com

Abstract. When using non-custodial cryptocurrency wallets such as Exodus (Bitcoin), Metamask (Ethereum), and Keplr (Osmosis), the private keys are directly stored on the user's device. Using such a wallet comes with the risk of losing all crypto assets when the device gets lost, stolen, or breaks down irremediably. Fortunately, most non-custodial wallets offer a way to recover the private keys by the mean of a "recovery phrase" also known as a "mnemonic seed phrase". That phrase is usually between 12 and 24 words and it is generated when the user creates the wallet. Indeed, this mnemonic phrase is a really sensitive piece of information since anyone knowing that phrase can get full control of the crypto assets held by the wallet. Usually, it is recommended to write this passphrase down on a piece of paper and store it in a "safe place". However, storing a physical object is still not ideal since it can get stolen, lost, or destroyed as well. In this paper, we propose a decentralized application that can be used to back up mnemonic phrases and recover them eventually using a simple email. This application is built on a privacy-preserving blockchain to store the confidential passphrase and protect the identity of its owner and the crypto assets holders.

Keywords: Blockchain · Smart Contracts · Decentralized Applications · Privacy · Wallets · Cryptography Protocol

1 Introduction

In the world of cryptocurrency, a *wallet* provides users with an interface to manage their crypto assets. Under the hood, those wallets store a set of private keys and use them to sign transactions. There are two types of wallets: "custodial wallets" in which the private keys are in the custody of a trusted third party and "non-custodial wallets" in which the private keys are directly stored on the user's device whether it is a computer, a mobile phone or a dedicated USB dongle. Using either of these types of wallets comes with inherent risks [1]. Using custodial wallets comes with the risk of losing all crypto assets when the trusted

G.-V. Jourdan et al. (Eds.): FPS 2022, LNCS 13877, pp. 355–370, 2023.
https://doi.org/10.1007/978-3-031-30122-3_22

entity goes bankrupt[1] and non-custodial wallets come with the risk of losing all crypto assets if the device gets lost, stolen, or irremediably breaks down.

Yet, non-custodial wallets (our focus here) such as Exodus (Bitcoin), Metamask (Ethereum), and Keplr (Secret Network) offer a way to recover the private keys through the mean of a "recovery phrase" also known as "mnemonic seed phrase". That phrase is usually between 12 and 24 words and it is generated when the user creates the wallet. Here is an example of such a phrase:

```
witch fox practice feed shame open
despair creek road again ice least
```

That phrase is important as it is used to generate the same private keys on demand (BIP39 standard [16]). It can be used as a backup or to import the wallet into a new device. Indeed, this mnemonic phrase is a really sensitive piece of information. Anyone who has access to this phrase would have full control over the crypto assets as explained in the *Metamask* Wallet FAQ page:

> *"MetaMask requires that you store your Secret Recovery Phrase in a safe place. It is the only way to recover your funds should your device crash or your browser reset. We recommend you to write it down. The most common method is to write your 12-word phrase on a piece of paper and store it safely in a place where only you have access. Note: if you lose your Secret Recovery Phrase, MetaMask can't help you recover your wallet. Never give your Secret Recovery Phrase or your private key(s) to anyone or any site, unless you want them to have full control over your funds."*

As written above, users are not supposed to remember that phrase like a password but instead write it down on a piece of paper and store it in a "safe place". However, storing physical objects is still not ideal since they can get stolen, lost, or destroyed as well. As a consequence, users do not always follow such a recommendation and put themselves at risk as studied in [19]. So, as an alternative, could we design a simple application that would take custody of that passphrase and would allow users to recover it based on some sort of authentication? Intuitively, that application could be something similar to a password manager but such a solution requires 1) that the service provider is trustworthy and 2) that the whole application is secured [10]. Moreover, a password manager is a centralized solution that goes against the idea of decentralized applications [4,5].

In this paper, we propose a decentralized application that can be used to back up mnemonic phrases protected with a new type of crypto asset, that we call a *Passphrase Lock*, that will be distributed to other users. When it is time to recover these mnemonic keys, the user can unlock the passphrase using a simple email. This application is built on a privacy-preserving blockchain [21] to store the confidential passphrase and protect the address of the Passphrase Lock holders. To better explain our idea, we will go through 3 iterations each more

---

[1] As popularized by the mantra from *Andreas Antonopoulos*: *"Not Your Keys, not Your Coins"*.

secure than the previous one. In the first iteration (Sect. 3), we aim at capturing the user experience but its overall design is rather naive and not secure. The attacker can retrieve the passphrase by stealing the user's wallet that was used for backing up the passphrase or by breaching the user's email. We fix those two shortcomings in the second iteration by introducing the concept of *Passphrase Lock* and by adding a second layer of encryption to ensure *perfect forward secrecy*. Finally, in the third iteration (Sect. 5), we improve the reliability by distributing the Passphrase Lock to multiple users and recovering the passphrase with only a subset of these users.

2   Background

Our Mnemonic Backup System is a decentralized application developed and deployed on a privacy-preserving blockchain called *Secret Network* [21]. Secret Network Smart Contracts enable storing and processing of private data directly on the blockchain. It relies on the Intel SGX (Software Guard Extension) Trusted Execution Environment (a.k.a Confidential Computing) [11] to prevent nodes from reading private data directly from memory during execution. To make sure that nodes protect data during transit, processing, and at rest on the blockchain, each node joining the network has to go through a bootstrap process as explained in [14]:

> *"Before the genesis of a new chain, there must be a bootstrap node to generate network-wide secrets that will empower all the privacy features of the Secret Network chain. When the first node joined the Secret Network, it went through a three-step process. First, the enclave of the bootstrap node generated a remote attestation proof to prove the TEE is genuine. Next, the node generated a random 256-bit number known as the consensus seed. The consensus seed is the most critical part of the Secret Network encryption schema as all other keys and therefore functionality of the protocol are contingent upon secure distribution of this originally generated consensus seed. Using HKDF-SHA256 the consensus seed, in combination with other context-relevant data, derived private keys for the process of registering a new node, I/O encryption, and state encryption. New nodes also use HKDF-SHA256 for key derivation using the original seed or second-generation seeds. Next, the consensus seed is sealed to the disk of the bootstrap node. Finally, the remote attestation proof, the public key for the consensus seed exchange, and the public key for the consensus I/O exchange are all published to the Secret Network genesis.json. Curve25519 is the elliptic curve used for asymmetric key generation and ECDH (x25519) is used for deriving symmetric encryption keys which are used to encrypt data with AES-128-SIV."*

In the remaining of the paper, we assume that an attacker cannot retrieve data during transport and execution without having the user's private key that was used to encrypt those messages. Moreover, we assume that the attacker cannot decrypt the data stored on the blockchain without getting the node consensus seed sealed with the Intel SGX. That said, it is good to acknowledge that several attacks against Intel SGX have been published in the past few years [3,7,13,15] but those vulnerabilities have been mitigated by Secret Network.

3   Iteration 1: The User Experience

Alice is a blockchain user that holds crypto assets in her wallet. She would like to have an online backup of her wallet's passphrase in case her device gets lost, stolen, or breaks down irremediably. When that doomsday comes, she would like to recover her passphrase using her email. In our first iteration, the user experience is rather simple:

– **When Alice wants to back up a passphrase**, she visits our Mnemonic Backup website and enters her email. After submitting her information, our application sends her an email with a confirmation code that she must copy onto the webpage along with her passphrase to finalize the backup process.
– **When Alice wants to recover a passphrase**, she visits our Mnemonic Backup website and enters her email. Our application sends her an email with a verification code that she must copy onto the webpage before getting her passphrase back.

This user experience is similar to existing security mechanisms used in traditional web applications where we must make sure that the user is the legitimate owner of the email address used for signing up, signing in (with two-factor authentication enabled), or resetting a password.

3.1   Architecture

For this first iteration, we implement our Mnemonic Backup System as a smart contract on the Secret Network that records the passphrase when backing up and restores that passphrase when recovering. However, our secret contract cannot send emails by itself, so we are pairing it with an off-chain Mailer Backend that sends emails to users. So, there are three entities in our system:

– **The Frontend Client** is the javascript code running in Alice's web browser that allows to back up and recover passphrases.
– **The Backup Contract** is the smart contract that stores users' email and passphrases. The Backup Contract is stored on the blockchain and is executed by one of the Secret Network nodes. The Frontend Client interacts with the Backup Contract by sending messages to one of the Secret Network nodes directly.

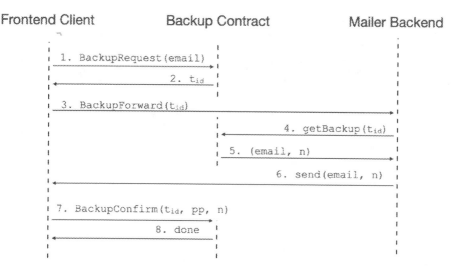

Fig. 1. Iteration 1 - Backup

- **The Mailer Backend** is the off-chain server that sends confirmation/verification codes to users by email. For security reasons, the mailer backend never handles the passphrase. The passphrase is always sent back and forth between Frontend Client (running in the browser) and the Backup Contract (running on the Secret Network)

3.2 The Protocol

For backup (see Fig. 1), the goal is to verify Alice's email address to eventually store her passphrase.

1. When Alice wants to back up her passphrase, she creates a throwaway wallet (different than the one she wants to back up), provision it, and visits the backup page of the Mnemonic Backup Website. Then, she enters her email and presses the submit button. A script running inside the webpage, called Frontend Client, is executed. The Frontend Client sends a transaction BackupRequest(*email*) to the Secret Network where a node executes the request using the Backup Contract code.
2. The Backup Contract generates a transaction id t_{id}, a random confirmation code n, stores the record $(t_{id}, email, n)$ in the backup dataset, and returns the transaction id to Alice.
3. The Frontend Client forwards the transaction id to the Mailer Backend.
4. The Mailer Backend queries the Backup Contract using that transaction id.
5. The Backup Contract returns the email and confirmation code n associated to the transaction id.
6. The Mailer Backend sends the confirmation code to Alice by email.

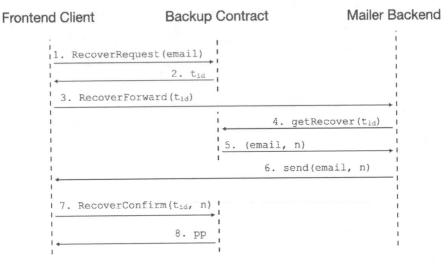

Fig. 2. Iteration 1 - Recovery

7. Alice opens her email and copies and pastes the confirmation code into her browser, and enters her passphrase pp. The Frontend Client sends a transaction BackupConfirm($email, pp, n$) to the Backup Contract.
8. The Backup Contract verifies the code and stores the record ($email, pp$) in the `passphrase` dataset.

For recovery (see Fig. 2), the goal is to verify Alice's email address to eventually, send her passphrase back.

1. When Alice wants to recover her passphrase, she creates yet another throwaway wallet (different than the ones she used for backup), provision it, visits the recovery page of the Mnemonic Backup Website and enter her *email*. The Frontend Client (running in the browser) sends a transaction RecoverRequest(*email*) to the Backup Contract (running on the Secret Network).
2. The Backup Contract generates a transaction id t_{id}, a random confirmation code, stores the record ($t_{id}, email, n$) in the `recover` dataset, and returns the transaction id to Alice.
3. The Frontend Client forwards the transaction id to the Mailer Backend.
4. The Mailer Backend queries the Backup Contract using that transaction id.
5. The Backup Contract returns the email and confirmation code n associated to the transaction id.
6. The Mailer Backend sends the confirmation code to Alice by email.
7. Alice opens her email and copies and pastes that verification code into her browser. The Frontend Client sends a query RecoverConfirm(*email, n*) to the Backup Contract.

8. The Backup Contract verifies the verification code, retrieves the corresponding record from the `passphrase` dataset, and returns the passphrase.

3.3   Security Analysis

There are two main security concerns in this first design. First, if the attacker breaches into Alice's mailbox or the Mailer Backend directly, he could retrieve the confirmation code. During the backup phase, the attacker could use the confirmation code to upload an arbitrary passphrase for Alice. This is a problem if Alice recovers what she believes is her original passphrase but another that the attacker can access. Then, any new asset that Alice puts in her wallet can be stolen by the attacker from now. During the recovery phase, it is even worst since the attacker could trigger and use the verification code to query the Backup Contract directly and get the passphrase back.

Secondly, if the attacker steals any of the private keys that Alice used for backing up or recovering her passphrase, he could recover the passphrase from the messages. As mentioned earlier, it is recommended that Alice use distinct throwaway wallets when backing up or recovering her passphrase. However, if the attacker steals any of these wallets afterward, he could decrypt the messages stored on the blockchain and recover Alice's passphrase. Said differently, the problem is that our protocol does not ensure the cryptographic property of *perfect forward secrecy* [8].

4   Iteration 2: Security Hardening

Our first iteration captures the right user experience but fails in terms of security. Two main security threats need to be addressed: 1) prevent the attacker from taking advantage of having access to emails and 2) prevent the attacker from recovering passphrases from compromised wallets. We are solving those two problems by introducing a second authentication factor and a second-layer of encryption.

4.1   A *Passphrase Lock* as a Second Authentication Factor

The first security problem is an authentication problem. Relying solely on emails to authenticate Alice is insecure if we assume that the attacker could breach Alice's mailbox, or worse, into the Mailer Backend directly. One way to prevent that is to add a second authentication factor, but this time, we want to rely on the blockchain directly. The idea is for Alice to create a crypto asset called a *Passphrase Lock* during backup and transfer that asset to her friend Charlie that will hold that lock. When doomsday comes, Alice should first ask Charlie to transfer the Passphrase Lock back to her before recovering the passphrase.

This Passphrase Lock is designed as a crypto asset that Charlie holds in his wallet before eventually transferring it back to Alice's recovery wallet when she needs it. This Passphrase Lock is similar to the concept of NFT [20] but different in its conception. First, Charlie cannot retrieve Alice's passphrase even if he holds that lock. Moreover, Charlie cannot transfer that crypto asset arbitrarily either. He can only transfer it back to its original owner, Alice, or to any other designated owner approved by Alice.

Going back to our original problem, we assume that the attacker can breach Alice's email. However, he would not be able to recover the passphrase without retrieving the Passphrase Lock in his wallet first. In addition, the attacker would not even know who holds Alice's Passphrase Lock since that information is encrypted in the Backup Contract. This is similar to the concept of confidential ownership introduced by Secret Network NFTs in which the owner's address is confidential contrary to other blockchain NFTs.

4.2   A Second-Layer Encryption for Perfect Forward Secrecy

The second security problem comes from the fact that messages sent back and forth between the Frontend Client and the Backup Contract are stored on the blockchain permanently. Unfortunately, these messages can be decrypted afterward by anyone holding the private key that was used to send those messages. This problem can be fixed by adding a second layer of encryption by establishing a session key between the Frontend Client and the Backup contract to encrypt sensitive information sent back and forth. The idea is to use the *Diffie-Hellman Key Exchange* protocol to agree on the session key without sharing it explicitly and so preventing it from being stored on the blockchain. That session key is meant to be forgotten as soon as the backup or recovery process is done.

The *Diffie-Hellman Key Exchange* protocol is a cryptography protocol that allows two parties, usually named Alice and Bob, that have no prior knowledge of each other, to securely agree on a shared key over an insecure channel [6]. That channel is considered as insecure because we assume that an attacker can eavesdrop on the communication and read all messages sent back and forth between Alice and Bob[2]. In a nutshell, Alice generates an asymmetric key pair (sec_A, pub_A) and sends the public one to Bob over the in-secure channel. In practice, we use the *Elliptic-curve Diffie-Hellman* (abbreviated ECDH) that relies on Elliptic-curve cryptography [2]. When Bob receives Alice's public key, he will also generate its own pair (sec_B, pub_b) and send his public key back to Alice. Once the public keys have been exchanged, Alice and Bob can combine the public key with their private key to generate the same shared secret value s. Alice computes $s = \text{ECDH}(sec_A, pub_A, pub_B)$ and Bob computes the same shared secret value $s = \text{ECDH}(sec_B, pub_B, pub_A)$. The security of the protocol resides in the fact that an attacker cannot compute that secret value s even if pub_A and pub_B are known but not either sec_A or sec_B. In practice, this shared secret value is usually

---

[2] We only consider message confidentiality here leaving aside authentication and message integrity that is ensured by the Secret Network protocol.

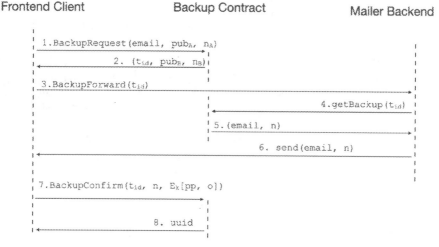

Frontend Client   Backup Contract   Mailer Backend

1.BackupRequest(email, pub$_A$, n$_A$)

2. {t$_{id}$, pub$_B$, n$_B$}

3.BackupForward(t$_{id}$)

4.getBackup(t$_{id}$)

5.(email, n)

6. send(email, n)

7.BackupConfirm(t$_{id}$, n, E$_X$[pp, o])

8. uuid

Fig. 3. Iteration 2 - Backup

not used as a cryptographic key directly. Instead, that shared value is given as input of a key derivation function such as the HMAC-based extract-and-expand key derivation function HKDF [9] that generates the same cryptographic key based on the secret value.

4.3 The Protocol

In addition to the two security measures discussed above, we are also adding additional security measures in both the backup and recovery protocols. First, we check that the request message and the confirm message are sent by the wallet address. Secondly, we limit the time between the request and confirm messages by saving the block Id (denoted b_{id}) after the request. Thus the time limit is calculated based on the number of blocks that have been validated between the request and confirm messages.

The new **backup protocol** shown in Fig. 3) goes as such:

1. When Alice wants to back up her passphrase, she creates yet a throwaway wallet, provision it, visits the backup page of the Mnemonic Backup website and enters her *email*. The Frontend Client generates an ECDH private and public key pair (sec_A, pub_A), a nonce n_A, and sends the transaction BackupRequest($email, pub_A, n_A$) to Backup Contract.
2. The Backup Contract generates a transaction id t_{id}, a new ECDH private and public key pair (sec_B, pub_B), a nonce n_B, and returns those values to the client. In addition, the contract calculates the ECDH secret $s = $ ECDH(sec_B, pub_B, pub_A), and derives the 128-bit AES symmetric key k using

the standard password-based key derivation function HKDF and the concatenation of n_A and n_B as a salt $k = \text{HKDF}(s, n_A \| n_B)$. Finally, the contract generates a confirmation code n, and stores the record $(t_{id}, email, k, n, @A, b_{id})$ in the backup dataset.

3. The Frontend Client calculates the ECDH secret $s = \text{ECDH}(sec_A, pub_A, pub_B)$, derives the AES symmetric key k using HKDF and the concatenation of n_A and n_B as a salt $k = \text{HKDF}(s, n_A \| n_B)$. Then it forwards the transaction id to the Mailer Backend.
4. The Mailer Backend queries the Backup Contract getBackup(t_{id}).
5. The Backup Contract checks that the query comes from the Mailer Backend wallet's address, retrieves the record from the backup dataset, and checks that the query has not expired based on the initial block id b_{id} and the current block id on the Secret Network. If not, it returns the $email$, and the confirmation code n to the Mailer Backend.
6. The Mailer Backend sends an email to Alice with the confirmation code.
7. Alice opens her email and copies and pastes the confirmation code into her browser, enters her passphrase pp and the address of Charlie @C that will receive the Passphrase Lock. Finally, the Frontend Client encrypts the passphrase and sends the transaction BackupConfirm($t_{id}, n, E_k[pp, @C]$) to the Backup Contract.
8. The Backup Contract checks that 1) the message comes from the same address as the request, 2) the query has not expired based on the initial block id b_{id}, and the current block id on the Secret Network and 3) that the confirmation code corresponds to the one stored. Finally, the contract generates a universally unique identifier, stores the record $(uuid, email, pp, @C)$ in the passphrase dataset, and returns the $uuid$ back to Alice for the record.

When Alice wants to recover her passphrase, she creates a new throwaway wallet and contacts her friend Charlie to transfer the Passphrase Lock back to her new recovery wallet following the newly created **transfer protocol** shown in Fig. 4):

1. Charlie visits the transfer page of the Mnemonic Backup website and selects the Lock Passphrase to transfer (identified by its $uuid$), enters Alice's new wallet address @A and the password pwd. The Frontend Client generates an ECDH private and public key pair (sec_A, pub_A), a nonce n_A, and sends the transaction TransferRequest($uuid, pub_A, n_A$) to the Backup Contract.
2. The Backup Contract retrieves the record $(uuid, email, pp, @C)$ from the passphrase dataset and checks that the Passphrase Lock owner C corresponds to Charlie's wallet address. Then, it generates a transaction id t_{id}, a new ECDH private and public key pair (sec_B, pub_B), a nonce n_B, and returns those values to the client. In addition, the contract calculates the ECDH secret $s = \text{ECDH}(sec_B, pub_B, pub_A)$, and derives the 128-bit AES symmetric key k using the standard password-based key derivation function

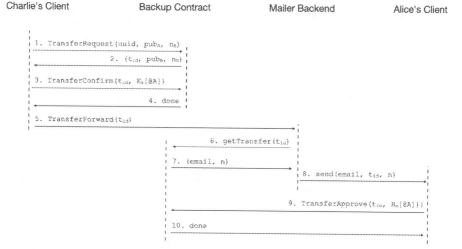

Fig. 4. Iteration 2 - Transfer

HKDF and the concatenation of n_A and n_B as a salt $k = \mathsf{HKDF}(s, n_A \| n_B)$. Finally, the contract generates a confirmation code n, and stores the record $(t_{id}, email, k, n, @A, b_{id})$ in the transfer dataset.

3. The Frontend Client calculates the ECDH secret $s = \mathsf{ECDH}$ (sec_A, pub_A, pub_B), derives the AES symmetric key k using HKDF and the concatenation of n_A and n_B as a salt $k = \mathsf{HKDF}(s, n_A \| n_B)$. Then, it encrypts the address of the new owner (Alice's address $@A$ here) and sends the transaction $\mathsf{TransferConfirm}(t_{id}, E_k[@A])$ to the Backup Contract.

4. The Backup Contract checks that 1) the address use for the confirmation is the same as originally recorded, 2) the query has not expired. If so, it decrypts the owner's address and updates the record in the backup dataset.

5. The Frontend Client forwards the transaction id to the Mailer Backend.

6. The Mailer Backend queries the Backup Contract $\mathsf{getTransfer}(t_{id})$.

7. The Backup Contract checks that the query comes from the Mailer Backend wallet's address, retrieves the record from the transfer dataset, and checks that the query has not expired. If not, it returns the *email*, the confirmation code n to the Mailer Backend.

8. The Mailer Backend sends an email to Alice with the confirmation code.

9. Alice opens her email and copies and pastes the confirmation code, goes to the transfer approval page on the backup mnemonic website, and enters the transfer code and the supposed address of the new owner (Alice's address $@A$ here). The Frontend Client uses the confirmation code to calculate a message authentication code h from the address $h = HMAC_n(@A)$. Finally, the Frontend Client sends the transaction $\mathsf{TransferApprove}(t_{id}, h)$ to the Backup Contract.

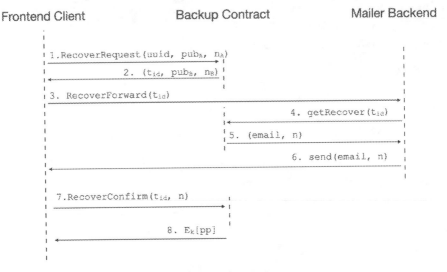

Fig. 5. Iteration 2 - Recovery

10. The Backup Contract checks that the query has not expired. If not, it checks the message authentication from the confirmation code and the address stored in the **transfer** dataset. If there is a match, the **passphrase** record $(uuid, email, pp, @A)$ is updated by changing the ownership of the Passphrase Lock to the new owner's address.

Once the protocol is completed, Alice owns the Passphrase Lock in her new wallet. Now she can use that wallet to recover her passphrase as shown in Fig. 5):

1. Alice visits the recovery page of the Mnemonic Backup website and she sees all passphrase records for which she actually hold the lock. She selects the passphrase record she wants to recover (identified by its $uuid$). The Frontend Client generates an ECDH private and public key pair (sec_A, pub_A), a nonce n_A, and sends the transaction RecoverRequest($uuid, pub_A, n_A$) to the Backup Contract.

2. The Backup Contract retrieves the record $(uuid, email, pp, @C)$ from the **passphrase** dataset and checks that the Passphrase Lock owner A corresponds to Alice's wallet address. If so, it generates a transaction id t_{id}, a new ECDH private and public key pair (sec_B, pub_B), a nonce n_B, and returns those values to the client. In addition, the contract calculates the ECDH secret $s = \text{ECDH}(sec_B, pub_B, pub_A)$, and derives the 128-bit AES symmetric key k using the standard password-based key derivation function HKDF and the concatenation of n_A and n_B as a salt $k = \text{HKDF}(s, n_A \| n_B)$. Finally, the contract generates a confirmation code n, and stores the record $(t_{id}, k, pp, email, n, @A, b_{id})$ in the **recover** dataset.

3. The Frontend Client calculates the ECDH secret $s = \text{ECDH}$ (sec_A, pub_A, pub_B), derives the AES symmetric key k using HKDF and the

concatenation of n_A and n_B as a salt $k = \mathsf{HKDF}(s, n_A \| n_B)$. Then it forwards the transaction id to the Mailer Backend.

4. The Mailer Backend queries the Backup Contract $\mathsf{getRecover}(t_i d)$.
5. The Backup Contract checks that the query comes from the Mailer Backend wallet's address, retrieves the record from the `recover` dataset, and checks that the query has not expired. If not, it returns the *email*, the confirmation code n to the Mailer Backend.
6. The Mailer Backend sends an email to Alice with the confirmation code.
7. Alice opens her email and copies and pastes the confirmation code into her browser. The Frontend Client sends the transaction $\mathsf{RecoverConfirm}(t_{id}, n)$ to the Backup Contract.
8. The Backup Contract checks that 1) the message comes from the same address as the request, 2) the query has not expired and 3) that the confirmation code corresponds to the one stored. Finally, the contract encrypts the passphrase with the key k, and returns it to the client.

Once the protocol is completed the Frontend Client decrypts the passphrase and displays it to Alice.

4.4 Security Analysis

First, if the attacker can steal any of Alice's private keys afterward, he cannot decrypt the passphrase sent back and forth between the Frontend Client and the Backup contract since the passphrase is always encrypted with the ECDH session key in both the backup and the recovery protocols. In addition, the attacker cannot know the address of Passphrase Lock owner since that information is always encrypted as well.

Now, let's assume the attacker has been able to breach Alice's mailbox or the Mailer Backend directly. During the backup, the attacker could get the confirmation code, however, he would not be able to upload an arbitrary passphrase without knowing Alice's private key. For recovery, the attacker cannot initiate the recovery process without first holding the Passphrase Lock. Even if the attacker holds the lock (if the attacker is Charlie for instance), he would not be able to recover the passphrase without also compromising Alice's email. Finally, it takes both the Passphrase Lock owner and the original email owner to work together to transfer the Lock Passphrase.

In the end, an attacker cannot retrieve the passphrase without obtaining the lock first **and** compromising the victim's email.

However, having a single individual holding Passphrase Lock introduces another problem: what if that person does not or cannot return the Passphrase Lock? The passphrase would be locked forever. We are improving this availability issue in our next and final iteration.

5   Iteration 3: Improving Availability

Having a unique friend holding Alice's Passphrase Lock can be a problem if that friend does not or cannot return it to her. A naive solution would be to duplicate the Passphrase Lock and send it to multiple friends. This solution is feasible but not ideal in terms of security since we are extending the attack surface. The attacker can now target multiple people to regain one of these Passphrase Lock. Instead, our idea is to split the passphrase into multiple parts that we call *Passphrase Lock Shares* and send each friend one of these shares. To recover the passphrase, not all shares are needed but a minimum of shares called the *threshold*. This is ideal from the usability perspective since the user does not have to collect all the shares back but only the minimum threshold required. Moreover, this is perfect from the security perspective since any attacker who can retrieve any number of shares less than the threshold will not be able to start the recovery process. This approach is similar to threshold cryptosystem such as *Shamir's Secret Sharing Scheme* [18].

5.1   The Protocol

The protocol is very similar to the previous iteration with two modifications:

- At step 7 in the **backup protocol**, Alice must specify a threshold number t, and provide the list of addresses that will receive one *Passphrase Lock Share* each. Indeed, the threshold number should be smaller or equal to the number of shareowners. The new backup protocol is shown in Fig. 6.
- At step 1 in the **recovery protocol**, the Backup Contract must check that Alice's wallet owns enough Passphrase Lock shares relatively to reach the threshold.

6   Related Work

Users must keep the wallet's mnemonic phrase safe because whoever gets access to that can access all of the crypto assets held in the wallet. To the best of our knowledge, there is only one significant proposal addressing the same issue. In [17], Rezaeighaleh and al. propose using a second wallet for backup. They propose a protocol based on Elliptic-Curve Diffie-Hellman to back up the private keys of the first wallet into a second wallet. They recommend having that secondary wallet be a "cold" wallet such as a hardware USB dongle or a smart card. This approach is technically sound but again relies on storing a physical object in a safe place which is hard in practice as shown in [19].

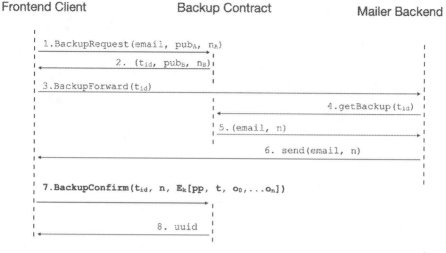

Fig. 6. Iteration 3 - Backup

7   Conclusion and Future Work

In this paper, we propose a Decentralized Mnemonic Backup system that anyone can use to give custody of any blockchain passphrase to a Secret Network smart and protect it using a new type of crypto asset that we call a Passphrase Lock. This Passphrase Lock is split into different shares and distributed to multiple users. When comes the time to recover the passphrase, the user should collect a subset of those shares to unlock the passphrase.

The key recovering system can be used outside of our Mnemonic Backup system. It can be used for more advanced cryptographic protocols that involve storing and managing secret keys on-chain with the option of recovering them using an email. For instance, this can be used to encrypt files on the InterPlanetary File System (IPFS) [12] and manage the access using a Secret Contract that would hold custody of the encryption key. Our system could be used to safely generate and manage the encryption key on the Secret Network and possibly have an email backup solution if such a feature is desired.

Acknowledgments. This work has been funded through a grant from the *Secret Network*.

References

1. Azar, P.D., et al.: The financial stability implications of digital assets (2022)
2. Bernstein, D.J.: Curve25519: new Diffie-Hellman speed records. In: Yung, M., Dodis, Y., Kiayias, A., Malkin, T. (eds.) PKC 2006. LNCS, vol. 3958, pp. 207–228. Springer, Heidelberg (2006). https://doi.org/10.1007/11745853_14

3. Biondo, A., Conti, M., Davi, L., Frassetto, T., Sadeghi, A.R.: The guard's dilemma: efficient Code-Reuse attacks against Intel SGX. In: 27th USENIX Security Symposium (USENIX Security 2018), pp. 1213–1227 (2018)

4. Buterin, V., et al.: Ethereum: a next generation smart contract and decentralized application platform (2013/2017). http://ethereum.org/ethereum.html

5. Cai, W., Wang, Z., Ernst, J.B., Hong, Z., Feng, C., Leung, V.C.: Decentralized applications: the blockchain-empowered software system. IEEE Access **6**, 53019–53033 (2018)

6. Diffie, W., Hellman, M.E.: New directions in cryptography. In: Democratizing Cryptography: The Work of Whitfield Diffie and Martin Hellman, pp. 365–390 (2022)

7. Götzfried, J., Eckert, M., Schinzel, S., Müller, T.: Cache attacks on Intel SGX. In: Proceedings of the 10th European Workshop on Systems Security, pp. 1–6 (2017)

8. Krawczyk, H.: Perfect forward secrecy. In: van Tilborg, H.C.A. (ed.) Encyclopedia of Cryptography and Security, pp. 457–458. Springer, Boston (2005). https://doi.org/10.1007/0-387-23483-7_298

9. Krawczyk, H., Eronen, P.: HMAC-based extract-and-expand key derivation function (HKDF). Technical report (2010)

10. Li, Z., He, W., Akhawe, D., Song, D.: The Emperor's new password manager: security analysis of web-based password managers. In: 23rd USENIX Security Symposium (USENIX Security 2014), pp. 465–479 (2014)

11. McKeen, F., et al.: Innovative instructions and software model for isolated execution. HASP@ ISCA **10**(1) (2013)

12. Muralidharan, S., Ko, H.: An interplanetary file system (IPFS) based IoT framework. In: 2019 IEEE International Conference on Consumer Electronics (ICCE), pp. 1–2. IEEE (2019)

13. Murdock, K., Oswald, D., Garcia, F.D., Van Bulck, J., Gruss, D., Piessens, F.: Plundervolt: software-based fault injection attacks against Intel SGX. In: 2020 IEEE Symposium on Security and Privacy (SP), pp. 1466–1482. IEEE (2020)

14. Secret Network: Secret network: a privacy-preserving secret contract & decentralized application platform. Technical report

15. Nilsson, A., Bideh, P.N., Brorsson, J.: A survey of published attacks on Intel SGX. arXiv preprint arXiv:2006.13598 (2020)

16. Palatinus, M., Rusnak, P., Voisine, A., Bowe, S.: Mnemonic code for generating deterministic keys (2013). https://github.com/bitcoin/bips/blob/master/bip-0039.mediawiki

17. Rezaeighaleh, H., Zou, C.C.: New secure approach to backup cryptocurrency wallets. In: 2019 IEEE Global Communications Conference (GLOBECOM), pp. 1–6. IEEE (2019)

18. Shamir, A.: How to share a secret. Commun. ACM **22**(11), 612–613 (1979)

19. Voskobojnikov, A., Wiese, O., Mehrabi Koushki, M., Roth, V., Beznosov, K.: The U in crypto stands for usable: an empirical study of user experience with mobile cryptocurrency wallets. In: Proceedings of the 2021 CHI Conference on Human Factors in Computing Systems, pp. 1–14 (2021)

20. Wang, Q., Li, R., Wang, Q., Chen, S.: Non-fungible token (NFT): overview, evaluation, opportunities and challenges. arXiv preprint arXiv:2105.07447 (2021)

21. Zyskind, G., Nathan, O., et al.: Decentralizing privacy: using blockchain to protect personal data. In: 2015 IEEE Security and Privacy Workshops, pp. 180–184. IEEE (2015)

IoT and Security Protocols

If-This-Then-Allow-That (to Phone Home): A Trigger-Based Network Policy Enforcement Framework for Smart Homes

Anthony Tam[1], Furkan Alaca[1(✉)], and David Barrera[2]

[1] Queen's University, Kingston, ON, Canada
{anthony.tam,furkan.alaca}@queensu.ca
[2] Carleton University, Ottawa, ON, Canada
david.barrera@carleton.ca

Abstract. The Internet of Things (IoT) has become entrenched in many users' networks due to the utility these Internet-connected objects provide. But this does not mean that users should unconditionally trust IoT devices on their networks. While several approaches exist for restricting network connectivity of IoT devices, these proposals typically identify legitimate traffic, and then permanently allow it to flow to or from the device. In this paper, we argue that this permanent access control can lead to privacy and security violations, and in many cases is not strictly required. We present If-This-Then-Allow-That (IFTAT), a framework that supports security policies that dynamically update network access control rules based on the type of access that is required at any given time. Device or environmental triggers such as motion sensors or mobile phone applications initiate the process of adding firewall exceptions, which are removed either automatically or after another trigger is activated. We describe a proof of concept implementation which shows how IFTAT can restrict the network access of untrusted IoT devices with little impact to the usability of these devices.

1 Introduction

Internet of Things (IoT) devices have been widely exploited by attackers to carry out malicious activities against their users and the Internet at large [1,7, 11,14,21]. The exploitation of IoT devices also threatens user privacy, since IoT devices often access and handle privacy-sensitive data such as audio or presence information. While evidence suggests [19] that users are interested in knowing what data their devices send over the network and why, users are often unaware of this information due to the lack of security and privacy tools that provide it. To mitigate the exploitation of IoT devices, prior research has proposed mechanisms to narrow the scope of allowable IoT device network traffic, e.g., by restricting allowable protocols or allowable source and destination ports and hosts [5,18,22]. Many proposed methods employ security policies to allow network traffic that matches pre-defined rules, but few of these methods update the rules in response

G.-V. Jourdan et al. (Eds.): FPS 2022, LNCS 13877, pp. 373–388, 2023.
https://doi.org/10.1007/978-3-031-30122-3_23

to contextually-relevant information. This means that a smart doorbell could upload audio or video to the cloud even while the user is not using the doorbell's mobile app, or that a motion sensor could report motion activity even when an alarm system is disarmed. We are thus motivated to rethink IoT network access control: we aim to provide users with greater control of when their IoT devices communicate over the network, and we do so by providing a means to mediate network traffic based on contextual events that reflect users' real-world usage patterns.

We propose the If-This-Then-Allow-That (IFTAT) framework, which introduces a new time-based dimension to network access control by allowing user-defined policies to update traffic mediation rules in response to trigger events. Trigger events can be generated by sources such as physical sensors, network traffic signatures, or software running on a user's device. User-defined policies specify rules for allowing or denying network traffic to or from a target device (e.g., a security camera, thermostat, doorbell, network-attached storage) in response to the occurrence of a trigger event (e.g., motion detection, light switch turned on, application launched on a user's smartphone). For example, a thermostat might only be allowed to communicate with a cloud service provider while there is a human user in close physical proximity to the thermostat; or a surveillance camera might only be allowed to stream video to the cloud while the owner of the camera has the companion app running in the foreground on their smartphone. IFTAT does not need to learn the network traffic patterns of IoT devices, but IFTAT policies can optionally use such patterns to enable more granular rules for allowing or denying network traffic. Figure 1 illustrates the timeline of events when executing a policy that applies a traffic mediation rule (e.g., allow a security camera to access the Internet) in response to a trigger event, followed by a change or reversal of that rule (e.g., by denying the security camera access to the Internet) in response to a subsequent trigger event.

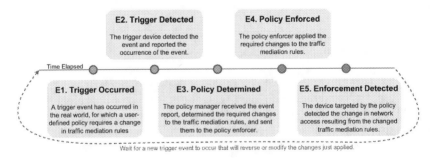

Fig. 1. The timeline of events that occur while detecting a trigger event (blue), applying a change in traffic mediation rules (green), and waiting for a new event to subsequently reverse or modify the previous change in traffic mediation rules (red). (Color figure online)

IFTAT is well-suited for protecting devices that have the characteristic of predictably and consistently requiring network access in response to specific trigger events that can be detected by other devices on the network. IoT devices in particular fit this general characteristic, since they are generally known to have specialized features that can be implemented by predictable and repetitive actions such as submitting sensor readings to a cloud service at a regular interval [22]. However, our system may also complement traditional firewall rules to reduce the attack surface on more general-purpose devices as well, particularly those that provide services over the network such as network-attached storage.

The contributions of this paper are as follows.

1. We present IFTAT, a framework for time-based network access control derived from user-defined trigger events.
2. We demonstrate the use and effectiveness of IFTAT on mainstream IoT devices and hardware through a proof of concept implementation. We propose and implement an initial set of trigger events.
3. We provide a discussion of how IFTAT defends against two distinct threat models that we define.

The remainder of the paper is structured as follows. Sections 2 and 3 outline the IFTAT security goals and system design, respectively. Section 4 discusses related work. Section 5 discusses and categorizes trigger events that we propose and that we identify from other work. Section 6 presents use cases that we implement with our instantiation of IFTAT using commodity hardware and software. Section 7 discusses security considerations and potential focuses for standardization effort, and Sect. 8 concludes.

2   Security Goals and Threat Model

IFTAT reduces the attack surface of IoT and other special-purpose devices by reducing the times during which they have unrestricted network or Internet access. This reduced network access is designed to serve as a defense against the following two threat models.

T1: Large-Scale Opportunistic Exploitation. IoT devices are prone to being targeted and exploited by large-scale operations. Large botnets have been created via automated device scanning and exploitation, and leveraged for malicious activities such as distributed denial of service (DDoS) attacks [1,7]. Residential proxies as a service leverage both volunteer users and compromised IoT devices as proxies to funnnel customers' traffic through residential Internet connections to evade measures such as bot detection or geoblocking [11]. These operations often exploit devices running firmware with unpatched vulnerabilities. Confining the network access of devices to only periods when the access is required would significantly narrow their window of exploitability (and, in the event of device compromise, would reduce the time windows during which they can be leveraged for malicious activities).

T2: Exfiltration of Privacy-Sensitive Data. IoT devices often handle privacy-sensitive data such as audio or presence information. Restricting devices' network connectivity reduces the potential for the exfiltration of privacy-sensitive data, whether due to exploitation as explained immediately above, device error (e.g., due to misinterpreting the user's intentions [13]), or the collection of tracking and usage data by device manufacturers [8].

3   System Design and Overview

The IFTAT framework specifies four device classes: untrusted devices, trigger devices, policy enforcers, and a policy manager. Figure 2 illustrates how these devices interact with each other: trigger devices report trigger events to the policy manager, which in turn sends instructions to policy enforcers for how to mediate network traffic to and from untrusted devices. IFTAT can function with multiple trigger devices, untrusted devices, and policy enforcers on the same network.

Fig. 2. Sequence of actions performed by each device following the occurrence of a trigger event. Each line represents a network connection, and is labelled with an action performed over that connection during events E2-E4 from Fig. 1. The dashed line at the policy enforcer denotes a network bridge, and the dashed lines leading to the cloud service denote an optional communication path used by some trigger devices.

3.1   Untrusted Devices

An untrusted device is a network-connected device designated by the user to have its network access mediated by the occurrence of user-defined trigger events. Untrusted devices may often be IoT devices, since they have simpler network traffic patterns [22] and often handle privacy-sensitive data, which may motivate users to ensure that such devices remain uncompromised [19]. Examples of such IoT devices may include security cameras, voice assistants, and door locks. General-purpose devices may also be designated as untrusted devices; e.g., a user may wish to restrict network access to their network-attached storage (NAS) device that performs backups of the user's other devices; the user may wish to allow network access to the NAS only in response to trigger events that indicate that a backup will take place (e.g., the user launching a backup application).

3.2   Trigger Devices and Trigger Events

A trigger device detects trigger events and reports them to the policy manager. Examples of trigger devices include special-purpose hardware devices such as motion sensors or light switches. A trigger device may also be a general-purpose device, such as a smartphone running a program that reports user actions, or a network traffic analysis device that reports the occurrence of device activities (e.g., streaming video, updating firmware) on the network [17]. Examples of trigger events are discussed further in Sect. 5. Depending on the context, a device may be both an untrusted device and a trigger device; for example, a motion sensor may report a trigger event to enable network connectivity for a light switch, and the light switch may in turn report a trigger event to enable network connectivity for a security camera.

Trigger events may have different delays between the events E1, E2, and E3 denoted in Fig. 1. The delay from E1 to E2 is the time elapsed between the event occurring and the detection of the event by the trigger device. For example, passive infrared (PIR) motion sensors typically report motion if it has been detected continuously for a period of time such as two seconds. In contrast, the opening of a mobile application can be detected virtually instantaneously when the user taps on the application icon. The delay between E2 and E3 is the time elapsed between the trigger device reporting an event and the policy manager receiving the report. This delay can be near instantaneous if the trigger device is on the local network and report events to the policy manager over the local network; if the trigger device instead reports events to a cloud service provider, additional delay will be introduced since the policy manager would need to poll the cloud service provider at a regular interval to identify the occurrence of an event. RTX-IFTTT [3] provides a technique to minimize this delay by sniffing outgoing cloud API calls made by IoT devices on the local network, which would eliminate the need for the policy manager to poll the cloud API.

3.3 Policy Enforcer

Policy enforcers mediate network access to and from untrusted devices. A policy enforcer may employ a packet filtering firewall to mediate access based on attributes such as IP address, protocol, and port number. Alternatively, it may employ an application-layer firewall, e.g., to mediate HTTP requests. Each policy enforcer receives instructions from a centralized policy manager for how to enforce network access restrictions. The instructions received will be tailored to the traffic mediation capabilities of the policy enforcer and the set of untrusted devices that are connected to the network through the policy enforcer.

3.4 Policy Manager

The policy manager performs the following key functions:

Policy Creation and Storage. An interface and syntax is provided for the creation of IFTAT policies. IFTAT policies define how to allow or block network access to or from an untrusted device when a specified trigger event occurs. Network access may be allowed or blocked either in whole or based on specified network packet header attributes or traffic patterns that the policy enforcer is capable of identifying.

Trigger Event Report Collection. An interface is provided for trigger devices to report that a trigger event has occurred. Trigger events can be reported by either local or remote trigger devices. Local trigger devices report events via a local interface such as USB, Bluetooth, Zigbee, or Z-Wave. Remote trigger devices report events over a network interface either directly to the policy manager or to a cloud service (e.g., over HTTPS) that the policy manager can poll to determine when a trigger event occurs.

Untrusted Device Designation. The policy manager retrieves the list of all devices connected to each policy enforcer, and provides an interface through which the user designates the devices that are untrusted.

Policy Translation and Distribution. The policy manager must translate IFTAT policies into instructions that can be enforced by the policy enforcer(s). For example, IFTAT policies can be converted into packet filtering rules or Software-Defined Networking (SDN) policies. When a trigger event report is received, the policy manager (i) identifies traffic mediation actions corresponding to any IFTAT policies triggered by the event; and (ii) sends the instructions necessary for executing the actions to the corresponding policy enforcer(s).

4   Related Work

Many systems for mediating IoT traffic have been proposed; e.g., machine learning classifiers can identify and block anomalous or malicious traffic [10,15]; or devices can be assigned network access policies based on general device categories [4] or specifications of intended network access patterns provided by device manufacturers [9]. Here, we discuss three systems in related work that modify or update their traffic mediation behaviour in response to events observed on the network; i.e., systems that employ what we refer to as trigger devices in IFTAT.

Table 1 summarizes and compares these three systems on the basis of how each of them implements functionality that falls within the responsibility of IFTAT trigger devices, policy enforcers, and policy managers. These systems can be implemented in IFTAT, since the framework allows for the implementation of different types of trigger devices and policy enforcers.

LeakyPick [13] uses a microphone-equipped security device to passively listen for selected "wake words" (e.g., "Alexa" or "Hey Google") to be spoken by the user nearby a smart voice assistant. The security device checks if the voice assistant connects to the Internet without the wake word having been spoken; this is intended to check whether the voice assistant is only active while the user intends it to be. The authors suggest that this technique could also be used to deny network access to the voice assistant unless the wake word is spoken.

HomeSnitch [17] classifies IoT device communication into actions (e.g., firmware update, video upload) using a classification algorithm on features extracted from network traffic. A policy language is also proposed, which can allow or deny specific device activities, or use a device activity as a condition to allow or deny other traffic. Since supervised learning is used to train the classifier on a manually-labelled dataset, it is proposed that a service provider would

Table 1. Comparison of IoT network traffic mediation systems proposed in related work. The systems are compared on the basis of how each system implements functionality that falls within the responsibility of each device class defined in IFTAT. We compare only systems that modify their traffic mediation behaviour in response to detected trigger events. We later propose and implement additional examples of how IFTAT device classes can be instantiated.

Related work	Trigger device	Policy enforcer	Policy manager
LeakyPick† [13]	**Trigger event:** User-spoken wake word **Detection method:** Monitor ambient sound with microphone	WiFi access point for untrusted devices denies traffic by default and forwards traffic when signalled by policy manager	**Policy syntax:** Rule to permit network access for an untrusted device when a specified trigger is detected **Policy source:** User-specified
HomeSnitch [17]	**Trigger event:** Activity performed by an IoT device **Detection method:** Identify activities using a classifier pre-trained on network traffic signatures	Network gateway that receives **OpenFlow** rules from policy manager	**Policy syntax:** Rule to permit an untrusted device activity when a specified trigger is detected **Policy source:** User-specified rules; signatures downloaded from 3rd party
SerenIoT [22]	**Trigger event:** Change in an IoT device's network traffic patterns **Detection method:** Identify packet signatures that were not previously observed	WiFi access point for untrusted devices that receives firewall rules from policy manager	**Policy syntax:** Packet signature to define allowable traffic for specified device **Policy source:** Proof-of-work blockchain; new packet signatures are submitted when trigger is detected

† LeakyPick does passive detection, but also suggests the option of active prevention.

be responsible for providing updated classifier models by collecting and labeling data to periodically re-train the classifier.

SERENIoT [22] uses a public proof-of-work blockchain that can be queried to retrieve the allowable network traffic signatures for a given IoT device. Nodes on the blockchain, called Sentinels, submit summaries of observed device behaviours that get added to the blockchain if the majority of nodes have also observed the same behaviour. New behaviours resulting from firmware updates would thus be observed by the majority of nodes and added to the blockchain, whereas malicious behaviour resulting from device compromise would not. Sentinels allow any newly-connected device on the network to send and receive all traffic for a one-minute period; this is used as a profiling phase to identify the device type if possible and to determine its required network traffic.

5   Trigger Events Identified and Proposed

Table 2 lists examples of trigger events that can be used in IFTAT. We categorize the examples by the source from which the trigger event is derived: (i) physical measurements; (ii) software-based determination that a condition has been satisfied; or (iii) signature- or heuristic-based detection. We list both generic techniques and techniques proposed in academic literature that are suitable for use as trigger events.

deGraaf et al. [2] propose a cryptographic protocol that operates via port knocking to authenticate users prior to allowing application traffic through the firewall. VibLive [23] is a secure continuous liveness detection technique, using a microphone and loudspeaker, to ensure the user is present when giving voice commands. We also propose a technique that, to the best of our knowledge, has not previously been used for access control decisions: detection of when a user opens or closes a specific application on their smartphone. He et al. [6] conducted a survey of techniques for using physical sensors to detect home contexts relevant to security-related decisions, such as user presence, user identity, or home emergencies—these techniques can also be used to define trigger events.

Table 2. Categorization of trigger events suitable for use in IFTAT.

Trigger source	Trigger event	Implementation
Physical	Motion detected	‡
	Door or window opened or closed	—
	Smoke detected, water detected, etc.	—
Software	Mobile application opened or closed	‡
	User authenticated (e.g., to WiFi network)	—
	Timer expired	‡
Signature	Phrase or word spoken by user	[13]
	Liveness detection	[23]
	Network traffic matched an activity signature	[17, 22]

‡ denotes trigger events implemented in this paper; — denotes trigger events listed as examples but not implemented.

6   System Implementation

We implemented a proof-of-concept of IFTAT on a small test network to demonstrate two use cases as follows.

UC1. A home owner wishes to deny network access to a smart doorbell except for while a person is physically present in front of the device. This reduces the time that the device is allowed outgoing network connections to align with the user's intended usage of the device (e.g., for communicating with a person at their front door). Human presence should be determined without relying on the untrusted device, so we use a separate motion sensor for this task.

UC2. A business owner wishes to deny network access to a security camera except for while an authorized user is using a mobile application to access the camera feed. This prevents the device from being accessible to the Internet while the user does not need to access it. The user's smartphone serves as the trigger device that reports when the user has launched the mobile app.

6.1 Hardware Overview

We use two Raspberry Pi 4 devices[1]: one of them running Home Assistant[2] to function as the policy manager, and the other running OpenWRT[3] to function as the policy enforcer. An Energizer Connect EOD1-1002-2002-SIL Smart Doorbell and a ReoLink RLC-410-5MP security camera are designated as untrusted devices. Two trigger devices are also implemented, an iPhone 12 Pro and a AM312 PIR motion sensor running ESPHome[4] firmware. Figure 3 depicts the network connectivity between all devices. The policy enforcer has three network interfaces (WAN, LAN, and WLAN) and performs routing, NAT, and packet filtering.

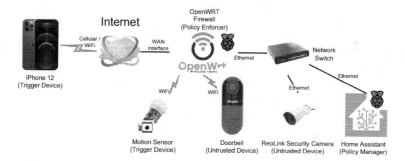

Fig. 3. Connectivity diagram of devices in the proof-of-concept implementation. Each device is labelled with its device class (untrusted device, trigger device, policy enforcer, or policy manager).

Devices are assigned a static IP address to ensure that security policies are applied to the correct untrusted devices. Alternative techniques can be used to identify untrusted devices dynamically, e.g., via device fingerprinting [10,12,22].

---

[1] https://www.raspberrypi.org/.
[2] https://www.home-assistant.io/.
[3] https://openwrt.org/.
[4] https://esphome.io/.

6.2   Policy Manager

We implement IFTAT policies in YAML using Home Assistant automation rules; for each rule we specify a trigger event and a corresponding traffic mediation action to be taken. Table 3 describes the policies we defined to implement **UC1** and **UC2**.

Table 3. Description of IFTAT policies used to implement proposed use cases **UC1** and **UC2**. The lettered suffixes distinguish between the two policies required for implementing each use case.

Rule	Trigger event	Traffic mediation action
UC1a	Motion detected near doorbell	Allow outbound connections from the doorbell to the Internet
UC1b	Ten minutes elapsed since motion detected near doorbell	Deny all outbound connections from the doorbell to the Internet
UC2a	User launched security camera mobile app	Allow inbound connections from the Internet to the security camera
UC2b	Ten minutes elapsed since security camera mobile app launched	Deny inbound connections from the Internet to the security camera

The traffic mediation actions are taken by issuing a command over an SSH connection to the policy enforcer. In a production-ready IFTAT implementation, the policy manager would automatically translate each action into a series of commands that the policy enforcer would understand. In our proof-of-concept implementation, we manually create a shell script for each action that enables or disables the iptables rules necessary to execute the action, e.g., allowing or denying network access to the camera. A sample policy in YAML format to implement **UC2** is shown in Fig. 4.

To allow remote trigger devices to report trigger events, we use webhooks on the policy manager. Each webhook is an HTTP URL with an embedded bearer token to ensure that only authorized trigger devices (e.g., the iPhone) can report trigger events. The webhook must be served over HTTPS to ensure that the bearer token cannot be eavesdropped. Trigger devices within the local network utilize Home Assistant's ESPHome integration to monitor the motion sensor's state over the WiFi network.

6.3   Trigger Events

We implement three trigger events, which are detected as described below.

Mobile Application Opened. This event is reported by the iPhone using the Shortcuts app. We create a shortcut that performs the following actions:

1. Send an HTTP POST request to the webhook exposed by the policy manager (using the "Get contents of URL" action).

```
alias:  Trigger  Security  Camera  Policy
trigger:
  - platform: webhook
      webhook_id:  trigger-security-camera-elS4xo2eEykNlqS0GrlXeCvr
action:
  - service: shell_command.enable_camera
  - delay:
      minutes: 10
  - service: shell_command.disable_camera
mode: restart
```

Fig. 4. A sample security policy to implement **UC2**.

2. Launch the VLC App (using the "Open App" action).

The first action allows the phone to notify the policy manager that the user intends to interact with the untrusted device (security camera) via the VLC app. This trigger causes the policy manager to modify the active policy on the policy enforcer to allow network access to the untrusted device. The second action launches the application.

Motion Present. This event is reported by the motion sensor. Home Assistant presents a binary state (i.e., "on" for motion present or "off" not present) for the motion sensor, which we monitor for changes from the "off" to the "on" state to determine when the event has occurred.

Timer Expired. This event was implemented in Home Assistant by configuring a timer to expire 10 min after either a **Mobile application opened** or **Motion present** event is detected. Each of these two event types has its own timer, which resets to 10 min if a new event of that type is detected before the timer expires.

6.4   Policy Enforcer

Traffic mediation actions are implemented using iptables rules and the OpenWRT UCI system. When blocking network access to a device, we ensure that any active connections are terminated immediately by blocking all ESTABLISHED connections as well. The ReoLink security camera and Energizer Doorbell are configured as untrusted devices and by default will have all network access denied unless the **Mobile application opened** or **Motion present** events are detected.

Mediating traffic between devices on the same LAN requires using different LAN segments (e.g., using separate VLANs) or using Software Defined Networking as in HomeSnitch [17]. In the absence of such mechanisms, devices within the same LAN segment can communicate with each other without restriction.

6.5   Performance Evaluation

The time delays between the events in Fig. 1 have practical implications for creating IFTAT policies, since trigger events should be detected and the resulting traffic mediation action should take effect before the untrusted device requires network access. To evaluate the practicality of the policies we implemented, we collected the following timestamps to compute the aforementioned delays:

1. When the trigger event is detected by the trigger device
2. When the trigger event report is received by the policy manager
3. When the traffic mediation instructions are received by the policy enforcer
4. When the change in network access is detected by the untrusted device

All devices were synchronized with the same NTP server to ensure consistent timestamps, and all delay calculations were averaged across ten runs. Figure 5 provides a timeline of events that includes the delays computed from the above timestamps that were collected for the enforcement of **UC1a**. We draw comparisons below with delays observed for the other policies.

Fig. 5. A timeline for enforcing security policies when a trigger is received for **UC1a**.

E1–E2. For **UC1a**, after motion occurs, there is a small delay before it is detected by the motion sensor; this delay is sensor-dependent. As per the AM312 datasheet, our motion sensor has an activation delay of 2.3 s. For the remaining three use cases (**UC1b**, **UC2a**, **UC2b**), this delay is negligible.

E2–E3. For **UC1a** and **UC2a**, this delay was ~300 ms. This is the time taken for Home Assistant to receive an external trigger and process the policy (e.g., see Fig. 4) to determine the command to send to the policy enforcer. For **UC1b** and **UC2b**, this delay is negligible since the timer trigger is implemented directly on the policy manager.

E3–E4. All four policies from Table 3 consistently resulted in a delay of ~250 ms; this is the time taken to establish an SSH connection to the policy enforcer and execute the shell script to enforce the policy.

E4–E5. For **UC1a**, a delay of ~2.2 s was measured before the Energizer mobile app (which tracks the doorbell status through a cloud backend) would identify the doorbell as online. In contrast, for **UC2a**, an RTSP connection could immediately be opened from the mobile app to the camera upon the policy being enforced, since the camera is accessed via a direct connection (i.e., the delay was negligible). For both **UC1b** and **UC2b**, a cloud provider may cause additional delay to identify the device as offline after failing to receive several consecutive heartbeat messages. For **UC1b**, connectivity to the doorbell resulted in immediate disconnection from the video stream, but the doorbell was not reported offline by the mobile app for ~2.5 s. In contrast, for **UC2b**, the camera was immediately identified as offline by the mobile application.

Finally, we investigate the impact of the firewall rule table being updated each time a trigger event report is received. To test whether network performance is impacted, we used iperf3[5] to send a fixed number of UDP packets at a rate of 75Mbps to the policy manager from outside the local network (i.e., through the WAN interface of the policy enforcer, which is the LAN-to-WAN gateway in our implementation). In a control test with no rule updates, the average measured round-trip delay and jitter between the policy manager and the external test device was 0.587 ms and 0.1106 ms, respectively; no packet loss occurred and the TCP state table was preserved. To measure the impact of rule updates, we run a shell script that updates the firewall rules by successively adding and removing the rules for **UC1** in a loop; we measured that the script executed 40 iterations of the loop per second, with each iteration taking ~25 ms to complete. We repeated the iperf3 test while the aforementioned shell script was running, and observed an average round-trip delay and jitter of 0.589 ms and 0.1134 ms, respectively; no packet loss occurred and the TCP state table was preserved. We thus conclude that even under an unrealistically high rate of firewall rule updates as described above, the impact on network performance is negligible.

7 Discussion

Herein we discuss how IFTAT can strengthen a network's security and we discuss avenues for standardization that would support the security objectives of IFTAT.

7.1 Security Considerations

We discuss how IFTAT can combat the spread and operation of IoT malware (refer to **T1**) and the exfiltration of privacy-sensitive data (refer to **T2**). We also discuss security considerations relating to the implementation of trigger devices.

Protecting Externally-Exposed Devices Against Compromise. This is the primary threat targeted by **UC2** with the ReoLink security camera. In this use case, IFTAT ensures that the device is only externally accessible when required by the user. Externally accessible devices are regularly targeted by botnets via IP scanning, causing any online and vulnerable devices to be infected by malware [1]. IFTAT reduces the likelihood of infection, as the device can only be scanned for a short period of time following a valid trigger event.

While home Internet gateway devices typically block incoming connections by default to all devices on the home network, they provide user interfaces to open ports to target devices. IFTAT offers the alternative of only openings ports on a temporary basis in response to trigger events that reflect a legitimate user's attempt to access the target devices. Moreover, IFTAT can leverage the following additional measures to further enhance the security of **UC2**:

i. The inclusion of an IP address in an allow list, ensuring only the mobile device which performed the trigger is able to access the camera, this reduces the risk to the levels of protection applied to the web hook bearer token.

---

[5] https://iperf.fr/.

ii. Incoming traffic to the policy enforcer targeting the untrusted device could be collected while the untrusted device has been denied network access. Using this data, signatures can be created representing traffic patterns sent to the untrusted device in the absence of trigger events. This signature can then be used to block potentially malicious traffic when the device is later allowed network access.

Preventing Leakage of Sensitive Information. This is the primary threat targeted by **UC1**. IFTAT restricts the device's outgoing network communication to only the time periods that align with the user's intended usage of the device. This reduces unnecessary opportunities for leaking sensitive information to the device manufacturer or third-party trackers [8], and prevents the device from performing other outbound malicious activities [1,11]. However, devices which are reliant the manufacturer's cloud service may react differently to being connected and disconnected from the Internet [16], e.g., by caching events locally and sending them to the cloud when connectivity is restored. Techniques employed by OConnor et al. [16,17] may be used to determine how devices behave when they lose connectivity, and this can inform the creation of IFTAT policies.

Importance of Countermeasures Against Trigger Device Spoofing. Should a trigger device be spoofed or compromised, it may be possible for an attacker to artificially signal the occurrence of a trigger event to allow network access to a target untrusted device. Thus, it is critical to secure the communication channel between the trigger devices and the policy manager. This can be achieved by reporting trigger events to the policy manager over an encrypted channel, e.g., a TLS connection, or over a channel that is inaccessible to untrusted devices, e.g., Zigbee or USB. This limits the attack surface that could be used by an attacker to compromise a trigger device and use it to allow network traffic to an untrusted device at will. However, the security of these channels may not be perfect, and the risk of trigger device spoofing remains present in Zigbee devices as well [20], especially if an attacker has physical access to the environment.

7.2   Standardizing IFTAT

Manufacturer Usage Descriptions (MUD) [9] provides a policy language that device manufacturers can use to define a profile of the network access (e.g., protocols, port numbers, destination IP addresses or hostnames) that the device requires. A device's MUD profile can then be used to restrict its network access and reduce its attack surface. Since MUD profiles are provided by the device manufacturer, they would be expected to be more accurate than network traffic profiles that are learned via traffic analysis as is done in aaa related work [17,22] discussed in Sect. 4. The primary obstacle in the use of MUD profiles is its limited adoption thus far by device manufacturers. Should MUD be more widely adopted, IFTAT can use them to enforce more granular policies: when a trigger event occurs, an untrusted device could be allowed only the network access as defined by its MUD policy (instead of allowing unrestricted access), thereby minimizing the attack surface of the device.

MUD could also be extended to support the concept of trigger devices. For example, a device's MUD profile could specify if certain types of network access is required in response to external trigger events. For example, the MUD may define the network access required by the device when a **New firmware published** or **Motion present** event occurs. The former can be detected by polling the manufacturer's website to monitor for announcements that a new firmware version has been released. The latter can be detected by allowing the user to select a motion sensor device on the network to use as the trigger device.

8   Conclusion

IoT users deserve more control over the devices they own. To gain this control, users must currently manage complex networking setups or manually add/remove firewall rules. Due to the dynamic nature of many IoT devices, this network management requires constant supervision and adjustment to not interfere with device functionality.

This paper presents IFTAT, a framework that gives users simple, granular, time-restricted control over the network connectivity of untrusted devices on their networks. Narrowing this connectivity time window substantially reduces the amount of information that can be leaked, as well as the exposure window during which devices are vulnerable to attack or misuse. As demonstrated, IFTAT can be deployed using existing IoT devices, hubs, and network infrastructure to create and manage policies, requiring no costly new equipment or backend cloud services. We hope that IFTAT and future time-based access control systems based on our framework offer users peace of mind when bringing new, potentially untrusted devices into their networks.

Acknowledgement. The second and third authors acknowledge funding from the Natural Sciences and Engineering Research Council of Canada (NSERC) through the Discovery Grant program.

References

1. Antonakakis, M., et al.: Understanding the Mirai botnet. In: USENIX Security Symposium, August 2017
2. de Graaf, R., Aycock, J., Jacobson, M.: Improved port knocking with strong authentication. In: Annual Computer Security Applications Conference (2005)
3. Dong, K., et al.: Real-time execution of trigger-action connection for home Internet-of-Things. In: IEEE INFOCOM 2022 - IEEE Conf. on Computer Communications (2022)
4. Goutam, S., Enck, W., Reaves, B.: Hestia: simple least privilege network policies for smart homes. In: ACM WiSec (2019)
5. Hamza, A., Ranathunga, D., Gharakheili, H.H., Roughan, M., Sivaraman, V.: Clear as MUD: generating, validating and applying IoT behavioral profiles. In: ACM SIGCOMM Workshop on IoT Security and Privacy (2018)

6. He, W., et al.: SoK: context sensing for access control in the adversarial home IoT. In: IEEE EuroS&P (2021)
7. Herwig, S., Harvey, K., Hughey, G., Roberts, R., Levin, D.: Measurement and analysis of Hajime, a peer-to-peer IoT botnet. In: NDSS Symposium (2019)
8. Huang, D.Y., Apthorpe, N., Li, F., Acar, G., Feamster, N.: IoT inspector: crowdsourcing labeled network traffic from smart home devices at scale. Proc. ACM Interact. Mob. Wearable Ubiquitous Technol. **4**(2), 1–21 (2020)
9. Lear, E., Droms, R., Romascanu, D.: Manufacturer usage description specification. RFC 8520, March 2019
10. Marchal, S., Miettinen, M., Nguyen, T.D., Sadeghi, A., Asokan, N.: AuDI: toward autonomous IoT device-type identification using periodic communication. IEEE J. Sel. Areas Commun. **37**(6), 1402–1412 (2019)
11. Mi, X., et al.: Resident evil: understanding residential IP proxy as a dark service. In: IEEE Symposium on Security and Privacy (2019)
12. Miettinen, M., Marchal, S., Hafeez, I., Asokan, N., Sadeghi, A.R., Tarkoma, S.: IoT sentinel: automated device-type identification for security enforcement in IoT. In: Conference on Distributed Computing Systems (ICDCS) (2017)
13. Mitev, R., Pazii, A., Miettinen, M., Enck, W., Sadeghi, A.R.: LeakyPick: IoT audio spy detector. In: Annual Computer Security Applications Conference (2020)
14. Newman, L.H.: An elaborate hack shows how much damage IoT bugs can do. WIRED, April 2018. https://www.wired.com/story/elaborate-hack-shows-damage-iot-bugs-can-do/
15. Nguyen, T.D., Marchal, S., Miettinen, M., Fereidooni, H., Asokan, N., Sadeghi, A.: DÏoT: a federated self-learning anomaly detection system for IoT. In: IEEE International Conference on Distributed Computing Systems, pp. 756–767 (2019)
16. OConnor, T., Enck, W., Reaves, B.: Blinded and confused: uncovering systemic flaws in device telemetry for smart-home internet of things. In: Conference on Security and Privacy in Wireless and Mobile Networks, pp. 140–150 (2019)
17. OConnor, T., Mohamed, R., Miettinen, M., Enck, W., Reaves, B., Sadeghi, A.R.: HomeSnitch: behavior transparency and control for smart home IoT devices. In: ACM WiSec (2019)
18. Ruiz, C., Pan, S., Bannis, A., Chang, M.P., Noh, H.Y., Zhang, P.: IDIoT: towards ubiquitous identification of IoT devices through visual and inertial orientation matching during human activity. In: IEEE/ACM International Conference on Internet-of-Things Design and Implementation (2020)
19. Seymour, W., Kraemer, M.J., Binns, R., Van Kleek, M.: Informing the design of privacy-empowering tools for the connected home. In: ACM Conference on Human Factors in Computing Systems (2020)
20. Talakala, G.H., Bapat, J.: Detecting spoofing attacks in Zigbee using device fingerprinting. In: IEEE Annual Consumer Communications Networking Conference (2021)
21. The Associated Press: Your smart fridge could be mining bitcoins for criminals. CBC News, June 2018. https://www.cbc.ca/news/science/bitcoin-hacking-smart-devices-1.4728222
22. Thomasset, C., Barrera, D.: SERENIoT: distributed network security policy management and enforcement for smart homes. In: Annual Computer Security Applications Conference (2020)
23. Zhang, L., Tan, S., Wang, Z., Ren, Y., Wang, Z., Yang, J.: VibLive: a continuous liveness detection for secure voice user interface in IoT environment. In: Annual Computer Security Applications Conference (2020)

Reducing Trust Assumptions with OSCORE, RISC-V, and Layer 2 One-Time Passwords

Konrad-Felix Krentz[1](✉) and Thiemo Voigt[1,2]

[1] Uppsala University, Uppsala, Sweden
{konrad.krentz,thiemo.voigt}@angstrom.uu.se
[2] RISE Computer Science, Kista, Sweden

Abstract. In the Internet of things (IoT), traffic often goes via middleboxes, such as brokers or virtual private network (VPN) gateways, thereby increasing the trusted computing base (TCB) of IoT applications considerably. A remedy is offered by the application layer security protocol Object Security for Constrained RESTful Environments (OSCORE). It allows for basic middlebox functions without breaking end-to-end security. With OSCORE, however, traffic is routed to IoT devices largely unfiltered. This opens up avenues for remote denial-of-sleep attacks where a remote attacker injects OSCORE messages so as to cause IoT devices to consume more energy. The state-of-the-art defense is to let a trusted middlebox perform authenticity, freshness, and per-client rate limitation checks before forwarding OSCORE messages to IoT devices, but this solution inflates the TCB and hence negates the idea behind OSCORE. In this paper, we suggest filtering OSCORE messages in a RISC-V-based trusted execution environment (TEE) running on a middlebox that remains widely untrusted. To realize this approach, we also put forward the tiny remote attestation protocol (TRAP), as well as a Layer 2 integration that prevents attackers from bypassing our TEE. Experimental results show our remote denial-of-sleep defense to be lightweight enough for low-end IoT devices and to keep the TCB small.

1 Introduction

Object Security for Constrained RESTful Environments (OSCORE) is a security protocol for the Constrained Application Protocol (CoAP), while CoAP in turn is a RESTful application layer protocol for Internet of things (IoT) devices [29,30]. The principle of OSCORE is to map a CoAP message to an OSCORE message at the sender side and to restore the original CoAP message at the receiver side. An OSCORE message is, again, a CoAP message. Unlike IPsec or Datagram Transport Layer Security (DTLS), OSCORE operates at the application layer and hence provides end-to-end security across CoAP proxies.

Unfortunately, OSCORE is vulnerable to remote denial-of-sleep attacks [7, 8,27,28]. Denial-of-sleep attacks generally aim to expend the typically limited charge of IoT devices [31]. What distinguishes local from remote denial-of-sleep

© The Author(s), under exclusive license to Springer Nature Switzerland AG 2023
G.-V. Jourdan et al. (Eds.): FPS 2022, LNCS 13877, pp. 389–405, 2023.
https://doi.org/10.1007/978-3-031-30122-3_24

attacks is that remote ones are carried out via the Internet. As for OSCORE, a remote attacker can just direct OSCORE messages to an IoT device. Though an IoT device discards inauthentic and replayed OSCORE messages, this only happens after having consumed energy for their reception and processing already.

A naive defense against remote denial-of-sleep attacks is to equip IoT devices with a pertinent detection mechanism and to enter an energy-saving sleep mode in the face of such attacks. We call this defense naive because, under remote denial-of-sleep attacks, all OSCORE clients will be blocked, rather than just malicious OSCORE clients. There are two approaches to avoid this denial-of-service (DoS) vulnerability. One is to install a trusted middlebox that performs authenticity, freshness, and per-client rate limitation checks before forwarding messages to IoT devices [8,27,28]. Authenticity and freshness checking is done for two reasons. For one thing, this filters out messages that do not originate from an authorized client. For another, this enables attributing forwarded messages to certain clients and thus rate-limiting compromised clients without affecting benign clients. Altogether, middlebox-centered remote denial-of-sleep defenses are effective, but their authenticity checking requires giving away end-to-end keying material to a middlebox. As long as the middlebox remains uncompromised, no issues occur. This is, however, a questionable assumption because such a middlebox may run a large amount of code, typically a whole Linux operating system (OS). Thus, the chance for a vulnerability is high. Another approach consists in adding one-time passwords (OTPs) to Layer 7 headers [7,8]. These OTPs are checked before parsing a message's payload, thereby accelerating the rejection of unwanted messages. Yet, that approach only offers a partial mitigation as the reception and partial parsing already consume energy.

The main contribution of this paper is to drastically relax the trust assumptions of the middlebox-centered approach. We achieve this by adapting the middlebox-centered approach to perform the filtering in a trusted execution environment (TEE). Consequently, unlike current middlebox-centered remote denial-of-sleep defenses, ours tolerates the compromise of most of the middlebox's software, including its OS, its host apps, as well as tenanted TEEs.

Moving the filtering to a TEE raises two practical hurdles. First, to enable the TEE to filter OSCORE messages without violating privacy, each IoT device should (i) convince itself that the middlebox runs trusted software versions on genuine hardware and (ii) establish a shared key with the TEE for sharing end-to-end keying material confidentially. Both can be done at once through a remote attestation [18]. However, the energy constraints of battery-powered IoT devices mismatch the design choices of present remote attestation protocols. In particular, the Diffie-Hellman (DH)-based remote attestation protocols of the Keystone, Sanctum, as well as Intel Software Guard Extensions (SGX) TEE technologies all require energy-consuming signature operations and do not optimize their communication overhead [11,18,19]. A second hurdle is to handle the situation when an attacker compromises untrusted parts of the middlebox. It is then key that the attacker cannot forward OSCORE messages without consent by the TEE. Bypassing the TEE should also be impossible by injecting or replaying OSCORE messages toward the to-be-protected IoT devices.

As part of our main contribution - a middlebox-centered remote denial-of-sleep defense with a significantly reduced trusted computing base (TCB) - we overcome both practical hurdles outlined above briefly as follows:

- Regarding the first hurdle, we propose the tiny remote attestation protocol (TRAP). TRAP builds on Fully Hashed Menezes-Qu-Vanstone with Confirmation (FHMQV-C) [25]. Switching from DH to FHMQV-C reduces the number of involved signatures to one. Also, TRAP keeps the communication overhead low, mainly by means of using CoAP as its transport protocol.
- Regarding the second hurdle, we integrate our remote denial-of-sleep defense with an emerging countermeasure against a set of local denial-of-sleep attacks, namely to embed OTPs in the Layer 2 headers of radio transmissions [9,13–16,35]. These Layer 2 OTPs enable receivers to quickly cancel the reception of unwanted radio transmissions, thereby avoiding energy loss. Through our integration, IoT devices are also able to cancel the reception of OSCORE messages that bypassed the TEE.

The rest of this paper is structured as follows. Section 2 completes our discussion on related work. Section 3 elaborates on our remote denial-of-sleep defense. Section 4 goes into implementation details. Section 5 gives an empirical evaluation. Section 6 concludes and suggests directions for future work.

2   Related Work

Our remote denial-of-sleep defense is inspired by TEE-based deep packet inspection (DPI) engines first proposed by Schiff et al. [26]. Basically, a TEE-based DPI engine operates as follows. A client C first initiates a remote attestation to ensure that a middlebox runs trusted DPI code inside a TEE T. A by-product of this remote attestation is a key K that C and T share. C then uses K to securely send its end-to-end keying material to T, thus enabling T to fully inspect packets from and to C. Unfortunately, however, all current TEE-based DPI engines rest on Intel SGX, which is susceptible to side-channel attacks. The known side-channel attacks against Intel SGX can broadly be classified into controlled channel, cache, and transient execution attacks [3,22]. Though there are meanwhile defenses against most of the known side-channel attacks against Intel SGX [22,23], those defenses address attack-specific privacy leaks. Conversely, our remote denial-of-sleep defense rests on the Keystone TEE technology, which follows a principled approach to protect against side-channel attacks [19].

Like Keystone, many other TEE technologies also build on open instruction set architectures (ISAs) so as to raise the confidence in their privacy preservation. Early open ISA-based TEE technologies used the OpenSPARC ISA [5,20]. Newer ones build on the more widespread RISC-V ISA [1,18,19,32,34]. Yet, three of the existing RISC-V-based TEE technologies, namely Sanctum, TIMBER-V, and SERVAS, require hardware modifications [18,32,34]. By contrast, Keystone and MultiZone use the newly specified hardware interface for Physical Memory Protection (PMP), thereby obviating hardware modifications [1,19].

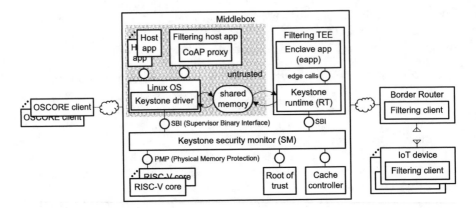

Fig. 1. Components and actors involved in our remote denial-of-sleep defense. Most of the middlebox's components are untrusted in our threat model.

As mentioned, two of the existing remote denial-of-sleep defenses follow the approach of adding OTPs to Layer 7 headers and to check these OTPs before parsing a message's payload [7,8]. In the context of local denial-of-sleep attacks, this concept was taken a step further by cancelling the reception of unwanted radio transmissions already during reception [2,4,6,9,13–16,35]. The approach there is to embed OTPs in Layer 1 or 2 headers and to check these OTPs during reception. However, whereas Layer 1 OTPs remained at a conceptual stage, Layer 2 OTPs are meanwhile part of a fully functional medium access control (MAC) layer, henceforth called HPI-MAC [13]. We use HPI-MAC for implementing our idea of coupling a local and a remote denial-of-sleep defense together.

3   Design of Our Remote Denial-of-Sleep Defence

In this section, we first introduce the components and actors involved in our remote denial-of-sleep defense. Subsequently, we define our threat model, detail TRAP, explain the filtering itself, and lastly analyze possible attacks.

3.1   Components and Actors

The central component of our remote denial-of-sleep defense is the *Filtering TEE*. It filters out unwanted OSCORE messages toward the to-be-protected IoT devices. To do so, it confidentially gets access to end-to-end keying material from the to-be-protected IoT devices. By virtue of building on the Keystone TEE technology, neither a compromised OS, nor a compromised host app, nor a compromised tenanted TEE can access the Filtering TEE's data. Figure 1 shows further components and actors involved in our remote denial-of-sleep defense:

- *OSCORE clients* communicate with IoT devices as per OSCORE. This communication goes via our middlebox, which acts as a CoAP proxy. That is, OSCORE clients direct their OSCORE messages to the middlebox and include a Proxy-Scheme option in each of their OSCORE messages.

– The middlebox itself has multiple subcomponents. The *Keystone security monitor (SM)* enforces security boundaries through RISC-V PMP and manages TEEs. The Keystone SM is loaded by a first-stage boot loader named *root of trust*. The Linux OS uses the *Keystone driver* to interact with the Keystone SM. Besides, the Linux OS may host multiple apps. A mandatory host app is the *Filtering host app*. It proxies OSCORE messages and also sends CoAP messages on behalf of the Filtering TEE. Before proxying OSCORE messages, however, the Filtering host app asks the Filtering TEE to inspect them. The Filtering host app and TEE communicate via shared memory. Like any Keystone TEE, the Filtering TEE comprises an enclave app (eapp) and a Keystone runtime (RT). While eapps implement application logic, RTs mediate with the Keystone SM and driver.

– The *border router* may run as another host app or be a separate device. It mainly relays CoAP messages between the middlebox and neighboring IoT devices. As part of our remote denial-of-sleep defense, the border router also embeds a *Filtering OTP* in each radio transmission that imparts an inbound OSCORE message. A Filtering OTP is generated with a pairwise key between the Filtering TEE and the next hop IoT device. Inbound CoAP messages without an OSCORE option, on the other hand, may carry TRAP traffic and are to be forwarded by the border router without a Filtering OTP. Those CoAP messages fall back on normal Layer 2 OTPs and hence require rate-limiting at the receiver side. Likewise, normal OTPs are still to be used for securing internal traffic, where rate-limiting at the receiver side is also required to mitigate compromises of the border router and of IoT devices.

– A *Filtering client* mainly performs a remote attestation at startup. This is to check whether the middlebox runs trusted versions of the Filtering TEE and the Keystone SM on a genuine root of trust. A by-product of the remote attestation is a pairwise key $K_{i,T}$ between the initiating Filtering client i and the Filtering TEE. Either side derives two keys from $K_{i,T}$. $K_{i,T}^{\text{OSCORE}}$, on the one hand, becomes an OSCORE Master Secret. The resulting OSCORE session, in particular, serves for sharing end-to-end keying material confidentially. $K_{i,T}^{\text{OTP}}$, on the other hand, serves for generating Filtering OTPs.

3.2   Threat Model

We consider the threat of remote denial-of-sleep attacks against IoT devices. To this purpose, the attacker may sniff, inject, modify, and block messages. Additionally, the attacker may compromise OSCORE clients, untrusted parts of the middlebox, the border router, as well as IoT devices. But, we do not aim to protect compromised IoT devices from remote denial-of-sleep attacks anymore. Local denial-of-sleep attacks must be mitigated by complementary measures.

As for the privacy preservation of the Filtering TEE, we inherit the threat model of Keystone [19]. Keystone TEEs resist physical and side-channel attackers. Physical attackers tamper with signals that leave the RISC-V processor

Table 1. Notations

Symbol	Meaning
PK_R, SK_R	the static public/private key pair of the root of trust
PK_i, SK_i	the static public/private key pair of Filtering client i
PK_M, SK_M	the public/private key pair of the Keystone SM
PK_C, SK_C	an ephemeral public/private key pair of a Filtering client
PK_T, SK_T	an ephemeral public/private key pair of the Filtering TEE
$K_{i,T}^{\mathrm{MIC}}, K_{i,T}$	FHMQV-C keys of the Filtering client i and the Filtering TEE
$K_{i,T}^{\mathrm{OSCORE}}$	a key derived from $K_{i,T}$ for use by OSCORE
$K_{i,T}^{\mathrm{OTP}}$	another key derived from $K_{i,T}$ for generating Filtering OTPs
HMIC(key, data)	a hash-based message integrity code (MIC) algorithm

package. Side-channel attackers may launch various side-channel attacks, namely controlled, cache, and transient execution side-channel attacks. The prevention of timing side-channel attacks, on the other hand, is at the responsibility of Keystone TEEs themselves. Depending on where the middlebox is being deployed, some of Keystone's protection mechanisms may be dispensable in favor of saving resources. For example, if physical access to the middlebox is restricted, Keystone's countermeasures against physical attackers can be disabled.

Further, while we protect the middlebox from DoS attacks, we do not aim to maintain service when untrusted parts of the middlebox get compromised.

3.3   TRAP: Tiny Remote Attestation Protocol

The protocol participants are the Keystone SM, the Filtering host app, the Filtering TEE, and an initiating Filtering client i. The goals of TRAP are (i) to assure the Filtering client i that the middlebox runs trusted versions of the Filtering TEE and the Keystone SM and (ii) to agree on the keys $K_{i,T}^{\mathrm{OSCORE}}, K_{i,T}^{\mathrm{OTP}}$ with the Filtering TEE. TRAP assumes each Filtering client to know the static public key PK_R of the root of trust, the hash of the initial state of the Keystone SM, and the hash of the initial state of the Filtering TEE. Also, it assumes the Filtering TEE to know the static public key PK_j of each Filtering client j. If this pre-configured information changes, a software update is necessary. For a summary of our notations, see Table 1. Figure 2 depicts the four phases of TRAP:

① **DoS Protection:** The Filtering client initiates a remote attestation by sending a CoAP request to the path "/kno" (short for knock). Yet, as serving a remote attestation is resource-intensive, attackers may cause DoS by initiating several remote attestations. Moreover, attackers may misuse the Filtering host app for launching amplification attacks. The idea of amplification attacks consists in sending initiation messages to a server in the name of a victim host, i.e., with a spoofed IP source address. If the server's responses are longer than the initiation messages, an attacker can amplify his or her bandwidth. This may thus enable DoS attacks. To prevent both these attack paths, TRAP incorporates

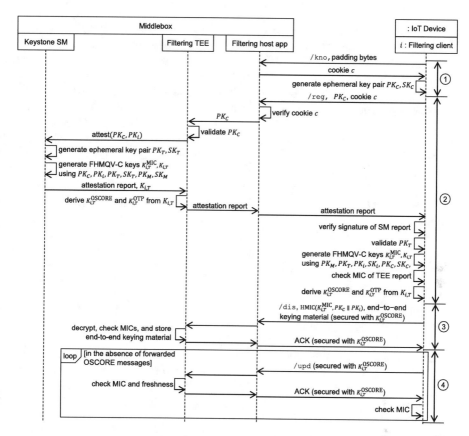

Fig. 2. TRAP's four phases, namely ① DoS protection, ② key agreement, ③ disclosure & confirmation, and ④ keep-alive messages

the respective countermeasure of DTLS [24]. Specifically, the Filtering host app maintains a secret value r that is regenerated at a regular time interval. When the Filtering host app receives a kno request, the Filtering host app initially challenges the initiator. The Filtering host app does so by returning a cookie $c = \mathsf{HMIC}(r, a)\|t$, where $\mathsf{HMIC}(\text{key}, \text{data})$ is a hash-based message integrity code (MIC) algorithm, a is the source IP address of the received kno request, t is the current time interval, and $\|$ denotes concatenation. By presenting the cookie in the subsequent phase, the Filtering client proves that it can receive data on its IP address.

② **Key Agreement:** On reception of the kno response with the cookie c, the Filtering client generates an ephemeral key pair (PK_C, SK_C). Next, the Filtering client sends a CoAP request to the path "/reg" (short for register). The payload of the reg request comprises PK_C and the cookie c.

DH-based Scheme: If c is valid, the DH-based scheme of Keystone and Sanctum would now proceed as follows. The Filtering TEE generates its ephemeral key pair (PK_T, SK_T) and asks the Keystone SM to generate an attestation report. In Keystone and Sanctum, an attestation report consists of an SM and a TEE report. The SM report contains the public key PK_M of the Keystone SM and a signature. This signature is generated using the static private key SK_R of the root of trust and covers both PK_M and a hash of the initial state of the Keystone SM. Note that when the root of trust loads the Keystone SM, it also generates the key pair (PK_M, SK_M), creates the SM report, and finally erases SK_R from random-access memory (RAM). The TEE report contains PK_T and another signature. That signature is generated with SK_M and covers PK_T, PK_C, as well as a hash of the initial state of the Filtering TEE. Before sending the attestation report to the Filtering client, the Filtering TEE generates the DH key $K_{i,T}$ with PK_T, SK_T, and PK_C. On reception of the attestation report, the Filtering client verifies both contained signatures. If valid, the Filtering client proceeds with generating $K_{i,T}$, too. Thus, the original DH-based scheme requires two signatures and lacks client authentication. Client authentication requires the client side to, e.g., sign PK_C with PK_i, but this entails another signature.

TRAP: TRAP's FHMQV-C-based scheme reduces the number of signatures to one despite adding client authentication [25]. While DH derives $K_{i,T}$ only from the ephemeral key pairs (PK_C, SK_C) and (PK_T, SK_T), FHMQV-C additionally entangles the long-term key pairs (PK_i, SK_i) and (PK_M, SK_M). Another change is that FHMQV-C generates two symmetric keys, namely the actual FHMQV-C key $K_{i,T}$ and the key $K_{i,T}^{\text{MIC}}$ for perfect forward secrecy. Concretely, if PK_C and c are valid, the Filtering TEE will ask the Keystone SM to generate an attestation report. Like in Keystone and Sanctum, an attestation report consists of an SM and a TEE report. We keep the SM report unmodified and only adapt the TEE report. The TEE report contains PK_T and a MIC. The MIC is generated with the FHMQV-C key $K_{i,T}^{\text{MIC}}$ and authenticates PK_M, PK_T, as well as a hash of the initial state of the Filtering TEE. Before sending the attestation report to the Filtering client, the Filtering TEE derives $K_{i,T}^{\text{OSCORE}}$ and $K_{i,T}^{\text{OTP}}$ from the actual FHMQV-C key $K_{i,T}$. On reception of the attestation report, the Filtering client checks its contents and finally derives $K_{i,T}^{\text{OSCORE}}$ and $K_{i,T}^{\text{OTP}}$, too.

③ **Disclosure & Confirmation:** The next interaction serves the dual purpose of disclosing end-to-end keying material to the Filtering TEE and of ensuring perfect forward secrecy. An exception is the border router, which does not share any end-to-end keying material. The potentially empty disclosed keying material is sent as a CoAP request to the path "/dis" (short for disclose). To secure the dis request, TRAP uses $K_{i,T}^{\text{OSCORE}}$ as an OSCORE Master Secret. Including $\text{HMIC}(K_{i,T}^{\text{MIC}}, PK_C \| PK_i)$ ensures perfect forward secrecy [25]. On reception, the Filtering TEE unsecures the dis request as per OSCORE, checks the FHMQV-C MIC, stores the end-to-end keying material (if any), and returns a CoAP ACK that is secured by the just established OSCORE session.

④ **Keep-Alive Messages:** The forth phase accounts for reboots of the middlebox. Note that if the Filtering client reboots, it will initiate another remote attestation and a new OSCORE session begins. By contrast, if the middlebox rebooted, this would go unnoticed by Filtering clients. Hence, the Filtering client sends, in the absence of forwarded OSCORE messages from the middlebox, CoAP requests to the path "/upd" (short for update). To secure upd requests, TRAP uses the established OSCORE session. A fresh authentic CoAP ACK signals that the middlebox is up. Otherwise, if an upd request remains unacknowledged, the Filtering client will initiate a new remote attestation.

3.4   Filtering of Inbound OSCORE Messages

The Filtering TEE filters out inauthentic and replayed inbound OSCORE messages and rate-limits remaining ones on a per client basis. Checking the authenticity of inbound OSCORE messages is possible since IoT devices disclose their end-to-end keying material to the Filtering TEE after the remote attestation. To detect replayed inbound OSCORE messages, the Filtering TEE keeps track of the sequence numbers used in authentic inbound OSCORE messages. As for the rate limitation, the Filtering TEE maintains per-IoT client leaky bucket counters (LBCs) like in prior work [8,27]. The main motivation behind rate-limiting this way is that the rate of forwarded inbound OSCORE messages may overshoot temporarily, while a maximum rate is still enforced in the long term.

If an inbound OSCORE message passes authenticity, freshness, as well as rate limitation checks, the Filtering TEE resecures it using the OSCORE session that was established with the addressed IoT device during remote attestation. This resecuring allows the addressed IoT device to ensure that the OSCORE message actually passed through the Filtering TEE. Furthermore, this already prevents remote denial-of-sleep attacks that depend on the middlebox to forward OSCORE messages. Yet, it does not cater for an attacker who bypasses the Filtering TEE by, e.g., injecting OSCORE messages on the path between the middlebox and the border router. This is why we integrate with Layer 2 OTPs.

Consider that the border router plans a radio transmission that conveys an inbound OSCORE message to a neighboring IoT device running Filtering client j. Such a radio transmission is to be prefixed with an OTP that is generated with an unusual key, namely the pairwise key $K_{j,T}^{OTP}$ between j and the Filtering TEE. Since $K_{j,T}^{OTP}$ is unknown to the border router, it retrieves a ready-to-use Filtering OTP from the Filtering TEE. To do so, the border router sends a CoAP request to the path "/otp". To secure this otp request, the border router uses its OSCORE session with the Filtering TEE. The otp request's payload contains (i) the wake-up counter of the next hop IoT device at the scheduled time of reception, (ii) the number of bytes of the radio frame, (iii) the MAC address of the next hop IoT device, and (iv) the two final bytes of the MIC of the inbound OSCORE message. While (i), (ii), and (iii) are inputs to the generation of an OTP as per HPI-MAC [13,15], (iv) allows the Filtering TEE to relate otp requests to relayed OSCORE messages, thereby enabling the Filtering TEE to detect a compromised border router who illegitimately requests Filtering OTPs. For signaling the use of a Filtering OTP rather than a normal OTP, we leverage an unused flag in HPI-MAC's header, allowing receivers to branch accordingly.

3.5   Security Analysis

DoS Attacks: A basic threat to the middlebox are DoS attacks, where an attacker either initiates several remote attestations or misuses the returned attestation reports to amplify his or her bandwidth. Owing to TRAP's cookie check, Filtering clients must prove address ownership prior to any remote attestation. This enables the Filtering host app to implement an IP-based rate limitation, e.g., using LBCs along with a hash-based lookup table. Amplification attacks, on the other hand, are complicated by the fact that they can only be launched from functioning source IP addresses. In this regard, there are two possible pitfalls. First, kno requests must at least be as long as kno responses so that the returned cookies do not enable amplification attacks themselves. Second, cookies must be invalidated by choosing a new value for the secret value r at regular intervals. TRAP attaches the current time interval to cookies so that the Filtering host app may choose to accept old cookies for a transition period.

Attacks on Key Agreement: FHMQV-C stands at the end of a series of improvements to the famous MQV protocol [17]. Sarr et al. showed HMQV, a more efficient version of MQV [12], to be vulnerable to impersonation and man-in-the-middle attacks when certain session-specific information leaks [25]. As a countermeasure, Sarr et al. proposed FHMQV, which is based on revised signature schemes [25]. FHMQV-C adds a confirmation message and MICs to FHMQV so as to attain perfect forward secrecy. FHMQV-C's confirmation message contains $\text{HMIC}(K_{i,T}^{\text{MIC}}, PK_C \| PK_i)$, which TRAP includes in dis requests. A preliminary to using FHMQV-C is to ensure the authenticity of the public key PK_M. TRAP does so by letting the root of trust generate the key pair (PK_M, SK_M), as well as letting the root of trust sign PK_M with SK_R. We remark that a protocol verification of TRAP using a pertinent tool, such as Tamarin, goes beyond the scope of this paper because adding support for MQV-based protocols to such tools is a subject of current research itself [10].

Attacks on Privacy Preservation: To ensure IoT devices that their communication is kept secret, their Filtering clients check if the Keystone SM and Filtering TEE were loaded properly and agree on an OSCORE Master Secret with the Filtering TEE. For this purpose, the root of trust hashes and signs the initial state of the Keystone SM. Hence, Filtering clients need to know the hash of the software version they trust. Further, as the signature also covers PK_M, PK_M can later serve to authenticate the hash of the initial state of the Filtering TEE in TEE reports. Thus, Filtering clients need to know that hash, as well.

Remote Denial-of-Sleep Attacks: Suppose an uncompromised IoT device with Filtering client i receives a radio frame and that the radio frame has the flag that signals the use of a Filtering OTP set. Let l denote the number of bits of a Filtering OTP. We argue that if the contained Filtering OTP does not originate from the Filtering TEE, there is only a probability of 2^{-l} that the radio frame is going to be fully received. Observe that $K_{i,T}^{\text{OTP}}$ is required for generating a Filtering OTP. Furthermore, $K_{i,T}^{\text{OTP}}$ is only known to the Filtering TEE and the IoT device itself. Thus, the compromise of IoT clients, other IoT devices, untrusted parts of the middlebox, and the border router does not reveal $K_{i,T}^{\mathrm{OTP}}$. This retains guessing and replay attacks. Replay attacks, however, do not work out because a Filtering OTP is only accepted as valid at the intended wake up.

4   Implementation

As for the implementation, preliminary steps concerned the CoAP, cryptographic, and OSCORE libraries. The CoAP library we opted for is libcoap, across all components where CoAP is needed. Concerning the Filtering host app, a minor complication was to cross-compile libcoap to RISC-V. By contrast, on our CC2538-based target IoT devices [33], we run Contiki-NG, an OS libcoap was not yet ported to. Our choice for Contiki-NG is motivated by the availability of an implementation of HPI-MAC for it [13]. As cryptographic library, we use existing C implementations of P-256 and SHA-256 in the Keystone SM and root of trust. On our CC2538-based target IoT devices, on the other hand, we implemented these cryptographic primitives by ourselves so as to leverage the hardware acceleration features of CC2538 chips. Finally, we implemented an OSCORE library for use by Filtering TEEs, Filtering clients, and test IoT clients. With these preliminary steps done, the implementation is rather straightforward since libcoap is convenient for realizing standard CoAP interactions. The main repository of our implementation is https://github.com/kkrentz/filtering-proxy.

5   Evaluation

Our empirical evaluation focuses on two probable concerns about the practicality of our remote denial-of-sleep defense. On the one hand, low-end IoT devices might be incapable of performing the involved elliptic curve cryptography (ECC) or of handling the communication overhead. On the other hand, the increase of the TCB might represent an unacceptable security trade-off. We shall conclude that neither of these concerns applies to our remote denial-of-sleep defense.

5.1   Overhead of TRAP vs DH-Based Remote Attestation

To quantify the overhead of TRAP vs the original DH-based scheme with client authentication, the following experiments were conducted. It was first measured how long it takes a CC2538-based IoT device to perform the involved ECC. For this, both remote attestation protocols were executed multiple times with and without hardware acceleration for the cryptographic primitives P-256 and SHA-256. During each protocol run, the durations for (i) generating (PK_C, SK_C), including, in the case of the DH-based scheme, signing PK_C, and (ii) checking the attestation report, including key derivation were logged. Next, the sizes of the CoAP messages that are exchanged during a remote attestation were determined via Wireshark. The disclosed end-to-end keying material comprised 16 bytes. Finally, the program memory and static RAM overhead of the Filtering client on

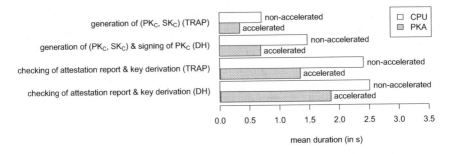

Fig. 3. Compared to the original DH-based scheme with client authentication, TRAP shortens the processing times noticeably. Enabling hardware acceleration for SHA-256 and P-256 further speeds up processing times.

a CC2538-based IoT device was measured. As a baseline, a Contiki-NG example of an OSCORE-secured CoAP server was first compiled without our remote denial-of-sleep defense enabled. Then, the example was compiled with our remote denial-of-sleep defense enabled and eventually both binaries were analyzed. In the same manner, the memory overhead of hardware-accelerated and software-only ECC was determined. As software implementation, Micro-ECC was used.

Figure 3 shows the measured processing times. A first observation is that enabling hardware acceleration for P-256 moves the bulk of the workload to the Public Key hardware Accelerator (PKA) of the CC2538. The PKA operates in the background while the CPU can proceed with other threads in the meantime. Since Contiki-NG has an event-driven kernel, this is highly beneficial. Specifically, in Contiki-NG, long-running tasks have to be split up since event handlers run to completion. Given that all involved cryptographic computations take quite long, Micro-ECC can actually not be used "as is" in Contiki-NG. Hardware-accelerated ECC circumvents this issue and, beyond that, accelerates processing times significantly. A second observation is that TRAP shortens the overall processing times due to FHMQV-C being more efficient. A third observation is that the processing times are still far from negligible. Hence, one should protect against attackers that provoke remote attestations, e.g., through jamming upd messages. Possible mitigations include rate-limiting remote attestations.

Figure 4 shows the sizes of the CoAP messages that are exchanged during a remote attestation. The kno and dis requests and responses are all small enough to fit in a single IEEE 802.15.4 frame, at least when using the 2.4-GHz IEEE 802.15.4 offset quadrature phase-shift keying (O-QPSK) physical layer (PHY) like us. This is because this PHY has a maximum transmission unit of 127 bytes. If an IPv6 packet does not fit within a single IEEE 802.15.4 frame, even after compressing it, Contiki-NG automatically fragments it as per 6LoWPAN [21]. This actually happens during the reg interaction. That said, TRAP exchanges much less data during the reg interaction due to obviating two signatures compared to the original DH-based scheme with client authentication. Furthermore,

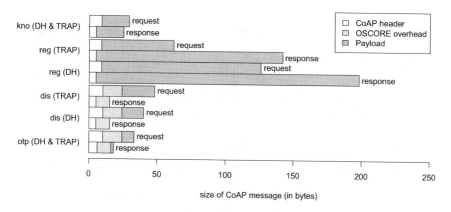

Fig. 4. Sizes of the CoAP messages that are sent while executing TRAP and the original DH-based scheme with client authentication. TRAP has a significantly reduced communication overhead due to obviating two signatures.

in our implementation of both protocols, we use public key compression, which saves 255 bits per transferred public key (3 in total). The `otp` interaction, on the other hand, occurs between the more capable border router and the Filtering TEE in order to retrieve a valid Filtering OTP for forwarding the `dis` response. Thus, this interaction does not consume any charge of any IoT device anyway.

Figure 5 shows the static RAM and program memory consumption of the Filtering client on CC2538-based IoT devices. As even the top version of the CC2538 only offers 512 KB of program memory and 32 KB of RAM, these figures are also important. The static RAM consumption of the Filtering client turned out to be small. TRAP consumes more RAM since some keys need to be kept in RAM for longer than in the original DH-based scheme. The program memory consumption, on the other hand, is rather high, whereof the code for ECC has a large share. That said, the program memory consumption is still well manageable for CC2538-based IoT devices. TRAP consumes slightly more program memory since the implementation of FHMQV-C is more complex.

5.2   Trusted Computing Base

Running additional code on the IoT devices, as well as trusting part of the code that runs on the middlebox may intolerably increase the TCB. However, as shown in Fig. 5b, the additional code that IoT devices must run is overseeable, even more so when ECC is required anyway. The TCB on the middlebox comprises the root of trust, the Keystone SM, and the Filtering TEE. As for the root of trust and the Keystone SM, Keystone is especially designed to keep their software thin [19]. As for the Filtering TEE, the code sizes shown in Fig. 6 were determined using a tool of the RISC-V GNU Compiler Collection (GCC) toolchain. We managed to decrease the TEE code by doing much of the CoAP and OSCORE processing in the untrusted Filtering host app. A large part of the

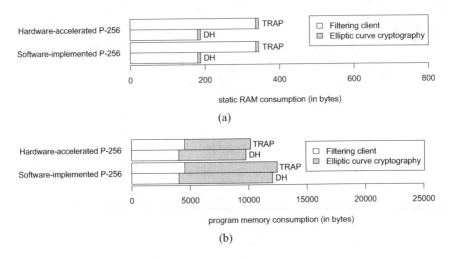

Fig. 5. Memory footprint of the Filtering client on CC2538-based IoT devices

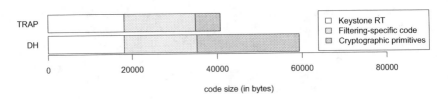

Fig. 6. Size of the trusted TEE code if compiled to 64-bit RISC-V

remaining TEE code implements the cryptographic primitives AES-128, SHA-256, and P-256. In the case of TRAP, the Filtering TEE does not need a P-256 implementation since all ECC-related processing is then performed by the Keystone SM, which requires ECC anyway. Overall, the Filtering TEE has 17 KB of application logic, which we deem an acceptable security trade-off.

6   Conclusions and Future Work

Remote denial-of-sleep attacks are easy to execute and incur severe repercussions in safety-critical IoT applications. In safety-uncritical IoT applications, it is, at least, desirable to prevent such attacks from the viewpoint of customer satisfaction and quality-of-service guarantees. The state-of-the-art defense is to install a fully trusted middlebox that filters out unwanted messages en-route. We have drastically reduced the trust assumptions on such a middlebox via the Keystone TEE technology. Notably, our solution does not depend on the middlebox to be placed on the path between OSCORE clients and IoT devices anymore. This is because it ultimately requires a Filtering OTP to wake up an IoT device and Filtering OTPs are only issued by the Filtering TEE. Another useful side effect is that it now suffices for an IoT device to establish an OSCORE session with the middlebox, rather than with every OSCORE client. A downside of our remote denial-of-sleep defense is that it requires a remote attestation, which we have addressed with the lightweight remote attestation protocol TRAP. For future work, we will be interested in the implications on latencies and throughput.

Acknowledgment. This work was carried out within the LifeSec project, which is funded by the Swedish Foundation for Strategic Research (grant 2017-045989).

References

1. MultiZone: https://hex-five.com/. Accessed 14 Nov 2022
2. Aljareh, S., Kavoukis, A.: Efficient time synchronized one-time password scheme to provide secure wake-up authentication on wireless sensor networks. Int. J. Adv. Smart Sens. Netw. Syst. **3**, 1–11 (2013). https://doi.org/10.5121/ijassn.2013.3101
3. Canella, C., et al.: A systematic evaluation of transient execution attacks and defenses. In: Proc. of USENIX Security, pp. 249–266. USENIX (2019)
4. Capossele, A.T., Cervo, V., Petrioli, C., Spenza, D.: Counteracting denial-of-sleep attacks in wake-up-based sensing systems. In: Proc. of SECON, pp. 1–9. IEEE (2016). https://doi.org/10.1109/SAHCN.2016.7732978
5. Champagne, D., Lee, R.B.: Scalable architectural support for trusted software. In: Proc. of HPCA, pp. 1–12. IEEE (2010). https://doi.org/10.1109/HPCA.2010.5416657
6. Falk, R., Hof, H.J.: Fighting insomnia: a secure wake-up scheme for wireless sensor networks. In: Proc. of SECURWARE, pp. 191–196 (2009). https://doi.org/10.1109/SECURWARE.2009.36
7. Gehrmann, C., Tiloca, M., Höglund, R.: SMACK: short message authentication check against battery exhaustion in the Internet of Things. In: Proc. of SECON, pp. 274–282. IEEE (2015). https://doi.org/10.1109/SAHCN.2015.7338326
8. Hristozov, S., Huber, M., Sigl, G.: Protecting RESTful IoT devices from battery exhaustion DoS attacks. In: Proc. of HOST, pp. 316–327. IEEE (2020). https://doi.org/10.1109/HOST45689.2020.9300290
9. Hsueh, C.T., Wen, C.Y., Ouyang, Y.C.: A secure scheme against power exhausting attacks in hierarchical wireless sensor networks. IEEE Sens. J. **15**(6), 3590–3602 (2015). https://doi.org/10.1109/JSEN.2015.2395442
10. Jackson, D.: Improving automated protocol verification: real world cryptography. Ph.D. thesis, University of Oxford (2020)
11. Knauth, T., Steiner, M., Chakrabarti, S., Lei, L., Xing, C., Vij, M.: Integrating remote attestation with transport layer security. arXiv preprint arXiv:1801.05863 (2018)
12. Krawczyk, H.: HMQV: a high-performance secure Diffie-Hellman protocol. In: Shoup, V. (ed.) CRYPTO 2005. LNCS, vol. 3621, pp. 546–566. Springer, Heidelberg (2005). https://doi.org/10.1007/11535218_33
13. Krentz, K.F.: A denial-of-sleep-resilient medium access control layer for IEEE 802.15.4 networks. Ph.D. thesis, Potsdam University (2019). https://doi.org/10.25932/publishup-43930
14. Krentz, K.F., Meinel, C.H.: Denial-of-sleep defenses for IEEE 802.15.4 coordinated sampled listening (CSL). Comput. Netw. **148**(15), 60–71 (2019). https://doi.org/10.1016/j.comnet.2018.10.021

15. Krentz, K.-F., Meinel, C., Graupner, H.: More lightweight, yet stronger 802.15.4 security through an intra-layer optimization. In: Imine, A., Fernandez, J.M., Marion, J.-Y., Logrippo, L., Garcia-Alfaro, J. (eds.) FPS 2017. LNCS, vol. 10723, pp. 173–188. Springer, Cham (2018). https://doi.org/10.1007/978-3-319-75650-9_12

16. Krentz, K.F., Meinel, Ch., Schnjakin, M.: POTR: practical on-the-fly rejection of injected and replayed 802.15.4 frames. In: Proc. of ARES, pp. 59–68. IEEE (2016). https://doi.org/10.1109/ARES.2016.7

17. Law, L., Menezes, A., Qu, M., Solinas, J., Vanstone, S.: An efficient protocol for authenticated key agreement. Des. Codes Cryptogr. **28**(2), 119–134 (2003). https://doi.org/10.1023/A:1022595222606

18. Lebedev, I., Hogan, K., Devadas, S.: Invited paper: Secure boot and remote attestation in the Sanctum processor. In: Proc. of CSF, pp. 46–60. IEEE (2018). https://doi.org/10.1109/CSF.2018.00011

19. Lee, D., Kohlbrenner, D., Shinde, S., Asanović, K., Song, D.: Keystone: an open framework for architecting trusted execution environments. In: Proc. of EuroSys, ACM (2020). https://doi.org/10.1145/3342195.3387532

20. Lee, R.B., Kwan, P.C.S., McGregor, J.P., Dwoskin, J., Zhenghong, W.: Architecture for protecting critical secrets in microprocessors. In: Proceedings of ISCA, pp. 2–13. IEEE (2005). https://doi.org/10.1109/ISCA.2005.14

21. Montenegro, G., Kushalnagar, N., Hui, J., Culler, D.: Transmission of IPv6 packets over IEEE 802.15.4 networks. RFC 4944 (2007)

22. Nilsson, A., Bideh, P.N., Brorsson, J.: A survey of published attacks on Intel SGX. Tech. rep., Lund University (2020)

23. Oleksenko, O., Trach, B., Krahn, R., Silberstein, M., Fetzer, C.: Varys: protecting SGX enclaves from practical side-channel attacks. In: Proc. of USENIX ATC, pp. 227–240. USENIX (2018)

24. Rescorla, E., Modadugu, N.: Datagram transport layer security version 1.2. RFC 6347 (2012)

25. Sarr, A.P., Elbaz-Vincent, P., Bajard, J.-C.: A secure and efficient authenticated Diffie–Hellman protocol. In: Martinelli, F., Preneel, B. (eds.) EuroPKI 2009. LNCS, vol. 6391, pp. 83–98. Springer, Heidelberg (2010). https://doi.org/10.1007/978-3-642-16441-5_6

26. Schiff, L., Schmid, S.: PRI: privacy preserving inspection of encrypted network traffic. In: Proc. of SPW, pp. 296–303. IEEE (2016). https://doi.org/10.1109/SPW.2016.34

27. Seidel, F., Krentz, K.F., Meinel, Ch.: Deep en-route filtering of constrained application protocol (CoAP) messages on 6LoWPAN border routers. In: Proc. of WF-IoT, pp. 201–206. IEEE (2019). https://doi.org/10.1109/WF-IoT.2019.8767262

28. Seitz, K., Serth, S., Krentz, K.F., Meinel, Ch.: Demo: enabling en-route filtering for end-to-end encrypted CoAP messages. In: Proc. of SenSys. ACM (2017). https://doi.org/10.1145/3131672.3136960

29. Selander, G., Mattsson, J., Palombini, F., Seitz, L.: Object security for constrained RESTful environments (OSCORE). RFC 8613 (2019)

30. Shelby, Z., Hartke, K., Bormann, C.: The constrained application protocol (CoAP). RFC 7252 (2014)

31. Stajano, F., Anderson, R.: The resurrecting duckling: security issues for ad-hoc wireless networks. In: Christianson, B., Crispo, B., Malcolm, J.A., Roe, M. (eds.) Security Protocols 1999. LNCS, vol. 1796, pp. 172–182. Springer, Heidelberg (2000). https://doi.org/10.1007/10720107_24

32. Steinegger, S., Schrammel, D., Weiser, S., Nasahl, P., Mangard, S.: SERVAS! secure enclaves via RISC-V authenticryption shield. In: Bertino, E., Shulman, H., Waidner, M. (eds.) ESORICS 2021. LNCS, vol. 12973, pp. 370–391. Springer, Cham (2021). https://doi.org/10.1007/978-3-030-88428-4_19
33. Texas Instruments: CC2538 SoC for 2.4-GHz IEEE 802.15.4 & ZigBee/ZigBee IP Applications User's Guide (Rev. C). https://www.ti.com/lit/ug/swru319c/swru319c.pdf
34. Weiser, S., Werner, M., Brasser, F., Malenko, M., Mangard, S., Sadeghi, A.R.: TIMBER-V: tag-isolated memory bringing fine-grained enclaves to RISC-V. In: Proc. of NDSS, USENIX (2019). https://doi.org/10.14722/ndss.2019.23068
35. Wood, A., Stankovic, J., Zhou, G.: DEEJAM: defeating energy-efficient jamming in IEEE 802.15.4-based wireless networks. In: Proc. of SECON, pp. 60–69. IEEE (2007). https://doi.org/10.1109/SAHCN.2007.4292818

Towards Characterizing IoT Software Update Practices

Conner Bradley[(⊠)] and David Barrera

School of Computer Science, Carleton University, Ottawa, Canada
connerbradley@scs.carleton.ca

Abstract. Software updates are critical for ensuring systems remain free of bugs and vulnerabilities while they are in service. While many Internet of Things (IoT) devices are capable of outlasting desktops and mobile phones, their software update practices are not yet well understood, despite a large body of research aiming to create new methodologies for keeping IoT devices up to date. This paper discusses efforts towards characterizing the IoT software update landscape through network-level analysis of IoT device traffic. Our results suggest that vendors do not currently follow security best practices, and that software update standards, while available, are not being deployed.

Keywords: IoT · Software Updates · Update Detection

1 Introduction

Consumer Internet of Things (IoT) devices have gained significant popularity in recent years, resulting in a revolution of IoT devices used in many applications. IoT devices are typically resource-constrained and require specialized operating systems and software stacks depending on their application [5]. Due to the unique resource constraints of IoT devices, device vendors have to either design their software update infrastructure and supporting applications from scratch or use an integrated third-party solution[1] which has historically shown to be inconsistent and vulnerable [30]. Software update systems are well understood and widely available on general-purpose computers and servers [4]; however, there is very little insight and research into how these vendor-specific IoT software update systems work due to a lack of standardization in the IoT space [6,31]. Our goal is to characterize how typical consumer IoT devices query for and retrieve software updates, and evaluate the security of these techniques as used by prominent IoT vendors.

A unique challenge for deployed IoT devices is their expected lifespan. Typical personal computers have a relatively short lifespan compared to an IoT device, which is expected to behave in an appliance-like fashion with minimal (if any) downtime. Personal computers may get replaced in 5–10 years if the hardware cannot keep up with current software demands. In contrast, an IoT device such

---

[1] Such as Microsoft Azure IoT, or Amazon Web Services IoT.

G.-V. Jourdan et al. (Eds.): FPS 2022, LNCS 13877, pp. 406–422, 2023.
https://doi.org/10.1007/978-3-031-30122-3_25

as a smart thermostat may be expected to run for decades before being replaced. With the constant evolution of technology, device vendors have the additional challenge of providing a secure implementation of their software on potentially outdated hardware.

We hypothesize that suboptimal update intervals from IoT device vendors may further weaken IoT update systems. For example, device libraries such as the crucial OpenSSL library were analyzed during a study of 122 IoT device firmware files, which revealed several vendors failed to patch OpenSSL in their IoT devices after critical vulnerabilities were released [32]. Device vendors took months to supply an updated system image with a patched OpenSSL version, and one vendor took nearly 1,500 days to patch the critical vulnerability. Failing to update critical libraries causes these devices to gain a larger attack surface that could potentially be leveraged by bad actors to trick the device into downloading malware [29] or to bypass security measures that are in place to prevent the device from loading modified firmware [6,9].

In recent years there have been many proposals for secure software update systems that are designed for IoT [7,11,32] and related cyber-physical systems [13,18]; however, there is no research (to our knowledge) aiming to broadly understand the IoT software/firmware update landscape in consumer IoT devices.

Our primary focus is identifying software updates being requested and taking place. The benefits of this can be leveraged in various contexts: Network-level update detection can be used as independent feedback to end users that their devices are being updated regularly – an IoT device vendor may promise to publish security patches for their IoT devices, but not deliver on that promise [32]. In an enterprise context, administrators may want to apply the principle of least privilege to fleets of IoT devices. Certain IoT devices do not need continuous access to the open internet as most devices can function exclusively with LAN connectivity to a central hub or other devices. The only edge case to this is checking for updates and downloading them. If an active firewall can detect update-related traffic from IoT devices, it can adjust rules to (1) allow the IoT device to download an update from the internet, and (2) log the update instance.

The research contributions in this paper are:

- The first in-depth analysis of consumer IoT network traffic to identify software update communications. We identified design patterns used in several IoT devices and found vulnerabilities that could be exploited.
- A case study of software update schemes and practices that we identified through our methodology. Devices featured in our case study distribute software updates over HTTP with no tamper-resistant protection mechanisms added on. One of the devices identified in the case study provides a happy medium between update transparency and security.
- An event-based characterization of when IoT devices update. We contextualize the various conditions that lead to an IoT device performing updates. For example, power cycling an IoT on is highly likely to trigger an update check.

2   Methodology

Our research objective is to understand and characterize how and when IoT devices perform software updates. To accomplish this, we build a network traffic analysis system that identifies and analyzes software update requests and responses from IoT devices. We aim for the system to be vendor-agnostic, requiring no *a priori* knowledge about the IoT vendor's infrastructure or devices. The system should also identify updates across multiple independent cloud vendors, which are relied upon heavily in IoT.

To accomplish this, we analyze network traffic from a 2019 Internet Measurements Conference (IMC) paper by Ren et al. [24] which actively captured traffic from 81 IoT devices. These 81 devices were located in two geographic regions; 46 in the US, 35 in the UK, and 26 common devices across both regions. In total, the dataset contains packet captures from 55 unique devices. Collected data was harvested at network gateways, but no form of middle-person attack was done on TLS traffic which precludes peering into an encrypted device communication. Therefore, in this paper, we rely exclusively on extractable HTTP traffic for identifying software updates. Additionally, we harvest metadata from the TLS handshakes to gain insight into the security of the secure communication channels used by these devices.

2.1   Data Extraction

In total, the dataset of packet captures from Ren et al. is 13 GB in size, which includes 37,744 packet captures recorded by the automated test system and 611 unsupervised experiment packet captures, yielding a total of 38,355 packet captures. We do not separate traffic by geographic region as Ren et al. found very negligible differences in region-specific traffic [24].

To identify network traffic related to software updates, we hypothesize that update interactions between an IoT device and vendor cloud follow a structured schema. If the schema is human-readable (e.g., JSON, XML, etc.) there will be keywords contained inside indicating some update-related information, such as a firmware version. We initially searched for a single keyword "update", which led us to build a corpus of update-related keywords: update, upgrade, firmware, software, and download.

These keywords will be the basis we use for identifying update-related traffic; however, manually searching through files will not scale to the number of devices we have. Therefore, we developed a parallel network traffic processing pipeline (see Fig. 1) that manages network traffic metadata and HTTP object extraction. The pipeline design is compatible with distributed data processing frameworks such as Apache Spark, and works on the dataset as follows:

Metadata Extraction: We extract metadata representing the packet capture. This includes the specific sub-dataset, region, experiment type (e.g., power on, interact with the device, etc.), and device name. The extracted metadata is saved to a metadata database and used for later steps in the pipeline.

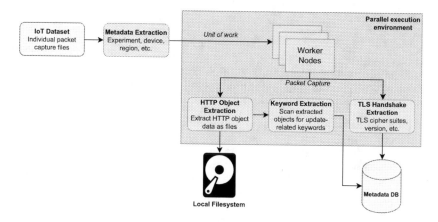

Fig. 1. Our data extraction pipeline: starting with the IoT packet capture dataset, we extract metadata for each packet capture to represent a given packet capture as a unit of work. We process each packet capture in parallel, extracting HTTP objects to the local filesystem, TLS Handshakes, and update-related metadata. All extracted metadata is stored relationally in a metadata database for further analysis, and HTTP objects are stored on the local filesystem.

Parallelization: We parallelize the extraction of metadata and HTTP objects on a per-packet capture basis. The parallelization is done by assigning each packet capture to a worker node, and the worker node performs the following steps on each packet capture individually. In practice a parallelization approach is not needed; however, passive analysis of a large amount of packet captures warrants the speedup gains of parallelization.

HTTP Object Extraction: We extract all HTTP payloads from a given packet capture. The HTTP payload data is of particular interest as it provides us insight into any files transferred along with any web service interactions.

TLS Handshake Extraction: We then extract TLS client and server hello data using a modified version of pyshark[2]. Our modified version of pyshark supports extracting an extended set of TLS handshake metadata, including the ciphers advertised in the TLS client hello and server hello handshake. In total, we return a list containing every TLS handshake, including the TLS version, TLS handshake type, and a list of cipher suites. The TLS cipher suite data is used to determine if devices are adequately securing communication channels against TLS-related attacks.

Keyword Extraction: For each of the extracted HTTP objects, we scan for the aforementioned update-related keywords by performing a case-insensitive search for all of the keywords. A keyword occurrence flags a packet capture related to a software update. Counts of keyword occurrences are saved to the metadata DB for future analysis.

---

[2] https://github.com/KimiNewt/pyshark.

The data-extraction pipeline operates per packet capture in parallel. On a test VM with 24 virtual processors, 64 GB of RAM, and a solid-state drive, we were able to run the extraction pipeline on 38, 355 packet captures in over 60 min, with approximately 10 packet captures processed per second. Without a parallel approach, our extraction pipeline would have taken over 24 h to complete.

2.2 Data Analysis

Using the metadata that corresponds to the packet capture, we can perform extended analysis on the packet capture that had been flagged as having update-related traffic. After identification of these packet captures, we inspect the HTTP response data to look for any update endpoints or update artifacts. Ideally, we should find no update-related artifacts in HTTP responses, as this would imply these files are transmitted over an insecure channel.

Device vendors *should* be protecting their firmware from being tampered with regardless of the transfer protocol being used: if a vendor uses only TLS to secure their updates in transit, the compromise of a single cryptographic key is the only requirement to jeopardize the integrity of the vendor's update system [26].

Analyzing IoT update interactions by raw traffic can be misleading as it does not consider the *context* that triggers a device to update, only that the device checked for an update. To further characterize update interaction, we look at event-related information to provide more context to the various conditions that cause IoT devices to update. All the packets captured from the Ren et al. study are labeled with various event-related information such as power events, app interaction, or idle events. Therefore, we analyze these crucial pieces of context to correlate events to update activity. For example, if an IoT device checks for an update when powered on, an adaptive firewall can use temporal data of an IoT device's network connectivity to provide more context to classify if an IoT device may be requesting and applying a software update.

Finally, we extract and analyze all TLS handshake data from all the packet captures (independent of update keyword traffic) to assess the overall strength of the communication channels in use. Our methodology only allows us to perform extended analysis on unencrypted traffic; however, if IoT devices send all of their traffic over an encrypted medium, it is a reasonable assumption that the devices will also perform firmware updates over these encrypted connections. If the TLS implementation on the IoT device is outdated or insecure will undermine the overall security of the IoT device, including the software update system. Whether TLS is explicitly or implicitly chosen for a design, using TLS is a design choice for IoT update systems.

To interpret the set of cipher suites advertised between clients and servers, we converted the cipher suite's hexadecimal value to the IANA cipher suite name by leveraging a cipher suite information API [25] which aggregates all IANA cipher suites along with IANA cipher suite security classifications. Cipher suites are then categorized into four buckets: insecure, weak, secure, and recommended. Insecure cipher suites have easily exploitable security flaws and thus should *never* be used, while weak cipher suites may have proof-of-concept vulnerabilities that are more difficult to exploit in practice. The classes of secure and recommended cipher suites have no known vulnerabilities, and all recommended cipher suites are a subset of secure cipher suites. The only differentiating factor is that recommended cipher suites support Perfect Forward Secrecy (PFS).

3   Results

In this section, we discuss our results in identifying update-related traffic. At the network level, software updates are difficult to detect if the update communications are taking place over an encrypted connection. TLS offloading may be an option in non-IoT contexts; however, attempting TLS offloading on IoT devices will require physically tampering with the device which may cause erratic behavior [24].

Our HTTP object extraction pipeline extracted HTTP objects from 5,766 of 38,356 packet captures, which is 15% of the packet captures in the dataset. In other words, 85% of packet captures use some form of encryption, or a protocol other than HTTP. We extracted HTTP data for 35 out of 55 devices[3], which is 63% of devices. Originally, Ren et al. attempted to measure encryption adoption with slightly different results: no device had more than 75% unencrypted traffic [24]. The key difference in our results is we focus on extractable HTTP objects, whereas Ren et al. attempted to guess if certain UDP traffic was encrypted or not by measuring byte entropy, which only concludes if certain packets are *likely* encrypted [24].

In the following sections, we describe our results for identifying software update keywords, characterizing software updates based on device interaction, and our TLS results. These results are summarized as follows:

- Section 3.1: Out of the 35 devices that did not encrypt all traffic, 9 (25%) checked for available software updates transparently.
- Section 3.2: Update-related traffic is correlated to power and idle events, but a small percentage of devices checked periodically (some as often as once per hour).
- Section 3.3: Update endpoints (where software update files are hosted) for devices in our set exist primarily in 3rd party cloud service platforms, or on content delivery networks (CDNs), which makes DNS-based identification difficult.
- Section 3.4: TLS is pervasively used in IoT communications, possibly including update-related traffic. Devices that only use TLS for communication could be vulnerable to key compromise if there are no additional protections in place [26].
- Section 3.4: The majority of our devices use secure TLS cipher suites which would not make them vulnerable to TLS downgrade attacks; however, there are devices that support vulnerable TLS cipher suites, which jeopardizes any update communications made through TLS.

---

[3] Originally, Ren et al. had 81 devices with 26 common devices between regions, thus 55 unique devices.

3.1 Update Keywords Results

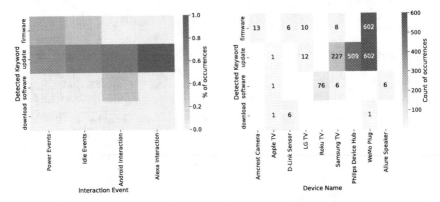

(a) Update keyword occurrences by interaction event. A lighter color indicates a higher percentage of occurrences. In the original study [24] there were 9 different Alexa interaction events, and 4 android interaction events, which we chose to merge into a single group for readability.

(b) Count of detected update keywords aggregated by device as a heatmap, where the number in the square corresponds to the number of keyword usage occurrences were found.

Fig. 2. Our results for update keywords by device and interaction event.

We successfully extracted several HTTP interactions between IoT devices and web services related to software updates. Our most prominent keyword is *update* with 1,351 occurrences among extracted HTTP objects, *firmware* with 639 occurrences, *software* with 89, and *download* appearing only 8 times.

The specific devices and the corresponding keywords they matched are shown in Fig. 2b. The heatmap shows the number of occurrences of the keywords in the rows for the devices in the columns, where a darker blue indicates more occurrences. We observed that certain devices exchange update-related information much more often than others, such as the Wemo plug and Phillips hub.

The Wemo plug device had the most occurrences of keywords, which means the Wemo plug was polling the most frequently for updates; however, this does not imply there may be a software update in progress. For example, the Wemo Plug exchanges firmware information in nearly every request which contributes to the high amount of keyword detection; however, we did not find any proof that the Wemo plug performed an update during the capture period. There is an update web service offered by the Wemo plug, which we discuss in detail in Sect. 4.3. By contrast, the Apple TV only has a single occurrence of exchanging update-related keywords, and we found that the Apple TV downloaded system firmware over HTTP, which would imply that the Apple TV installed the aforementioned firmware, which we discuss in Sect. 4.2. This contrast shows that our

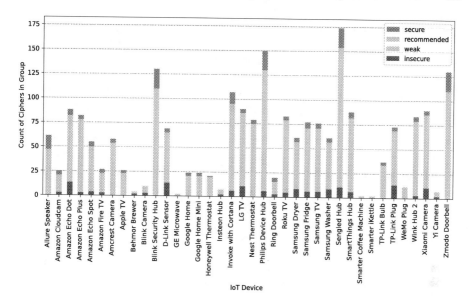

Fig. 3. Count of TLS cipher usage on a per-device basis. Each bar is represented by insecure, weak, secure, and recommended cipher suites.

heuristic does not guarantee a device is performing an update, but it is enough to detect traffic that *might* be update related.

Aside from being able to detect firmware downloads in real-time, an unexpected result from our heuristic was it picks up current updates and firmware versions in 7 of the 9 devices. This is because these 7 devices report their firmware version as an HTTP request, or as part of a service discovery response. This is valuable information for both defensive and offensive applications. A potential application for this in defensive security is an active firewall appliance that can scan IoT devices and fetch firmware versions from them, if a CVE is released for that particular firmware the firewall can automatically quarantine the affected devices. This assumes that the firmware version is accurately reported, which may not be the case for malicious devices. For offensive security applications, an attacker could perform reconnaissance by identifying vulnerable firmware versions of devices that actively advertise these versions.

3.2   Update Events Results

Our results for event-related update activity are shown in Fig. 2a. The heatmap shows the number of update keyword occurrences in the rows for the interaction event in the columns, where a lighter color indicates more occurrences. Due to the granularity of the experiments from Ren et al., Android-related events (e.g., taking a photo, controlling a device from an app, etc.) and Alexa interactions (e.g., invoking Alexa, changing color, etc.) were merged into two respective categories. Aside from these events, all 9 of the IoT devices in Fig. 2b exchange update-related keywords on power events, and even more on idle events. Examples of update traffic events include devices reporting their *firmware* version to an update service, then receiving an *update* response in return.

When idle, we found some IoT devices that exchange update-related traffic between one another. This is out of the ordinary, as independent IoT devices should not be issuing or exchanging update commands to one another when idle – these communications should only occur between the device and the vendor's update platform. We investigated these inter-device occurrences and found that as part of service discovery protocols (e.g., SSDP, UPnP) there is an exchange of firmware information. Certain devices even advertise endpoints for invoking update behavior manually which is ripe for exploit by bad actors or rogue IoT devices. Section 4.3 for more information regarding these endpoints.

Other than power and idle events, Alexa interaction events contribute the most to our heatmap. Alexa devices do not exchange detectable update-related traffic; however, the Philips hub exchanged update-related information when being controlled by Alexa. Additionally, the Roku TV, Samsung TV, and Wemo plug exchanged update-related data when controlled remotely by Android interaction events. We believe there is no correlation between these interactions and update traffic: these devices exchange the same information when not being controlled by Alexa or Android.

3.3 Observed Update Design Patterns

We analyzed the extracted HTTP interactions flagged as being update-related to attempt characterizing common designs or behaviors between device vendors. Unfortunately, no common architecture or strategy was used between the 9 devices we identified. The heterogeneity of the designs and schemas involved provide great motivation for standardized update system designs, such as RFC 9019 and RFC 9124 [14,15]. While there is no common schema among different device vendors, we noticed some common patterns among certain device manufacturers.

No Security: The D-Link movement sensor, Amcrest camera, and Wemo fetch firmware update metadata from a web service that returns a complete URL for downloading the firmware image. What is concerning about this is there is no tamper-protection in place for any of these devices. To make matters worse, both of these devices fetch data from public S3 bucket endpoints over HTTP. We examined firmware images served through these endpoints and found no forms of tamper-protection such as checksums, digital signatures, etc. built into the firmware.

Out-of-Band Security: While insecure device update schemes are certainly concerning, there are update techniques that allow authentication and integrity verification even over HTTP. The Apple TV exchanged all update-related traffic over HTTP, including web service interactions for downloading the firmware and related metadata. What sets the Apple TV apart is it exchanges digital signatures and certificates over HTTP to validate the responses. Apple's design provides a happy medium of ensuring the integrity (assuming the signatures and certificates are validated) of the update through cryptographic means while giving us insight into specific details that can be leveraged by a network appliance, such as specific firmware and information assuming that the network appliance can parse the XML schema Apple uses.

Full TLS: The remaining devices encrypted all cloud-destined communications using TLS. It is reasonable to expect that, if implemented, a software update mechanism would also use one of the available TLS channels. While communication encryption is advantageous for security and privacy, we believe transparency in software update implementations (perhaps implemented with an out-of-band scheme as described above) can be beneficial for providing transparency and security, as we described in Sect. 1. Additionally, we note that exclusive reliance on TLS for software updates is known to be insufficient in protecting against many update-specific attacks [26].

3.4 Cipher Suite Results

We see a larger amount of devices with extractable TLS cipher suites, which is expected as many IoT devices use TLS as a means of interacting with the web services they depend on. In Fig. 3 we observe there were a total of 16 insecure cipher suites used between IoT devices. All 16 cipher suites have significant vulnerabilities that when combined with a downgrade attack could allow an attacker to perform a machine-in-the-middle (MITM) attack; however, among the 24 devices that advertise insecure cipher suites, we estimate 4 of them would be vulnerable to a downgrade attack. This is because the *secure* and *recommended* cipher suites would take precedence over the weak and insecure cipher suites, and the cipher suites contained in secure and recommended classes contain measures to prevent downgrade attacks.

We have only discussed the TLS cipher suites in the context of IoT devices. To see these results in perspective to other applications that require secure communication, we searched for a dataset of TLS cipher suite support in web browsers. While we did not find a comprehensive dataset that summarized recent browsers, we did find a service that provides us with what our browser supports [22]. Using this service, we found modern browsers (Firefox 94, Chromium 96) support far fewer cipher suites with none of them being insecure – although roughly half of the cipher suites supported were deemed to be "weak". This can be used to offset the large amount of IoT devices that also offer large amounts of "weak" cipher suites, as these may only be present for backward compatibility. In this context, the weak cipher suites used by IoT devices do not strictly increase the attack surface as compared to modern web browsers; however, insecure cipher suites when not using TLS 1.3 do increase the attack surface.

3.5   Limitations

We found 11 devices that did not have extractable HTTP data or extractable TLS data. By manually inspecting packet captures we found several devices that stream data over UDP, which is a consistent finding with the Ren et al. study [24]. The data was not meaningful, as it was either encoded using some vendor-specific encoding or a stream of application-specific data (e.g., a video stream) that can not easily be deciphered. While these edge cases are technically possible to extract, it is challenging to do so at scale given the wide breadth of devices and a large amount of packet captures.

A limitation of our study is TLS encrypted traffic, which is consistent with other large scale IoT analysis papers [20,21]. A potential workaround for TLS-encrypted edge cases is an alternative heuristic: for example, another approach that is agnostic to the protocol in use is to look at response sizes. If a device exchanges a large amount of data in a short burst, assuming that this burst of traffic is abnormal for the device based on regulapproach is not ideal as there is no way to verify if traffic is update-related – this only identifies large bursts of abnormal traffic. Furthermore, even if we could deduce that encrypted traffic is a device update, there is no meaningful extractable information from an encrypted payload such as firmware version which is crucial to our motivation for detecting IoT software updates.

Another potential heuristic is to analyze traffic patterns temporally. O'Connor et al. developed a simple yet effective methodology for classifying various IoT subsystems without any form of decrypting or inspecting packet payloads, instead opting to analyze traffic frequency and size over a long period of time [19]. This temporal approach proved effective for identifying IoT device telemetry, and in an active measurement context, O'Connor et al. were able to derive various attacks based on a temporal analysis of IoT device traffic. While this approach is novel, it is not ideal for a large-scale passive analysis of traffic.

Regarding the keyword-based analysis, our heuristic which associates terms such as "firmware" and "software" to update-related events can produce false positives. For example, some devices report a current firmware version to a web service contained as an HTTP payload. While this is not an update request, our pipeline will flag it as such and require manual removal. Future work will investigate the use of additional heuristics to improve the accuracy of identification of updates without requiring manual verification. Adding checks for outbound traffic, inbound traffic, and schema verification would greatly assist in avoiding false positives.

4   Case Studies

In this section, we discuss our findings by analyzing select update practices and firmware files that we extracted through our methodology. First, we look at the firmware update interactions from the D-Link Camera, which we use to illustrate harmful practices that undermine the device's security. We then contrast this approach with the firmware update interactions we observed against the Apple

TV, which combines several distinct tamper-resistant mechanisms with update transparency. Finally, we conclude our case studies with a vulnerable WeMo update service, that allows for unsigned code to be uploaded from an arbitrary source.

4.1 D-Link Camera Firmware

The D-Link camera is an example of the **No Security** pattern, as it exchanged firmware update information through HTTP. Based on the identified traffic, we extracted a firmware update endpoint and also a firmware image. The firmware update endpoint is a web service that accepts a device model and returns an XML response containing firmware metadata information along with a URL to the latest firmware download. We were able to download the latest firmware image as it is being hosted by a static file store which does not require any prior authorization. The firmware update endpoint does not return any checksum or signature to validate that the firmware image was not tampered with. Using the `binwalk` utility[4] we analyzed the firmware image and found the following:

1. A μImage header, indicating that the OS is Linux built for a MIPS CPU. This is likely a boot loader for the next item
2. LZMA compressed data, likely the kernel image to be executed by (1)
3. A SquashFS filesystem, which is the root filesystem

The image header indicates that the OS is a Linux Kernel from roughly 2014 (6 years old at the time of writing). Looking at the kernel image (2) we extracted the image version, which is Kernel version 2.6.31 released in 2009 [27]. While we did not find any notable CVEs for this particular version (*2.6.31*) of the kernel [10], we did find CVEs for the parent minor version (*2.6*) which allow for arbitrary code execution through multiple buffer overflows [16]. It is likely after 2014 the device reached the end of its "service life", thus D-Link stopped updating it. This is unfortunately a fairly common occurrence amongst IoT devices [23].

Theoretically speaking, the D-Link camera is vulnerable to MITM attacks as shown in Fig. 4b: the communication between (1) the update service and (2) the image repository is unauthenticated and does not have any integrity protection. For (1), an on-path attacker can intercept traffic between the IoT device and the vendor's cloud. In this case, the message responded by the vendor's cloud contains the full URL to the firmware image being hosted on an S3 bucket (also on HTTP). A second MITM attack (2) could occur if an attacker intercepts HTTP traffic between the IoT device and the S3 bucket. With this in mind, it is highly likely an attacker can leverage (1) to give the D-Link camera the URL of a different S3 bucket hosted on the "malicious cloud instance" which would then serve the modified firmware. An attacker could build and distribute modified firmware trivially, as the original firmware file is not signed digitally or otherwise clearly authenticated.

---

[4] https://github.com/ReFirmLabs/binwalk.

4.2   Apple TV Firmware

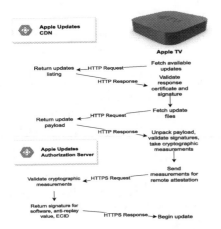
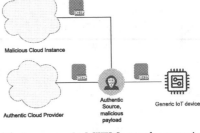

(a) AppleTV update process between Apple's content delivery network and update authorization server. There are two distinct stages to the update process: first downloading the update bundle via the Apple Updates CDN, then validating and authorizing the update through remote attestation.

(b) An example MITM attack scenario that the D-Link camera is vulnerable to. The attacker would appear as an authentic source that provides a malicious payload, such as a download link to a modified firmware version being hosted by the attacker.

Fig. 4. Our results for update keywords by device and interaction event.

In a contrast to the D-Link camera, the Apple TV's update behavior combines security and transparency, making it an instance of the **Out-of-Band Security** pattern. The complete update flow of the Apple TV is shown in Fig. 4a. Similar to the D-Link Camera update metadata is exchanged over HTTP; however, there are several additional measures to harden communications against attackers.

The Apple TV first connects to a central update repository over HTTP. Although the connection for update metadata happens over HTTP, we found the API response contains a certificate and signature field, which is used to validate the responses integrity [3]. We found the certificate was issued by the "Apple iPhone Certification Authority", with a common name of "Asset Manifest Signing". This suggests that the certificate is purpose-made specifically for signing these update manifest responses. Unfortunately, the certificate expired in 2018, and the API response indicated updates from as recently as 2020.

Downloading the update files also takes place over HTTP. To protect against tampering there is an additional field containing a validation measurement for the update file. If the update file is downloaded and does not match the measurement, the update is invalid and rejected. This behavior is consistent with

Apple's platform security documentation which details the measures taken to secure device updates [3].

Using the Apple Repository response, we reconstructed the firmware download URL and acquired the firmware image for the Apple TV. When unpacked, the firmware contains a file tree for distributing software updates. Without having the source code to the software responsible for performing updates on Apple devices, we are unable to determine how exactly the update is performed; however, combining an analysis of the directory tree with prior reverse engineering efforts [12] along with Apple's platform security documentation [3] gives us good insight into how the update is performed past this point.

After the AppleTV validates the update payload, the AppleTV must perform remote attestation with the Apple Updates Authorization server to fetch keys that are required to perform the update. According to our packet captures, this communication takes place over HTTPS (as pictured in Fig. 4a), so we do not have concrete knowledge of what exactly is being exchanged. According to Apple's platform security documentation, cryptographic measurements of the bootloader (iBoot), kernel, operating system image, and exclusive chip ID (ECID) are sent to the update authorization server [3]. The server validates all the measurements sent by the device, and if they are valid, the update server returns the signature for the software, an anti-replay value, and the device's ECID [3].

4.3   WeMo Update Service

The Belkin WeMo plug largely communicates using Simple Service Discovery Protocol (SSDP), which is a protocol used to advertise services and consume them in a standardized way [1]. SSDP uses HTTP as its underlying communication protocol, therefore all SSDP activity was captured by our passive analysis. We observed amongst the various device management services listed is one for firmware updates. The firmware update service advertised various methods for firmware management, one of particular interest is the "UpdateFirmware" method, which accepts various parameters describing the new firmware – one such parameter allows for an unsigned image to be uploaded, which has been historically shown to be exploitable [8,17]. An attacker could have a local or remote firmware repository and upload a modified firmware image to the device. Due to the lack of authentication and authorization on this SSDP endpoint, this is an instance of the **No Security** pattern.

We cannot test the viability of uploading arbitrary firmware to the WeMo update service as we are passively analyzing packet captures; however, previous efforts aimed at exploiting this update endpoint have proven to be successful, leading to arbitrary firmware uploads to the WeMo device [8]. An attacker could have a local (or remote) firmware repository, and upload a modified firmware image to the WeMo device. The only difference between the exploit used in the D-Link camera and the WeMo plug is the attacker has the ability to trigger device update behavior by interacting with an endpoint, whereas the D-Link camera has no such functionality.

5   Related Work

To our knowledge, this is the first work attempting to analyze and characterize how consumer IoT devices perform software updates at the network level. There have been recent works focusing on the different network-level analysis of IoT devices: Prakash et al. analyze the update practices of IoT vendors by tracking software versions listed in the user-agent header included in HTTP requests made by IoT devices [21]. The conclusions found by Parakash et al. do not characterize and analyze how IoT update systems work, rather, they conclude that IoT device vendors are slow to update their devices when new vulnerabilities are found.

We identified pervasive use of TLS, which precludes the identification of update-related traffic without additional data analysis. Related work here includes Alrawi et al., who provide an excellent SoK of the overall security of home IoT devices by systematizing the current state (as of 2019) of IoT vulnerability literature and then evaluating 45 devices, a subset of the security evaluation involves looking at various encryption qualities that would make the device vulnerable [2]. More recently in 2021, Paracha et al. performed a deep dive into IoT TLS usage patterns which ultimately found 11/32 IoT devices are vulnerable to interception attacks [20]. If IoT devices are relying on TLS to secure communications to backend APIs and endpoints for software updates, any vulnerabilities in the TLS transport layer will undermine the overall soundness of how these devices perform updates.

An encouraging finding is the high amounts of TLS usage among devices; however, there is a caveat to this high TLS usage: it is only one line of defense. If a private key is compromised, this could jeopardize the integrity of update-related services if there are no additional lines of defense. Samuel et al. present a novel design for an updated system that allows for key compromise in update systems [26].

Due to the previously discussed challenges, there are several opportunities to explore and innovate IoT software update designs. Related work in this space consists of proposed designs for IoT update systems relating to firmware updates and library management. Zandberg et al. present a prototype for a firmware update system on IoT devices by leveraging various open-source libraries and standards [31]. Zandberg et al. leverage SUIT, a new IETF standard that provides *encrypted* firmware update files with encryption keys provided by hybrid public-key encryption [28]. The SUIT standard appears as if it may not work on resource-constrained IoT devices, but Zandberg et al. have their reference implementation built on IoT devices with less than 32 KB of RAM and 128 KB of storage [31].

6   Conclusion

Using a passive measurements approach and a dataset from one of the largest IoT information exposure studies to date [24] we identified and characterized several design patterns used by IoT devices to perform updates. There is no common schema or design pattern behind various update systems, which provides additional motivation for standardizing IoT software updates [15]. Additionally, we characterized events related to when an IoT device may update, which is useful for building data-driven models for real-time update identification. In our analysis of update systems, we found vulnerable devices that provide no mechanisms for securing firmware updates. We observed that many devices use encrypted connections to secure communications: 60% of devices support insecure TLS cipher suites, while 10% of devices are vulnerable to downgrade attacks.

In the future, more comprehensive studies can follow by performing active measurements during software updates. This can reveal more IoT update endpoints, allow us to develop more accurate heuristics for identifying when a device is updating, and therefore gain a better understanding of these walled gardens.

Acknowledgements. This research is supported by the Natural Sciences and Engineering Research Council of Canada (NSERC) through a Discovery Grant.

References

1. Albright, S., Leach, P.J., Gu, Y., Goland, Y.Y., Cai, T.: Simple service discovery protocol/1.0. Internet-Draft, Internet Engineering Task Force (1999)
2. Alrawi, O., Lever, C., Antonakakis, M., Monrose, F.: SoK: security evaluation of home-based IoT deployments. In: IEEE S&P, pp. 1362–1380 (2019)
3. Apple Inc: Secure software updates (2021). https://support.apple.com/en-ca/guide/security/secf683e0b36/web
4. Bellissimo, A., Burgess, J., Fu, K.: Secure software updates: disappointments and new challenges. In: First USENIX Workshop on Hot Topics in Security (2006)
5. Bellman, C., Van Oorschot, P.C.: Analysis, implications, and challenges of an evolving consumer iot security landscape. In: 2019 17th International Conference on Privacy, Security and Trust, pp. 1–7. IEEE (2019)
6. Bettayeb, M., Nasir, Q., Talib, M.A.: Firmware update attacks and security for IoT devices: survey. In: Proceedings of the ArabWIC 6th Annual International Conference Research Track, pp. 1–6. ACM Press (2019)
7. Boudguiga, A., et al.: Towards better availability and accountability for IoT updates by means of a blockchain. In: IEEE Euro S&PW, pp. 50–58 (2017)
8. Buentello, D.: Belkin wemo - arbitrary firmware upload (2013). https://www.exploit-db.com/exploits/24924
9. Cui, A., Costello, M., Stolfo, S.: When firmware modifications attack: a case study of embedded exploitation. NDSS (2013)
10. CVE Details: Linux 2.6.31 rc3: Security vulnerabilities. https://www.cvedetails.com/version/446073/Linux-Linux-Kernel-2.6.31-rc3.html
11. He, X., Alqahtani, S., Gamble, R., Papa, M.: Securing over-the-air IoT firmware updates using blockchain. In: Proceedings of the International Conference on Omni-Layer Intelligent Systems (COINS 2019), pp. 164–171. ACM (2019)
12. iPhone Wiki: Apple OTA updates. https://www.theiphonewiki.com/wiki/OTA_Updates
13. Karthik, T., et al.: Uptane: securing software updates for automobiles. In: The 14th ESCAR Europe, pp. 1–11 (2016)

14. Moran, B., Tschofenig, H., Birkholz, H.: A manifest information model for firmware updates in internet of things (IoT) devices. RFC 9124 (2022)
15. Moran, B., Tschofenig, H., Brown, D., Meriac, M.: A firmware update architecture for internet of things. RFC 9019 (2021)
16. National Vulnerability Database: CVE-2008-4395
17. National Vulnerability Database: CVE-2013-2748
18. Nikitin, K., et al.: CHAINIAC: proactive software-update transparency via collectively signed skipchains and verified builds. In: 26th USENIX Security Symposium, pp. 1271–1287 (2017)
19. OConnor, T., Enck, W., Reaves, B.: Blinded and confused: uncovering systemic flaws in device telemetry for smart-home internet of things. In: 12th WiSEC Conference, pp. 140–150. ACM (2019)
20. Paracha, M.T., Dubois, D.J., Vallina-Rodriguez, N., Choffnes, D.: IoTLS: understanding TLS usage in consumer IoT devices. In: Proc. of the Internet Measurement Conference, pp. 165–178 (2021)
21. Prakash, V., Xie, S., Huang, D.Y.: Software update practices on smart home IoT devices (2022). http://arxiv.org/abs/2208.14367
22. Qualys Inc.: Qualys SSL labs. https://www.ssllabs.com/
23. Rahman, L.F., Ozcelebi, T., Lukkien, J.: Understanding IoT systems: a life cycle approach. Procedia Comput. Sci. **130**, 1057–1062 (2018)
24. Ren, J., Dubois, D.J., Choffnes, D., Mandalari, A.M., Kolcun, R., Haddadi, H.: Information exposure from consumer IoT devices: a multidimensional, network-informed measurement approach. In: Proceedings of IMC, pp. 267–279. ACM (2019)
25. Rudolph, H.C., Grundmann, N.: TLS ciphersuite search. https://ciphersuite.info/
26. Samuel, J., Mathewson, N., Cappos, J., Dingledine, R.: Survivable key compromise in software update systems. In: 17th ACM CCS, pp. 61–72 (2010)
27. Torvalds, L.: Linux 2.6.31 released (2009). https://www.linux.com/news/linux-2631-released/
28. Tschofenig, H., Housley, R., Moran, B.: Firmware Encryption with SUIT Manifests. Internet-draft, Internet Engineering Task Force (2021)
29. Wang, A., Liang, R., Liu, X., Zhang, Y., Chen, K., Li, J.: An inside look at IoT malware. In: Chen, F., Luo, Y. (eds.) Industrial IoT 2017. LNICST, vol. 202, pp. 176–186. Springer, Cham (2017). https://doi.org/10.1007/978-3-319-60753-5_19
30. Yu, J.Y., Kim, Y.G.: Analysis of IoT platform security: a survey. In: International Conference on Platform Technology and Service (PlatCon), pp. 1–5 (2019)
31. Zandberg, K., Schleiser, K., Acosta, F., Tschofenig, H., Baccelli, E.: Secure firmware updates for constrained IoT devices using open standards: a reality check. IEEE Access **7**, 71907–71920 (2019)
32. Zhang, H., Anilkumar, A., Fredrikson, M., Agarwal, Y.: Capture: centralized library management for heterogeneous IoT devices. In: USENIX Security Symposium (2021)

Two-Layer Architecture for Signature-Based Attacks Detection over Encrypted Network Traffic

Omar Tahmi[1([envelope])], Chamseddine Talhi[1], and Yacine Challal[2]

[1] École de technologie supérieure, Montreal, Canada
omar.tahmi.1@ens.etsmtl.ca, chamseddine.talhi@etsmtl.ca
[2] University of Doha for Science and Technology, Doha, Qatar
yacine.challal@udst.edu.qa

Abstract. The rapid development of network function virtualization (NFV) technology on a large scale and the explosive growth of network traffic in enterprises has made it necessary to move to the paradigm of middlebox services (MB) in the cloud. Intrusion detection system (IDS) is one of these middlebox services that needs to be deployed in the cloud. However, with the growth of network attacks, redirecting enterprise traffic to external middleboxes inevitably raises new concerns related to packet content security and unauthorized access to the ruleset used for detection. To address these concerns, many research efforts targeted the design and development of IDS that operate over encrypted traffic (secure IDS) by looking for ways to make matching possible over encrypted data (aka secure/encrypted pattern matching) without any leakage while maintaining the same level of efficiency. However, most of the existing designs are communication inefficient and too slow to be deployed to support 5G network traffic that requires high throughput. Furthermore, the majority of real network traffic is legitimate and needs to be filtered quickly. Therefore, in order to improve the inspection delay, we propose in this paper a fast and efficient secure IDS that performs detection over encrypted network traffic based on the Searchable Encryption (SE) class of methods using a two-layer architecture in which the first layer is used to quickly filter out the majority of legitimate traffic and the second layer is used to further inspect only unfiltered malicious traffic. We implemented our solution and a recent powerful secure IDS and showed how our approach provides better results and outperforms it.

Keywords: Secure middlebox · Searchable encryption · Intrusion detection · Homomorphic encryption · Signature-Based detection · Secure pattern matching

1 Introduction

Several enterprises have transformed their network services into middleboxes (e.g., firewalls, network address translators, load balancers, and deep packet inspection) through the large-scale adoption of network functions virtualization, which facilitates the realization, deployment, and management of advanced network functions as well as cost reduction. But due to the increase of network traffic and the rapid evolution of cloud services, these companies have started to outsource their middleboxes to the cloud.

© The Author(s), under exclusive license to Springer Nature Switzerland AG 2023
G.-V. Jourdan et al. (Eds.): FPS 2022, LNCS 13877, pp. 423–440, 2023.
https://doi.org/10.1007/978-3-031-30122-3_26

Despite the benefits of cloud services, this transformation brings new constraints in terms of security and privacy of enterprise data, as its traffic is redirected to an untrusted environment. In this work, we aim to implement an IDS in the form of a middlebox deployed on the cloud for packets inspection without revealing confidential data.

According to Poh et al., 2021 [6], many companies use a simple approach called MitM (Man-in-the-Middle) to inspect their traffic on a third party. The idea is to encrypt the content of the traffic before sending it to the cloud, and then decrypt it on the MB in order to perform the inspection. However, this approach can easily lead to eavesdropping attacks. With this traditional way of outsourcing IDS, cloud servers could have access to all the rules and packets in the MB. Exploiting the packets can provide sensitive data about the company's infrastructure and exploiting the rules can allow attackers to escape the inspection.

To address these issues, a class of methods called searchable encryption (SE) is proposed. It allows to inspect the packets of encrypted traffic against encrypted rules directly, so that the packets and the rules remain protected. The objective of this work is to build signature-based intrusion detection system by protecting both the signatures and the packets.

1.1   Limitations of Prior Works

A recent work in the SE class called SHVE+ proposed by Lai et al., 2021 [4] used the SHVE scheme to inspect encrypted packets against encrypted rules directly in a different way to avoid tokenisation in order to enable encrypted pattern matching with constant and moderate communication overhead. To speed up the process, they designed encrypted SHVE filters (secure filter system) to further reduce the number of accesses to SHVE+ during the matching process. However, the number of vectors in these filters is very large, which makes them very expensive to traverse, affecting the overall performance of the system. In addition, according to Ren et al., 2020 [7], 99% of the real network traffic is legitimate that should be filtered quickly without passing through thousands of SHVE filter vectors. Therefore, such filtering cannot filter packets quickly.

Another recent work called EV-DPI [7] proposed a scheme with two-layer, one is a TFS (token filtering server) and the other is an RMS (rules matching server). The first layer filters out quickly the most of legitimate packets using an encoded token filter (ETF), which is a Bloom filter containing all the encoded keywords extracted from the DPI rules. The second layer performs exact rules matching using SHVE scheme [3] to inspect only malicious traffic. However, the RMS splits patterns that contain multiple words which require a tokenisation of the packets. Such tokenisation introduces a considerable communication overhead which makes these types of designs are communication inefficient since traffic content must be transformed into variable size tokens. As a result, long latency is introduced, which is not acceptable in most networked applications [4].

1.2   Our Contributions

To tackle the above limitations, in this paper, we aim to propose our scheme where we combined the advantages of the previous two systems to build our fast and efficient secure IDS without any data leakage. We achieve this goal by using a completely separate two-layer architecture inspired by the scheme of Ren et al., 2020 [7] and we use the same fast filtering layer as in the TFS in a different way to quickly filter the majority of the traffic. For the second layer, we used the SHVE+ pattern matching system of Lai et al., 2021 [4]. Our contributions can be summarized as follows:

- In order to improve the performance of the scheme proposed by Lai et al., 2021 [4] for attacks detection over encrypted traffic, we have modified the scheme to a completely separate two-layer architecture: the "Fast filtering" layer and the "Exact pattern matching" layer. The first is used to quickly eliminate the majority of legitimate traffic. We used a Bloom filter for this layer. The second is used to perform exact pattern matching using the scheme of Lai et al., 2021 [4] only for the unfiltered packets in the possible matching positions received from the first layer.
- We implemented our approach and evaluated it by comparing it with the previous pattern matching scheme of Lai et al., 2021 [4] and we show how our architecture can improve the overall performance using the first layer.

2   Related Works

According to the survey of Poh et al., 2021 [6], signature detection methods over encrypted network traffic can be classified into four main categories: Searchable Encryption (SE), Access Control (AC), Machine Learning (ML) and Trusted Hardware (TH). Our work is based on the SE class of methods (aka cryptographic solutions). Here we give a brief overview of some of the works in this class. We present them by order of appearance.

2.1   BlindBox by Sherry et al., 2015

BlindBox (the name indicates that the middlebox cannot see the content of the traffic) is the first DPI scheme that preserves traffic privacy using the SE class. BlindBox supports four entities: the sender (S), the receiver (R), the middlebox (MB) and the rules generator (RG). The general idea is that the sender generates the tokens by tokenising the payload, then encrypts them with a key k and sends them over a second connection, apart from the SSL/TLS connection. The MB hosts the rules, generated by RG, and then encrypts them in the same way as the sender, by using a garbled circuit hard-coded with the same key k. The MB then tries to match the tokens with the encrypted rules. If there is a match, then the traffic is considered malicious. The MB must not know the value of k and both the sender and receiver should not have access to the IDS rules. Therefore, they used an exchange scheme called "obfuscated rule encryption". However, Sherry et al., 2015 [8], did not consider preservation of inspection rules against the MB. BlindBox is the first step towards a general protocol, based on the SE class, that aims to solve the MitM problem. However, it is computationally costly.

2.2   Yuan et al., 2016

Yuan et al., 2016 [10] remarked that BlindBox is still not suitable for the context of outsourced middleboxes, as it does not consider rule protection against middleboxes.

They also found that BlindBox is currently not ready for practical deployment due to its expensive initialisation phase. For these reasons, they proposed a scheme that is more efficient using a high-performance encrypted filter (secure filter). They formulated the problem as encrypted token matching based on homomorphic encryption. As in Blindbox, the payload must be divided into tokens so that they can be encrypted (but in this work, they used hashing to encrypt the tokens). Meanwhile, patterns and actions are extracted and encrypted (hashed) as key-value pairs - by the RG - to be used to create the secure filter. This filter allows MB to perform DPI over the encrypted traffic without knowing the content of packets and the inspection rules. It is based on one of the efficient hash table designs [1]. They transformed an efficient hash table, which stores only the encrypted actions, into an encrypted index while preserving its original performance characteristics. Cuckoo hashing [1] is applied to make the filter extremely compact where the actions can be moved to different gaps so that the filter can achieve a high fill rate.

2.3   Hidden CrossTags (HXT) by Lai et al., 2018

HXT is a cryptographic scheme used for conjunctive queries without revealing data based on two cryptographic primitives: Hidden Vector Encryption (HVE) and Bloom filter. HVE [2] is a public key encryption paradigm that allows testing membership over encrypted data, without the need to decrypt it, thanks to the use of homomorphic encryption. It supports conjunctive, equality and comparison queries. For efficiency reasons, Lai et al., 2018 [3] exclude public key HVE and replace it with their symmetric key HVE scheme (SHVE) which uses a symmetric key encryption scheme. The general idea of HXT is to compare two Bloom filter vectors using SHVE.

2.4   EVDPI by Ren et al., 2020

Neither of the previous schemes support packet filtering. Ren et al., observed that most of the packets are legitimate (more than 99%). Therefore, the most of packets should be filtered quickly. Thus, legitimate packets filtering and exact rules matching should be performed separately. By doing so, the efficiency of DPI can be improved. To this end, they proposed the EV-DPI scheme [7] based on HXT scheme to implement a DPI using a two-layer architecture deployed on two separate servers. The first layer filters legitimate packets by filtering encrypted tokens using an encrypted Bloom filter and sends only malicious packets to the second layer which performs exact pattern matching using the scheme of Lai et al., 2018 [3].

2.5   SHVE+ by Lai et al., 2021

According to Lai et al., 2021 [4] these designs are communication inefficient due to traffic tokenisation. They observed that variable size tokenisation introduces a considerable communication overhead, which can reach more than 100 times the original packet size. As a result, high latency will be introduced, which is not acceptable in large network applications. Recently Lai et al. in 2021, proposed an efficient solution that is based on their SHVE scheme [3] to build an efficient pattern matching scheme over encrypted network traffic without going through the traffic tokenisation step. However, the SHVE scheme cannot be used directly for packet inspection because inspection rules are composed of patterns and the corresponding actions whereas the goal of packets inspection is to reveal a message in case of a match (i.e., the corresponding action), not only to test the membership by using the SHVE. For this purpose, the actions must be considered as encrypted messages. Therefore, they have replaced the SHVE scheme with a new one called SHVE+ which supports encryption of actions to reveal them in case of a match. They have also built a secure filter (based on SHVE) to filter out legitimate traffic and perform pattern matching only on malicious traffic. The construction of their filter is based on the S-PATCH scheme [9]. This filter provides an improvement in the overall performance of pattern matching because, for each rule, instead of using all encrypted patterns for matching, only those matched during the filtering need to be examined in the exact pattern matching using only possible match positions. However, the size of this filter is very large, which limits the overall performances. Thus, this filter is not suitable for fast traffic filtering.

Therefore, we built our system in two layers, the first designed to quickly filter legitimate traffic and the second to further inspect malicious packets. In the following sections, we will present the detailed design and development of our solution and in the Sect. 5 "Experiment and Evaluation" we provide a comparison which shows that our proposed design outperforms the existing cryptographic solution of Lai et al., 2021 [4] in terms of inspection time.

3   Overview of the Solution Based on SHVE+ Scheme

3.1   System Architecture

Our design uses the same architecture/entities as all existing searchable encryption systems, which we present in Fig. 1. There are four entities: the sender (S), the receiver (R), the middlebox (MB) and the rules generator (RG). We use the term "endpoints" to denote both S and R. The simple use case we rely on is that the sender aims to inspect all traffic in a third-party middlebox MB service (deployed in the cloud service provider) against malicious activities, and then forwards only the legitimate traffic to the receiver. The Rules Generator (RG) is the part that endpoints rely on to inspect their traffic. It generates the rules that allow the middlebox to perform the inspection without knowing neither the traffic content (packets) nor the rules. We will present the general process of preparing rules and packets as well as the inspection process in detail later.

3.2   Threat Assumption

As our system is based on the searchable encryption (SE) category, we follow the same security model where the middlebox is (semi-)honest (i.e., it honestly participates in the detection system but aims to learn the contents of the private encrypted traffic or the encrypted rules) and one of the endpoints should be honest. According to Sherry et al., 2015 [8], under this threat assumption, there will be two types of attackers against this

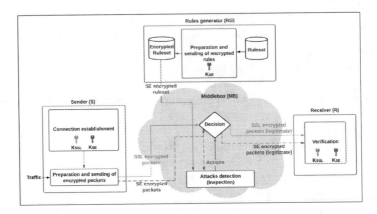

Fig. 1. System architecture

system which are: The original attacker considered by any traditional IDS and another attacker who aims to learn data from both encrypted packets/rules. Therefore, MB is considered semi-honest. The main goal here is to detect anomalies caused by the first attacker by letting the MB inspect the encrypted traffic using the encrypted rules, while preserving data privacy (both traffic and rules) from the second attacker.

3.3 Building Blocks

In order to facilitate the understanding, we will first talk about the building blocks on which our system is based before moving on to explain the general flow of the system.

Basic Cryptographic Tools

- Sym: Is a symmetric key encryption system. It consists of three basic functions defined as follows:
  - $k \leftarrow KeyGen(.)$: To generate the secret key k.
  - $c \leftarrow Enc(k,m)$: To encrypt the message m by the symmetric key k.
  - $m \leftarrow Dec(k,c)$: To decrypt the ciphertext c by the encryption key k.
- PRF: It is a function in which the set of possible outputs is not effectively distinguishable from the outputs of a random function. The existence of one-way functions is sufficient to construct this type of function. Formally, a pseudorandom function is a function $F : K * X \longmapsto Y$ where K represent the key space, $K * X$ represents the domain of the function and Y its image. The associated security definition is given by the fact that any polynomial adversary is unable to distinguish between the output of F and the output of a random function on the same domain, conditional on the choice of the key k [5].

SHVE+. We have based our work on the symmetric key HVE scheme version which also supports message encryption called SHVE+ [4]. It uses a symmetric key encryption Sym to generate the secret key k, encrypt the message m by the symmetric key k and decrypt the ciphertext c by the same key used for encryption. The SHVE+ scheme consists of four probabilistic polynomial-time algorithms.

- $k_{SE} \leftarrow$ SHVE+.$Setup(\lambda)$: This function is used to generate the key k_{SE} (used for the searchable encryption) and it takes as input a security parameter λ.
- $\mathbf{C} \leftarrow$ SHVE+.$Enc(k_{SE}, \mathbf{X})$: It takes as input the key k_{SE} and the packet represented as a vector, byte by byte, $X = \{x_1, \cdots, x_n\}$ to produce the ciphertext, byte by byte, vector $\mathbf{C}$ (associated to the vector $\mathbf{X}$) where $\mathbf{C} = \{c_i = F_0(k_{SE}, x_i||i)\}; \forall i \in [n]$. F_0 is a PRF used to encrypt each byte x_i concatenated with its position i ($x_i||i$).
- $T = \{P_{NW}, d_0, d_1\} \leftarrow$ SHVE+.$KeyGen(k_{SE}, \mathbf{V}, Action)$: It takes as input the key k_{SE}, a pattern (of a rule) placed at a predicate vector $\mathbf{V} = \{v_1, \cdots, v_n\}$ (such that $|\mathbf{V}| = |\mathbf{X}| = n$) in a specific positions called non-wildcard positions P_{NW} where the search of this pattern should be applied on the packets. The unfilled positions are called wildcard positions and are denoted by the symbol "*" which means don't care about these positions. It also takes as input a message $Action$ which represents the action associated to the pattern in order to encrypt it as d_1 (using Sym) and then hide the key inside an homomorphic encryption calculation d_1 with the ciphertext of the vector $\mathbf{V}$ on the non-wildcard positions. The algorithm generates the triplet $T = \{P_{NW}, d_0, d_1\}$ corresponding to the predicate vector $\mathbf{V}$ such that:
  - $P_{NW} = \{l \in [n]; v_l \neq *\}; l_1 < \cdots < l_{|P_{NW}|}$
  - $d_1 = Sym.Enc(K, Action); K \leftarrow Sym.KeyGen(.)$
  - $d_0 = \oplus_{j \in [|P_{NW}|]} (F_0(k_{SE}, v_{l_j}||l_j)) \oplus K$
- $Output \leftarrow$ SHVE+.$Query(T, \mathbf{C})$: The Query algorithm used for the test. It takes as input a trapdoor/triplet $T = \{P_{NW}, d_0, d_1\}$ and a ciphertext $\mathbf{C}$. As a result, it can extract the key K from the homomorphic encryption calculation d_1 iff the pattern matches the encrypted packet in the non-wildcard positions P_{NW} (i.e., $\forall j \in [1, n], x_j = v_j$ ou $v_j = *$) and then reveal the corresponding $Action$ as $Output$. Otherwise, it outputs $\perp$. More formally, the algorithm performs an homomorphic encryption calculation $result$ as follows:

$$result = \oplus_{j \in [|P_{NW}|]} c_{l_j} \oplus d_0$$

By replacing d_0, we obtain:

$$result = \oplus_{j \in [|P_{NW}|]} c_{l_j} \oplus_{j \in [|P_{NW}|]} F_0(k_{SE}, v_{l_j}||l_j) \oplus K$$
$$= \oplus_{j \in [|P_{NW}|]} F_0(k_{SE}, x_i||i) \oplus_{j \in [|P_{NW}|]} F_0(k_{SE}, v_{l_j}||l_j) \oplus K$$

If ($\forall j \in [1, n], x_j = v_j$ ou $v_j = *$) then:

$$\oplus_{j \in [|P_{NW}|]} F_0(k_{SE}, x_i||i) = \oplus_{j \in [|P_{NW}|]} F_0(k_{SE}, v_{l_j}||l_j)$$

As a result:

$$result = K$$

Otherwise:

$$result \neq K$$

Bloom Filter. The Bloom filter is a probabilistic data structure used essentially to test the membership of elements to the vector V of N elements represented as fellows $V = \{s_1, s_2, \cdots, s_N\}$. The idea is to choose k independent hash functions, $\{H_i : V \longmapsto [m]\}; 1 \leq i \leq k$. The filter consists of a binary vector b of m bits, all initialized to 0. In order to establish a BF of V, for each element $s \in V$, the bits at positions $\{H_i(s)\}; 1 \leq i \leq k$ are changed to 1. To test the membership of an element q, we check if b has 1 in all positions $\{H_i(q)\}; 1 \leq i \leq k$, and if it is the case, we conclude that $q \in V$ with a high probability. If not, we conclude that $q \notin V$ with a probability of 1. If $q \notin V$ and the membership test returns 1, we call it a "false positive" event.

3.4 SHVE+ System Architecture

Returning to Fig. 1, our system is based on SHVE+ system architecture in which the general flow process for secure packet inspection involves three phases: preparation and sending of encrypted rules (initialisation), preparation and sending of encrypted packets (preprocessing) and inspection. We can also add one more phase for verification when receiving traffic by the receiver (R) as in BlindBox [8].

Preparation and Sending of Encrypted Packets. Before starting, a connection establishment session is required where the sender establishes an SSL connection with the receiver (using the SSL encryption key k_{SSL}) which passes through the middlebox for forwarding encrypted legitimate packets. Then, the sender and the rules generator establish a searchable encryption key k_{SE} (generated using the SHVE+.$Setup()$ algorithm). When this session is executed at least one time, the sender then prepares the packets by encrypting them by the use of the key k_{SE} using the SHVE+ method in order to allow the detection later. Each packet $\mathbf{X}$ is encrypted (hashed) byte by byte using the SHVE+.$Enc(k_{SE}, \mathbf{X})$. The hashing is performed using a PRF F_0 function that concatenates each byte x_i with its position i to link it to it and generate the hashed bytes c_i of the hashed packet $\mathbf{C}$ as shown on the Fig. 2(a). The sender then sends the two flows (the SE flow beside the SSL flow) to the MB for the inspection.

Preparation and Sending of Encrypted Rules. On the other hand, the rules generator prepares the set of encrypted inspection rules E by encrypting rules (patterns) using the key k_{SE} (the same key used for hashing the packets) with SHVE+.$KeyGen(k_{SE}, \mathbf{V}, Action)$ algorithm. The latter generates a triplet $T = \{P_{NW}, d_0, d_1\}$ for each (pattern, action) in each rule. We will now explain the process of generating a triplet T for each vector $\mathbf{V}$ with an example using this snort rule:

---

alert tcp \$HOME_NET any $\rightarrow$ \$EXTERNAL_NET any (msg:"MALWARE-BACKDOOR Infector.1.x" ; flow: established , to_client ; **content:"WHATISIT"** , **offset 2 , depth 9**; metadata:impact_flag red , ruleset community ; reference:nessus , 11157; classtype:miscactivity ; sid:117; rev:17;)

We are only interested in 4 fields which are the **Content/Pattern: "WHATISIT"** to search for, the **Offset: "2"** for the starting position, the **Depth: "9"** of the search and the **Action: "alert"** to be triggered in case of a match. The pattern will be duplicated j times ($j = end - |pattern| - beg + 2$) in the form of a set of vectors $V_1, ..., V_j$ such that:

$$beg = \begin{cases} offset, & offset > 0 \\ 1, & else \end{cases} \qquad end = \begin{cases} beg + depth, & depth > 0 \\ |paquet|, & else \end{cases}$$

Each V_i represents a pattern insertion (byte by byte) at a specific position such that V_{i+1} is a one-byte shift to the right compared to V_i. The first vector V_1 inserts the first byte of the pattern at the position "offset", and then the other bytes are inserted in succession just after the first byte of the pattern. All other empty positions of the vector are filled with the wildcard character "*" and the positions where the pattern is placed represent the set P_{NW}. After generating the V_i vectors, the algorithm $KeyGen(k_{SE}, V_i, Action)$ encrypts them to obtain the corresponding T_i of each as shown on the Fig. 2(b). The collection of T_i triples represents the set of encrypted inspection rules E that the rules generator sends to the MB to perform the inspection.

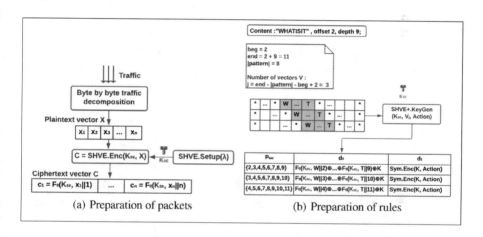

Fig. 2. Preparation of packets and rules (SHVE+) [4]

Inspection. The MB traverses the encrypted (hashed) ruleset E vector by vector and compares it to the encrypted (hashed) packets **C** using the SHVE+.*Query* algorithm which uses the Sym.*Dec* to decrypt $d1$ (the encrypted *Action*) using the key K found in case of match as follows:

$$SHVE + .Query = Sym.Dec(result, d_1) = \begin{cases} Action, & result = K \text{ "MATCH"} \\ \perp, & else \text{ "MISMATCH"} \end{cases}$$

If the packet is legitimate, the MB allows the SSL connection to pass to the receiver side. Otherwise, it blocks the SSL connection and acts as an IPS by applying the security actions corresponding to the matched rules (e.g., dropping the packet). The MB also sends the legitimate hashed packet to the receiver to verify the inspection.

The process of pattern matching proposed by Lai et al., 2021 [4] is performed in two phases: the filtering phase then the exact pattern matching phase. The filtering phase uses two filters FC and FL to filter out some patterns. The creation of these filters is also carried out by using SHVE+.*KeyGen* algorithm. FC contains the set of vectors Ti associated to short patterns ($|pattern| \leq 3$ Bytes) that use the subchain "pattern[0] | | pattern[1]" instead of using the full pattern. It is used to filter out rules with short patterns based on the first two bytes only. FL contains the set of vectors Ti associated to long patterns ($|pattern| > 3$ Bytes) used to filter out rules with long patterns based on the first fourth bytes only instead of using the full pattern. It contains two successive sub-filters FL12 (contains the first and second byte) and FL34 (contains the third and fourth byte). The filtering is performed before the exact pattern matching process using the SHVE.*Query(Filter,C)* algorithm to eliminate unmatched patterns and keep the first position of only matched patterns in a vector called "possible match positions". This vector is later used as input to perform exact pattern matching process (to check the remaining bytes for each matched pattern) on the packets at the collected positions only. The Fig. 3 summarizes SHVE+ scheme of Lai et al., 2021 [4].

Verification. The receiver must verify the detection results by decrypting the SSL connection flow using the k_{SSL} key and re-encrypting it with the same encryption algorithm used by the sender (hashing it using the k_{SE} key) and compare it to the legitimate hashed packets received from the MB. In case of mismatch of any packet, it indicates that the detection process is escaped.

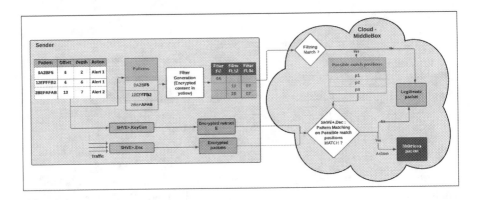

Fig. 3. SHVE+ with filtering [4]

4   The Proposed System

The problem with the filter of Lai et al., 2021 [4] scheme is that the size of the two filters (FC and FL) together is very large almost equal to E that contains a very large number (thousands) of T_i vectors, which makes traversing this set very costly. Therefore, the same applies to traversing the two filters (FC and FL) in the filtering phase. Moreover, according to Ren et al., 2020 [7] 99% of real network traffic is legitimate and needs to be filtered out quickly without going through thousands of SHVE+ filter vectors. Therefore, the filtering phase of Lai et al., 2021 [4] is not designed in a way that helps filter out such legitimate packets quickly. To solve this problem, we need a filter that quickly eliminates the majority of legitimate traffic. Therefore, we proposed a completely separate two-layer architecture, inspired by the Ren et al., 2020 scheme [7]: **"Fast filtering layer"** and **"Exact pattern matching layer"**, as shown in the Fig. 4. The objective of the first layer (Fast filtering) is to filter out the majority of legitimate traffic. The filtering must not produce any false negatives (i.e., it must not miss any possible matches). It must also produce less than 50% false positives in order to filter out the majority of incoming traffic. The objective of the second layer (Exact pattern matching) is to further inspect unfiltered packets from the first layer using an exact pattern matching process only in the possible match positions provided by the first layer. In the following, we provide details on each of them.

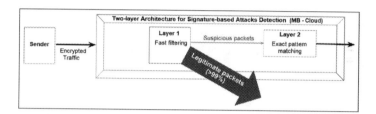

Fig. 4. Two-layer architecture

4.1   Layer 1: Fast Filtering

For this layer, we have chosen the tokens filtering server (TFS) of the EVDPI scheme [7], which is based on ETF (Bloom filter of encoded keywords/tokens). The main idea is to associate each encoded token/keyword *etk* (extracted from DPI rules) to specific locations in the Bloom filter ETF, of size m, using k hash functions to avoid collisions. Then, to test the membership (for the filtering) of a given encoded token *etk* (generated from a packet using tokenisation), the TFS computes the k hash functions as follows: $loc_i = h_i(etk) \bmod m; 1 \le i \le k$. Then, the token is matched only if $ETF[loc_i] = 1; \forall i \in [1,k]$. This layer must check all tokens and if no match is found, the packet must be sent outside the network. In our conception, we used the first two bytes of each pattern concatenated with the offset as a token to be searched. We encrypt the token by a PRF F_0 using another key k_{BF}. Thus, our *etk* is calculated as follows: $etk = F_0(k_{BF}, pattern[0]||pattern[1]||offset)$ for each pattern. This filter is generated at the level of the rules generator RG. Thus, the filtering process is the same as in TFS. The Fig. 5 illustrates the design of this layer. The probability of a false positive of a bloom filter is $P_e \le (1 - e^{(-k \cdot N/m)})^k$ (N is the number of elements in the set). Bigger m and k allow to avoid collisions, which reduces the false positive rate. But a small k is preferable because it reduces the computational cost (fast hashing). A smaller m is also preferable so that the search can be performed in the lower levels of the cache.

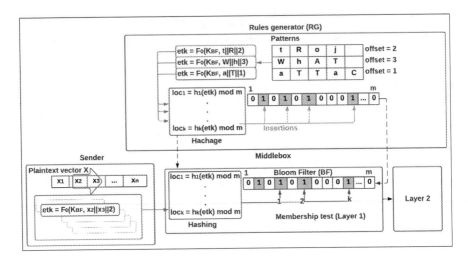

Fig. 5. Preparation and fast filtering of the first layer

4.2   Layer 2: Exact Pattern Matching

For this layer we have used the SHVE+ scheme. However, in our case (when using the first layer) it is necessary to remove the two filters FC and FL12 because they become useless in the presence of the Bloom filter which processes the first two bytes of each pattern in the previous layer (layer 1). The advantage of our proposed scheme compared to the Lai et al., 2021 scheme [4] is that in the latter, for each packet of maximum 1500 bytes, the filtering algorithm has to go through thousands of vectors just to decide if the packet is legitimate or not, and thus requires a deep inspection of all the bytes after the filtering process. In contrast, in our design, with the use of the bloom filter (in the first layer) of fixed size m, which does not increase with the number of patterns unlike the SHVE filters, the first layer filtering algorithm traverses the packet instead of the $SHVE$ filters. This means that the algorithm uses a fixed size sliding window of 2 bytes to generate 1499 tokens of fixed size, for each packet, to test the membership of each of them in the bloom filter and collect the possible match positions. Thus, in next layer, for packets that require further inspection, the algorithm only checks the possible match positions found in the first layer. In summary, we prefer to traverse a packet of 1500 bytes through a 2-bytes sliding window instead of traversing a set containing thousands of vectors to just filter out the legitimate packets.

5   Experiment and Evaluation

To evaluate the performances of our solution, we have implemented 4 different inspection methods. The first two Method 1[1] and Method 2[2] are those of Lai et al., 2021 [4]

---

[1] Method 1: SHVE+ without SHVE filtering.
[2] Method 2: SHVE+ with SHVE filtering.

(SHVE+ without and with SHVE filter, respectively) and the other two Method 3[3] and Method 4[4] are our two-layer architecture without and with the use of FL34 SHVE filter in the second layer, respectively. Figure 6 represents a summary of the conception of each. The objective of this section is to compare the four implemented inspection methods between them and show how the size of the Bloom filter improves the inspection time. To do that, we present the results of two tests. The first one "**Methods comparison**" is to compare the methods and the second one "**Parameters optimization**" to see the effect of the Bloom filter size. The execution time was used as a metric for these tests. We want to mention that we used the programming language Python for the implementation which is very slow compared to other languages like C++ with a very remarkable difference. Therefore, we will compare our conceptions with the SHVE+ methods that we implemented in our environment under the same conditions. For inspection performance evaluations, we used a machine equipped with Intel®Core™i7-5500U CPU @ 2.40 GHz and 8 GB RAM. We used Snort[5] as a ruleset for the inspection.

5.1 Test 1: Methods Comparison

For these tests, we used five rulesets R0[6], R1[7], R2[8], R3[9], R4[10] (ordered from the smallest to the biggest, respectively) to inspect 40 packets where only 2 are malicious, giving a percentage of 5% of malicious packets (which is high compared to the real world). We present in Table 1 the inspection time of each method, of 40 packets, using the five rulesets. Then, we present in Fig. 7 the relation between the inspection time of each method and the number of packets. For this first test, we used a Bloom filter of 1000 elements (BF_{1000}).

Table 1. Inspection time of 40 packets through 5 rulesets using the four implemented methods

Ruleset	Method 1	Method 2	Method 3	Method 4
Ruleset0	0.15 s	0.14 s	1.58 s	1.59 s
Ruleset1	11.39 s	10.56 s	7.41 s	7.56 s
Ruleset2	22.88 s	21.37 s	15.04 s	17.10 s
Ruleset3	45.68 s	43.6 s	27.2 s	33.24 s
Ruleset4	214.14 s	192.10 s	116.84 s	143.33 s

---

[3] Method 3: Bloom filter in Layer 1 with SHVE+ without filtering in layer 2.

[4] Method 4: Bloom filter in Layer 1 with SHVE+ and SHVE filter FL34 in layer 2.

[5] Snort, "Snort community ruleset", 2019. [Online]. Available: https://www.snort.org/downloads.

[6] Ruleset0 (70 KB), 1 rule, 64 vectors.

[7] Ruleset1 (3.7 MB), 9 rules, 4951 vectors.

[8] Ruleset2 (8.4 MB), 9 rules, 10085 vectors.

[9] Ruleset3 (19 MB), 17 rules, 20544 vectors.

[10] Ruleset4 (86 MB), 107 rules, 88360 vectors.

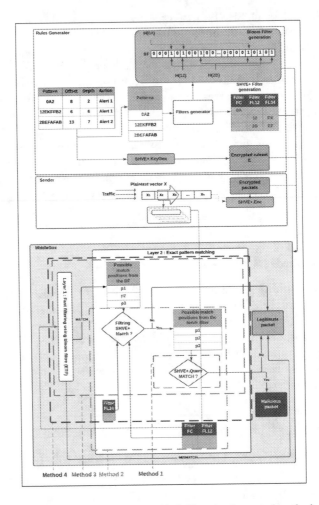

Fig. 6. The overall conception with the four implemented methods

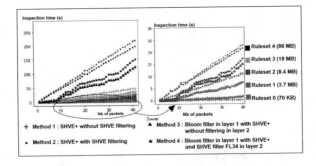

Fig. 7. The relation between the inspection time and the number of packets (using BF_{1000})

We obtain for a small set of rules (Ruleset0):

$$T(Method2) < T(Method1) < T(Method3) < T(Method4)$$

The method 2 is faster than method 1, making it interesting to use the SHVE+ filter, instead of using SHVE+ alone to avoid inspecting all bytes of each pattern as mentioned in Lai et al., 2021 [4]. We also remark that when the number of vectors is very small, the SHVE+ methods (methods 1 and 2) becomes fast compared to our conception (methods 3 and 4) which performs a membership test of 1499 tokens of fixed size for each packet, which is logical. However, when the number of patterns increases, we obtain:

$$T(Method3) < T(Method4) < T(Method2) < T(Method1)$$

When the number of vectors becomes large, the SHVE+ filtering becomes very time consuming. To avoid this, it is necessary to quickly filter legitimate packets in the first layer with the membership test of 1499 fixed size tokens, which makes it very fast compared to passing through a set that contains thousands of vectors. Therefore, the methods that use the fast filtering layer give a better inspection time than those that use only the second layer. As the ruleset becomes larger, the difference in inspection time between the methods becomes larger as shown in Fig. 8 which shows the relation between inspection time and ruleset size for the four methods.

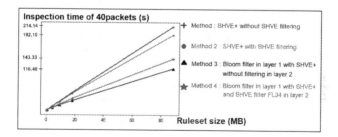

Fig. 8. The relation between the inspection time and the size of the ruleset (using BF_{1000})

We notice that for Method 3, the inspection time increases when the number of patterns increases, while normally this is not the case (because normally the size of the ruleset is independent of the filtering time in the first layer, as the filtering time of the Bloom filter is basically completely dependent on the computation time of the hash functions). This is due to the fact that the Bloom filter used has a very small number of elements ($m = 1000$) which means that there are many legitimate packets that pass the Bloom filter (the problem of collisions during insertions leads to many false positives). To solve this problem, it is necessary to increase the number of elements m in the filter. However, Method 3 gives us the best results, despite the use of a Bloom filter with a very small number of elements. We will see later the improvement of this method by increasing the number of elements.

5.2 Test 2: Parameters Optimization

In this second test, we will first show the difference between using a 1000 elements bloom filter "BF_{1000}" and a 10000 elements bloom filter "BF_{10000}". For that, we used 8 packets with the ruleset "Ruleset2" and the Method 3 for inspection as shown in Fig. 9. Then we will compare the four methods again and show the big difference using the filter BF_{10000} instead of BF_{1000}. From Fig. 9 we remark that there is a big difference between the two cases and this is due to the fact that in the first case, when the number of elements is small, the Bloom filter suffers a lot of collisions and consequently more legitimate packets pass to the second layer (more false positives) which increases the inspection time. In contrast, when there is enough space in the Bloom filter, it lets only suspicious packets pass for further inspection (less false positives), making the inspection time at layer 2 very fast.

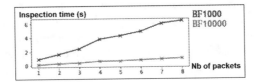

Fig. 9. The difference between using "BF_{1000}" and "BF_{10000}" according to the inspection time

We now present, in Fig. 10, the difference between the inspection time of the four methods with the use of "BF_{10000}" for methods 3 and 4. We can see this time that our methods (methods 3 and 4) give us a better inspection time and incomparable to the other methods especially when the set of rules becomes bigger and this thanks to the use of the Bloom filter of 10000 elements which minimizes the false positive rate in the first layer.

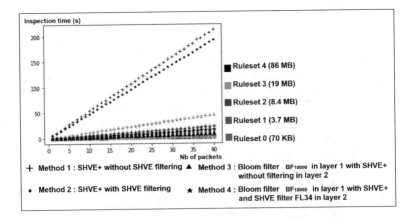

Fig. 10. The relation between the inspection time and the number of packets (using BF_{10000})

We present in Table 2 the inspection time results obtained using Method 3 with the Bloom filter "BF_{10000}" for the inspection of 40 packets. We also give the inspection throughput and the gain obtained compared to methods 1 and 2 (abbreviated as Gain % M12) and method 3 with BF_{1000} (abbreviated as Gain % M3$_{1000}$). The most important thing to observe is that the larger the ruleset, the greater the gain of the Bloom filter compared to other methods that don't use this filter. As the IDS needs a very large number of rules to work efficiently, this filter will be very useful, especially when the percentage of malicious packets becomes very low where they get filtered by the Bloom filter, which saves a lot of inspection time. Moreover, we show in Fig. 11 that by using a Bloom filter of 10000 elements, we obtained an inspection time almost independent of the size of the ruleset due to the sufficient space of this filter which reduces the collisions and so the false positive rate. It is important to choose the number of elements m carefully to maximize the efficiency of the filter without degrading the performances. Increasing the value m leads to a risk of degrading performances when the Bloom filter size surpasses the cache size.

Table 2. Inspection throughput, gain and inspection time of 40 packets using Method 3 (our conception) based on BF_{10000}

Ruleset	Inspection time	Gain % M12	Gain % M3$_{1000}$	Throughput
Ruleset0	1.57 s	loss	1%	25 Packets/s 38 Bytes/ms
Ruleset1	1.78 s	≥83%	76%	22 Packets/s 34 Bytes/ms
Ruleset2	2 s	≥91%	87%	20 Packets/s 30 Bytes/ms
Ruleset3	2.53 s	≥94%	91%	16 Packets/s 24 Bytes/ms
Ruleset4	8.52 s	≥96%	93%	5 Packets/s 7 Bytes/ms

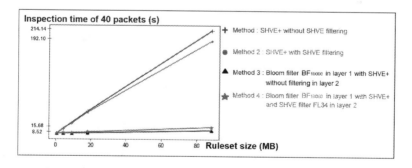

Fig. 11. The relation between the inspection time and the ruleset size (using BF_{10000})

6 Conclusion and Future Work

In this work, we have built a fast secure IDS that performs intrusion detection over encrypted traffic within a very interesting inspection time due to the use of a two-layer architecture that allows to quickly filter out the majority of legitimate traffic using a very powerful filter. This filter saves a lot of unnecessary computations and lets the pattern matching process to treat only the unfiltered malicious traffic. We proved that our solution outperforms one of the best recent searchable encryption works in terms of inspection time. We showed how fixed-length tokenisation can improve the performance of the secure IDS. We also presented how our solution becomes more important as the number of rules gets larger and larger.

As an extension of this work, we will study how to minimize the extra bandwidth overhead without losing the power of our solution. We will also try to improve more and more the inspection time by playing on the number and parameters of the fast filter. Cuckoo hashing is also an interesting way to be considered in order to enhance the filtering.

Another future goals is to study how to extend our system to support other inspection rules such as multi-pattern rules, regexes and scripts as well as other rulesets.

References

1. Fan, B., Andersen, D.G., Kaminsky, M., Mitzenmacher, M.D.: Cuckoo filter: practically better than bloom. In: Proceedings of the 10th ACM International on Conference on emerging Networking Experiments and Technologies, pp. 75–88 (2014)
2. Iovino, V., Persiano, G.: Hidden-vector encryption with groups of prime order. In: Galbraith, S.D., Paterson, K.G. (eds.) Pairing 2008. LNCS, vol. 5209, pp. 75–88. Springer, Heidelberg (2008). https://doi.org/10.1007/978-3-540-85538-5_5
3. Lai, S., et al.: Result pattern hiding searchable encryption for conjunctive queries. In: Proceedings of the 2018 ACM SIGSAC Conference on Computer and Communications Security, pp. 745–762 (2018)
4. Lai, S., et al.: Practical encrypted network traffic pattern matching for secure middleboxes. IEEE Trans. Dependable Secure Comput. 19(4), 2609–2621 (2021)
5. Paillier, P.: Paillier encryption and signature schemes (2005)
6. Poh, G.S., Divakaran, D.M., Lim, H.W., Ning, J., Desai, A.: A survey of privacy-preserving techniques for encrypted traffic inspection over network middleboxes. arXiv preprint arXiv:2101.04338 (2021)
7. Ren, H., Li, H., Liu, D., Xu, G., Cheng, N., Shen, X.S.: Privacy-preserving efficient verifiable deep packet inspection for cloud-assisted middlebox. IEEE Trans. Cloud Comput. 10, 1052–1064 (2020)
8. Sherry, J., Lan, C., Popa, R.A., Ratnasamy, S.: BlindBox: deep packet inspection over encrypted traffic. In: Proceedings of the 2015 ACM Conference on Special Interest Group on Data Communication, pp. 213–226 (2015)
9. Stylianopoulos, C., Almgren, M., Landsiedel, O., Papatriantafilou, M.: Multiple pattern matching for network security applications: acceleration through vectorization. J. Parallel Distrib. Comput. 137, 34–52 (2020)
10. Yuan, X., Wang, X., Lin, J., Wang, C.: Privacy-preserving deep packet inspection in outsourced middleboxes. In: IEEE INFOCOM 2016-The 35th Annual IEEE International Conference on Computer Communications, pp. 1–9. IEEE (2016)

Short Papers

A Decision-Support Tool for Experimentation on Zero-Hour Phishing Detection

Pavlo Burda[✉], Luca Allodi, and Nicola Zannone

Eindhoven University of Technology, Eindhoven, The Netherlands
{p.burda,l.allodi,n.zannone}@tue.nl

Abstract. New, sophisticated phishing campaigns victimize targets in few hours from attack delivery. Some methods, such as visual similarity-based techniques, can spot these zero-hour attacks, at the cost of additional user intervention. However, more research is needed to investigate the trade-off between automatic detection and user intervention. To enable this line of research, we present a phishing detection tool that can be used to instrument scientific research in this direction. The tool can be used for experimentation on assisting user decision-making, evaluating user trust in detection, and keeping track of users' previous "bad" decisions.

1 Introduction

Research and industry have identified an increasing sophistication of phishing attacks in the last years [4,8,13]. The adoption of innovative detection evasion techniques and the velocity at which phishing attacks arrive and change form make it challenging to design early detection systems able to warn users of the suspicious nature of a visited website. New and unknown attack instances take their toll in the first few hours since delivery (hence *zero-hour* phishing), and attempt to bypass detection systems by fingerprinting user agents or concealing features of cloned pages in embedded objects, while preserving the visual similarity needed to persuade the end user they are indeed on the legitimate webpage [7,15]. For example, Fig. 1 shows a phishing website in which no textual reference to the Office 365 brand in the HTML page, or in single image resources, is present. This makes it hard to automatically extract relevant features by just relying on image resources or textual features from the Document Object Model (DOM).

To counteract evasion techniques, automatic detection methods can identify relevant visual features of a suspicious page (e.g., a logo) and find the corresponding legitimate page using search engines, without relying on slow-to-update block-lists [7]. Such systems, however, are less reliable than allow/block-lists (too many false alarms) and, therefore, require human intervention to effectively counter such attacks [5]. Yet users are often not considered in the design of the tools themselves [2,12]. On the other hand, humans may not heed the generated

G.-V. Jourdan et al. (Eds.): FPS 2022, LNCS 13877, pp. 443–452, 2023.
https://doi.org/10.1007/978-3-031-30122-3_27

Fig. 1. Phishing website imitating Microsoft Office 365

Fig. 2. Example of splitting an image of the PayPal logo to evade detection

warnings for many reasons, such as lack of trust in the decision support system or additional user interface fatigue, with consequent detrimental habitual patterns [14]. Moreover, the amount, type and even content of warnings can depend on the employed detection system and, consequently, affect warning effectiveness.

Assisting users in taking decisions on website legitimacy is in essence the goal of phishing detection and warning effectiveness research. However, gaps in this direction are mainly addressed separately by extant research, for example by improving detection accuracy through the usage of visual features in [7], or by investigating different warning types, as reported in [3]. As a consequence, existing methods and tools are often limited in applicability to experiments that capture the full process where the interaction between the phishing webpage and the user unfolds. For example, even the best detection methods can be ineffective when users do not trust and follow the tool's advice [6]. On the contrary, pitfalls of detection tools, such as false positives or long run-times, can be mitigated with effective risk communication. We argue that these limitations narrow the research possibilities where technology and automation can support individuals in avoiding phishing attacks. To address them, we need an *integrated research approach* that puts both phishing detection and Human Computer Interaction (HCI) ingredients together for an experimental tool to evaluate, characterize, and refine the interaction between zero-hour phishing decision support, and the final user.

In this work, we propose a new experimentation approach to conduct research on zero-hour attack detection and to inform users about related risks. In particular, we present a tool, implemented as a browser extension, to support users in the detection of zero-hour phishing websites, with a particular focus on websites aiming to steal user credentials. The tool relies on a visual similarity-based method for detection and leverages various warning methods for user notification. Thus, our tool enables an integrated research line on zero-hour phishing that allows, for instance to:

– Assess user aids supporting decision-making on website legitimacy.
– Evaluate user trust in a detection system's risk advice.
– Explore new risk communication methods by keeping track of past decisions and associated risks.

2   Need for Zero-Hour Phishing Detection Experimentation

According to industry reports [1,13], a significant fraction of phishing attacks are zero-hour, i.e., when deployed with a variation on previously-observed features (e.g. domains or DOM elements), they cannot be easily linked back to previously-seen attacks (e.g. a similar phishing landing page). Several approaches have been proposed to detect phishing attacks and to communicate risk advice to users. Next, we review existing methods and discuss their drawbacks w.r.t. zero-hour attacks, and argue on the need for more experiments (involving end-users) to investigate their actual effectiveness.

Warnings. Warnings are the primary means to communicate security risks to users [14]. Two main categories are often employed in web browsers: *passive warnings*, which warn users without blocking the content area of a webpage, and *active interstitial warnings*, which block the content area and require an active interaction from the user to be bypassed [10]. Active warnings are more likely to be heeded by users than passive ones and, therefore, considered more effective in averting phishing attacks. Nonetheless, more experiments are needed to understand the effects of these warnings, which still suffer clickthrough rates between 9–18% for the phishing warnings and up to 70% for SSL related warnings [3]. Active warnings carry the risk of disrupting applications' usability too often, to a point where users can develop habitual and detrimental behavior patterns (such as overriding security settings), nullifying warning effectiveness altogether [14]. Moreover, user compliance is very sensitive to the context where warnings are triggered; for example, higher compliance was observed in online banking than in an e-commerce context [6]. Recent work has investigated how to nudge users to pay attention to warnings, for example, with *just-in-time, just-in-place* tooltips that elicit a more systematic cognitive response without blocking users completely [17]. This recent line of research integrates multiple disciplines and yields promising results, further signalling the need of new and innovative experimentation in this direction. Overall, research on warnings tends to disregard the internal mechanisms of phishing detection methods. On the other side, users are often not considered in the design of such methods. This has the side effect of limiting methods and tools' applicability to experiments that capture the full process where the interaction between phishing webpages and users unfolds.

Phishing Detection. Automated detection methods of phishing websites can be broadly grouped into three main classes: list-based, heuristic-based, and visual similarity-based [9]. List-based approaches operate by comparing the URL a user visits against a (*block*) list of known phishing websites or an (*allow*) list of legitimate websites. These lists are typically maintained and updated by relying on external crowdsourcing or reputation systems sources, such as PhishTank and Google Safe Browsing. While these solutions have proven to be effective against known threats, they face significant limitations when URLs are yet unknown (new or compromised websites) [7], or due to the time it takes to update block lists [15]. Especially the slow update of such lists (approximately nine hours [15]) makes these methods ineffective against zero-hour attacks, which trigger victim responses in the first few hours since delivery [5,15]. On the other hand, heuristic-based approaches analyze features extracted from the webpage using predefined rules to determine its legitimacy. These approaches often rely on features such as SSL certificates, anomalies in the DOM or URL, etc. [9] which have however proven to be unreliable as attackers can forge relevant features invisible to heuristic rules [9,10].

These issues are addressed by visual similarity-based approaches, which use content rendered in the browser to determine the (non)legitimacy of a website. These techniques use features such as the logo, the screenshot of the webpage or other features to compare two websites and determine whether one imitates the other [2,11,12]. The advantage of visual similarity-based techniques is that the replacement of text by other objects (such as images and other embedded objects) cannot circumvent the detection technique [7]. However, their ability to detect phishing attacks depends on their ability to find the impersonated legitimate website [10,11]. This important limitation is evident in the state-of-the-art [2,11,12] where it is often addressed by narrowing the scope to a predetermined target list of sites or brands that covers specific classes of phishing attacks.[1]

Zero-Hour Detection. Whether previous work use corpora of predetermined URLs, webpages, screenshots or combinations thereof, these approaches are fundamentally limited in detecting zero-hour attacks not present in the given corpus [10]. Therefore, the identification of a page resembling the page under analysis has to be performed using external sources. Visual similarity-based approaches often apply keyword extraction methods to extract relevant terms from the webpage metadata (e.g., title-tag) and image resources (e.g., logos) in the DOM, which are then fed to a search engine [7]. The underlying assumption is that search engines place benign websites on top [16]. However, the brand name cannot be detected when it occurs only in embedded objects, as it is the case for the webpage in Fig. 1. Similarly, adversaries can compose images from several sub-images as in Fig. 2 or generate them with CSS. Therefore, more robust ways of extracting search terms, which goes beyond applying text mining or extracting images from the DOM for a reverse image search, are needed to effectively enable zero-hour detection capability.

Need for Experimentation. Overall, most of the research in phishing detection deals with improving accuracy and devising new methods for attack detection. However, this often happens without integrating the constraints of the human in the loop. As a consequence, the proposed methods and tools are often limited in applicability to experiments that capture the full cycle of a phishing attack. For example, when (re)producing experiments with such tools, end-user components

---

[1] Password managers can act as detection methods by flagging mismatched locations of used credentials; however, they are not the de-facto authentication method and still act similarly to an allow-list of previously saved websites.

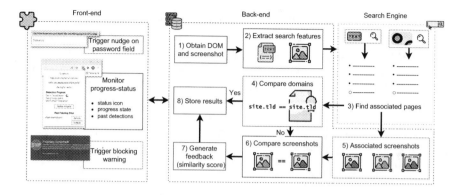

Fig. 3. Overview of the phishing website detection tool

that should connect to the phishing detection method, e.g. browsers or other UI components displaying warnings, are often not provided. This gap affects the possibility to measure or manipulate human-computer interaction (HCI) factors, also in relation to tool capabilities and warning features. When experimenting with phishing detection, we need an integrated research approach that puts all ingredients together in an experimental tool that allows to investigate the complex interaction between users and (risk-based) decision support tools for zero-hour phishing detection.

3   A Tool for the Early Detection of Phishing Websites

To enable experimentation in the context of early phishing detection, we designed and developed a tool that employs a visual similarity-based phishing website detection method as the backend and leverages a variety of warning mechanisms to inform the user about the identified risks posed by the webpage they are visiting. An overview of the overall tool architecture is presented in Fig. 3. The tool is available at: https://github.com/paolokoelio/zerohour-decisionsupport-phishing.

3.1   Backend

The backend of our tool implements the machinery for early detection of phishing websites, which operates on a remote server exposing a REST-like API. In particular, we extended and enhanced a visual similarity-based detection approach that employs *both* textual and visual features of an arbitrary webpage as search terms for the identification of the original webpage from [7]. The overall idea is to combine textual and visual features extracted from a screenshot of the rendered webpages and to evaluate an unknown webpage against the results of the search engines. The output of the evaluation is then used to generate feedback to the user (see Sect. 3.2). Figure 3 (Backend) illustrates how the approach operates. By relying on search engines and the visual features of a *rendered* webpage (rather than only on features of the DOM), the tool allows a zero-hour protection by avoiding the maintenance of benign allow-lists, and is robust against resource evasion techniques, such as image splitting (Fig. 2), image replacement by pure CSS and image distortions.

As shown in Fig. 3, our approach takes as input a website and obtains the DOM and a screenshot of the rendered webpage (1). Textual features are extracted from the DOM (e.g., title-tag) in a similar fashion to other techniques (cf. Sect. 2). On top of it, visual regions potentially containing identifiable information are extracted from the screenshot (2). These features include, but are not limited to, logos, slogans, parts of header images, and other visual information that is likely to be found in the corresponding legitimate website. Such visual regions are extracted by means of serial image processing steps that rely on region characteristics, such as saliency and high contrast with other elements in a webpage. Region extraction can return several regions, where some of them might not contain information useful to identify the mimicked website. To retain only regions with relevant information, we employ a random forest classifier to filter regions based on regions' features, such as dimensions, coordinates on the page, color properties, and energy-entropy characteristics. The rationale for using certain properties stems from their ability to store "constant" brand/logo-like characteristics [18]. We also rely on the Clearbit public API as an additional region candidate. This API allows to retrieve the logo of a company by sending a request with a URL.

Together with the title-tag, the extracted regions are used as (reverse) search terms to find websites similar to the current webpage through a search engine (*associated pages* in step 3). Based on the intuition that search engines most likely place benign results at the top [16], the top results of both searches are marked as candidate associate pages and used to determine whether the current page is legitimate or not. To determine the legitimacy of the current website, its domain name is checked against the domain names listed in the "Subject Alt Names"-field of the associated pages' SSL certificates (4) (this field contains domain localizations of the current website, e.g., amazon.com, amazon.co.uk, etc.). If the current domain is in this list, the website is marked as "legitimate". Otherwise, a screenshot of the associated pages is obtained (5). Each screenshot is automatically compared with the screenshot of the current webpage using a number of image similarity algorithms (Earth Moving Distance, Discrete Cosine Transformation, etc.) (6) and, depending on their degree of similarity, it is classified as "phishing" or "legitimate". The similarity scores are then used to generate feedback about the legitimacy of the current webpage (7).

3.2   Frontend

To enable experimentation in which the human is in the loop, we also realized a frontend interface as a Chromium browser extension. This allows to include HCI factors in the experimentation ingredients and facilitate experiment deployment. The modules of the plug-in are shown in Fig. 3 (Frontend).

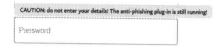

Fig. 5. Passive, just-in-place tooltip when selecting a password field

Fig. 4. Extension status pop-up (past phishing sites are displayed)

Fig. 6. Active, full-screen blocking warning upon a successful detection

The extension is configured to only scan pages that contain a password field, given the focus on phishing websites aiming to steal user credentials. Upon visiting a page, the detection process starts in the background (cf. Sect. 3.1), and a traffic light icon in the address bar signals the current status, as shown in Fig. 4. The user may click on the icon for more details. On the top, the current URL is displayed together with the outcome, the center contains information on the progress, i.e., the textual/image search and image comparison steps, and the bottom shows the past phishing discoveries.

Whenever users select the password field, the extension triggers the just-in-time just-in-place passive warning in Fig. 5 to remind that the detection in not complete. Researchers can personalize the warning behavior to steer user attention with different designs or impede certain actions by, e.g., temporarily blocking the "Submit" button. When a webpage is detected as a phishing webpage, a full-page blocking warning (Fig. 6) blocks the user if she is still on that page, akin to current browsers' behavior. To ignore this active warning or remember this choice the user must click locate and click on the respective links. Contents and design of the message can be customized to, for example, embed information on the used search features or alter interaction paths to dismiss the message.

To cover cases where the user acts on the webpage before the analysis is complete, past phishing websites are displayed in a retrospective fashion, as shown at the bottom of Fig. 4: even if the user navigates away from the not-yet-detected phishing page, the system will alert the user retrospectively in the status icon and in the pop-up of a detection. Users can dismiss or label as "legitimate" a previously detected phishing URL. The displayed information and interactive elements of the pop-up can be altered to give less or more insights and control to the user, such as near real-time data, history of detection or (de)activation of features.

4   Discussion and Conclusions

As zero-hour phishing detection methods can generate false positives, human intervention is often needed in the decision making process. This, however, places additional burden on the user. To this end, research should assess the best ways to avoid too much strain on the user while keeping them safe. Our work presents a visual similarity-based phishing detection tool that enables this line of research. The tool is packaged into a usable and upgradable browser extension and a web API. This allows an easy deployment of experiments with a scalable number of participants to investigate research gaps in this area. We identify three main research directions that could be supported, experimentally, by the proposed tool:

Assessing User Aids Supporting Decision-Making on Website Legitimacy. Thanks to prior research in usable security, passive indicators have been replaced with blocking warnings. Nonetheless, new experiments can shed light on the gaps not filled by active warnings, such as the circumstances of warning triggering. Our tool can be used to evaluate (types of) warnings in the context of different website categories, such as e-commerce, social media or banking. Similarly, different implementations of nudges, such as dynamic notifications or timed blocking of the "Submit" button, can be tested in various circumstances. For example, experiments can be set up within an organization's embedded phishing training, thus allowing warning efficacy to be tested in an ecologically valid setting.

Evaluating User Trust in a Detection System's Risk Advice. The efficacy of decision-support systems depends on the balance between system's capabilities and users trust [6]. Our tool can help investigating the calibration between the perceived trust and the tool's risk advice by dynamically customizing the warning contents. For example, effects of user calibration on the final decision can be measured by presenting further details on where, how and when a warning has been generated or by displaying the tool's detection statistics. Research on indicator proxies for the inner processes of the tool, such as progress bars or status indicators, has the potential to steer user perceptions and, eventually, improve user choices. Experiments can benefit from the dynamic interaction of the plug-in and the underlying detection logic where, for example, experiment designs may vary the content and placement of status indicators in the browser UI at detection run-time.

Exploring New Risk Communication Methods by Keeping Track of Past Decisions and Associated Risks. Whereas visual similarity-based detection tools are able to detect zero-hour attacks, they have typically long runtimes, which can significantly affect a user's reliance on such tools. Our implementation takes an original approach to this problem: instead of blocking users before the detection is complete (as done by, e.g., Microsoft SafeLink), users are notified retrospectively of the past phishing encounter and, thus, can remediate 'bad' decisions by changing their credentials. While a similar approach has been successfully applied against credential stuffing attacks, it is unclear if this concept is effective in a near real-time setting. Our tool enables further research in this direction, for example, user studies on the efficacy of retrospective notifications to reduce attack success rates.

Acknowledgment. The authors thank Ardela Isuf and Sam Cantineau for the implementation of the tool. This work is supported by the ITEA3 programme through the DEFRAUDIfy project funded by Rijksdienst voor Ondernemend Nederland (grant no. ITEA191010).

References

1. APWG: Phishing activity trends reports. https://docs.apwg.org/reports/apwg_trends_report_q2_2022.pdf
2. Afroz, S., Greenstadt, R.: PhishZoo: detecting phishing websites by looking at them. In: Int. Conference on Semantic Computing, pp. 368–375. IEEE (2011)
3. Akhawe, D., Felt, A.P.: Alice in warningland: a large-scale field study of browser security warning effectiveness. In: USENIX Security, pp. 257–272 (2013)
4. Allodi, L., Chotza, T., Panina, E., Zannone, N.: The need for new antiphishing measures against spear-phishing attacks. IEEE Secur. Priv. **18**(2), 23–34 (2020)
5. Burda, P., Allodi, L., Zannone, N.: Don't forget the human: a crowdsourced approach to automate response and containment against spear phishing attacks. In: European Symposium on Security and Privacy Workshops, pp. 471–476 (2020)
6. Chen, Y., Zahedi, F.M., Abbasi, A., Dobolyi, D.: Trust calibration of automated security IT artifacts: a multi-domain study of phishing-website detection tools. Inf. Manag. **58**(1), 103394 (2021)
7. van Dooremaal, B., Burda, P., Allodi, L., Zannone, N.: Combining text and visual features to improve the identification of cloned webpages for early phishing detection. In: International Conference on Availability, Reliability and Security, pp. 1–10. ACM (2021)
8. Google: Understanding why phishing attacks are so effective and how to mitigate them (2019). https://security.googleblog.com/2019/08/understanding-why-phishing-attacks-are.html
9. Jain, A., Gupta, B.: Phishing detection: analysis of visual similarity based approaches. Secur. Commun. Netw. **2017**, 1–20 (2017)
10. Khonji, M., Iraqi, Y., Jones, A.: Phishing detection: a literature survey. IEEE Commun. Surv. Tutor. **15**(4), 2091–2121 (2013)
11. Lin, Y., et al.: Phishpedia: a hybrid deep learning based approach to visually identify phishing webpages. In: USENIX Security, pp. 3793–3810 (2021)
12. Liu, R., Lin, Y., Yang, X., Ng, S.H., Divakaran, D.M., Dong, J.S.: Inferring phishing intention via webpage appearance and dynamics: a deep vision based approach. In: USENIX Security, pp. 1633–1650 (2022)
13. Microsoft: Microsoft digital defense report (2021). https://www.microsoft.com/en-us/security/business/microsoft-digital-defense-report-2021
14. Modic, D., Anderson, R.: Reading this may harm your computer: the psychology of malware warnings. Comput. Hum. Behav. **41**, 71–79 (2014)
15. Oest, A., et al.: Sunrise to sunset: analyzing the end-to-end life cycle and effectiveness of phishing attacks at scale. In: USENIX Security, pp. 361–377 (2020)
16. Panum, T.K., Hageman, K., Hansen, R.R., Pedersen, J.M.: Towards adversarial phishing detection. In: Cyber Security Experimentation and Test Workshop, p. 7 (2020)

17. Volkamer, M., Renaud, K., Reinheimer, B.: TORPEDO: TOoltip-poweRed Phishing Email DetectiOn. In: Hoepman, J.-H., Katzenbeisser, S. (eds.) SEC 2016. IAICT, vol. 471, pp. 161–175. Springer, Cham (2016). https://doi.org/10.1007/978-3-319-33630-5_12
18. Ye, Q., Jiao, J., Huang, J., Yu, H.: Text detection and restoration in natural scene images. J. Vis. Commun. Image Represent. **18**(6), 504–513 (2007)

Deep-Learning-Based Vulnerability Detection in Binary Executables

Andreas Schaad[(⊠)] and Dominik Binder

Offenburg University of Applied Sciences, Offenburg, Germany
{andreas.schaad,dominik.binder}@hs-offenburg.de

Abstract. The identification of vulnerabilities is an important element in the software development life cycle to ensure the security of software. While vulnerability identification based on the source code is a well studied field, the identification of vulnerabilities on basis of a binary executable without the corresponding source code is more challenging. Recent research [1] has shown how such detection can generally be enabled by deep learning methods, but appears to be very limited regarding the overall amount of detected vulnerabilities. We analyse to what extent we could cover the identification of a larger variety of vulnerabilities. Therefore, a supervised deep learning approach using recurrent neural networks for the application of vulnerability detection based on binary executables is used. The underlying basis is a dataset with 50,651 samples of vulnerable code in the form of a standardised LLVM Intermediate Representation. Te vectorised features of a Word2Vec model are used to train different variations of three basic architectures of recurrent neural networks (GRU, LSTM, SRNN). A binary classification was established for detecting the presence of an arbitrary vulnerability, and a multi-class model was trained for the identification of the exact vulnerability, which achieved an out-of-sample accuracy of 88% and 77%, respectively. Differences in the detection of different vulnerabilities were also observed, with non-vulnerable samples being detected with a particularly high precision of over 98%. Thus, our proposed technical approach and methodology enables an accurate detection of 23 (compared to 4 [1]) vulnerabilities.

1 Introduction

Identifying vulnerabilities is an important element of the software development process to ensure the security of software. In the early stages of development, this can be done by testing the code and performing static analysis based on the source code. The identification of vulnerabilities, however, becomes more challenging when analysing applications without knowledge of the associated source code. This usually occurs when analysing legacy applications, proprietary

This work has been funded by the German BMBF under Grant Number 16KIS1403.

G.-V. Jourdan et al. (Eds.): FPS 2022, LNCS 13877, pp. 453–460, 2023.
https://doi.org/10.1007/978-3-031-30122-3_28

software or other forms of black-box pentesting scenarios. In these cases, black-box tests can be used to identify vulnerabilities based on the behaviour of an application without knowing its internal workings.

Unfortunately, black-box analysis methods have a number of disadvantages. Vulnerability detection methods such as fuzzing are very time-consuming, offer low code coverage and have high resource requirements. Furthermore, the success of these methods depends heavily on the specification of the test and the completeness of the test cannot be proven [2]. Since in an analysis scenario without the presence of the source code, the application would still be available in the form of assembly code, this code could be used for an analysis to avoid the disadvantages of a black-box analysis. However, due to its complexity a manual analysis of assembly code performed by humans may hardly be feasible for larger applications.

The analysis of assembly code is therefore particularly interesting in the form of an automated analysis. Since the creation of a program for automated analysis is not a trivial task due to the complexity of the code, this demanding programming task in the field of binary code analysis can be accomplished by using machine learning techniques [3].

This paper aims to analyse whether deep learning-based models can be used to sufficiently identify vulnerabilities (categorised by CWEs) in binary executables. The adopted methodology is based on the approach from [1], and extends this in both implementation and scope. Therefore, the following objectives are examined:

- Can the approach shown in [1] be reproduced and significantly extended beyond identification of only four vulnerabilities?
- To which of the 118 vulnerability types (categorised by CWEs) in the used dataset (SARD) can the approach be extended and how well are they identifiable?
- Is such a model able to identify the exact type of vulnerability or is it more efficient at identifying the presence of an arbitrary vulnerability?
- Which architectural design decisions influence the result?

Based on the defined objectives, this paper first provides an overview of related research (Sect. 2). Then, the creation of the dataset used and the training process based on that data is described in detail (Sect. 3 and Sect. 4). Afterwards we discuss our findings, its implications and possible improvements (Sect. 5 and 6).

2   Related Work

Previous work on machine learning based vulnerability detection can be divided into static versus dynamic analysis approaches. When considering static analysis methods, those can be further divided on static analysis of the source code and analysis techniques in which no source code is available.

In the area of vulnerability detection through static source code analysis, research has been conducted to determine a code similarity order of a fingerprint to already known vulnerabilities. A number of publications have shown how algorithmic solutions can be used to detect reused vulnerable code fragments on the basis of the source code [4–7]. Limitations of these approaches were found in the detection of new vulnerabilities that were not a direct copy of known vulnerabilities or were heavily modified. A detection of new vulnerabilities requires a deeper understanding of the code to be analysed, which can be implemented by deep learning. VulnDeePecker [8] uses such a deep learning based detection method on program slices, derived from the SARD dataset [9], to detect bidirectional LSTM neural network API function calls related vulnerabilities, resulting in F1-scores between 86.6 and 95%. VulDeeLocator [10] demonstrated how the use of an intermediate code representation and an associated reduction of the code of interest can be used for detection, which enabled the detection of vulnerabilities with an F1-score of 90.2% to 96.9%.

Another subarea of static analysis is in the area of vulnerability detection without using the source code, which will also be the focus of this work. In [11], it was shown how similarity-based binary detection methods can be used under consideration of cross-architecture. For this purpose, binary code from ARM, MIPS and x86 CPU architectures was analysed by first translating them into an intermediate representation and later deriving a similarity score of the translated samples. Another similarity-based detection method that does not require the use of source code is discovRE [12]. Here, a k-nearest neighbor algorithm was used to identify similar functions based on numerical features, which were filtered based on the similarity of control flow graphs. The authors of [13] showed how a detection based on decompiled ASM code can be performed using of natural language processing (NLP) methods. In their work, only stack-based buffer overflows collected from public repositories were considered, resulting in perfect classification results reported both in-sample and out-of-sample. Vulnerability detection based on an intermediate representation of the code extracted from binary executables, was presented in [1]. In this work a total of 14,657 code fragments were used for detecting the four vulnerability types CWE-134, CWE-191, CWE-401 and CWE-590 of the SARD dataset. Six different variants of recurrent neural networks were trained to perform a classification with the bidirectional simple recurrent neural network giving the best result. The results were only presented graphically but based on the reported accuracy, a range of 98–100% could be deduced.

3   Data Gathering and Preprocessing

The approach adopted in this paper follows the methodology reported in [1], where we initially replicate the reported results and then extend their approach to cover 19 additional CWEs and required preprocessing steps. This approach can be defined using the taxonomy introduced in [14] as supervised deep learning using recurrent neural networks for the application of vulnerability discovery.

Therefore, code-base features on a token-level are embedded by using a word-to-vector model. The steps for generating and preprocessing our dataset follow those of [1] and are outlined in Fig. 1 and detailed in the following.

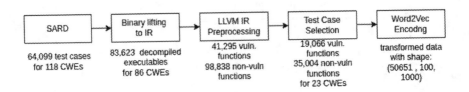

Fig. 1. Data gathering and preprocessing steps

We used the Juliet Suite for v1.3 C/C++ containing 64,099 artificially generated non-flawed and a flawed test cases[1], categorised following the Common Weakness Enumeration (CWE). Since we do not want to process the source code for further processing, but rather in the form of a black-box-based approach, the code first gets compiled into binary executables using already public code from the [15] repository. A decompilation of the binary executables to LLVM IR is performed using *RetDec*[2]. The decompiled IR functions are then preprocessed by standardising variable and function names, decomposing numerical values into individual digits and marking line ends with individual tokens. The selection of relevant weaknesses is narrowed down by selecting functions directly related to the respective weakness, having more than 500 samples per weakness and having a minimum length of 300 tokens per sample. The preprocessed samples were encoded using a Word2Vec model with 100 dimensions, a context size of 3, and a downsampling rate of 1e−3 padded to a maximum sequence length of 1000 using zero padding.

4   Machine Learning - Training and Evaluation

Using train-test-validation split (70/15/15%) we trained a selection of LSTM, GRU and SRNN neural networks to perform binary (flawed vs non-flawed functions) and multi-class (exact vulnerability) classifications. The selection includes unidirectional and bidirectional variants of the model, different numbers of RNN layers (up to 3), followed by ordinary fully connected feed forward layers and a unit size of 64 for all RNN layers, using a *tanh* activation function. Training was performed with a batch size of 64 to optimise categorical cross entropy, with early termination occurring after 15 epochs without loss improvement.

For binary classification the single layer unidirectional SRNN model performed best on the test set and achieved an out-of-sample accuracy of 88% using the validation set. This model was also able to detect non-flawed classes

---

[1] https://samate.nist.gov/SARD/resources/releaseJuliet1.3Doc.txt.

[2] https://github.com/avast/retdec.

with a precision of 96%. The experiment was repeated under same conditions for the multi-class classification using 24 classes (23 types of vulnerabilities and one for non-flawed samples). Here, a bidirectional SRNN with three hidden layers and the unit size of 128 gave the best results with an out-of-sample accuracy of 78%. In both the unidirectional and bidirectional implementations, it can be observed that the models with more hidden layers clearly outperform the smaller models. The results of the multi-class training iterations are shown in Fig. 2.

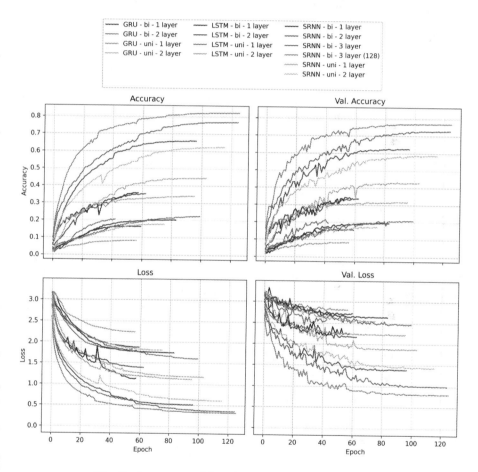

Fig. 2. Accuracy and loss for multi-class classification

5 Discussion

We examined the improvement of a supervised deep learning approach using recurrent neural networks for the application of vulnerability detection based on binary executables [1]. The existing approach has been extended in both implementation and scope, in terms of test case selection, pre-processing and the actual training process. We aimed at analyzing if additional vulnerabilities can be detected, if the exact type of vulnerabilities can be identified and which architectural changes of a recurrent neural network are relevant for the learning process.

As part of the test-case selection, we expanded the test case selection and justified this selection resulting in the use of 23 weaknesses and 50,651 samples in total. In the preprocessing step, existing methods were extended to standardise numerical values in the form of individual digits. We expect this step to be essential for the detection of memory allocation related vulnerabilities.

When examining the suitability of an exact identification of the weakness type, a binary classification was compared with a multi-class classification, which achieved an accuracy of 88% and 77% respectively. In addition, the learning effects and accuracy of detecting flawed code were both better with multi-class classification, identifying the exact type is thus more useful.

However, we were not able to determine from [1] whether the classifications performed consider classes in isolation and thus binary classify each of the flawed and non-flawed samples of a single CWE. We are actually concerned that such a sample selection could introduces a bias, since the isolated consideration of single vulnerabilities does not reflect the real use case of vulnerability detection, where several vulnerabilities have to be considered. For that reason our work explicitly details the implementation of both approaches.

5.1   Limitations

Limitations of the approach used mainly arise from the dataset used, which consists of synthetically generated test cases of selected CWEs. It can be presumed that this data set has different properties in terms of structure and complexity than real code, which would deviate the detection rate in real use cases. Furthermore, the approach used at the function level has the disadvantage that it is not suitable for identifying weaknesses that extend across several functions.

5.2   Future Work

In order to overcome the limitations discussed we propose the expansion of the training dataset by using more realistic data for further enhancement. In addition a combination with taint analysis methods could be used to be able to identify vulnerabilities spreading across multiple functions. To not only identify a vulnerability, but also to find out how this vulnerability can be exploited and how the respective code location would be reached, a combination of our approach with fuzzing techniques would be possible. In the first step, possible vulnerable functions could be identified, and then fuzzing would be used to determine the most ideal way to reach them. For finding the correct execution branch, existing research has already impressively shown how the use of machine learning methods can also accelerate this process [16].

6   Conclusion

This paper aimed to analyse whether deep learning-based models can be used to sufficiently identify vulnerabilities in binary executables. We have shown how the approach introduced in [1] can be extended from 4 to 23 types of identified vulnerabilities and how additions to the preprocessing process allow for better processing of numerical values in particular. These differences in preprocessing and our extended scope meant that it was not possible to reproduce the work precisely.

We also showed that our approach can be transferred to other types of vulnerabilities and that false negatives in particular can be excluded, thus generously reducing the scope of an analysis. In the extended model selection, the findings from the work [1] regarding the result that SRNN produce the best results could be confirmed.

Based on these findings, we can recommend the general analysis approach and state that deep learning methods are able to identify a variety of practically relevant vulnerabilities. However, in terms of practical application, it was noted that it is unclear how accurately the relationships learned from synthetic data can be recognised in real applications.

A reasonable next step for further research would therefore be to apply the investigated approach to realistic data in order to prove its added value for finding weakness with regard to real applications. For this purpose, a comparison with other methods discussed, such as the similarity-based analysis of binaries or the common methods of static analysis, would also be useful. Finally, the possibility of combining the presented approach with alternative analysis methods was discussed. We consider such a combination to be reasonable due to the possibility of precise narrowing of the scope of analysis of a binary file based on the detection methodology presented in this work.

References

1. Zheng, J., Pang, J., Zhang, X., Zhou, X., Li, M., Wang, J.: Recurrent neural network based binary code vulnerability detection. In: Proceedings of the 2019 2nd International Conference on Algorithms, Computing and Artificial Intelligence, ser. ACAI 2019, Sanya, China, pp. 160–165. Association for Computing Machinery (2019). https://doi.org/10.1145/3377713.3377738. ISBN 9781450372619
2. Li, J., Zhao, B., Zhang, C.: Fuzzing: a survey. Cybersecurity 1(1), 1–13 (2018)
3. Arakelyan, S., Arasteh, S., Hauser, C., Kline, E., Galstyan, A.: Bin2vec: learning representations of binary executable programs for security tasks. Cybersecurity 4(1), 1–14 (2021)
4. Li, Z., Zou, D., Xu, S., Jin, H., Qi, H., Hu, J.: VulPecker: an automated vulnerability detection system based on code similarity analysis. In: Proceedings of the 32nd Annual Conference on Computer Security Applications, ser. ACSAC 2016, Los Angeles, California, USA, pp. 201–213. Association for Computing Machinery (2016). https://doi.org/10.1145/2991079.2991102. ISBN 9781450347716

5. Jang, J., Agrawal, A., Brumley, D.: ReDeBug: finding unpatched code clones in entire OS distributions. In: 2012 IEEE Symposium on Security and Privacy, pp. 48–62 (2012). https://doi.org/10.1109/SP.2012.13

6. Liu, Z., Wei, Q., Cao, Y.: VFDETECT: a vulnerable code clone detection system based on vulnerability fingerprint. In: 2017 IEEE 3rd Information Technology and Mechatronics Engineering Conference (ITOEC), pp. 548–553 (2017). https://doi.org/10.1109/ITOEC.2017.8122356

7. Kim, S., Woo, S., Lee, H., Oh, H.: VUDDY: a scalable approach for vulnerable code clone discovery. In: IEEE Symposium on Security and Privacy (SP), pp. 595–614 (2017). https://doi.org/10.1109/SP.2017.62

8. Li, Z., et al.: VulDeePecker: a deep learning-based system for vulnerability detection. In: Proceedings 2018 Network and Distributed System Security Symposium (2018). https://doi.org/10.14722/ndss.2018.23158

9. Black, P.E., et al.: SARD: thousands of reference programs for software assurance. J. Cyber Secur. Inf. Syst. Tools Test. Tech. Assur. Softw. Dod Softw. Assur. Community Pract. 2(5) (2017)

10. Li, Z., Zou, D., Xu, S., Chen, Z., Zhu, Y., Jin, H.: VulDeeLocator: a deep learning-based fine-grained vulnerability detector. IEEE Trans. Dependable Secure Comput. 1 (2021). https://doi.org/10.1109/tdsc.2021.3076142. ISSN 2160-9209

11. Pewny, J., Garmany, B., Gawlik, R., Rossow, C., Holz, T.: Cross-architecture bug search in binary executables. In: IEEE Symposium on Security and Privacy, pp. 709–724 (2015). https://doi.org/10.1109/SP.2015.49

12. Eschweiler, S., Yakdan, K., Gerhards-Padilla, E.: DiscovRE: efficient cross-architecture identification of bugs in binary code. In: NDSS, vol. 52, pp. 58–79 (2016)

13. Dahl, W.A., Erdodi, L., Zennaro, F.M.: Stack-based buffer overflow detection using recurrent neural networks (2020). arXiv:2012.15116 [cs.CR]

14. Xue, H., Sun, S., Venkataramani, G., Lan, T.: Machine learning-based analysis of program binaries: a comprehensive study (2019). https://doi.org/10.1109/ACCESS.2019.2917668

15. Gutstein, B., Richardson, A.: Juliet test suite for C/C++ (2019). https://github.com/arichardson/juliet-test-suite-c

16. Wang, Y., Wu, Z., Wei, Q., Wang, Q.: NeuFuzz: efficient fuzzing with deep neural network. IEEE Access 7, 36 340–36 352 (2019). https://doi.org/10.1109/ACCESS.2019.2903291

Robustness of Affine and Extended Affine Equivalent Surjective S-Box(es) Against Differential Cryptanalysis

Shah Fahd[1]([✉]), Mehreen Afzal[1], Dawood Shah[2], Waseem Iqbal[1],
and Atiya Hai[3]

[1] National University of Sciences and Technology, Islamabad 44000, Pakistan
sfahd.phdismcs@student.nust.edu.pk,
{mehreenafzal,waseem.iqbal}@mcs.edu.pk
[2] Quaid-i-Azam University, Islamabad, Pakistan
[3] University of Surrey, Guildford, UK

Abstract. A Feistel Network (FN) based block cipher relies on a Substitution Box (S-Box) for achieving the non-linearity. S-Box is carefully designed to achieve optimal cryptographic security bounds. The research of the last three decades shows that considerable efforts are being made on the mathematical design of an S-Box. To import the exact cryptographic profile of an S-Box, the designer focuses on the Affine Equivalent (AE) or Extended Affine (EA) equivalent S-Box. In this research, we argue that the Robustness of surjective mappings is invariant under AE and not invariant under EA transformation. It is proved that the EA equivalent of a surjective mapping does not necessarily contribute to the Robustness against the Differential Cryptanalysis (DC) in the light of Seberry's criteria. The generated EA equivalent S-Box(es) of DES and other 6×4 mappings do not show a good robustness profile compared to the original mappings. This article concludes that a careful selection of affine permutation parameters is significant during the design phase to achieve high Robustness against DC and Differential Power Analysis (DPA) attacks.

Keywords: S-Box · Permutations · Block Ciphers · Cryptography · Differential Cryptanalysis · Differential Uniformity · Affine Equivalence

1 Introduction

Al-Kindi cracked the thousands-year-old Ceaser cipher by exploiting the frequency of occurrence problem in a natural language. The US intelligence agencies broke the language redundancy problem aroused due to misuse of the Russian One Time Pad (OTP) [1]. To suppress the statistics of plaintext in the resultant ciphertext, Claude Shannon coined the idea of information entropy in his landmark papers [2–4]. He proposed the concepts of Confusion and Diffusion achievable by networking substitution and permutation in a block cipher. Research

G.-V. Jourdan et al. (Eds.): FPS 2022, LNCS 13877, pp. 461–471, 2023.
https://doi.org/10.1007/978-3-031-30122-3_29

on the design and security of the substitution layer is maturing [5,6]. The engineering of S-Box remains an area of focus for the cryptographic community. A cryptanalyst intends to find the statistical vulnerabilities in its design [7–9], and a side channel analyst exploits the cryptographic implementations [10]. An S-Box is generated in multiple ways, i.e., Mathematical processing (Finite Field Inversion [11–13]), random generation [14,15] and heuristic-based approach [16,17]. The mathematical generation of S-Box needs rigorous research, but it promises an optimum cryptographic profile, i.e., Differential Uniformity (DU) [8] and Linearity [9]. The mathematician focuses on the Affine, or Extended Affine (EA) equivalent, to copy the cryptographic profile of the parent candidate [18,19]. Seberry et al. [20,21] discussed the idea of Robustness against the DC (later on will be called Robustness throughout the document) rather than focusing on the highest coefficient in the Difference Distribution Table (DDT) alone. The robustness is upper bounded by $(1 - 2^{-n+1})$ for $(n \equiv 1 \mod 2)$ and $(1 - 2^{-n+2})$ for $(n \equiv 0 \mod 2)$ for an n-bit (finite field inversion based) bijection. However, the Robustness of an $m \times n$ surjective S-Box is interesting in this regard, upper bounded by $\frac{2^{n+m-1} - 2^m - 2^{n-1} + 1}{2^{n+m-1}}$. The realistic values deviate from the lower or upper bounds. The AE and EA equivalent S-Box retains the distribution of differential probabilities at different locations in the DDT compared to the parent profile. Evaluating Robustness in the surjective substitution layer is crucial rather than focusing on the DU alone. This article identifies and addresses the robustness problem in the AE and EA equivalent surjective mappings.

Paper Organization: Section 2 explains the preliminary mathematical notations used throughout the document. In Sect. 3, we have discussed the types and design strategies of S-Box mappings. Section 4 outlines the robustness against differential cryptanalysis. Our results are elaborated in Sect. 5, and the paper is concluded in Sect. 6.

2   Preliminaries

Definition 1. *Given two positive integers $(m, n \geq 2)$, an S-Box is a vectorial boolean function of the form $\beta : \mathbb{F}_2^m \to \mathbb{F}_2^n$, mapping an m-bits to n-bits. For $m = n$, S is a bijection, and $m > n$ is a surjective mapping.*

Definition 2. *An S-Box is deferentially δ-uniform ($\delta \equiv 0 \mod 2$), if for all $a \in \mathbb{F}_2^m \setminus 0$, $x \in \mathbb{F}_2^m$ and $b \in \mathbb{F}_2^n$ in a $2^m \times 2^n$ Difference Distribution Table (DDT), δ is the maximum number of occurrences for which Eq. 1 is satisfied.*

$$N_B(a, b) = \{\beta(x) \oplus \beta(x \oplus a) = b\}$$
$$\delta = \max_{\Delta a \neq 0 \in \mathbb{F}_2^m, \Delta b \in \mathbb{F}_2^n} N_B(\Delta a, \Delta b) \tag{1}$$

Definition 3. *An $m \times n$ S-Box is differential R Robust, if for δ, and the frequency ψ of non-zero entries in the DDT for $a \neq 0$ and $b = 0$.*

$$R = (1 - \frac{\delta}{2^m})(1 - \frac{\psi}{2^m}) \tag{2}$$

Definition 4. *Two m-bit S-Box(es), β and β^* are affine equivalent (AE) if there exists an affine permutation $L \in \mathcal{A}_n$ and $z \in \mathbb{F}_2^m$ [18, 19]*

$$\beta^* = L \circ \beta(x) \oplus z \tag{3}$$

Definition 5. *Two m-bit S-Box(es), β and β^* are extended affine (EA) equivalent, if there exists an affine permutation $K, L \in \mathcal{A}_n$, for some $A, c, x, z \in \mathbb{F}_2^m$ and affine function $Z(x) = A \cdot (x) \oplus z$ [18, 19]*

$$\beta^* = K \circ \beta(x) \circ L \oplus Z(x) \tag{4}$$

3   Design of S-Box(es)

The information-theoretic security of an FN or SPN block cipher mainly depends upon an S-Box; therefore, heinous efforts are made on the design level strategies [5]. Since its inception, high-end research is contributed to its optimal design. These strategies are grouped into three (03) classes, i.e., Mathematical objects, Random Generation and Heuristic Techniques. A cryptographer expects a profile with lower δ from an S-Box. The probability distribution of differentials in a DDT is estimated in [22–24] and Theorem 9.1.1, Eqn 9.1 and 9.2 in [25]. The mathematical function-based cryptographic mappings are (not limited to) Finite Field inversion [26–31], Finite Field exponentiation [32,33], Modular Ring Exponentiation [34], and APN functions [35,36]. Like Finite Field inversion [11], not all the mathematical functions are promising for optimal cryptographic profile, $\delta = 128$ for SAFER [34] and $\delta = 10$ for E2 [37].

Based upon the results in (Theorem 9.1.1 and Eqn 9.1 [25]), the probability that a random $m \times n$ mapping will be differentially 4 uniform is negligible. For any 6×4 random mapping, the probability that it will be an APN is very low compared to any other 6×4 random mapping with $\delta = 12$. Random mappings available in the literature [38–41], key-dependent S-Box generation [42] lies in this cluster as well. A randomly generated S-Box does not guarantee an optimal cryptographic profile.

The heuristic-based mappings are the refined version of the pseudo-random mappings. A randomly generated S-Box is filtered for some set of cryptographic properties. The S-Box is accepted if the desired profile is achieved; otherwise, a new mapping is generated. The S-Box in Kuznyechick [43] was claimed to be heuristically generated but turned down by Perrin in [25]. The permutation in Anubis [44], Skipjack [45], and Kalyna [46] is the outcome of the Hill climbing technique.

The differential uniformity [11], linearity [9], Algebraic Degree [18], balancedness and linear structures [47] remains invariant under the affine equivalence. The differential branch number and linear branch number [48], Differential Power Analysis (DPA) Signal to Noise Ratio (SNR) [49], Transparency Order (TO) [50] does not remain invariant under the affine and extended affine equivalence. Lower values of DPA-SNR and TO guarantee the resistance of an S-Box against DPA attacks.

4   Robustness of Surjective S-Box(es)

Seberry explained the reasons for the weaknesses of the Data Encryption Standard (DES) against the differential Cryptanalysis [20]. The author argued that only the largest coefficient in the DDT table does not matter, and the frequency of non-zero entries in the first column of DDT is also important. For an n-bit bijection, the frequency of zero entries for the first column is $2^n - 1$, and R is upper bounded by $1 - 2^{-n+1}$. The number of non-zero entries is not strictly unitary in the DDT of $m \times n$ mapping (Page 62 - [8]). For surjective mappings, the robustness is quite interesting and bounded by $(1 - \frac{1}{2^m})(1 - 2^{-n+1})$. The robustness deviates from the lower or upper bound as proposed in [20,21].

Proposition 1. *Robustness against the differential cryptanalysis is invariant under affine equivalence.*

Proof: For any positive $x, \alpha \in F_{2^n}$, the derivative of $S(x)$ in the direction of α is $D_\alpha S(x) = S(x) \oplus S(x \oplus \alpha)$. For an affine matrix L over F_2 and $z \in F_{2^n}$, let $S^*(x) = L \cdot S(x) \oplus z$ be the affine equivalent S-Box. The directional derivative of $S^*(x)$ can be computed in the following manner,

$$
\begin{aligned}
D_\alpha S^*(x) &= S^*(x) \oplus S^*(x \oplus \alpha) \\
&= L \cdot S(x) \oplus z \oplus L \cdot S(x \oplus \alpha) \oplus z \\
&= L \cdot S(x) \oplus L \cdot S(x \oplus \alpha) \\
&= L \cdot (S(x) \oplus S(x \oplus \alpha)) \\
&= L \cdot (D_\alpha S(x))
\end{aligned}
\tag{5}
$$

Since the robustness profile in Eq. 2 only considers the frequency of non-zero entries in the first column (which is $\beta = 0$, equivalently $D_\alpha S(x) = 0$) of DDT, An S-Box's affine preserves the distribution of coefficients (with altered positions) in the DDT. The frequency of non-zero entries in the first column remains unchanged. The affine equivalence changes the positions of coefficients in the DDT rows according to the affine matrix. The affine constant z does not play any role in managing DDT coefficients. The affine permutation parameters do not affect δ and ψ, thus preserving the values of R in Eq. 2 accordingly.

Proposition 2. *Robustness against the differential cryptanalysis is not invariant under extended affine equivalence.*

Proof: For two affine matrices A_1, A_2 over F_2, let $S^\Delta = A_1 \cdot S(A_2(x \oplus b_1)) \oplus b_2 \oplus A_3(x) \oplus b_3$ be EA equivalent S-Box of S. The directional derivative of S^Δ can be computed in the following manner,

$$
\begin{aligned}
D_\alpha S^\Delta(x) &= S^\Delta(x) \oplus S^\Delta(x \oplus \alpha) \\
&= A_1 \cdot S(A_2(x \oplus b_1)) \oplus b_2 \oplus A_3(x) \oplus b_3 \oplus A_1 \cdot S(A_2(x \oplus \alpha \oplus b_1)) \oplus b_2 \oplus A_3(x \oplus \alpha) \oplus b_3 \\
&= A_1 \cdot S(A_2(x \oplus b_1)) \oplus A_1 \cdot S(A_2(x \oplus \alpha \oplus b_1)) \oplus A_3(x) \oplus A_3(x \oplus \alpha) \\
&= A_1 \cdot S(A_2(x \oplus b_1)) \oplus A_1 \cdot S(A_2(x \oplus \alpha \oplus b_1)) \oplus A_3(\alpha) \\
&= A_1 \cdot (S(A_2(x \oplus b_1)) \oplus S(A_2(x \oplus \alpha \oplus b_1))) \oplus A_3(\alpha)
\end{aligned}
\tag{6}
$$

From Eq. 6, it is evident that the directional derivative is affected by the affine permutation parameters, thus affecting the values of the directional derivative for α. The changing frequency of non-zero entries in the first column of DDT results in the variation of the Robustness profile of EA equivalent mappings.

The higher values of δ and ψ lead to weakened S-Box(es) against the differential cryptanalysis. The designer focuses on importing the exact cryptographic profile rather than stressing the affine permutation parameters. The selection of affine permutation parameters and functions is crucial in this regard. Those affine permutation parameters are of the utmost importance, which can lower the value of ψ, resulting in higher robustness. The preceding section shed some light on the actual test cases of the real-world ciphers, and optimal mappings in the 4-bit class [51,52].

5 Results

For evaluation of robustness, the S-Box(es) from a well-known cipher DES, analyzed in [20], are compared to the affine equivalent S-Box(es) for different affine permutation parameters. The 4-bit S-Box(es) with optimal cryptographic properties from [51] are combined to get 6-bit S-Box(es) of the form $\beta_1 : \mathbb{F}_2^6 \to \mathbb{F}_2^4$. The three 5-bit non-linear mappings from [47] are combined for achieving $\beta_2 : \mathbb{F}_2^6 \to \mathbb{F}_2^5$. For β_1 and β_2, R is upper bounded by 0.861 and 0.923 respectively. We have also randomly generated (6×5) and (6×4) mappings and their associated affine equivalent candidates[1]. The lower values of R against the affine equivalent of the DES Substitution layer in (Table 1, from [20]) is a clear indication of the weakness against DC. For the sake of convenience, the affine equivalent mappings are represented as $i, j \in [0 \dots ord(\mathcal{A}_n) - 1]$ for an affine matrix $M_i, M_j, \in \mathcal{A}_n$, for all $i \neq j$.

Following the proof in Proposition-1 and Eq. 5, the robustness profile of affine equivalent mappings in Table 3, 2 and 1 remains invariant for all the S-Box(es) under consideration. The results from Proposition-2 prove that the robustness profiles for the extended affine equivalent in Table 3, 2 and 1 do not remain invariant for the surjective mappings. For EA-S0 (EA equivalent of S0), the R values drastically drop to 0.1289 from 0.316 in Table 1. In Table 2, the values of R decline to 0.063 for EA-O3 and EA-O4. The R values for EA equivalence are not promising as the parent mappings in Table 3.

According to [49], the upper bound of DPA-SNR for 6×4 S-Box is 2^3. The higher values of DPA-SNR make an S-Box vulnerable to the DPA attack. DPA-SNR of A-S0 (5.0360) is higher than the parent S-Box DPA-SNR (3.6110). Similarly, the DPA-SNR profile of EA-S7 shows smaller values than S7 and A-7, making it more resistant to DPA attacks. The TO profile of S-Box(es) in Table 1 is altered by the affine parameters as compared to the parent mappings;

---

[1] The S-Box(es), their equivalent mappings and detailed cryptographic profile is available at https://drive.google.com/drive/folders/1-6DNsVdZWT_kkdhJEpZgM-A0Pjtv8wtQ?usp=sharing.

the lower value of TO against all the S-Box(es) is minimized to 2.0079 for EA-S2. The lower value of TO for the S3 in Table 1 is maximized from 2.0634 to 2.0674 in EA-S3. The values of DPA-SNR for EA-O1 and EA-O5 in Table 2 are drastically higher and approaching the higher bound, making them vulnerable to DPA attacks.

For 6×5 mappings, the DPA and TO profiles show considerable variations in Table 3. The DPA-SNR of S54 is lowered from 5.0531 to 3.729 in A-S54. On the other hand, the EA map amplifies the values against S51 and EA-S51. The TO values are maximized for EA-S54, and EA-S52 are lowered accordingly.

Table 1. Robustness Profile of DES and its Equivalent S-Box(es)

S-Box	S0	S1	S2	S3	S4	S5	S6	S7
ψ	37	33	37	24	31	33	35	36
δ	16							
R	0.316	0.363	0.316	0.469	0.387	0.363	0.340	0.328
DPA-SNR	3.6110	4.503	0.316	3.855	3.855	3.0836	4.6618	4.2188
TO	2.063492							
Affine Equivalent S-Box(es) of DES								
S-Box	A-S0	A-S1	A-S2	A-S3	A-S4	A-S5	A-S6	A-S7
ψ	37	33	37	24	31	33	35	36
δ	16							
R	0.316	0.363	0.316	0.469	0.387	0.363	0.340	0.328
DPA-SNR	5.0360	4.3813	4.3787	4.7819	4.3120	3.4148	4.8906	4.0236
TO	2.063492							
Extended Affine Equivalent S-Box(es) of DES								
S-Box	EA-S0	EA-S1	EA-S2	EA-S3	EA-S4	EA-S5	EA-S6	EA-S7
ψ	53	44	52	44	49	45	48	44
δ	16							
R	0.1289	0.2344	0.1406	0.2344	0.1758	0.2227	0.1875	0.2344
DPA-SNR	4.57711	4.3813	4.9506	3.3795	4.2350	4.7970	3.9806	3.05629
TO	2.03571	2.0555	2.0079	2.0674	2.05158	2.0238	2.0555	2.04761

Table 2. Robustness Profile of 6×4 Equivalent S-Box(es)

S-Box	O1	O2	O3	O4	O5
ψ	18	11	15	21	21
δ	46	54	54	48	44
R	0.2021	0.1294	0.1196	0.168	0.210
DPA-SNR	3.1459	3.2825	2.8857	3.1067	3.2356
TO	2.063492				

Affine Equivalent 6×4 S-Box(es)

S-Box	A-O1	A-O2	A-O3	A-O4	A-O5
ψ	18	11	15	21	21
δ	46	54	54	48	44
R	0.2021	0.1294	0.1196	0.168	0.210
DPA-SNR	4.4216	4.0	2.5217	2.3717	3.3288
TO	2.063492				

Extended Affine Equivalent 6×4 S-Box(es)

S-Box	EA-O1	EA-O2	EA-O3	EA-O4	EA-O5
ψ	46	38	38	45	46
δ	46	54	54	48	44
R	0.079	0.063	0.063	0.0742	0.0879
DPA-SNR	7.3292	5.8362	5.2277	5.0695	6.2719
TO	2.0436	2.01984	2.05157	4.0	2.0198

Table 3. Robustness Profile of 6×5 Equivalent S-Box(es)

S-Box	S51	S52	S53	S54
ψ	18	21	25	21
δ	34	32	32	32
R	0.3369	0.3359	0.3042	0.2734
DPA-SNR	4.1367	4.8013	4.5584	5.0531
TO	4.06394	4.0555	4.0158	4.0834

Affine Equivalent 6×5 S-Box(es)

S-Box	A-S51	A-S52	A-S53	A-S54
ψ	18	21	25	21
δ	34	32	32	32
R	0.3369	0.3359	0.3042	0.2734
DPA-SNR	5.0800	4.2156	3.8318	3.7290
TO	5.0000	4.0198	5.0000	4.0119

Extended Affine Equivalent 6×5 S-Box(es)

S-Box	EA-S51	EA-S52	EA-S53	EA-S54
ψ	31	27	37	29
δ	34	32	32	32
R	0.2417	0.2891	0.2109	0.2734
DPA-SNR	5.3692	5.0838	5.4433	4.9637
TO	4.0158	4.0079	4.0476	5.0000

6   Conclusion

An S-Box is designed to achieve specific cryptographic properties to satisfy the notions of information-theoretic security. The affine equivalent mappings import the desired cryptographic profile. During the importing process, the cryptographic engineer may overlook the robustness of surjective mappings. The affine permutation choices drastically affect the robustness of a surjective mapping. In our analysis, none of the 6×4 and 6×5 EA equivalent S-Box achieved good robustness compared to the parent mapping. Neglecting affine parameters may lead to a weakened mapping against the differential cryptanalysis irrespective of the parent differential uniformity. The choice of affine parameters also affects the security of an S-Box against DPA attacks. Therefore, a careful selection of affine equivalence parameters is as essential as the cryptographic profile.

References

1. Hankin, C.: Project VENONA: breaking the unbreakable code (2020)
2. Claude Elwood Shannon: A mathematical theory of communication. Bell Syst. Tech. J. **27**(3), 379–423 (1948)
3. Shannon, C.E.: Communication theory of secrecy systems. Bell Syst. Tech. J. **28**(4), 656–715 (1949)
4. Shannon, C.E.: Prediction and entropy of printed English. Bell Syst. Tech. J. **30**(1), 50–64 (1951)
5. Kam, J.B., Davida, G.I.: Structured design of substitution-permutation encryption networks. IEEE Trans. Comput. **28**(10), 747–753 (1979)
6. Adams, C., Tavares, S.: The structured design of cryptographically good s-boxes. J. Cryptol. **3**(1), 27–41 (1990). https://doi.org/10.1007/BF00203967
7. Heys, H.M., Tavares, S.E.: Substitution-permutation networks resistant to differential and linear cryptanalysis. J. Cryptol. **9**(1), 1–19 (1996). https://doi.org/10.1007/BF02254789
8. Biham, E., Shamir, A.: Differential cryptanalysis of des-like cryptosystems. J. Cryptol. **4**(1), 3–72 (1991)
9. Matsui, M.: Linear cryptanalysis method for DES cipher. In: Helleseth, T. (ed.) EUROCRYPT 1993. LNCS, vol. 765, pp. 386–397. Springer, Heidelberg (1994). https://doi.org/10.1007/3-540-48285-7_33
10. Zhou, Y., Standaert, F.X.: S-box pooling: towards more efficient side-channel security evaluations. In: Applied Cryptography and Network Security Workshops. ACNS 2022. LNCS, vol. 13285, pp. 146–164. Springer, Cham (2022). https://doi.org/10.1007/978-3-031-16815-4_9
11. Nyberg, K.: Differentially uniform mappings for cryptography. In: Helleseth, T. (ed.) EUROCRYPT 1993. LNCS, vol. 765, pp. 55–64. Springer, Heidelberg (1994). https://doi.org/10.1007/3-540-48285-7_6
12. Cruz Jiménez, R.A.: Generation of 8-bit s-boxes having almost optimal cryptographic properties using smaller 4-bit s-boxes and finite field multiplication. In: Lange, T., Dunkelman, O. (eds.) LATINCRYPT 2017. LNCS, vol. 11368, pp. 191–206. Springer, Cham (2019). https://doi.org/10.1007/978-3-030-25283-0_11

13. Canright, D.: A very compact s-box for AES. In: Rao, J.R., Sunar, B. (eds.) CHES 2005. LNCS, vol. 3659, pp. 441–455. Springer, Heidelberg (2005). https://doi.org/10.1007/11545262_32

14. Arı, A., Özkaynak, F.: Generation of substitution box structures based on blum blum shub random number outputs. In: 2022 IEEE 16th International Conference on Advanced Trends in Radioelectronics, Telecommunications and Computer Engineering (TCSET), pp. 677–682. IEEE (2022)

15. Artuğer, F., Özkaynak, F.: A method for generation of substitution box based on random selection. Egypt. Inform. J. **23**(1), 127–135 (2022)

16. Freyre-Echevarrıa, A.: On the generation of cryptographically strong substitution boxes from small ones and heuristic search. In: 10th Workshop on Current Trends in Cryptology (CTCrypt 2021), p. 112 (2021)

17. Opirskyy, I., Sovyn, Y., Mykhailova, O.: Heuristic method of finding bitsliced-description of derivative cryptographic s-box. In: 2022 IEEE 16th International Conference on Advanced Trends in Radioelectronics, Telecommunications and Computer Engineering (TCSET), pp. 104–109. IEEE (2022)

18. Canteaut, A., Roué, J.: On the behaviors of affine equivalent sboxes regarding differential and linear attacks. In: Oswald, E., Fischlin, M. (eds.) EUROCRYPT 2015. LNCS, vol. 9056, pp. 45–74. Springer, Heidelberg (2015). https://doi.org/10.1007/978-3-662-46800-5_3

19. Fuller, J.E.: Analysis of affine equivalent Boolean functions for cryptography. PhD thesis, Queensland University of Technology (2003)

20. Seberry, J., Zhang, X.M., Zheng, Y.: Systematic generation of cryptographically robust s-boxes. In: Proceedings of the 1st ACM Conference on Computer and Communications Security, pp. 171–182 (1993)

21. Seberry, J., Zhang, X.-M., Zheng, Y.: Pitfalls in designing substitution boxes. In: Desmedt, Y.G. (ed.) CRYPTO 1994. LNCS, vol. 839, pp. 383–396. Springer, Heidelberg (1994). https://doi.org/10.1007/3-540-48658-5_35

22. Daemen, J., Rijmen, V.: Probability distributions of correlation and differentials in block ciphers. J. Math. Cryptol. **1**(3), 221–242 (2007)

23. O'Connor, L.: On the distribution of characteristics in bijective mappings. J. Cryptol. **8**(2), 67–86 (1995). https://doi.org/10.1007/BF00190756

24. Hawkes, P., O'Connor, L.: XOR and Non-XOR differential probabilities. In: Stern, J. (ed.) EUROCRYPT 1999. LNCS, vol. 1592, pp. 272–285. Springer, Heidelberg (1999). https://doi.org/10.1007/3-540-48910-X_19

25. Perrin, L.P.: Cryptanalysis, reverse-engineering and design of symmetric cryptographic algorithms. PhD thesis, University of Luxembourg, Luxembourg (2017)

26. Daemen, J., Rijmen, V.: The rijndael block cipher: AES proposal. In: First Candidate Conference (AeS1), pp. 343–348 (1999)

27. Aoki, K., et al.: Camellia: a 128-bit block cipher suitable for multiple platforms — design and analysis. In: Stinson, D.R., Tavares, S. (eds.) SAC 2000. LNCS, vol. 2012, pp. 39–56. Springer, Heidelberg (2001). https://doi.org/10.1007/3-540-44983-3_4

28. Daemen, J., Knudsen, L., Rijmen, V.: The block cipher square. In: Biham, E. (ed.) FSE 1997. LNCS, vol. 1267, pp. 149–165. Springer, Heidelberg (1997). https://doi.org/10.1007/BFb0052343

29. Guo, J., Peyrin, T., Poschmann, A.: The PHOTON family of lightweight hash functions. In: Rogaway, P. (ed.) CRYPTO 2011. LNCS, vol. 6841, pp. 222–239. Springer, Heidelberg (2011). https://doi.org/10.1007/978-3-642-22792-9_13

30. Shirai, T., Shibutani, K., Akishita, T., Moriai, S., Iwata, T.: The 128-bit blockcipher CLEFIA (extended abstract). In: Biryukov, A. (ed.) FSE 2007. LNCS, vol. 4593, pp. 181–195. Springer, Heidelberg (2007). https://doi.org/10.1007/978-3-540-74619-5_12

31. Diffie, W., Ledin, G.: SMS4 encryption algorithm for wireless networks. Cryptology ePrint Archive (2008)

32. Perrin, L.P., Udovenko, A.: Exponential s-boxes: a link between the s-boxes of belt and kúznyechik/streebog. IACR Trans. Symmetric Cryptol. **2016**(2), 99–124 (2017)

33. Agievich, S., Afonenko, A.: Exponential s-boxes. Cryptology ePrint Archive (2004)

34. Massey, J.L.: SAFER K-64: a byte-oriented block-ciphering algorithm. In: Anderson, R. (ed.) FSE 1993. LNCS, vol. 809, pp. 1–17. Springer, Heidelberg (1994). https://doi.org/10.1007/3-540-58108-1_1

35. Bilgin, B., Bogdanov, A., Knežević, M., Mendel, F., Wang, Q.: FIDES: lightweight authenticated cipher with side-channel resistance for constrained hardware. In: Bertoni, G., Coron, J.-S. (eds.) CHES 2013. LNCS, vol. 8086, pp. 142–158. Springer, Heidelberg (2013). https://doi.org/10.1007/978-3-642-40349-1_9

36. Matsui, M.: New block encryption algorithm MISTY. In: Biham, E. (ed.) FSE 1997. LNCS, vol. 1267, pp. 54–68. Springer, Heidelberg (1997). https://doi.org/10.1007/BFb0052334

37. Kanda, M., et al.: E2-a new 128-bit block cipher. IEICE Trans. Fundam. Electron. Commun. Comput. Sci. **83**(1), 48–59 (2000)

38. Scott, R.: Wide-open encryption design offers flexible implementations. Cryptologia **9**(1), 75–91 (1985)

39. Rose, G.G., Hawkes, P.: Turing: a fast stream cipher. In: Johansson, T. (ed.) FSE 2003. LNCS, vol. 2887, pp. 290–306. Springer, Heidelberg (2003). https://doi.org/10.1007/978-3-540-39887-5_22

40. Kaliski, B.: The MD2 message-digest algorithm. Technical report (1992)

41. Das, I., Nath, S., Roy, S., Mondal, S.: Random s-box generation in AES by changing irreducible polynomial. In: 2012 International Conference on Communications, Devices and Intelligent Systems (CODIS), pp. 556–559 (2012)

42. Kazlauskas, K., Kazlauskas, J.: Key-dependent s-box generation in AES block cipher system. Informatica **20**(1), 23–34 (2009)

43. Dolmatov, V.: GOST R 34.12-2015: block cipher kuznyechik. Technical report (2016)

44. Barreto, P.S.L.M.: The anubis block cipher. NESSIE (2000)

45. Knudsen, L., Wagner, D.: On the structure of skipjack. Discret. Appl. Math. **111**(1–2), 103–116 (2001)

46. Oliynykov, R., et al.: A new encryption standard of Ukraine: the Kalyna block cipher. Cryptology ePrint Archive (2015)

47. Bannier, A.: Combinatorial Analysis of Block Ciphers With Trapdoors. PhD thesis, École Nationale Supérieure d'Arts et Métiers (2017)

48. Sarkar, S., Syed, H.: Bounds on differential and linear branch number of permutations. In: Susilo, W., Yang, G. (eds.) ACISP 2018. LNCS, vol. 10946, pp. 207–224. Springer, Cham (2018). https://doi.org/10.1007/978-3-319-93638-3_13

49. Guilley, S., Hoogvorst, P., Pacalet, R.: Differential power analysis model and some results. In: Quisquater, J.-J., Paradinas, P., Deswarte, Y., El Kalam, A.A. (eds.) CARDIS 2004. IIFIP, vol. 153, pp. 127–142. Springer, Boston, MA (2004). https://doi.org/10.1007/1-4020-8147-2_9

50. Li, H., Zhou, Y., Ming, J., Yang, G., Jin, C.: The notion of transparency order, revisited. Comput. J. **63**(12), 1915–1938 (2020)

51. Leander, G., Poschmann, A.: On the classification of 4 bit s-boxes. In: Carlet, C., Sunar, B. (eds.) WAIFI 2007. LNCS, vol. 4547, pp. 159–176. Springer, Heidelberg (2007). https://doi.org/10.1007/978-3-540-73074-3_13
52. Zhang, W., Bao, Z., Rijmen, V., Liu, M.: A new classification of 4-bit optimal s-boxes and its application to present, rectangle and SPONGENT. In: Leander, G. (ed.) FSE 2015. LNCS, vol. 9054, pp. 494–515. Springer, Heidelberg (2015). https://doi.org/10.1007/978-3-662-48116-5_24

Author Index

G.-V. Jourdan et al. (Eds.): FPS 2022, LNCS 13877, pp. 473–474, 2023.
https://doi.org/10.1007/978-3-031-30122-3

Printed in the United States
by Baker & Taylor Publisher Services